Reveille in Washington

Reveille in Washington
1860-1865

by MARGARET LEECH

RTP

TIME *Reading Program Special Edition*

Time-Life Books Inc., Alexandria, Virginia

Time-Life Books Inc.
is a wholly owned subsidiary of
TIME INCORPORATED

TIME Reading Program: *Editor,* Max Gissen

For information about any Time-Life book, please write:
Reader Information, Time-Life Books,
541 North Fairbanks Court, Chicago, Illinois 60611

Editors' Preface

A CENTURY AFTER secessionist guns fired on Fort Sumter, the Civil War is still the most evocative event in United States history. Soldiers who have themselves fought in climactic battles of two world wars and in Korea read with undiminished interest about Gettysburg and Bull Run, but can take or leave alone a book about Château-Thierry, the Battle of the Bulge or the Marine retreat from the Chosin Reservoir. Almost certainly this does not arise from a trick of time, from the luster given by the patina of the past as against the patent discomfort of what still disturbs the living memory. Before the Civil War there was, of course, the War of the Revolution, and after that the War of 1812, the Mexican War and the Spanish-American War. These wars, too, live in the American consciousness, but only in the minds of their special buffs do they glow. All these conflicts had their continuing consequences, but alone of them the Civil War created passions that can still be fired by the pages of a book.

One has only to think of the men who figured greatly in those other wars to measure the feelings set in motion by the Civil War. For all their dash, Andy Jackson, Winfield Scott, Teddy Roosevelt and George Patton pale before the compulsive excitement that can still be evoked by such names as Grant, Lee, Sherman and Stonewall Jackson. And as the years pass, Lincoln grows in stature and human interest even when tried in the magisterial company of Washington, Adams, Jefferson and Madison. All this is no accident: for if ever a nation came through a traumatic wringer, it was the United States during the Civil War. In modern times, only the Spanish Civil War has evoked anything like the same intransigence, the same hatreds, the same sorrows and the same compassions.

Of books about the Civil War there is no foreseeable end. Since the last shot was fired, it is estimated that there has been published, on an average, one a day. Of these, many are trivial and as many pointless: dull, badly written diaries, paste-and-scissors cullings from old volumes which were suspect even when they were fresh. But solid research never ceases and first-rate books about the war have become a commonplace. One book alone, a very expensive one at that, sold over 300,000 copies since its publication in 1960.

In the face of such industry and such genuine national interest, it might seem almost presumptuous to select a single book as an introduction to so massive a literature. Yet *Reveille in Washington, 1860-1865* by Margaret Leech has claims that attach to no rival volume. For what she has done is to view the war from the most sensitive point of all during the conflict: the nation's capital. Washington was more than the seat of government: it was a southern city in which loyal men labored to save the Union while secessionist neighbors openly jeered at their efforts. It was at once a seat of bumbling bureaucracy, a training ground for raw recruits, a giant hospital, the habitat of Confederate spies and, finally, the scene for the assassination of the one man who might have diminished the residue of the war's bitterness.

That *Reveille in Washington* won its author the Pulitzer Prize occasions no great wonder since the book so richly deserved it. What was surprising was that she had written it at all. She had tried her hand at writing novels and had published three which she would now, quite understandably, prefer to forget. With Heywood Broun she had collaborated on a biography of the scourge of pornography, *Anthony Comstock: Roundsman of the Lord,* a sophisticated, factual account of the famous vice crusader. (She and Broun wrote alternate chapters.) Collaborating with Beatrice Kaufman (wife of playwright George Kaufman), she wrote a play called *Divided by Three.* Even so great an actress as Judith Anderson could not save it. As Margaret Leech herself described her foray into the theater, she and her collaborator "had every advantage there was, except talent."

At this point, it would have been fair to expect that Margaret Leech would go on being the charming New York hostess who gave delightful dinners for brilliant conversationalists and savored the good life in the most congenial surroundings. It was then that publisher Cass Canfield of Harper put an idea into her head. Why not write a book about Washington during the Civil War? To another woman the suggestion might have seemed preposterous. Margaret Leech knew no more about the Civil War than any other college graduate, had no training in historical research and had no notion of where to begin. Later she was to admit that at the outset "ignorance, like inexperience, seemed to me a defect supremely easy to remedy."

It never occurred to her "that I should struggle longer than the Federal army before I brought those blue-clad boys marching in triumph up Pennsylvania Avenue." It was, in fact, five years before *Reveille* became a book.

To write *Reveille*, Margaret Leech tackled masses of material that might have intimidated the most doughty professional historian. For she had attempted many things in one. Not only did she show Washington at the center of war, a sleepy capital suddenly become the chaotic headquarters from which issued orders that sent unprecedented numbers of men to their deaths; she undertook to describe it as a prototype of a divided nation which bumbled from despair to despair until the very succession of defeats put the iron in its soul necessary for the ultimate effort.

Published in 1941, *Reveille* was an immediate success. It was fine and vivid writing, yes, but it was more. Said one review: ". . . behind the writing there has been the selection and the amalgamation, and behind that there has been the assimilation which is the requisite of a truly living, as of a scholarly, book. In years of study of her material Miss Leech has made her mind the channel of its living quality. *Reveille in Washington* is not merely good because it is well written, it is well written because it is good. . . . This book of the Civil War comes to us with enlightenment and wit, brilliance in scene and universality in insight."

Margaret Leech's Washington is an incredible city, a war capital seemingly without control of its own resources. Filthy, ugly and unfinished, it swarmed with prostitutes, dead horses rotted in the streets and only a brave and well-armed man would think of going out after dark. Confederate cavalry contemptuously galloped around the city. Lincoln once went out to Fort Stevens and stood on the parapet to watch a Confederate charge, whereupon young Oliver Wendell Holmes barked at the President: "Get down, you fool!" It is Lincoln, almost without seeming intention on author Leech's part, who emerges not only as the hero of *Reveille* but also as a very great human being for whom the war was a continuous succession of heartbreaks. Margaret Leech is almost casual in the handling of the book's greatest moments, and it is precisely this quality that gives *Reveille* a continually astonishing air. When Lincoln first meets a shabby, uneasy little man named Grant at the White House, the drama is intense because no drama is attempted. Here is Miss Leech's account:

"Near the door of the Blue Room the advance of the column of callers was suddenly checked. The President, after cordially wringing the hand of one visitor, detained him in conversation. He was a short, scrubby officer, stooped and sunburned, with rough, light-brown whiskers, and he appeared scarcely worthy of signal attention. There was something seedy about him; the look of a man who is out of a job, and takes too much to drink. The stars on his shoulder straps were tarnished. But a buzz ran through the Blue Room. Everyone began to stare at the man who stood awkwardly looking up at the President, while arriving guests jostled in confusion outside the doorway. General Grant and Mr. Lincoln were meeting for the first time.

"Seward hurried to the rescue. He presented the general to Mrs. Lincoln, and led him through a lane of eager faces into the crowded East Room. Grant's entrance turned the polite assemblage into a mob. Wild cheers shook the crystal chandeliers, as ladies and gentlemen rushed on him from all sides. Laces were torn, and crinolines mashed. Fearful of injury or maddened by excitement, people scrambled on chairs and tables. At last, General Grant was forced to mount a crimson sofa. He stood there bashfully shaking the thrusting hands that wanted to touch success and glory—Donelson, Vicksburg, Chattanooga—personified in a slovenly little soldier, with a blushing, scared face."

And when Miss Leech describes the assassination of Lincoln, it is almost as if it were a natural and inevitable consequence of all that had gone before. *Reveille* makes the reader wonder how the North managed to win the war at all, while making it effortlessly clear that of course it would.

THE EDITORS

For Susan Pulitzer

Contents

I *The General Is Older than the Capital*

THAT WINTER, the old General moved from the rooms he had rented from the free mulatto, Wormley, in I Street to Cruchet's at Sixth and D Streets. His new quarters, situated on the ground floor—a spacious bedroom, with a private dining-room adjoining—were convenient for a man who walked slowly and with pain; and Cruchet, a French caterer, was one of the best cooks in Washington.

In spite of his nearly seventy-five years and his increasing infirmities, the General was addicted to the pleasures of the table. Before his six o'clock dinner, his black body servant brought out the wines and the liqueurs, setting the bottles of claret to warm before the fire. The old man had refined his palate in the best restaurants in Paris; and woodcock, English snipe, poulard, capon, and *tête de veau en tortue* were among the dishes he fancied. He liked, too, canvasback duck, and the hams of his native Virginia. Yet nothing, to his taste, equaled the delicacy he called "tarrapin." He would hold forth on the correct method of preparing it: "No flour, sir—not a grain." His military secretary could saturninely foresee that moment, when, leaning his left elbow on the table and holding six inches above his plate a fork laden with the succulent tortoise, he would announce, "The best food vouchsafed by Providence to man," before hurrying the fork to his lips.

From his splendid prime, the General had retained, not only a discriminating palate, but the defects suitable to a proud and ambitious nature. He had always been vain, pompous, exacting, jealous and high-tempered. Now that his sick old body could no longer support the racking of its wounds, his irascibility had dwindled to irritation, and his imperiousness to petulance. His love of flattery had grown, and he often declared that at his age compliments had become a necessity. While taking a footbath, he would call on his military secretary to remark the fairness of his limbs. In company, he spoke of the great commanders of history, and matched with theirs his own exploits at Chippewa and Lundy's Lane, at Cerro Gordo and Chapultepec. Near his desk stood his bust in marble, with shoulders bared; classical, serene and idealized. The walls were brilliant with his portraits at various ages, from the young General Winfield Scott who had been victorious over the British in 1814 to the already aging General-in-Chief who had defeated the Mexicans in 1848. They were arresting figures, those generals on the walls; handsome, slender, heroic, with haughty eye and small, imperious mouth. Gold gleamed in spurs, in buttons and embroidery and huge epaulettes, in the handle of the sword which had been the gift of Virginia; and one portrait showed the superb cocked hat, profusely plumed, that had earned for Scott the sobriquet of "Fuss and Feathers." He stood six feet, four and a quarter inches in height, and had been wont to insist on the fraction. But, swollen and dropsical, he spoke no longer of his size. He pointed instead to the bust, to the portraits, to show what he had been.

Such was the commanding general of the Army of the United States in December of 1860, but not so did his compatriots see him. His eye had lost its fire and he could no longer sit a horse, but in huge epaulettes and yellow sash he was still his country's hero. Europe might celebrate the genius of Napoleon; the New World had its Winfield Scott. For nearly half a century the republic had taken pride in his achievements as soldier and pacificator; and, if he now lived in a glorious military past, so did his fellow-countrymen. He was the very figure to satisfy a peaceful people, fond of bragging of its bygone belligerence. The General was as magnificent as a monument, and no one was troubled by the circumstance that he was nearly as useless.

Smugly aloof from the dissensions of Europe, the young nation scorned the large standing armies of the Old World. It was wary of the political danger of a large military class; and, regarding high rank as perilous to democratic liberties, looked uneasily on West Point as a breeding ground for aristocrats. Save for George Washington, Winfield Scott alone had held the rank of lieutenant-general, and in his case Congress had conferred it only by brevet. To guard its far-flung borders and fight its Indian wars, the United States maintained an army of sixteen thousand soldiers, scattered for the most part over the Pacific coast, Utah and the Southwest.

This small establishment offered a limited opportunity for military preferment, and in the twenty years of Scott's command he had shown a marked partiality for advancing Southern officers. To favor gentlemen from the slave States, with their martial spirit and their "habit of command," had been as natural to the old Virginian as a daily perusal of the Richmond *Enquirer*. Of the six Army departments, only the Department of the East was commanded by a Northerner, General John E. Wool. The five Western departments, in which the mass of the Army was stationed, were all headed by officers of Southern birth. Scott found the "Southern rascals" not only meritorious, but congenial. The only Northern aide on his staff was his military secretary, Lieutenant-Colonel E. D. Keyes, and the appointment had first been offered to a Virginian, Colonel Robert E. Lee. Since the nation's political destinies had long been controlled by the statesmen of the slave States, there had been no interference with the General's predilections. For twelve years, the War Department patronage had been in Southern hands. A Southern clique ruled the Army, and many ambitious Northerners who had shown promise at West Point —Halleck, McClellan, Hooker, Burnside, Sherman, Rosecrans—had felt sufficiently discouraged to resign their commissions and return to civil life.

In spite of his sentiment for the South, General Scott was no believer in State sovereignty; he was strongly attached to the Union. In the Presidential election of 1852, he had been the last standard-bearer of the dying Whig party, overwhelmingly defeated by the Democratic candidate, Franklin Pierce, a New Englander of Southern sympathies. Scott had spent much time in the North, and, when Pierce took office, he moved his headquarters from Washington to New York. There, growing old and feeble, he had remained, while North and South, with increasing bitterness, disputed the question of the extension of slavery to the territories, and abolitionists vied with fire-eaters in a chorus of recrimination and hatred. In 1856, the anti-slavery Republican party entered the national lists, captained by the gallant adventurer, Frémont. Again a Democrat, James Buchanan, was elected President; but the North's growing antipathy to slavery was written in the large Republican vote. The canvass of 1860 revealed a disastrous sectional division. The Democratic party split into two factions, each of which nominated a candidate, and the success of the Republicans in November appeared to be assured. After the October elections, the cotton States began to agitate for disunion. South Carolina threatened immediate secession, if the Republican candidate, Abraham Lincoln, should be elected. In late October, General Scott wrote the President a letter containing his views. He advised Buchanan that the Southern forts should be strongly garrisoned to prevent a surprise attack. It was the advice that the General had given President Jackson during the nullification troubles in South Carolina, when Scott himself had gone to Charleston and executed his mission with firmness and diplomacy.

Scott was no longer the man he had been in 1832. His letter maundered off into arguments for peaceable disunion, and he presented the suggestion that the nation might solve its problems, not simply by splitting in half, but by dividing into four confederacies. A week after he had sent his letter, Abraham Lincoln was elected President of the United States. Four days later, South Carolina called a convention with the view of seceding from the Union. There were wild political demonstrations in the cotton States; and, as Southern trade with the North fell off and markets fell and banks called in their loans, the free States, forgetful of their recent enthusiasm for the limitation of slavery, grew despondent. Northern merchants and manufacturers, chilled by the prospect of bankruptcy, were eager to make concessions. Some people thought that the only course was to permit the separation of the sections; but the great majority still refused to take the threats of disunion seriously. At every election for the past twenty years, the Southerners had been gasconading about secession. Few Northerners had any comprehension of the crisis, and almost none faced the possibility that it might end in civil war.

In December, the General was boosted into a railway car, and started on his journey to Washington. It was a hardship for him to travel, he had been ill in bed; but the President had sent for him, and like a good soldier he was ready to do his duty. The dirty, rattling cars wound slowly down through Maryland, and, leaning on the arm of his military secretary, the General entered the nation's capital, a town of sedition and dismay.

The North might worry over tumbling markets; in Washington there was revolution, and men feared for democratic government. A very young man of the Adams family, who was attempting that winter what he called an education in treason, observed "the singular spectacle of a government trying to destroy itself." The conspiracy for disunion was not confined to the States, but permeated the highest councils of the nation. It was unique among revolutions only in its impunity. Southern senators and representatives made no secret of their disloyalty to the Union. Three members of the President's Cabinet had been deeply implicated: Howell Cobb of Georgia, Secretary

of the Treasury; John B. Floyd of Virginia, Secretary of War; and
Jacob Thompson of Mississippi, Secretary of the Interior. Clerks in
the Government departments sported secession cockades on their coats,
and loudly over their whisky at Willard's bar vowed that Lincoln
should never be inaugurated.

Uneasily in the Presidential chair sat James Buchanan of Pennsylvania, like a nervous gentleman on a runaway horse, longing for
the ride to be over. A commonplace politician of nearly seventy, he
was conscientious, evasive and irresolute. He was a staunch Democrat;
Southerners were his friends and closest political associates. He had
belatedly become aware that his allegiance might carry him into presiding over the disruption of his country. General Scott's repeated
advice to strengthen the Southern forts had no more effect on him
than on his secessionist War Secretary, Mr. Floyd. Mr. Buchanan was
not oblivious of the problem of the forts. In conference with his divided Cabinet, he was considering little else than the question of the
policy to be pursued in Charleston harbor. Major Robert Anderson,
stationed with a small garrison at Fort Moultrie, was appealing to the
Government to take a stand; if it was intended to hold the forts,
Anderson begged for reinforcements. Dreading a collision, the President felt obliged to follow a policy so noncommittal that it produced
the impression of being no policy at all. However dull ears might be
at the North, Mr. Buchanan had heard the roar of the deluge, and
to the induction into office of his successor, Mr. Lincoln, he was looking forward with the keenest anticipation.

Washington was in a turmoil. Its very existence as the Federal
City seemed threatened. Geographically the situation of the District
of Columbia was precarious. If the slave States of Virginia and Maryland were both to secede, they would carry Washington with them.
Sympathy with secession was strong in a large group of the city's
residents, and it was feared that they would participate in any seditious enterprise. Men in public life found their mail heavy with
threats and warnings, and General Scott's ears were soon ringing with
stories of conspiracy.

The General had made the journey to Washington for a consultation with the President. It was evident that he would be obliged to
remain. Scott was no Republican, but, baffled by Mr. Buchanan, and
cold-shouldered by Mr. Floyd, he wished to God that Mr. Lincoln

were in office. For Army headquarters, space was presently found in Winder's Building in Seventeenth Street, opposite the small brick structure of the War Department, and the General-in-Chief took up his duties at the divided and jeopardized seat of Federal Government.

It was as a symbol that the capital was valued; it had no other importance. Built to order at the dawn of the century, it gave after sixty years the impression of having been just begun. "As in 1800 and 1850, so in 1860," wrote Henry Adams, "the same rude colony was camped in the same forest, with the same unfinished Greek temples for workrooms, and sloughs for roads." European travelers, doing their tour of the United States, looked superciliously on Washington. They were accustomed to capitals which were the rooted centers of the cultural and commercial life of their nations. Washington was merely a place for the Government. It was an idea set in a wilderness.

All too typical of the young republic, the town was pretentious and unfulfilled. It had been ambitiously laid out over an area extending from the Potomac and the Eastern Branch or Anacostia River as far as Rock Creek on the west and Boundary Street—later to be known as Florida Avenue—on the north. Vast sums, by the standards of the day, had been spent on the public buildings, but they were widely spaced, unrelated and, for the most part, incomplete. In sixty years, men may construct a compact city; not Rome. The very grandioseness of the capital's conception called forth ridicule, and the often-quoted tribute, "a city of magnificent distances," had become a favorite jibe.

The vaunted buildings of Washington were the Capitol, the General Post-Office, the Patent Office, the Treasury, the Executive Mansion and the Smithsonian Institution; and, despite the distances, the tour could be made in a forenoon. First in importance was the classic Capitol, with its historical paintings and statuary and its Library of Congress; above all, with its great marble Extension, progressing toward completion after nearly ten years of work. In the two new wings, only recently occupied by the legislators, visitors now might gaze on the splendid Senate Chamber and the ornate red and gold Hall of Representatives. There was no doubt that the interior decorations were gorgeous, though Americans thought them gaudy and foreign: but on the outside imagination was needed to envision an imposing architectural effect. The original dome had been removed, and only the base of the new cast-iron dome, topped by scaffolding and a towering crane, surmounted the old sandstone building in the center. At either end, the glittering marble wings stretched bare and unfinished, devoid even of steps. Of the hundred Corinthian columns needed for the completion of the porticoes, only three had been crowned by their capitals and set in place. Columns and capitals, blocks of marble, keystones, carvings, lumber and iron plates lay strewn about the grounds, which were further defaced by workmen's sheds and depots for coal and wood. Visitors lingered on the east portico to admire the colossal statues, especially Persico's Columbus, with his ball; and all paused to stare at the Greenough statue of Washington which sat, godlike amid the litter, in the eastern park. Modeled on the Roman conception of Jupiter Tonans, the figure of the Father of his Country was naked to the waist, with his limbs swathed in draperies; and even Philp's guidebook was constrained to remark that Washington was "scarcely recognizable, in this garb, to his countrymen."

Diagonally across from each other, at Seventh and F Streets, were the marble palaces of the Post-Office and the Patent Office. The latter, which was not quite finished, contained a display of models and curiosities, and provided space for the entire business of the Department of the Interior. On Fifteenth Street, the Treasury Department occupied an immense edifice, the Extension of which was still under construction. Next door, on the future site of the north end of the Treasury, was the little brick State Department. It attracted no more attention than did the Army and Navy Departments, which were installed in similar old-fashioned houses on the western side of the Executive Mansion, whose wooded lawn extended, without intervening streets, to the four department buildings.

By travelers from overseas, the mansion itself was dismissed as an ordinary country house, wanting in either taste or splendor; but it was an object of deep interest to Americans, who roved through the spacious public rooms, admiring the large mirrors, the flowered carpets and the sparkling chandeliers. At either end, the mansion straggled out into low sheds, which were used for household purposes, and the extension on the west was surmounted by a conservatory which communicated with the first floor. With its outbuildings, greenhouses, fruit trees, and flower and kitchen gardens, the place had an appearance of prosperous untidiness, like that of a Southern plantation house. In front of the mansion, there was an iron fence with large gateways, and another fence enclosed the grounds on the south; but the lawns were traversed by interior paths between the departments, and that which crossed the north side of the house was freely used by the public. In the circle before the north portico stood a statue of Thomas Jefferson in bronze, a material which was thought to have imparted a negroid appearance to the statesman's features. On the other side of Pennsylvania Avenue, the bronze equestrian statue of Andrew Jackson embellished Lafayette Square. It was the work of Clark Mills, a talented young plasterer from South Carolina. There had been many criticisms of the prancing horse, with its lifted fore-feet. Charles Sumner, the cultured senator from Massachusetts, found the Jackson statue grotesque, and was humiliated at having to conduct British visitors past it.

The great disadvantage of the President's House was its un-healthy situation near the Potomac flats, which were held responsible for the prevalence of malaria in Washington during the summer and autumn months. At the foot of the President's Park, as the unkempt tract south of the mansion was called, there was an unsavory marsh which had formerly been an outlet for sewage. This bordered on the opening of the town's great nuisance, the old city canal, formerly an inland waterway between the Potomac and the Eastern Branch, but now fallen into disuse, save as a receptacle for sewage and offal. To reach the Mall and the southwest section of Washington, it was neces-sary to cross this unsightly and odorous channel, which was spanned at intervals by high iron bridges.

In the half-developed park of the Mall arose the red, fantastic towers of the Smithsonian Institution, surrounded by prettily planted grounds which, like those of the Capitol and the White House, had been planned by the famous horticulturist, Andrew J. Downing. Its large library and museum of natural history were considered well worth visiting. West of Fifteenth Street and directly south of the Executive Mansion, though separated from it by the wide mouth of the canal, stood a truncated shaft, intended to commemorate the Father of his Country. Here sentimental patriots might wander among the stone carvings which lay piled on the ground, and meditate on the ingratitude which had suffered the subscriptions to lapse. Another memorial of Washington, a rigid equestrian statue by Clark Mills, was solitarily situated in Washington Circle, at the intersection of Penn-sylvania Avenue and Twenty-third Street.

These were the sights of the Federal Metropolis—six scattered buildings, a few dubious statues and one-third of an obelisk—and, barring an inspection of the Government greenhouses, or a drive to the Navy Yard, the Arsenal or the Observatory, there was nothing more to be seen within the city limits.

Northwest from Capitol Hill ran the city's main thoroughfare, Pennsylvania Avenue—"the" Avenue. It had been conceived as a broad and imposing boulevard, along which the Capitol should confront the Executive Mansion, but the great bulk of the Treasury had necessitated a bend in the Avenue, and from the Capitol the vista now terminated, not in the White House, but in the red-brick barn which President Buchanan had erected in the grounds. Devoid of fine buildings, the wide, neglected street wore an air of desolation. Its thin cobble pavement had been broken up by faulty drainage and the traffic of the heavy omnibuses which plied between the Capitol and Georgetown. In dry weather, the ruts and hollows were iron traps, covered with thick dust. Rain turned the roadbed into a channel of mud, underlaid by areas of treacherous gravel. The south or "wrong" side of the Avenue was lined with dingy buildings, and its only place of popular resort was the Center Market, an agglomeration of sheds and shacks which backed on the open sewer of the canal. The restaurants and the shops and the big hotels were all on the north side, where the brick sidewalk constituted the town's promenade.

The hotels were a recent development in a capital whose politicians had emerged only in mid-century from a background of small taverns and boardinghouses. The large, ugly buildings were the chief attractions of the Avenue, enlivening its dullness with their uniformed attendants, their ranks of hacks and the bustle of arriving and departing guests. When Congress was in session, their halls and parlors, dining-rooms and bars were crowded. The din was frightful, the prices were high, and the clerks were haughty and disobliging; but, to see and to be seen, to establish contact with the political personages of the day and feel the pulse of Government, it was necessary to go to the hotels.

Two of them were situated on opposite sides of Sixth Street: the National, a huge caravansary, and the marble-fronted pile of Brown's, later known as the Metropolitan. Because of their convenience to the Capitol, these houses were much patronized by members of Congress, especially by Southerners. The slaves of the planter-politicians loitered on the sidewalk of the Avenue, while their masters, in broad-brimmed hats, conferred in the corridors, or called for bourbon and juleps in

the bars. At the time of Mr. Buchanan's inauguration, the National
had suffered an eclipse, because of an outbreak of an intestinal malady
among its guests. The new President was one of the many who became ill, and his nephew died of the National Hotel disease. In extreme pro-Southern circles, the epidemic was declared to have been
the result of a Republican plot to poison the leaders of the Democratic party; but most people accepted the explanation that it had been
caused by sewer gas, and after a brief closure for repairs the National
had regained its former popularity.

The Kirkwood, on the corner of Twelfth Street, had its devoted
clientele, as did two or three smaller houses on the Avenue. The most
famous of all the hotels, however, was Willard's at Fourteenth Street.
Formerly a small and unsuccessful hostelry, its failure had been
ascribed to the fact that it was too far uptown. Its reputation had been
made·under the efficient management of the Willard brothers, who
hailed from Vermont; and, enlarged and redecorated, Willard's had
become the great meeting place of Washington. Much of the business of Government was said to be done in its passages and its bar.
From eight to eleven in the morning—for Washingtonians were not
early risers—a procession of celebrities might be observed passing to
the breakfast table. The huge breakfast, which included such items
as fried oysters, steak and onions, blanc mange and *pâté de foie gras,*
was succeeded by a gargantuan midday dinner; by another dinner at
five o'clock; by a robust tea at seven-thirty; and finally by supper at
nine. Englishmen, themselves no inconsiderable feeders, were appalled by the meals that the American guests, ladies as well as gentlemen, were able to consume.

The British visitors hated Willard's. Its very architecture offended
them. Accustomed to snug inns with private parlors, they could find
no decent seclusion in this rambling, uncomfortable barracks. American hotel life was gregarious, and a peaceful withdrawal from an atmosphere of "heat, noise, dust, smoke, expectoration" was the last
thing that the natives appeared to be seeking. After breakfast, as after
dinner, the guests hastened to mingle in the public rooms. At
Willard's, the parlor furniture was occupied by the same sallow, determined men, the same dressy ladies and the same screaming, pre-
cocious children that travelers observed elsewhere in the United
States.

Yet, when the secretaries at the British legation had finished their work, it was to Willard's bar that they ran. There was life in the masculine voices that clamored in the blue cigar smoke; and the youngsters had formed "the pernicious local habit of swallowing cocktails." Lord Lyons, the red-faced British minister, wrote that Washington was a dreadful place for young men; it had no clubs and no good restaurants, no permanent theatre or opera. There were, however, saloons in profusion, and a suitable complement of brothels; while, behind discreetly curtained windows on the Avenue, gentlemen were able to wile away an evening at faro, without any serious interference from the Washington police.

The area immediately north of the Avenue, between the Capitol and the Executive Mansion, was the only part of Washington which was sufficiently built up to warrant the description of a city. Here were houses and churches and a few inadequate school buildings, and here, on Seventh Street, was the principal business section. The government of the seven wards, into which Washington was divided, was administered from the stucco City Hall on Judiciary Square, which contained the office of the mayor and the rooms used by the Boards of Aldermen and Common Council. This building also held the circuit and criminal courts and the office of the United States marshal of the District. Behind the City Hall was the town's only general hospital, the E Street Infirmary; and still farther north on the square, which extended as far as G Street, was the ancient county jail.

The city's business—in contrast to that of Federal Government, which required a setting of porticoed immensity—seemed all to be done in a small way. Ugly blocks of offices had been hastily run up as a speculation. Shabby boardinghouses, little grocery shops, petty attorneys' offices and mean restaurants and saloons served the fifteen hundred clerks who were employed in the departments. The clerks were too poorly paid, and, in the unceasing scramble for appointment, too insecure to bring their families with them; and, since so many bachelors in single rooms required a large number of individual fires, they were also responsible for the unusual quantity of woodyards, which plied an untidy trade in almost every other square.

It was a Southern town, without the picturesqueness, but with the indolence, the disorder and the want of sanitation. Its lounging Negroes startled Northern visitors with the reminder that slaves were held in the capital. Hucksters abounded. Fish and oyster peddlers cried their wares and tooted their horns on the corners. Flocks of geese waddled on the Avenue, and hogs, of every size and color, roamed at large, making their muddy wallows on Capitol Hill and in Judiciary Square. People emptied slops and refuse in the gutters, and threw dead domestic animals into the canal. Most of the population still depended on the questionable water supply afforded by wells and by springs in the hills behind the city. Privies, in the absence of adequate sewage disposal, were plentiful in yards and dirty alleys, and every day the carts of night soil trundled out to the commons ten blocks north of the White House.

Outside the area in which the population was concentrated were lonely tracts of woodland and commons, broken at intervals by large estates, planted and bowered in trees, and by settlements which had pushed out from the expanding center of the town. The effect of this random development reminded one foreign observer of "a frame of Berlin wool work in which the fair embroideress has made spasmodic attempts at a commencement." The elaborate paper plan of the capital gave no indication that within the city limits the labeled streets and avenues were country roads, which crisscrossed in the wilderness.

> There is a map of Washington accurately laid down [wrote that genial traveler, Anthony Trollope]; and taking that map with him in his journeyings a man may lose himself in the streets, not as one loses oneself in London between Shoreditch and Russell Square, but as one does so in the deserts of the Holy Land, between Emmaus and Arimathea. In the first place no one knows where the places are, or is sure of their existence, and then between their presumed localities the country is wild, trackless, unbridged, uninhabited and desolate. . . . Tucking your trousers up to your knees, you will wade through the bogs, you will lose yourself among rude hillocks, you will be out of the reach of humanity. . . . If you are a sportsman, you will desire to shoot snipe within sight of the President's house.

The oldest of the village communities which had developed in Washington was situated near the Navy Yard on the Eastern Branch, and was the home of the mechanics, laborers, carpenters and office workers who were employed at the yard. Neighbored by the Marine Barracks, it was rural and self-contained, although it was connected with the rest of the city by an omnibus line. At the foot of Eleventh Street, an infirm wooden structure, the Navy Yard or Eastern Branch Bridge, gave access to the Government Insane Asylum and to the Maryland countryside. Farther east of the yard was the Congressional Cemetery, city property, in spite of its name; while the bend of the river was bordered by the extensive grounds in which stood the poorhouse and the smallpox hospital. The Eastern Branch was not navigable for ships of war above the Navy Yard, and commerce with Bladensburg, once lively on its waters, had become a thing of the past.

Southwest Washington, divided from the other sections of the city by the old canal, was familiarly known as the Island. On Greenleaf's Point, the angle of confluence of the Potomac and the Eastern Branch, was situated the United States Arsenal, with the Penitentiary a little to the north. The Island had some reason for local pride and ambitions for further development. It included the Mall, with the Smithsonian Institution and also the militia armory. At the foot of Sixth and Seventh Streets were the wharves for the steamboats and sailing vessels which connected the capital with the railroads at Alexandria and Aquia Creek; or made longer voyages by way of Chesapeake Bay and the sea. From the end of Maryland Avenue ran the Long Bridge, the thoroughfare from Washington to Virginia, and the great mail road between the Northern and Southern States.

The good name of the Island, however, was tarnished by the disorder that frequently broke out in its tangle of poverty-stricken alleys. The less populous parts of the city harbored, not only ill-famed resorts, but gangs of rowdies who disturbed good citizens by their lawlessness, and had even started riots during municipal elections. The respectable settlement of the Northern Liberties, located above G Street, had its sordid districts. Other plague spots were Negro Hill far out on North Tenth Street; English Hill, east of the City Hall; and Swampoodle, an Irish colony in a marshy tract near North Capitol Street.

It was a courageous man who ventured to walk alone by night in the ill-lighted streets of the capital of the United States. The inefficiency of the Washington police was as notorious as the prevalence of its footpads and hoodlums. The municipality supported a day force of fifty patrolmen; while the fifty members of the night force were paid by the Government. The chief duty of the latter, however, was the protection of the public buildings; while the city's appointments were made as a reward for services in the local elections. Both forces, remarked Philp's guidebook, "contrary to the usages of other cities, do not separately patrol the entire city, but are to be found in bodies at the most public places."

The town's outstanding grievance, as well as its great pride, derived from the fact that it was the seat of Federal Government. Toward Congress, the supreme authority in the District, it maintained the attitude of a neglected and fretful stepchild. In truth, the grand scale of the city's design was responsible for most of its deficiencies. The fitful Federal appropriations for improving the streets were at no time the equivalent of a tax on the Government property; and, except for the grounds around the Capitol and the President's House, the national authorities had done little to beautify Washington.

From the viewpoint of Congress, the demands of the city were insatiable. Enormous sums had been appropriated to build the aqueduct which would eventually carry over Rock Creek a supply of pure Potomac water adequate for the city's needs. In making this outlay, the legislators had been prompted, not only by considerations of health, but by a desire to reduce the fire hazards. The Washington fire companies, however, were controlled by gangs of toughs, and the frequent conflagrations raged unchecked, not only because of a scarcity of water, but because of rowdyism, confusion, and stone and pistol fights. In every department of civic life in which Congress lent aid to Washington, it encountered the inefficiency of the ward system of municipal government, common in towns of that day.

From its close association with the Government, Washington derived the peculiarity of its seasonal character. It was a winter resort. After the quiet drowse of a long, unhealthy summer, the town awakened each autumn to prepare for the opening of Congress. The dismal railway depot welcomed travelers from North and West. The wharves were busy with the Southerners, arriving by steamer from Aquia Creek. In the train of the legislators followed office seekers, claimants, lobbyists, delegations, inventors and reporters. Minstrel shows came, and opera companies; and famous stars, Joe Jefferson and Charlotte Cushman, Edwin Forrest and Edwin Booth, played at the dingy old Washington Theatre at C and Eleventh Streets. There was a stealthy invasion of pickpockets, confidence men and vagrants. By · the end of November, the town was lively. The desolate Avenue hummed with hacks, with the elaborate carriages of the legations and the blooded horses of the Southerners. Shops furbished their windows. Hotels and boardinghouses filled up, and so did the E Street Infirmary, the poorhouse and the county jail. Practical motives dictated the presence of all the winter sojourners. There were no parties of idle, amusement-seeking tourists. The townsfolk entertained their friends and relatives, and every winter a bevy of pretty girls came for the festivities of the social season; but, apart from these negligible few, Americans did not visit Washington for pleasure. Although it had many churches, an active Young Men's Christian Association and a dignified official society, the city bore an unwholesome name among the pious folk of the nation. It was darkly imagined as a sink of iniquity, where weak-minded bachelors were exposed to the temptations of saloons, gambling hells and light women; and the prevalence of hotel life was instanced as a proof of the city's immorality.

Such was the capital of the United States in December of 1860, the sprawling and unfulfilled embodiment of a vision of national grandeur. Unfinished though it was, it perpetually evoked comparisons with remote antiquity. Henry Adams would recall a boyhood impression of "the Post-Office and the Patent Office which faced each other . . . like white Greek temples in the abandoned gravel pits of a deserted Syrian city." An Army officer, Colonel Charles P. Stone, thought that the Treasury would make the grandest Palmyra of them all. Anthony Trollope was also reminded of the ruins of Palmyra by the framework of the new Capitol dome; and a popular designation of Captain Montgomery Meigs of the engineers, often seen superintending the work on the Capitol Extension, was "Meigs among the ruins of Carthage."

It was a mere ambitious beginner, a baby among capitals. Its defects were those of youth and energy and inexperience. Yet people were ready to fancy it moldering and abandoned, a relic of an optimistic moment of history when men had essayed an experiment called democracy. Dissolution was heavy in the air; and even the rising monuments of the republic wore the image of ruin and decay.

The presence of the old General was reassuring to the worried residents of Washington: to those who were used to living in the capital; who depended on their jobs in it; owned property in it; saw it hopefully, not as it was, but as it might grow to be; and even cherished, some of them, the ideal of a permanent Union of the States. As Scott limped to Winder's Building from his low coupé, drawn by a powerful horse, the passers-by lined up, removed their hats, and cried, "God bless you, General."

II "The Union, Sir, Is Dissolved"

THERE WERE PEOPLE who loved Washington, not alone with an habitual affection for warm firesides and growing gardens, but because they found enjoyment in the particular life the town afforded. They derived a vicarious excitement from the proximity of Government, and from the many rumors of which Washington was the sounding box. They watched with pride and pleasure the progress of the public buildings, attended the improving lectures at the Smithsonian Institution, danced at the hops at the big hotels, and ran pell-mell to the fires.

In spite of many diversions, living was leisurely and almost rustic in character. After church on Sunday, friends went to hospitable houses to dine, sometime between the hours of four and seven, on the excellent and varied fare provided by the markets. There were agreeable evening tea parties in the parlors. From lamp-lit windows came the sound of piano music, or the deliberate slap of the cards in a game of euchre or whist. Like villagers, the townsfolk went to the depot to welcome visitors, or speed them on their way. Sportsmen caught rock bass at the Little Falls, and gunned for duck and reedbird in the Potomac marshes. Along Rock Creek in springtime, the Judas trees unfolded their purplish-pink blossoms. Everyone feasted on shad and strawberries, and in the dimming light white dresses gleamed on the doorsteps. The city's children shuffled in the dry gray slush of the poplar plumes, and April gave place to May, not only as mud is succeeded by dust, but as hyacinths and snowdrops and lilacs yield to woodbine and clematis and a wilderness of roses.

In fine weather, there were many outdoor excursions. Lodges and societies danced and picnicked at pavilions in the groves near the town. People voyaged by steamboat to Alexandria and Fort Washington and the dilapidated countryseat of George Washington at Mount Vernon. Columbian College on the pretty eminence of Meridian Hill was a favorite place to visit. North of Washington, too, were the fine estates of Eckington, Harewood and Kalorama. Three miles beyond the crossing of the city boundary and Seventh Street was a wooded hill on which stood the Soldiers' Home, founded by a part of the tribute which General Scott had levied on Mexico City. A long drive out on the Seventh Street Road, beyond the District line, led to Silver Spring, the summer home of the venerable statesman, Mr. Francis P. Blair. Across the Long Bridge, the pillared mansion of Colonel Robert E. Lee crested the Arlington Heights. Carriages were always rolling across Rock Creek to Georgetown, with its dignified streets of old-fashioned, red-brick houses. The duty of paying calls involved an arduous amount of travel, for ladies were expected to leave their *cartes de visite,* not only in Georgetown, but even in distant Bladensburg.

The town had its aristocracy. It was, said the *New York Herald,* "the abode of a very slow and respectable people, who cool themselves during the hot weather by the delightful remembrance that they are of gentle blood." Prominent residents were allied to the statesmen of the South through family connections in Maryland and Virginia, and during the Pierce administration the official society was Southern in tone. In its inner circle were included the members of the diplomatic set, as well as Northern Democrats who had shown themselves tolerant of slavery. Other notable gentlemen from the free States were courteously, if formally received.

It was a society which permitted an unusual freedom to ladies. Moving breathlessly and without privacy in a shower of white kid gloves and calling cards, they had a role to play in the parlors; and might still enjoy homage at an age when in other American cities they would have been relegated to knitting by the fireside. The galleries of the "sacred" Capitol were bright with their bonnets. They thronged its corridors, sending in their cards to summon acquaintances from the floor of Senate and House. If her husband were occupied, it was considered correct for a lady to be escorted to a levee by one of his friends. Failing a female companion for a tour of the public buildings, she might with decorum accept the attendance of a child. In the H Street mansion of Mr. W. W. Corcoran, there was an octagonal alcove, hung with red velvet, where the famous statue of the *Greek Slave* stood, protected by a gilded chain. It was nakedness, but it was art, and even ladies looked and admired.

The social season opened on New Year's, which throughout the country had become a day of great jollification, of paying calls and making presents and drinking eggnogs and hot punch. In Washington, the hospitable custom of keeping open house prevailed in official as well as private circles, and on New Year's Day was held the first of the winter receptions at the Executive Mansion. No refreshments were offered at these functions, but the general public—or at least the part of it that was white and respectably dressed—circulated freely in the mansion, and shook the President's hand.

After the first of January, the round of entertainment began. The morning and afternoon levees, the "at homes" and dinners and musicales were but preludes to the splendor of the balls and the big evening parties with music and supper. By night, gloomy streets resounded with the restless stamping of horses, the crack of whips and the shouts of coachmen, as the carriages moved slowly into line, and before some lighted residence discharged their freights of ladies, shaped like great bells. The fragile, low-cut evening dresses of the 1850's were fashioned of gauze and illusion, and garlanded with roses, white clematis, water lilies, violets or scarlet honeysuckle; and headdresses matched the blossoms that swelled on the corsage and trailed on the distended skirts.

Save for a few old-fashioned fellows, invulnerable to the new craze for mustaches, almost all the gentlemen had ceased to shave their upper lips. Southerners wore their hair in long, flowing locks. American men made as yet no strict distinction between daytime and evening dress, wearing impartially their best black or blue broadcloth swallowtails with bright buttons. Many of them, even in the exclusive circles of Washington society, were not yet aware that in London a white neckcloth was considered indispensable for evening, and sported large colored cravats above their brocaded and embroidered waistcoats. The foreign ministers were resplendent in court costumes, trimmed with gold and silver lace and sparkling with orders. In the radiance of the gaslight from cut-glass chandeliers, ladies and gentlemen promenaded arm in arm, danced vivacious quadrilles and waltzes and germans, and partook heartily of the supper supplied by the fashionable French caterer, Gautier. There were oysters and lobster and terrapin, wild turkey and partridge and quail; and Gautier excelled in satisfying the eye as well as the appetite by his table decorations of confectionery towers, castles, pyramids and pagodas.

By 1856, the halls of Congress were noisy with angry debates over the admission of the territory of Kansas. Free-Soil and slavery men were aligned in violent opposition; but the controversies were still blandly ignored in the parlors. Through the pretense of polite oblivion sounded the thwacks of Preston Brooks's cane, raining blows on the head of Senator Sumner, as he sat writing at his desk in the Senate Chamber. Sumner, a moralistic anti-slavery crusader, had made an intemperate speech on the jangling question of Kansas. Brooks, a congressman from South Carolina, took it upon himself to reply by breaking Sumner's head. Washingon society was well acquainted with the handsome, cultured and priggish senator from Massachusetts. He had been fond of earnestly discoursing to Southern ladies on suitable subjects—laces, intaglios and the history of dancing. All his courtesy and erudition had been of no avail. Preston Brooks was the great hero of the Southern chivalry. Northerners, on the other hand, were indignant over the assault, which critically injured Sumner's spine, and kept him for three and a half years from active duty in the Senate.

Less than a year after Brooks made his attack, Washington welcomed Mr. Buchanan of Pennsylvania with open arms. The new President, though tall, ruddy and silver-haired, had one badly squinting eye, which he kept habitually closed, and he held his head stiffly inclined toward his left shoulder. Old Buck's head, said Major B. B. French, a prominent Washington Republican, was "all askew like a cow with the horn-ail." His admirers, however, thought that Mr. Buchanan had a fine presence. His political views were congenial to the best people of the capital, and he was very fond of society.

The President's habits, like those of Washington, were simple. As though he had not recently returned from the court circles of England, where he had served as United States minister, he walked every day for an hour on Pennsylvania Avenue, affably greeting his acquaintances. In summer, for the sake of his health, Mr. Buchanan accepted the use of a modest stone cottage at the Soldiers' Home, but he did not otherwise use his coach and horses a dozen times a year. On Saturday afternoons, when Scala's Marine Band played in the President's Park, he mingled with the populace on the lawn. He invited friends to sit for a neighborly afternoon at the Executive Mansion, and often at small dinners carved the roast himself. He always wore a big old-fashioned standing collar with a starched white choker, like a poultice around his neck.

Buchanan was a bachelor. His niece, who had been with him in London, presided over the Executive Mansion. Though youthful, Miss Harriet Lane had poise and social experience, and she was vastly admired. Lace berthas became the fashion because she wore them, a revenue cutter was given her name, and a new song, "Listen to the Mocking Bird," was dedicated to her. Tactful, correct and violet-eyed, Miss Lane had strict ideas of etiquette. Dinner guests at the mansion were formally presented before moving to the dining-room. In spite of the French cooking and the nutty old Madeira, the President's parties were stiff. Mr. Buchanan was anecdotal, but cold. Miss Lane's "gracious chill" added the last austerity to appointments which were considered far from lavish. No flowers ornamented the dinner table, there were no bouquets at the covers. Indeed, there were so few flowers in the house that a stand of potted plants and a small palm rose conspicuously out of a circular divan in the Blue Room. Jefferson Davis is said to have compared Mr. Buchanan's administration to an elegant republican court, and a colonial bleakness breathes from the admiring phrase.

The President was not niggardly. To pay his household expenses, he was obliged to supplement his salary of twenty-five thousand dollars by drawing on his private purse. Washington society, however, was growing increasingly competitive in extravagant entertainment, and its leaders were immensely rich. William M. Gwin, the pro-slavery senator from California, was believed to be spending seventy-five thousand dollars a year on the maintenance of his mansion at Nineteenth and I Streets; and two Cabinet members lived on the same scale—Mr. Jacob Thompson of Mississippi, and Mr. Aaron Brown of Tennessee, who was Postmaster General during the first years of the administration. One of the wealthiest Washington residents was the banker, Mr. Corcoran. His palatial residence on H Street contained an art gallery whose treasures were destined for the public in the building which he was erecting at Seventeenth Street and the Avenue. Mr. Corcoran was famous for his hospitality and his Johannisberg, and there were also splendid parties at the homes of other Washingtonians, the Riggses, the Parkers and the Tayloes. Their friends, Secretary Cobb, Mr. Justice Campbell of the Supreme Court and Senator Slidell of Louisiana all entertained handsomely. The wife of the senator from Georgia, Mrs. Toombs, though she was a sober lady with but one daughter, spent twenty-one thousand dollars a year.

In an unimproved section, I Street west of New Jersey Avenue, Senator Stephen A. Douglas, the popular Democratic leader of the free States, had built one of the finest houses in the capital. Vice-President John C. Breckinridge of Kentucky and Senator Henry M.

Rice of Minnesota built on adjoining lots, and the three new houses were known as Minnesota Row. Douglas had made his residence, with its elegantly furnished parlors and steam-heated greenhouse, a suitable background for the loveliness of his young bride, who had been Adele Cutts, a famous Washington belle. With her favorite japonicas in her hair and in huge bouquets, Mrs. Douglas gave many levees, which were thronged by the fashionable company of the capital. The pressure of their social engagements was quite exhausting to the ladies of Washington. To prepare herself for the evening, after a strenuous day, pretty Mrs. Clement C. Clay was refreshed by charges from an electrical apparatus, operated by her capable maid, for whom the senator from Alabama had paid sixteen hundred dollars.

In an atmosphere of unremitting gaiety, the intercourse between Southerners and all but a few Northerners became increasingly ceremonious. At the very outset of Mr. Buchanan's term, the agitation over slavery had been doubled by the opinion of the predominantly Southern Supreme Court in the case of the slave, Dred Scott. The aged Marylander, Chief Justice Taney, had taken this occasion to affirm that Congress had no power to prohibit slavery in the territories, and Free-Soil men roared a protest at the subservience of the Federal judiciary to the slaveholders. Insulting and inflammatory speeches were made on both sides, as Congress continued to be rocked by partisan struggles for the control of "bleeding Kansas." In the city, the political lines were drawn through neighborhoods, churches and families. Senator Douglas broke with Buchanan's pro-slavery administration, and was henceforth regarded by the chivalry as little better than a Black Republican.

In the autumn of 1859, John Brown's raid on the United States arsenal at Harper's Ferry jarred the South like an explosion, and raised the cry that Republicans were instigators of lawlessness and murder. The Virginia town at the confluence of the Shenandoah and the Potomac was only fifty-five miles from Washington, and the slaveholding community shared the alarms of its neighboring State. Even after the insignificance of the old fanatic's force was realized and the fear of attack had passed, there was dread of a Negro uprising in the capital. Typical of Washington's Southern viewpoint was the apprehension with which the city regarded its colored population. As a result of anti-Negro riots fourteen years before, an effort had been made to revive the District militia, but in 1859 only four small companies were in existence. The United States military force in the District, one hundred and six marines, had been rushed to Harper's Ferry, under the command of Colonel Robert E. Lee. The mayor secured arms from the War Department, and stationed mounted men on the roads leading into the city. Colored people were forbidden to congregate while the excitement lasted. Washington, sharply aware of its defenseless condition, made another effort to build up its militia. A number of recruits came forward, but soldiering was never popular with the citizens.

When Congress opened that winter, the Capitol rang with the name of John Brown. In the Senate, the discussion was all of the irrepressible conflict and the impending crisis. Southern hotspurs were shouting for State sovereignty and disunion, and the taunt was often heard that Northern men were cowards and would not fight. Political differences had led to rancorous personal animosities. Charles Sumner, returning to his seat after his long illness, was welcomed by no Democratic senator. In the House, there were violent quarrels in which blows were barely averted. Many Republicans buckled revolvers under their coats, and escorted less bellicose colleagues to and from the Capitol, to protect them from assault. Senator Zachariah Chandler of Michigan took muscular exercise and practiced marksmanship. The story was told that Benjamin F. Wade of Ohio carried a brace of horse pistols into the Senate, and laid them on the lid of his desk, looking around with his sharp little eyes and his grim smile until he was sure they had been noticed.

In any mixed social gathering, politics had become a forbidden subject. With doubt and bitterness in their hearts, people conversed on neutral topics: the disturbances in Italy, or the figure of Armed Freedom which the late Thomas Crawford had modeled for the Capitol dome; Tennyson's poems, or Thackeray's new book, *The Virginians*, or *Adam Bede* by the young Englishman, George Eliot, whose novels were the latest literary discovery. The friends of the administration, the Slidells, the Toombses, the Gwins, the Clays and the Jefferson Davises formed a tight little clique. Small parties had become strictly sectional. Foreign ministers consulted the map of the United States in making up their dinners.

Among the impassioned Southern ladies, there was one who continued to receive Republicans. This was Mrs. Rose O'Neal Greenhow, a native of Maryland and the aunt of Mrs. Stephen Douglas. As the wife of a scholarly Virginian, Robert Greenhow, she had long been a leader in the society of the capital. Since his death, she had lived with her daughters in a small house on the corner of Sixteenth Street, across from St. John's Church. Mrs. Greenhow was no longer young, but she had the reputation of being the most persuasive woman in Washington. To her cosy parlors, divided by a red gauze, came many important personages, and she was on intimate terms with the President himself. A few weeks after John Brown was hanged, Mrs. Greenhow had the temerity to invite Senator Seward of New York and Congressman and Mrs. Charles Francis Adams of Massachusetts to a dinner party otherwise composed of Southerners. Mrs. Adams was tactless enough to speak in praise of John Brown, and her hostess answered her with emphasis and heat. Mrs. Greenhow decided that she would not mix her dinner parties again; but she continued to see much of Senator Seward, and also of another Republican whose antislavery views had made him highly offensive to Southerners, Senator Henry Wilson of Massachusetts.

In the spring of 1860, Scott's military secretary, Colonel Keyes, accompanied the General on a visit to Washington, and attended a number of dinner parties, at which he heard much talk about the national crisis. One night he sat next the Detroit merchant, Zach Chandler, "full of war and blood—in a whisper." On other occasions, flirtatious Southern ladies disturbed him by "the incandescence of their treason." Mrs. Greenhow tried to discourage Keyes from taking any part in the coming war by arguing that the Southern coasts were sickly in the summer. He felt that she showed her woman's weakness by prescribing remedies against the miasmas. Keyes was a strong Union man, but he was a romantic widower of fifty. He confessed that, though he was never diverted from his loyalty to his country, the blandishments of the ladies from the slave States often lured him "to the brink of the precipice."

The exciting prospect of secession preoccupied the society of the capital. Southerners realistically faced the possibility that it might lead to civil war; but they were convinced that the cowardly Yankees would soon be beaten. Soldiers were drilling and arming in the slave States, and Washington belles discussed the military preparations and the forts at dinners and balls and supper parties. Festivities were touched with the exotic splendor of the Orient, when the Japanese ambassadors visited Washington with a large suite. The representatives of the Tycoon, with their fantastically dressed hair, their fans and their richly embroidered robes, girt by two swords, made a great stir in the capital. Everyone turned out to see them received with ceremony at the Executive Mansion, and they were entertained at private parties. Even the recess of Congress in the summer of 1860 was not without variety. The corps of Chicago Zouaves came to Washington in August in gaudy Algerian uniforms which appeared almost as outlandish as the costumes of the Japanese. Young Colonel Elmer E. Ellsworth, who had drilled them and taken them on tour, had awakened enthusiasm for the formation of Zouave companies throughout the country. By invitation, the Chicago Zouaves performed their eccentric drill on the White House lawn in the presence of Mr. Buchanan and Miss Lane.

The social season opened with unwonted earliness that year, for in October Mr. Buchanan was host to Baron Renfrew, the name assumed on his travels by Albert Edward, Prince of Wales. This "peachy-cheeked, beardless boy" was already a model for diplomats. At a reception, he immediately removed his gloves when he saw that the President wore none. On observing that Mr. Buchanan shook hands with those who were presented, the Prince hastened to shake hands, too. Conducted on the revenue cutter, *Harriet Lane,* to the ruinous house at Mount Vernon, he stood uncovered before George Washington's tomb, and obligingly planted a small tree in its vicinity. Mr. Buchanan was able to write the Queen that her son had made an excellent impression on "a sensitive and discriminating people."

The cloud of the Presidential election hung heavy over the capital. Out on Minnesota Row were domiciled two of the candidates: Douglas, standard-bearer of the Northern Democrats, and Breckinridge, who was the choice of the South. Though the people of the District wanted a voice in the national decision, they were energetic in forming partisan associations. Clubs had been organized to support the leaders of both the Democratic factions, as well as the candidate of the conservatives, John Bell, and the Black Republican, Abraham Lincoln. The National Volunteers, a Democratic organization which stood for Southern rights, competed in their parades with Republican Wide Awakes, wearing glazed caps and capes, and brandishing torches. Feeling ran high, and on the night of Lincoln's election a mob attacked the local Republican wigwam, and partially wrecked the building before being dispersed by the police.

From Charleston, waving with palmetto banners instead of the Stars and Stripes, there were echoes of artillery and cheers and calls to arms. Already the Federal courts were suspended in South Carolina. The senators from that State did not come to the Capitol in December. On either side of the splendid new Senate Chamber, the extremists of North and South were drawn in hostile ranks. In the chair sat the ultra-Democrat, Breckinridge. The business of the nation was taken up in the harsh lull of the deadlock in which the sections were implacably joined. Under the leadership of two Democrats who had risen above partisan feuds, the venerable Crittenden of Kentucky, and Douglas of Illinois, moderate-minded men were still hoping to arrange some compromise.

The senators from the cotton States sat in the Capitol of the Union, dreaming of a new empire which would make the Gulf of Mexico a western Mediterranean. There was no hope of compromise with boisterous, swaggering Toombs of Georgia, or his truculent colleague, Iverson; with insolent Slidell of Louisiana, or Judah P. Benjamin, with his purring, musical voice and his lawyer's subtleties; with sick, defiant Clay of Georgia, or Wigfall of Texas, with his fierce, scarred face. Most influential among them was a cold, fastidious man, Jefferson Davis of Mississippi. He was a graduate of West Point, who had served with distinction in Mexico, and had been Secretary of War during the Pierce administration. In his military bearing and romantic conceptions of honor, he symbolized the Southern ideal which had produced this revolution. Such men would listen to no appeals to patriotism. "You cannot save this Union by making 4th of July speeches," sneered Senator Wigfall. "Whipped syllabub is not the remedy for the patient. You have got to come down to your work, and you have got to do something practical."

On the other side of the Senate Chamber sat men who were no less unyielding, the men who had grown strong with the rise of the young Republican party; men who denied State sovereignty, hated slavery and loved power. No concessions to the South would come from bluff Ben Wade, or from Zach Chandler, who thought the Union would be the better for a little bloodletting; from Hale of New Hampshire, Fessenden of Maine, Trumbull of Illinois, or Grimes of Iowa; from Henry Wilson of Massachusetts, or the cultured crusader, Sumner, who could be surprisingly vulgar in the passion of controversy. The leader of the Republican party, William H. Seward of

New York, was a different person altogether. He was bland and mysterious and equivocating. He had made no public declaration of his views, and the radical Republicans were beginning to draw away from him because he was supposed to be in favor of conciliating the South.

While the galleries applauded the sentiments of secession, and the mediators worked to save the country, like a bucket brigade at a conflagration, a solitary Southern senator arose to speak on behalf of the Union. Andrew Johnson of Tennessee was no kin of the cavaliers. He was a demagogue, coarse, honest and courageous, and he did not mince his words in condemning secession. The seizure of Federal property in South Carolina was treason, he said, and nothing but treason.

A few days before Christmas, the President attended a fashionable wedding. As he wearily sat in the parlor, breathing the fragrance of unseasonable roses and lilies, he was startled by a hubbub in the hall. He asked Mrs. Roger Pryor, wife of the disunionist congressman from Virginia, whether the house were on fire. She might imaginatively have answered, yes. The shouts were those of rejoicing over a telegram announcing the secession of South Carolina. The President called for his carriage.

Congress received the expected news calmly, but there was contention at the War and Navy Departments, where voices angrily resounded long after the offices were closed. As the brief afternoon darkened in a drizzle of rain, the tidings reached the hotels. It was the late dinner hour, and dining-rooms and corridors were shaken with excitement, as men with the blue cockades of the secessionists brushed jubilantly past those who wore the colors of the Union. One man thought that there was as much treason talked in Washington as in Charleston. That evening, Southern leaders, after celebrating in the parlor of Senator Jefferson Davis, went to call at the Executive Mansion. Mrs. Davis preceded them, hastening impetuously ahead to share the good news with the President.

Across the joyous emblems of Christmas fell the shadow of the palmetto and the rattlesnake. In hopes of stimulating the lagging holiday trade, the small shops dressed their windows, and inserted their notices in the newspapers. Gifts were enticingly suggested for every variety of taste: shaving cases and motto coffee cups and albums; glove boxes, odor stands and *tête-à-tête* tea sets; backgammon boards and battledores and wax dolls with moving eyes. Gautier was ready to take orders for Christmas cakes, both pound and fruit. Madame Delarue announced a shipment of full-dress bonnets and Jouvin's gloves, just received from Paris. Some of the advertisements sounded a timely note. "Readers, the Union is in danger, but by buying your holiday presents at Lammond's, you *may* save it." After Christmas, there were new alarms in the capital, and Galt, the jeweler, marked down his watches and silverware to "panic prices."

Fears for the security of Washington had sharpened with secessionist agitation in Maryland and Virginia. On the floor of the Senate, Iverson of Georgia had suggested that Washington might be the capital of the Southern confederacy. On Christmas Day, the Richmond *Examiner* had boldly called for Maryland men to join with Virginians in seizing the Capitol. There were persistent rumors of a secret secessionist organization in Washington, which was plotting to capture the city and the public archives, and assume control of the Government. Senator Seward, who was no alarmist, wrote the President-elect in late December that such a conspiracy was forming, and that it had its accomplices in the public councils. So great was the anxiety for the Capitol building that guards were placed at the main entrances, and the cellar was searched nightly for explosives.

At the same time, there was a fresh crisis in South Carolina. As though the Union were a precious substance, held in delicate equilibrium, Mr. Buchanan had been fearful of making the slightest movement. Ironically, he was thrown off balance by the act of a Southern sympathizer, committed on behalf of the Federal authority. Major Anderson, who commanded the United States forts in Charleston harbor, was a Kentuckian with a stern sense of duty. Fearing an attack on his untenable position at Fort Moultrie, he dismantled it, and transferred the little garrison to Fort Sumter, which commanded the harbor. South Carolina interpreted Anderson's move as an act of aggression. It immediately assumed the proportions of a vexing incident, and Mr. Buchanan was aghast at the news of it.

Three South Carolina commissioners, arrived in Washington to treat with the Government like envoys of a foreign power, pressed Mr. Buchanan hard, telling him that his personal honor was involved. The President dodged and hedged and pleaded for time. Before making any important decision, he told them, he always said his prayers. The interview was succeeded by a demand that United States troops should be entirely withdrawn from Charleston harbor. Buchanan would have yielded to the influence of his Southern friends, had it not been for the recent shift in the sentiment of his Cabinet. Cobb had gone, to lead the secession movement in Georgia, and the Virginia disunionist, Floyd, would soon be forced to resign. As Secretary of War, he would be succeeded by the Postmaster General, Joseph Holt of Kentucky, who had swung to a firm national policy after the secession of South Carolina. Although Jacob Thompson of Mississippi still lingered at his post, men of Union sympathies were in the ascendancy in the President's council, and they persuaded him to an assertion of authority. At last, he wrote the palmetto commissioners that the United States garrison would remain where it was, and he granted permission to General Scott to reinforce Fort Sumter. The President's decision cut short the social activities of the commissioners, who had rented a fine house as a suitable ambassadorial background. They had been cordially welcomed by the chivalry, but on the night before their departure the police were called out to prevent a tin-pan serenade which less fashionable elements in Washington were proposing to offer to the gentlemen from South Carolina.

During the days of painful suspense, when the attention of the country was fixed on the conclaves at the Executive Mansion, Mr. Buchanan had received a call from Benjamin F. Butler, a Breckinridge Democrat from Massachusetts. In the President's office, they sat face to face, but not eye to eye, for Butler, too, had a startling squint. He was a stout, crafty-looking, forceful little man, and he had his own plan for solving the country's predicament. He advised Mr. Buchanan to have the South Carolina commissioners arrested and tried for treason before the Supreme Court, the judgment of which would determine the rights of secession. Mr. Buchanan, blanching at the very mention of such bold action, could only reply that it would lead to great agitation.

Ben Butler heard from Southern men in Washington that the North would never fight, but he told them that it would, and he would fight with it. He was a brigadier-general of militia in Massachusetts, which had several enthusiastic organizations of citizen soldiers. He was hopeful that the nation might find some remedy, but, after he had taken tea with Senator Davis, he saw that war was inevitable.

Mr. Buchanan later protested that during this period his mood had been serene, and that he had "not lost an hour's sleep or a single meal." Unsympathetic observers, on the other hand, described him as a broken old man, who did nothing but cry and pray. The first picture seems nearly as exaggerated as the second. He had ordered a day of national prayer and humiliation, and was preparing a special message to Congress which reflected his despair at the progress of revolution. At Charleston, the palmetto banner waved over Fort Moultrie and Castle Pinckney, as well as the United States arsenal and other Governmental property. The fever of secession was spreading through the cotton States. There were scandalous irregularities in the disunionist administration of the War and Interior Departments; while the Treasury was in a state that threatened financial ruin to the country. Among the rumors with which the capital was humming was the story of a plot, headed by Senator Wigfall, to kidnap the President, and install Breckinridge in his place. At his New Year reception, Mr. Buchanan's face was haggard. The calls were fewer than usual. The East Room seemed almost deserted. Many of the visitors, wearers of Union and secession cockades alike, refused to shake the President's proffered hand.

The old politician from Pennsylvania was timid, not treacherous. In ordinary times, he might have retired with honor at the close of his term. He had been caught in the glare of a crucial moment of history. Even his Southern friends, to whom he had conceded so much, had turned against him. At a dinner party at Mr. Corcoran's, General Scott witnessed the passionate outbursts of Senator Toombs and Senator Benjamin, who cursed the President, along with Major Anderson and the Union. In the end, his sundered country was united only in the opinion that Mr. Buchanan was a coward and a fool. Sinking heavily into a chair in Scott's headquarters, he exclaimed, "The office of President of the United States is not fit for a gentleman to hold!"

With the New Year, the temper of the North was growing increasingly conciliatory. In answer, the news of secession came, like hammer strokes, from the cotton States. Mississippi was the first to follow the lead of South Carolina. Florida and Alabama hurried close behind; then Georgia, Louisiana and Texas. The seceded States seized United States property within their borders—forts, arsenals, customhouses, revenue cutters. The Government made no effort to reclaim them, and its passivity was matched by that of the free States.

Their people were so apathetic that there was no great indignation when South Carolina guns fired on the Union flag, and drove off the *Star of the West,* carrying reinforcements to Fort Sumter. Late in January, however, there was a sign that Northerners were discouraged and leaderless, rather than indifferent to the fate of their country. John A. Dix, a reactionary Democrat from New York, who had been appointed Secretary of the Treasury, was incensed by the continued seizure of revenue cutters in Southern ports. He telegraphed a revenue official at New Orleans, "If any one attempts to haul down the American flag, shoot him on the spot." The words sounded like a trumpet call from the timorous silence of Washington, and the North applauded the Government official who had dared to speak out for the nation.

In the Senate, Mr. Seward of New York had made his long-awaited speech. He was the idol of the masses of the Republicans. Before the nomination of the Westerner, Lincoln, it had been taken for granted that he would be the Republican candidate for President. In January, it was known that he would head the Cabinet of the new administration; would, in short, be President in all but name. Many looked to him to save the country.

Governor Seward, as he was usually called, was a complex personality. He was gentlemanly, subtle and smiling, but not quite elegant or effete; there was too much of western New York for that. He was brilliant and cynical, but not quite a polished trifler; he was too much the man of the party machine, the intimate of the astute political manager, Thurlow Weed. In spite of his sixty years, he attracted young men by his warmth and kindness, and by the unassuming simplicity of his manner. Although his doctrine of "the irrepressible conflict" between free labor and slavery had made him hated throughout the South, he was considered a man without convictions, a Jesuit and an opportunist; he was the affectionate friend of Jefferson Davis; and not Mr. Buchanan himself was more earnest in the cause of propitiating the slave States.

Seward's policy was one of temporizing and conceding, of delaying hostilities until the Republicans should have time to organize in March. Working outside the Government, he had established a network of secret alliances which extended deep into the slaveholding States. He was informed of the proceedings of Buchanan's Cabinet by one of its members, who, save for a talent for intrigue and a strong sentiment for the Union, was Mr. Seward's antithesis. This was Edwin M. Stanton, a domineering, cross-grained Washington lawyer, able but without national reputation, who had been given the office of Attorney General in December. That winter, he was conferring with two other politicians who were peculiar confidants for a Breckinridge Democrat—Zach Chandler and Charles Sumner. To prevent suspicion, Stanton's reports to Seward were always made through a third man, and, except for one chance encounter in F Street, they did not meet during the Buchanan administration.

When, on January 12, Seward arose in the crowded Senate Chamber, he seemed the only tranquil person there. As he had already publicly pronounced that all would be right in sixty days, he was believed to have developed some clever, guarded plan; and before this slender, slouching figure in a gray frock coat, Northerners and Southerners sat hushed and tense. No expectation of eloquence moved them, for Seward was an indifferent speaker. He delivered his carefully prepared addresses in a perfunctory way; and his husky voice had been weakened by excessive cigar smoking and the use of snuff. But he represented the new administration and the unknown quantity at Springfield. Optimistic and debonair, he represented hope. In a time of chaos, it was reassuring that a man could know so much and still smile.

Seward's affability was impenetrable; it had covered many thoughts. He had smiled when Southern ladies refused to meet him, and when hotheaded young senators from the slave States had ignored his greeting. He had smiled after he had lost the Republican nomination for President, the crowning ambition of his career. Too much had been expected of one adroit politician. His vague and conciliatory phrases antagonized radical Republicans and disunionists alike. Events were moving with an inexorable speed. As States seceded, their delegates withdrew from Senate and House. Representatives, for the most part, left quietly, but in the Senate there were oratorical ebullitions of defiance and farewell. The senators from Florida, Alabama and Mississippi pronounced their valedictories on the same day, while trembling Southern ladies packed the galleries, sitting on the floor and crowding the doorways. As the speeches were delivered, they waved their handkerchiefs and cried out in sympathy with secession. Even Republican ladies wept at the pathetic close of Senator Jefferson Davis's address. In a voice strained by emotion, he expressed the hope that the relations between North and South would be peaceful; if, in the heat of debate, he had given offense to any senator, he offered his apologies. The senator from Mississippi spoke without bravado. He cherished the bold dream of a new confederacy; but, more than most of his Southern colleagues, he counted its probable cost. He thought that only fools doubted the courage of Yankees, and that, if war should come, it would not soon be over.

The dawn of 1861 had cheered General Scott by bringing him into a close relation with the Government. He had promptly been called into consultation by Holt, under whose control the War Department had ceased its favors to the revolutionary senators and representatives. After the unhappy expedition of the *Star of the West*, the reinforcement of Fort Sumter was held in abeyance. Major Anderson was as solicitous as the administration to avoid any act which might precipitate hostilities; and the secessionist leaders, to gain time for their political and military preparations, exercised a restraining influence on the South Carolina hotheads. An informal truce was arranged, not only in the case of Sumter, but also of Fort Pickens in Pensacola harbor, which by Scott's orders had been occupied by United States troops. These and two forts at the southern tip of Florida, whose garrisons Scott strengthened, were the only property which the Government held in the then seceded States. Small detachments of soldiers were also sent to a few military points in the border slave States, including Fort Washington, on the Maryland side of the Potomac, across from Mount Vernon. Although the fort, fallen into rust and rot, was useless for defense, it was vulnerable to occupation by a hostile force. Its entire garrison, before a company of marines was sent there from the Washington barracks, consisted of one old Irish pensioner, and General Scott said that it might easily have been taken by a bottle of whisky.

After the problem of the forts, the most pressing question before the General-in-Chief was the maintenance of order in the capital. It was feared that an uprising might occur during the count of the electoral vote in February, and there were convincing rumors that March 4 would be the occasion for a seditious outbreak. Men in high political positions had declared that Lincoln's inauguration should never take place. The *Constitution*, the local disunionist newspaper, which received the patronage of the Government, had advised preventing the inauguration by armed force. It was believed that Mayor James E.

Berret, a Breckinridge Democrat, was in accord with the secessionists.

From his Democratic associates, Ben Butler had heard much of the treasonable talk which was current in the capital. One evening a Washington acquaintance, after dining with Butler at his hotel, proposed a walk. Taking their cigars, the two men strolled west on K Street, and stopped near some low buildings, like market sheds. In the wall of one of them was a hole, through which Butler peered at a company, drilling with arms. They were getting ready for the fourth of March, his friend told him.

"Drilling a company of the District militia to escort Lincoln?" Butler asked.

The Washington man laughed. "Yes, they may escort Lincoln," he said, "but I guess not in the direction of the White House."

Early in January, in his special message to Congress, the President felt it necessary to mention that the capital would be adequately protected at the coming inauguration. General Scott was working in co-operation with Senator James W. Grimes of Iowa and Congressman Elihu B. Washburne of Illinois, who composed an investigating committee, appointed by Congress. These gentlemen appealed to the New York chief of police, and detectives in long beards and slouched hats, chewing tobacco and damning Yankees, went to work in Washington, Baltimore, Richmond and Alexandria.

Scott had called in an Army officer, Charles P. Stone, who had served under the General in Mexico; and, after Stone had outlined an acceptable plan for the defense of the capital, he was assigned to the duty of organizing and drilling the District militia. He entered energetically on his work, for after several months' residence in Washington he had become convinced that two-thirds of the population would sustain the Government in defending it.

The four existing organizations of citizen soldiers, three in Washington and one in Georgetown, were already supplied with arms. The Georgetown company, though it contained some dubious members, seemed in the main well-disposed; while the Washington Light Infantry and the National Guard Battalion were old and dependable establishments. The third and most fashionable militia organization in Washington, the National Rifles, was a hotbed of disloyalty. It was commanded by Captain F. B. Schaeffer, an employee of the Department of the Interior, who had formerly been a lieutenant in the United States Artillery. Schaeffer had more than a hundred men, mostly Marylanders, on his company's rolls, and they were remarkably well armed and drilled. Colonel Stone was surprised to find that, in addition to rifles and ammunition, they possessed a supply of sabers and revolvers and two mountain howitzers, with harness and carriages, all drawn from the United States Arsenal. When he complimented Schaeffer on the excellence of the company's drill, the militia captain remarked that he supposed he should soon have to lead his men to the Maryland frontier, to keep the Yankees from coming down to coerce the South.

Through a detective who enlisted in the company, Stone obtained reports on the new recruits, many of whom were avowed secessionists. He ordered Schaeffer to deposit in the armory the howitzers and other unsuitable armament, and the order was obeyed. Eventually, the captain resigned, taking the elite of his men with him to serve in the South.

A company of the semi-political National Volunteers, who had agitated for Southern rights during the Presidential campaign, was also holding nightly drills. The Washington *Evening Star* attacked the National Volunteers in January as a disloyal organization, whose intention was to prevent Lincoln's inauguration. One of Stone's detectives reported that the seizure of the city was openly discussed at their meetings. A committee of five, appointed by the House to inquire into the rumors of conspiracy, questioned Mayor Berret, who endorsed the National Volunteers as a non-political body, composed of respectable citizens. Their senior officer, a secessionist called Dr. Cornelius Boyle, assured the congressmen that the association was not secret and had no unlawful purpose. Although the committee uncovered much disloyal activity, it cautiously reported that it had found no evidence to prove the existence in the District of an organization hostile to the Government; and that, if such a combination had been projected, it had been contingent on the secession of Maryland or Virginia, or both.

Before granting the National Volunteers' application for arms, Colonel Stone demanded their muster roll. Soon after the list was turned over, the leaders left for Richmond. Stone had no trouble in raising new volunteer companies for the preservation of order in the District. The alarmed citizens of Washington were anxious to protect their property. Prominent gentlemen lent their influence. Fire companies enrolled, and so did groups of artisans and German turners. By the middle of February, Stone had fourteen companies, over nine hundred men, ready for service; and he asserted that the number could be doubled on a week's notice. The only opposition he had encountered had come from the mayor, who refused to deliver the names and addresses of the city police.

General Scott was too old a soldier to place full reliance on citizens in an emergency. Aware that undisciplined men could not be trusted to hold their fire under a shower of stones and brickbats, he had felt it indispensable to order some regulars and especially some flying artillery to the city. Only eight companies could be spared from the Army to safeguard Washington. Three were brought from Kansas, and one from Plattsburg, New York; there were two companies that had been driven out of arsenals in Louisiana and Georgia; and two were taken from West Point.

Though Mr. Buchanan had been forced to yield to the representations of Scott and Holt, the idea of calling in soldiers filled him with perturbation. Washington was the most unmilitary of capitals. Apart from the handful of marines at the barracks, its only uniforms were those worn by a few naval officers and the doddering old generals at the War Department bureaus.

In late January, there was an especial reason for the Government to appear pacific and benign. With the defeat of plans for compromise in Congress, Virginia, most influential of the border States, was initiating a Peace Conference, to be held in Washington on February 4. The slave States of Maryland,. Kentucky, Tennessee, North Carolina, Missouri and Delaware accepted Virginia's invitation. If, in conference with the delegates of the free States, they could work out some amicable adjustment, it was hoped that the secession fever might abate, and the cotton States be persuaded to return to the Union. In readiness for the emissaries of peace, Mr. Chandlee, who had the card-writing stand at Willard's, advertised a line of cockades, "suitable for all shades of political sentiment." The arrival of armed forces, in Mr. Buchanan's opinion, would raise the cry of coercion, inflame the secessionists and irritate the border slave States.

The only available quarters for troops were the barracks at the Arsenal and the militia armory on the Mall. Arrangements were made for lodging companies in the Treasury Extension, in Judiciary Square, and on E Street. New barracks and stables were hastily erected on Capitol Hill, and in a lot west of the War Department. Arriving a few at a time, without fanfare or music or parade, the eight companies of hardy, well-drilled regulars were a sensation in Washington. Their gear encumbered the little depot; the saddles alone made a monument of baggage. Horses of cavalry and artillery, restless after the confinement of the boxcars, kicked up their heels in the streets. Brass fieldpieces stuck in the mud, and were dragged out with shouts that brought the crowds running. A battery of light artillery sent the city into a panic by firing a salute of thirty-four guns in honor of the admission of the free State of Kansas to the Union. The residents mistook the thundering volleys for an attack by secession troops from Virginia; while disunionist ladies at the National, apprehensive of Federal belligerence, began to pack their trunks for a hasty retreat. On a dark early morning, drum taps in E Street frightened good citizens from their beds. Hoisting windows and thrusting their nightcapped heads into the fog, they discovered that the uproar was not revolution, but reveille. Mounted soldiers pounded up and down the Avenue, exercising the horses. The Government reservations were muddy; and perhaps the regulars enjoyed cutting a figure in the national capital. It does not, for example, seem necessary for exercising horses that one company of artillerymen should have worn their old hats with the red plumes, which made a fine appearance and aroused much admiration.

The Peace delegates from the border slave States glowered under their slouched hats, and Mr. Buchanan must have winced when he took his constitutional. He might have regretted the weakness that had made him send for General Scott, for here, in every gun and plume and prancing horse, was the logical consequence of becoming involved with a soldier. Scott took no stock in peace congresses, regarding them as collections of visionaries and fanatics. In this instance, he was wrong, for among the delegates were many eminent gentlemen. On the very day that representatives of the seceded States met at Montgomery, Alabama, the Peace Conference foregathered in a large, bare room, a former Presbyterian church, which had been assimilated by the spreading structure of Willard's. Before a fine portrait of George Washington, loaned by the mayor, a quavering, suave old man, ex-President John Tyler of Virginia, occupied the chair. Reporters were excluded from the meetings; and, with moderate secrecy, the sections collided behind closed doors. Presently, "with the solemnity of a funeral procession," they marched to the Executive Mansion, where Mr. Buchanan received them with streaming eyes, and implored them to arrange some compromise.

General Scott's adherence to the Government had not passed un-noticed in the South. His mail was growing heavy with threats of assassination. He had been burned in effigy at the University of Virginia, and representatives of his native State had denounced him on the floor of the House as an ungrateful and parricidal son. The General was in agreement with Hobbes, that war is the natural state of man; but he had not been thinking of civil war. It was his greatest wish to keep the peace. His many visitors were, however, impressed with his firm intention to suppress insurrection in the capital. An emissary, sent by the President-elect to sound out his loyalty, was completely reassured. The General, suffering from an attack of dys-entery, received the Illinois man in bed, and declared that he would be responsible for Lincoln's safety whenever he was ready to come to Washington. If necessary, he would plant cannon at both ends of Pennsylvania Avenue, and blow to hell any Maryland and Virginia gentlemen who showed their heads.

Meanwhile, in mansions and hotels, the dark-skinned maids had packed their mistresses' dresses. The body servants had laid out their masters' traveling shawls. "We must make concessions!" cried the North; but the steamers bound for Aquia Creek were laden with the chivalry. Through the streets rattled baggage wagons, piled high with trunks and boxes. Houses were closed and dark. Broad-brimmed hats and blooded horses disappeared from Pennsylvania Avenue. The Toombses' coachman ran away, and the senator and his sober wife had to drive in a hired hack. Jefferson Davis left behind his tiny Japanese dog, "to be reclaimed when convenient." The Sardinian minister begged Mrs. Clement Clay not to weep, since it was but a revolution. Some journeyed South in proud expectation of the empire of King Cotton; some, in scorn for the Yankee traders and crude Westerners who would supplant them; some, in sorrow for lost friendships and old ambitions. A regime had ended in Washington.

The town was filling up with new arrivals, and among them were many Southerners. Baltimore plug-uglies, secessionist rowdies who were the allies of the Washington gangs, were filtering into the city. The atmosphere was tense with foreboding. Men scowled and mut-tered in the hotel lobbies, and groups stood whispering on the street corners. A young artist, Thomas Nast, who had come down to make sketches for a New York illustrated paper, would shudder at the memory of those weeks in Washington.

Early on the morning of February 13, crowds began to move up Capitol Hill. The regulars were at their posts. Horses and harness and guns were ready for an attack. At the entrances of the Capitol, soldiers turned away the general public, and admitted only those who held tickets. One hundred special policemen in plain clothes mingled with the arriving spectators in the gilded corridors. Many fashionable ladies decorated the galleries of the Hall of Representatives, fluttered about the cloakrooms, and even occupied seats surrendered by gallant members on the floor of the House. It was after twelve when the doorkeeper announced the Senate, and the defeated candidate, Breckinridge, entered at its head. Without untoward incident, the tellers opened and registered the electoral votes, and Breckinridge with pale-faced formality announced that Abraham Lincoln of Illinois had been elected President of the United States.

After the Senate had withdrawn, there were howls of disapproval from the floor and the galleries. Southerners cursed old Scott for a "free-State pimp," and protested at the presence of his "janizaries" about the Capitol. Outside, the crowd lingered on Capitol Hill. The saloons were full, and that night the city was noisy with street fights. In Republican eyes, every quarrelsome drunkard was a traitor, and every jostling rowdy was an armed invader; but no one dignified the brawling and disorder by the name of insurrection. The noisy Southern sympathizers were the scum of the secessionists, and had no relation with the reputable, hotheaded and personally ambitious gentlemen who were organizing the government of the Confederate States at Montgomery, Alabama.

One crisis was safely past, but another was to come. For the inauguration, General Scott was bringing a few more regulars to the city; and every day Republicans, eager for their first chance at the spoils of Federal patronage, were arriving in Washington. Sunburned, countrified, heavy-stepping Westerners were beginning to be familiar figures in the streets. In the anteroom of Mr. Buchanan's office, Republicans now waited to see him. Always an industrious worker, the President spent arduous hours at his desk; an Old Public Functionary (as he had once been unwise enough to call himself) in a dressing gown and slippers, with an unlighted cigar in his mouth. At White House receptions, it had been remarked that the attendance of Republicans was increasing; and, as their numbers mounted, Mr. Buchanan's levees grew in popularity. With his white cravat on his wry neck, the

President stood before the newcomers like a decadent patrician facing the hordes of the Vandals. His court was now in another sense Republican; but elegant it could by no stretch of the imagination be called. At the last reception in mid-February, five thousand people were present. Scala's Marine Band, discoursing music for the occasion, began its program with "Dixie" and closed with "Yankee Doodle." It was an epitome of Mr. Buchanan's administration.

III *Arrival of a Westerner*

WHILE PREPARATIONS were being made for the inauguration of Jefferson Davis as president of the Confederate States, Abraham Lincoln was traveling eastward from Illinois. He was accompanied by his wife and three sons, and by a suite of State politicians, personal friends, relatives by marriage, secretaries and newspaper correspondents; and he also had a military escort of four Army officers appointed by the War Department. One was a friend, Major David Hunter, an honest, anti-slavery paymaster, with a dyed mustache and a dark-brown wig. Young Captain John Pope was the son of an Illinois judge, while Colonel Edwin V. Sumner was a good old white-haired cavalry officer from Massachusetts.

The militia system was represented by Colonel Elmer E. Ellsworth, the Zouave drillmaster, who was entrusted with the responsibility of passing the President-elect through the crowds at his stopping places on the route. The man on whom Mr. Lincoln placed most dependence, however, was Ward Hill Lamon, a younger lawyer who had been associated with him in practice on the circuit. Lamon, a native of Virginia, resembled the chivalry in his long hair, defiant eyes and drooping mustaches. He had brought his banjo in his baggage, and amused the party with Negro songs. Of these, *The Blue-Tailed Fly,* a buzzing ballad, was a favorite with Mr. Lincoln; and he loved to listen to many other simple tunes, both sad and comical, that Lamon sang. In addition to the banjo, Lamon carried an assortment of pistols and knives, a slingshot and brass knuckles. He was powerfully built and fearless, and he considered himself especially charged with Mr. Lincoln's safe-conduct to Washington.

It was a tour and a progress, rather than a journey. The special trains, preceded by pilot engines, ran on carefully arranged schedules between the big cities where the President-elect had appointments for speeches and receptions. Past cheering miles of people, in a confusion of bonfires, parades, salutes and handshakings, Mr. Lincoln moved to the ovation in Philadelphia. After a trip to Harrisburg on February 22, he was to proceed to Washington, where he was expected late on the following afternoon. Among the invitations with which he had been deluged, none had come from Maryland. The omission was the more conspicuous, since a slow transit through the city of Baltimore, where the cars were separately drawn by horses between the depots, was unavoidable in journeying by rail to the capital from the North.

This impending passage through a disaffected community had been a source of considerable anxiety to Mr. Lincoln's friends. The Baltimore gangs were notoriously lawless, and Maryland was boiling with secession agitation. There, as in Washington, military companies of suspect loyalty had been drilling; and threats had been heard that Mr. Lincoln would never go through Baltimore alive. The President of the Philadelphia, Wilmington and Baltimore Railroad, Mr. Samuel M. Felton, not only felt the responsibility of conveying the President-elect across a hostile State, but he had been disturbed by reports of conspiracies to destroy railroad property. Some weeks earlier, he had sent for a trusted Chicago investigator, Allan Pinkerton, a Scottish barrelmaker who had founded one of the first private detective agencies in the United States. Pinkerton, who was also in the pay of Mr. Lincoln's Illinois advisers, placed spies in the military companies and secret societies in and about Baltimore. On receiving confirmation of the rumored plots to interrupt the railroad, Felton organized and armed some two hundred guards, whom he distributed in the guise of workmen along the line between the Susquehanna and Baltimore.

The dangers attendant on Mr. Lincoln's journey to Washington, as well as on his inauguration, had been recognized in Congress by the appointment of another committee of two, on which Congressman Washburne again represented the House, while Mr. Seward was the member for the Senate. As in the case of the committee on which Washburne served with Senator Grimes, there was close co-operation with General Scott. On February 21, Colonel Stone received a report from detectives he had placed in Baltimore that there was serious danger that Mr. Lincoln might be assassinated in passing through the city. Scott sent Stone posthaste to Seward, who agreed with the General's opinion that Mr. Lincoln should change his announced traveling schedule. To persuade him to do so, Seward dispatched his son, Frederick, to Philadelphia with a warning letter, enclosing Stone's report.

The Republicans of Washington were, in view of the ominous rumors, a stouthearted lot. They were erecting a large edifice in back of the City Hall for the inauguration ball. With eager anticipation, they were looking forward to receiving Mr. Lincoln at the depot on the afternoon of February 23, and they had prepared a quantity of banners with which to deck their wigwam. Meantime, the city was agog over the prospect of a military parade on Washington's Birthday. Early in the morning, the Avenue was cluttered with the wagons and drays of the country folk who had driven in to see the spectacle. By the market house, the City Hall and other vantage points, vendors set out tables of pigs' feet and gingerbread. Boys, with lettered placards on their breasts, offered patriotic songs for sale, and there were many flags with patriotic legends. Mr. Seward, since the New Year, had been agitating for a display of the national colors in the capital, and his efforts were rewarded on Washington's Birthday by an unusual show of red, white and blue. In the morning, the *National Intelligencer* carried the War Department's confirmation of the news for which everyone had been hoping, that the regulars would march, as well as the District militia.

At breakfast, however, General Scott had received an order countermanding the participation of the United States troops. The Virginian, John Tyler, was averse to this provocative exhibition of military force, and his protests had overwhelmed Mr. Buchanan. The militia proudly paced the Avenue, but there were no blue-clad regulars, no flying artillery nor plunging horses. Disappointment clouded the people's holiday spirits, as the rumor spread that the soldiers would not, after all, appear. The prevailing indignation was shared by Representative Daniel E. Sickles of New York, a close friend of the President. Two years earlier, Sickles had won great notoriety by shooting Mr. Philip Barton Key for trifling with his pretty wife. Key, the son of the author of "The Star-Spangled Banner," had been the District Attorney, and a popular figure in Washington society. His murder and the ensuing trial had made a tremendous sensation. Mr. Edwin M. Stanton, who conducted Dan Sickles's defence, had pleaded the unwritten law, and the verdict of acquittal had been cheered in the courtroom and received with delight by the President.

This impulsive congressman was enthusiastic for celebrating Washington's Birthday, and he rushed hotfoot to the War Office, where Secretary Holt was in conference with the President. Sickles's remonstrances induced Mr. Buchanan to change his mind, and Holt hurried off to General Scott's headquarters. The General felt a natural irritation. It was by this time midday. The officers had doffed their dress uniforms, and the soldiers had been dismissed. While a diminished force was hastily rounded up, Mr. Buchanan penned a note to ex-President Tyler, excusing himself for permitting Federal soldiers to be in evidence in the capital. In the afternoon, the people were appeased by a second parade. The artillery drill proved to be the high point of the exhibition. All were startled and amazed by the rapidity with which the guns were manned and prepared for action; and verisimilitude was lent to the martial scene by the dust of the Avenue, which floated about men and guns like the smoke of battle.

At six o'clock next morning, when the train from Philadelphia pulled into the Washington depot, the conductor might have been surprised at the sudden recovery of a sick gentleman, who on the preceding night had been quietly hustled into a berth at the end of the last car. The gentleman, in a soft, slouched hat, a muffler and a short, bobtailed overcoat, descended spryly to the platform. His tall and lanky figure would have made him an oddity in any gathering, and he had a plain, dark-skinned, melancholy face, with a stiff new crop of chin whiskers. He was closely attended by two companions, one of whom was big and heavily built, with bulges under his coat in every place where a man might carry arms; while the other was a short, bearded fellow, with a wary, peasant face. As they passed along the platform in the stream of sleepy-eyed travelers, they attracted attention from only one person in the depot, a man who had planted himself behind a pillar, and was peering out with a sharp, worried expression. As the lanky stranger passed, this man seized hold of his hand. "Abe," he cried in a loud voice, "you can't play that on me!" "Don't strike him," the stranger hastily told his escorts. "It is Washburne." The President-elect had arrived in the capital of the United States.

The warning which Frederick Seward had carried to Philadelphia had already been sounded in a report from Detective Pinkerton of an assassination plot in Baltimore. Doubly disquieted by a second alarm, Lincoln's friends had prevailed on him to alter his published program. After his trip to Harrisburg, he had slipped secretly on the night train, accompanied only by Ward Hill Lamon and a Mr. E. J. Allen, otherwise known as Pinkerton. Frederick Seward had returned with the message that Mr. Lincoln might be early expected in Washington, and Congressman Washburne had hurried to the depot in the winter dawn. The three travelers climbed into Washburne's carriage, and drove off to Willard's.

The original plan, that Mr. Lincoln should occupy a rented house during the pre-inauguration period, had been changed on the advice of Thurlow Weed, the political manager of New York State. In a hotel, the incoming President would be accessible to the people, and Mr. Weed himself had written to Willard's to make the reservation. The best rooms in the house were, however, occupied when Mr. Lincoln made his unexpectedly early appearance, and a New York capitalist had to be hastily dislodged from the suite connected with Parlor Number 6, a large corner apartment on the second floor, overlooking the Avenue and the grounds of the Executive Mansion.

Mr. Seward was waiting at Willard's to receive the President-elect and congratulate him on his safe arrival. He was somewhat chagrined, Washburne thought, that he had not been up in time to go to the depot. At eight o'clock, however, the senator and the congressman sat down in high elation to breakfast, loading their plates with the first run of Potomac shad. Mr. Lincoln had retired to his rooms to rest. He did not share the exultation of his friends. He had yielded to the advice to change his plans, but he had not taken stock in the story that he risked assassination in Baltimore. Since his nomination, he had constantly received letters threatening his life. He believed that he was destined to suffer a violent death, had expressed the feeling that he would not return alive to Springfield; but Mr. Lincoln's apprehensions, though they may have been quickened by the menaces of his enemies or the nervous solicitude of his friends, were the shadowy alarms of premonition and anxiety, and the prospect of actual danger left him unmoved. For the rest of his life, he would regret the secret journey to Washington. It exposed him to bitter criticism from friends and enemies alike; and it seemed to many to cast reproach on a Government already sufficiently dishonored. Mr. Seward would laughingly agree with the detractors, and say that he had not believed in the Baltimore assassins, though General Scott had done so.

Mr. Lincoln breakfasted alone at nine in his parlor, and did not appear until eleven, when he left the hotel under the escort of Mr. Seward. Those solitary morning hours were the quietest he was ever to know in Washington. He would live thereafter at the mercy of the people, advancing eternally toward him in a jerking procession of faces.

The first duty of the President-elect was to pay his respects at the Executive Mansion. A special meeting of the Cabinet was in session, when the doorkeeper handed Mr. Buchanan a startling card. "Uncle Abe is downstairs!" the President cried, and hurriedly descended to the Red Room. He soon returned with the two Republicans. Mr. Lincoln was presented to the Cabinet, and paused for a few minutes' conversation before leaving to call on General Scott. One of the members, Attorney General Stanton, had a sneering contempt for Mr. Lincoln. Some years earlier, they had been associated as counsel for the defense in a famous case, a suit brought for infringement of patent rights by Cyrus McCormick, the inventor of the reaping machine. Stanton had snubbed and humiliated the backwoods lawyer, and Lincoln had not forgotten his mortification; but he had also retained a vivid impression of Edwin M. Stanton's abilities.

Mr. Lincoln was familiarly acquainted with Washington, where he had served a term as congressman from Illinois, but the capital could not return the compliment. In spite of his extraordinary figure, no one glanced a second time at the ungainly Westerner, as he walked with Mr. Seward through the streets. Rumors that he was in town caused unprecedented sales of the *Evening Star,* which was out in the early afternoon with a description of his arrival at Willard's. Many people still remained skeptical. Republicans declared that the story was a dodge to keep them from the cars; and, mounting on top of a big furniture wagon laden with their banners, they proceeded to decorate their wigwam to impress Mr. Lincoln on his way from the depot. Later, "squads of the incredulous" surged through the rain to meet the special train, and the Fourteenth Street entrance to Willard's was surrounded. The crowds were rewarded by the sight of the weary Presidential party, oppressed by the gloom of the Maryland threats and Lincoln's sudden departure. Mrs. Lincoln had become hysterical over the separation from her husband. Colonel Edwin Sumner was a very angry old soldier, thwarted in the performance of his duty; and Colonel Ellsworth had expected their train to be mobbed in Baltimore. To counteract the depression, Bob Lincoln had led the party in a rendition of "The Star-Spangled Banner," as the cars crossed the Maryland line.

Leaning on the arm of Mr. Seward, Mrs. Lincoln entered the

hotel, and was received in the thronged hallway by the Messrs. Willard in person. Upstairs, the President-elect sprawled in an arm-chair with a beaming face, while his two spoiled boys, Willie and Tad, climbed over him. He had had a busy afternoon, for the tide of visitors had already set toward Parlor Number 6. General Scott, whom he had missed in the morning, had returned his call in full uniform, sweeping his instep with the yellow plumes of his hat as he bowed. Headed by Stephen A. Douglas, the Illinois senators and congressmen had paid their respects. Old Francis P. Blair had come in with his hatchet-faced son, Montgomery, who was hoping to be appointed Postmaster General. The Blair family, father and two sons, were a power in the Republican party. They were a fighting clan from the border slave States, Democrats who had swung into opposition to slavery. The elder Blair, formerly a famous newspaper editor and a member of Jackson's Kitchen Cabinet, was an acute politician who still wielded great influence behind the scenes. Frank, junior, former congressman, recently re-elected, was a Free-Soil leader in Missouri; while Montgomery, like his father, now lived and intrigued in Mary-land. Mr. Lincoln reposed great confidence in the senior Blair, and submitted to him, as well as to his chief adviser, Mr. Seward, a copy of his inaugural address.

Soon after his family's arrival, Lincoln was informed that the delegates to the Peace Conference desired to wait on him. He ap-pointed the hour of nine to receive them, and drove off to a seven o'clock dinner at Seward's, where the Vice-President-elect, Senator Hannibal Hamlin of Maine, was also present. The long parlor hall at Willard's was lined with people when he returned; and, shaking hands on both sides, he was so interested, said the *New York Herald,* that he forgot to remove his shiny new silk hat.

Ex-President Tyler and the Honorable Salmon P. Chase of Ohio led the Peace delegates up the stairs to Parlor Number 6. Chase was as pompous as General Scott, and very nearly as antipathetic to slavery as Senator Sumner. Re-elected to the Senate after serving as governor of his State, he was the most prominent of the former Democrats in the Republican party. His rumored appointment to the Cabinet would satisfy the radicals, who were disgruntled with the conciliatory Seward. He was tall, imposing and handsome, with the noble brow of a states-man. As he stood beside Mr. Lincoln, presenting the delegates, it was

Chase who looked the part of President of the United States, and Chase would have been the first to think so.

Curious and prejudiced, Easterners and men from the border slave States scrutinized the phenomenon from the prairies. The long, lean, sallow frontier lawyer was a shock to people who were unused to the Western type; and his homely phrases and mispronunciations grated on Eastern ears. It was impossible that Lincoln should have inspired confidence or admiration; but some saw shrewdness, honesty and even a natural dignity in his face. Its ugliness was partially redeemed by his eyes, though their dreamy, meditative expression did not bespeak either firmness or force. He had a pleasant, kindly smile, and was thought to be not so ill-favored and hard-looking as his pictures represented him. Chatting informally with the delegates, remembering like a good politician their claims to fame and their middle initials, Lincoln made on the whole a not unfavorable impression.

The next day was Sunday, and Mr. Lincoln attended St. John's Church with Mr. Seward. Under the same guidance he visited the Senate and the House on Monday, and also the Supreme Court; but almost his entire time during the pre-inauguration week was spent in the big, crowded parlor of the hotel suite. Willard's held an unprecedented collection of men notable in public affairs, civil, military and naval. Republican leaders were there to confer, and delegations to press their advice on the administration's policies and Cabinet appointments. The Peace Conference was winding up its session with resolutions that satisfied no one, and border slave State men came to beseech guarantees that there would be no Federal coercion. Past the new President, from early morning until late at night, streamed minor politicians, place seekers, editors, reporters and handshakers. He was still unknown to the passer-by in the street, but hundreds became familiar with his features in Parlor Number 6. Mr. Lincoln assured Mayor Berret and the Common Council of Washington, who called to tender a welcome, that he had kindly feelings toward them, and meant to treat them as neighbors. It was, he remarked, the first time since the present phase of politics that he had said anything publicly in a region where slavery existed. Again, in responding to a serenade by the Washington Republicans, Mr. Lincoln voiced his awareness of his peculiar situation in the capital city, whose population was almost entirely opposed to him in politics.

The new President had formed an inflexible determination to entertain no compromise on the extension of slavery, and to defend the Constitution, as his oath of office required. None of the multitude who, since his departure from Springfield, had casually met him or heard his speeches had been able to discern either his decision or his anxiety. In his public utterances, Mr. Lincoln had depreciated the seriousness of the crisis. His placid manner, the "jocular freedom" of his conversation, and his unceasing fund of anecdote gave the impression that he had but a shallow and provincial understanding of national affairs. Among the Republican leaders, none was more puzzled than Senator Charles Sumner. Mr. Lincoln had an amiable weakness for measuring heights with other tall men, and outraged Sumner's dignity by making the proposal to him. Sumner excused himself with the heavy pleasantry that it was a time for uniting their fronts and not their backs. The Washington Republican, Major French, who was chief marshal of the inauguration parade, declared that they all liked Old Abe, but wished "he would leave off making *little* speeches. He has not the gift of language," French went on, "though he may have of *western gab*."

With the appointment of Montgomery Blair as Postmaster General, the slate of Lincoln's Cabinet was complete. At the head of his advisers was Mr. Seward, balanced by the radical Mr. Chase, who was to be Secretary of the Treasury. Two selections had been virtually forced on Lincoln by bargains which his managers had made at the Republican convention which had nominated him. One was Caleb B. Smith of Indiana, the Secretary of the Interior, a prosaic-looking, lisping conservative. The other was Senator Simon Cameron of Pennsylvania, whom Mr. Lincoln had with much reluctance appointed Secretary of War. Cameron was the Republican leader in his own State, but his reputation for unscrupulous political practices shed no luster on the new Cabinet.

As a sop to New England, Mr. Lincoln had made Gideon Welles of Connecticut his Secretary of the Navy. He was tall and "venerably insignificant," with a flowing beard and a huge gray wig. Welles had been a newspaperman in Hartford, and did not know the stem from the stern of a ship, but he was an industrious and capable administrator. He was also very irritable, and those who undervalued him did not know that, with a pen dipped in gall, he kept a diary. In one respect, Welles was unique among the Cabinet members—he did not think himself a better man than the President.

The Attorney General, Mr. Edward Bates of Missouri, had been one of Mr. Lincoln's earliest selections. He was a former slaveholder, worthy, legalistic and reverential of the Constitution. The choice of the Marylander, Montgomery Blair, gave Lincoln two advisers from the border slave States. Blair was courageous, and had won abolitionist acclaim by acting as counsel for the slave, Dred Scott. However, while scarcely anyone could object to polite old Mr. Bates, the pinched and vindictive Montgomery had a host of enemies. He was detested by the radical wing of the Republicans, and disliked as an uncompromising and warmongering extremist by the moderates. He had plenty of secessionist relatives, and voiced his Union sympathies with challenge and defiance.

With the notable exception of sympathy with disunion, the President's advisers represented, like Mr. Chandlee's cockades, all shades of political sentiment. Four members of the Cabinet, Seward, Chase, Cameron and Bates, had been candidates for the Presidential nomination at the Republican convention, and for the first two the failure to secure it had been a rankling disappointment. It was not to be expected that these dissentient personalities should work together in harmony. Mr. Seward could foresee that it would be difficult to act as premier of the composite council. He sent in a last-minute resignation just before Mr. Lincoln's inauguration, but withdrew it in response to the President's firm request.

In spite of the pall of the national crisis, the President's party was not wanting in high spirits. Besides his oldest boy, Bob, a Harvard student of eighteen, it included three young men who had been law students in Mr. Lincoln's Springfield office, and he was on warmly affectionate terms with them all. John George Nicolay, capable, Teutonic, nearly thirty, was the private secretary. John Hay, the assistant secretary, was a clever, flippant, good-looking college graduate of twenty-two. The handsome little Zouave, Ellsworth, was not much older, and he had a magnetic boyish enthusiasm. He had worked out a plan for reforming the State militia system, and bringing it under Federal control; and he was hoping to be appointed to the chief clerkship of the War Department. Bob Lincoln had been educated at Phillips Exeter, and showed in speech and manner that he had enjoyed more advantages than his father. As a pendant to the campaign publicity for the rail splitter, Bob had been facetiously nick-named "The Prince of Rails." Some people inevitably called him proud and affected, but he conducted himself sensibly during a pro-longed ordeal of popular attention and flattery.

Nicolay thought that the bevy of ladies in the parlors made it seem like having a party every night. He was, however, occupied with the President's correspondence, while Ellsworth, though schoolgirls sighed over his black curls, was a moralist and a Spartan. John Hay and Bob Lincoln were the merry, carefree members of the party. Hay made a new friend in Henry Adams, another private secretary, who would soon be going off with his father to the Court of St. James's. In the evening, Bob sometimes tarried downstairs in the smoking room, listening to the music of the harpists and enjoying a cigar with the other men. Some disunionists, on one of these occasions, induced the musicians to play "Dixie," which Secessia had adopted as its national air; but the harpists quickly followed it with "Hail, Columbia." In Parlor Number 6, Mrs. Lincoln, attended by her sister, Mrs. Ninian Edwards, her two nieces and her cousin, Mrs. Grimsley, received a deferential throng in her stylish Springfield toilettes. The President's Kentucky wife was arrogantly pleased with her position, fancied her-self of great importance in politics, and referred in company to Mr. Seward as a "dirty abolition sneak."

Every night, the new squads of militia were drilling in the open spaces of the city, but the fears of revolution had largely subsided. Many patriotic men thought that it would be ill-advised to make an ostentatious display of armed force at the inauguration. The threats to his own life, however, had convinced General Scott that the cere-mony was a hazardous undertaking, and he prepared to guard the incoming President with every soldier in the city. He now had, exclu-sive of the marines at the Navy Yard, six hundred and fifty-three regulars at his command. He thought of Mr. Lincoln's drive from Willard's to the Capitol as a movement, and he planned to place a picked body of men, the sappers and miners from West Point, in the van. A squadron of District cavalry would ride on either side of the Presidential carriage, and infantry companies of militia would march in its rear. Squads of riflemen and a small number of United States cavalry were ordered to posts along the route. The main force of the regulars, headed by Scott in his coupé, was assigned to "flanking the movement" in F Street.

While one battery of artillery was situated near the Treasury building, two were stationed outside the north entrance to the Capitol grounds. At this latter important point, Scott himself proposed to remain during the ceremonies, and there, too, would be Major-General John E. Wool, the thin little old man who was the commander of the Department of the East.

On Saturday and Sunday, strangers, almost all men, were pouring into town in anticipation of the ceremonies on Monday. Baltimore plugs, tippling and shrieking their rallying cries, were but a noisy minority in the swelling influx of the Republicans. There were dignitaries among them—twenty-seven governors and ex-governors of States, and many former senators and congressmen—and there were also militia and civic organizations. Largest by far in number, however, were the plain men of the West—a type only recently familiar to Washington—who dodged forlornly about the city in travel-stained clothes, looking for a place to sleep. Hotel rooms were all preempted. The best accommodation to be had was a cot or a mattress in a parlor. The newcomers were not a spendthrift lot. Bonifaces noted that they were a cold-water army. Hack drivers and porters complained that they were given to walking and carrying their own carpetbags, reluctant to part with a quarter-dollar.

Sunday, with its roving crowds, did not seem like the Sabbath. In the morning, there was a rush to Fourteenth Street to see the President-elect depart for church. So many people congregated around the ladies' entrance to Willard's that police had difficulty in clearing a passage on the sidewalk. All tall men of only moderately good looks, said the tactful *Star*, were closely scanned, as they passed from the hotel. Uncle Abe, however, did not appear, and the sight-seers had to content themselves with the spectacle of the pugilist, John Morrissey, promenading in a stovepipe hat.

Willard's dined fifteen hundred on Sunday, and a thousand feasted at the National. In the evening, laborers were industriously scraping the entire width of the Avenue between the Capitol and the White House, a herculean assignment which they had been unable to finish on Saturday night. The wind whirled the thick dust into clouds, and, though there was now a water supply sufficient for the purpose, the city had no system for dampening the streets. At dusk, crowds of manifestly secular intention were walking toward the lighted Capitol, where the Senate flag was flying. Hundreds of homeless visitors slept on market stalls and lumber piles, or strolled about the streets all night. Orderlies and cavalry platoons rode through the dark. A rumor had reached Scott's headquarters that an attempt would be made to blow up the platform which had been erected at the east portico of the Capitol. A guard was placed under the floor of the stand, and at daybreak a battalion of District troops marched to form a semi-circle around the foot of the steps.

The city was early astir with unaccommodated strangers, assembling to perform their toilets at the public fountains. People began to turn out for the parade. Boys screamed the morning newspapers, and there were lithographs of Uncle Abe's features, damp from the press. The sidewalks of the Avenue were filled from building line to curbstone. In the crush, Newton Leonard, aged four, with blue eyes and a full face, dressed in a plaid suit with tight knees, strayed from his parents, and was advertised for next day in the *National Intelligencer*.

In spite of bright sunshine, it was a raw, disagreeable day. Whipped by the gusty wind, the people stood waiting, while soldiers and District militia formed in line. It was not a festive gathering. The city seemed anxious and depressed. Few buildings had been decorated in honor of the inauguration. Some houses along the route had closed shutters, and many unfriendly faces frowned from balconies and windows. The story was being whispered that, if Mr. Lincoln were inducted into office in good order, a company of Virginia horsemen intended to dash across the Long Bridge and take the President captive at the Union Ball that evening.

Among the groups of spectators on the housetops, militiamen with loaded rifles moved to their posts overlooking the Avenue. It was a little after twelve when the word to present arms was passed along the line of cavalry on Fourteenth Street and infantry on the Avenue in front of Willard's. A band struck up "Hail to the Chief," and Mr. Buchanan and Mr. Lincoln emerged arm in arm from the side door of the hotel, and took their seats in an open barouche. In an hour, an Old Public Functionary would be free of a position which had covered him with ignominy and scorn. The Westerner at his side would be the man to trip over the obstacle of Fort Sumter, to guide, under the blows of hatred, an unruly country from which seven States had withdrawn. Mr. Buchanan sat in silence, as the barouche rolled toward the Capitol. His withered face was pale above his white cravat. Only four years before, he had taken this drive through cheering lanes of people, moving between two pretty floats, the Goddess of Liberty on her pedestal and a full-rigged ship, manned by sailors from the Navy Yard. Now, compact and short, the inaugural procession advanced like a military expedition, fearful of attack. There was little enthusiasm on the packed sidewalks. The spectators could scarcely see the new President through the escort of dancing cavalry. Colonel Stone, riding alongside, was digging his mount with his spurs, and he thought that he succeeded in making the militiamen's horses so uneasy that it would have been hard for even a good shot to take aim at the occupants of the carriage.

One hundred mounted marshals, with their trappings of orange, pink and blue, did their utmost to give the parade a garish air of holiday; but, after the disciplined ranks of the regulars and the sizable guard of militia, the civic procession looked straggling and insignificant. There were five hundred Washington Republicans in line, and a few delegations from the States. Thirty-four girls rode in a triumphal car, and were all later kissed by Mr. Lincoln. The *Star* made fun of the pegged boots of the New Englanders, cracking like air guns in the pauses of the Marine Band. No other startling sounds disturbed the progress on the Avenue. The rowdies had foregathered in the liquor shops. A few drunken men tried to obstruct the march of the soldiers, and one of them shouted insults at a delegation of Republicans from Virginia, and proposed three cheers for the Southern Confederacy. In the eastern park of the Capitol, a little man with red whiskers sat high in a tree and addressed the crowd with oratorical flourishes. These were, however, minor disturbances, soon silenced by the police. Chief Marshal French, after a long day on horseback, would be exultant over the perfect success of his arrangements.

The official party entered the Capitol by the north door, through a passage enclosed by a high, boarded fence, guarded by marines. While the ceremonies took place in the Senate Chamber, and Vice-President Hamlin and a few senators were sworn in, the multitude silently waited in the eastern park. They saw the spreading structure of the Capitol, with its unfinished dome surmounted by gaunt derricks braced with ropes of steel. The model of the statue of Armed Freedom, destined for its apex, stood in the grass among the littered and ruinous marbles. In every window of the stark new wings, two riflemen were posted; and Colonel Stone, looking from one of the windows, was satisfied that they perfectly flanked the steps. At last, the door opened, and the dignitaries took their places on the platform, over the heads of the fifty armed men concealed beneath it.

Silver-haired and eloquent, Mr. Lincoln's old friend, Senator Edward D. Baker of Oregon, stepped forward to introduce the new President. There was a faint ripple of cheers, as Lincoln made his way to the rickety little table provided for his address. Burdened with his gold-headed cane and glossy silk hat, he paused in embarrassment. As he laid his cane under the table, Senator Douglas smilingly reached out his hand for the hat. All the people could see Douglas, seated at the front of the platform, holding Lincoln's hat as a public profession of faith in a united country. In the background, Senator Wigfall of Texas leaned with folded arms against the Capitol doorway, watching the inaugural scene with contempt on his fierce, scarred face.

In a resonant, high-pitched voice, trained in the open-air meetings of the West, Mr. Lincoln began to speak. While his audience stood hushed in a painful silence, a tall man with a shrewd, impassive countenance detached himself from the crowd. Like one whom much familiarity backstage has robbed of interest in the play, Mr. Thurlow Weed of Albany turned his back on Mr. Lincoln, and wandered from the Capitol park. Perhaps he was too grieved to stay and see the sad-faced Westerner in the place where he had dreamed and schemed to put a subtle, smiling man. Mr. Weed was the most skillful political manager of his day, but he had failed in his fondest ambition, to manipulate the nomination of Seward by the Republican party.

As he walked north on Capitol Hill, Mr. Weed came upon two batteries of light artillery. Near one of them, General Scott drooped in splendid decay. Beside the other was General Wool, prim and perpendicular, in his high, choking collar. Like Scott, he bore in his stiffening body the scars of 1812. Mr. Weed started forward. In 1812, this cynical politician had been a drummer boy. Nearly half a century before, he had seen the two old generals, one so fat and the other so thin, as dashing, buoyant young officers. He hastened to present himself to them, and respectfully shake their hands.

Behind him, Mr. Lincoln's voice rang out, across the unenthusiastic multitude, across the sundered nation. "We are not enemies, but friends. . . . Though passion may have strained, it must not break our bonds of affection." The voice ceased. There was the noise of applause. Chief Justice Taney tottered forward, a cadaver in black silk. The old regime and the new faced each other, and a Bible lay between them, a pretty book, gilt-clasped and bound in cinnamon velvet. Mr. Lincoln solemnly swore to defend the Constitution of the United States.

There was a thundering salute from the batteries. Mr. Weed had been deeply moved by his chance encounter with the two commanders. He did not remember De Tocqueville's warning, that the army of a democracy tends to become weakened by a burden of old and unfit officers. Effulgent with that sentimentality to which the corrupt are prone, he gazed with veneration on the heroes of his boyhood; and failed to see in the antique tableau on Capitol Hill a presentation of the Union's unpreparedness for long and bloody war.

IV Deserted Village

"THE 4TH OF MARCH has come and gone, and we have a *live, Republican* President," wrote a female clerk in the Patent Office, Miss Clara Barton, "and, what is perhaps singular, during the whole day we saw no one who appeared to manifest the least dislike to his living." After the strain of the inauguration, Washington awoke on Tuesday with a feeling of anticlimax and a suspicion that there had been something slightly ludicrous in the exaggerated military precautions.

The Union Ball had been held without disturbing incident in the "white muslin Palace of Aladdin" behind the City Hall. The palace was actually a temporary plank structure, divided into rooms for dancing and for supper, and dependent for dressing-rooms on the City Hall, ladies in the Common Council chamber, and gentlemen in the courtroom. Mr. Lincoln, looking exhausted, and worried by his white kid gloves, led the grand march arm in arm with Mayor Berret, while his wife followed with a former admirer, Senator Douglas. The ladies who revolved to the strains of Scala's Marine Band had discarded the ruffled and garlanded dresses of the fifties in favor of the fashion for stiff and heavy materials, richly braided and trimmed with lace. Crino- lines had grown enormous, and, to avoid appearing pinheaded, the ladies crowned themselves with labyrinthine creations of blonde, feathers, velvet and flowers. Mrs. Lincoln, who danced a quadrille with Douglas, was observed to be dressed all in blue, with a necklace and bracelets of gold and pearls. Most of those who had purchased tickets to the ball were strangers to the society of the capital, and they took an innocent pleasure in the muslin decorations, the large gas chandeliers and the elegant pyramids which Gautier had contrived for the supper table. Henry Adams thought it a melancholy function.

Mr. Lincoln had come to Washington with a heavy heart, sick of his office before he had assumed it. In taking up his terrible respon- sibilities, he was distracted by two extraneous duties—the social demands of his position and the distribution of appointments.

The Lincolns were uninstructed in the rules of official Washington etiquette; and for their information the State Department furnished a detailed memorandum on formal functions, the order of precedence and the use of visiting cards. The President and his wife were warned not to address a titled foreigner as sir, and advised that state dinners should take place at seven o'clock, although the family might dine privately at six. There was a pointed admonition that gentlemen, for evening affairs, should never wear frocks. In matters of protocol, Mr. Seward was the President's guide and guardian. One of his early duties was to arrange an audience for the Chevalier Bertinatti, the diplomatic representative of Sardinia, who had been appointed minister of the new kingdom of Italy. Mr. Lincoln dutifully made smacking, violent bows to the gorgeous Chevalier, with cocked hat, silver lace and sword; and, in response to a long address, pulled from the pocket of his wrinkled black suit a proper little speech.

A few days after the inauguration, the President and Mrs. Lincoln held their first evening levee in the Executive Mansion. Measured by the numbers in attendance, it was a monstrous success. At seven o'clock, an hour before the doors opened, the great driveway was blocked with carriages. Senator Charles Sumner arrived in the sartorial perfection of English evening dress; there were military and naval officers, and a number of the foreign ministers presented themselves as a diplomatic, if disagreeable duty. From eight until ten-thirty, the President shook hands without pause, often using his left hand, too, to pass the visitors along. He wore his inauguration suit, and fresh white kid gloves. Ward Hill Lamon stood beside him. Mr. Lincoln intended to nominate his friend as District marshal, one of the Washington appointments which were a Presidential prerogative. It was an office which super-added to the duties of sheriff the occasional role of court chamberlain, for the marshal, who had charge of the county jail and was partially responsible for the preservation of order in Washington, also traditionally presented the guests to the President at White House receptions. A similar attendance on the President's lady was required of the Commissioner of Public Buildings. Around Mrs. Lincoln clustered the female relatives who had accompanied her from Springfield: her sister, Mrs. Edwards, in brown and black; the two nieces, in lemon color and crimson, respectively; Mrs. Grimsley in blue watered silk. There were also two half sisters who had arrived in season for the inauguration, and one of them, Mrs. Clement White of Alabama, was a secessionist. The function broke up in a disorderly scramble for wraps. During the Buchanan administration, an attempt had been made to check them in the hall, but it had not been popular. At the Lincoln's first levee, coats and hats, casually discarded, became inextricably confused. Perhaps not one person in ten, in the opinion of the *Star,* emerged with his own outer garments.

The place seekers, ravenous for post-offices, consulates and Indian agencies, had immediately taken possession of the White House. They occupied the parlors and halls, and loitered on the portico and lawns. At all hours of the day, two queues moved on the broad staircase, one going up, the other going down. The anteroom of the President's office and the second-floor corridor were filled with restless applicants, bristling with credentials.

The arrangement of the mansion might have been designed to preclude all decent privacy for the President. Executive business was transacted in three rooms on the east end of the second floor, at the head of the main stairway. The family's sleeping quarters were situated at the other end of the same hall—Mr. Lincoln occupying the small, southwest bedroom and his wife the larger adjoining chamber, while the two little boys were across the way. In passing between his office and his bedroom or the dining-room, the President was obliged to struggle through the lines of office seekers, some of whom grabbed him, holding out their papers. Only a doorkeeper was on duty at the Executive chamber. The conditions in his new home contrasted strangely with the precautions taken in bringing Lincoln to Washington and in guarding the inauguration. All anxiety for his life had apparently been forgotten as soon as he became President; yet he was still receiving threatening letters, and there were cranks among the strangers who occupied the White House. His secretaries wrote that madmen frequently reached the anteroom, and sometimes even entered Lincoln's presence.

To loyal men, in Congress and out of it, there was a bitter incongruity in the administration's preoccupation with patronage at a time of national emergency. The Confederate States were aggressively preparing for war. Late in February, General David Twiggs, U.S.A., had delivered nineteen Army posts to the rebel authorities of Texas, wearing the uniform of his country while he made the surrender. The newly appointed superintendent of West Point, Captain Pierre G. T. Beauregard of Louisiana, had resigned to become a Confederate brigadier, commanding at Charleston. Many experienced officers of the higher grades in both Army and Navy had offered their services to the rebellion. The resignations were accepted without question, and the officers were given honorable discharges. Some who remained at their posts were known to be unfaithful.

The air of Washington was thick with treason, and with the suspicion of treason. The Adjutant General, Samuel Cooper of New Jersey, resigned in March to go with the Confederacy. The Quartermaster General, Joseph E. Johnston, was a Virginian, disloyal to the Union. The old Surgeon General's disaffection was nullified by his infirmity, but the acting head of the Medical Bureau, Robert C. Wood, was Jefferson Davis's brother-in-law by the latter's first marriage. The dandified Virginia captain, "Prince John" Magruder, who commanded the First U. S. Artillery, brought for the defense of the capital, was well known to be a secessionist. Commodore Franklin Buchanan, commander of the Washington Navy Yard, was a disunion sympathizer from Maryland, and most of his subordinate officers were unreliable. All the executive departments retained large quotas of unfaithful clerks and messengers. Judge John A. Campbell of the Supreme Court was in active correspondence with the Montgomery authorities, and would eventually cast his fortunes with the South. At the short extra session of the Senate which followed the inauguration, all the slave States save six were represented, in many cases by disunion leaders. The senators from Texas continued to sit in the Capitol, although the State had sent delegates to the Confederate congress. Washington heard the echo of Wigfall's threats of war on the Senate floor, and his boast that he owed no allegiance to the Government. A motion was made to expel him, but no action was taken.

An irresolute Republican Cabinet convened in the White House, instead of an indecisive council of Democrats—that was nearly the only visible difference between Government in March and in February. Public opinion in the North was lethargic and divided, and the decadence of patriotic feeling was increased by the inaction of the new administration. In journeying up from the deep South, the traveler passed from an atmosphere of unanimity and martial excitement into a region of apathy and indifference. Early in March, the contrast was noted by a former Army colonel, a red-headed, quick-tempered nervous man named William T. Sherman. He was one of the Northern officers who, despairing of a future in the service, had gone into civil life. For the past year and a half, he had been acting as superintendent of a military academy in Louisiana. Colonel Sherman liked the place and the people, but he could no longer with honor remain there, and he was returning to his home in Ohio to look for another position.

Sherman knew that war was coming, but he did not suppose that it would give him any employment that would provide for his wife and children. In Washington, however, he had a young brother, John, a Republican congressman from Ohio, who had just been appointed to the Senate, in place of Mr. Chase. John Sherman believed in his brother's military ability, and he persuaded him to visit Washington. The colonel went, but he was disgusted with everything he saw. There was no appointment waiting for him, and he was by nature impatient. One day, John took him to the White House and introduced him to the President, explaining that his brother was just up from Louisiana and might have some useful information. The colonel began to tell his grim story, that the South was preparing for war. "Oh, well!" said Mr. Lincoln, "I guess we'll manage to keep house." Colonel Sherman closed his lips. Outside the President's office, he broke out and damned the politicians. "You have got things in a hell of a fix," he told his brother, "and you may get them out as you best can." The country was sleeping on a volcano that was ready to burst, and William T. Sherman wanted no part in it, and went off to accept a job in St. Louis.

Washington residents were of two minds about the national crisis. A large minority, which included the fashionable set, looked forward to the exodus of the Black Republicans, and the return of "nice people" to the capital. Secession badges continued to be sold at the doors of the hotels. When the Confederate flag was designed, a few windows flaunted the Stars and Bars, and some women appeared in a symbolic costume—a short skirt broadly striped in red and white, and a blue sacque with seven stars on the bosom. Society regarded the Republican interregnum flippantly. Ladies circulated merry stories about the vulgarity of Mrs. Lincoln, and laughed at the rail splitter for coming to Washington disguised in a Scotch cap. They made fun of dismal parties, at which Republicans did not enjoy themselves amid "the hardly stifled grumbling and growling" of those who were asked to meet them. A letter from the Gwins went to South Carolina—by courtesy of the United States postal service—with the message, "They say Washington offers a perfect realization of Goldsmith's Deserted Village."

While the mass of the inhabitants viewed the overthrow of the Government with apprehension, their fears had been allayed by the orderly passing of Inauguration Day. There was nothing very alarming in the military manuals with which the bookshops were stocked, or in the sight of an occasional squad of District militia drilling in one of the vacant lots. Strangers still crowded the hotels, and wandered about the public buildings. Twice in one week, it was necessary to employ a second steamboat to accommodate all who wished to visit Mount Vernon. Otherwise, life in Washington jogged along as usual. The hungry customers at Harvey's kept twenty men busy opening oysters and scalding them in steaming cauldrons. Joe Jefferson delighted audiences at the Washington Theatre with his performance of *Rip Van Winkle*. Some people went to see Duprez and Green's Original New Orleans and Metropolitan Double Minstrel Troupe; some attended lectures at the First Presbyterian Church on Madame de Maintenon, Pascal and Galileo. Others sat at home, and read *Elsie Venner*. Elmer Ellsworth, now commissioned a second lieutenant in the Army, caught the measles from the Lincoln boys. A valuable Negro man was put up for auction at the county jail, by order of the Orphans' Court. There was much distress among the unemployed mechanics in the city. The tulip trees around the Capitol put forth tender green leaves. The purple lilacs budded. Dry-goods shops sold their winter remnants to make room for organdies, mozambiques, mull muslins, straw bonnets and sun umbrellas.

Throughout the month of March, Washington was tranquil. There was a general expectation that the crisis would be averted without any serious trouble. Mr. Lincoln, in his inaugural address, had declared his intention of holding the property and places belonging to the Government; but a week afterward it was the universal opinion in Washington that both Forts Sumter and Pickens would shortly be abandoned. All knew the conciliatory views of Mr. Seward, the Secretary of State and the most influential man in the administration. Three Confederate commissioners had been sent to Washington to treat for a peaceful settlement, to which the surrender of all Federal property in the seceded States was an indispensable condition. Mr. Seward declined to receive the commissioners, but through intermediaries, one of whom was Judge Campbell, he conveyed the assurance that Fort Sumter would be evacuated. The fort in Charleston harbor had little military value, and Mr. Seward was opposed to making an issue of holding it.

In believing that he spoke for the administration, Mr. Seward was guided not only by his own egoism, but by the opinion of General Scott. The old man had lost his earlier enthusiasm for strengthening the Southern forts. During Lent, he dined often alone. When the meal was ended, and his body servant had turned his wheel chair and lifted his feet, he sighed, "A dull man would be the death of me now!" In Virginia, the movement for disunion was rapidly spreading. The General shrank from the thought of war, long and devastating, against the seceding States. A phrase had formed in his mind: "Wayward Sisters, depart in peace!" It stood impressively at the close of a letter containing his views on the crisis, which he had prepared for Mr. Seward.

The President, while he listened to the prayers of aspiring postmasters, was haggard with the problem of Fort Sumter. On assuming office, he had received a report that Major Anderson's provisions were running low. The fort was menaced by Beauregard's batteries, and the decision, to relieve or not to relieve, was at once set squarely before the new administration. General Scott gave the opinion, in which the Chief Engineer, old General Joseph G. Totten concurred, that evacuation was almost inevitable. Day after day, the dismayed gentlemen of the Cabinet assembled in the President's office with its worn carpet and plain, heavy furniture. They sat around a long oak table, covered with a green baize cloth, and listened to the advice of the experts: Army officers, who discouraged the relief of Fort Sumter; Navy men who believed that it could be successfully carried out. Even granted that an expedition was feasible, it was not an easy matter to resolve to undertake it. The Sumter question had become a powder magazine, and only one of the President's advisers, Mr. Montgomery Blair, was eager to drop a match in it. High above the fireplace, an old engraving of Andrew Jackson stared down on Lincoln and his Cabinet.

Down in Pensacola harbor, Fort Pickens was still in Federal possession and it, too, was menaced by hostile batteries. The President, however, was hopeful that this fort could hold out, for he had jogged General Scott into sending orders to strengthen it with troops that were on shipboard in the harbor. Although Lincoln was in frequent conference with Scott and had seen his letter to Seward, he had not wholly realized the conciliatory drift of the General's sentiments. On receiving from Scott a statement that Fort Pickens, as well as Fort Sumter, should be abandoned, Mr. Lincoln was greatly agitated.

That evening, March 28, the Lincolns were giving their first state dinner for the Cabinet ministers and Vice-President Hamlin and their ladies. Among the guests of less official importance was Mr. William Howard Russell of the London *Times*, a portly, graying and quietly dandified Briton, given to fiddling with his eyeglasses, which hung on a chain about his neck. All unknown to himself, he was the forerunner of a line of lean, fluent and adventurous gentlemen. He was the first of the war correspondents. His dispatches from the Crimea and from India had already made a name for him in England, and he had now been sent by his newspaper to report on the troubled situation in the democracy overseas.

Mr. Russell did not find the arrangements for the state dinner remarkable for their ostentation, and he was not, for the most part, impressed by the company. The epaulettes of one old naval officer provided the only glitter, for, though General Scott had been invited, he was unable to be present. Some of the gentlemen—wanting the benefit of Mr. Seward's supervision—were attired in frock coats. Mrs. Lincoln, in a bright-colored dress, sat indefatigably waving her fan, while her guests were presented. Mr. Russell had been regaled with the malicious gossip of Washington, and he was pleasantly surprised in the President's wife, whom he thought homely in manners and appearance, but desirous of making herself agreeable. It was evident that Mrs. Lincoln was eclipsed by the brilliance of a very young lady of her "court," Miss Kate Chase. The Secretary of the Treasury had been three times a widower. Of the two daughters who composed his family, the elder was his close companion, his confidante and his official hostess. As little more than a child, Kate had taken her place at the head of her father's table, and entertained his many visitors with her wit and her astute political comments. At twenty-one, she was a girl of imperious beauty. Hypercritical persons might carp that her little nose was too tilted, or her graceful figure too slender; but none could deny the loveliness of her queenly head, her bronze hair, large hazel eyes and marble-white complexion. Perhaps, that evening, Mrs. Lincoln was able to divine that the most popular parties in Washington would not be those given at the White House, but at the Secretary of the Treasury's mansion at the corner of Sixth and E Streets.

The President, entertaining the company with his funny stories, gave no impression of a man in distress of mind, save to the members of his Cabinet, whom he drew apart for a brief conference; but he did not sleep that night. He felt that national destruction was the alternative to an assertion of the Federal authority, at one point or the other. He had not firmly decided on relieving Fort Sumter, but after the Cabinet meeting next day he signed an order to make ready an expedition, to be used if necessary. In the plans for a similar expedition to Fort Pickens, Mr. Seward was the moving spirit, and all knowledge of this project was withheld from the other Cabinet officers, including the Secretaries of War and the Navy. The resultant inefficiency and confusion of orders impaired the preparations for Fort Sumter, and damaged the morale of the Cabinet. Mr. Lincoln soon saw the mistake he had made in permitting his Secretary of State to override the authority of his colleagues. Clever Mr. Seward, with his air of "a refined New York criminal lawyer enacting Richelieu," assumed that his abilities entitled him to perform all the executive duties of the Government, and he soon wrote Mr. Lincoln a letter which contained a plain intimation of his alacrity to discharge the functions of President. Mr. Lincoln composed a courteous reply which put Mr. Seward in his place. The Secretary of State played the role of Richelieu on a smaller scale thereafter; but he did not, as a pettier man would have done, bear Mr. Lincoln a grudge for the deflation of his ambition. His mind was supple and his nature generous, and two months later he would write his wife, "The President is the best of us."

As every movement of the Federal authorities was promptly reported to the South, the preparations for both expeditions were carefully guarded from the public; but from the New York wharves a flock of rumors presently arose like sea gulls, and the opinion began to be expressed in Washington that Fort Sumter might not after all be evacuated. The Confederate commissioners agitatedly dispatched to Montgomery telegrams which retailed the conjectures of the Avenue, and Judge Campbell accused Mr. Seward of bad faith. The President made an appearance at Mrs. Lincoln's Saturday afternoon levee on April 6. Among the callers were several Indians, accompanied by their white-bearded friend, Father Beeson, who was holding meetings on behalf of the Red Man; and Larooqua, the Indian Jenny Lind, entertained the company with song. The President, chatty and unceremonious as usual, had that day written a notice to the governor of South Carolina that an attempt would be made to supply Fort Sumter, peaceably, if possible. The expedition to Fort Pickens had already started from New York. The two fleets comprised the entire available naval force north of the Chesapeake.

After a month of relaxation Washington was again uneasy. It was said that a band of five hundred men, led by the Texas ranger, Ben McCulloch, planned to raid the capital from Richmond. According to some, their object was to carry off the President and the Cabinet. Mr. Stanton wrote Mr. Buchanan that McCulloch had made a scouting trip to the capital, spending the night at the Gwin mansion, and telling his friends that he expected to be in possession of the city before long. There was a strong national sentiment in Virginia, and Mr. Lincoln's initial policy of forbearance and delay had been influenced by the hope that the State would adhere to the Union. The governor, however, was hostile to the North, and the enthusiasts for secession were active. As an emissary to Charleston they sent a United States congressman, Roger A. Pryor, a young fire-eater with an impassioned and truculent face, and long, straight hair, brushed back behind the ears. The message that Pryor carried was "Strike a blow!" If blood were shed, he told the excited crowd in Charleston, in less than an hour by Shrewsbury clock, Virginia would join the Confederacy.

Mr. Seward, still exuding confidence, said that the national crisis would be over in three months; but Washington scented danger. Of the soldiers brought to the city for the count of the electoral vote, scarcely more than half remained. General Scott was expecting reinforcements, but, as the fleet set out for Fort Sumter, he began to fear that they might come too late. In order to furnish guards for the public buildings, the President called out ten companies of the District militia.

There was a stir of excitement, as the men assembled at their armories to be inspected by Colonel Stone. The muster-in of six companies began immediately in the yard in front of the War Department. Some of the bystanders urged the militia not to take the oath of allegiance to the Government, and only one company proved ready to do so. Out of thirty volunteers who presented themselves in the reorganized National Rifles, eighteen promptly resigned. About twenty men of the Washington Light Infantry refused to be sworn in. Seventeen members of the Potomac Light Infantry of Georgetown left the ranks when required to take the oath. As they marched back to their armory, some persons hissed them, but other residents of the Washington suburb applauded the dissenters and hissed the loyal soldiers. District troopers, however, serenaded General Scott at his lodgings in the evening. Scott made them a little speech about "rallying round," and "dying gloriously" and "old flag of our country"; and the band played "Yankee Doodle." On the suggestion of Mr. Seward, who was dining with the General, "The Star-Spangled Banner" and "Hail, Columbia" were also rendered, before Scott and his guests sat down to Cruchet's excellent dinner, with wines from France, Spain and Madeira.

The muster-in had been initiated with an arbitrary abruptness that would have startled a more patriotic town. The nation was not at war. The militiamen, assembled on a half-hour's notice, had been left in ignorance of the length or the character of the service expected of them. Many of the men had refused to take the oath because of fear that they were to be sent outside the District. Things went better on the second day of the enrollment, when the citizens understood that they had been called out for guard duty. Major Irvin McDowell, the Assistant Adjutant General, explained that their services would be required within the District limits, and that the enlistment period was for three months only. Half-a-dozen rifle companies promptly swore allegiance, and the Washington Rifles took the oath so heartily that unionist spectators around the War Department fence broke into applause.

Squads of militia were placed on nightly duty at the public buildings, while United States cavalry pickets were stationed at the Long Bridge, at the Navy Yard and Rock Creek bridges, and at other approaches to Washington. One of the most important points outside the city limits was the Chain Bridge, which spanned the Potomac three miles above Georgetown. In spite of its old-fashioned name, it was a strong wooden structure, resting on piers of masonry. It connected Washington with the Virginia turnpike which led by way of Leesburg to Harper's Ferry.

The administration, in great anxiety, awaited news from Charleston. The unceasing tramp of the office seekers' feet in the White House corridor was beginning to get on Mr. Lincoln's nerves. Senator Douglas imparted to Mr. Welles his positive knowledge that the rebels would fire on Fort Sumter. On Friday, April 12, Washington heard that General Beauregard had demanded the surrender of the fort, and that Major Anderson had refused. Next day, the headlines proclaimed that the bombardment of Fort Sumter had started on the preceding day. Newspaper offices were raided, and the presses could not supply the demand. Late in the evening, the *Star* posted on its bulletin board the dispatch which told that the fort had surrendered. All day Sunday, in the big hotels and on the street corners, people gathered to discuss the news. There was some skepticism about its reliability. Many held the opinion that the report had been put out to affect the decision of Virginia. On Monday, the President's proclamation was published, calling out seventy-five thousand militia for three months.

Suddenly, it was impossible to deprecate or parry the crisis any longer. Civil war was upon the nation. The bonfire kindled by the politicians had lighted a great blaze of rebellion. Washington looked anxiously toward the heights beyond the Long Bridge.

Roger Pryor had been a true prophet. The guns that battered Sumter swept Virginia into the Confederacy; but neither he nor any man could have foretold that, in less than an hour by Shrewsbury clock, they would arouse the North. The flag that fluttered earthward in defeat sent the men of the loyal States thronging to the recruiting offices. There was a hearty clamor of bells and bands and cheers. People ran into the streets with a strange new look on their faces—a kind of desperate joy, as if they were relieved to feel passionately again. It had not been so when South Carolina guns fired on the *Star of the West*, nor when in State after seceded State other forts had been seized by the rebels. In the same fervor and exaltation and unreason, it would not be so again in that war.

From sixteen States, telegrams and letters flooded into Washington, offering men, money, arms. The volunteers far exceeded the number called by the President. Six border slave States sent angry refusals, and one of these was Virginia. A hesitant reply came from Governor Hicks of Maryland. He was a Union man of the stamp of Mr. Buchanan, patriotic but timid; and his State, split into warring factions, was a microcosm of the national problem. Some Marylanders employed in the Government departments had moved into town because they feared trouble. Like the Baltimore gangs, the Maryland militia companies were secessionist.

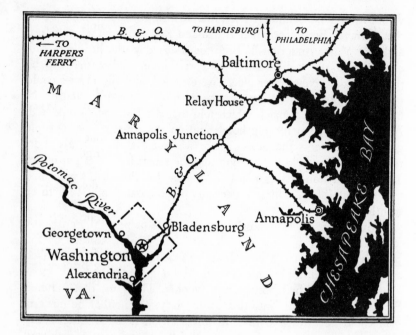

The boundaries of the District were lines traced in the soil of Maryland, and Virginia's relation to Washington by bridge and ferry was nearly as close. The Potomac, the water route to the capital, was bordered by the territory of both States. Baltimore was the terminus of the two great railroads from the North, one from Philadelphia, the other from Harrisburg; while at the Relay House, eight miles south of Baltimore, the railroad from the Ohio River and the West formed a junction with the Washington line. Washington, dependent on Maryland and Virginia for its communications with the rest of the country, was the scene of no enthusiastic demonstrations for war. Even the unionist population faced the outbreak of hostilities with doubt and reserve.

In the eyes of the North, Washington was a cherished symbol of the nation's power, to be held and defended at all costs. To the South, the capital was a great prize whose capture would enhance the prestige of the rebellious government, and surely bring it recognition by foreign powers. The Confederate Secretary of War publicly boasted that before the first of May the Stars and Bars would float over the dome of the Federal Capitol. Richmond secessionists were panting for the attack, and the *Enquirer* called on Virginia volunteers to be ready to join the march of a Southern army on Washington. The confidence of the disloyal residents of the capital increased the impression that the danger was imminent and acute.

On Monday morning, two important Pennsylvania Republicans, Governor Curtin and Mr. McClure, anxiously questioned General Scott in the course of a conference at the White House. Scott acknowledged that the capital was not defensible, and that Beauregard commanded a large army; but he insisted that Washington was not in danger and could not be taken, and both Curtin and McClure came to the conclusion that the General was in his dotage. While they talked, Mr. Lincoln sat twirling his spectacles. He quaintly remarked that it seemed to him that, if he were Beauregard, he would take Washington. From the windows of the President's office, a sloop of war, on which General Scott set great value, could be seen making a solitary little cruise between Alexandria and the Long Bridge.

The defense of Washington, in spite of the British invasion of 1814, was not a subject which had been studied by Army engineers, who were versed in the topography of the environs of Paris and other European capitals. The city, sprawling in its marshy valley, covered too wide an area to be easily defended, and no natural features in its vicinity were well adapted to fortifications. One neglected fort, twelve miles down the river, was the only protection that had been devised for Washington. The reliance of the city was on man power.

Massachusetts, the only Northern State that was fully prepared for the crisis, was promptly sending four regiments, under the command of Benjamin F. Butler, brigadier-general of militia, and three had been ordered direct to Washington. Two companies of weary regulars had come in from Texas before the fall of Sumter, and at least one more was soon expected. Pending the arrival of reinforcements, more citizen soldiers were called out in the District. Every day the muster-in proceeded in the yard of the War Department. The National Rifles had been hustling for new recruits, and, purged for a second time, this company was sworn into the service. The chiefs of the Treasury bureaus met to organize a regiment of clerks and messengers. Office seekers were routed out of their hotel rooms to listen to fiery speeches from two veterans of the Mexican War: Cassius M. Clay, a picturesque Kentuckian who had had vice-presidential aspirations, and

General James H. Lane, Kansas border fighter and senator-elect. In a pinch, these strangers in Washington would at least prove dependably loyal—they were Republicans, to a man.

The Government had been assured that in a few days numerous militia regiments would arrive, and to all save professional soldiers militia meant an army. Even civilians, however, recognized the difficulty of finding competent officers of the higher grades. Among those who remained faithful, none save Scott and Wool had had command of a brigade. "What are we to do for generals?" Mr. Seward inquired of Scott.

Half an hour's ride away, in his pillared mansion on Arlington Heights, was a handsome officer for whose abilities Scott had an almost idolatrous admiration. Colonel Robert E. Lee, a man who believed secession to be revolution and anarchy, had been ordered to Washington from Texas in February. On his return home, he had paid his respects to General Scott, and the two Virginians had been closeted together for nearly three hours. Scott's secretary, Keyes, felt certain that the General had offered to resign in favor of the younger officer. Keyes had observed that, after the interview, Scott had been silent and "painfully solemn"; and he also remembered Lee's chill and formal evasion of an inquiry regarding Twiggs's surrender.

On the morning of Thursday, April 18, Lee again rode across the Long Bridge to Washington. He had appointments with old Mr. Blair and General Scott, and he went first to Montgomery Blair's yellow house on Pennsylvania Avenue. At the instance of the President, the elder Blair that morning made Colonel Lee an unofficial offer of the command of the Federal army. Whether Lee hesitated to reply or at once gave a firm refusal, in the afternoon he rode for the last time from Washington to his home on Arlington Heights. Behind him, he left a city uneasy with rumors of the secession of Virginia. Militiamen were moving to their posts. Carts, laden with iron jars of cartridges and grapeshot, were distributing ammunition. Pickets, with bundles of hay on the high pommels of their saddles, galloped through the streets, their blue capes flying. In preparation for an attack, artillerymen manned guns at the Washington end of the bridge by which Colonel Lee crossed the Potomac. Captain William B. Franklin of the engineers, in charge of the construction work at the Treasury, was placed in command of that building. Guards were posted, and preparations made to transform the Treasury into a strongly defended citadel, flanked by the State Department and protected by an additional guard in the Riggs Bank building. The Capitol, Major Irvin McDowell commanding, was ready for an assault. Boards and stones and casks of cement blocked the doors and windows. Pictures and statues were covered with heavy planking. Firewood was stacked in the basement arches; and iron plates, intended for the dome, formed breastworks on the porticoes. In the wings, amid the anticipation of destruction, workmen still chipped at columns and tinkered with carvings.

From group to group in the public rooms of Willard's, the rumors spread that Virginians were marching on Washington. The mail train was late, and treason was feared in Baltimore. Half of the faces in the crowd at Willard's were Southern; and, while loyal men loudly declared their sympathies, and impatiently asked, "Why don't the troops come on?" there were many who stood apart, whispering or listening. The dependable boarders were assembled in the large hall adjoining Willard's, and messengers were sent to bring in guests from the other hotels. They were divided into the Clay Battalion and the Frontier Guards, headed respectively by Cash Clay and Jim Lane, and were placed under the command of an Army officer—Mr. Lincoln's friend, Major David Hunter. The two companies were motley groups of vigilantes rather than military organizations. Senator-elect Pomeroy of Kansas joined up with the applicants for office in the Frontier Guards. Among the Republican place seekers in the Clay Battalion was Count Adam Gurowski, a former Polish revolutionary leader, who was the author of several books and knew everyone of prominence in Washington. Gurowski had a snarling and cross-grained disposition, and one of his pet detestations was slavery. He gladly took an oath of fidelity, and signed a pledge to defend the capital. When these formalities had been completed, the men were supplied with muskets, and Major Hunter stationed Clay's company at Willard's, with orders to patrol the streets all night, while he took the Frontier Guards to the Executive Mansion.

At about seven in the evening a train drew into the depot, carrying one company of regulars from Minnesota and four hundred and sixty volunteers from Pennsylvania. A mob had hooted and stoned the soldiers, as they passed through Baltimore. The Washington Artillery of Pottsville had brought an old Negro, known as Nick Biddle, who was fond of tagging along on their outings. He had put on a uniform for this grand excursion, and blood still oozed from the rags around his head, where the stones of the rowdies had found a mark. Nick Biddle was the first casualty of the war to enter Washington. He told people that he was not afraid to fight, but he never wanted to go through Baltimore again.

The Pennsylvanians marched to the Capitol to be reviewed by Major McDowell, and assigned to temporary quarters in the building, whose north wing was already occupied by a company of District militiamen. Despite the anxiety for the arrival of the volunteers, no preparations had been made for their reception. The two companies installed in the luxurious committee rooms of the north wing would willingly have exchanged Brussels carpets and marble washstands for a heartier meal than the sides of bacon which were presently served out in the basement. The chandeliers and furnace were hastily lighted in the unoccupied south wing, and the smell of broiling and frying meat was wafted through the Hall of Representatives. Pennsylvania had been prompt in its patriotism, but a hodgepodge of five companies, wanting in regimental organization and almost entirely unarmed, could give no immediate assistance to the capital. A member of one of the companies, Mr. James D. Gay, who happened to be in Washington on business, went to visit his friends, and then returned to Willard's. In the office he met Captain Magruder, and, pulling him into the street, pointed to the lighted Capitol, and said that two thousand soldiers had arrived there, armed with Minié rifles. Mr. Gay wanted to do his part toward saving Washington, and he hoped that Prince John believed him.

General Jim Lane, a bold Kansas ruffian, with "the sad, dim-eyed, bad-toothed face of a harlot," strode into the East Room of the White House, brandishing his shiny new sword. Behind him marched his earnest and awkward following of jayhawkers and a few Easterners, in citizens' dress, with muskets on their shoulders. In the blaze of the crystal chandeliers, ammunition boxes were opened, and cartridges distributed. Colonel Stone, when he came to inspect the District sentries who were posted every night around the mansion, was startled by the loud voices and the ringing of rammers in musket barrels which proceeded from the East Room; but he was assured by Mrs. Lincoln's cousin, Captain Lockwood Todd, that it was all right.

The Frontier Guards practiced drilling for a while, and then composed themselves to sleep on the velvet carpet, with Major Hunter beside them.

It was quiet on the second floor of the White House, where Mr. Lincoln had retired early. John Hay was enjoying the excitement hugely. A pretty lady who called to see the President turned out, to Hay's infinite delight, to be Jean M. Davenport, an actress who had been his idol in his "stage-struck salad days." This lovely creature— once the object of Mr. Stanton's admiration, in the interval between his two marriages—was now the wife of Colonel Frederick W. Lander, a civil engineer who had made important Government surveys in the West. She had a little tale to tell of an encounter with a swaggering young Virginian, who had vaguely boasted of a great, daredevil thing that was to be done within forty-eight hours. Mrs. Lander, blushing at the impropriety of her visit, although she was accompanied by an older and plainer lady, was fearful that Virginians were plotting to assassinate or capture Mr. Lincoln. John Hay went to his chief's bedside, and told him the yarn. The President "quietly grinned."

During the evening, the Government received verification of the report that the Virginia convention, which had been deliberating in Richmond since mid-February, had adopted an ordinance of secession. Aside from the threat to the capital itself, the secession of Virginia endangered three points of consequence: Harper's Ferry, with its arsenal and armory; the navy yard at Norfolk, with its ships and materials; and Fort Monroe, which guarded the entrance of Chesapeake Bay. The fort was of primary importance as a base for both military and naval operations. It had a small garrison, and General Scott had already ordered one of the four Massachusetts regiments to reinforce it. From the three remaining regiments, he had considered sparing one for the defense of Harper's Ferry. On Friday morning, however, it was learned that the little Federal garrison, attacked by Virginia militia, had demolished the arsenal and burned the armory building.

At the same time, Secretary Welles received disturbing news from Norfolk. The scarcity of both soldiers and seamen had made it impossible either to protect the navy yard, or to bring away the ships. Only recently, Welles had been able to assemble enough sailors to remove the most valuable vessel there, the *Merrimac*; and he now learned that the old commandant of the yard, overborne by treacherous subordinates, had refused to permit the ship to leave. An expedition was hastily rushed to Norfolk. The prospect of losing valuable ships was a heavy one. Of the Navy's ninety vessels, more than half were ancient and useless, and most of the serviceable ships were scattered at foreign stations. In answer to a program of privateering announced by the Confederacy, the President published a proclamation of a blockade of the rebel ports from South Carolina to Texas. Even with a powerful navy, it was a long coast line to patrol.

On Friday, the Cabinet had grim news from Maryland, as well as from Virginia. An official dispatch brought word of fearful excitement in Baltimore, of a collision between citizens and Northern troops. Rumors that the capital's reinforcements had been attacked were flying through the city. By five o'clock, the depot was surrounded with anxious people. The regular afternoon train was followed by a special, which stopped just outside the station. Uniforms descended from the cars, and the crowd hailed with a cheer the Sixth Massachusetts Regiment, the first armed volunteers to come to the defense of Washington. They were soldierly figures in their dark-gray overcoats, with neat knapsacks and new rifles; but their young faces were dirty and haggard. They had fought their way through a mob, hurling stones and firing guns, in the streets of Baltimore. Their casualties were four dead and thirty-one wounded. As the stretchers were carried out, some ladies sprang forward to dress the wounds with handkerchiefs. Their leader was the Patent Office clerk, Miss Clara Barton of Massachusetts—a shy little spinster, who forgot her timidity in her earnestness to assist the boys from her home State. The injured men were placed in hacks and removed to the E Street Infirmary, and the crowd escorted the regiment as it marched to the Capitol. The soldiers were fasting and exhausted, and it was late before they were handed one ration each of bacon, bread and coffee, and stumbled down to cook it on the furnace fires in the basement. Their camp was the Senate Chamber, and wrapped in their blankets, with knapsacks for pillows, they flopped heavily on the carpeted floor, the gallery seats, and the cold tiles of the corridor.

Now the capital was ringed by rebellion. The northbound trains were packed. All night the pickets were vigilant at the roads and bridges, and a sharp watch was kept by the militia at the public buildings. The sentries of the Frontier Guards patrolled the White House porticoes. Major Hunter was still faithfully stretched on the East Room floor. All Washington looked for an attack before morning; but

Secretary Cameron, sleeping on a sofa in the War Department, was disturbed only by the intrusion of a Baltimore committee, urging that no more soldiers be sent through their city. Its disaffection had been whipped into a frenzy by the casualties among the citizens, on whom the Massachusetts troops had fired, and armed secessionists were in control. At midnight, the Baltimore authorities decided on a plan for keeping the Yankee soldiers out of their town. While Simon Cameron turned over for another nap, the word was going out in Maryland to burn the bridges of the railroads to Philadelphia and Harrisburg. Washington awoke on Saturday, to find itself without railway communication with the loyal States, without mail or newspapers from the North. Until Sunday night, the telegraph faltered on. Then rioters seized the Baltimore office, and the capital was left in silence, isolation and fear.

Over the week end, women and children were sent away. Hotel guests fled the city. Office seekers scurried home. Travelers piled on board the trains that ran irregularly to Baltimore; for that city might be in the hands of a mob, but it sounded safer than Washington. Vehicles were hired at extravagant prices. Every sort of conveyance was pressed into service to carry the refugees. A long, disorderly line of traffic moved up Seventeenth Street—carriages, wagons, drays and trucks, loaded with little children and household goods. Some started out on foot, pushing carts and baby wagons filled with groceries and clothes, or wheelbarrows stacked with baggage.

Across the Potomac, secession sympathizers went in droves, carrying the story of Washington's helplessness and alarm. Travelers to Aquia Creek were chagrined at the Government's seizure of several large river steamers, an act which not only interfered with transportation to the South, but deprived Virginia of the ships. Army and Navy officers were leaving for the Confederacy by scores, and civil servants by hundreds. Quartermaster General Joseph E. Johnston sent in his resignation on Monday, and Captain Magruder took his sleek hair and fine manners to Virginia the same day. Magruder had made repeated protestations of fidelity to the President, who was shocked and pained at learning of his defection. On Monday, too, Commodore Buchanan resigned, together with most of the officers of the Navy Yard. Commander John A. Dahlgren, a brilliant ordnance officer and the inventor of the cannon which was the chief armament of the Navy, succeeded Buchanan in command. A more loyal heart than

Franklin Buchanan's never throbbed, the *National Intelligencer* still asserted, and it published an affecting description of his workmen, with tears running down their bronzed cheeks, as they listened to the Commodore's farewell admonitions to be faithful. It was soon discovered that large quantities of bombshells manufactured at the yard had been filled with sand and sawdust instead of explosives.

Some of the citizens, called on for assistance in the departments, which the exodus of clerks had left shorthanded, refused with the explanation that they would be criticized when the Virginians took possession of the capital. Unionist Washington was incredulous and baffled. The confusion of patriotic citizens was partly caused by their failure to understand that Virginia was irretrievably committed to the Confederacy. They at first interpreted the warlike movements across the Potomac as the acts of a rebellious minority and clung to the hope that secession would be repudiated by the people of Virginia. General Scott cherished no such illusion. Now he spoke of the soil of his native State as enemy's country, repeating the strange phrase over and over again. Scott had been persuaded to move from Cruchet's to Mrs. Duvall's boardinghouse on the Avenue above Seventeenth Street. People nervously observed that the General was keeping close to the War Department, with a guard of soldiers posted in the yard around his lodgings. No man dared trust his neighbor, and Scott was a Virginian. There were whispers that he was unfaithful. The day after the Baltimore attack, a committee from Richmond had called on Scott to offer him the command of the forces of Virginia, and it was announced in a Charleston newspaper and joyfully credited in the South that the General had offered his sword to his State. But Scott had served under one flag for more than fifty years, and he would die a Union man. The command of Virginia's army was given to Robert E. Lee.

The old General's gout was so bad that, when he drove to the White House for a conference, Mr. Lincoln came down and stood beside his coupé in the driveway, to spare him the pain of climbing the stairs. Troops must somehow be rushed to the capital. They might be ordered to fight their way through Baltimore—and men like Major Hunter and Kansas Jim Lane were ready to see the rebellious city laid in ruins. Mr. Lincoln, however, wanted to avoid bloodshed, and conciliate the timid Union sentiment in Maryland. The spreading turbulence in the State soon led him to abandon the hope of marching the troops around Baltimore. Scott had promptly endorsed a route, suggested on Friday by the railroad authorities—by steamer from Perryville on the north shore of the Susquehanna to Annapolis, which had a rail connection with the Washington branch line. In spite of rumors of rebel batteries on the Potomac, it was also expected that troops might come by the river route. On Sunday, the Government received the cheering news that General Benjamin F. Butler was off Annapolis with the Eighth Massachusetts Regiment, and the Seventh New York and a Rhode Island Regiment were believed to be close behind. Scott could not spare a body of cavalry to establish communication with his reinforcements, only forty miles away, but was forced to rely on scouts, who, like the Government's couriers, had difficulty in traversing the unfriendly territory of Maryland. On Monday, a letter was received from Governor Hicks, protesting against landing soldiers at Annapolis. It was known that the town was disloyal, and that the twenty miles of rails which joined it with the Washington line had been torn up. Scott, however, thought that, with good management, the soldiers could be landed and marched to Washington.

Word of the Maryland uprising had set the whole South clamoring for an immediate advance on Washington. The only news the capital received came through Baltimore and Alexandria. In the dearth of reassuring information, the rumors had full sway. Wherever men looked, they saw the shapes of danger—on the river, on the Virginia heights, on the Seventh Street Road, and on the Bladensburg Turnpike. The Prussian envoy, Baron Gerolt, placed an identifying sign, lettered in large German script, over the entrance of his legation. He had intended to make a display of his national colors, but the railroad had been interrupted before he could procure them from New York. There were stories that secessionists would start fires all over Washington, so that it might easily be overrun by invading mobs. The click of hammers in the Treasury, where workmen were fitting the doors with iron bars, gave rise to a sensational report that mines were being laid under the building.

The city looked deserted. Shops had shuttered windows, and dust gathered on the steps and railings of vacant houses. Many offices and all places of amusement were closed. Silence had fallen on the big hotels. The servants' feet waked echoes in the empty halls of Willard's. There was a short-lived alarm of famine, as provisions ceased to come in from Maryland and Virginia, and speculating grocers raised the price of flour from seven dollars and a half to twelve and fifteen dollars a barrel. During the preceding week, the Government, anticipating the arrival of thousands of soldiers, had laid in a large quantity of salt meat and other army stores, and on Sunday thousands of barrels of flour had been confiscated at the Georgetown mills. Ships and warehouses had been taken over by the militia, and all Sunday afternoon and night cartloads of barrels, trailing fine threads of flour, had moved to the Capitol, the Treasury and the Post-Office. Housewives ceased to hoard their rations and profiteering prices dropped, when it was announced that the city was provisioned for a siege.

The unchallenged arrival of two steamers on Monday had proved the rumor of a blockade to be unfounded; but no troops came by the Potomac. At noon on Tuesday, as the Cabinet sat in the White House, two more steamers were reported. There was a flash of hope which quickly died. The Norfolk expedition had returned with the news that the navy yard was lost—the buildings had been burned and the ships scuttled. That day, the Government placed a guard at the railroad depot. All cars and locomotives were seized and dispatched to Annapolis Junction.

Every day people collected at the depot, longing for the sight of soldiers. They walked aimlessly away, with apathetic and discouraged faces. The general opinion was that the South was prepared, and the North was not; and those who declared their faith in the power of the Union were met with smiles of incredulity. Looking up at the iron skeleton of the Capitol dome, one Washington resident despondently remarked, "I wonder if it will ever be finished!" "Yes, ma'am!" a Yankee voice emphatically replied. It came from a sentry of the Sixth Massachusetts, the spokesman of the spirit of the awakened North. Somehow, on Tuesday, a belated New York mail found its way to Washington. The newspapers were avidly seized. The hero of Fort Sumter, Major Anderson, had been greeted with wild enthusiasm in New York. The Seventh New York Regiment had departed in a storm of cheers. Governor Sprague of Rhode Island had sailed with a regiment from his State. The columns blazed with enlistments, orders, proclamations, flag raisings. But the newspapers were three days old, and the patriotism of the North seemed a senseless mockery. From the President to the last despairing property holder, the cry went up from Washington, "Why don't they come!"

The number of enrolled militia companies in the District mounted to thirty-three in the days of the capital's isolation, and one company of cavalry was nearly ready to be mustered in. French and Italian residents met to organize for defense. Elderly men formed the Silver Grays' Home Guard. The veterans of 1812 tottered out to offer their services. Colonel Stone admired the spirit of the District volunteers, but his enthusiasm was not shared by the rest of Washington. People looked askance at the awkward squads of civilians. Even the best trained companies seemed to be composed of underfed clerks and flat-footed German and Irish laborers. Many were of dubious fidelity. Over in Georgetown, the Potomac Light Infantry disbanded until peace should be restored, and one of its members proposed the toast: "The P. L. I., invincible in peace; invisible in war."

General Scott invited Colonel Stone to dine with him. When the meal was ended, the old General and the young Colonel sat staring at each other over their glasses of sherry. Scott recapitulated the disasters of the past few days—Harper's Ferry, the Norfolk navy yard, the burned bridges.

"They are closing their coils around us, sir!"

"Yes, General."

Stone produced his plan for the defense of Washington. His centers were three: the Capitol; the City Hall hill, with the Patent Office and Post-Office; and the Executive Square, including the mansion and its neighboring departments. Three centers were too many, the General said. They must concentrate their little force on holding the Executive Square. Its citadel was the Treasury, with every opening barricaded, and breastworks made of sandbags on the portico. It had a supply of good water, and two thousand barrels of flour in the basement. In the last extremity, the President and the Cabinet members would have to take up their quarters there. "They shall not be permitted to desert the capital!" the General said.

The President's placid manner concealed the strain he suffered. His nerves played tricks on him, as the suspense was prolonged almost beyond endurance. One day he heard a sound like the boom of cannon. None of the White House attendants had noticed anything, and Mr. Lincoln walked out to see for himself. He walked on and on to the south, until at last he stood before the Arsenal. The gunfire had been a phantom sound, but the open doors of the Arsenal were real. Mr. Lincoln saw that there were no guards on duty. Anyone could have helped himself to the arms.

The same trancelike mood which had sent the President wandering the whole desolate length of the Island was expressed in the words he spoke to some of the wounded of the Sixth Massachusetts, who came with their officers to visit him on Wednesday. "I don't believe there is any North. The Seventh Regiment is a myth. Rhode Island is not known in our geography any longer. *You* are the only Northern realities." There was an unusual irony, too, in Mr. Lincoln's tone. Since midnight on Saturday, reinforcements had been only forty miles from Washington.

Next day, the spell was broken. The sight of a train, filled and covered with soldiers, set the militia at the depot cheering. At the Capitol, the Sixth Massachusetts raised a shout. Crowds came running, and housetops, windows and balconies swarmed with people. Reviving at the sight of its deliverers, the Federal City warmed its chill faith at the fires of the North. For six days at the very outset of hostilities, it had shivered at its fate—a border town, divided within itself, and nakedly exposed to danger in a time of great rebellion.

V *Home of the Brave*

THE DELIVERANCE of Washington was effected in style. It was relieved by the Seventh New York, the kid-glove militia corps of the North. In spick-and-span gray uniforms with pipe-clayed crossbelts on their breasts, the young gentlemen had had several days' experience of the inconvenience of war—dirty, crowded ships and coarse rations, long marches and hard labor. The sandwiches, prepared for them under the supervision of Delmonico, had long ago been eaten; and they had had to leave at Annapolis a thousand velvet-covered camp stools. All night long, they had trudged the miles from Annapolis to the Junction, helping the Eighth Massachusetts to repair the track, sharing their rations with hungry, resolute sailors and mechanics. The New Yorkers had suffered all their hardships without complaint—even fellows who would send back a *turban de volaille aux truffes* at Delmonico's, if the truffles happened to be tough. They had come to save the capital, and were proudly aware of their own pluck and perseverance. As they marched in perfect step to the White House, with flags flying and bands playing, and rifles and little brass howitzers shining in the sun, they accepted the welcome of the Washington population as their rightful due.

"We are here," wrote Private Fitz James O'Brien, an Irish author, who was at home in the best circles of New York City, ". . . we all feel somewhat as Mr. Caesar Augustus must have felt when he had crossed the Rubicon."

After saluting the President, the Seventh paraded back along the Avenue to the Capitol. Through the dust, they looked at their quarters as they went up the hill, and joked about their Big Tent ready pitched. The top of the dome, of course, had been left off for ventilation.

This was dramatic business, Private Theodore Winthrop thought. He was a Winthrop of Connecticut, a thin, shy man, with luminous eyes and waving hair and side whiskers. His tastes and talents were literary; but, though he had published novels and travel sketches, he had not quite made his mark at thirty-two. There was a touch of the

dilettante about Winthrop—something refined and anemic and ineffectual. A friend observed in him the "curious critical introspection
. . . which paralyzes action." Henry Adams would have understood
him. They had been pruned by the same sharp culture.

Yet, in the rough and tumble of American life, Theodore Winthrop had suddenly discovered direction and deep meaning. He had
been living on Staten Island when the President called for volunteers,
and he had lost no time in presenting himself at the Seventh Regiment
armory. It had all happened very quickly after that—the new gray
uniform, the thousand comrades, the cheering New York crowds,
the journey, the fellowship with the Eighth Massachusetts at Annapolis and on the march. Now the Seventh was climbing the very
steps of the national Capitol, entering the crimson and gold Hall
of Representatives. Bayonets, Winthrop thought as he surveyed the
seats, were taking the place of buncombe.

Desks and gallery benches were allotted to the men. The leftovers
occupied corners and lobbies. The staff used the committee rooms.
The colonel took the Speaker's parlor. Commenting favorably on the
congressmen's lavatories, the Seventh washed; and then, formed in
companies, they marched down the hill to dine at the big hotels.
This regiment was never obliged to put up with a ration of bacon
and biscuit in the furnace room, but ate three times a day on the
Avenue during the week it spent in the Capitol.

Early the next morning, soldiers from Massachusetts and Rhode
Island came tramping into Washington. Troop ships were gathering
in a cloud outside the port of Annapolis, whose tenuous little railroad
now formed the connecting link between the capital and the North.
Brigadier-General Ben Butler was assigned to the command of the
newly formed Department of Annapolis. He vigorously expedited the
forwarding of regiments to Washington, but his jealous quarrels with
the colonel of the Seventh New York had been a factor in delaying
the arrival of the first troops. Butler was a military amateur, puffed
up with self-importance. His stout body was encased in a gorgeous,
gold-embroidered militia uniform, his crossed eyes flashed authority
and he gave his orders as curtly as a general on the stage. Although
he claimed for the Eighth Massachusetts full credit for repairing the
tracks, there were also skilled workmen on the job. At the request of
Secretary Cameron, Mr. Thomas A. Scott, vice-president of the Pennsylvania Railroad, had hastened to Annapolis with a corps of assist-

ants. His former private secretary and personal telegrapher, a dapper little flaxen-haired Scotchman named Andrew Carnegie, had pitched in with the laborers and militia, and was the engineer of the first train which carried soldiers to Washington over the reconstructed line from Annapolis. On the way, he stopped the train to repair the telegraph line, which had been torn down and pinned to the ground. As he pulled up the stake, the released wires lashed his face, and Carnegie was bleeding profusely when he arrived at the capital.

The Eighth Massachusetts was quartered in the well-ventilated Rotunda of the Capitol, between their comrades of the Sixth and their new-found friends of the Seventh New York. Drums beat, feet tramped and guns clanked in the marble halls. In both wings, mock sessions of Congress were the favorite diversion. The uproar started every morning with the rattle of reveille. A self-appointed presiding officer rapped for order. The galleries shouted to the floor, and the floor bawled back. There were pompous speeches and burlesque debates, greeted by howls of applause and hoots of derision. In the midst of the racket, some men were always writing letters. The militia thought it comical to sit at the legislators' desks and use the stationery of House and Senate; and their prolific correspondence did not even entail the expense of three cents' postage, for the letters all were franked.

The Capitol park was a pleasant drill ground, fragrant with snowballs and horse-chestnut blossoms. Soldiers stretched on the grass in the shade to watch the evolutions of the other regiments. In ancient committee rooms in the basement, a huge bakery was being established, and, as the May days passed, smoke belched from queer little chimneys that dotted the west terrace. Soldiers lost themselves in the caves and crypts, with barrels of flour in every one of them. Even after taps had sounded, the basement of the Capitol was lively. Men in paper caps moved around the enormous troughs and ovens. Sentries stood at their posts, their guns gleaming in the gaslight, and the relief awaited its turn in the guardroom. Toward morning, the smell of fresh bread drifted warmly through the cellar damp. The wagons began to back up to receive their loads of brown loaves for the regiments.

The men of the First Rhode Island had spread their bunks beside the cabinets of curiosities in the Patent Office. They were likely troops in simple coarse uniforms—gray pants, dark-blue flannel shirts and

Army hats, turned up at the side—and across their shoulders they slung the scarlet rolls of their blankets. The absence of smart trappings made the Rhode Island militia look fit and ready for business, though the regiment was noted for the social standing of some of its private soldiers. John Hay, who had attended Brown University, and knew Providence well, was impressed by the spectacle of men of wealth and breeding, quietly doing their duty amid the litter of Company C's quarters in the Patent Office. "When men like these leave their horses, their women and their wine," he wrote with that accent of youthful snobbery which oddly accords with his admiration for Lincoln, "harden their hands, eat crackers for dinner, wear a shirt for a week and never black their shoes,—all for a principle—it is hard to set any bounds to the possibilities of such an army."

The First Rhode Island was commanded by a graduate of West Point, Colonel Ambrose E. Burnside, who had started out in life as a tailor in Indiana. He had resigned from the Army to go into business. Burnside was that rarity in the militia organizations, a professional soldier; and he was, in addition, a splendid military figure. His big, imposing presence, bright, dark eyes and honest, genial manners won everybody's admiration; and he had a set of old-fashioned Army whiskers—forming the letter W on the upper lip and jowls—whose beauty and luxuriance would put his name in Webster's Dictionary. William Sprague, the Boy Governor of Rhode Island, dwindled into insignificance beside the hearty colonel. His importance was derived from the family cotton mills—he had the reputation of being the richest man in New England. Small, thin and stooping, with an amiable, eyeglassed face, Sprague had accompanied the troops from his State, wearing military dress and a yellow-plumed hat. It was soon observed that the lovely Miss Kate Chase was frequently in his society, and appeared to be acting in the capacity of hostess at the Rhode Island quarters. Even General Scott took an interest in the gossip, and watched the young lady narrowly when the Boy Governor, during a military display, went to the Chases' carriage to pay his respects.

The Rhode Islanders had brought four women with them—a laundress and three relatives, charming ladies, who, said the *Star*, "utterly refused to be left at home." One of them was immediately married to a soldier. Her bridal dress was Turkish—a blouse of cherry-colored satin, blue pants and a felt hat with white plumes. Another was Kady Brownell, a stern-faced girl with long, flowing hair, who was the wife of a sergeant. Kady had a passion for military life, and she wore a modified uniform, with a skirt covering the trousers to the knee, a sash with big curtain tassels, and a sword. She was presently made color-bearer of her husband's company.

The Fifth Massachusetts was encamped in the Treasury, cooking and eating in the courtyard. An open shed near by served as both barracks and stable for a company of United States dragoons. There were regiments sleeping in warehouses and in the Center Market, on the waxed floors of the Assembly Rooms on Louisiana Avenue, and in the white muslin Palace of Aladdin behind the City Hall. The Seventy-first New York was sent to the Navy Yard, and huts were built for the Twelfth New York in Franklin Square.

A high board fence was built at the depot to protect the troops from the welcoming crowds. Every day, the population turned out to see the parade on the Avenue. "It seemed," wrote Theodore Winthrop, "as if all the able-bodied men in the country were moving, on the first of May, with all their property on their backs, to agreeable, but dusty lodgings on the Potomac." Soldiers in gray and soldiers in blue, garish companies of Zouaves, chasseurs and firemen carried their presentation flags past the White House. The legions of the New Yorkers mingled with regiments from Pennsylvania, from Connecticut, Vermont, New Jersey, and Michigan. The full brigade from New Jersey, thirty-two hundred strong, was the largest body of men that Washington had ever seen in line; but the record soon was broken by a single afternoon's parade of four thousand men, their bayonets glittering all the way from Sixth to Fifteenth Streets. They comprised six regiments from three different States, arriving so close together that they formed a continuous procession.

Some of the regiments had made circuitous voyages, and others had been detained on guard duty along the railroad. In varying degrees, all had endured hunger and exposure. Their privations had been partially mitigated by the prompt action of Mr. James S. Wadsworth of western New York, who had dispatched a steamer loaded with provisions to Annapolis. The War Office was not even organized to take efficient care of the troops when they reached the capital. Its bureaus were accustomed to the leisurely, red-tape formalities of a small peacetime establishment, and the post of Quartermaster General was still vacant. Every regiment was greeted like an unexpected guest, for whose entertainment no provision has been made. The Commissary Department laid in large quantities of food supplies, but had no organization for distributing them. Horses and wagons were lacking. Some days passed before cooking facilities were introduced into buildings where thousands of men were quartered. Tents, cots, mattresses, blankets, clothing, stoves and kitchen utensils were immediately needed on a scale beyond the wildest imagination of the functionaries. Orders were hurriedly placed by the Government and by State authorities, almost without regard to price or quality. The Medical Bureau had no means of caring for the many cases of accidents and illness, and did not devise any, beyond reserving forty beds at the Washington Infirmary on E Street. Later, the old Union Hotel at Georgetown was taken for a Government hospital, but most sick and injured men were cared for by their own regiments or by private charity.

The War Department was incapable of making the living arrangements necessary for a large convention; but the thousands arriving in Washington were soldiers, and, save for a few regiments who had rifles, they needed arms. The Northern arsenals contained a small number of improved weapons. In the main, however, they were stocked with old flintlock muskets of Revolutionary days, altered by the addition of the percussion cap and rifling. These rusty and clumsy guns, frequently defective, were handed out to the militia. The Ordnance Department, as hidebound as the other bureaus, planned for the future, not by ordering a large supply of breech-loading rifles, but by purchasing the antiquated arms of Europe, of various calibres and patterns.

As the well-equipped regiments received their baggage, they were sent to make their camps on the hills around the city. While in some new organizations the men did not possess even a change of underwear, the established militia regiments of the East had towering piles of tents, bags, haversacks, knapsacks, overcoats, blankets and hammocks. They staggered under loads of parting gifts—pipes, tobacco, pills, needlebooks, Bibles, books, magazines, patent knives, towels, soap, slippers, water filters and portable writing desks. The food and other luxuries which were sent to them at Washington swamped the post-office and the express company. In suitability for army life, it was difficult to choose between regiments that were destitute, and those which required from twenty-five to fifty wagons to transport their baggage.

The Irishmen of the Sixty-ninth New York marched out with emerald colors flying to the grounds of Georgetown College. They were loyal to a man to their narrow-faced commander, Colonel Michael Corcoran, who had refused to order them to parade in honor of the Prince of Wales during his visit to New York. Corcoran had been court-martialed for his disobedience, but the charges were dismissed to permit him to lead his command to the seat of war. The Southern students all were gone from Georgetown College, and others had been withdrawn by their parents in apprehension of disturbances in the District. About seventy, however, still remained, and the courses of instruction proceeded while the Sixty-ninth New York occupied the campus.

The New Jersey Brigade camped on Meridian Hill, in the neighborhood of the Seventh New York. The regular dragoons were sent out the Seventh Street Road. The First and Second Connecticut went to Glenwood, W. W. Corcoran's fine estate two miles north of Washington. The Rhode Islanders occupied huts, roofed in felt, in the vicinity of Glenwood Cemetery. The entrances had curtains of red, white and blue, and several soldiers, with Yankee ingenuity, dug cellars underneath the floor, to keep their provisions cool. Some regret was expressed that they did not reach camp in time to get in a patch of vegetables.

By the middle of May, vast loads of freight were coming to Washington by rail and by the Potomac. The Navy Yard was filled with steamers, schooners, screw packets and tugs, carrying thousands of blankets and tons of coal, hard bread and groceries. A herd of cattle, ordered to provide fresh beef for the soldiers, was put to pasture in the grounds of the Washington Monument, and presently fell into the canal. It took a day and a half to drive them back ashore, and six fine beeves were drowned. Washington began to be familiar with the army of the profiteering contractors, who packed Secretary Cameron's office to compete for a fat cut of the Government funds, in return for sleazy blankets, shoddy uniforms and shoes and knapsacks that fell to pieces. By degrees, through some superhuman exertion of the Quartermaster's Department, enough camp equipage arrived to outfit most of the unprovided regiments, and a semicircle of encampments formed on the hills behind the city.

The apprehensions of the Washington population had been immediately dissipated by the arrival of troops. Confectioners, oyster-men and barbers were delighted with their trade, and all but die-hard secessionists rejoiced to find that war, which had been heralded by such great alarms, had turned out to be a holiday outing of militia. Two days after the Seventh New York reached the city, its band played on the lawn south of the White House. A gaily dressed and carefree crowd strolled through the grounds, to the strains of "Yankee Doodle," "Upidee," "The Girl I Left Behind Me," and "Columbia, the Gem of the Ocean." The Saturday afternoon concerts of the Marine Band were offered, just as in normal times, and there were many novel diversions—a variety of regimental concerts and serenades, drills, dress parades and flag raisings. There was a grand celebration at the Patent Office, where the President hoisted the big new flag contributed by the clerks of the Interior Department. The Rhode Island troops cheered manfully, and, after performing some military evolutions, marched into their quarters, singing "Our Flag Still Waves." At the Navy Yard, the band of the Seventy-first New York gave a matinee concert, with singing, before a large and distinguished audience. One of the great cast-iron Dahlgren guns was fired at targets in the river, and the Seventy-first New York marched in dress parade.

> Strangers began to come in to see the show [wrote Joseph Bradley Varnum], children were everywhere seen playing at soldiers in the streets—the ladies were delighted with the officer-beaux, and the strains of music from the numerous military bands. There seemed to be one continual drumbeat. People were awakened by the reveille, walked with measured tread during the day, and were lulled by the tattoo at night. All seemed more like a grand gala season than a serious work of war.

Patriotic citizens of Washington rallied to the aid of the soldiers. The Y.M.C.A. held services, and handed out Bibles and tracts. Ladies carried delicacies to the sick, and gathered to make havelocks, the headdresses which had been designed for troops in India by the British general, Sir Henry Havelock. They were made of heavy white drilling, and hung in long flaps over the soldiers' necks. As havelocks were declared to be a perfect protection from sunstroke, they were made in enormous quantities by ladies who longed to be of service. All over the Union, bales of white drilling piled up in church sewing circles, and soon the volunteers, wearing a faintly Bedouin air, were enduring the heat of the havelocks, as well as the rays of the sun.

After the Seventh New York pitched its tents on a level clover field on Meridian Hill, the Fourteenth Street Road was lively every evening with carriages and horsemen on the way to the dress parade. Sometimes Cabinet ministers were among the spectators: smiling Mr. Seward, with "a head like a wise macaw"; or Mr. Welles, who looked like an exasperated Santa Claus; or Mr. Cameron, his thin face marked by "a thousand political bargains." Major Robert Anderson, feted and serenaded in Washington, rode out one afternoon to review the famous Seventh. Hundreds of brightly bonneted ladies leaned on their escorts' arms on the pretty terrace shaded by oak trees. Below them, warm in the evening light, lay Washington—"ambitious Washington, stretching itself along and along like the shackly files of an army of recruits."

When the dress parade was over and the carriages went bumping back along the Fourteenth Street Road, when the last horseman had jounced away and the soft light had faded, then the Seventh relaxed and was at ease in its neat village of tents, with marquees, barbershops, offices and kitchens. Each tent became "a little illuminated pyramid," and the cooking fires burned bright along the company streets, labeled with droll and fanciful names.

> At last, when the songs have been sung and the hundred rumors of the day discussed [wrote Private Winthrop], at ten the intrusive drums and scolding fifes get together and stir up a concert, always premature, called tattoo. The Seventh Regiment begins to peel for bed. . . . At taps—half-past ten—out go the lights. . . . Then, and until the dawn of another day, a cordon of snorers inside a cordon of sentries surrounds our national capital. The outer cordon sounds its "All's well"; and the inner cordon, slumbering, echoes it.

Another regiment of New Yorkers attracted quite as much attention as the Seventh, though for totally different reasons. Elmer Ellsworth, discouraged in his aspirations to a War Department post by the jealous antagonism of Army officers, had hurried up to New York to recruit a regiment from the volunteer fire departments. He returned early in May with a gang of roughs, dressed in gray, scarlet and blue Zouave costumes, armed with rifles and huge bowie knives, and encumbered with handsome presentation flags.

Heavy-shouldered, hard-faced, spoiling for a fight, the Fire Zouaves were a new type of hero. They tumbled off the cars, asking for Jeff Davis and growling over the fact that they had been brought by way of Annapolis. "We would have gone through Baltimore like a dose of salts," one of them told the *Star* reporter. As they marched up the Avenue, the Franklin Hose Company reel dashed past them on the way to a fire, and the Zouaves hailed the apparatus with a yell of recognition. Ellsworth was indignant that no preparations had been made for the regiment. Sitting in Hammack's restaurant with John Hay, he could not enjoy his tea because his Zouaves had not been fed. Like them, he wore his hair shorn to the scalp under a little red cap, and carried a knife a foot long. His face was thin, his voice was hoarse, but he was in command of men, and he was happy.

The regiment was soon installed in the old and new Halls of Representatives. In their gaudy fancy dress, the brawny firemen sat about the floor, smoking, reading, sleeping or playing cards. They swung themselves down on ropes from the cornice of the Rotunda, walked around the outside parapets and hung like monkeys from the edge of the dome. One day, some of the men contrived to have the fire bell rung, ran to the Franklin engine house on the Avenue opposite Willard's, and "snaked out" the engine and hose reel which had been provided by Federal funds for the protection of the public buildings. After a gallop around town, they returned to their quarters, steaming hot and satisfied.

The Fire Zouaves had great respect for their little colonel, but they were as wild as wharf rats. Some seized a wandering pig, cut its throat and ate it. One Zouave pushed another through thirty-five dollars' worth of plate-glass window. They bought new shoes at a fashionable bootmaker's, and asked that the bill be sent to Old Abe. Dinners and suppers, cigars and transportation were charged to Jeff Davis. The firemen chased secessionists, and frightened old ladies. There was a horrible story of seduction which terrified "the maiden antiques" of the town. The regiment was superbly able-bodied and pugnacious, and it had enlisted, not for a paltry three months, but for three years. The *Star* treated the Fire Zouaves with indulgence, called them the Pet Lambs and thought their antics very funny. Washington citizens were, however, not amused. No crime was believed too dreadful for "those awful New York Zouaves," and a straw-stuffed effigy of Jeff Davis, playfully suspended from a buttonwood tree in the Capitol park, gave rise to a rumor that they had hanged one of their victims. Colonel Ellsworth sent the most recalcitrant soldiers home, put a few rascals in irons and dramatically adjured the rest to noble conduct. His speech was greeted with affectionate shouts of "Bully for you," and he privately expressed the opinion that most of the criticisms of his command had originated in the inventive brains of the reporters.

After the Fire Zouaves had spent a week at the Capitol, they had an opportunity to distinguish themselves. Early one morning, a fire broke out in a tailor shop next door to Willard's. As the Washington fire companies were notorious for letting buildings burn to their foundations, Colonel Joseph Mansfield, commanding the Department of Washington, gave orders to call out a detachment of the New Yorkers. Colonel Ellsworth detailed ten men from each company, and led them on a run down the Avenue. They broke down the door of the Franklin engine house, and dashed across the street, followed by most of the remaining members of the regiment, who had knocked down the sentries at the doors and leapt from the windows of the Capitol at the cry of fire. A large crowd on the Avenue, including the guests of the hotel in varied wardrobes, watched the Zouaves expertly mounting lightning rods, and climbing into windows. They formed themselves into human ladders for passing up water buckets, and one man was suspended head first from the burning roof to reach the hose line. Suddenly, a Union flag on the roof quivered and fell. Secessionists in the crowd made mocking comments, but some Zouaves caught the flag and waved it, and Willard's hastily ran up two flags in a roar of cheers. With an exhibition fire drill and a patriotic demonstration, a calamity was averted. The tailor shop was in ruins, but Willard's was saved.

By breakfast time, in spite of a smell of smoke and some water damage, the hotel was doing business as usual. Servants cleaned the floors and washed the windows, while in the dining-room the Zouave heroes breakfasted with the guests, on Mr. Joseph Willard's invitation. Colonel Mansfield had complimented them. They had been profusely thanked by all hands. Intoxicated by applause, they amused themselves during the morning by pulling down the walls of the burned building "in the presence of a large assemblage of both sexes." That day, the Pet Lambs had things their own way. They seized engines and hose reels and ran in all quarters of the city, followed by "the usual fire-engine crowd." A purse of five hundred dollars was made up for them, and even Mayor Berret chipped in ten dollars. Nevertheless, the Zouaves had succeeded in clouding the admiration of Washington for the volunteers. War, it began to be realized, brought out not only the best, but the worst—the idle and vicious, as well as the gallant. Probably no one was sorry, and doubtless there were many who thought the camp site appropriately chosen, when the New York firemen were moved to the vicinity of the Government Insane Asylum.

The newspapers of Washington, in recording the daily life of the city, were reporting matters of unprecedented interest to the nation. The *National Intelligencer,* lofty, conservative and, in the old-fashioned sense, Southern, had seldom condescended to local items. Its proprietor, Mr. W. W. Seaton, aged eighty, had acquired an interest in the newspaper shortly before the office was burned by the British. On the day that the Seventh New York arrived in Washington, the *Intelligencer* contained a rather petulant editorial on national insanity, and a long article about the disappearance of salmon fishing in England. It was a feeble voice of elderly moderation in the rising chorus of war; but it did its best to praise the volunteers. It observed that, so strict was the Seventh's regard for propriety, that during the encampment on Meridian Hill the soldiers did not disturb a fence rail, nor even pull a flower. It described divine service at the Patent Office, and temperance and prayer meetings in Franklin Square; and printed a pious anecdote about some New Jersey volunteers' presenting a handsome Bible to an old lady who had given vegetables to one of their sick comrades. Concerned for the reputation of the capital, the *Intelligencer* scoffed at reports that the best possible order did not prevail in Washington; and it was closely seconded by the *National Republican,* the rather undistinguished organ of the new party in power, in portraying Washington as a military Utopia.

The *Evening Star* was a saltier sheet altogether. It was owned and edited by Mr. W. D. Wallach, a lively and keen-witted journalist, and it had the largest circulation of any local newspaper in the District. Wallach, in spite of Southern connections and ultra-Democratic sympathies, strongly supported the administration. But the *Star* printed the news; and its columns gave a picture, not of Utopia, but of a city which was gradually being driven to distraction.

Washington's prayers for soldiers had been answered with a vengeance. The country town had been turned into a great, confused garrison, and the entertaining novelty had soon begun to pall. Quiet residential neighborhoods were in an uproar. Soldiers were drilling and bugling and drumming all over the place. In spite of excellent discipline in the Twelfth New York, the encampment in Franklin Square and the surrounding regimental hospitals made the neighborhood so unpleasant that Mr. Stanton was obliged to move his family out of their house on K Street.

As irresponsible as children, the soldiers fired their weapons in any direction, causing accidents in streets and even in houses. Ladies were frightened to cross the canal bridges or enter the Smithsonian grounds, which had been selected as suitable spots for target practice. Militiamen were accustomed to handling muskets or rifles, and country boys knew about squirrel guns. Almost none, however, had had any experience with pistols or revolvers. The volunteers regarded small arms as amusing toys, skylarked with them, dropped them and snapped caps on them to kill flies. The result was a long casualty list.

Keyed to a pitch of high patriotic excitement, the Yankee boys suffered from anticlimax in Washington. The city itself was a disappointment. They had not expected it to be like Boston or New York or Philadelphia, but they were depressed at seeing that the national capital was a ramshackle town, dirty and unpaved. "Hardly worth defending, except for the éclat of the thing," one volunteer remarked. Washington citizens, though they charged high prices for their milk and butter and strawberries, seemed slow-paced and indolent to the Northerners. The only energetic inhabitants appeared to be children— little white newsboys, shrilling the *New York Herald,* at twenty-five cents a copy, small darkies crying "Shine your boots for half a dime with the Union polish." Even more astounding than the general slovenliness of dust and bad smells, lounging Negroes and marauding pigs, was the emotional lethargy of the population. After the war fever of the North, the soldiers found the quiet of Washington bewildering. "It is as if we were here separated by a screen from the universal excitement," wrote Carl Schurz, a German-American, who had taken an active part in campaigning for Lincoln's election. For all its guards and barricades, the town did not appear to be in danger. The volunteers stared in amazement at the workmen fluting the columns and carving the cornices of the Capitol Extension.

Many young crusaders reacted to boredom and discomfort by going on drunken sprees. While no other regiment was composed of such lawless elements as the Fire Zouaves, and it was admitted that most of the soldiers conducted themselves decently, the riotous minority was large enough to destroy the peace of Washington. Intoxicated playboys whooped it up in the streets, and fought with each other and with their officers. The city police had never been able to cope with the offenses of normal times, and public confidence in its efficiency was not encouraged by the widespread disaffection to the Government which existed in both the day and night forces. A provost guard was soon formed to patrol the town at night. The soldiers were ordered to be in their quarters at nine-thirty, and Mayor Berret closed the drinking places at the same hour; but the provost guard was still kept busy carrying delinquents to the station houses, where they were often subjected to the punishment of the shower bath, a stream of cold water played from a hose on their naked backs.

Still more disturbing to the capital was the antagonism which some of the troops developed toward the residents. They brashly insulted many families, and brawled with civilians who incurred their displeasure. Sometimes, the soldiers may have been justified in their belligerence. There was the case of a private of the Twelfth New York whom a Washington man called a Northern son of a bitch. Outraged at discovering sympathy with secession in the capital they had come to defend, the volunteers arrested a number of citizens and hauled them off to prison. Most of the cases were discharged for want of evidence, or released on taking the oath of allegiance. Yankee patriots were confused to find that the arrests were frowned on as high-handed displays of military authority.

For the most part, the soldiers were entirely unprepared for shifting for themselves. The best of the militia regiments had had no real experience of camp life. They were merely social clubs which made a hobby of drilling, and enjoyed parading in their fine uniforms on national holidays. Ben Butler admitted that even the handy boys of the Eighth Massachusetts did not know how to cook, because they had

always taken caterers with them on the glorified picnics of their encampments. They looked with a laughable uncertainty at the salt beef
and hard bread and cords of wood which were distributed to them.
Every regiment was surrounded by sutlers, and the men made themselves sick on tainted pies and cakes and candy. Many of them, like
small boys escaped from their mothers, neglected to change their
underwear for weeks at a time, and some had no underwear to change.

Certain regiments showed remarkable initiative in creating comfortable camps, with well-organized kitchens and bakeries, and tidy
rows of tents, decked with green boughs. They were, however, entirely
uninstructed in matters of hygiene, placed the tents too close together,
did not provide drainage, and usually thought it unnecessary to dig
latrines. In the city, the sanitary conditions were appalling. Washington, with its river flats, its defective sewage system and its many
privies, had always been odorous in warm weather. In May of 1861,
it was as sour as a medieval plague spot. The ill-ventilated buildings
were stale. Squares festered. Alleys stank. The barracks of the Fourth
and Fifth Pennsylvania Regiments, at the rear of the City Hall and
at the Assembly Rooms, were public nuisances. "Are we to have
pestilence among us?" asked the *Evening Star,* and the query was
echoed by the worried citizens. The comatose Board of Health aroused
itself to a protest, the Surgeon General made inquiries and the War
Department conducted an investigation.

The town was growing murmurous with complaints, directed not
so much against the men as against the officers. It was evident that
decent camps and orderly conduct were the rule in regiments whose
officers were conscientious. Militia colonels owed their positions to
their personal popularity, and the colonels of the newly formed regiments—usually appointed by the governors of their respective States—
were chosen, not on the basis of military aptitude, but because of their
influence, political services or ability to raise recruits. All other officers
were elected by the soldiers themselves. Under this system, shoulder
straps conferred no authority, and the officers had to win the respect
of their commands by their qualities of decency, industry and intelligence.

It required no small application to master the varied details of
Army regulations, and to organize regimental commissary, quartermaster and medical departments, while boning up on unfamiliar
manuals of drill and tactics. Out of the many random selections, some

officers were stupid and incompetent, and a few were downright dishonest. Many were lazy and indifferent, and preferred lounging around the Washington bars to attending to the training and welfare of their men. There were regiments which were getting almost no rations at all, while others complained of measly pork and musty biscuits. The food provided by the Commissary Department was mainly sound enough, though coarse and without variety. The soldiers soon understood that their own officers were to blame if they fared worse than their fellows, and the disaffection in some camps mounted almost to mutiny.

Even men who held their officers in high esteem had no intention of giving implicit obedience to comrades on whom they had conferred rank. Democratically resentful of the notion of a military caste, privates slapped their company officers on the back, called them by their first names and thought that saluting them was pure nonsense. These soldiers were independent Americans who had sprung to arms at their country's call, and they were ready to fight, but not to submit to a lot of strait-laced discipline and irksome military formalities.

The system of electing officers was acceptable, not only to the volunteers themselves, but to the American people. It was supposed that the technical side of war could be easily mastered, and that resourceful Yankees would soon develop into competent military leaders. Only Army men looked with contempt on the volunteer organizations. The election of untrained officers was encouraged by General Scott's policy of retaining professional soldiers in command of regulars, on whom he depended for the brunt of the fighting. The three months' men were enlisted for too short a period to be made into soldiers before the time came to muster them out. Since the fall of Sumter, Scott had faced the fact of war. He was counting on the blockade to close the Southern ports—for, as Gideon Welles remarked, Scott was always ready to put the burden on the Navy. Then, in time, when the regular Army had been enlarged and a large force of three years' volunteers had been trained, Scott planned to send an expedition down the Mississippi to complete the strangulation of the Confederacy. He discouraged the organization of volunteer artillery and cavalry. Carl Schurz was full of enthusiasm for raising a cavalry regiment of New York German-Americans. He had been appointed minister to Spain as a reward for his campaign services, but he won consent to deferring his mission, although Scott frowned on his project. If there were to be any war at all, the General impatiently told Schurz, it would be over long before volunteer cavalry could be made fit for service in the field.

Mr. Seward and a few others were saying that the war would be very short, and the President thought that they might be right; but he was not entirely sanguine. Virginia was in arms. North Carolina, Tennessee and Arkansas were going with the Confederacy. Maryland, Kentucky and Missouri were torn by internal dissension. On the question of the three months' militia, the Government at least partly concurred with Scott. The War Department had refused to accept any more men for a short term of service, and the President had widely exceeded his powers by calling out volunteers for three years, and by adding ten regiments to the regular Army and eighteen thousand seamen to the Navy. In the absence of Congress, Mr. Lincoln had assumed the war powers of the Government. Appalled at their own audacity, the gentlemen of the Cabinet had sanctioned acts which, in Mr. Seward's opinion, might bring them all to the scaffold. One of these had been the proclamation of the blockade, now also applied to the coasts of Virginia and North Carolina. Mr. Lincoln had also authorized Scott to suspend the writ of *habeas corpus* along any military line between Washington and Philadelphia. This order would bring charges of military despotism against the administration, but Mr. Lincoln would not hesitate to extend it ruthlessly, as he felt the public safety should require.

For nearly four weeks after troops had begun to arrive for the defense of Washington, the only change in its situation was the subsidence of secessionist agitation in Maryland. The most virulent disunionists went off to join the rebel forces at Harper's Ferry and Richmond. Three weeks after the attack on the Sixth Massachusetts, some thirteen hundred regulars were transported across south Baltimore without disturbance.

Ben Butler had been chafing for drastic action in Maryland. Shortly before the resumption of the usual train service between Washington and Philadelphia, he conceived a dramatic plan. To forestall an attack from Harper's Ferry, he had been stationed by General Scott at the Relay House, the junction of the Baltimore and Ohio Railroad with the Washington line. Taking the Sixth Massachusetts and a few other troops, Butler made a surprise movement on Baltimore, and planted his artillery on Federal Hill. As he had expected, he met with no opposition, and he was highly pleased with himself for having brought Baltimore into subjection.

Butler was soon informed that he was to be promoted to the rank of major-general and placed in command of an important post, Fort Monroe. He was, however, deeply wounded at being relieved of the command of the Department of Annapolis, and by a censorious communication which he had received from General Scott, who had been as surprised as Baltimore. A fort was not as large as a department, and Butler felt that the transfer disgraced him, and was ready to quit the Army and go home. He took the cars to Washington and had a furious quarrel with Scott. While he was in the General's presence, he did not even wink, but on his return to his rooms at the National he threw himself on the lounge and burst into a flood of tears.

A lifetime of political manipulation had well qualified Secretary Cameron to understand that the loss of the adherence of a leading Democrat was not one to be taken lightly by the administration; and his efforts to mollify General Butler were warmly abetted by the President and Secretary Chase. Furthermore, Butler's boldness had won him much popular acclaim. There were consoling items in the press, and he was waited on at the National by many friends and serenaded by Withers's Brass Band. After all, he concluded to give in and be a major-general, and take command of Fort Monroe. Before he left Washington, he had an agreeable conference with General Scott, who congratulated him on the assignment, which he said was very fortunate at that season on account of the soft-shell crabs and the delicious hogfish.

On the Virginia side of the Potomac, the situation was still menacing. With a spyglass, a Confederate flag could be plainly seen on the roof of the Marshall House, a tavern in Alexandria; while along the shore the campfires of General Lee's forces pricked the evening dusk. Hope had slowly died in Washington that the population of Virginia would adhere to the Union, although it was not until May 23 that the formality of a popular ratification of secession showed that the only loyal counties lay west of the Allegheny Mountains. The capital, protected by its large garrison, was not apprehensive. Traffic moved peaceably across the bridges. After some interruption, farmers once more brought their crops to the city markets, and soldiers occasionally strolled over to have a look at Virginia.

Army officers, however, did not share the opinion that the defense of Washington had been accomplished by overrunning the town with men. The white-bearded Inspector General, Colonel Mansfield, had advised the occupation of the Virginia shore of the Potomac immediately after taking command of the Department of Washington. Mansfield was an engineer, and he saw the importance of holding the Arlington Heights, which were only two miles distant from the low-lying executive offices and Government buildings. The range of artillery fire had recently been increased to three or even four miles. For the security of Washington, redoubts were needed at the south end of the Long Bridge and the Chain Bridge, and also of the Aqueduct, which carried the Chesapeake and Ohio Canal over the river from Georgetown. Finally, to protect the navigation of the Potomac, the decayed old port of Alexandria must be occupied by Federal troops.

Mansfield's recommendations were accepted, but they could not immediately be carried out. It was not until the morning after the people of Virginia voted for secession that the soldiers of the Union advanced.

One column was to march before daybreak by the Long Bridge, another by the towpath over the Aqueduct. Colonel Ellsworth and the Fire Zouaves were to move in two steamers from Giesboro' Point, opposite the Arsenal, to Alexandria. Rumors of the movement had been whispered in Washington. The troops were packed and ready for the word that went toward midnight through the encampments. The drum beat on Meridian Hill, and the Seventh New York fell into ranks and marched through the trees to the highway. It was very still as they passed the lonely pile of Willard's. "A hag in a night-cap," wrote Private Winthrop, "reviewed us from an upper window as we tramped by."

Squads of cavalry posted across to hold the Virginia ends of the bridges. Under command of Colonel Stone, companies of District militia, including the National Rifles, advanced on scouting and patrol duty. South through the sleeping Island went boys from New York, New Jersey and Michigan. Other New Yorkers converged on the Aqueduct from the Georgetown Heights. There was no sound of drum or fife. Officers gave low-voiced commands. Artillery rumbled above the heavy irregular tread of men marching in broken step. The moon made a white path on the Potomac, and tipped the rows of bayonets with sparkling points of light.

On the Virginia shore, the regiments established their outposts and engineers traced lines of fortifications. The Seventh New York sprawled out for a rest. As the sun rose high, guns were stacked, with blankets draped over them for shade. "Nothing men can do," thought Private Winthrop, "—except picnics, with ladies in straw flats with feathers—is so picturesque as soldiering." He lay watching his comrades, as they lounged or slept or nibbled at their rations. It was hot, and he nodded. A rattle of horse's hoofs aroused him. Before he had grasped the shouted words, that Colonel Ellsworth was dead, the rider was gone, galloping on to the bridge, to carry the news to Washington.

The city was horror-struck, and at first incredulous. At ten o'clock, the tolling of the bell of the Franklin engine house confirmed the news. The flag of the fire company was lowered to half-mast, and then all the Union flags in Washington, great and small, drooped slowly in honor of young Ellsworth.

Carried on a litter of muskets, his body was taken by boat to the Navy Yard, and laid on a bench in its neat little engine house. Thousands came that day to look at the remains. At the mess of the Seventy-first New York, on duty at the yard, sat Private Francis E. Brownell of the Fire Zouaves, with blood on his gaudy uniform. Over and over again, he had to tell the story: how Ellsworth had gone to the roof of the Marshall House in Alexandria and torn down the Confederate flag; how the innkeeper had shot him, as he came down the stairs; how he, Private Brownell, had shot the innkeeper. His lip was bitten nearly through in his effort to keep from crying aloud. Ellsworth had understood the command of men. He had disciplined his New York roughs, played ball with them, fathered them, won their love and respect. As rage succeeded the first shock of grief, the Fire Zouaves threatened to burn the town of Alexandria, and it was thought prudent to confine them for the night on a steamer anchored in the middle of the Potomac.

The President had suffered a personal bereavement, and Ellsworth's funeral services were held in the Executive Mansion. More thousands filed through the East Room, where he lay in state, dressed in his uniform, with white lilies on his breast. On the casket, Mrs. Lincoln had placed his picture, framed in a waxen laurel wreath. Single-minded, courageous and austere, he was the ideal figure of a fallen hero. It was told that a medal he wore, a golden circle inscribed

"Non nobis, sed pro patria," was driven into his heart by the shot that killed him.

When the services were over, the flag-draped coffin was placed in a hearse drawn by four white horses. The military escort marched with arms reversed and colors shrouded. Directly behind the hearse came an unarmed company of Fire Zouaves, and among them Private Brownell drew all eyes, for he carried the darkly splashed Confederate flag for which Ellsworth had given his life. The President, with bowed head, drove in the cortege to the depot.

On the Avenue, the pendant flags were tied with crape. The crowds were out, but there were no cheers, only silence and tolling bells. From the capital, sorrow spread in a wave over the Union. It was as if the people of the republic, so inexperienced in war, had closed their eyes to the purpose for which their young men had been sent to Washington; as if Ellsworth's death had for a moment undeceived them, and a premonition passed, like a shudder, over all hearts.

There had been rumors of heavy fighting across the Potomac, and correspondents telegraphed alarming stories to their newspapers; but the rebel garrison had left Alexandria as the Union troops arrived, and on the heights men from New York and New Jersey, assisted by a force of laborers, were quietly engaged in "shovelling up Virginia. . . ." Lee's mansion, which had been vacated by the family, was used for army headquarters.

While the advance movement had been planned by Colonel Samuel P. Heintzelman, U. S. A., who had been called to Washington from the West, the commanding officer was an old lawyer, Charles W. Sandford, who for many years had headed New York City's large militia organization, in which he held the rank of major-general. Sandford, however, was soon superseded in command of the forces in Virginia by the Army officer, Irvin McDowell, who had an influential friend in Secretary Chase. McDowell was made a brigadier-general of volunteers, having declined the rank of major-general because he feared to excite the jealousy of his brother officers. He was a sensitive man, forty-three years old, robustly built, with cropped dark hair and narrow beard of iron gray. He had received an excellent education in France, and possessed a wide theoretical knowledge of military affairs. His hobby was architecture, and he loved music and landscape gardening. There was nothing convivial about McDowell. He neither drank nor smoked. His manners were frank and simple, but not winning. He spoke with "rough indifference" to his subordinates, and was too reserved to be popular. He had a poor memory for names and faces, and seemed absent-minded, lost in thoughts of his own, while people were talking to him.

McDowell immediately learned that his appointment was displeasing to General Scott, who twice sent messages asking him personally to request the Secretary of War not to send him across the river. The General was "cool for a great while," because the new brigadier felt too insecure to make this presumptuous application. McDowell thought that Scott was irritated because his assignment placed Sandford in an equivocal position, and especially because he resented the slight to Mansfield, who as colonel and former Inspector General outranked McDowell. Mansfield was also made a brigadier of volunteers, but the post in Virginia was more important than the command of the Department of Washington. McDowell, facing ever heavier responsibilities, keenly felt a want of co-operation. In the first weeks after he took command, nothing at all was sent across the river.

Some of the regiments which had advanced were withdrawn from Virginia. The Seventh New York, after bearing its part in a two days' chore of digging, had returned to the encampment on Meridian Hill. The regiment had volunteered for only thirty days, and its service was over. Its final perfect gesture was to contribute one hundred and three dollars to the Washington Monument—that abbreviated shaft, beside which a Government slaughterhouse was now established, with the offal rotting two and three feet deep.

Impeccable and self-satisfied, the Seventh had not accomplished very much; and it could scarcely be said that the country's need of soldiers had ended. Yet it was true that some grace departed from Washington when they trundled their little brass howitzers to the depot. More significant than the easy admiration of the crowds was the friendship they had won from the honest fellows of the Eighth Massachusetts. Affection breathed from every line of the testimonial they had inscribed to "the generous, gallant, glorious Seventh." The fervent words somehow make clear that there were kind and brave hearts under those pipe-clayed crossbelts, that those were manly hands that never dislodged a fence rail nor picked a flower on Meridian Hill.

When the Seventh took the cars for New York, Private Winthrop did not go with them. War was his destiny—he had found himself at last. At Annapolis, he had caught the attention of General Ben Butler, and a place on Butler's staff, with a major's commission, awaited him at Fort Monroe.

Having disgorged its thousands, Washington turned lazily in the warm sun, and began to prepare for the special session of Congress, which the President had convened. At the Capitol, soap and sand removed the grease, tobacco and filth of the soldiers' occupancy. It was remarked that the furniture and draperies, the mirrors, chandeliers and frescoes remained as bright as new. In spite of the well-known whittling propensities of Yankees, no cuts were found on the gallery seats. When the scrubbing was finished and the carpets had been taken up and cleaned, there was little to remind the visitor that the Capitol had been a crowded bivouac. To complete the renovation, artists were employed to decorate the red and yellow ceiling of the Hall of Representatives in less garish colors.

An alien activity was imposed on the slow life of the city. Its rough pavements were noisy with the clatter of army wagons, the screams and curses of the drivers, and the crack of their long whips. Every hotel and every house was filled. Sutlers had taken all the vacant shops. Business revived. Even property holders felt encouraged. The depot and the wharves knew a ceaseless passing of horses, cattle, wagons, ambulances, provisions, arms, equipments, uniforms—all the multiple requisitions of a Government at war. The movement around the big new stables, barns and warehouses began to give the town almost a Yankee air of bustle and trade.

The application of the modern invention, the telegraph, to military uses was strikingly apparent in Washington. Immense reels of insulated wire were among the supplies which the Government had ordered, and the War Department had been connected with the Navy Yard, the Arsenal, the Capitol, the depot, the Chain Bridge and the outlying encampments. The wires were now carried into Virginia, and a corps of operators, mainly drawn from employees of the Pennsylvania Railroad, took up their duties in and around the capital. The Executive, Thomas A. Scott, was placed in charge of Government railways and telegraphs. His right-hand man, Andy Carnegie, was stationed at Alexandria to organize military transport.

Washington was startled to learn that another scientific invention, the balloon, might be used for military observations. Professor Thaddeus S. C. Lowe, an enterprising aeronaut of twenty-nine, was sponsored by Professor Joseph Henry, the director of the Smithsonian Institution. He made several captive ascensions from the grounds of the armory on the Mall. The President and Secretary Cameron were impressed, but the experiments did not enlist the interest of General Scott. To illustrate the speed with which observations could be reported, Lowe carried aloft a telegraphic apparatus, attached by a long wire to the Executive Mansion. Mr. Lincoln received the message, "The city, with its girdle of encampments, presents a superb scene." Professor Lowe then soared over the terrain of Virginia, and reported scattered camps and a huge cloud of dust near Fairfax Court-House. He claimed an ascent of five hundred feet, though the correspondent of the *Star* thought the elevation not more than two hundred.

Washington was satiated with spectacles. It had grown blasé. No one heard the band music any longer, or the racket of fife and drum. A passing regiment evoked no more attention than a Georgetown omnibus. The First New Hampshire arrived with eighty horses and sixteen baggage wagons, a brass band with a major in a bearskin hat, a hospital wagon and a contingent of nurses in gray traveling dresses and straw flats. The First Ohio strode by with its West Point colonel, Alexander M. McCook, of the clan of the "Fighting McCooks." The Second Maine panted in, sweating in heavy overcoats. The Seventy-ninth New York, commanded by Secretary Cameron's brother, succeeded in fluttering the ladies with the thrill of seeing Highlanders in kilts; and everyone stared at Louis Blenker, the German émigré who was colonel of the Eighth New York, one of four German regiments. Blenker was a soldier of fortune, who had fought in Greece and in the German revolution of 1848. If his past was rather dubious, he was a magnificently martial figure, as he rode through Washington in his red-lined cape. Another soldier who never failed to attract attention was Captain Thomas Francis Meagher of the Sixty-ninth New York, who strutted along the Avenue in a gorgeous Zouave uniform covered with gold lace.

The regiment which completely captivated the flagging attention of Washington was a picturesque collection of foreign scamps, recruited in New York and known as the Garibaldi Guard. It was made up of Hungarians, Germans, Italians, French, Spanish and Swiss, mixed with a few Cossacks, Sepoys, Croats and English deserters, all romantically attired in red blouses and *bersaglieri* hats; and beside the companies marched vivandières in feathered hats, jaunty red jackets and blue gowns. The *Intelligencer* informed its readers that the vivandières had husbands in the ranks; but the *Star* reported that two of them were runaways from Jersey City, presently pursued and carried back to their homes. The *Star*, however, praised Colonel D'Utassy, the theatrical commander of the Garibaldi Guard, and ascribed his idiosyncrasies to his mercurial foreign temperament. D'Utassy was an adventurer, who was reputed to have been a dancing master and a circus rider prior to entering the service of the Union. He played a splendid part in the Washington pageant of 1861, but he would eventually land in Sing Sing for embezzling and cheating and persuading soldiers to desert.

The summer heat of the capital was hard on Northern boys. Fifteen or twenty men of the Second Michigan dropped in the ranks as they went through Georgetown. There were cases of dysentery in the camps. On both sides of the river, soldiers stifled in their tents. The water was like pea soup, with snakes in it, and a man was dirtier after bathing than before. The night closed in with swarms of mosquitoes and an infinite consumption of bad whisky. Rations were sometimes poor and insufficient, and a few regiments rebelled against their officers. James Jackson of the Ninth New York—a mutinous organization—refused to be mustered into the service, and was drummed out of his regiment. Disrobed of his uniform and clad in a suit of common tweed, he was released and started to run. There had been many to encourage the District volunteers who balked at the oath of allegiance; but feeling had changed in the capital. James Jackson's defection came a good six weeks too late. A crowd pursued him, hooted and kicked and stoned him. At last a justice of the peace took Jackson under his protection, and concealed him until he could escape from town.

In June, the exasperation against the irresponsible officers was flaming high in Washington. "Of soldiers the country is full," said the *Star*. "Give us organizers and commanders. We have men, let us have leaders. We have confusion, let us have order. . . ." There were black sheep in the fine-appearing Eighth New York and the Garibaldi Guard. Late in the month, when the troops received their pay, drunken pandemonium broke out in the capital. Fire Zouaves raced

up and down the Avenue, brandishing pistols and exchanging their
red caps for the hats they snatched from the heads of the passers-by.
Boys from New York and New Jersey went on the rampage, and broke
up bars and restaurants. Some volunteers wrecked a bawdy house on
the Island, carrying off china and alabaster ornaments. Others, refused
admittance to Julia Deane's brothel in Marble Alley, fired pistols at
one of the inmates, Nelly Mathews, who pluckily returned their fire.
Nelly, however, was not a good shot, and the ball entered the thigh of
a colored woman. The *Star* tried to excuse the inadequacy of the police
on the ground that they were in bad odor with the soldiers. The force
was, in any case, too small to control the vast disorder.

Early in June, a smart cavalry skirmish at Fairfax Court-House
had killed and wounded a few men. Washington had seen its first
prisoners of war—Virginia boys, who were taken to the Navy Yard.
They did not seem to realize their position, observed the *Star*, but
were entirely unconcerned, having a jolly time with cards. The country
had grown wildly impatient for news of a decisive battle. Richmond
had been made the capital of the Confederate States, and the rebel
congress was to meet there on July 20. Horace Greeley's influential
newspaper, the *New York Tribune*, had sent the cry of "On to Richmond" ringing through the North. Confederate forces were concentrated at Manassas, less than thirty miles west of Alexandria, on a line
due north from the new Confederate capital. The magnificent Federal army must rout and scatter them, and march in triumph on
Richmond, to end the rebellion for good and all.

Beyond the Alleghenies, Virginia unionists were welcoming troops
from Ohio, who had defeated a small rebel force in that district; but
from eastern Virginia came only reports of skirmishes mainly disad-
vantageous to the Federal arms. Toward the middle of June, distress-
ing news had come from Big Bethel, on the road between Hampton
and Yorktown. There, under the command of Prince John Magruder,
the Confederates had made an entrenched camp, with a masked battery. An expedition had set out from Fort Monroe to capture it. From
the start it was badly managed. The attack was blundering and irresolute, and presently, with some losses, the Federal forces retreated.

Near the close of the engagement, so near the battery that the
Confederates could distinguish his slender, gallant figure, a Union
officer tried to rally the wavering lines. In the hand that was formed

for a pen, he held a sword. Theodore Winthrop was on his great adventure. He had forgotten, in the exaltation of battle, the critical introspection that paralyzes action. Mounting a log, he raised his sword and called to the men to come on. A Carolina sharpshooter took careful aim, and Theodore Winthrop fell—a meaningless casualty of a day already lost.

VI *Excursion in Virginia*

AS SOON AS the Washington train pulled out of Baltimore, the traveler began to see the pickets guarding the railroad tracks, and the pale blotches of the camps, growing ever larger and denser as the cars moved south. The waste land around the capital seemed to have flowered in a profuse and gigantic crop of tents, guns, caissons and white-covered wagons. Passing through the Washington depot in late June, a man felt the war like a blast of furnace heat. The embattled North was filled with flags and bands, drilling soldiers and ladies' sewing circles. In the garrisoned capital, there was a grimmer reality. The main Confederate army, General Beauregard commanding, was entrenched a day's march from Washington.

The gentlemen of the Thirty-seventh Congress were assembling for the special session convened by the President's proclamation. The withdrawal of the delegations of the seceded States had diminished their numbers, placing the ambitious Republican leaders in control of both Houses. Not disaffection, but death had vacated one Democratic senator's seat. The sudden passing of Stephen A. Douglas early in June had deprived the administration of the support of the powerful little demagogue from Illinois. Among the handful from the border slave States, two senators were outstanding—Andrew Johnson of Tennessee and John C. Breckinridge of Kentucky. Tennessee had seceded, but no one doubted Johnson's staunch adherence to the Government. Kentucky had not seceded, but there was wide distrust of Breckinridge's patriotic professions. He had not come to Washington to uphold the war measures of the administration. Many doubted whether he had come for any good reason at all. His graceful presence and winning manners seemed oddly out of place in the capital from which his friends had departed.

New Englanders would head the four powerful Senate committees which shaped wartime legislation. Charles Sumner of Massachusetts was chairman of Foreign Relations, and his colleague, Henry Wilson, would preside over Military Affairs. Hale of New Hampshire would rule Naval Affairs, and Fessenden of Maine, Finance. These men and others like them—Wade of Ohio, and Chandler of Michigan —were the radicals of their party, to whom war offered an opportunity to punish the hated South and put an end to slavery. Equally vindictive was the crippled old leader of the House, Thaddeus Stevens of Pennsylvania, a brilliant and bitter antagonist of the region below the Mason and Dixon line, and of its peculiar institution. Stevens would hold the purse strings of the nation as chairman of the Committee on Ways and Means, which included jurisdiction over appropriations.

At dawn on Independence Day, the small fusillades in the Washington streets mimicked the rumble of artillery from the entrenchments across the river and the Rhode Island battery north of the city. Major-General Sandford had ordered a parade of the New York regiments which remained on the District side of the river. Over twenty thousand soldiers marched the broiling length of the Avenue that morning. It was the first grand army that Washington had ever seen. The twenty-odd regiments from New York were but a fraction of the man power in the immediate vicinity of Washington, where sixty-four regiments were concentrated, in addition to twelve hundred regulars.

Holidaymakers filled Lafayette Square and the President's grounds, and were massed along the Avenue. On a platform, canopied with flags, in front of the White House, the President and the General-in-Chief were stationed with Cabinet members and staff officers to receive the marching salute of the regiments. As the Garibaldi Guard passed by, each man tossed a spray of flowers or evergreens toward the platform, while a bouquet was thrown from the head of each company. A pretty carpet was spread before the dignitaries, and the old General was garlanded with blossoms. The graceful ceremony, with its foreign flavor, evoked the admiration of all but the owners of the ravaged gardens in the neighborhood of the Garibaldians' encampment.

For the capital's residents, Independence Day had always been the occasion for excursions and picnic parties. This year, all the groves and springs had been pre-empted by the encampments. Columbia Spring, a favorite picnic place at the Virginia end of the Long Bridge, was now Fort Runyon, with horses stabled in the ten-pin alley and a commissary in the dancing pavilion. People were reduced to the far from novel entertainment of listening to the military bands, which blared to the deafening accompaniment of the fireworks. Many gathered to watch the animated scene in Franklin Square, where the men of the Twelfth New York, off duty for the day, were idling in their municipal encampment, and devouring pies and cakes around the sutlers' booths. Chinese lanterns hung in trees and on poles, and were suspended between the huts. In the warm dusk, Franklin Square glowed with colored lights, and paper balloons, brilliantly illuminated, rose in the dark-blue sky. The band played tirelessly. There were speeches and singing and, finally, a dance. Colonel Daniel Butterfield, a handsome little businessman, with chiseled Greek features and jet-black hair and mustache, had a taste for military life. He had his regiment well in hand, and, although he had given the men freedom for the day, only fourteen were missing at tattoo. The holiday, on the whole, was celebrated in an orderly fashion. The restaurants and bars were cautious in dispensing liquors. There were few casualties, and the provost guard vigilantly cleared the streets of drunken soldiers who exceeded their leave of absence. The explosions and the shouting subsided and the capital settled into a repose invaded only by the odors of its drains and the whine of its myriad mosquitoes.

To the Republican lawmakers, assembling in the scoured Capitol, the grand army of the New Yorkers had been a dazzling exhibition of numbers, fine physique, drill, unparalleled equipment. Army men might not share their enthusiasm, but there was little sympathy with West Point at the Capitol. From its foundation, the republic had looked with aversion on the standing armies of paid mercenaries which supported the despotic governments of the Old World. The volunteers were the embodiment of an article of the American faith. In the varied uniforms on Pennsylvania Avenue, the politicians had seen marching the tradition of the stockade, Lexington, the prairie wagon.

The spectacle had acted as a spur to an already restless impatience. Instead of parading and throwing flowers at General Scott and imbibing spirituous liquors, this magnificent army should sweep to Richmond and stamp out the rebellion. The movement must be made without delay, for the time of the three months' men was running out, and the Union forces would soon be depleted by many thousands.

"They think," wrote Mr. Russell, the correspondent of the London *Times,* "that an army is like a round of canister which can be fired off whenever the match is applied."

Russell had returned from a tour of the South to the turbulence of a city almost incredibly altered since his departure in April. Looking about Washington with his prominent, light-blue eyes, he observed much military activity and not a little disorder. Next door to the lodgings he had taken on the Avenue was a wine and spirits store, noisily frequented by privates and officers. Uniformed men wandered about the streets, begging for money to buy whisky. Russell began to feel doubts about the Federal army. When he had asked certain specialized questions about artillery and cavalry and transport, his doubts grew increasingly serious. He was quickly made aware of the low estimation in which the regular Army officers held "this horde of battalion companies—unofficered, clad in all kinds of different uniform, diversely equipped, perfectly ignorant of the principles of military obedience and concerted action. . . ." General McDowell spoke openly of his difficulties. He had formed an unfavorable impression of volunteer soldiers in Mexico, and said at breakfast at Mr. John Bigelow's that some of the officers were "more than suspected" of lining their own pockets by selling rations and taking money from the sutlers.

McDowell was about to advance. The urgency of the country had induced the Government to anticipate the convening of Congress by giving the order. Originally, it had been General Scott's intention to send a large expedition to Harper's Ferry, but that point had already been recaptured with surprising ease by the Federals. Scott had ordered the head of the Pennsylvania militia, Major-General Robert Patterson, to threaten Harper's Ferry with a force from his State, augmented by troops from Washington. In the face of Patterson's cautious approach, the Confederate commander, General Joseph E. Johnston, late Quartermaster General of the United States, had retreated up the Shenandoah Valley to Winchester. Patterson was one of the antique major-generals of militia whose rank the Union had perforce accepted with the largest State contingents. He was not, however, without military experience, for he had commanded troops in the War of 1812 and in Mexico, and Scott was satisfied that Patterson had the situation in the lower Valley well in hand.

Viewing the war as a soldier, not as a politician, Scott was still looking toward a grand campaign of encircling the Confederacy in the autumn. An immediate invasion of Virginia would be "a little war by piecemeal," which would settle nothing conclusively. In vexation at the turbulent clamor of the public and the press, and the interference of President Lincoln and Secretary Cameron in military affairs, he had nevertheless been forced to yield, and he had requested McDowell to prepare a plan for a movement toward Manassas. Late in June, at a military council composed of the President and the Cabinet and a number of Army officers, McDowell had spread his map on the table and demonstrated his project with clearness and precision.

The Confederate position had been well chosen strategically. It guarded the junction of the Orange and Alexandria Railroad with the branch line running to the Shenandoah Valley, and the forces at Manassas and Winchester could thus be speedily concentrated at either point. An essential condition of McDowell's plan was that this combination should be prevented, and General Scott gave assurances that Patterson would detain Johnston in the Valley, and sent him sufficient reinforcements to enable him to fight.

One day in June, a thin, redheaded soldier had turned up in Washington to get his colonel's commission. William T. Sherman had not been easy in his job with a St. Louis street railway company. Even his best friends had begun to wonder about his loyalty, and he had written the Secretary of War that he was ready to serve his country, if he could be given a command for three years. He had been appointed colonel of one of the new regiments of regulars, and, while it was being recruited, he was ordered on inspection duty with General Scott. At the end of the month, when McDowell received permission to put his regiments into brigades, Sherman was placed in command of one of them.

The inexperienced officers of the regular Army were Napoleons in comparison with the politicians who were being given high rank. One of McDowell's brigadiers was Robert C. Schenck of Ohio, prepared for military life by a career as congressman, minister to Brazil and Republican campaigner. Another Republican, Nathaniel P. Banks, former Speaker of the House and governor of Massachusetts, was made a major-general of volunteers. The party's first Presidential candidate, John C. Frémont, was commissioned major-general in the regular Army and placed in command of the important Department of the West. The Democrat, John A. Dix, lately a member of Buchanan's Cabinet, was rewarded by the rank of major-general of volunteers for his active co-operation in raising New York regiments.

General Scott, overburdened by his duties and suffering severely from his gout, had failed in the last few months. At his headquarters, he lay on a lounge drawn into the center of the room, and pointed with a long reed to the military maps on the wall. After dinner, under

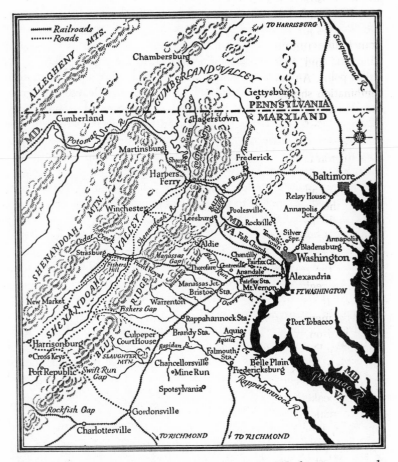

The Virginia terrain across the Potomac from Washington was the
scene of many battles and skirmishes. The Shenandoah Valley was the
path of Confederate invasion of the North.

the tropical blaze of a six-burner gas chandelier, he dozed in his chair in his shirt sleeves, with a servant at his back, brushing off the flies. Two aides supported him as he hobbled to and from his carriage, but the secretary, Keyes, was no longer on his staff. Eager for an active part in the war, Keyes had incurred Scott's displeasure by working on the plan for the relief of Fort Pickens. McDowell, who badly needed officers, placed him at the head of a brigade.

Scott's manifest infirmity did not disturb the popular faith in his leadership. There was a rumor that he had gone up in Professor Lowe's balloon, and discovered Jeff Davis, Lee and Beauregard breakfasting together, with eighty thousand men encamped around them. Many believed that he would command the army in person. It was said that a light carriage was kept always ready for a swift journey to Virginia. Scott himself gave Colonel Sherman the impression that he intended to take the field when he had organized a grand army, of which the regulars would constitute the "iron column." Meanwhile, he had grown reconciled to the idea of the piecemeal war in Virginia, and was confident that the movement would succeed.

At his headquarters at Lee's abandoned mansion, McDowell was troubled by deep misgivings. Since assuming the command in Virginia, he had met with a hundred obstacles. He was expected to weld a mass of raw regiments, belatedly straggling across the Long Bridge, into an army. Many of them were not sufficiently organized to obtain their own rations. At night, every wind that stirred the trees was taken for an advance of the enemy, and the nervous pickets aroused the camps with false alarms of attack. The Federals showed no respect for the rights of Virginia civilians, arrested them and broke into their houses; and in some regiments there was a wanton tendency to loot and plunder. Near the Aqueduct, there were farmhouses that had been completely sacked. McDowell had begged Mr. Cameron and Mr. Chase not to force him to organize and discipline and march and fight all at the same time. He felt that it was too much for any person to do. In the Mexican War, he had been acting adjutant general of Wool's column. Now he was going to command an aggressive movement of thirty thousand men. McDowell had seen large bodies of soldiers abroad, in reviews and marches, but he had never handled them himself—no officer in the Army had. He wanted time. "You are green," he was told, "it is true; but they are green, also; you are all green alike."

McDowell's thirteen brigades were organized into five divisions, one of which was designed to guard the roads in the rear of the army. The four divisions which would take the field were headed by Colonel Samuel Heintzelman, Colonel David Hunter, Colonel Dixon S. Miles, who had been called from duty in Kansas, and Colonel Daniel Tyler of the First Connecticut, an elderly West Point graduate who had resigned from the Army in 1834 with the rank of first lieutenant.

When McDowell had one body of eight regiments reviewed together General Scott censured him, as if he "was trying to make some show." Some of his troops had not yet crossed the river. The Garibaldi Guard marched over, carrying their rations of bread on their bayonets in the French style. Out went the Third Maine, singing "I wish I was in Dixie." Some regiments were eager to see action, but others were thinking of going home, and rejoiced that their time was nearly up, and that they had protected Washington "without a fight." There were cases of dissatisfaction because of the disparity between the time when regiments had enrolled and the date of their muster-in at the capital. The New York Sixty-ninth, part of Colonel Sherman's brigade, had been one of the first to enlist, but before reaching Washington it had been detained on guard duty in Maryland. Colonel Corcoran and the other officers wanted to engage in the coming battle, but the men grumbled over the decision that their enlistment period had not expired.

The correspondent of the London *Times* obtained a pass from General Scott, and set out on a hired horse to see the Virginia camps for himself. He noted the weakness of the rudimentary fortifications at the end of the Long Bridge; and marked the filth of the camps, the officers' ignorance of company drill, and the different calibers of the artillery. The headquarters of the army consisted of four small tents pitched near Arlington House, and in front of one of them McDowell sat, studying plans and maps. He had been unable to procure a decent map of Virginia, and had no officer capable of conducting a reconnaissance.

Russell also visited Fort Corcoran, the earthwork constructed and garrisoned by the Sixty-ninth New York at the Virginia end of the Aqueduct. The camp was neatly laid out inside the fort, with pine boughs sheltering the tents from the sun. There was a little door, like the entrance to an icehouse, half buried in the ground, which one soldier was showing to a friend. A sergeant came running. "Dempsey!"

he called. "Is that you going into the 'magazine' wid yer pipe lighted?" Russell lost interest in Fort Corcoran, and rode hastily away. On a subsequent and more extensive tour of the camps, he flatly concluded that the Federal army was a rabble. The Northern newspapers which described it as a magnificent force, disciplined, equipped and effective, were grossly ignorant of what an army should be. The dispatches which Russell had written during his tour of the South had earned him some unpopularity in the Union, but he was not disturbed by it. He cared little for the eminent senators, who reminded him of a gathering of bakers or millers in "slop-coats and light-colored clothing and felt wide-awakes." He cared nothing at all for the tradition of Lexington. He knew the world and its armies, and had won fame as a correspondent by writing the truth, as he saw it. As the London *Times* entertained small sympathy for the Union cause, he was untroubled by an incentive to write anything else.

McDowell had worked hard on his fine paper plan. He was serious and painstaking, and he had welcomed the opportunity of distinguishing himself. Yet, in the hot days of early July his soldierly figure moved against the garish Washington scene—walking alone through streets filled with troops too careless or ignorant to salute him, in spite of the gold star on his shoulder straps—like a man under the compulsion of a tragic destiny. His friend, John Bigelow, visiting him at Arlington, saw that he was greatly depressed. "This is not an army," McDowell said. "It will take a long time to make an army." Bigelow pitied him as he had never in his life pitied any man.

Over the telegraph, the news winged to the Union that at last there was going to be an advance. On July 8, the *Star* remarked that, as the subject had been aired in the Northern press, it might mention that General McDowell's line would probably move in the course of the week. An attempt at military surveillance of the telegraph had been ineffectual, and Scott issued an order, confirmed by Secretary Cameron, that henceforward it would convey no dispatches concerning army operations which were not permitted by the commanding general. On the Government's undertaking to publish prompt official accounts of all battles, the correspondents grudgingly consented to yield obedience to this order, but the bargain would be kept on neither side.

Files of Northern newspapers were regularly sent from Washington to the headquarters of McDowell's West Point classmate, Beauregard. The Confederate forces were not, however, obliged to depend for their information on newspaper stories, distorted by patriotic boasting, crazy rumors and bare-faced inventions. It was not hard to travel quietly between Washington and the enemy lines. There were plenty of people along the Potomac who were glad to serve as clandestine ferrymen. Around the departments, there were men who watched and listened. Military maps and plans sometimes unaccountably disappeared. The secessionist ladies of the capital were not all innocent sentimentalists of the old regime. There were resolute spirits among them, who would stop at nothing to aid the Southern cause. The most important of these was the elegant widow, Mrs. Rose O'Neal Greenhow, who was also the most persuasive woman in Washington, with a taste for politics and a talent for intrigue. During the Buchanan administration, she had known everyone of official consequence, and was regarded as a person of influence, to whom people went for help in getting introductions and appointments. Statesmen, soldiers and diplomats had mingled in her parlors. They dined at her table, escorted her on promenades, paid her evening—sometimes late evening —calls.

After the outbreak of hostilities, Mrs. Greenhow's Southern sympathies had not prevented her enjoying the society of Union officers. She was not estranged from her friends among the Republican leaders. She still received Secretary Seward, and commented that she found him convivially loquacious after supper. Senator Wilson of Massachusetts was frequently a guest in her little house across from St. John's Church. That plebeian abolitionist had none of Mr. Seward's social grace, but he was a powerful figure in the Senate. He was chairman of the Committee on Military Affairs.

Mrs. Greenhow later avowed that her relations with the Republicans had been prompted by a desire to learn their plans, in order to make herself useful to the South. "To this end I employed every capacity with which God had endowed me," she wrote, "and the result was far more successful than my hopes could have flattered me to expect." In May she had been approached by a friend, Captain Thomas Jordan of the United States Army, on the subject of sending information to the Confederate forces. Jordan had lingered in the capital long after his allegiance was given to the rebellion. Before he changed his blue coat for a gray one and went off to become colonel and adjutant general in Beauregard's army, he provided Mrs. Greenhow with a cipher code. Behind his earthworks at Manassas, the little Creole general had reason to appreciate the happy foresight which Jordan had shown before departing from Washington.

Because of the recent death of one of her daughters, Mrs. Greenhow was not going out in society that spring and summer; but she continued, as usual, to receive her good friends. She entertained callow aides and clerks, who blabbed the Government's secrets in her sympathetic ear; and conferred with the Washington secessionists, many of whom, in spite of Republican replacements, still remained in the executive departments. Among the items which Mrs. Greenhow claimed that she forwarded to the Confederates was the map used by the Senate Committee on Military Affairs, with red dotted lines showing the proposed route to Manassas.

According to General Beauregard, it was about July 10 when he received his first message from Mrs. Greenhow concerning the Federal advance. It was delivered by a Washington girl, Miss Bettie Duvall, to the South Carolinian, General M. L. Bonham, at Fairfax Court-House. Bonham saw in Miss Duvall the beautiful spy of romance, with glossy black hair and dark, sparkling eyes. On the preceding day, she had crossed the Chain Bridge in a market cart. At the house of Virginia friends, she had changed her "peasant dress" for a neat riding costume, and posted off to Fairfax on a borrowed horse. Admitted to Bonham's headquarters, Miss Duvall took out her tucking comb, and from beneath the tumbling masses of her hair drew a package the size of a silver half-dollar, sewn up in black silk. It contained the information that the Federals would advance by way of Fairfax Court-House and Centreville, and that an attack might be expected by the middle of July. This news was confirmed by other reports and by newspaper accounts, and it also verified statements made by a Federal prisoner, a regular soldier who had been engaged in compiling the army returns in McDowell's adjutant general's office. Beauregard immediately began to prepare for the attack, and dispatched an aide to Richmond to advise the Confederate authorities.

July 9 had been the date set for McDowell's movement, but it was only by great exertion that he was able to get his army under way a week later. Meanwhile, the country was electrified by the news that in western Virginia young Major-General George B. McClellan—lately an Army captain of engineers, who had resigned to go into railroad management—had inflicted defeats on the rebel forces. The loyal section beyond the Alleghenies was reclaimed for the Government; and, assured by the press of the superlative effectiveness of McDowell's army, the Union looked with exultant expectation toward the campaign in eastern Virginia.

On the morning of Tuesday, July 16, there was intense excitement in Washington. For the last two days, troops and wagon trains and ambulances had been going across the Potomac. They were still going on the day the army marched. At the Navy Yard, the Seventy-first New York cheered its marching orders, and through hurrahing crowds started for Virginia with other last-minute additions to an army already in movement. For transport, McDowell had only ambulances and munition wagons. Tents and baggage and rations would have to follow later.

The extension of the Federal pickets had interfered with the underground communication between the Confederates and their friends in Washington. During the night of July 15, a man named Donellan was secretly ferried across the Potomac at a point below Alexandria, and in the morning he entered the capital, rumorous with the army's advance. Donellan knew the city well, for until recently he had been a Government clerk, and he had no trouble in finding "a certain house . . . within easy rifle-range of the White House," in General Beauregard's phrase. The credentials which he handed to Mrs. Greenhow consisted of a small scrap of paper on which the words, "Trust bearer," were written in Colonel Jordan's cipher. Mrs. Greenhow, in the same cipher, wrote nine words, "Order issued for McDowell to march upon Manassas tonight." By her own account, she had been able to obtain a copy of the order.

Donellan was sped in a buggy, with relays of horses, down the eastern shore of the Potomac to a Confederate ferry in Charles County, Maryland, a district of slaveholding planters strongly secessionist in sentiment. On the Virginia side, the message was handed to a cavalry courier, and galloping relays carried it to Manassas. At nightfall, Beauregard had the nine words which Mrs. Greenhow had written—momentous words to him. Within half an hour, he had ordered his outpost commanders to fall back before the enemy to already designated positions. Next morning he sent an urgent telegram to Richmond, asking that General Joe Johnston's forces in the Valley be permitted to join him, and was promptly assured that not one army, but two would confront the Federals at Manassas.

Mr. Russell had gone on a trip to Fort Monroe, and, returning on the train from Annapolis on the evening of July 16, he was surprised to see General McDowell alone on the platform, looking anxiously into the cars. He was in search of two batteries of artillery, and was obliged to look after them himself, for his small staff was engaged at his headquarters. "You are aware I have advanced?" he asked. The general offered Russell a seat in his carriage. He spoke confidently, but did not seem in good spirits. He was having great trouble in getting any information about the enemy, and observed that they had selected a very strong position.

The appearance of General Scott at the President's levee that evening was hailed with much enthusiasm. When it was whispered in the East Room that he was there, everyone rushed to see him. Many people still believed that the old man was about to take the field in person. He left early, to the sound of handclapping, and huzzas greeted him outside the mansion.

On Wednesday, the army straggled into Fairfax Court-House, and twenty-four hours later into Centreville. In its wake followed visitors who had been attracted to the county capital by the interesting prospect of a battle. Parties on horseback and in carriages succeeded in making their way to the head of the advancing column. As the rebel outposts fell back, Northern newspapers exulted over a Confederate retreat. On to Fairfax! On to Centreville! The soldiers were as joyous, said the Boston *Transcript*, as if bound on a clambake. Civilians, once more in a majority on the Washington streets and in the bars and offices of the hotels, collected to listen to stories of desperate fighting. "I was rather amused," wrote Russell on Wednesday, "by hearing the florid accounts which were given in the hall of Willard's by various inebriated officers, who were drawing on their imagination for their facts, knowing, as I did, that the entrenchments at Fairfax had been abandoned without a shot on the advance of the Federal troops." Though all were confident of success, one observer thought that the civilians were taking a serious attitude toward the war. Even among the drinking crowds, there was less bluster and hilarity than usual. Some facetious fellow told that Beauregard had sent for a thousand barrels of tar and was going to dip his soldiers into it so that they would stick. The joke fell flat, turning into a perplexing rumor that the Confederates had ordered tar for some incomprehensible military purpose.

At Centreville, McDowell's force faced the main army of Beauregard, which was entrenched beyond Bull Run, a winding, sluggish stream bordered by steep, wooded banks. On the hot morning of Thursday, as the London correspondent went into the department headquarters on the Avenue, Mansfield dashed out of his room. "Mr. Russell, I fear there is bad news from the front." "Are they fighting, General?" "Yes, sir. That fellow Tyler has been engaged, and we are whipped." Messengers and orderlies, aides and civilians were running in and out of the departments, the Executive Mansion and the Capitol. On the Avenue, an Army officer shouted as he rode, "these confounded volunteers have run away." From the Capitol, smoke could be seen rising in Virginia, and people thought it came from cannon, though it was evidently from burning houses and campfires.

Senator Sumner was radiant with the assurance of a great success, and spoke of taking Richmond by Saturday night. There were other smiling faces on the Avenue, but they were all secessionists. Ladies were exchanging meaningful little nods and smiles with the tradespeople, as they sauntered past their shops. "Beauregard has knocked them into a cocked hat," one shopkeeper cried. "Believe me," said his wife, "it is the finger of the Almighty is in it. Didn't he curse the niggers, and why should he take their part now with these Yankee abolitionists, against true white men?" They had their own underground railway, they said, for getting information from Virginia.

In the evening, an overheated, hurrying man crossed the Avenue, near the Treasury. It was Mr. Lincoln, "striding like a crane in a bulrush swamp among the great blocks of marble, dressed in an oddly cut suit of grey, with a felt hat on the back of his head, wiping his face with a red pocket-handkerchief."

At army headquarters, word had been received that the divisional commander, old Colonel Tyler, ordered to make a reconnaissance of the lower fords of Bull Run, had brashly exposed a large part of his force to heavy fire, under which the men had retreated in confusion. The major engagement had been postponed. McDowell remained at Centreville, seeking to obtain information about the difficult terrain, and to concentrate his half-organized command. There had been much burning and pillaging at Fairfax Court-House. The men were wearied by their march in the terrible heat, and shaken in spirit by Tyler's blunder. On Thursday night, they were starving, for they had devoured or thrown away the rations in their haversacks, and commissary wagons did not reach Centreville until Friday morning.

Stories of desperate fighting and immense losses continued to circulate in Washington on Friday; yet the confidence of the unionist population remained unshaken. With such an army as McDowell's, the dislodgement of the Confederates from their works, said the *Star*, could only be a question of hours. There was a reassuring dispatch which described the skill with which Tyler had maneuvered his infantry; the men had wheeled back from the fire of the enemy's batteries with the coolness and precision of a dress parade. Everyone was impatiently waiting for the action to be renewed. People gathered in the shade of the ailanthus trees on the Avenue, conjecturing what news was brought by the dusty orderlies coming in from Virginia. The July sun glared from a brazen sky. Early in the day, a troop of regular cavalry rode exhausted through the city, horses and men flagging in the heat. Some rebel prisoners were marched to General Mansfield's headquarters, and sat down on the pavement and the steps, while Mansfield determined what to do with them. Laggard Federal soldiers wandered idly through the streets, without fear of arrest, and skulking officers were numerous in the barrooms and restaurants. In the evening, General McDowell and two or three staff officers were ushered into General Scott's quarters. McDowell had completed his reconnaissance, and the great battle would be fought on Sunday.

Washington received the news with rejoicing. "Before the battle," wrote "Sunset" Cox, a Democratic congressman from Ohio, "the hopes of the people and of their representatives are very elate and almost jocosely festive." Already at Centreville, the carriages of the visitors gave the bivouacs "the appearance of a monster military picnic." On Saturday, there was a great rush to obtain passes to Virginia for the fighting next morning. The day selected for the excursion was a scandal to the godly, but many churchgoers could not resist taking advantage of the unique opportunity. Republican senators were exhilarated by a dispatch stating that McDowell had carried Bull Run without firing a shot. The House adjourned, said Cox, with "jocund levity." An exception was John A. Logan of Illinois, whose black hair and dark skin showed Indian blood. Logan had already gone to join the ranks of the Second Michigan.

The demand for picnic lunches was tremendous. "The French cooks and hotel-keepers," Russell wrote, ". . . have arrived at the conclusion that they must treble the prices of their wines and of the hampers of provisions which the Washington people are ordering to comfort themselves at their bloody Derby." All the carriages, gigs, wagons and hacks in Washington had been hired at advanced rates. There was not a decent saddle horse to be had, for officers, cavalry and sutlers had bought up all the droves that came in.

As a Britisher and the correspondent of an organ hostile to the Union cause, Russell enjoyed none of the facilities offered to the representatives of the American press, who were welcomed as guests of the officers in the field, and accompanied the army on horses and in wagons belonging to the Government. He was forced to make a day's outing on Sunday, like any idle amusement seeker. He hired a gig with two horses, promising to pay their full value in case they were destroyed by the enemy; and at the last minute he also managed to rent a fiery black Kentucky saddle horse, which he planned to mount at Centreville. Russell did not sleep well that night. The moon shone brightly through the mosquito curtains of his bed, and once he started up and walked into the next room, where he fancied he saw General McDowell standing by the table in the light of the guttering candle.

At dawn, Russell put on an outfit he had worn in India, and gathered up a revolver, an assortment of flasks, and a paper of stale ham and sausage sandwiches put up for him by his German landlady. The gig, with a driver who felt great reluctance for the expedition, and the Kentucky nag, ridden by a Negro boy, were punctually on hand; but the other member of the party, an attaché of the British legation, was not an early riser, and they were late in starting. "You'll find plenty of congressmen on before you," said the sentry at the Long Bridge, with a grin.

In the tranquil loveliness of the summer morning, the army of the sight-seers crossed the silver Potomac, and drove through the wooded hills, the deserted farms and the ripening cornfields of the Virginia countryside. The gentlemen were dressed in thin summer clothing. They carried spyglasses, rifles and revolvers. In their comfortable carriages, they had stowed rich lunches, bottles of wine and flasks of Monongahela and bourbon. There were a few adventurous ladies among them. Negroes looked from the doors of their cabins, as they jolted over the road plowed up by artillery and army wagons. The muffled pounding of artillery began to be heard in the distance, growing heavier and louder as the carriages rolled toward Fairfax. Out of a cloud of dust came a shambling body of troops, with carts laden with baggage and chairs and tables. They were the men of the Fourth Pennsylvania. Their time was up, and with the Eighth New York Battery, they had been discharged at Centreville the day before. Talking and laughing, they hurried on to Alexandria, with the battle roaring at their backs.

Among the senators on the road to Centreville were some of the Republican leaders who had been loudest in their demand for an advance—Henry Wilson and Ben Wade and Zach Chandler. The holiday mood of the partisans was enriched by the anticipation of seeing the rebels run for Richmond. Congressman Albert G. Riddle of Ohio had a sentimental duty to his constituents. He had promised "our Grays" that, if a battle were fought near Washington, he would join them and share their fortunes on the field. It was as simple and informal as that. Another congressman, the Honorable Alfred Ely of New York, also felt an obligation to the soldiers of his district—the Thirteenth New York from Rochester. In a white linen coat, Ely set off in high spirits with his party of friends. He had paid twenty-five dollars for a carriage for the day, and the price impressed him, but it was a double carriage with fine horses, and he was satisfied.

Matthew Brady, the fashionable photographer, drove to Centreville, lugging his huge camera and plateholder. He was a bushy-haired little Irishman, with a pointed beard and a big nose, and he wore a long, light duster and a straw hat. His wagon was shrouded with black cloth and fitted with chemicals, for Brady was obsessed with the idea that he could do something which no man had ever done before—make a photographic record of a battlefield.

In a thin black suit, a straw hat, low-cut shoes and white stockings, Andrew J. Clement, a boy from Chelsea, Massachusetts, jogged out in an army wagon. He had a brother in the First Massachusetts, enlisted for three years. On arriving in Washington with a box of dainties from home, Andrew had been crest-fallen to discover that the army had started on the march to Richmond. He had eagerly snatched at an opportunity to go along, too. Filled with innocent excitement over his trip to the Confederate capital, Andrew did not reflect that this was a highly unsuitable day on which to go in search of a soldier at the front.

On the hill at Centreville which overlooked Bull Run, the carriages were drawn up like those of spectators at a country race. There was one lady with an opera glass. It was not possible to make out what was happening on the thickly wooded plain, clouded with dust and smoke; but a battle was certainly taking place, with deafening artillery and rolling musketry, and the Federal soldiers, by all reports, were driving the enemy back.

Meantime, in Washington, the Sunday streets were quiet. There was a feeling of strong suspense, but no alarm. A quiet throng stood all day in front of the Treasury, listening to the dull rumbling of the distant guns. After church, Mr. Lincoln studied the unofficial telegrams that were coming in from the vicinity of the battlefield. He went to call on General Scott, and aroused the veteran from an afternoon nap. Scott still expressed confidence of success, and composed himself to sleep again.

Later in the afternoon, a reassuring report was received at Scott's headquarters. The dispatches all declared that the Federals were pressing forward; and, with a feeling of relief, the President ordered his carriage. He had not returned from his drive when at six o'clock Mr. Seward came to the White House, haggard and hoarse-voiced. He asked the private secretaries where the President was, and whether they had any late news. They had the reports of a Federal success. "Tell no one," Mr. Seward said. "That is not true. The battle is lost. The telegraph says that McDowell is in full retreat, and calls on General Scott to save the capital. . . ."

At first, Scott received the adverse news with incredulity, but it was confirmed by a dispatch from McDowell himself. The President and the Cabinet gathered in Scott's quarters. They sat gravely in their black coats among the old pedantic War Department generals and the fledgling staff officers with brass spurs and rakish kepis. Orderlies ran across from the War Department with the telegrams. The acting Adjutant General, Colonel E. D. Townsend, sat near the door to receive them, and read them aloud. Once he faltered—after the words, "Colonel Cameron." Townsend looked for a moment at the Secretary of War, whose brother was at the front with his Highland regiment; then he whispered the rest of the sentence, "was killed."

At first, McDowell declared his intention of holding Centreville. In a later dispatch, he said that he would try to make a stand at Fairfax. At last, word came that he was forced to fall back on the Potomac. Retreat, retreat, the telegraph reiterated, the day is lost—save Washington—the routed troops will not re-form. Soldiers and civilians listened with white faces. Above the hissing of the gas jets, louder than the murmur of Townsend's voice, another sound seemed to fill the bare little room—the roar of a mob in flight.

Since eight o'clock, people had been returning who had seen something of the action early in the day. Those who had left in mid-afternoon were convinced of a Federal victory. Still, in anxiety for definite news of the outcome, the Washington crowds, many women among them, lingered abroad. Before Willard's blazing windows, the pavement was packed, and every arrival was closely scanned and questioned. Hundreds went to the War Department, but no bulletin was issued. Late-comers gave vague or guarded answers to questions about the battle. The traffic on the Long Bridge was growing heavy. The night air was cool after the burning day, as the sight-seers clattered home in the moonlight to the capital. A few soldiers came. With his face wrapped in a bloody handkerchief, David Hunter was carried in a wagon, attended by a little escort. Ambrose Burnside galloped in without a hat, dashed up to Willard's and dismounted. Thurlow Weed was standing at the curb. He asked no question—it was not necessary. His shrewd old eyes were skilled in reading faces, and disaster was written on Burnside's.

All those who returned toward midnight had been in the tumult and dust and terror of the retreat, the smashing, tumbling torrent of carriages, army wagons, sutlers' teams and running soldiers. Some people who had driven out in the morning did not come back that night because their carriages had been wrecked, or commandeered to carry the wounded. Mr. Russell's gig had departed without him while he was off having a look at the battle, and he had been obliged to ride all the way to Washington. "Stranger, have you been to the fight?" called the soldiers at the city end of the Long Bridge. A crowd surrounded his horse, and cheered his opinion that the army had fallen back on Centreville to reorganize for a new attack.

Russell had formed an attachment for the black Kentucky nag, and determined to buy it, regardless of expense. The proprietor of the livery stable knocked a hundred dollars off the price. He was in good heart, he explained, because twenty thousand Union soldiers had been killed and wounded.

Ben Wade and Zach Chandler drove into Washington with set and angry faces. Near Fairfax, their carriage and Congressman Riddle's had blocked the road and stopped the rush of panic-striken soldiers. Ben Wade had threatened the runaways with his rifle. He and Chandler made straight for the White House.

Back came the other Republicans: Senator Trumbull, feeling dreadfully mortified; Senator Wilson, who had been obliged to mount a stray army mule; Senator Grimes, who had escaped capture by less than a minute, and resolved that this was the last battlefield he would ever visit voluntarily. Congressman Riddle returned, shaken by a knowledge of the depths of his own nature. Examining the body of a dead Union soldier, he had discovered in himself "a brutish desire to kill." He would gladly have plunged into the fight with his Remingtons, but the battle had moved on, and no rebel was in sight. He was a teetotaler, but he admitted that he took a long drink of whisky.

Back came Congressman Ely's expensive carriage and his friends who had started out in such fine spirits that morning; but Congressman Ely was not with them. While taking shelter from the firing behind a tree, he had been seized by Confederate soldiers, and that night, in his linen coat, he lay shivering on the filthy floor of a barn near Beauregard's headquarters. Ely's wife had often admonished him that breaking the Sabbath would surely bring disaster, and his wife had proved to be right.

Rumors of catastrophe were sweeping through the streets. Hour after hour, the crowds stood around, worried, waiting. Congressman G. W. Julian of Indiana, called from bed by the calamitous news, found the Avenue solidly packed from the Capitol to the Treasury. In the small hours of the morning, they were still there; the population of a doomed city, listening for the thundering guns, the pounding cavalry, the shouts of the victorious rebel army.

On a lounge in his office, the President received the spectators of the battle. Some thought that the soldiers had been infected with panic by the frightened sight-seers, some thought the civilian teamsters were to blame. Others cursed the want of morale among the three months' men, who were thinking only of getting home. All decried the volunteer officers who had deserted their commands and run to save their necks. Lincoln listened in silence. He did not go to bed all night. Clouds swirled across the face of the moon, the sky darkened, and a sullen morning dawned in a drizzle of rain; and with daylight came the soldiers—not the victorious rebel army, but the defenders of the Union. Across the Long Bridge and the Chain Bridge and the Aqueduct, they scrambled back to Washington; to safe, familiar streets, to shops and houses, to a place where they had had rest and rations and letters from home.

By six o'clock, the tramp and splash of their feet and the murmur of their voices rose loudly above the drumming of the rain. Awakened by the noise, Russell looked out on the Avenue, then threw on his clothes and ran downstairs. A pale young officer, who had lost his sword, told him that the army was whipped, and that he was going home, for he had had enough fighting to last his lifetime. "I saw the beaten, foot-sore, spongy-looking soldiers," Russell wrote, "officers and all the *debris* of the army filing through mud and rain, and forming in crowds in front of the spirit stores. Underneath my room is the magazine of Jost, *negociant en vins*, and he drives a roaring trade this morning. . . ."

Occasionally, a regiment marched in order. The men still bore their arms, and had the look of soldiers. Most of the groups were conglomerations of squads, broken companies and stragglers, mingled in disorder. They did not appear to be soldiers, said an excellent observer, Frederick Law Olmsted, so much as "a most woe-begone rabble, which had perhaps clothed itself with the garments of dead soldiers left on a hard-fought battle-field." Their bright militia uniforms were smoke-stained, muddy and sopping. Guns, coats, caps, shoes, and haversacks had been lost or thrown away. Some wore black grins, sketched in cartridge powder across their faces. Many had walked forty-five miles in thirty-six hours, without counting the action on the battlefield. They staggered through the staring city like sleepwalkers, dropped on the steps of houses, crumpled on the curbstones with their heads against the lampposts, stretched full-length in the flooded gutters. Artillerymen and officers slept on their horses, as they rode.

There were many slightly wounded men in the streets, and more were lying strewn along the road from Fairfax Court-House. A hospital had been set up in Alexandria, and Andy Carnegie had got a sunstroke superintending the transport of the wounded on the cars, but ambulance-loads were coming into Washington, as well. A little wagon drove along the Avenue, with Judge Daniel McCook in the driver's seat. In the back he had the body of his son, Charles, a boy of seventeen, who had enlisted in the Second Ohio. Before Mrs. Parris's boardinghouse, across from Brown's Hotel, a sympathetic crowd gathered, while they carried the body in. Two years later, the old judge himself would fall in a skirmish in the West.

Henry Villard, a clever young German-American, who was acting as correspondent for several newspapers in different cities, all at the same time, had trotted into the capital at dawn. Two other correspondents were still sound asleep at Centreville. They arrived later in the day, much elated at the adventure of having found rebel officers on the veranda when they came down for breakfast. Mr. Matthew Brady came forlornly back to his photographic studio on the Avenue. He had lost everything—wagon, camera, equipment. His duster was badly wrinkled, and under it he wore a sword which he had been given by some Fire Zouaves who had found him lost in the woods near Bull Run.

In his summer suit and straw hat, Andrew J. Clement limped along the Avenue. He was glassy-eyed with fatigue, and there were blood blisters on his feet, but he was carrying a musket which a Union soldier had thrown away. Just as he had planned, Andrew had found his brother, but it had not been an easy matter; for the First Massachusetts had been in action on Sunday morning, lying in the woods, supporting a battery. Andrew had crawled around in the woods, shaking hands with about a hundred Chelsea boys whom he had known all his life. On his way back to Centreville, he had been caught in the retreat. He had eaten a fine supper of roast chicken and sweet biscuits and sherry wine—the first wine he had ever tasted— from an abandoned sutler's wagon along the way; and over a road paved with muskets, mess kettles and knapsacks, he had stumbled back to Washington. He went to his hotel and had a hot bath, and fell into bed. The defeat had not discouraged Andrew. Not all the soldiers had run, he told people. He would enlist for the duration, when he got home to Chelsea.

All day, McDowell's army streamed into Washington. They stood in the wet streets around smoldering fires built of boards pulled from the fences, and told fearful stories of masked batteries, black horse cavalry and regiments cut to pieces. A gaudy handful of men, grouped in front of the Treasury, claimed to be the only survivors of the Fire Zouaves. General Mansfield opened many of the buildings where regiments had previously been quartered. The National Rifles filled their armory in Temperance Hall with stragglers. Soldiers were begging for food at the doors of the houses. Ladies stood in the rain, handing out sandwiches and coffee. Citizens sent their carriages across the river to carry wounded and exhausted men into town.

Washington's secessionists, on the other hand, made no pretense of concealing their sympathies. The *Star* said that their exultation at the Federal defeat was undisguised. They loudly claimed that they would be in possession of the city in twenty-four hours; and exhibited "inhuman joy" at the sufferings of the wounded, as they passed through the streets. Among those unable to hide their satisfaction was "a person named Roberdeau." He tantalized patriotic ladies standing before the mansion of the late Senator Douglas, by removing his hat and giving three cheers for the rebels. "Who'll hoist your stars and stripes now!" he shouted. "Seventeen thousand of your party killed!" A wounded Rhode Island lieutenant seized his pistols, and ran after the fellow. But he escaped into a house near by, and the females shut the door in the Rhode Island officer's face.

As evening drew in, the shopkeepers looked with alarm at the mob on the Avenue. Some of Mr. Russell's visitors thought it dangerous to move abroad. He was assured that the whole contest was over, but he reflected that the gentlemen of Washington had Southern sympathies. When at length he locked his door and sat down to write his story, he was distracted by the uproar in the streets. Soldiers interrupted him, begging for drink and money; and it was three o'clock before he handed the messenger the dispatch which was destined to earn for him the sobriquet of Bull Run Russell, and the envenomed hatred of the Union.

Helplessly stretched in the mud, Washington awaited capture in the morning; but no invasion came. The rebel army, too, was made up of volunteers. They had been as disorganized as the Federals by their unexpected victory. Across the Long Bridge came only the wagon trains which had slowly disputed the narrow road from Centreville—white-covered supply wagons, boxlike ambulances, country carts and sutlers' vans. By noon on Tuesday, the Long Bridge was solidly blocked from end to end. The cries of the wounded could be heard above the shouts of the drivers.

A large part of the army had retreated in fair order to the camps across the Potomac. At Mansfield's and Scott's headquarters, an effort was made to assemble the demoralized soldiers at rendezvous appointed for the various regiments. Scott's aides tried to round up the officers who were "doing duty at the Washington hotels." As mounted patrols cleared the streets, the great exaggeration of the Union losses was apparent. Some regiments had seen hard fighting and had suffered casualties, but none was cut to pieces. On Arlington Heights, Colonel Sherman had his brigade well in hand. Colonel Corcoran, with his narrow face and drooping mustaches, was missing, and the Sixty-ninth New York was more mutinous than ever. On every train the three months' militia were taking their departure from Washington. In their torn and smoke-stained uniforms, they hurried home to tell their fearful stories and receive the welcome of heroes.

The sight of Confederate prisoners awakened fierce resentment, for stories of atrocities to the Federal wounded had spread through the city, and were believed. Some were spattered with mud and cursed, as they marched from Mansfield's headquarters to the Old Capitol on First Street, where it had been decided to confine them. Soldiers and citizens, gathered in front of the Treasury, assailed one party of prisoners with cries of "Kill them!" and the escort of marines had hard work to keep the crowd back with their bayonets. However, the Southerners presently discovered that they had friends in Washington. Mrs. Greenhow, who had been in New York over the week end, returned to visit them, and to raise a fund to supply them with food and clothing. In this work, she was assisted by Mrs. Philip Phillips, wife of a Washington attorney who had formerly been a member of Congress from Alabama; and, according to the *Star*, Senator Breckinridge of Kentucky also went to the Old Capitol to see the Confederate prisoners. A few days later, however, visitors were excluded. Mrs. Greenhow was especially named in the order.

The hotels were filled with anxious friends and relatives of soldiers who had been in action. The new drama of *Eily O'Connor* packed every nook and cranny of the Washington Theatre. Wyman, "the unrivalled necromancer and ventriloquist," held audiences spellbound at Odd Fellows' Hall. The Board of Aldermen unanimously passed a resolution of regret at the repulse of the army. Naming no names, but arousing much resentment among persons in the walks of life specified, the *Star* declared that treason had been manifested by well-known jewelers, bankers, wood dealers, dry-goods merchants, criminal lawyers, magistrates, court criers and assistant market clerks; and that the very grocers who furnished the army stores were disloyal. The optician, M. I. Franklin, inserted a card in the newspapers to announce that the battle could never have been lost if every captain had been provided with one of his good field glasses. Mrs. Kady Brownell made her way back to Arlington Heights, after having been fired on six times while carrying her company's colors, and worried about her husband until he turned up. Miss Annie Etheridge, a daughter of the Second Michigan, armed with two pistols, had also been under fire at the Bull Run fords and at Manassas. Miss Augusta Foster of the Second Maine had had a horse shot from under her, but was learned to be safe and well at Alexandria, where she was acting as a ministering angel to the wounded. People spoke in the past tense of Congressman Ely of Rochester, citing the achievements of his career. Ely, however, was not dead. Like Colonel Corcoran, he had been carried off to Richmond. He was the only one of the impatient politicians who reached that destination.

To the sanguine expectations of the North, the reverse had been a cruel disappointment. In spite of bitterness and angry criticism, the Union did not flag in its determination to carry on the war. Even as the militia hurried North, new regiments of three years' volunteers tramped through the depot, to form and march in Washington. The hurrah of their arrival resounded amid the confusion and the defeat. Up the Avenue went their serious young faces, their dapper officers, rich flags and bleating bands. For a second time, the nation was rising in force to defend its capital and its cause.

On the banks of Bull Run, more had been lost than the battle, more than pride and honor. The tradition of Lexington had suffered an eclipse. The notion was spreading which for weeks had been voiced in Washington, that gallant hearts were not enough, that training, too, was needed to make an army. American volunteers had been whipped, and shamefully whipped, and the country's blame fell heavily on their officers. Many of them had been among the first to run. Soldiers had been left leaderless on the field. Two hundred officers sent in their resignations after the battle. Others filled the Washington barrooms, drinking, defeated, sick of the war, indifferent to their orders and their men. "There you are, shoulder-straps!—" Walt Whitman wrote, "but where are your companies? where are your men? . . . Sneak, blow, put on airs there in Willard's sumptuous parlors and bar-rooms, or anywhere—no explanation shall save you. Bull Run is your work. . . ."

In the chorus of recrimination, the higher officers suffered as well. West Pointers were derided. A scapegoat was needed for the humiliating blunder of the battle, and General McDowell was proclaimed incompetent. The most unjust criticisms were made of him. He was accused of having been drunk, and the same charge, apparently with more justification, was leveled against Colonel Miles, commanding a division. Quiet and self-possessed, McDowell sat at his headquarters on Arlington Heights, trying to reorganize the broken army. He wrote John Bigelow that it was his chief consolation that his friends seemed warmer to him than ever. He had welcomed the opportunity of distinguishing himself. No one knew better than he how disastrously—and how fortuitously—he had failed.

General Patterson had weakly permitted Johnston's army to join Beauregard. The old three months' general from Pennsylvania had had too great a responsibility in the Valley. He was mustered out in a storm of obloquy. Even General Scott was suspected of being in part responsible for the mismanagement of the battle. He lost his temper and blamed the politicians, and called himself the greatest coward in America; and across his magnificent figure a shadow fell. It was cast by the stocky young major-general who was summoned from western Virginia to supersede McDowell and Mansfield in command of all the troops at Washington. The nation which hailed George B. McClellan had learned that no summer excursion of militia would end that war.

IF HE CAME to the capital at a propitious season, when rash counsels had ended in disaster and were for the moment still, McClellan had also some advantages in his own right. He was youthful, vigorous and self-confident; and, crowned with the laurels of his recent victories, he was a hero for a crowd which sorely needed one. His appearance was stalwart. Under a thick Roman nose, a ragged, reddish mustache concealed his mouth. Rather short in stature, he had a sturdy, muscular figure, with broad shoulders and a massive throat; and the tilted French kepi suited his well-shaped head. There was a dramatic quality about him. He had imagination. With that audacity of conception which subdues or inspirits timid minds, he began at once to discuss his command in terms of three hundred thousand men.

The chaos of Washington inspired McClellan to an almost frenzied activity. Convinced that the city was about to be attacked by an overwhelming force, he spent twelve and fourteen hours a day on horseback, and worked at his desk until early morning. At a press conference which he called soon after his arrival, the *Star* reporter noticed that his blouse was so sweated through on his linen by a hot day's work that it was hard telling whether his shirt were faded blue or stained white. He wore a plain blue wool uniform, without shoulder straps, and was not at first recognized by some of the correspondents as "the young Napoleon" of their dispatches. It was the only recorded occasion on which McClellan was inconspicuous in the capital. The shaken little world of Washington received him with flattering respect. The President and the Cabinet—General Scott himself—deferred to him. When he visited the Senate Chamber, gray-haired men gathered around this general who was not quite thirty-five years old. "I almost think," he wrote his wife, "that were I to win some small success now I could become Dictator or anything else that might please me—but nothing of that kind would please me,—*therefore* I *won't* be dictator. Admirable self-denial!"

"For the first time since the armaments, I enjoyed a genuine

military view," Count Gurowski wrote in his diary. "McClellan, surrounded as a general ought to be, went to see the army. It looks
martial. The city, likewise, has a more martial look. . . . It seems
that a young, strong hand holds the ribbons."

With McClellan's arrival, the uniformed vagabonds disappeared
from the thoroughfares. Beggars hovered in dusty byways, or rushed
across Rock Creek to escape arrest. A Rhode Island volunteer, Professor Sweet, who walked a tightrope stretched across the Avenue
from the roof of the National to the roof of the Clarendon, must
have had the approval of his brigade commander tucked in his flesh-
colored tights, for permits to visit Washington were strictly regulated,
and McClellan's provost guard stopped every soldier to examine his
papers. The guard was composed of regulars—about one thousand
infantry, a battery and a squadron of cavalry—and the provost marshal
was an experienced officer, Colonel Andrew Porter, who had commanded a brigade at Bull Run.

Congress also came to the aid of Washington by passing a bill
creating the Metropolitan Police, to consist of a superintendent, ten
sergeants and one hundred and fifty patrolmen. The unsatisfactory
Federal night guard was abolished, and the city council immediately
discontinued the day police. While the new force was being organized, the provost guard was the only agency for maintaining law
and order in Washington. One of its hardest duties was the enforcement of the act of Congress prohibiting the sale of liquor to soldiers. In
little fly-by-night shops, drink was sold without the formality of a
license, and many respectable hotels and restaurants opened secret
bars. Willard's, the Metropolitan, Hammack's and Gautier's had their
stocks confiscated and held, until they promised future compliance
with the law. Vigilant sentries seized wine, brandy and bourbon at
the Long Bridge. The soldiers, however, showed much ingenuity in
smuggling their purchases. Whisky bottles were hidden in sacks
of flour, cornmeal barrels, tea chests and cheeses. Medicine chests contained vials of brandy. Longnecked demijohns were fitted with two
corks, one at the bottom and one at the top of the neck, which was
filled with table syrup; and a similar deception was practiced with the
spouts of milk cans.

Another act of Congress which was of importance to Washington
was the appropriation for repairing the Long Bridge. Half earth
embankments, half rotten timbers and broken planks, the bridge was

incapable of supporting the heavy movement of men and guns and wagons. Furthermore, a railway connection with Alexandria was necessary for military transport, and the strengthened bridge would carry tracks, extended from the Baltimore and Ohio by way of Maryland Avenue, across the Potomac. A supplementary military route was made by shutting off the water from the Aqueduct of the Chesapeake and Ohio Canal, and converting the trough into a wagon road. The tracks laid over the Long Bridge did not prove a success, for the structure was too weak to bear the weight of the trains, and eventually a railroad bridge was built.

Before adjourning early in August, Congress also voted the men and money for carrying on the war; and, with some muttering about the increase in the regular Army and the suspension of the writ of *habeas corpus,* upheld the orders and proclamations of the President. It had been a brisk and businesslike session, which offered little fireworks for the galleries. On the first of August, however, there was a dramatic scene in the Senate. Breckinridge, opposed to all war measures, was making one of his obstructive speeches when Baker of Oregon entered in uniform. He was colonel of a regiment of Californians which he had raised in the East, and divided his time between the Capitol and the field. Laying his sword across his desk, he listened in silence; then, with his face glowing under his silver hair, he sprang to his feet to assail the sentiments of Breckinridge as "words of brilliant, polished treason." Baker was a superb orator, and his eloquent attack fixed public attention on the position of the gentleman from Kentucky. To the end, he protested that he had "never uttered a word or cherished a thought that was false to the Constitution and Union"; but somehow he was able to reconcile this opinion with joining the Confederate forces in the autumn.

With the departure of the legislators, Washington entered on an era of military efficiency. McClellan had a brilliant aptitude for organization, and, as a member of a military commission sent to observe the operations in the Crimea, he had studied European armies at first hand. He was exact, methodical and interested in detail. In Washington, he saw that there were two things for him to do. He had to fortify a city. He had to forge a weapon—the Army of the Potomac.

McClellan was the man in the saddle—and even the saddle bore his name. No one looked at the President, walking through the streets or driving in his carriage in his gray suit and slouched hat. All eyes were on the young commander. He was as different from modest McDowell, walking alone on Pennsylvania Avenue, as from obese, magnificent Scott. Every street lounger knew his stocky, high-booted figure. His passing, in clouds of dust or fountains of mud, was an event, a clatter, a cavalcade. Round the corner, hell for leather, he posted on his favorite horse, Dan Webster, with his staff and escort of dragoons hard put to follow him. He delighted in wearing them out, and thought nothing of a dash from the Chain Bridge all the way to Alexandria, through the Virginia encampments which made a continuous military city, more populous than the capital. McClellan wanted his troops to know and trust him. The latest raw recruits were familiar with their general's face, called him "Our George" and "Little Mac," and joined lustily in the shouts which greeted him.

McClellan's affection for his soldiers was tempered by stern parental discipline when they proved insubordinate. There were discontented regiments, which had volunteered for three years in the spring and wanted to go home with the three months' men. In mid-August, McClellan had two mutinies on his hands, in the Second Maine and the Seventy-ninth New York. He put them down with firmness, ordering the ringleaders sent to the Dry Tortugas, off the southern tip of Florida, to serve out their term at hard labor. In the case of the New Yorkers—the late Colonel Cameron's Scots—McClellan blamed the officers. He took away the regimental colors, and kept them in the hall at his headquarters, until the Highlanders, by subsequent good behavior, earned the right to have them restored.

The new three years' volunteers, who were pouring into Washington under the President's call for half a million men, showed more resolution than the three months' men, but they were as evasive of discipline as children and as unprepared for the work of war. Examining boards weeded out the most incompetent regimental officers, while those who were serious and intelligent gradually learned their duties. Even the best of them seemed slipshod and undignified to West Pointers. It was hard for professional soldiers to feel much faith in an army, in which a colonel felt free to ride companionably down the Avenue with a private, both smoking cigars.

McClellan's commanders of brigades and divisions were almost all men of military training, educated to Army standards of discipline and obedience in the days when the gold star on their shoulder straps had been only a dim aspiration. Notable exceptions were the impulsive

congressman, Dan Sickles, who had raised the Excelsior Brigade of
New Yorkers, and the landed gentleman, James S. Wadsworth, who
was made a brigadier as a reward for good service as aide to McDowell
at Bull Run. West Point officers had all been trembling over their
part in the defeat. "By ——— it's all a lie!" Heintzelman had said
in his nasal voice, when the list of promotions was brought to the big
room which the officers used in the Lee mansion. "Every mother's
son of you will be cashiered." But Heintzelman, Sherman, Franklin,
Burnside, Keyes and Andrew Porter were among the new brigadiers.
Several were detached from the Army of the Potomac. Sherman went
to serve in the West, and so did Alex McCook, who was also promoted. Burnside was chosen to head an expedition to the coast of
North Carolina. McClellan, however, received accessions of high
quality. The names of Meade, Hooker, Buell, Sedgwick, Hancock,
Reynolds, Kearny, Fitz-John Porter, Edwin Sumner and W. F. Smith
would all stand in newspaper headlines before a year had passed.
These capable West Point graduates enabled McClellan to make
great progress in organizing the volunteers. Some, like Kearny and
Sedgwick and Hancock, had personalities which won the love and
loyalty of their troops. Others were as unpopular as McDowell, who
now commanded a division. Charles P. Stone was too strict and
formal in manner to find favor with his brigade. The severe discipline
of W. F. Smith, known in the Army as Baldy, was resented by his
soldiers.

It was in Smith's brigade that a Vermont boy, William Scott, fell
asleep on sentry duty at the Chain Bridge. He was tried by court-
martial, and sentenced to be shot. The case awakened much sympathy,
and Scott was pardoned by the President. The first execution in the
Army of the Potomac took place in December, when William H.
Johnson, a private in the Lincoln Cavalry, was shot for desertion. The
death penalty, however, was seldom carried out in the first years of
the war. Soldiers were imprisoned, or, since flogging had been
abolished in the Army, subjected to minor camp tortures. An offender
was gagged and "bucked"—trussed in a sitting position, with his knees
up and a gun or stick thrust beneath them—or loaded down with a
knapsack of bricks and made to stand on a barrel. "Tying up" was
a summer punishment, which pinioned a man bareheaded in the sun,
with his arms and legs stretched apart. The icy stream of the Washington shower bath was a dreaded infliction in winter.

McClellan stationed his strongest brigades across the river, where the line of defense formed an arc extending from Alexandria to the Chain Bridge. Directly in front of the Federals lay the Confederate army. An enemy outpost was established behind earthworks on Munson's Hill, and the stars and bars again waved in sight of the capital.

New regiments were formed into provisional brigades, and encamped in the Washington suburbs until they were equipped and sufficiently disciplined to be sent to Virginia. Troops enlisted for the artillery and the cavalry were placed in special instruction camps, respectively directed by General William F. Barry and General George Stoneman. A surprising fact was elicited by the belated call for these two branches of the service—in the East, the buggy had so far supplanted the saddle that men had forgotten how to ride. Cavalry recruits were awkward figures, bumping up and down, with their knees out, in a manner "terribly killing to their animals." Out of ignorance or indifference, they treated their horses badly, laming and foundering them. The remarkable thing was not that many mounts were used up—for the wastage was enormous—but that large numbers were hardy enough to survive.

To guard the District, brigades were posted on the Bladensburg and Seventh Street Roads; and north of Georgetown—at the Chain Bridge, and at Tennallytown, where the roads from Rockville and Poolesville met. In Maryland, Stone's brigade acted as a corps of observation and a guard on the upper Potomac. McClellan succeeded in breaking down the system of military departments favored by General Scott, and the Army of the Potomac included the force near Harper's Ferry, which had been placed under the command of the Massachusetts politician, Banks, as well as the troops in Baltimore, under General John A. Dix.

The soldiers in the vicinity of Washington had at once begun the arduous labor of building earthworks. On both sides of the river, the farmers were ruined. Not only were their orchards and vegetable gardens trampled and their fields filled with tents, but the very face of their land was changed, as its soil was shifted into high mounds and deep ditches. In his decision to surround the capital with fortifications, McClellan was motivated by a desire to free his army for action in the field; and he was undaunted by the fact that the circumference of the city, including the heights across the river, measured thirty-seven miles. With all the enthusiasm of his engineer's training, he endorsed plans for a system of forty-eight works—forts, lunettes, redoubts and batteries, mounting three hundred guns. His chief engineer, who had served McDowell in the same capacity, was John G. Barnard, a quiet, middle-aged officer, extremely deaf and highly competent.

Experienced staff officers were a rarity in an army which needed every trained soldier for the command of troops, and McClellan himself had few of them. His large and showy staff was headed by his father-in-law, Randolph B. Marcy, a steady old Army man of only moderate ability. For a brief time, Senator Wilson of Massachusetts was one of McClellan's aides. He had been a brigadier-general of militia, and, after Congress adjourned, he raised a regiment and brought it to Washington. Probably Wilson thought of staff duty as an agreeable patriotic interlude between sessions at the Capitol. Nearly fifty, fat-bellied and unaccustomed to riding, he took to his bed after his first gallop around the defenses, and promptly resigned his position.

Another volunteer aide was the rich New Yorker, John Jacob Astor, who lived luxuriously in a well-appointed house, with his own valet, steward and chef. McClellan also welcomed a number of foreign visitors, French, German and English. Two of the Frenchmen were distinguished additions to Washington society, for they were princes of the House of Orléans—the Comte de Paris and the Duc de Chartres. Exiled in the regime of Napoleon III, they had come to the States to offer their services to the Union cause. They were unassuming, cheerful young fellows whom everyone liked. Donning the blue uniform, they were known to their fellow officers as Captain Parry and Captain Chatters. The Comte de Paris, pretender to the throne of France, was tall, awkward and handsome. He had an Assyrian profile, and his dark hair curled thickly around his kepi. He took a keenly intelligent interest in the army and the democracy, and even grew a beard and mustache in the style favored by Americans. The Duc de Chartres was a lanky, lively boy, who liked the war and enjoyed a trooper's joke.

The princes lived in a house in Washington, and were attended by their personal physician and a big captain of *chasseurs à pied*. They were vigilantly supervised by their uncle, the Prince de Joinville, whose young son had been placed in the Naval Academy, now removed from Annapolis to Newport. De Joinville became intimate with McClellan, and acted as an unofficial staff member. Like Barnard, he was very deaf. The changes in his fortunes he had met with resignation. It was natural for McClellan to speak of him as "the dear old Prince de Joinville," though his age was only forty-three. A sad-faced, bearded, uncomplaining man, he amused himself by making clever little sketches of ludicrous things he observed.

From the first, some people thought it strange that McClellan did not live in camp. He had established his headquarters on the Avenue, near the Old Clubhouse, the mansion which Mr. Seward occupied on the east side of Lafayette Square. In a house on H Street, diagonally across the little park, he was installed in bachelor comfort, while he waited for his wife and new baby girl to join him. His conspicuousness in Washington was due to the fact that he never stayed with his troops, but was always galloping to and from the camps.

Of all his duties, McClellan most enjoyed his visits to the division of foreign regiments, mainly Germans, in command of which he had placed the adventurer, Louis Blenker. The depredations of the Europeans, who could not be restrained from looting the countryside, made Blenker's name a byword, but in soldierly aspect they were McClellan's show troops. When he rode into their camp, the ravaged Virginia landscape became the background of a scene from a romantic opera. With his scarlet-lined cloak wrapped around him, Blenker stood in the center of his polygot collection of officers, who wore uniforms of every color of the rainbow. His tent was made of double folds of bluish material, restful to the eye. He loved ceremony, and received the commanding general with the most formal courtesy. Soon he would shout, "Ordinanz numero eins!" It was the signal for the appearance of champagne. The foaming bottles were set on tables loaded with fruit and cake; and while the officers drank, the band played Italian music and sometimes they sang. The soldiers had an abundance of lager beer, and McClellan apparently had no objection to the relaxation of the rules against drink. He found the procedure in the other divisions matter-of-fact by contrast.

In the crisp, cool days of autumn, McClellan began to stage the grand reviews of the Army of the Potomac. McDowell had been censured for assembling eight regiments before Bull Run, but week after week whole divisions paraded at McClellan's command. Hundreds of sight-seers were drawn to the capital by the fame of these military spectacles. Ladies in wide crinolines and tiny bonnets sat marveling in their carriages, and little boys and girls stared popeyed at the white gloves and glistening bayonets, the flags, the polished brass, the cannon smoke. Driving back to Washington in heavy traffic one evening, a party of Bostonians beguiled the tedium by singing. "John Brown's Body," a favorite with the Massachusetts regiments, was among the songs. One of the party, Mrs. Julia Ward Howe, was a writer, and she had vaguely wished to set some new words to the tune. At dawn next morning, she awoke in her room at Willard's, with long lines of verse swinging through her brain. She jumped out of bed, and with an old stump of pencil scrawled in the semidarkness the stanzas of "The Battle Hymn of the Republic."

The favorite parade ground was on the commons east of the Capitol; but on a raw November day of mud and wind, a monster review of fifty thousand men was held at Bailey's Cross Roads in Virginia, eight miles from Washington. Since Bull Run, a stricter system of passes had regulated the casual traffic of civilians across the Potomac. For this occasion all restrictions were lifted, and early in the morning the Washington population began its exodus into Virginia. General McClellan arrived, attended by his staff and escorted by eighteen hundred regular cavalry. In his gallop along the columns, he was accompanied by the President and by Secretaries Seward and Cameron. The Comte de Paris thought it curious to see these civilians "boldly caracoling at the head of a brilliant military cortege." To thousands of uncritical onlookers, the sight was imposing beyond anything they had ever imagined. The divisions extended for miles over the plain. Until twilight veiled the muddy fields, troops passed in review. Faintly, from the direction of Fairfax, came the sound of heavy, irregular firing; for the enemy, always accurately informed of Federal plans, was trying to create the impression of an attack, and throw the review into confusion.

The enemy was the one blot on McClellan's achievement. Three things had occurred to shake Washington's wholehearted faith in the young Napoleon: the blockade of the Potomac, the withdrawal of the Confederates from the city's front, and an engagement upriver in Virginia.

The capital had been proud of its busy wharves, where twenty new storehouses had been built, and the schooners from New York and Philadelphia had awaited their turn in a splendid vertical confusion of masts. Trade had begun to languish with the erection of the first rebel batteries on the lower Potomac. Navy men, in bitter humiliation, tried to deny the existence of the blockade. McClellan had refused to co-operate with them in demolishing the batteries. The Washington wharves grew dull. Many articles were highpriced, some things were not to be had at all. Sometimes bearing a strange freight of fugitive slaves, a ship would come in like a heroine. Only the little pungies arrived with regularity, and Harvey's Oyster Saloon advertised that its boats ran the blockade daily.

At first, there had been repeated alarms from the capital's line of defense in Virginia. The sound of practice guns sent old ladies scut-tling from the Center Market with half-filled baskets. The cannonade of a reconnaissance brought people to their roofs to watch the puffs of smoke rising above the treetops. As each report sounded, there was a confirmatory murmur, "There, do you hear that?" A decisive battle was believed to be taking place; and, prematurely elated, loyal citizens waved the Stars and Stripes, and rejoiced in a victory for the Union arms.

The late summer days, however, had unfolded no action of any consequence. McClellan possessed little information about the Confederate forces. Professor Lowe's new silk balloon, inflated at the gasometer in the First Ward, went reeling across the Aqueduct to ride majestically above the Virginia hills. Mr. John La Mountain made an ascent of nearly two miles, without moorings. In spite of observations and reconnaissances and prowling Union spies, the enemy remained mysterious. McClellan's secret service bureau, headed by Allan Pinkerton, gave reports that Washington was menaced by immense numbers, and the general believed them. He had assumed command with the spirited intention of crushing the rebels in one campaign, but the passing weeks found him hesitant, absorbed in the perfection of elaborate plans and of his army's organization.

At the end of September, the disappearance of the enemy's flag informed the capital that the Confederates had fallen back on Fairfax. The Union lines were advanced, and civilians journeyed out to ex-amine Munson's Hill. Surprise was felt, together with a little chill of doubt, on discovering that the Union forces had been defied by a few Quaker guns made of logs and pasteboard. Presently, there was news of a farther withdrawal, to Centreville and Manassas. Enveloped in awe-inspiring stories of masked batteries, Manassas had taken on a

quality of legend; and before its strong defenses people envisioned
the bloody battleground on which the Army of the Potomac would
show its mettle. When there was news of an engagement, however,
it came from the upper Potomac, where General Stone was in command. A detachment, sent across the river toward Leesburg under the
command of Colonel E. D. Baker, met with disaster at Ball's Bluff.
Near sunset of a lovely autumn day, a newspaper correspondent heard
the insistent clicking of the telegraph in the inner room at McClellan's
headquarters, and saw Mr. Lincoln stumble out, with tears rolling
down his face. Baker, with that gallantry which effaces a want of
discretion, had been killed at the head of his battalion.

The eloquent senator from Oregon had become popular in
Washington, and his funeral was a great occasion. As Mrs. Lincoln
had turned the White House topsy turvy with upholsterers, the
services took place in the H Street house of James Watson Webb,
recently a newspaper proprietor in New York and soon to be minister
to Brazil. Baker's eminent friends gazed at his handsome face, which
seemed—a triumph of embalming—to be that of a sleeping soldier.
The flag-draped coffin, loaded with wreaths of white flowers and evergreens, was carried to the hearse by six colonels, and a large military
procession escorted the bier through the streets.

Retarded by the censorship, the details of Ball's Bluff gradually
reached the country. The Federals had been trapped between the
cliff and the river, without enough boats to make good their return
to the Maryland shore. A great part of the force had been captured,
while some had been shot in the water, and others drowned. There
were bodies on the flooding waters of the Potomac which roared down
in early November to shake the infirm structure of the Long Bridge.
A soldier in light blue lay on a near-by pile of driftwood. One nearly
naked corpse was washed against the wharf at the foot of Sixth Street.
Others were recovered at the Chain Bridge, and near the Georgetown
wharves. Opposite Fort Washington, they found a private of the
artillery, with a testament, a round looking glass and a lock of hair
in his pocket.

Something more senseless than the habitual use of war was seen
in the fate of these drowned men. Ball's Bluff had been a small engagement, but it spread dismay in the Union. Baker's friends called
his death a sacrifice to military bungling, and their fingers pointed
at General Stone. Like McClellan, Stone was a Democrat. In relations

other than military, he was tolerant and courteous, and, toward the slaveholding people of Maryland, he had shown no more disposition to be tyrannical than toward the people of the District. Slavery-hating Republicans listened to stories about Stone, and found it hard to discriminate between tolerance and treason.

In October, there were premonitory signals of the opening of Congress. Wade and Chandler and Trumbull were in Washington, calling on the President and conferring with McClellan. They demanded an advance, declaring that a defeat was no worse than a delay. McClellan assured them that General Scott was the principal barrier to action, and they promised to try to have him retired at once.

From the first, McClellan had treated Scott with contemptuous neglect. Only four years before, the young commander had resigned from the Army with the rank of captain. He was now unable to endure the fact that the General-in-Chief was his superior officer. He considered Scott either "a dotard or a traitor," and pushed him aside, in vexation at finding a clumsy obstacle in his path.

After his first taste of his junior's arrogance, Scott had sent in his resignation. The President had persuaded him to withdraw it; but his importance was gone.

"Hard is the fate of those who serve republics," wrote Mr. Russell in September. "The officers who met the old man in the street today passed him by without a salute or mark of recognition, although he wore his uniform coat, with yellow lapels and yellow sash; and one of a group, which came out of a restaurant close to the General's house, exclaimed, almost in his hearing, 'Old fuss-and-feathers don't look first-rate today.'"

While Scott limped home, supported by two aides, General McClellan dashed along the lines of his troops, in a roar of cheers almost as deafening as the salvos of artillery. When he rode back to the city in the hazy autumn twilight, his train streamed behind him—generals, adjutants, aides, orderlies, politicians, citizens, sight-seers. It was like the triumphal procession of a conquering hero. Crowds clustered about McClellan's door, while, within, the leaders of the nation waited on him, and even President Lincoln often sat cooling his heels in the parlor. Never in the life of the republic had such adulation been paid to any man.

At four o'clock one rainy November morning, the voices of orderlies and the stir and snuffle of horses sounded before the house. A squadron of cavalry came pounding up, to wait in the darkness. General McClellan and his staff, cloaked and hooded in black rubber, hurried down the steps, and rode away, with the cavalry at their heels. No guns roared on the Potomac, it was a matter of etiquette which called them from their beds. They were going to escort General Scott to the railroad station. The young aides chatted as they rode along, speculating about the fortunes of their commander. "It would have been easier," wrote the Comte de Paris, "to pierce the night and fog which enveloped us." In the dimly lighted depot McClellan and his staff gleamed like knights in black armor, their hidden swords clanking. General Scott took a courteous leave of the man who had made his last months of service as disagreeable as possible. He sent kind messages to Mrs. McClellan and the new baby; and said that his sensations were very peculiar on leaving Washington and active life. McClellan wrote his wife that the sight of this feeble old man was a lesson to him; and asked her, if ever he became vainglorious and ambitious, to remind him of it. Whatever served him for ambition had now been realized. While retaining the command of the Army of the Potomac, he succeeded Scott as general-in-chief. The President ventured to suggest that the increased responsibilities might be too much for one man. "I can do it all," McClellan told him quickly.

In honor of McClellan's promotion, the soldiers of Blenker's division organized a grand torchlight parade. Many other soldiers, and a concourse of citizens, joined in the procession, as with torches held aloft it traversed a line of march marked by red, white and blue lights. Before McClellan's house, the bands played a lively serenade, and he was loudly called for. He appeared for an instant, bowed and retired. Fireworks flared and crackled in the streets, rockets burst the national colors high in the moonlit sky, but McClellan did not see all of the display. He was obliged to attend "a pseudo Cabinet meeting." The Cabinet "bored and annoyed" him—there were "some of the greatest geese" in it that he had ever seen. Only Simon Cameron, the Secretary of War, won his approval, for he "occupied himself solely with contracts and political affairs," and left the war alone.

The removal of Scott and his own elevation to the chief command had not satisfied McClellan. His inflated self-esteem required that he should not be crossed or even questioned by anyone. His nerves were flayed by the fact that he had to deal, not only with his cheering troops, but with men in power. A touchy vanity lay at the base of McClellan's arrogance. He liked only subordinates and un-critical admirers, and could find comfort in the approval of his horse, writing that "he, at least, had full confidence in his master."

A far more dangerous tendency, however, had also developed in McClellan's thinking. In his political opinions, he was opposed to the party in power. With some vague benevolence toward Negroes, he cared nothing about abolishing slavery. His ultra-Democratic friends and supporters, by placing a grandiose construction on McClellan's influence and power, had encouraged him to think of himself as a superman with a mission. He devoutly believed that God was on his side, and that he was the only patriot in Washington. It occurred to him that he might "cheerfully take the dictatorship," as people were calling on him to do—not, of course, from selfish motives, but to save the country.

The Democratic lawyer, Mr. Edwin Stanton, was very friendly with McClellan. Stanton had a gift for vituperation, and he lavished it freely on the Republican party, and on President Lincoln, in par-ticular. His favorite joke was that du Chaillu was a fool to go to Africa in search of something that he could so easily have found at Spring-field—"the original gorilla." McClellan said that Stanton shocked him by such talk; but he adopted the phrase in writing about the President to his wife. As a railroad executive in Illinois, McClellan had known Lincoln, and more than once in out-of-the-way towns he had spent the night in front of a stove, listening to the country lawyer's anec-dotes. The President, always informal in his manners, felt at ease with an old acquaintance, and often called on McClellan. Sometimes he would appear before breakfast. Frequently he came at night, to learn the latest news before he went to bed. His pockets bulging with papers—for he was trying to post himself all at once on military strategy and naval warfare—he would enter the parlor, where the officers sat smoking, writing and reading newspapers. Was George in? he would ask the aide. It was not necessary to send up, he would wait; he thought he would take supper with him.

Lincoln deferred to McClellan, with a civilian's respect for a military specialist. But the general, who disdained him for his ignor-ance, despised him for his deference. McClellan was something of a snob. The son of a Philadelphia doctor, he had enjoyed a liberal education. He had read widely in several languages, was interested in archaeology and collected old china. While he addressed the President with ceremonious deference as "your Excellency," he privately derided his homely phrases and manners.

One November evening, Lincoln called at the general's house in company with Secretary Seward and John Hay. They were told that McClellan had gone to an officer's wedding, and sat down in the parlor to wait. After nearly an hour, McClellan returned. Without heeding the orderly's announcement that the President was there, he went upstairs. Thinking that there must be some mistake, Mr. Lincoln sent a servant to his room. The answer came that the general had gone to bed. John Hay thought that "this unparalleled insolence of epaulettes" was "a portent of evil to come." Mr. Lincoln quietly passed it over; but he let McClellan come to him thereafter.

McClellan's military supremacy, to which Mr. Lincoln had quietly assented, was plainly threatened by the opening of Congress in December, but the general appeared oblivious of the fact. He could no longer plead the excuse that Scott was in his way, but he made no movement to advance. Drilling continued, recruits came in, and Thanksgiving Day was celebrated with drunkenness in the camps.

It was true that McClellan's troops were not completely disciplined or even equipped after four months' exertions. Montgomery Meigs, a capable captain of engineers, who had organized the expedition to Fort Pickens, had been appointed Quartermaster General; but Secretary Cameron's awards of contracts were scandalously inefficient. Late in the winter, McClellan's inspectors condemned twenty-five thousand infantry coats, costing the Government $167,750, in a single day.

A special correspondent of the *New York Tribune* might have been writing a brief for McClellan's defense, when he described the military procession at Colonel Baker's funeral. Standing on a horse rack for a better view, the correspondent found himself among a group of down-Easters. Along the line rode a tall man in civilian clothing, with black cloth pantaloons rumpling up halfway to his knees. He was wearing an army cap, and his saddle and trappings were military.

First Down-Easter: Who's that chap?
Second Down-Easter: Guess he's the colonel.
First Down-Easter: What sort of a way is that for a colonel to rig himself?
Second Down-Easter: Morphodite rig, I guess.

Third Down-Easter: He ain't no colonel; he's one of the new brigadier-generals that hain't got his uniform yet.
First Down-Easter: Half general and half minister.
Second Down-Easter: Well, I said he was a morphodite.

In drill and training, the soldiers were far from precise. Infantrymen, standing at salute while Baker's coffin was carried to the hearse, were looking over their shoulders, talking aloud, lounging on one leg, wriggling and scratching. Their guns were pointed in all directions, and some held them like fish poles. In the grand military procession which escorted the bier, some companies were all in a muddle, and at times ran to keep up with the men ahead. The troopers and their horses looked rough and uncouth. "No Cossack or Bashi Bazouk," wrote the *Tribune* man, "was ever half so rude, raw, undisciplined and uncivilized in appearance as this cavalry selected for a purpose of ceremony."

Still, the Army of the Potomac was the greatest organization that the Union had ever seen. In November, McClellan had an aggregate of two hundred thousand men in the District and in Virginia. These troops were not expected to face the professional soldiers of Europe, but another volunteer army. They had unbounded confidence in their commanding general, and were ready to follow him anywhere. Even a small success would have appeased the politicians and delighted the country. There had been great joy because joint military and naval expeditions had taken Fort Hatteras and Port Royal in the Carolinas. If McClellan had silenced the rebel batteries on the Potomac, he would have been wildly acclaimed; but he felt no need for conciliating either the people or the politicians. The Republican radicals assembled in a dismal city, surrounded by a large and impotent army, commanded by a messianic Democrat.

The senators and congressmen elbowed their way through a motley crowd. European soldiers of fortune had come running to war, like boys to a fire. McDowell had commented that a man need only "prove that he once saw Garibaldi to satisfy us in Washington that he is quite fit for the command of a regiment." But foreigners had recently grown so numerous that there were not even staff appointments enough for all of them. Veterans of the Crimea jostled Garibaldians in the lobbies. Most of the former claimed to have been members of the Light Brigade, and someone said that their numbers were extraordinary, in view of the well-known high mortality in that organization. An English correspondent at Willard's found himself constantly reminded of the Hotel Victoria in Naples in the Garibaldian days, not only by the military atmosphere and the babel of languages, but because he kept seeing many of the actual people he had known at the camp before Capua, and in the Neapolitan cafés.

Washington was packed with the varied concourse of people attracted by the great army. Contractors, inventors and cranks infested the bureaus. Officers used their furloughs to seek promotion. There was a joke about a boy who threw a stone at a dog on Pennsylvania Avenue, and hit three brigadier-generals. Correspondents were there to scribble, and artists to sketch. Soldiers' relatives mingled with sight-seeing tourists. A delegation of Creek, Seminole and Chickasaw Indians, after inspecting the camps and forts and witnessing two reviews, expressed unlimited confidence in the success of the Union cause. Counterfeiters and confidence men assembled from all sections of the country. Petty thieves and pickpockets, "from the genteel, fashionable 'dip' down to the vagabond handkerchief picker," slid through the crowds and kept the Metropolitan Police on the run. Embalmers arrived—for, even when an army does not fight, some men sicken and die. To entertain the legions of the living came dancers and singers and comedians, prize fighters and gamblers, vendors of obscene literature and proprietors of "rum-jug shops." Apparent on every street was the secret invasion of the women of the town; gay light-o'-loves who swished into the music halls on the officers' arms, whores who beckoned the drunken teamsters to shanties in the alleys. In the wake of the women, followed doctors, blatant in their promises. Dr. Schuman (all diseases of a private nature, permanent cure or no charge) had arrived early to set up his Southern Medical House in the Clarendon Hotel, but he was soon obliged to compete with "certain swindlers in the back streets." Dr. La Bonta had two offices, open at all hours, with an assistant in each; and advertised a permanent cure for gonorrhea in three days, as well as syphilis in all its forms, without interference with business or the use of disgusting drugs.

The first evening levee at the White House opened the winter social season in mid-December. There was a large company, brilliant with feathers and spangles and jewelry, with brass buttons and epaulettes and swords. General McClellan was the lion of the occasion. On his arm was his wife, Nell, recently come to Washington.

She was delicate and hazel-eyed—"not what a sickly stripling fresh from college would call handsome," wrote the *Herald* correspondent. Others found Mrs. McClellan a pretty and vivacious woman. She adored her young general, and was glad to be with him and sympathize with his vexatious troubles with the Republican politicians.

The radicals had started in full cry after General McClellan. Senators and representatives asked angry questions about Ball's Bluff, about the blockade of the Potomac, about the inactivity of the great army. They were scarcely less enraged at the President for interfering with their plan to turn the war into a crusade against slavery. Lincoln had revoked a proclamation of military emancipation which the flamboyant abolitionist, Frémont, had issued in Missouri. Frémont had shown such complete unfitness for command that the President had been obliged to remove him. He was in Washington in December, a storm center for the powerful anti-slavery faction. To assert the power of the legislative branch of the Government, Congress appointed a joint committee—the Committee on the Conduct of the War.

The threat of war with England hung heavy over the city, like the winter fogs. Confederate commissioners to Great Britain and France—men well known in Washington, Senator Mason of Virginia and Senator Slidell of Louisiana—were imprisoned at Fort Warren in Boston harbor. Their forcible removal by the American naval commander, Captain Wilkes, from the British mail steamship *Trent* had been the occasion for great jubilation in the Union, angered by England's recognition of the Confederacy as a belligerent power. Captain Wilkes returned to his residence on H Street in December, to be cheered and serenaded and hailed as "the hero of the *Trent*." The diplomatic corps fluttered with disapproval, and some of the ministers, said the *New York Herald*, expressed "passion and prejudice." Their sentiments were ascribed by that newspaper to "the poison of the last administration." Just before Christmas, Lord Lyons presented to Mr. Seward the demand of his government, outraged at the insult to the British flag, for the liberation of the commissioners. Over the holiday, the Cabinet struggled with the question, and reached the conclusion that Wilkes's rash and popular act must be disavowed.

Work serenely progressed on the dome and the Extension; and on the wall of the staircase of the House a red-bearded painter named Leutze industriously limned a mammoth picture, "Westward the

Course of Empire Takes Its Way." The Honorable Alfred Ely, ex-changed after five months in a Richmond prison, returned with gloomy stories of the misery of his fellow captives. After a quiet Christmas, New Year's brought the President the traditional bout of handshaking. The Indian agent from New Mexico, in a full suit of buckskin, presented Mrs. Lincoln with a red, white and blue Navajo blanket; and the President's old friend, Orville H. Browning, appointed to Douglas's seat in the Senate, had his pocket picked at the White House reception.

The President seemed weary and depressed. The Hutchinson family, popular abolitionist minstrels from New Hampshire, gave a concert for the guests at one of the receptions. While they sang, Mr. Lincoln twice closed his eyes and appeared to fall into a drowse. His heavy burden of anxiety was augmented by the ordeal of standing for hours, smiling automatically on the jostling visitors, enduring the painful pressure of hundreds of hands.

Anthony Trollope, paying a visit to Washington, found it a melancholy place. The end of a prolonged Indian summer had dis-couraged all hope of an advance. People laughed sardonically at the bulletin which was telegraphed to the country each morning—"All quiet on the Potomac." No orders to go into winter quarters had been issued to the army, but the men were making themselves as snug as possible in their chilly tents and huts; and the French princes were planning to leave on an excursion to Niagara Falls.

The city was despondent, but it was also indifferent; and Trollope felt that the loss of faith was worse than the loss of hope. Belief in McClellan was slipping away. No one had any confidence in the administration. The President did nothing. A congressional committee had blazoned the War Department's mismanagement of contracts. As the nation slid toward bankruptcy, the capital presented the spectacle of waste on an imperial scale. The peculations of the contractors and the frauds and thievery in the Commissary Department vied with the grotesque shiftlessness of foundered horses, spoiled rations, and broken bales of hay, on which along the railroad tracks the lean Swampoodle cattle were growing fat and sleek. The people of Washington shrugged their shoulders. Even in their hostility to England, Trollope thought that they were cynical rather than passionate. "We are splitting into pieces," he fancied a Washington man as saying, "and of course that is gain to you. Take another cigar."

"I hardly dare tell you what cloud we are walking in here," Mr. Seward wrote home. The carcasses of dead horses in the streets were a blight upon the city. The big droves purchased by the Government were served by civilian teamsters, rough, drunken and cruel. In the corrals which occupied the vacant lots near the Observatory, thousands of horses and mules were packed together, untended, diseased and covered with sores. One evening, a light in the sky brought people running to the flimsy pine stables. A fire had broken out, and rapidly spread. Soldiers and citizens pitched in to cut the halters of the terrified animals. Two hundred of them were burned to death. A thousand others rushed into the darkness, toward the common along Rock Creek, and into the Washington streets. The northern part of the city was filled with running horses. A herd galloped furiously down the dim length of Massachusetts Avenue. Many of them succeeded in passing over the canal bridges into the Seventh Ward. Some ran into holes or gullies, and were killed or broke their legs; others had been so badly burned that, in humanity, they were shot. The next morning, scorched and blackened horses were lying all about the streets. There was a dead horse in the southern enclosure of the Treasury.

Early in January, Private Michael Lanahan of the Second Infantry, United States Army, was hanged for killing his sergeant. The scaffold was erected on the commons between O and P Streets, near Vermont Avenue. Detachments of regulars escorted the hack, with drawn curtains, in which Lanahan was driven to the place of execution. He was accompanied by two guards and a priest. On the box with the driver, a soldier sat holding the rope. The troops formed a hollow square on the commons. Snow lay on the ground, and from the lowering sky a few flakes were still falling. In the distance, soldiers could be seen standing in dark patches on the white slopes of Meridian Hill. Close at hand, mounted on sheds and outhouses for a better view, about a thousand spectators were gathered. One or two artists sketched the scene as Lanahan, his hands pinioned at his sides, walked firmly from the hack with the priest and the two guards. Before mounting the steps, he said in a loud voice, "Good-bye, soldiers, good-bye." Curiosity hunters divided the rope, and chipped pieces from the scaffold.

The dejection of the capital was matched by the dreariness of the winter scene. Day after day, the rain poured down. The streets were running channels of liquid mud. At the corners, to enforce an order against fast riding, sat shivering, spattered dragoons, with dirty woolen comforters around their ears. People tipped street sweepers to clear a path at the crossings. Ladies' dresses were pulled up over heavy red or blue woolen petticoats by a patent arrangement of hooks and loops. Bootblacks abandoned their trade, and stood at the corners with pails and sponges, offering to wash the boots of the pedestrians. The roadbed of the Avenue was so treacherous that troopers took to riding on the brick pavements. Outside the city, the roads would have been considered impassable, had it not been imperative to use them for subsisting the army. Half-loaded wagons wallowed laboriously through the sloughs, and in the camps they told the story that, when a wagon sank near Arlington, the horses had been pierced through by the bayonets of a regiment that had gone under the day before. In ragged uniforms and blankets, the soldiers were bearing the exposure and the inactivity with spirit. "Under the organization of General McClellan we are an army now," General Blenker told the Committee on the Conduct of the War; "we were not before. The patriotism was as much before, but there has been a great deal done in this time."

General McClellan had fallen sick in December. The newspapers called it a cold, but the fact leaked out that he had the symptoms of typhoid. At his headquarters, all work was at a standstill. He had not delegated his powers, and no one could act in his name. The radical leaders pressed the President hard. Even the fact that McClellan had called in a homeopathic doctor was instanced as proof of his bad judgment. Mr. Edwin Stanton went to the general's sickroom to murmur, "They are counting on your death. . . ."

Montgomery Meigs, the Quartermaster General, was getting settled in his new office in Winder's Building, when the President visited him in great distress. He had been unable to gain admittance to McClellan's sickroom. Sitting down in a chair before the open fire, Mr. Lincoln said, "General, what shall I do? The people are impatient; Chase has no money and he tells me he can raise no more; the General of the Army has typhoid fever. The bottom is out of the tub. What shall I do?" Meigs advised him to consult with army officers, and Lincoln sent for McDowell and Franklin. They reached an agreement, in which Meigs concurred, that the army was now strong enough to make a movement on Manassas. This decision, imparted to McClellan by Mr. Stanton, hastened the general's convalescence. Three days after it had been impossible for the President to see him, McClellan came to a White House conference attended by Seward, Chase, Blair and the officers whom Mr. Lincoln had consulted. The atmosphere was strained. McClellan bore no ill will to Franklin, who was his close friend, but he believed that McDowell was intriguing for his position, and plainly showed his antagonism. He resented the attitude of Mr. Chase, who blurted out a demand that McClellan explain his plans.

McClellan was in a difficult position. He considered the Virginia roads impassable for army trains and artillery, and thought it impracticable to make an advance on Manassas before spring. It was unreasonable to expect him to take all official Washington into his confidence. There was much leakage of information, and the knowledge that he did not plan to move would have been of the greatest value to the Confederates. Moreover, he was considering a new line of advance—transporting his army by way of the lower Chesapeake to the neighborhood of Richmond. McClellan was justified in reticence; not in a haughty silence. Meigs privately appealed to him to speak, to promise some movement toward Manassas. The general replied that, if he told his plans to the President, they would be in the *New York Herald* the next morning. He added that Mr. Lincoln could not keep a secret—he would tell Tad. McClellan, still a sick man, was in a morbidly distrustful frame of mind. He scented a conspiracy. His suspicion of McDowell may have been sharpened by the fact that the latter was the protégé of Chase. There was in fact one conspiratorial figure in the case. It was that of Mr. Edwin Stanton. Apparently befriending McClellan, he was secretly in league with the radical Secretary of the Treasury. Mr. Stanton was a force to reckon with. The President had just appointed him Secretary of War.

The removal of Cameron was an important step in restoring public confidence in the administration. There was some murmuring among the antislavery faction, for Cameron had attempted to make an official recommendation that the slaves should be armed, and had been forced by the President to withdraw it. The country applauded the appointment. In Buchanan's Cabinet, Stanton had made a reputation as a strong Union man. Although since the outbreak of war he had condemned the Republican administration and vilified the President, he was intimate with Mr. Seward, with whom he had

intrigued during the Buchanan administration. It soon appeared that
he would act in wholehearted co-operation with the Republican
radicals. Stanton was energetic, impatient and entirely ignorant of
military affairs. He brought pressure on McClellan for an immediate
advance, and the Committee on the Conduct of the War was delighted with him.

Anthony Trollope had felt sorrowful at the impotence of Congress. It might vote committees of inquiry, might ask questions without end—but it had no power, Trollope mused. The army had thrown
the legislators out of favor, "the rough-shod generals were the men of
the day." The genial Englishman discounted the self-preservative in-
stinct of demagogues, and he had had scant opportunities of knowing
men like Ben Wade and Zach Chandler.

The Committee on the Conduct of the War sat in a room in the
Capitol basement, and to its door the generals marched like schoolboys
summoned for a secret examination. Ben Wade was in the chair, a
grand inquisitor coarse and shrewd, with sharp little jet-black eyes.
At the corners of his mouth, the upper lip doubled down over the
lower one, giving him a ferocious look. His questions poked and pried
into all the affairs of the army; they invited the officers to criticize, to
make their own recommendations. Some were flattered, and enthusiastically spilled out pet plans of campaign. Others answered stiffly,
resenting these infringements of military regulations.

". . . We must stir ourselves," Ben Wade said, "on account of
the expense." He made another explanation: "We are endeavoring to
see if there is any way in God's world to get rid of the capital besieged,
while Europe is looking down upon us as almost a conquered people."
Enmity to McClellan dictated most of the questions. If they had a
Napoleon at the head of the army, they might feel easy. "But," cried
Ben Wade on an almost Biblical note, "how can this nation abide the
secret counsels that one man carries in his head, when we have no
evidence that he is the wisest man in the world."

McClellan was summoned before the Joint Committee, and par-
ried questions about his plans. He made a long discourse on military
methods, and remained courteous under a sarcastic examination. After
it was over, Chandler told Wade that the delay in advancing appeared
to be a case of "infernal, unmitigated cowardice." McClellan had
further angered the radicals by barring the Virginia camps to the
melodious Hutchinson family, whom Secretary Cameron had per-

mitted to give concerts to the soldiers. The Army of the Potomac was not a force of abolitionists. Many of the men disliked the anti-slavery songs the Hutchinsons sang. The *Star* protested against turning the camps into "arenas for political pow-wowing." It was, however, an unfortunate moment for McClellan to add fresh fuel to the suspicions of his enemies. He might have been warned by the speed with which the whispers against another Democrat, Charles P. Stone, had swelled to an accusing chorus of treason.

Ben Wade and his colleagues passed judgment on Stone in January. Unfriendly officers had come down from the upper Potomac to blacken Stone's name with the charge of disloyalty. Republicans lent a willing ear to the slander of a general who had been lenient in his treatment of Maryland slaveholders. In his absence, Stone was tried, condemned and sentenced in the star-chamber court, and Mr. Stanton issued an order for his arrest. At McClellan's request that Stone might be heard in his own defense, he was called before the Joint Committee. None of his detractors confronted him. The vague accusations of communicating with the enemy were repeated; and Stone sat staring at the committee, a reserved and fastidious man, who, save for the droop of his mustaches and a nervous rigidity of carriage, resembled a portrait by Van Dyck. In his outrage, his words tumbled over each other. "That is one humiliation I had hoped I never should be subjected to," he cried to Ben Wade. "I thought there was one calumny that could not be brought against me . . . I raised all the volunteer troops that were here during the seven dark days of last winter. . . . I could have surrendered Washington." He had hardly been out of his clothes for the last year, he went on. Guarding the outposts of the capital, he got into his blankets every night without undressing. The most he had ever done was to pull off his boots.

"If you want more faithful soldiers you must find them elsewhere. I have been as faithful as I can be. . . ." General Stone might have saved his breath. He was arrested and sent to Fort Lafayette.

Late in January, the President took the unusual course of issuing an order that the land and naval forces of the Union should move on February 22. This was shortly followed by an order specifically directing that the Army of the Potomac, after providing for the defense of Washington, should make an expedition against Manassas. It was common talk among the army officers that McClellan's star was setting, and that nothing but a victory could save him.

In Kentucky, a victory had been gained by Union troops commanded by General George H. Thomas, a Virginian whom Lincoln had rather reluctantly promoted on Sherman's recommendation. Good news came from Burnside's expedition which, in co-operation with a naval force under Admiral Goldsborough, took Roanoke Island, valuable to the Federals in tightening the blockade. In prompt compliance with the President's order, another military and naval expedition, General Grant and Commodore Foote commanding, soon won highly important successes in the West. The capture of Fort Henry on the Tennessee was followed by the surrender of Fort Donelson on the Cumberland, opening western and central Tennessee to Federal occupation. These victories, after months of discouragement, were hailed with joy through the loyal States. The unknown brigadier, U. S. Grant, became overnight the hero of the Union. He had sent a terse dispatch to the Confederate commander at Donelson. "No terms except an unconditional and immediate surrender can be accepted. I propose to move immediately upon your works." The decisive words won a nation's applause. Grant spoke like a soldier, and he was acclaimed with proud nicknames. The initials, U. S., stood for United States, Uncle Sam, Unconditional Surrender.

The Army of the Potomac dawdled around Washington, polishing its buttons and stirrups. The perfection on which McClellan insisted was extravagantly exemplified in his personal preparations for taking the field. Twenty-four wagons and two traveling carriages, drawn by four finely matched bay horses, had been provided for the commanding general and his staff. The carriages were ingeniously fitted for sleeping, eating and writing *en route*.

Even before his wife joined him at Washington, McClellan had relaxed his program of unremitting work. Late in November, he had entertained a large gathering at his quarters with a display of the magical powers of the conjuror, Professor Hermann. Mr. Russell had remarked at the time that the general's party would be "aggravating news to the bloody-minded, serious people in New England." All of McClellan's social activities were scrutinized by bloody-minded, serious people in Washington. It was observed that he took his meals luxuriously at the restaurant of Wormley, the mulatto caterer, and gave elaborate dinners, with a variety of wines, almost every afternoon. There would be twenty guests at least, and they were not friends of the administration, either. "This army has got to fight or run away," wrote Mr. Stanton; "and while men are striving nobly in the West, the champagne and oyster suppers on the Potomac must be stopped." Mrs. McClellan gave a large reception in February, shortly after a grand party at the White House had set the abolitionists raging at the unsuitability of extravagant entertainment in Washington.

Mr. Stanton had cleared the swindling contractors from the War Department, and the new uniforms were made of wool, instead of shoddy. Save for the Zouave organizations, the entire Army of the Potomac was being clad in light-blue trousers and a tunic of dark blue. A mark of red distinguished the artillery; the cavalry had a note of yellow. Most regiments wore the kepi, though some had hats of soft black felt. McClellan's soldiers looked like an army, and they felt the change and were proud of it.

Around Fort Donelson, the blood of men in shoddy reddened the snow. Republican politicians looked with a jaundiced eye at the Army of the Potomac. Its accouterments were shining. There was a glimpse of snowy collar above the good wool tunics. Many soldiers had white gloves, some wore white gaiters. The force of bootblacks at Willard's had been trebled. Officers tied crimson sashes about their tightly fitted coats. The West Point generals were splendid in gold-embroidered shoulder straps and gauntlets and plumed felt hats. One of the finest was General Fitz-John Porter, a cold, autocratic, accomplished soldier, very intimate with McClellan. Another superb military figure was General Joe Hooker, with blue eyes shining in his florid, handsome, conceited face. General Phil Kearny, who had fought with the French in Algiers and Italy, clipped his beard to a point, and slanted his kepi in the French manner. His look of lean distinction was enhanced by an empty coat sleeve, for he had lost an arm in the Mexican campaign. Mounted on horses with costly trappings, followed by smart retinues of aides, the generals of the Army of the Potomac increased the disquiet of the gentlemen of Congress. The aristocratic traditions of West Point paraded in Washington in glory and power. McClellan was ruling the army with a little clique of professional soldiers, confiding his plans to his special pets, the arrogant Fitz-John Porter, and the quiet, cautious Franklin. Dazzled with prejudice and frightened by swank, the Republican radicals were reaching the conclusion that McClellan had traitorous intentions.

In fact, since the order for a movement on Manassas, McClellan had been ceaselessly urging on the President and the Secretary of War his plan to move on Richmond by way of the lower Chesapeake. Mr. Lincoln's order had proved to be only a full-sounding pronunciamento. He did not like McClellan's idea of stripping the capital of its great army, but he listened to it, and invited the general to justify his project. Mr. Stanton, though entirely opposed to the plan, made arrangements for transports and supplies. If the Army of the Potomac was to be removed from Washington, there were two things that must be done, the President told McClellan. One was to clear the rebel batteries from the Potomac. The general agreed. He was even more co-operative in his response to the President's second requirement, that he should open the line of the Baltimore and Ohio Railroad, repeatedly attacked by the enemy. McClellan intended to make a demonstration on the upper Potomac, reinforcing General Banks for a movement from Harper's Ferry on the Confederates at Winchester in the Valley. To carry troops and supplies across the river, a strong bridge was needed, and McClellan decided on a bridge constructed of canal boats. He entered on his preparations with energy, sent large numbers of boats up the Chesapeake and Ohio Canal, went himself to Harper's Ferry and ordered up additional troops. At the last moment, however, it was discovered that the boats were six inches too wide to pass through the lift lock from the canal to the river. McClellan countermanded the reinforcements, made a reconnaissance, and returned, well satisfied, to Washington. The expedition to Winchester, said Mr. Chase, ponderously essaying a witticism, had died of lockjaw.

On February 22, the military routine of the encampments was undisturbed by the President's order for a movement on Manassas. Crape hung on the White House door, and in the Green Room the undertakers were busy, for Willie Lincoln had died of typhoid fever. The illuminations, ordered for Washington's Birthday in honor of the Union successes in the West, were hastily canceled. Some private houses displayed colored lanterns, and others had busts of General Washington, crowned with flowers, in the windows. Cheated of their celebration, the children set off Chinese crackers, and ran that night in the streets with transparencies and torches.

They buried Willie Lincoln on a day of great wind, that tore the roofs off houses and slashed the flags to ribbons. The father drove, unseeing, through the wreckage in a carriage with Robert and the two Illinois senators, Trumbull and Browning. Mrs. Lincoln was too ill to attend the funeral services.

Early in March, the capital saw another funeral cortege. General Frederick W. Lander—the husband of the lovely actress whom John Hay admired—had been in command in western Virginia, and during the winter his skirmishes with the Confederates had been the only military movements in the neighborhood of Washington. Lander had sickened, died at his post. Now his body came jolting through the mud, to be drawn on a caisson with military pomp. McClellan was one of the pallbearers. An observer noted that his face was "shaded by grief"; but General Franklin told General Meade (who wrote it to his wife) that McClellan had said to him that he almost wished he was in the coffin, instead of Lander.

In the moist air, there was a premonition of spring. Still, beyond the narrow, mired roads, Manassas waited. McClellan firmly refused to go against that stronghold, and the transports were gathering to take the Army of the Potomac to a Virginia battlefield of their general's choosing. He had won consent to his plan, but there was thunderous disapproval. Lincoln, distracted by sorrow for his dead boy, was almost overwhelmed by the clamor for McClellan's removal. At seven-thirty in the morning, he sent for the general, and between the two men the word *traitor* flashed like a drawn sword. McClellan sprang to his feet, demanding that the President retract the expression. In agitation, Mr. Lincoln disclaimed that the idea was his own. He was merely repeating what others said, that the plan of withdrawing the army from the defense of Washington had a traitorous intent. McClellan suggested that he should be careful in his language. The President again apologized.

At terrible cost to his own prestige, Lincoln retained McClellan in command, and permitted him to embark his troops, but his war orders revealed how deeply his confidence was shaken. Without consulting or even informing McClellan in advance, he directed that the twelve divisions of the Army of the Potomac should be formed into four corps—an organization which had been urged by the Committee on the Conduct of the War, but which McClellan had wished to postpone until he had tested his generals in the field. The President himself specified the corps commanders—McDowell, Heintzelman, Edwin Sumner, and Keyes, who had been secretary to General Scott. Not one was a favorite with McClellan. At a military council, recently called at the President's instigation, all save Keyes had expressed themselves as opposed to the movement by the lower Chesapeake, and Keyes had qualified his assent to McClellan's plan by saying that the Potomac batteries should first be reduced. Another Executive order substantiated the point which Keyes had made, and appointed the date of March 18 for the army's movement—"and the General-in-Chief," the order continued, "shall be responsible that it moves as early as that day." Most important of all to the capital was the President's decree that a force adequate to protect Washington should be left behind. The corps commanders were to be consulted regarding the size of this force.

On Sunday morning, March 9, Gideon Welles rushed over to the White House where he found the President and Mr. Stanton in great alarm. There was bad news from Hampton Roads. For some time, the Government had been informed that the Confederates had been making ready an ironclad ship. They had raised the United States frigate *Merrimac* from Norfolk harbor, found her hull and engines serviceable, and fitted her with an iron ram and a roof of iron plates. Now there was a telegram saying that the *Merrimac* had come down from Norfolk to spread destruction in Hampton Roads. Wooden ships had been helpless before the armored monster, the *Congress* and the *Cumberland* shot and rammed, the *Minnesota* driven aground. "If she sinks our ships," Captain Gustavus Fox, the Assistant Secretary of the Navy, had previously said to Lincoln, "who is to prevent her dropping her anchor in the Potomac . . . and throwing her hundred-pound shells into this room, or battering down the walls of the Capitol?" "The Almighty, captain," Lincoln had replied. The event found the President wanting in tranquil faith. In his nervously overwrought condition, he showed uncharacteristic excitement, sent his carriage for his friend, Browning, and drove off with him to the Navy Yard to fetch Commander Dahlgren. He wanted a professional opinion on the possibility that the *Merrimac* might attack Washington, but Dahlgren could give him "little comfort," and referred him back to Mr. Welles. Stanton, Seward, Chase, McClellan, Meigs and other officers stood around the President's office, while the Secretary of the Navy explained that there was a ray of hope. The United States ironclad *Monitor,* barely completed, had reached Hampton Roads on the preceding night. Designed by the Swedish inventor, John Ericsson, she was a new experiment in fighting vessels—a queer little craft, with a low armored deck, surmounted by a revolving turret. She had been condemned by all the older naval officers; but Captain Fox had been enthusiastic about giving the design a trial, and Mr. Welles had taken the risk of bringing censure and ridicule on his department. That Sunday morning, while Washington tremblingly awaited the news from Hampton Roads, the old newspaperman from Hartford was made uncomfortably aware of the great responsibility he had assumed. There was no one to stand by him. Dahlgren offered no support, and the vigorous Captain Fox was at Hampton Roads. Mr. Welles calmly expressed his confidence in the *Monitor*. When he said that she had two guns, against the ten carried by the *Merrimac*, Mr. Stanton gave him a "mingled look of incredulity and contempt. . . ." It was beyond the powers of Mr. Welles to describe that look, or the sneering tone of Mr. Stanton's voice.

There were fearful men in the President's office that Sunday, but the most frightened of all was the Secretary of War. As he paced the room, he foretold the destruction of the United States Navy the capture of Fort Monroe, the capitulation of Boston and New York. Burnside's expedition would be taken, McClellan could not sail for the Virginia Peninsula. Stanton dashed off telegrams to governors and mayors, advising them to obstruct their harbors. He kept running to the window and looking down the Potomac for a sight of the *Merrimac* on her way to shell the Capitol and disperse Congress. His alarming predictions kept the President at the window, too. Mr. Welles remarked that the *Merrimac*'s draft of water was such that she could neither pass up the Potomac, nor reach the Burnside expedition, and that, with her heavy armor, she would probably not venture outside Hampton Roads.

Mr. Welles was passing one of the most unpleasant days of his life, but it was not entirely devoid of secret satisfaction. He was taking the measure of the new Cabinet member, Stanton, "as he ran from room to room, sat down and jumped up after writing a few words, swung his arms, scolded and raved." Mr. Stanton was a physical coward. Fear drove him to bluster, sneer and rage. Mr. Welles just sat quietly looking at Stanton. There was an expression in his big, luminous eyes which he thought that the War Secretary could not fail to read. The next day, he would have a sharp argument with Stanton for trying to override his authority by ordering Dahlgren to sink canal boats, loaded with stone and gravel, in the Potomac channel. Mr. Welles won that battle, and asserted his authority and kept the Potomac open. Mr. Stanton took his measure, too, and always treated him with courtesy thereafter.

On Sunday night, the telegraph clicked out a message which changed despair into exultation, and vindicated the judgment of the Secretary of the Navy. The little *Monitor* had forced the *Merrimac* to retire to Norfolk. It had been a drawn battle, but its effect was that of a victory. Naval history had been written in Hampton Roads, and all men read the portents of change in the battleships of the world. The foreign ministers were eager to learn the details of the combat that they might transmit to their governments the facts concerning armor-plated ships. The Swedish minister, Count Piper, was bursting with pride—the inventor Ericsson was of Swedish birth, and Dahlgren, who had devised the guns on the *Monitor,* was the son of a Swede.

Two other messages were received in Washington on that momentous Sunday evening. The first disclosed that the rebel batteries on the Potomac had been abandoned. The other brought the tremendous news that the Confederates had evacuated Manassas. Incredulous, McClellan posted across the river. That night he ordered an advance of the whole army.

A friend slapped the Prince de Joinville on the shoulder, shouted into his sealed ears, *"Vous ne savez pas? l'ennemi a évacué Manassas, et l'armée part demain!"* Word that the rebels had skedaddled aroused the camps. The next morning, Washington was in commotion. Artillery, cavalry and wagons blocked the streets, moving toward the Potomac. The two balloons were made ready, and the new portable gas generators, which permitted them to be inflated in the field, were loaded on their twenty trucks. On the sidewalks, officers were tenderly bidding farewell to weeping ladies, while through the streets the army passed in strong and steady ranks. Blue-clad infantry and gaudy Zouaves marched with shining rifles, smartly slung blanket rolls and haversacks, new canteens and cartridge boxes. Regimental bands blared their brassy tunes. The generals rode in splendor with their staffs. But the rain poured down in torrents; and Washington, which had cheered so many raffish regiments, showed little enthusiasm on the day that the Army of the Potomac advanced.

Silently, efficiently, General Joe Johnston had withdrawn his troops beyond the Rappahannock. The march of the Federals was no more than a promenade, an exercise in the neglected business of making an advance. Beyond the battlefield of Bull Run, where General McDowell could not restrain his tears at the sight of the bleaching bones, the ramparts of Manassas proved to be no more than rude earthworks, with Quaker guns in the embrasures; and a fantastically minded man named Hawthorne thought of the old tales, in which great armies are kept at bay by the arts of necromancers.

As he crossed the Long Bridge, the Prince de Joinville had met General McClellan. In the midst of several batteries, which were slowly defiling across the shaky structure, the general was riding alone, without aides, attended only by a few troopers. He appeared anxious. The Prince thought that there was bitterness in his soul. Nearly eight months had passed since the young Napoleon had come out of the West, crowned with the laurels of his little victories. He had not fought a battle. Yet perhaps in that moment he was aware that he was already defeated.

VIII Ladies in Durance

THE EARLY WINTER NIGHT had fallen on the park to the east of the Capitol, and behind the stripped trees the white stones glimmered in the gas lamps, when a carriage splashed through First Street, and stopped before a corner building of dingy brick. Its imposing doorway, surmounted by a triple window, was the mark of an obsolete importance. Behind that great arched window had sat the senators of the infant nation. The building had been erected for the use of Congress in 1815, while the prouder edifice across the park, burned by British soldiers, was being restored. On this January evening of 1862, the windows, great and small alike, were disfigured by horizontal slats of wood, through which light feebly twinkled. Armed sentries paced their rounds on First Street, and around the corner, along a rambling series of extensions on A Street. The Old Capitol had been turned into a military prison.

In the anteroom, officers loitered with an air of expectation, as a lady and a little girl stepped from the carriage, and were escorted across the threshold. Like an eager host, Superintendent Wood hurried to meet them. It was his custom to do the honors to new arrivals. "Hello, Gus; you're back again. You couldn't stay away from us very long," he would say to a Virginia farmer, repeatedly arrested for refusing to take the oath of allegiance. "I'm always glad to see your countrymen *here*," he once greeted an Englishman, taken up while attempting a visit to Richmond via the Federal lines. Gentlemen he was in the habit of receiving, but a lady was a novelty in the Old Capitol. Mrs. Rose O'Neal Greenhow, standing, dark and handsome, in the anteroom, had not only been a prominent figure in the social life of the capital; she was considered the most important Confederate spy arrested by the Government. She noted that the superintendent received her with "great *empressement*," and seemed "sensible of the honor" of being her custodian.

"You have got one of the hardest little rebels here that you ever saw," piped young Rose. She was her mother's daughter; and five months of romping with detectives and soldiers cannot have been conducive to mending her manners. Of Mrs. Greenhow's entrance speech, there is no record. Perhaps she did not condescend to reply to the jailer's courtesies. Her admiration for Southern institutions embraced the conception of caste; and she understood the theatrical value of a disdainful silence.

Mrs. Greenhow knew the Old Capitol well. For years, it had been a boardinghouse—kept, some said, by her aunt. One famous lodger, her husband's friend, John C. Calhoun, had hallowed this house for her. The South Carolina statesman had been Mrs. Greenhow's idol. He had formed her political philosophy. The bare room to which she was taken, while she waited to be shown to her cell, was the room in which Calhoun had died. There, with his black eyes burning in his wasted face, he had uttered to the last his defense of State sovereignty and his prophecies of disunion. Rose Greenhow had sat by his bedside and ministered to his wants, while she listened. After twelve years, his influence had brought her back to his room again. But, if she thought of this, it was without qualm or regret. Hers was the happy arrogance of a convinced superiority. In the dreary jail, she sat like Marie Antoinette, with whom she was fond of comparing herself.

The rout of Bull Run had filled Mrs. Greenhow with the exultation of a personal triumph. While she carried presents to the Confederate prisoners and schemed to deliver Washington into the conquering Beauregard's hands, she had continued to send her dispatches to Colonel Jordan. They contained, she herself declared, "verbatim reports" of the Cabinet meetings and the Republican caucuses, exact drawings of the Washington fortifications, and the "*minutes* of M'Clellan's private consultations, and often extracts from his notes." Mrs. Greenhow may have exaggerated her information, but it was extensive and valuable to the enemy. Some men who were privy to the councils of the Union, or wore its uniform with apparent honor must have trembled at the news of her arrest.

After Bull Run, Rose Greenhow's activities were soon curtailed. Suspicion fell on her almost at once, and on the sultry morning of August 23—five months before her removal to the Old Capitol—she took her last promenade in Washington. She had been warned. She knew that she was being watched and followed. On her walk, she was joined by "a distinguished member of the diplomatic corps," and it was not until she reached her door that two men stepped forward, with some mumble of verbal authority, to arrest her. One of them was in uniform, and called himself Major E. J. Allen. Among the miscellaneous bits of information which Mrs. Greenhow was skillful in collecting, was the knowledge that he was Allan Pinkerton, the Scottish barrelmaker turned detective who headed McClellan's secret service.

The house was filled with men. Downstairs, in the parlors divided by a red gauze, Mrs. Greenhow coolly waited while the detectives searched beds, drawers and wardrobes, tumbled out soiled clothes and ransacked the papers in her library. All was quietly done in the hope that, if no alarm were raised, some accomplices might call. But little Rose ran out to climb a tree in the garden and shout to the passers-by, "Mother has been arrested!" Detectives issued from the house, and dragged the eight-year-old rebel from the tree, in tears. In spite of her warning, a number of Confederate sympathizers presented themselves, and were promptly taken into custody.

That August day another clever Southern woman, Mrs. Philip Phillips, was also imprisoned in her own house. During the night, the mayor of Washington, James G. Berret, was arrested by the provost guard. No one suspected Berret of being a spy. However, as an ex-officio member of the Metropolitan Police Board, he had balked at repeating the oath of allegiance. His past record and his associations smacked of sympathy with secession, and Beret was whisked off on the early morning train to Fort Lafayette in New York harbor.

For the first week of her imprisonment in the Sixteenth Street house, Mrs. Greenhow was under continual surveillance. All privacy was denied her. Pinkerton had a number of women operatives, for he had brought the entire staff of his Chicago agency to Washington; but a man peered through the open doors at the intimacies of Mrs. Greenhow's toilet. When she lay down, a man sat by her bed. At the end of August, she was relieved of these intrusions. It had been decided to turn her house into a female prison. Mrs. Greenhow was confined to her chamber, and other occupants were installed in the remaining rooms. A detachment of General McClellan's bodyguard, a Chicago company known as the Sturgis Rifles, took the place of the detectives.

A War Department clerk sorted the torn scraps of letters which the Pinkerton detectives had found in Mrs. Greenhow's stove. Some contained militiary information evidently intended for the enemy. There was also a letter from Donellan, the messenger who had carried the news of McDowell's advance. Mrs. Greenhow had succeeded in destroying the key to Colonel Jordan's cipher, but the amateurish cryptograms were soon translated by experts. Several of her recent dispatches, moreover, had fallen into the hands of Secretary Seward. The Government was amassing ample evidence to support its contention that Rose Greenhow was a "dangerous, skillful spy."

The Sturgis Rifles were more considerate guards than the Pinkerton detectives. Lieutenant N. E. Sheldon, a good-looking New Yorker, proved to be an indulgent jailer. Mrs. Greenhow recorded that he was obliging enough to undertake to send her dispatches to the rebels. She made no allusion to the fact that he actually delivered them to the provost marshal; but Sheldon was the only helpful army officer whose name she betrayed when she came to write her story. She repeatedly expressed her gratitude for his kindness. She was provided with writing materials, and permitted to use her library. Sheldon protected her from the unwelcome visits of Brigade-Surgeon Stewart, who had been ordered by the provost marshal to make a daily inspection of her "sanitary condition." For some reason—perhaps for purposes of espionage—one of the prisoners, a Mrs. Onderdonk of Chicago, was allowed to eat with Mrs. Greenhow. But, as the latter protested at the outrage of holding intercourse with "a woman of bad repute," Sheldon restricted Mrs. Onderdonk to her own room. Finally, as Mrs. Greenhow could not eat the prison food, this solicitous officer bought delicacies for her out of his own pocket, until she discovered the generous deception and put a stop to it.

Mrs. Greenhow had a gift for interesting men, and winning their confidence. When, as Rose O'Neal, she had first come to Washington from her home in Maryland, she had been a girl so fresh and lovely that she had been called "the Wild Rose." But now she was over forty, and her smoothly parted hair was threaded with gray. Her photograph, taken by Brady in the yard of the Old Capitol, shows a handsome, resolute, time-worn face. Her heavy mourning silk has little ruffles of net, and full, transparent sleeves. She wears short black kid gloves, and a veil falls from the back of her sleek head. There is something indomitable in the picture of the finery, the dignity and the pride, seated in a kitchen chair before a barred window in a whitewashed wall. One arm encircles little Rose, who stands, in crisp muslin crinoline and pantalettes, resting her head against her mother's. Mrs.

Greenhow's dark eyes, looking steadfastly into Brady's camera, are still fine. But the portrait is that of a woman who has passed the age of sexual conquest.

Some radiance must have lighted her lined face when she spoke with men, for Rose Greenhow triumphantly maintained a reputation for allure. The *National Republican* romanticized her as "the beautiful rebel of Sixteenth Street" and "the fascinating female rebel." In the cold, official pages of the war records is written Pinkerton's tribute to "her almost irresistible seductive powers." She had not used them in vain, he reported to General Andrew Porter, on the officers of the army; she had unscrupulously exerted them on "persons holding places of honor and profit under the government," in order to obtain intelligence for the enemy.

Five years after the war ended, Hamilton Fish, then Secretary of State, heard a curious story from a fellow New Yorker, the newspaper proprietor and diplomat, James Watson Webb. It was the account of a confidence made to Webb by General Thomas Jordan, of the late Confederate army. Jordan told Webb that, at the outbreak of the war, he had found that an intimacy existed between Senator Wilson and "one Mrs. Greenhow." He, Jordan, had established "the same kind of intimacy" with her, and then induced her to obtain official information from Wilson, and forward it in cipher to the Confederates. It was from the Massachusetts senator, as Webb repeated the story to Fish, that Mrs. Greenhow obtained the news of McDowell's advance.

That Jordan gave Mrs. Greenhow a cipher, that she used it to communicate with the Confederates and that she advised Beauregard of McDowell's movement are matters of record. Mrs. Greenhow was bent on involving Henry Wilson in her disloyal activities. In her book, *My Imprisonment*, published in London in 1863, she definitely stated that he was implicated in certain of her intercepted dispatches. Several Republican officials, she said, were summoned to give an account of themselves before the Cabinet, Scott and McClellan. Wilson's was the only name she mentioned.

Moreover, in destroying much of her correspondence, Mrs. Greenhow carefully preserved a packet of love letters, which fell into Federal hands. They were signed with the initial, H. One of them, dated January 30, 1861, is written on stationery stamped with the seal of the United States and the heading, Thirty-sixth Congress. Two letters refer to the consideration of the Pacific Railroad bill, in which Wilson

Washington City 30th Jany 1861

Your note is rec'd — Believe me or
not you cannot be more wretched
than I am. I cannot now
explain. Let it suffice until
we meet that for the last few
days *every* movement and act
of mine have been watched with
Hawkeyed vigilance. For your
sake more than my own I
have been compelled to be
cautious. But tomorrow at
10 A.M. I will see you at
all hazzards

Yours &c
H

One of the letters, signed H—, seized by the Federals at Mrs. Greenhow's residence. The original is in the files of intercepted correspondence of the Civil War, at the National Archives, Washington, D. C.

took an active interest. They are hastily written notes, filled with ardor and frustration—the frustration of a man too busy to indulge his passion, and also fearful of exposure of a secret relationship.

Manuscript experts have pronounced that these letters are not in Wilson's handwriting. The internal evidence, combined with Mrs. Greenhow's published statement, awakens the suspicion that, if he did not write them, she intended them to be taken as his.

Henry Wilson, the hero of an American success story, started life as a farm laborer, and learned the trade of shoemaking. He achieved his political eminence through hard work and driving ambition. With his set, scowling farmer's face, his comfortable stomach, his ample yards of black broadcloth and his humpty-dumpty collar, he was not a figure of romance. Few of Mrs. Greenhow's friends saw her after her arrest, but Wilson visited her room in the Old Capitol. It does not seem the act of a guilty or fearful man. If he was named as an informant in her treasonable dispatches, he must have been able to make a convincing explanation. The authorities had the letters signed H— and Wilson was a married man, whose reputation would have been blasted by an intrigue, even if the lady had not been a spy for the enemy. No cloud fell on Wilson's political fortunes. Until the end of the war, he remained the zealous chairman of the Senate Committee on Military Affairs. In 1872, he was elected Vice-President of the United States.

Mrs. Greenhow's arrest brought her wide notoriety. Even a less theatrical woman might have fancied herself a heroine. Her house, nicknamed Fort Greenhow, was one of the sights of the capital, and tourists came to stare at it, in hopes of catching a glimpse of the famous female spy. For a short while, Mrs. Greenhow divided the honors with Mrs. Philip Phillips, who was moved from her own house to Fort Greenhow with her two eldest daughters and her sister, Miss Levy. This family was presently sent beyond the Union lines, and went to New Orleans. After the Union occupation of that city, Mrs. Phillips was accused of training her children to spit on Federal officers. In the summer of 1862, she stood laughing on her balcony while the funeral of a Northern lieutenant passed; and General Ben Butler, then commanding in New Orleans, ordered her sent to Ship Island, where she was confined for more than two months.

The other women who came and went in Mrs. Greenhow's cheerless house were, according to its deposed mistress, "generally of the lowest class." She was much annoyed by the presence of a Miss Poole, arrested in western Virginia on the charge of corresponding with the rebels. Miss Poole was allowed the freedom of the house, and ingratiated herself with the Government by making reports on everyone, from little Rose to the soldiers of the guard. As her room adjoined Mrs. Greenhow's, the latter was cut off from conversation, and obliged to receive "all knowledge of the outer world" in writing.

Another objectionable fellow-prisoner, an elderly divorcée called Mrs. Baxley, reached Fort Greenhow at the end of December. She had been arrested on returning to Baltimore after a visit to Richmond. Her garrulousness on the truce boat had been her undoing. She had boasted to her fellow-passengers that she had obtained for Dr. Septimus Brown of Baltimore a commission as surgeon in the Confederate army. She also claimed to have "nuts from President Davis's table" and a letter for Mrs. Greenhow. The latter disgustedly ascribed these vaunts to "a disordered imagination." However, the United States authorities, after examining the papers found inside the lining of Mrs. Baxley's bonnet, took a serious view of her Richmond excursion. The commission for Dr. Brown was among them, and the unfortunate physician was hustled off to Fort McHenry.

Clamorous in her desire to be set free, Mrs. Baxley wrote Seward a series of letters, explaining that she was too insignificant to be detained. Her nature, she assured him, was "nervous, impulsive and frank," and no one would entrust her with important papers. She had gone to Richmond merely to gratify "a pardonable curiosity . . . to see Jeff Davis," and carried back only "a few friendly letters" in her bonnet. In spite of these protestations, Mrs. Baxley made no show of loyalty to the Union, and refused to sleep under blankets on which "U. S." was stamped. Mrs. Greenhow said that "she raved from early morn till late at night, in language more vehement than delicate," and that her shrieks and imprecations were unfit for the ears of little Rose. Both Mrs. Baxley and Miss Poole were subject to fainting fits, signalized by a loud cry and a heavy thud on the floor. The sentinel would give the alarm. Soldiers would come running to the rescue, with the attentive Lieutenant Sheldon "bringing up the rear . . . conspicuously flourishing a brandy bottle. . . ."

In the midst of these distractions, Mrs. Greenhow remained aloof, and somehow contrived to keep up a steady communication with her friends on the outside. In her book, she vaguely alluded to a "vocabulary of colors," introduced into the wools of her tapestry work. She also had an intermediary, known as "my little bird," and under the noses of the guard she actually succeeded in sending dispatches to the Confederacy. The Federal authorities had evidence of the weakness of Fort Greenhow; for a copy of a letter which Mrs. Greenhow wrote to Secretary Seward, bitterly detailing the outrages of her imprisonment, was printed in a Richmond newspaper. No immediate repercussions followed, and late in December the lady wrote Colonel Jordan that she expected to be sent South. This communication also was success-fully sent and delivered. At this date Mrs. Greenhow began to note a change in the attitude of her jailers. The press printed a story that a missive, containing plans for her escape, had been discovered in a cake sent to her at Christmas. In early January, after she had addressed a second angry letter to Seward, her library was searched, the window was boarded up, and all paper was removed from her desk. It was presently announced that the female prison would be closed. Of the inmates who remained, only Mrs. Greenhow and Mrs. Baxley were detained, and they were transferred to the Old Capitol.

When, in July of 1861, the Old Capitol had become a makeshift jail, no effort had been wasted on the task of strengthening its decayed walls, broken partitions, or creaking doors and stairways. Wooden slats were nailed across the windows, and high board fences filled the spaces between the buildings which casually bounded the inner quadrangle of the yard. The obstacles to the prisoners' escape lay not in the rambling structures, but in the military guard which paced the streets outside, and clanked and shouted in the corridors.

But, if the Old Capitol wanted the character of a stronghold, in gloom and filth and discomfort it belonged to an ancient tradition. Lice and bedbugs abounded in the rooms, and spider webs festooned the soiled whitewash of the walls. Unsavory pork and beef, half-boiled beans and musty rice made up the bill of fare. The atmosphere of the whole prison was soured by the effluvia of the open, uncleaned sinks, situated behind the cookhouse in the yard.

Some of the prisoners enjoyed special privileges. A few were admitted, by card, to the two enclosed sinks used by the officials. If they had friends in the capital, they were allowed to accept gifts of food. Indeed, when their means permitted, they were not obliged to partake of the miserable prison fare, but might form independent messes in their rooms. The food was sold to them, at profiteering prices, by the commissary of the jail, where tobacco and other luxuries could also be purchased.

The Old Capitol had originally been intended only for prisoners of war, but, though Confederate soldiers continued to form the largest single group, the building soon housed a motley assortment of inmates. The political prisoners ranged from spies to persons vaguely suspected of disloyal sentiments. Rebel mail carriers, smugglers and blockade-runners were confined in the Old Capitol. There were also Federal military offenders. A large house at Thirteenth Street and the Avenue had been taken for an army prison, and later the Central Guard-house was used for the same purpose. However, the Old Capitol continued to have its quota of Union officers, many of them incarcerated for talking against the Government. The extraordinary number of offenses committed by the military in Washington was ascribed to the influence of bad liquor, illegally purveyed throughout the war.

In the first months, a section of the Old Capitol was reserved for the Negro contrabands—former slaves of rebel masters. These destitute persons were kept in the jail as an act of charity. If they could find jobs, they were free to leave. Otherwise, the Government employed the able-bodied men at burying dead horses and other heavy labor. Some worked as servants in the institution, and for a consideration prepared the food for the private messes of the prisoners.

In spite of its dreariness, the jail was a sociable place. Save for the cells of the guard-house, to which recalcitrant inmates were sent for punishment, there was little solitary confinement. Separation of the prisoners was impossible in the crowded building, in which there were few small, single rooms. When their work was done, the Negroes skylarked with their women in the yard. The main occupation of the other inmates was card playing. Week after week, except on Sundays, the interminable games went on from early morning until roll call at nine in the evening. Bluff poker, with one-cent pieces for chips, was the favorite diversion. Muggins—or Old Capitol, as this game of dominoes was locally called—was also popular. Smoking, singing and horseplay enlivened the five large second-story rooms, formed from the chambers which had been used by Congress. One was occupied by Federal officers, while three were usually filled with Virginia farmers. The central room, Number 16, was allotted to political prisoners. Through the broken and dirty panes of the great arched window which had formerly lighted the proceedings of the Senate, citizens of the Union looked out on the skeleton of the Capitol dome, and cursed the Black Republicans beneath it. Like the neighboring rooms, Number 16 was equipped with a triple tier of bunks. It was furnished with a large cylinder stove, three or four iron bedsteads, some stools and benches, and two pine tables. The principal mess of the prison was in Number 16. There, the elite of the political prisoners devoured a ham bone or a piece of commissary beef, in sight of their less fortunate associates. The bunks were so infested with bedbugs that they were chiefly used to store a litter of belongings—valises, pots and pans, newspapers, pipes, empty bottles and remnants of food. At night, the tables were turned into beds, and the floor was strewn with shakedowns.

The rebel officers were confined in rooms on the north side of the building. The unhappy lot of prisoners of war had many alleviating circumstances in the Old Capitol. There was a coal fire in each room. Whisky was easily procured through the contrabands or the guard. Like the other inmates, the Confederates had cards and newspapers. They enjoyed the additional advantage of being excellently fed, for a committee of Washington sympathizers provided them with every delicacy. For the most part, they gave little trouble, and submitted quietly to their confinement. In the early days, prisoners of war looked forward to a speedy exchange, and their psychological condition was far better than that of the political prisoners. Like hundreds of their kind in Fort Warren, Fort Lafayette, Fort McHenry and elsewhere, persons of suspect loyalty had no assurance of an end to their captivity. The guarantees of the Constitution had vanished since the President had tampered with the ancient privilege of the writ of *habeas corpus* by suspending it along the military lines between Washington and Philadelphia. Chief Justice Taney, sitting in the circuit court in Baltimore, had handed down the opinion that the President had no constitutional power to suspend the writ, nor authorize a military officer to do so. The venerable judge had become embroiled in the case of John Merryman, confined for treasonable activities in Fort McHenry. The soldiers at the fort would neither yield the person of John Merryman, nor admit the United States marshal to serve an order against their commanding general for contempt. Taney's decision provoked much discussion, but he was an aged man of Southern bias. The conservative Attorney General, Mr. Bates, sustained the President. The majority of loyal men at first accepted the arbitrary arrests as necessary to the nation's struggle for survival, even when in September of 1861 General Dix and General Banks rounded up secessionist legislators of Maryland, and clapped them into prison.

Mr. Lincoln moved slowly in abrogating a cherished safeguard of the Constitution. In May, 1861, he authorized the suspension of the writ on a small section of the Florida coast; in July, on the military line north of Philadelphia, as far as New York; in October, for soldiers in the District of Columbia. Not until the autumn of 1862 did he deny the privilege to all persons imprisoned by military order. Still another year passed before, on authority given him by Congress, he found it necessary to suspend it throughout the Union. Yet the Bill of Rights had proved to be a fragile document, torn in pieces by the first rough touch. In 1861, the system of arbitrary arrests had already spread far and wide. Frequently they were made by the War Department or by some army officer, and the prisoners were always held in military custody. At first, however, all political prisoners were under the control of the State Department. The ambitious Mr. Seward, prone to meddle in the affairs of the other departments, had illogically assumed responsibility for suppressing disloyalty in the Northern population, and maintained a large force of detectives for that purpose. He was said to have bragged of the far-flung arrests he could order by touching his little bell, and was hated and feared for exercising the powers of a dictator. Suspects were carried off to military prisons, often secretly, by night. Their houses were searched, their valuables seized. In most cases, they were not even informed of the charges against them. They were not permitted to have legal advice, and no expectation of trial by jury mitigated the discomforts of their detention. The State Department had no intention of prosecuting the political prisoners, and did not even proceed to accumulate evidence against them. They could only hope that the pressure of their claims might call them to the department's attention, and win them a special examination. Often when this was held, it developed that there had been insufficient grounds for the arrest. The worst misery in the Old Capitol was the helplessness and uncertainty which made the men in Number 16 dull their minds with endless games of bluff poker, and toss wakefully at night on their shakedowns on the floor.

Washington saw a spectacular instance of military rule, exercised under the State Department, when one John Murphy tried to secure the release of his son, James, who had enlisted in the army under the legal age of eighteen. Judge William M. Merrick, a Marylander appointed by Buchanan to the United States circuit court, issued a writ of *habeas corpus* against the provost marshal, General Andrew Porter, just prior to the suspension of the privilege for soldiers in the District. Porter refused to respect the writ. Shortly after, the attorney who had served it was arrested on the provost marshal's order, and placed in the guard-house. Returning home one evening, Judge Merrick found an armed sentinel stationed at his door by the authority of the Secretary of State. He did not appear in his place on the bench next day. His indignant associates issued a contempt order against Porter, but the deputy marshal was forbidden by the President to serve it. There had been no proclamation of military law in the District, and the circuit court had not been advised of the suspension of the writ. Possibly the surveillance to which Merrick was subjected for several days was justified in Mr. Seward's mind by a report that the judge had written a disloyal letter to Chicago, but no accusation was communicated to Merrick himself.

In singular contrast to the arbitrary arrests was the retention of many doubtful unionists in the Government departments. The House had found this situation so disturbing that during the special session it had appointed a Select Committee on Loyalty of Clerks. It was headed by John F. Potter, a belligerent Wisconsin Republican, who two years earlier had been challenged to a duel by Roger A. Pryor of Virginia, and had turned the affair into a joke by choosing bowie knives as the weapons. As an agency for secret accusations, the Potter Committee formed a sounding board on which every whisper of suspicion was magnified during the latter half of 1861. In the offices, clerks trembled for their jobs, and spied and tattled on their fellows. Some five hundred and fifty charges were made to the committee, which examined nearly four hundred and fifty witnesses under oath. Workers at the Navy Yard, the Arsenal and the White House were among those whose fidelity was challenged.

Congress had passed an act requiring all Government employees to take a strong oath to support the Constitution, but many bureau heads had been slack in complying with the law. After studying the evidence, the Potter Committee concluded that over two hundred employees were in sympathy with the rebel cause, and it contended that even the suspicion of disloyalty should debar a man from holding a Government post. Wanting in any authority to remove the suspects, the congressmen sent detailed information to the department heads, and a number of dismissals and resignations resulted. The *Star* said that much of the evidence appeared to be "a bundle of malicious perjuries." The publication of the committee's report, giving the names of the witnesses and the substance of their testimony, brought the ill feeling in Washington to a crisis. One of the witnesses was beaten up near the Capitol, and a number of talebearers hurried out of town, to avoid facing the persons against whom they had testified.

In spite of the commotion raised by the House, the secessionist sympathizers of Washington were treated with remarkable leniency— they were "tolerated there," declared the Democrat, Horatio King, "with a degree of patience . . . scarcely compatible with the public safety." Only in extreme cases were they subjected to arrest and imprisonment. Some of those on Potter's black list remained in their positions, claiming that they had been unjustly accused. On taking office, Mr. Stanton found many "rat-holes" in the War Department, and stopped them by discharging clerks and officials and arresting army officers. The department mail pouch, which hung in the hall, had been freely used by rebel sympathizers for the transmission of information to Richmond.

Soon after Stanton was made War Secretary, the jurisdiction over the political prisoners passed from the State to the War Department. If Mr. Seward had ever had a little bell, it tinkled no more. There were large-scale deliveries from the overcrowded bastilles of the Union. The most obvious victims of injustice—there were many cases for which the State Department had no record of the charges—were released on parole. A commission composed of two prominent New Yorkers, General Dix and Judge Edwards Pierrepont, was appointed to examine the prisoners who remained in custody. It was the forerunner of many exclusively military commissions which would hold lengthy sessions in Washington and other cities. At the head of the Bureau of Military Justice, clothed in extraordinary authority, would rise the figure of a tall, gray-haired, courteous Kentuckian—Joseph Holt, Mr. Buchanan's War Secretary, who was appointed Judge Advocate General. Like his fellow Democrat, Stanton, Holt would prove an eager convert to radical Republican aims. The tyranny of the State Department had been casually and incapably exercised. Mr. Stanton would bring to the suppression of disloyalty an efficiently organized ruthlessness. The arbitrary arrests and the military trials of civilians would develop into a vast and despotic system, productive of great hostility to the administration. Over thirteen thousand persons were arrested by the War Department as political offenders in the course of the war.

Under the new dispensation, the Old Capitol bore an especially close relation to the War Department. Both Secretary Stanton and his stout, red-headed Scottish Assistant Secretary, Peter H. Watson, were lawyers practicing in Washington. In spite of the great pressure of national affairs, they were prone to busy themselves with local details. William P. Wood, the superintendent of the Old Capitol, was known to both of them. A native of Alexandria, Wood was a model-maker by trade, and in 1854 he had been an expert witness in the famous patent case, McCormick vs. Manny, in which both Stanton and Watson had acted as counsel for the defense—the same case in which Stanton had rudely edged out an obscure associate, Abraham Lincoln. Cyrus McCormick lost the case, which turned on an alleged infringement of patents for his reaping machine. When he was an old man, Wood made an affidavit that he had used trickery to aid the defense—altering the design of an early model of the McCormick reaper which was introduced in evidence. The court records do not show that his chicanery influenced the decision. Wood stated that Stanton never knew of the deception. The jailer, however, was reputed to have unusual influence with the War Secretary. Young Major William E. Doster, who became the Washington provost marshal when the Army of the Potomac took the field, said that Wood "was deeper in the War Office than any man at Washington, and it was commonly said that Stanton was at the head of the War Office and Wood at the head of Stanton."

Wood had been a private in the regular Army, and, as civilian administrator of the Old Capitol, seemed to take pleasure in con-temptuously disregarding the orders of all military officers. His im-pudence was particularly galling to Andrew Porter, who had been captain of the company in which Wood served. Watson told Doster that Porter once came to the War Department in a rage, because his orders had been rescinded by " 'that dog of a citizen Wood,' whom he used to tie up by the thumbs in New Mexico." After hearing Porter's demand for Wood's dismissal, Mr. Stanton gave the general "the alternative either of being insulted by Wood or resigning his commis-sion." Doster evoked this anecdote by visiting the War Department with a complaint of his own about the superintendent's disobedience. He concluded "that it was dangerous to interfere with Wood."

Stanton later made the jailer a colonel of cavalry. Wood also served as an agent of the War Department, and was sent on several confidential missions to the South. In the fall of 1862, he was severely censured by army officers for his activities while accompanying prisoners to the Confederate post of exchange at City Point, Virginia. He exceeded his authority by entering into general negotiations for exchange, and persuaded the Confederate commissioner, Robert Ould, a native of Georgetown and former District Attorney and popular clubman in Washington, to send him to Richmond, under ostensible arrest. The storm of protest from the Federal commissioners forced the War Department to recall Wood. He refused to report to General Dix, then in command at Fort Monroe. Dix made such an indignant report that Mr. Stanton replied that Wood should have been sent to the guard-house. The War Secretary, however, continued to place great reliance on the jailer, who retained his wide authority at the Old Capitol until the close of the war.

Though Wood was an undersized man of more than forty years, he had great physical strength. On one occasion, he shook a prisoner— a constable of the District marshal's force—"almost out of his clothes," because he had presumed to write the military governor about the secessionist proclivities of the gentlemen whose room he shared. As the inmates were well aware, the Old Capitol was riddled with paid informers. Detectives, in the guise of prisoners, were planted in the rooms, and joined the groups that gathered at mealtimes in the yard. The talebearing constable was a self-appointed spy, and had made the mistake of competing with Wood's established system.

In making up his reports for the Secretary of War, the superintendent also depended on winning the confidence of the prisoners. Though his manners were uncouth—he prided himself on his plebeian extraction—he was indulgent and obliging. When he chose, he could treat his prisoners with flattering respect; and he succeeded in convincing them that he was their friend, while higher authorities were responsible for their worst discomforts. He protected his charges from impertinent servants and insolent guards. He did his best to put through their letters, all subject to a rigid inspection. The fresh baker's bread, which was the only praiseworthy item on the prison bill of fare, was ordered on Wood's responsibility. At least, he told the prisoners

this, and they believed him. All accounts of life in the Old Capitol
—even Mrs. Greenhow's—bear testimony to Wood's good nature. He
was crafty and hypocritical, but his kindness was genuine. When one
of the prisoners was shot dead by a sentinel, this rough ex-soldier could
not conceal his agitation and dismay. His face went white. His voice
came hoarsely through his trembling lips.

Nevertheless, Wood was regarded with anything but affection in
the Old Capitol. His abolitionist views and his loyalty to the administration would have been enough to earn him the animosity of most of
the inmates. They hated him, moreover, for his detective system; and
were convinced that he accepted bribes and drew large profits from
the swindling prison commissary, in which his nephew was a partner.
Pious minds were shocked by the fact that the superintendent was an
infidel. In a day when religious nonconformity was a scandal—Lincoln
and his supporters had hushed up the President's early adventures in
skepticism—Wood, who had been reared in the Roman Catholic faith,
was an acknowledged doubter. On one occasion, when he appeared
as a witness in the criminal court of the District, his testimony was
thrown out by the judge, because he would not avow a belief in a
personal existence after death. Mrs. Greenhow said that "his desire
to make proselytes to his own *want of faith* was the ruling passion of
his soul"; and that, if anyone in the prison asked him for a book, he
was sure to produce a scrapbook of his own anti-religious writings,
or the works of Tom Paine.

On a pleasant Sunday morning in August of 1862, Wood went
bawling, like a town crier, through the Old Capitol corridors: "All ye
who want to hear the Lord God preached according to Jeff Davis, go
down to the yard; and all ye who want to hear the Lord God preached
according to Abe Lincoln, go down to Number 16." One prisoner
astutely observed that this was the jailer's way of holding up both the
Gospel and the credulous to ridicule. The fact remained that, while
an abolitionist preacher and his skinny wife discoursed in Number 16,
the yard was treated to an attack on New England fanaticism by a
Confederate chaplain who was among the prisoners. This performance
was repeated on subsequent Sundays. There were no such broad-
minded doings at Fort Lafayette or Fort Warren. Wood had a charac-
teristic surprising in a jailer—a sense of humor. He could listen to
violent arraignments of the administration "with a twinkle of amusement in his shrewd cynical eyes." He replied to one of Mrs. Green-

how's bombastic letters—he had offered to help her obtain her private papers, and wanted a power of attorney to receipt for them—with the request, "be kind enough to dispense with the God and Liberty style in your *pronunciamento.*" But the excellent criticism was wasted.

Among the frequent visitors to the prison was a lean, muscular, taciturn man, with bright-brown hair and beard, and cold, searching gray eyes. This was a former mechanic, La Fayette C. Baker, a native of western New York who had done good service as a member of the San Francisco vigilantes. Early in the war, he had been sent as a spy to Richmond by General Scott, and had shown great ingenuity in performing his hazardous mission. After being arrested by the rebels and holding three conversations with Jefferson Davis, he had escaped and returned to Washington with a fund of information about the Confederate army and capital. On Scott's recommendation, the State Department had employed Baker as a detective, and he was taken over by the War Department, after the February reorganization. He had made an excellent impression on Mr. Seward as a patriotic and zealous agent—truthful, though perhaps indiscreet—and both Stanton and Watson reposed great confidence in him. As chief of a large force of War Department detectives, organized under Watson's supervision, Baker was to become a sinister figure whose extraordinary powers and oppressive acts would make him feared and execrated throughout the nation.

Eventually, like Wood, Baker was given a colonel's commission. His command was the First District Cavalry—an organization which, for want of Washington recruits, was chiefly composed of companies from Maine. Prior to winning rank and notoriety, he was an obscure agent, operating mainly in Washington, Alexandria, Baltimore and lower Maryland, central points for the clandestine trade and communication with the Confederacy. In Washington, Baker was immediately marked as a scoundrel. Among the prisoners in the Old Capitol, his venality was a byword. Watson himself admitted to Doster that the employment of Baker was a case of "set a rogue to catch a rogue." Doster found that the Pinkerton detectives and the Washington police also had a bad opinion of Baker, and that Wood was of the same mind. Yet, in the superintendent's office, Baker and Wood were already beginning those secret examinations of prisoners which, later in the war, were to become a notorious procedure in the solitary cells of the Old Capitol annex, Carroll Prison.

Mrs. Greenhow was lodged in a back room on the second floor of the Old Capitol's A Street wing, where, General Andrew Porter said, she was "quite retired." This seclusion was prompted in part by fear that she would signal from her window to secessionist sympathizers. The ease with which she had outwitted the guard at the Sixteenth Street house had given her a reputation for superhuman ingenuity. Her only outlook was the prison yard, and she was forbidden to approach the barred window. Food was carried to her room, which she was not permitted to leave, even for exercise. Porter's opinion that the room was "fixed up . . . quite comfortable" was not shared by its occupant, who viewed with distaste the wooden chairs and table, the diminutive looking glass, and the straw bed which she shared with little Rose. Major Doster thought the furnishings suitable to a room in a second-class boardinghouse—praise never bestowed on any other quarters in the Old Capitol. Mrs. Greenhow had a sewing machine and a desk, books and writing materials. Lieutenant Sheldon had helped her "to rescue some few cherished memorials." She also had her pistol, though the ammunition had been removed.

From the Old Capitol, the lady sent out a stream of letters, complaining to everyone she knew about the military authorities. She tantalized the guards, made impossible demands, and resented every prison regulation. Her Southern blood boiled at her proximity to the contrabands. Like Marie Antoinette, she was an aristocrat persecuted by the rabble; and she addressed the Yankee officers with theatrical dignity, accenting her words with an unnatural distinctness of enunciation. "Greenhow enjoys herself amazingly," wrote a fellow-prisoner, Mrs. Morris. Porter once exclaimed that he would prefer to resign, rather than continue the irksome duty of having Mrs. Greenhow in charge. With Major Doster, on the other hand, she always talked freely; and he spoke of her treating her keepers with flattery and coquetry. This young officer wasted no pity on the lady. He thought that the moment of her arrest had been the happiest of her life.

Mrs. Greenhow's chief aversion at the Old Capitol was Brigade-Surgeon Stewart, the portly prison physician whose ministrations she had managed to avoid at her own house. She described him as "a vulgar, uneducated man, bedizened with enough gold lace for three field marshals," and said that his calls were prompted by an ambition to brag of having talked with her. The surgeon, whose pompous loyalty to the Union made him unpopular with secessionists, was under orders to visit all prisoners, but Mrs. Greenhow haughtily refused to permit him to attend either herself or Rose.

Little Rose had been taken to the Old Capitol at her mother's request; yet Mrs. Greenhow contrived to convey the impression that the child's confinement was an added proof of the administration's cruelty. "My little darling," she said to Rose, soon after their arrival, "you must show yourself superior to these Yankees, and not pine." "O mamma, never fear," Rose replied; "I hate them too much." But even a proud spirit cannot sustain an imprisoned child. Rose seldom left the small, dark room. Her chubby face grew thin and pale. She could not eat the prison meals of greasy beans and fat junk, and often cried herself to sleep from hunger. Though Mrs. Greenhow was reputed to be rich, and though after her release she engaged in cotton and tobacco speculations in Richmond, her means were apparently straitened at this time. It seems scarcely possible that she was too poor to purchase food; and, if she was, she could certainly have obtained it from the bountiful Washington secessionists. She said, however, that only the edibles sent her by Confederate officers in the Old Capitol kept her from starving; and under her eyes, as the weeks passed, little Rose continued to pine. She caught camp measles, which was epidemic in the prison. At length, she became so ill that her mother grew alarmed, and wrote the provost marshal to demand the services of a physician. A few hours later, Brigade-Surgeon Stewart burst into the room, burning with the injustice of the reprimand he had received for neglect of duty. It was one of Mrs. Greenhow's most dramatic moments in the Old Capitol, and she described the scene with relish. Her insults drove the surgeon into an apoplectic rage. He insisted on examining the child, but Mrs. Greenhow pushed herself between him and the bed, where Rose lay bright-eyed with fever. "At your peril but touch my child," she cried. "You are a coward and no gentleman, thus to insult a woman." The unfortunate surgeon attempted to fight it out, but he was no match for "the Wild Rose." When Mrs. Greenhow's poundings on the door had brought the officer of the guard, Brigade-Surgeon Stewart "slunk out," defeated. The authorities called in a doctor whose political views made the mother willing to have him attend the little girl.

Soon after, Mrs. Greenhow was allowed to take little Rose for a half-hour's daily exercise in the mud of the prison yard. She declined to associate with her fellow-prisoners, Mrs. Baxley and Mrs. Morris, and declared that their company was "but a shade less obnoxious" than that of the Negroes. The excitable Mrs. Baxley endured her detention with an ill grace. She was called "the most defiant and outrageous of all the female prisoners," and once engaged in a fist fight with a guard. She tried to push past him. He cursed her. She gave him a bloody nose. He knocked her down and kicked her. To Mrs. Greenhow, the fracas was a personal humiliation.

Mrs. Augusta Morris, a gay and pretty little woman, was equally detested by Mrs. Greenhow, and ascribed this hostility to jealousy and "mean ambition." Though reticent about her birthplace, Mrs. Morris liked to encourage the impression that she was French. Major Doster, who found her "exceedingly fascinating," said that she was the daughter of an Alexandria baker. She had been married in Paris to Dr. J. F. Mason, a native of Virginia. They had separated, and in the autumn of 1861 Mrs. Morris, having resumed her maiden name, had come with her two small sons from Richmond to Washington. She visited the State Department and offered to reveal the Confederate army signals for ten thousand dollars; and she discussed the same proposal with McClellan's father-in-law and chief of staff, General Marcy. If she hoped, as she said, to disarm suspicion that she was a rebel agent, she was mistaken in her course. Pinkerton's men were watching her closely. They discovered that she was in correspondence with Thomas John Rayford—Colonel Jordan's pseudonym, by which Mrs. Greenhow, too, addressed him—and had even received a visit from him at Brown's Hotel, where she was boarding "in style." So vigilant were the detectives that they attended the burial of Mrs. Morris's baby, who died early in February. The following morning, at four o'clock, she was arrested, by order of General McClellan, in her bed at the hotel. But she maintained that the general had acted too late. "I already had gotten his plans, as laid before the military committee, from one of the members," she wrote her estranged husband, who was now a captain in the Confederate army.

Mansfield T. Walworth, a clerk in the Adjutant General's office, was arrested in company with the charming grass widow. He was the erratic son of a distinguished father, the Honorable Reuben H. Walworth, chancellor of New York State. Through his wife's family, Mansfield Walworth had influential connections in the South, and for months he had aspired to be a secret agent of the Federal Government. He had received some encouragement from Secretary Seward, who was his father's friend; but he protested that his ambitions had been recently balked by General Marcy, because he had reported to Seward that Marcy had taken an undue interest in little Mrs. Morris. Walworth was a literary man, the author of a number of sensational novels which had a wide circulation. No evidence of disloyalty was found against him. Pinkerton reported that he seemed merely to have been "mixed up with Mrs. Morris socially to some extent, like several other parties." But the acquaintance, possibly reinforced by the fact that a Confederate lieutenant's uniform had been found in his trunk, cost Walworth two months' imprisonment in the Old Capitol.

Mrs. Morris's three-year-old boy, Frank, accompanied her to prison. His large hobbyhorse did not console him for the loss of freedom. He kicked against the door, and shouted to the guard, "Let me out, you damned Yankee." On the mother's protests that he should be allowed exercise like "the other gentlemen that are now confined here," Superintendent Wood promised to arrange airings for Frank. Mrs. Morris submitted to detention more gracefully than her son. She was supplied with every comfort by Washington sympathizers, and at first had no fault to find with prison life, save for the fact that it interfered with her work. Her lively, jesting manners covered a sore heart, for she was bitter against her husband for his desertion, and angrily resented her mother-in-law's hostility. She thought it a duty to be cheerful, and made herself very popular at the Old Capitol. "They only keep me here," she flippantly wrote, "because they hate to part with me." Scrawled above the mantel of her room were the opening lines of Byron's *Prisoner of Chillon;* but Mrs. Morris's defiance of her Yankee captors was always merry and sweet-tempered.

Of the other women who were at this time briefly detained in the Old Capitol, the most conspicuous was Mrs. L. A. McCarty of Philadelphia. Mrs. McCarty was originally confined under the name of John Barton, because of the disgraceful circumstance that she was dressed as a man. Throughout the war, Washington saw a procession of gallivanting transvestites—smooth-faced, slender lads in uniform, whose rounded figures and fluting voices quickly betrayed them to the police or the provost guard. Usually they were given skirts and packed out of town. Only Mrs. McCarty was suspected of being a spy. Her trunk was found to contain a quantity of opium, morphine and quinine, as well as a revolver, a pair of military spurs and an iron projectile. This last item was her husband's invention, which she had intended to proffer to the Confederate authorities at Richmond. Mrs.

Greenhow took a fancy to Mrs. McCarty, and declared that she "admired her spirit and independence." As their intercourse was held through the keyholes of a double door, Mrs. Greenhow had small opportunity to be shocked by the wanton display of trouser legs.

If the lady, as Major Doster asserted, had "looked forward to the notoriety of a public trial," she was presently disillusioned. On a dark, raw day toward the end of March, she was taken before Mr. Stanton's commissioners, who were sitting in ex-Senator Gwin's mansion at Nineteenth and I Streets, now appropriated for the use of the military governor and the provost marshal. Memories of its former elegance came back to Mrs. Greenhow, as she mounted the filthy stairs. She was kept waiting for an hour in a room without a fire. In a mood of high irritation, she was at last conducted to the examination, informally held around a long table, behind closed doors. "The most highbred courtesy marked the interview," she wrote; but it was "merely an amusing conversation." She openly sneered at the "mimic court," made elaborately sarcastic answers and asked almost as many questions as Judge Pierrepont.

Judge Pierrepont: "You can make any reply you desire to the charges."

Mrs. Greenhow: "Charges! How many have you? Now isn't this a farce! Isn't it solemn! It's a perfect farce!"

Judge Pierrepont: "You can make any reply you please to the charges."

But the replies that Mrs. Greenhow pleased to make threw no light on the investigation of her case. She demanded proof that she had ever corresponded with the enemy. When told that she was particularly charged with giving information about the Federal army before the battle of Bull Run, she said that she was not aware of having done so; she was not in a position to get important information. Otherwise, she would certainly have given it, as "a holy duty to my friends."

There ensued a long discussion as to whether Mrs. Greenhow would like to go South. Pierrepont supposed that it was hardly worth while to ask her to take the oath of allegiance, or give a parole not to aid the enemy. "You would blush to do that," the lady replied.

"General," said Pierrepont to his fellow-commissioner, "I think you had better talk to Mrs. Greenhow. You are an old friend of hers."

"I don't know as I have anything to say," General Dix responded, lamely. But he went on to make some inquiries about Mrs. Green-how's cipher, which she blandly declared she had invented during an illness, but had never used.

Conspicuously absent from the commissioners' questions was any curiosity about the origin of Mrs. Greenhow's information. "If I gave the information that you say I have," she remarked to Judge Pierre-pont, "I must have got it from sources that were in the confidence of the government. I don't intend to say any more. I merely throw this out as a suggestion." She reopened the subject with General Dix, by a reference to "traitors as you call them," within the Republican party. "If Mr. Lincoln's friends will pour into my ear such important infor-mation, am I to be held responsible for all that?" Here she suggested that she might be departing from the rules of strict examination.

"We don't wish to limit you at all, Madame," said Pierrepont. "You are at liberty to state anything you wish."

"There is no restriction," put in Dix.

The examination of Mrs. Greenhow was getting nowhere at all. Dix pleaded that he and the Judge would be "much better pleased" to see her exonerated from the charges. "I don't think you are bent so much on treason as on mischief," Pierrepont indulgently hinted. Dix didn't think there were any more questions.

Mrs. Greenhow was justified in thinking that hers were the honors of this polite engagement. "In these war times," she told the two gentlemen, as she took her leave, "you ought to be in some more important business, than holding an inquisition for the examination of women."

The commissioners had a brief session with Mrs. Baxley, who emphatically declined to take the oath or give a parole, and had strong objections to going South. They took quite a time over pretty little Mrs. Morris. In marked contrast with the sarcastic Mrs. Greenhow, Mrs. Morris was vague and feminine and appealing. Her method was equally effective in discomfiting the courtly commissioners.

Mrs. Morris: "Even if I could have committed treason, I don't know as I should have cared to do it."

Judge Pierrepont: "I don't know as I understand your remark perfectly?"

With wide-eyed innocence, she listened to the charges against her. "Now, I ask you," she said, "where could I get such information?" She said that General Marcy was the only Federal officer she knew.

Judge Pierrepont: "He didn't give you anything?"

Mrs. Morris: "I shouldn't suppose he would. Do you think he would?"

Judge Pierrepont: "I do not suppose he would."

But what harm, begged Mrs. Morris, could "a poor delicate, fragile woman" do? The Judge spoke of her offer to give the Confederate army signals. She was selfish, Mrs. Morris explained, and she had no particular desire to serve either side. She would have given the signals for ten thousand dollars.

Judge Pierrepont (triumphantly): "Then you see a poor, delicate, fragile woman can be of help to a government."

Mrs. Morris (who had been unable to make the sale): "They can when they have the chance."

Judge Pierrepont: "These little fragile, delicate women can sometimes be of great service, in aiding strong men, and strong governments."

When it came to the disposal of her case, Mrs. Morris showed unexpected firmness. She could not take an oath of allegiance "or anything like that." The Judge coaxingly alluded to "what we call a parole of honor." She couldn't even give that. She felt revengeful, she explained, because she had been so badly treated. The officers at the prison had been kind, and Superintendent Wood had behaved "like a gentleman." But the regulars had been outrageous, and the volunteers were "the worst men in the world."

Neither was Mrs. Morris willing to be sent South. She had had domestic troubles, of which she preferred not to speak; and living was expensive in the Confederacy. "I insist upon being put back in Brown's Hotel where you found me," she told Judge Pierrepont, who promised to talk to the President about letting her go free. He thought it possible that Mrs. Lincoln might help her. On this hopeful note, the examination closed. "I bid you all good morning, gentlemen," said Mrs. Morris. "I shall remember you with pleasure."

More than eighty political prisoners were examined by Dix and Pierrepont during the time they sat in Washington. Of these, sixty-five—including Walworth and Mrs. McCarty—were discharged on taking the oath or giving a parole not to aid the enemy. The commission had no power to acquit or punish, but could only release. The three recalcitrant ladies of the Old Capitol were ordered to be conveyed beyond the Union lines into Virginia, if they consented to go;

and they were there to be set free, on giving a parole not to return North during the war.

Mrs. Greenhow was at first very angry over the decision. Her temper had been growing sharper, and her disdainful airs gave place to rages, as her hope of further usefulness to the Confederacy faded. She had become a side show for Yankee tourists, of whom she professed to be in terror, declaring that they made her think of the fish women of Paris during the French Revolution. She longed to revenge herself on the "Black Republican dogs." "I fear now that my capacity of hate will over-shadow every other feeling," she wrote her niece, Adele Douglas.

A rumor that she was to be sent to Fort Warren in Boston harbor inspired Mrs. Greenhow with a vivid desire to go to Virginia. The spring days dragged by in suspense. It was not in the lady's nature to be entirely dull. She could always point her empty pistol at a guard's head, or run up a Confederate flag on her sewing machine, and hang it from the window. She loosened a plank in her closet floor, and lowered little Rose into the arms of rebel officers, who shared their fresh fruit with the child. One day, followed by the other female prisoners, Mrs. Greenhow climbed into Wood's market cart, and drove rapidly around the yard, shouting "I am off for Dixie!" She enjoyed the panic and confusion of the guard. But these moments of excitement were poor compensation for the loss of her importance.

After the commissioners left to visit other military prisons, inmates once more accumulated in the Old Capitol. The jail, Doster said, "operated like a rat-trap—there was only a hole in but no hole out. . . ." Stanton and his assistant secretaries, Baker and other detectives, the military governor and the provost marshal could all make arrests; "but none of them," said Doster, "could discharge without running great risk of getting into trouble with some or all of the others."

Late in April, a prisoner was shot dead by a guard because he refused to obey orders to go away from the window. In May, another was wounded in the thigh, while trying to escape, and died next day, after an amputation. The whole prison knew that the sentinel who shot the second man had agreed to accept a bribe to let him go free; but, after a short period in the guard-house, the soldier was returned to duty. Mrs. Greenhow was suspected of having connived at the attempted escape. She had been permitted some visitors, among them the Honorable Alfred Ely of New York, in whom a friendly feeling for prisoners had been inspired by his own detention in Richmond. But now all her friends were barred. In solitude, she began to lose heart. The exploits of Stonewall Jackson in the Shenandoah Valley gave her a burst of hope; but Jackson never came to set the prisoners free. Abruptly, a few days later, Wood notified Mrs. Greenhow that she was to leave for Virginia at once. There was barely time to pack. The captain of the guard conducted her through the prison to bid her fellow-captives good-by. Outside, the guard was drawn up under arms. There was, in addition, a mounted guard, as well as a special escort, a cavalry lieutenant and six men, "dressed in full uniform, with sword and carbine in hand." Mrs. Greenhow, sensible of the attention paid her, thought it "quite a military display." As an afterthought, she added that "the woman Baxley and Mrs. Morris or Mason were sent at the same time."

The door of the Old Capitol opened, and the ladies stepped into the street. For a moment, fearful of Yankee duplicity, Mrs. Greenhow hesitated. She asked the chief of escort if his orders were to conduct her to a Northern prison. He declared, on his honor, that they were bound for Fort Monroe; and, reassured by his answer, she entered the carriage. At the Washington depot, soldiers held off a throng of Southern sympathizers, but at Baltimore things were better arranged. Wood, who accompanied the party, permitted the ladies to receive their friends at the Gilmore House, where they spent the night. A story that they held "a regular levee" appeared in the *New York Herald*, and was indignantly denied by one of General Dix's aides.

The Baltimore secessionists gave the ladies an ovation, waving handkerchiefs and calling "God bless you!" as they embarked on the Old Point boat. General Dix, who was a fellow-voyager, on his way to take command at Fort Monroe, came on board with less notice. The journey was made by night, and the prisoners lay offshore for most of the following day. The tedium of the delay was relieved by the gentlemanly captain of the boat, who gave the ladies a luncheon, with iced champagne. Under the guns of Fort Monroe, Mrs. Greenhow raised her glass to the health of President Davis and the success of the Confederate cause. She said that the toast was drunk by all present. The chief of escort discreetly kept out of the way.

On the sacred soil at last, Mrs. Greenhow flounced off, with little Rose in her wake, and a large Confederate battle flag concealed beneath her shawl. She was free from Yankee tyranny, safe in the Confederacy she had ardently served. It must have been exasperating that, in the suspicious fashion of wartime, half the people in Richmond persisted in taking her for a Federal agent. Men who knew the secrets of the Confederate high command at Manassas were quick to come to her defense. She proudly recorded Jefferson Davis's greeting, when he visited her on the evening after her arrival. "But for you," he said, "there would have been no battle of Bull Run."

It was late July and the Old Capitol was blanketed in heat and stench and bedbugs, when another female spy arrived at the prison. Belle Boyd was as defiant and theatrical as Rose Greenhow; but she was young and strong and unembittered, and she played her role of Southern heroine with zest. She was the darling of the Old Capitol.

Belle had become famous during Stonewall Jackson's raid in the Shenandoah Valley. Her home was at Martinsburg, a convenient base for her operations. The legend of her coquetry and her daring horsemanship had preceded her to Washington. Everyone had heard that her talent for fascinating Federal officers had redounded to Jackson's advantage, and some gave her the credit for a Federal defeat at Front Royal. Belle was not beautiful. She had a mature, sharp-featured face with prominent teeth. But she was only nineteen, her slim figure was graceful, and there was charm in her vivacious personality, with its "air of joyous recklessness."

Superintendent Wood received Belle cordially, and conducted her to a second-floor room on A Street, scrawled with the names of former occupants, including that of Mrs. Morris. As she was urged to ask for anything she wanted, Belle demanded a rocking chair and also a fire, which she found cheerful, even in midsummer. She was soon given an opportunity to show her colors. A detective, introduced by Wood, suggested that she should take the oath of allegiance. Belle made a scornful speech, and ordered the detective to leave. Through the open door came the sound of cheers from the other rooms along the corridor. When she had been left alone, a small white object fell at her feet. A note, enclosing a tiny nut-shell basket, painted with Confederate flags, had been tossed by an English prisoner across the hall. Belle tossed back a reply. That night, looking from her window at the shanties of Swampoodle and the distant fields silvered by the moonlight, she felt almost happy in prison.

Save for the want of exercise, Belle suffered no privations. At every meal she enjoyed a variety of choice dishes, supplied by the Washington secessionists and served to her in her room by a contraband whom Wood had assigned to her as a servant. The first time that Major Doster called on Belle, he found her reading *Harper's* and eating peaches. "She remarked she could afford to remain here, if Stanton could afford to keep her. There was so much company and so little to do. Besides, it was an excellent chance to brush up her literature and get her wedding outfit ready."

At this time, Belle was affianced to a Confederate officer; according to one account, he was a handsome fellow prisoner, Lieutenant McVay. But her engagement by no means discouraged the attention of other admirers. From both side walls of her room and from the ceiling came the sound of knives scooping holes in the plaster. She was showered with notes and tokens, while the billets-doux of Lieutenant McVay rolled across the threshold, wrapped around a marble. When Belle sat in the hall, as in the evening she was sometimes permitted to do, the Confederate officers crowded at their doorways. On the stairs, the third-floor inmates—prisoners of state and Fredericksburg hostages, who were left unguarded—craned and scuffled for a glimpse of her face.

Belle was fond of singing, and often treated the company to an evening concert. Her favorite selection, which she rendered with much pathos, was "Maryland, My Maryland." In the last stanza, pathos gave way to exultation, as Belle pealed out, "Huzza! she spurns the northern scum!" A chorus of male voices made a deep and hearty accompaniment. The guard would stop pacing the corridor to bid Belle to hush up. "I shan't do it," Belle would answer, warbling the offensive line again; and, in illustration of the point, she would seize a broom, and sweep off the part of the floor on which the guard had stepped.

This nineteen-year-old girl had not gone gallivanting about the camps in the Valley without starting malicious gossip. Controversies raged about her chastity. It was reported that at the Old Capitol she talked with abandon, and wore a dress that exposed her neck and arms. She was fond of shouting insults from her window at passing soldiers, and did not shrink when they replied with "coarse jests and the vilest slang of the brothel," or bawled, "Hush up, you damn bitch, or I'll shoot you." Among the prisoners, however, she awakened not only devotion, but profound respect. When on Sunday mornings she descended to the yard to hear the Lord God preached according to Jeff Davis, the Southern chivalry put on their courtliest manners. Mr. Dennis Mahony, the white-bearded editor from Dubuque, Iowa—confined in the Old Capitol because of the anti-administration tone of his newspaper—was impressed by Belle's entrance. In the bosom of her dress, she wore a small Confederate flag. As she swept to her place, "with a grace and dignity which might be envied by a queen," she extended a gracious hand to the rebel captives, who stood with doffed hats in the blaze of her glowing glances, while the Northern prisoners of state stared enviously.

Belle reigned at the Old Capitol for a month, before she, too, was sent to Dixie. She screamed with joy when Wood brought her the news. Concealing on her person two gold saber knots, for Jackson and Joe Johnston, she bade tender farewells to her admirers. ". . . There was not a gentleman in the Old Capitol," wrote old Mr. Mahony, "whose emotions did not overcome him as he saw her leave. . . ." A fund was raised to buy her a gift; and presently in a Richmond boardinghouse a Confederate officer handed Belle a gold and enamel watch and chatelaine, richly set with diamonds, as a token of the affection and esteem of her fellow-prisoners.

Washington had not seen the last of Belle, who would return to Carroll Prison the following year. Meantime, a pretty girl from Fauquier County, Virginia, was the only female prisoner who attracted attention at the Old Capitol. The incarceration of Miss Louisa P. Buckner was brief and uneventful. It was notable because she was the niece of the Postmaster General.

With her mother and a minister, known as Buck Bailey, Miss Buckner drove up from Virginia on a shopping trip. Montgomery Blair loaned his relatives five hundred dollars to purchase groceries and other necessaries in Washington. The little party was well vouched for, with a packet of passes and recommendations, including a note from the President; but Stanton's chief detective, La Fayette C. Baker, was no respecter of persons and he ordered a careful watch kept on Blair's sister-in-law and niece. The information that they had visited three drugstores and purchased six hundred ounces of quinine was followed by a report from a Negro servant that Miss Buckner was making herself a skirt, formed of long pockets lined with oiled silk.

Baker waited until the party had started on the return journey.

Then he called on Montgomery Blair, who listened impatiently to his accusations, and declared his relatives to be as loyal as the detective himself. They were overhauled near Chantilly, and Baker went out to Fairfax Court-House to make a personal examination of Miss Buckner's skirt. It was packed with quinine, and a quantity of contraband drugs was also found in a false body of the wagon. Major Doster's name was signed on the military governor's pass, and at one o'clock he was called from bed to answer to Stanton for passing quinine through the army lines. With a dishonorable dismissal hanging over his head, the young provost marshal spent the rest of the night searching the pigeonholes in his office. At last, the memorandum of Blair's recommendation turned up, and Doster was cleared. On Stanton's order, the quinine, the horse and wagon and the groceries were confiscated by the Government.

Miss Buckner was quietly released, after a short stay in prison, leaving Buck Bailey to pay a longer penalty. But the legend of the Quinine Lady was not quickly forgotten in Washington. The iron hand of Mr. Stanton was turned against all enemies of the Union. It closed even on a pretty girl who had an uncle in the Cabinet.

IX Two Civilians and General Halleck

EVERY MORNING, in the reception room of the War Department, Mr. Stanton gave an hour to the public. With a quick step, he came through the door and took his stand behind a high writing desk which reached to his shoulders. There, like an irritable schoolmaster, he darted his eyes, large and piercing behind steel-rimmed spectacles, over the waiting petitioners. He had an hour to give—no more. He estimated the number of the crowd, and allotted the time he would be able to spend on each case. "He would lean his left arm on the desk, settle his spectacles, and wait for people to come and state their business—a peppery little man who looked as though he had not slept well, and as if it would not give him much pain to refuse your most urgent request."

The room was silent. People conversed only in hurried whispers. Clerks and orderlies moved on tiptoe. By the door stood a redheaded cavalryman of the provost guard, who well knew that most of the applicants were wasting their time. Politicians, contractors, job seekers and army officers were obliged to present their requests in brief, direct terms, audible to the entire room. The procedure was a novelty in Washington. There was no opportunity for suavity, persuasion, influence. Mr. Stanton was acquainted with no one whose claims of friendship or of favor he felt bound to recognize at the Government's expense. To each, in his low, soft voice, he brusquely gave his decision, and the line moved on.

All sorts of people stood waiting for their moment with the Secretary of War. The greedy and the ambitious mingled with sick and wounded soldiers, cashiered officers, friends of persons accused of disloyalty, chaplains, prostitutes, weeping wives and faltering old fathers. They were not invariably received in the order of their coming. Now and then, sometimes from caprice, Mr. Stanton would call an individual from his place. But, rich or poor, old or young, no one was permitted to delay the march of the procession. Across the stammered entreaties, Stanton's arbitrary answer dropped like a sledge hammer. At the end of the hour, the reception room was empty.

The Secretary of War had become the most hated man in Washington. Aggressive and pugnacious, he gloried in the enmity he aroused. To the eyes of his petitioners each morning, he must have seemed the incarnation of grim and implacable authority. His figure, with its round body and short legs, looked like that of a powerful gnome. He had a dark, mottled complexion; and a tendency to asthma intensified the irascibility of his face. His naked upper lip lay exposed in a thick, rubbery Cupid's bow above the profuse chin whiskers, which seemed to have been tied, like a false beard, to his large ears. To the chaos of the War Department—unpaid bills, swindling contracts, idle army officers, leakage of official information, and deficient armaments, equipment and supplies—Stanton brought a driving energy. For days on end, he scarcely left his desk, getting to work on important papers at midnight, falling asleep over them at dawn. In the morning hours, his wife would come to take him home, but often he would not go. Twice a week, a War Department messenger shaved his upper lip in his office. He rarely answered personal letters. He never took a vacation, cared little for social life, did not enjoy the theatre. The only outing he permitted himself was a visit to the Center Market, to purchase the provisions for his own table. The cash, on each occasion, was handed him by his confidential secretary and former law clerk, Major A. E. H. Johnson, who drew Stanton's salary. The War Secretary carried no money on his person, and had no watch. Neither time nor money existed for a man whose life had been turned into a crusade against the twin abominations of treason and corruption.

In his tremendous efficiency, Stanton had steeled himself not only against peculation and malingering, but against appeals to human pity. Arrogance and despotic oppression were the food on which he subsisted. Yet such food, however sustaining, leaves its own bitter aftertaste. Stanton was not actually so impervious as he appeared. When he returned to his office, after his public reception, he often washed his face and perfumed his whiskers with cologne, in a fastidious disgust with the emanations of the crowd. Once, when the hour was over, he had a nosebleed so severe that a doctor was called to stop it with cracked ice. There was a troubled melancholy in his sharp eyes. They "always conveyed to me," wrote Congressman Riddle of Ohio, "some mysterious message that I could never quite understand." A friend, returning unexpectedly after a private interview with the War Secretary in his office, found him with his head on the desk, sobbing.

Stanton was a man of violent emotions. They had not always found a stern expression. As a young lawyer in Steubenville, Ohio, he had been desperately in love with his wife, Mary. Their first baby died, and after a year Stanton had the little remains exhumed, and placed the ashes in a metal box, which he kept in his own room. Later, when Mary, too, died, he became hysterical with grief. He insisted that in her coffin she should resemble his bride of seven years before, and the seamstress was obliged to alter the grave clothes several times. In transports of sorrow, he flung into the coffin Mary's wedding rings and other trinkets he had given her. These were removed, but the little box which contained the baby's ashes was buried with the mother. Crying and moaning, Stanton walked the floor by day, and at night lay sobbing in bed, with Mary's nightcap and gown on his pillow.

In time, Stanton took another wife, Ellen, a handsome woman, with shining hair dressed wide over the ears, and brows that lifted like wings above dark, brooding, heavy-lidded eyes; "a pretty wife," wrote John Hay, "as white and cold and motionless as marble, whose rare smiles seemed to pain her." The second Mrs. Stanton wore a fine lace collar on her silk dress, which was fastened down the front with braided and tasseled bowknots; and her breast pin and earrings had delicate sprays of mosaic flowers. But, when little James died in the summer of 1862, there is no story that the father cherished a box of ashes in his room. By then, Stanton was burning with that passion which has great power as its object; and an abhorrence of all traitors, the excitement of harsh authority, and a fanatical hatred of General McClellan had replaced in his bosom the tender excesses of sentiment.

Soon after assuming office, Stanton took over the military telegraph, which had been centered at the headquarters of the Army of the Potomac. While McClellan was briefly absent from Washington, the outfit and the records were unceremoniously removed to the War Department, and the operators were installed in the library on the second floor. McClellan's aide in charge of the telegraph, Captain Thomas T. Eckert, was retained at the head of the office, and became one of Stanton's most trusted assistants.

Government censorship of the telegraph, recently controlled by the State Department, was also shifted to the War Department. The surveillance of dispatches, instituted a few days after the outbreak of war, had been irritating, but ineffective. The wires to the North, in a hum of rumors, alarms and inaccuracies, had carried information advantageous to the enemy. The House Judiciary Committee, directed to make an investigation of the telegraph censorship, reported that "the censor has manifested want of both care and judgment in the exercise of his duties." While important news slipped through, there was often complete suppression of dispatches made up of paragraphs clipped from Washington newspapers, already in circulation. To the indignation of the correspondents, their stories were often slashed into a jumble of nonsense. In a small room, high up a flight of badly lighted stairs at the National Hotel, the censor sat importantly surrounded by soft lead pencils, heavy pens, black ink, scissors and mucilage pots. Frequently the correspondents were obliged to hunt up this potentate at whisky shops or at the Canterbury music hall in order to get his signature of approval on telegrams for the afternoon newspapers.

Stanton appointed the president of the American Telegraph Company, Colonel E. S. Sanford, military supervisor of telegrams, and provided penalties of arrest and imprisonment for careless administration of the censorship. Washington newspapers received sharp notice of the War Secretary's severity, when he ordered the arrest of the editor of the *Sunday Morning Chronicle*—a first-class Washington weekly newspaper, soon to develop into one of the important dailies of the country—for printing information of army operations. On the editor's expressing regret and explaining that the paper had gone to press at a late hour without his supervision, the order of arrest was suspended. The publisher of the *Chronicle* was a prominent Democratic supporter of the administration, Colonel John W. Forney, proprietor of the Philadelphia *Press*, formerly clerk of the House, and recently elected secretary of the Senate.

Under the new dispensation, the censorship was more drastic, but no more intelligent than under the State Department. Stanton's suppression, distortion and delay of war news was the despair of the correspondents. The latest military reports were feverishly awaited in all parts of the Union. The war had enormously developed the sale and distribution of newspapers, to the reading of which, as all foreign observers had noted, Americans had always been inordinately addicted. The *New York Herald* alone had sixty-three war correspondents. Newspapers also had a large circulation in the camps, for the Union produced armies of readers. The Washington city post-office was nearly swamped, during the encampment of the Army of the Potomac in its vicinity, by the tons of newspapers and letters which the troops received. Newsboys visited even the battlefield, and, after one engagement on the Virginia Peninsula, the Prince de Joinville was startled to observe wounded soldiers raising themselves up to buy the latest New York papers.

Military information was issued at Stanton's pleasure to Government officials and major-generals, as well as to the public. Only the President had access to the dispatches. There was no telegraph at the Executive Mansion, and Lincoln formed the habit of going to the War Department for the news. Day and night, he crossed the wooded lawn, passed through the turnstile, and followed the path to the side door of the small brick building on Seventeenth Street. All dispatches, including the President's own, were copied in carbon on yellow tissue paper. One set was handed direct to Stanton. Major Johnson filed these tissues by date, fastening them with the spring clips then used for clothespins, and kept them in open boxes. Another set of the latest telegrams was laid in the drawer of the cipher desk in a room directly adjoining Stanton's, where the messages were decoded. Here Lincoln examined the telegrams, sometimes lingering with the young cipher operators, telling stories, or looking over their shoulders while they worked. There were other nights when he lay silent on the couch in Stanton's office. Out of shared responsibilities and anguish of spirit, an intimacy developed from an acquaintance that had inauspiciously begun between the two lawyers. The President admired Stanton, and depended on him. The War Secretary, in his own perfidious and intractable way, yielded loyalty and respect to Lincoln.

After the Army of the Potomac made its promenade to Manassas, the President issued a war order which won the approval of Stanton and his new allies, the Republican radicals. Lincoln's patience had been exhausted by McClellan's failure to anticipate the withdrawal of the Confederates, and the ease with which the Federals were able to march forward on an expedition without profit. He removed McClellan from the chief command of the armies. No successor was named. The commanders of the military departments were ordered to report to Stanton, who at once seized the papers in the War Office rooms which had been McClellan's headquarters in his capacity of general-in-chief.

The war order was printed in the *National Intelligencer* on the morning after it was issued. At Fairfax, McClellan learned the news, not through official channels, but from one of his aides, who read the published item and telegraphed him. Although he was indignant at "the rascals" for "persecuting" him behind his back, he wrote the President a letter which was a model of patriotic self-abnegation. His attitude was such as a high-minded man might assume in a personal feud. To remove himself and his army from "that sink of iniquity," Washington, to carry his campaign to the inaccurately mapped reaches of the peninsula between the York and the James Rivers, was the enterprise on which he was stubbornly set; and he gave no sensible consideration to the fact that his elaborate strategy had been made subject to a supervision which was not only inexperienced, but hostile.

The Joint Committee on the Conduct of the War had resolved on a visit to Manassas. The Virginia countryside was disfigured by shattered trees, blackened ruins and rudely marked graves. The litter of the retreating Confederates strewed the roads. Fences had been demolished; and the wheat fields were trampled plains of earth, covered with rebel soldiers' huts. Yet the excursion was not without its pleasurable aspect. It proved to be far more agreeable than the outing which two of the committee members, Ben Wade and Zach Chandler, had made the preceding summer. As the carriages rolled along in the pale March sunlight, the white tents of McClellan's army gleamed through the pine trees. Troops of cavalry were in motion. To the sound of martial music, soldiers were drilling in the open spaces, while others were amusing themselves by running races or playing ball. Congressman Julian of Indiana said that it was "delightfully exhilarating," especially to men who had been confined all winter at the long hearings in the basement of the Capitol. Centreville and Manassas must have been more exhilarating still, for they afforded the committee members that high moral pleasure which is to be found in the justification of a strong animosity. An inspection of the Quaker guns confirmed their suspicions of General McClellan's good faith. "They were certain, at all events," as Julian euphemistically phrased it, "that his heart was not in the work."

The gentlemen of the Joint Committee were not the only ones who were curious to visit the battlefield, now that it was restored to Federal occupation. Washington livery-stable keepers and hackmen were reaping a harvest from the trippers. A Saturday excursion train was inaugurated, while two stages made the run on three days of the week, in charge of drivers who had been taken prisoner by the rebels and were therefore qualified to act as guides. The collection of souvenirs was a craze. A commercial motive animated some of the tourists, for war curiosities found a ready market. At Fairfax, where the courthouse stood neglected, with open doors and ancient papers scattered over the floor, the excursionists carried off documents, some of which dated from the reign of George III. On the field of battle, trophies were hard to find, for everything had been picked over by the Union soldiers. Near Bull Run, the Confederates had erected a marble tablet to the memory of General Bartow, who had fallen in the battle; and Northern vandals busied themselves in chipping off pieces of the slab as mementoes. Cartridge boxes and haversacks, Bibles, horseshoes, rifle bullets and scraps of iron were eagerly salvaged. Now and then, industrious searchers were rewarded by a scabbard, a crooked saber or a bent gun barrel; and, stowing the treasure under the carriage seat, they drove back to Washington in triumph. Often their elation was short-lived. Government property was liable to seizure, and daily at the depot the provost guard removed from citizens between ten and a hundred pieces of swords, muskets and side arms. At the end of April, visits to Manassas were brought to a close by a report that three civilians on horseback had been captured by rebel cavalry. Guerrilla parties were said to be still hovering around that vicinity, and tourist travel was prohibited.

The old brick town of Alexandria was another mecca for sightseers. At the Marshall House, where young Ellsworth had been killed, souvenir hunters tore the paper from the walls at the foot of the stairway; and, attacking with their pocketknives the woodwork around the spot where the colonel had fallen, they demolished the stairs, the balustrade and the adjacent doors and door frames. In March, a new life and movement came to Alexandria, for in the Potomac a great fleet was gathering. The warehouses were closed; it was an activity alien to the secessionist town that crowded the shabby wharves. Schooners and brigs, many with stalls fitted for horses on their decks, lay along the shores, or moved from pier to pier in the wake of puffing little tugs. The big river steamboats made a colony of floating houses, white-painted and galleried with decks.

Under the sullen eyes of the Alexandria inhabitants, the divisions of the Army of the Potomac marched in to make their camps on the bleak hills near the little port. The words of their general's address rang in their ears, and it would have been hard to convince them that this was the speech of a traitor.

> The moment for action has arrived, and I know that I can trust in you to save our country . . . I am to watch over you as a parent over his children, and you know that your General loves you from the depth of his heart. . . . I shall demand of you great, heroic exertions. . . . We will share all these together; and when this sad war is over we will return to our homes, and feel that we can ask no higher honor than the proud consciousness that we belonged to the Army of the Potomac.

Night and day, at Alexandria and at the Washington wharves, the vast quantities of stores, the horses, mules and wagons, the heavy guns, the bales of hay, the pontoon bridges and the telegraphic materials were loaded on the ships. The banks of the river were lined with spectators, staring at the embarkation of an army. Regiment after regiment, the soldiers marched on board the transports; and, as the huge paddle wheels revolved and the steamers turned toward the south, the faces on the river bank were troubled. The great army had been like a burdensome shield before the breast of Washington. When it had sallied to Manassas, it had still been interposed between the city and the enemy. Now it was disappearing down the Potomac, and, for all its new earthworks, the capital felt bereft of protection.

The advance on Richmond by the water route had taken on new disadvantages since the appearance of the *Merrimac*. The James River was closed to Federal ships. It had by no means been established that the *Monitor* could handle the big Confederate ironclad, whose re-emergence from Norfolk was awaited with keen apprehension. Fort Monroe had become a precarious base for McClellan's operations on the Virginia Peninsula—it was, however, the base on which the administration insisted—and the Navy Department sent down a fleet of vessels to protect the Union transports, and prevent the *Merrimac* from entering the waters of the York River.

The President and Mr. Stanton were now committed to the

business of running the war. Civilians, without the slightest experience in military matters, they felt the need of professional advice; and they turned to a retired Army officer in poor health—Ethan Allen Hitchcock, a grandson of the Revolutionary hero whose name he bore. This clean-shaven old soldier, with bluff and forthright manners, had a record of forty years of honorable service, but he was not primarily interested in military matters. He had gone to West Point because friends of the family thought the career of a soldier an appropriate one for Ethan Allen's grandson. He was a student of philosophy, a devout pantheist, who delighted in metaphysical researches and wrote fat volumes on alchemy and other recondite subjects. He was obsessed by a belief that many writers clothed their true meaning in symbolism; and in Dante, Shakespeare and the Gospels he had, after much toil, discovered an esoteric philosophy not discernible to the ordinary reader.

Mr. Stanton's first interview with Hitchcock took place at the veteran's bedside. On reaching Washington, he had been prostrated by a severe hemorrhage from the nose, a disability to which he was subject. The War Secretary suggested his serving in an advisory capacity—giving the benefit of his experience. This duty did not sound arduous, and Hitchcock at length decided to accept a commission of major-general of volunteers. A few days later, Stanton abruptly asked him if he would take command of the Army of the Potomac. The invalid student of the occult was amazed, and at once refused. "Now—what is to come of this?" he wrote, in some perturbation, in his diary. "I want no command. I want no department. . . . On the whole, I am uncomfortable. I am almost afraid that Secretary Stanton hardly knows what he wants, himself."

There was one thing that Stanton wanted, and knew very well that he wanted. Behind closed doors, he apprehensively breathed into Hitchcock's ear "the most astounding facts" about General McClellan's incompetency. When the recital was ended, Hitchcock "felt positively *sick*." He shared to the full the fears of disaster. "I do not wonder, now," he wrote, "that the Secretary offered even me the command of this Army of the Potomac." The details of the sickening revelations he did not commit to paper; but Stanton, with dark references to the influence of Jeff Davis, was making no secret of his fears that McClellan would not be willing to do anything "calculated greatly to damage the cause of secession."

The extent of political interference in army affairs was drastically conveyed to McClellan by the depletion of his command. As he was on the point of sailing, he learned that Blenker's German division had been transferred to General Frémont. That staunch, if somewhat tarnished Republican had been given another chance to win honors in the war. A new command had been created for him, the Mountain Department in western Virginia. Since this loyal section had been abandoned by the Confederates, it was arranged that Frémont was to undertake a campaign across the mountains into eastern Tennessee. He had many supporters in the Republican party, and the President wrote of "pressure," when he notified McClellan of the loss of ten thousand men.

McClellan was already in the field when he received the news that he was to be deprived of a full army corps, on which he was counting for a flank movement on Yorktown. To the capital's politicians, the protection of Washington was of paramount importance, overshadowing all questions of military strategy; and recent events in the Valley had served to quicken their anxiety. McClellan had intended to interpose Banks's corps between Washington and the enemy. The main body of this force was to be stationed at Manassas, with infantry guards and cavalry detachments posted in the surrounding country. The railway was to be repaired from Alexandria to Manassas, and thence to the Shenandoah Valley, thus giving the Federals the advantageous communications which had proved so useful to the Confederates at Bull Run. It was a good plan, but, before McClellan sailed, it was upset by General Thomas J. Jackson, already known by the sobriquet of Stonewall, whose rebel command had been left in the Valley. Jackson made a daring attack on the Federal troops at Kernstown, near Winchester. It was repulsed, but the noise of battle beyond the Blue Ridge frightened Washington. McClellan, forced to detain Banks in the Valley, made no further effort to reinforce Manassas, guarded only by insignificant detachments.

The President had repeatedly stipulated that a sufficient force should be left behind to ensure the safety of Washington. The number and character of the troops thus vaguely defined had not been settled by a definite agreement; but McClellan's corps commanders, meeting in council soon after their appointment, had required full garrisons in the forts on the Virginia side (some twelve thousand men), the occupation of the forts on the District side (about three thousand men), and a covering force of twenty-five thousand. The total was not greatly in excess of the estimate of thirty-five thousand men made by McClellan himself in the preceding autumn. However, in his overmastering desire to perfect an army for the field, McClellan neglected the claims of Washington. In its growing apprehensions he had no interest at all. They were the apprehensions of unmilitary persons, and, as an expert, he was sure that his campaign against Richmond constituted the best defense of the capital. Mr. Lincoln's secretaries observed that McClellan never feared an attack on Washington, unless he happened to be there himself. He had ringed it with fortifications, but he had never provided enough artillerymen to handle the ordnance; and, in preparing to advance, he had withdrawn regiment after regiment from the disciplined troops stationed there.

Nevertheless, McClellan believed that the command of Washington was of primary importance. Mansfield had gone to serve in the Department of Virginia, centered at Fort Monroe. A military District of Washington had been created, under command of a military governor, and McClellan had suggested his great friend, General Franklin, for the place. Franklin was a capable officer, who enjoyed McClellan's confidence, and would have worked in full co-operation with him. Political considerations, however, determined the selection of the rich and influential Republican, James S. Wadsworth, to whom McClellan made the single, but insuperable objection that he was not a trained soldier. From the outbreak of war, Wadsworth had been notable for his patriotism. At fifty-three, he was still lean and active. Snowy hair and side whiskers framed his narrow, handsome face, and he wore the carved saber of antique pattern which his grandfather had carried in the Revolutionary War. To his new career of soldier, he had brought the qualities of energy, honor and courage. A landed proprietor of political interests, he resembled in many ways the Southern planters who had dominated Washington before 1861. There was one conspicuous difference. Wadsworth was an ardent abolitionist, unsympathetic to the slaveholding population of the capital. From the moment of taking command, he showed an intense distrust of McClellan—who expressed the opinion that Stanton had inspired this antagonism. On the other hand, Major Doster gathered from Wadsworth and his staff that there had been ill feeling for some months between the New Yorker and McClellan, because Wadsworth, officially and in conversation, had expressed himself in favor of an advance in Virginia.

Wadsworth's new duties included the command of all troops stationed in and about the capital, and he had promptly ridden out to make an inspection. Ten days before McClellan sailed, the military governor reported to Mr. Stanton that the force was "amply sufficient." But a belated letter from McClellan—who did not make a statement of the troops he intended to leave behind, until he was on board the steamer, ready to depart—changed Wadsworth's opinion, and drove him to indignant remonstrances that the capital had only a bare nineteen thousand soldiers, many of them entirely untrained. Stanton's worst suspicions were confirmed. General Hitchcock and Adjutant General Lorenzo Thomas agreed that the force was inadequate. Other War Department generals shook their white heads and concurred. Ben Wade's committee, starved since the Quaker guns of Manassas for a definite grievance, raised an outcry. McDowell's corps of thirty-five thousand men had not yet sailed, and an order, detaching it from the Army of the Potomac and retaining it for the defense of Washington, was issued by Stanton under the direction of the President.

A wiser and less arrogant man than McClellan might have anticipated this result. He had not done so. His plans were disarranged, and he indignantly protested that it would now be necessary to lay siege to Yorktown. The War Office saw only that McClellan still had an army of over one hundred thousand men. Smaller armies, with vastly inferior equipment, had been winning important victories, and this fact Stanton proceeded to emphasize in an order giving thanks for the successes of the Union arms. Thanks were due, specifically, to General Henry W. Halleck, commanding the Department of the Mississippi, in which the territory from the Allegheny to the Rocky Mountains had been unified, for the success of all the military operations in the West; to Generals Samuel R. Curtis and Franz Sigel and their forces for their gallantry at Pea Ridge, Arkansas, where they had won a decisive victory; to Generals Ulysses S. Grant and Don Carlos Buell and their forces for the repulse of the rebels at Pittsburg Landing; to General John Pope and his officers and soldiers for their bravery and skill in the operations which had captured Island Number 10 in the Mississippi. From this roster, General McClellan and his officers and soldiers, beginning to sicken in the swamps before Yorktown, were conspicuously absent.

There was a latent irony in the gratitude expressed for the repulse at Pittsburg Landing, better known to the Union as bloody Shiloh. The slaughter of two days of fighting had appalled a nation unprepared for long casualty lists. On the first day the Federals had been driven back; it was said that Grant had been taken by surprise, and that only the arrival of reinforcements under Buell had saved him from a disastrous defeat. Sherman emerged with brightened fame from the engagement; but Grant was no longer hailed as the hero of Fort Donelson. The news of Shiloh enraged the country, and Grant was denounced as incompetent in the press and in Congress. For a second time, the President jeopardized his popularity by retaining a general whose removal was vehemently demanded. There had been reports from Halleck that Grant was drinking, that he was negligent and disobedient. Sitting before the fire in his office, with his feet on the marble mantel, Lincoln listened to the Pennsylvania Republican, McClure, pleading with him that, in justice to himself, he must immediately relieve Grant from command. "I can't spare this man; he fights," Lincoln told McClure at last.

The President had issued a proclamation recommending that at their places of public worship the people should thank their Heavenly Father for the signal victories of the land and naval forces, and the Protestant Episcopal Bishop of Maryland backed this up by a letter to the clergy under his charge. In the Washington churches, the suggestion was not universally welcomed. Secesh were numerous among the capital's Episcopalians, and feeling was running high on the subject of giving thanks. A few weeks before, the Bishop had transmitted a special prayer to be used by his clergy, blessing and magnifying the name of the Lord "more especially for the deliverance of this city and district from the terrors of blockade and siege." The Reverend Doctor Pinckney of the Church of the Ascension, the Reverend Mr. Syle of Trinity, and the Reverend Mr. Morsell of Christ Church at the Navy Yard, to the high indignation of their unionist communicants, had all omitted the prayer. At the Ascension, things came to such a pass that the church was closed by order of the provost marshal, and the embattled congregation was obliged to disperse. The vestry of Trinity was split into two factions, one of which clamored for the severance of Mr. Syle's connection with the church. After the President's proclamation, Syle ventured to give thanks for the western victories, omitting, as unnecessarily exasperating, the reference to the blockade and siege of the District. The mention of Union successes, however, proved too much for a portion of his congregation, and several irate secessionists swept from the church, "head and tail up," as the prayer was being delivered. The Reverend Dr. Hall of Epiphany Church, who had complied with the bishop's instructions, told his congregation that he had urged his superior not to compose any more forms of prayer without a consultation. He concluded his remarks by "a hasty and dainty allusion to loyalty as the abstract duty of all of us."

"Glorious news come borne on every wind but the South Wind," wrote John Hay. ". . . The little Napoleon sits trembling before the handful of men at Yorktown afraid either to fight or run. Stanton feels devilish about it."

Word of the devilishness of Stanton's feelings was all abroad. Late in March, he had sent for the Joint Committee on the Conduct of the War, arraigning General McClellan's blunders to sympathetic ears and declaring that among his commanders there were traitors, eight of whom should have been dismissed on the discovery of the Quaker guns at Manassas. On a Sunday in mid-April, there was another conference, in which Mr. Stanton included Senators Wilson and Fessenden, and Congressmen Stevens and Blair. Frank Blair, Junior, had been made chairman of the House Military Committee. He was a tall, soldierly-looking man, with reddish hair and heavy mustache, who early in the war had taken a leading part in saving Missouri for the Union. He found himself in hostile company at Stanton's conference of radical leaders. Old Thad Stevens, a gaunt, spectral figure in a dark-brown wig, dragging his club foot, and embellishing his comments with profanity, remarked to Stanton that "not a man in the Cabinet, the present company excepted, was fit for his business." Fessenden heartily endorsed this statement, and all glanced slyly at Frank, to observe his reception of this hit at his brother, Montgomery. Thad Stevens went on to say that he was tired of hearing damned Republican cowards talk about the Constitution. He was in favor of stripping the rebels of all their rights, and giving them a reconstruction that would end treason forever. Stanton assured Stevens that this had been his policy from the beginning. Save for the outsider, Blair, the radicals had a love feast, denouncing slave catching in the army and McClellan's refusal to listen to information brought in by Negroes. McClellan was still king, remarked Ben

Wade, and the country was a long way yet from a vigorous war policy.

While Stanton's conferences with the radicals were held in secret, the trend of his opinions was well understood. Democratic newspapers, sympathetic to McClellan and his faction, had not failed to turn to political advantage the War Secretary's enmity. It was intimated that the movement at Yorktown was imperiled by interference from Washington. There were also rumors that Stanton would resign; and some newspapers suggested that General Hitchcock should be appointed in his place. Soon after, Stanton for the first time became "a little impatient" with Hitchcock. The Secretary's bullying of army officers was notorious. His low, musical voice could send white-haired generals flushed and trembling from his presence. But Hitchcock was the grandson of the hero of Ticonderoga, and he had not come to Washington to be insulted. When Stanton spoke rudely to him, he sat down and wrote out his resignation. It precipitated "a scene of it." As always, when people defied him, Stanton backed down. "If you send in that paper," he cried to Hitchcock, "you will destroy me." He reproached himself, lamented his faults of temper, and pleaded his overwhelming responsibilities. In the end, Hitchcock went up to Stanton's room, and put his resignation in the fire; but he was far from satisfied. Though he was publicly regarded as the military adviser of the War Department, both Stanton and Lincoln ignored his suggestions. As time went on, he was mortified at being associated with the strategy which emanated from the White House and the War Office. At length, he was permitted to take a long leave of absence, and returned for the summer to "the tranquility of hermetic speculation."

For Lincoln, the success of McClellan's campaign was a matter of increasingly desperate importance. The radicals were clamoring for more drastic war measures, for an immediate emancipation of the slaves. With his party split and his prestige endangered, Lincoln sorely needed the justification of a great victory for the Army of the Potomac. The country, too, showed wild impatience—the impatience which hope and confidence engender. Stanton—presumably from motives of economy—had ordered recruiting discontinued; and this fact, together with the victories in the West and the fame of McClellan's army, produced a feeling of optimism, and a belief that the war would be ended by midsummer. Late in April, the news of a great victory

resounded from the Gulf of Mexico. New Orleans, the chief commercial port of the South, had surrendered to an attacking squadron
commanded by Flag Officer David G. Farragut. He was a Southerner,
born in Tennessee. His wife was a Virginian, and at the outbreak of
war he had been on duty at Norfolk, surrounded by secessionist in-
fluences. Farragut had served under the Union flag as long as General
Scott, for he had gone to sea at the age of ten, and he was a veteran
of over sixty when he had his first opportunity to distinguish himself.
Commander David D. Porter accompanied the expedition with a fleet
of mortar boats. Though a Northern man, Porter had been friendly
with the secessionist politicians of Washington, and he was one of
the naval officers on whom Gideon Welles had looked with suspicion
in the spring of 1861. The capture of New Orleans brought both
Farragut and Porter into prominence, and the country rang once
more with the praise of wooden ships.

The single flaw in the triumphant advance of the Union cause
in the spring of 1862 was the delay of the Army of the Potomac
before Yorktown. The main body of the Confederate army had had
time to reach the Peninsula, and McClellan was confronted by a
considerable force. To his embittered mind, the enemies at his back
seemed scarcely less formidable. Three other Union generals were
operating in Virginia outside McClellan's control, responsible only to
the Secretary of War: Frémont, in the Mountain Department; Mc-
Dowell, whose corps had been transformed into a separate command,
the Department of the Rappahannock; and Banks, for whom the Department of the Shenandoah had been created. As he brooded over
his wrongs, McClellan was convinced that "the abolitionists and other
scoundrels" were sacrificing the Army of the Potomac out of personal
spite; and his dispatches cried without ceasing for more men and more
guns. Franklin's division was detached from McDowell's command,
and sent to the Peninsula. Before the reinforcements had disembarked,
before McClellan's bombardment had commenced, Yorktown fell into
the possession of the Federal forces. The process was already familiar.
To the surprise of McClellan, Joe Johnston had evacuated the city.

The country rejoiced to learn that the Army of the Potomac was
moving at last. After a bloody encounter at Williamsburg, it continued to advance. Federal gunboats and transports passed up the York
River, and shiploads of forage, provisions and ammunition moved to
McClellan's base at White House Landing on the Pamunkey. Slowly

and cautiously, the great army crawled forward through the mud. It was two weeks before it was encamped in the swamps of the Chickahominy River, eleven miles from Richmond. The health of the troops was reported to be good. Thoughtful persons might have paused over the news item that two rations of whisky and quinine were daily issued to the troops.

Steamers from Fort Monroe were arriving at the Sixth Street wharf. Some brought men released from Richmond prisons on parole —happy men who were bound for home. Cheering the Stars and Stripes and singing patriotic songs, they marched to the Soldiers' Retreat, the eating house erected at the depot. Other steamers carried quieter men from the army hospital at Yorktown. Most of the wounded had been taken to Northern cities. These were soldiers wasted by camp fever, by typhoid and consumption. Around their stretchers on the wharf hovered relatives and friends, as well as curious strangers and vendors of eggs and fruits, eager to profit from their necessity.

At Shillington's Book Store, Confederate bank notes taken at Bull Run were still on sale, and one of the Quaker guns from Centreville was exhibited under Hammack's Restaurant at the Avenue and Fifteenth Street. The capital did not lack new trophies, those tangible souvenirs which lend reality to great events and put them within the grasp of common men. In Mr. Hood's jewelry store on the Avenue was displayed a part of a steel vest which a Confederate captain had worn at Williamsburg. It was ironically described as bulletproof—the hole made by the fatal ball could be plainly seen. A sailor, John E. McKay, sold some broken scraps of wood and iron, and made such a good thing of it that he fell to treating his shipmates, and ended up in the guard-house. There was magic in the rubbish, for it was all that remained of the dreaded *Merrimac*. The rebels had abandoned Norfolk, and the ironclad, left without a harbor, had been blown up by her own men.

Released from the stalemate in Hampton Roads, Federal gunboats steamed up the James River. Only the Chickahominy and the Confederate forces lay between the Army of the Potomac and Richmond. On the Rappahannock, across from Fredericksburg, McDowell awaited his orders to march to McClellan's assistance. By any test of lines drawn on a military map, Richmond seemed doomed to fall. But in the Federal plans, there was a weak spot—the capital of the Union.

It was apprehensive, it was endowed with a profound symbolical importance, and for generalissimos it had only two civilians.

Stonewall Jackson's band of rebels in the Valley was the only enemy force in the vicinity of the capital; but it was one of Stanton's more subtle criticisms of McClellan that, though the Army of the Potomac threatened Richmond, he feared the Confederates might feel free to march in force on Washington. In April, he had made a little experiment. Over Wadsworth's protests, he had insisted on assuming an attack on the capital, and directing the troops within the city limits to assemble at the Chain Bridge and the Aqueduct. About three hours after the command was given, four thousand men had gathered, some with inadequate ammunition, some with no ammunition at all.

Jackson, the War Office learned, had received large reinforcements. His movements were all the more alarming because they were mysterious. There were contradictory stories of his whereabouts and intentions. Frémont, west of the Valley, reported that Jackson was threatening a part of his force—the Federals were actually attacked and driven back. McDowell heard that Jackson might be expected in his front. Stanton was convinced that, wherever Jackson might be, he was on his way to the capital. "Washington is the only object now worth a desperate throw," the War Secretary wrote Banks. Mulling over his reports, Mr. Stanton came to the conclusion that Jackson was withdrawing from the Valley to the south. He detached a division from Banks's command, and hurried it to the support of McDowell, who was ordered to join McClellan in reducing Richmond. With McDowell's advancing army interposed between Washington and the Confederates, the strategy of the War Department seemed to leave nothing to be desired; and it appeared—as Stanton must have suspected all along—that the business of generals was one that a pair of industrious lawyers could master in no time. That General Banks had been left a single division with which to defend the Valley was a source of anxiety only to General Banks.

In attempting to outguess Jackson, Mr. Stanton had drawn all the wrong conclusions. The rebel general was not moving south. With the handles of their frying pans stuck in their gun barrels, his ragged troops traveled as fast and light as foxes. Jackson was a black-bearded Presbyterian ascetic who packed his haversack with a supply of lemons and three books—the Bible, Webster's Dictionary and Napoleon's

Maxims of War. With all his fanatical soul, he hated Yankees, and he was a bold and brilliant soldier. Doubling back from the mountains west of the Valley with a speed undreamed of by the Federals, Jackson swept through Front Royal. On Saturday evening, May 24, the President and the War Secretary came back from a pleasant farewell visit to McDowell's army, to find the telegraph instruments snapping dots and dashes of alarm. Sunday morning brought news that Banks had been routed at Winchester. Though Jackson would not mail a letter so that it traveled on the Lord's Day, he did not let Sabbatarian scruples interfere with fighting. Often in the saddle he raised his face to his God (who also hated Yankees) to implore guidance in his campaign. Divine interposition could scarcely have scattered the Federal forces more perfectly to Jackson's advantage than had those amateurs of war, Mr. Stanton and Mr. Lincoln.

With the rebels pressing hard behind them, the soldiers of Banks's solitary division fled across the upper Potomac. There was no longer any mystery about Stonewall Jackson's whereabouts. He was within easy reach of the capital. Every man that could be spared from Washington and Baltimore was rushed to Harper's Ferry; and Stanton—as nervous, General Wadsworth said, as an old woman—telegraphed appeals for help to the Northern States. The newsboys' treble cry, "Washington in danger!" rang through the cities of the Union. The whole Confederate army was reported to be advancing on the Potomac. Amid general apprehension that senators and representatives were about to be seized as prisoners of war, militia and home guard regiments hurried down to the rescue.

They had come on a fruitless errand. Jackson did not attempt to cross the Potomac. The alarm fell flat, as the capital learned that the rebels were swiftly retreating up the Valley. The "big scare" was over, but Jackson had accomplished his object. McDowell's advance on Richmond had been promptly suspended. Military opinion was forced to yield to the Government's anxiety for the capital. McDowell protested as vehemently as McClellan, but one of his divisions was ordered to Washington, and another to the Valley. Without ever confronting McDowell's army—that army which might have turned the tide at Richmond—Jackson had effectively dispursed it. For some time, the hope persisted in the Union that his daring raid had led him into a trap, and that his army would be destroyed by the forces sent to intercept it. Slipping between the Federal armies at Strasburg,

Jackson executed a successful retreat, winning two more victories at Cross Keys and Port Republic before he joined the army before Richmond.

Meantime, from McClellan's forces straddling the Chicka-hominy, came the bloody news of Fair Oaks. It was hailed in Northern newspapers as a great Union victory, but the tale of the losses was long and sorry. In the lobby of Willard's, Zach Chandler was drunk—"a bad habit," wrote Attorney General Bates, "that has lately crept upon him"—and abused McClellan before the crowd, calling him a liar and a coward. Though the radicals raged, the country had not lost confidence. The Federals had made a hard and gallant fight. After the battle, the rebels were said to have retired "in a sort of Bull Run panic." Joe Johnston had been badly wounded. The Army of the Potomac was only five miles from Richmond. Nerved by the strong excitement of war, the people of the Union resolutely faced the casualties and delays, and looked forward to the fall of the Con-federate capital.

More troops were sent to McClellan—another fine division of McDowell's corps and ten picked regiments from Fort Monroe, as well as a number of new regiments. The June days lengthened, but there was silence on the Virginia Peninsula. Rumors circulated in Washington that Richmond had been captured, and Jeff Davis had committed suicide. The only reliable news was borne by the hospital ships, discharging their cargoes of fevered men from the Chicka-hominy swamps. Several excursion parties from the capital had visited White House Landing on the Pamunkey. McClellan had received Secretaries Seward, Welles and Bates, Commander Dahlgren, Mrs. Frederick Seward, the wife and daughter of Admiral Goldsborough and other ladies, who had taken a pleasant cruise on the steamboat, *City of Baltimore*, accompanied by the caterer Wormley and his assistants. The general had had ambulances harnessed up to drive them around the camps, and a hospital nurse wrote home about the visits of ladies "in silks and perfumes and lilac kid gloves." In late June, however, after greeting several groups of sight-seeing politicians, McClellan forbade a party of congressmen to visit his front lines, and they returned to spread an evil report of the general and all his works. Washington was excited by a rumor of heavy fighting on the Penin-sula, of a bad reverse for McClellan. The *Star* traced the story, not to the usual secessionist inspiration, but to an employee of the Capitol, who had it on the authority of members of Congress. This mischievous report had, in the *Star's* opinion, "been set afloat in a spirit of revenge by some of the junketing marplots who were so deservedly set to the right about by General McClellan, on their endeavor to penetrate to his front, on their late visit to the Peninsula."

Only a few days later, the noise of battle came at last from the neighborhood of Richmond. Through the roar of the cannonade sounded the obscure names of little, sleepy, fever-ridden places. Mechanicsville, Gaines's Mill, Savage's Station, White Oak Swamp stood blood-spattered in the headlines; and men tried to divine from the ambiguous and censored stories what new approach to Richmond had dictated this series of engagements. Three days of silence followed. When the news of Malvern Hill broke the suspense, and it was learned that the base of the Army of the Potomac had been changed from the Pamunkey to Harrison's Landing on the James, there could no longer be any doubt that McClellan's movement had been a retreat. In vain, the press protested that the battles of the Seven Days had been Union victories, and that a removal to the line of the James had been accomplished by the most masterly strategy. Marking the places on their big war maps, the people of the Union could plainly see that Harrison's Landing was nearly twenty-five miles from Richmond; and, at last, after the strong hope that had survived the delays and the terrible waste of men, despondency spread through the country like a sickness.

In the second summer of the war, the Union again faced disaster. Recruiting, discontinued by Mr. Stanton in April, had been resumed in June; but the failure on the Virginia Peninsula, startling the Government out of its satisfaction with an army of half a million men, made a new call for troops imperative. During the uncertainty of the Seven Days, the necessity was indirectly presented to the country. Mr. Seward secretly arranged with the governors of the Northern States to request the President to make the call, and in compliance with this inspired demand, Mr. Lincoln asked for three hundred thousand men. The country received the proclamation staunchly, if without enthusiasm. To attract recruits, cash bounties were offered, States and localities chipping in to increase the premiums.

In his personal campaign against McClellan, Stanton had long since succeeded in enlisting the full co-operation of Chase. In some measure, he had influenced all the Cabinet members against the general, who had, Welles remarked, "failings enough of his own to bear without the addition of Stanton's enmity to his own infirmities." To McClellan himself, however, the War Secretary made many professions of devotion, and after the Seven Days he wrote him letters that were fulsome with love and loyalty. No man, he wrote, ever had a truer friend than he had been to McClellan; the general was seldom absent from his thoughts, and he would make any sacrifice to aid him. When General Marcy came up from Harrison's Landing, Stanton invited him into his private office, put his hand on his knee and assured him, as a proof of his desire to serve McClellan, that he "would be willing to lay down naked in the gutter and allow him to stand upon my body for hours."

If he hoped to allay McClellan's resentment, Stanton was mistaken in his man. In the general's eyes, he was "the vilest man," "the most unmitigated scoundrel," and "the most depraved hypocrite and villain." McClellan wrote his wife: "I think that (I do not wish to be irreverent) had he lived in the time of the Savior, Judas Iscariot would have remained a respected member of the fraternity of the Apostles, and that the magnificent treachery and rascality of E. M. Stanton would have caused Judas to have raised his arms in holy horror. . . ."

While his superlatives were reserved for Stanton, McClellan raged with scarcely less fury against the rest of "those hounds in Washington." In his grandiose self-justification, and his ideas of persecution, he had become almost irrational, and the terrible Seven Days had driven him to the verge of an emotional breakdown. After Gaines's Mill, he had sent Stanton an agitated dispatch, charging his defeat to the Government because it had not sustained him. "If I save this army now," he wrote in conclusion, "I tell you plainly that I owe no thanks to you or to any other persons in Washington. You have done your best to sacrifice this army." McClellan knew that these were unforgivable words—he lashed out hysterically, too far gone to care for the consequences. It happened, however, that Stanton did not read the accusation. The dispatch fell under the horrified eye of Colonel E. S. Sanford, who took it upon himself to delete the sentences, thus turning the censorship on Stanton.

When the troubled President went down with Stanton to Harrison's Landing, there was little to reassure him in McClellan's state of mind. In his desperate situation, the general had found time to concern himself with politics. He had written a long letter advising Mr. Lincoln on his duties—especially, the avoidance of any pronouncement against slavery—and, with incomparable brass, he handed this to the President, who read it and remarked that he was obliged to him.

The Army of the Potomac had fought magnificently. In the fires of Fair Oaks and Gaines's Mill, McClellan had forged his weapon. Never inspirited by great success, as the Federal armies in the West had been, the Eastern soldiers had remained resolute in defeat; and, at the end of the searing week of their retreat, they had driven back the enemy from the slopes of Malvern Hill. They were not the sturdy, spandy boys who had sailed from Washington at the end of March. Before the toll of the Seven Days, the brigades had been decimated, not only by fighting, but by disease. On the other hand, McClellan had often been reinforced during his campaign, and was still receiving fresh troops. He had formed two new army corps, the Fifth and Sixth, and had won consent to appointing to their command his friends, Fitz-John Porter and Franklin. After all his losses, McClellan still had over eighty-six thousand men present for duty. He was crying for one hundred thousand more. His large force was penned in a hostile and unhealthy country, huddled beside the James in the shelter of the Union gunboats; and like another enemy the July sun blazed down on the crowded camp at Harrison's Landing.

While barrooms and hotel lobbies buzzed with rumors of Cabinet disputes over the army, major-generals congregated in the capital. There seemed something portentous in their presence. "They are not here on a mere visit of recreation," remarked the *Star*.

Washington had seen two Western generals, Franz Sigel and Lew Wallace. Sigel, the hero of Pea Ridge, had been received with acclaim. He was a German émigré, a neat, morose-looking man with a sparse mustache and beard. Among the large German population in the North, "I fights mit Sigel" had become a rallying cry, and his countrymen were thick in the crowd that serenaded him at Willard's. Indianians turned out to serenade Lew Wallace, lawyer, politician and Mexican War veteran of their State, who had commanded troops at Fort Donelson and Shiloh. In a vigorous speech, Wallace called for a draft, Negro soldiers, and confiscation of rebel property by the army.

General Dan Sickles arrived to tell the correspondents that the Excelsior Brigade of New Yorkers had been badly cut up in the

battles on the Peninsula. Marcy and Andrew Porter both declared
that the Seven Days had been a succession of Union victories. Handsome Joe Hooker told a different story. So did Phil Kearny, who came
to Washington wearing the "Kearny patch"—the scarlet badge of his
division—in his slanted kepi. At Wadsworth's headquarters, the correspondents of the great dailies heard Hooker and Kearny telling the tale
of the disasters on the Peninsula. A frequent visitor was the Polish
exile, Count Gurowski, who scribbled in his diary his detestation of
the moderate Republicans, Seward among them, although Gurowski
was employed as a translator in the State Department. Shabby and
spiteful, the count would sidle in, his one eye leering behind green
goggles. He admired Hooker and Kearny, Heintzelman and Edwin
Sumner—thought that they and other officers would have fought and
won, had it not been for the incompetence of "McNapoleon." Washington, like the rest of the Union, was divided into two disputing
factions—one upholding Stanton and the other, McClellan. Wadsworth's office in the old Gwin mansion was a little center for Stanton
sympathizers. In June, however, the War Secretary had deprived
Wadsworth of the greater part of his command. The troops in the
fortifications had been placed under a West Pointer, General S. D.
Sturgis, who had been called from the West. Wadsworth retained
the post of military governor, but his command was reduced to a
brigade comprising the provost guard and numbering about three
thousand men.

Major-General Burnside's strapping figure and beautiful whiskers
appeared again on Pennsylvania Avenue. After the Seven Days, he
had been ordered to bring a large part of his troops to reinforce Mc-
Clellan. Burnside had gained great popularity from the success of his
expedition, which had given the Union control of the interior coasts
of North Carolina; and his repeated visits to the War Office were
the subject of keen speculation. He was, in fact, offered the command
of the Army of the Potomac, and flatly refused it. He was a man of
simple virtues, honest, modest and loyal. The intrigues of Washington
distressed him. McClellan was his old and good friend. ". . . I do
know, my dear Mac, that you have lots of enemies," he ruefully
wrote in a letter to Harrison's Landing.

Outstanding among the generals in Washington was a youngish
Westerner, with a vain, slender face, an upturned nose and a stiff
rectangle of beard. This was Major-General John Pope, renowned

for his victories on the Mississippi. Late in June he had been summoned to take command of the newly created Army of Virginia, formed by a consolidation of the armies of Frémont, Banks and McDowell, and also including the force under Sturgis at Washington. Frémont refused to serve under Pope, who was his junior. He had won no honors in western Virginia or in the Valley, and few regrets attended the termination of his military career. Franz Sigel was appointed to the command of Frémont's corps in the Army of Virginia, and was enthusiastically received by the German-American troops. McClellan's former show regiments were in a pitiable state—depleted in numbers, exhausted by long marches, ragged and ill-equipped, demoralized by plundering the Virginia country. Most of them were included in two small brigades, which were commanded by Carl Schurz, who had hurried home from Spain to receive a brigadier's commission.

Pope had immediately proceeded to concentrate the greater part of his forces between the Blue Ridge and Manassas, where they were in position to meet an advance from Richmond, as well as in close proximity to the Valley. There were other disorganized brigades besides the Germans, and the cavalry and artillery horses were badly broken down. By mid-July, however, the Army of Virginia was in fair condition to move, and Pope issued orders pushing his lines farther to the south. In Washington, it was anticipated that their gradual advance would detach a considerable rebel force from the neighborhood of Richmond, weakening the army opposed to McClellan.

While his army advanced, General Pope tarried in Washington, at the President's request. He was often in attendance at the White House. Besides the weight of his recent successes, he had a background of friendliness with Lincoln, who had been well acquainted with his father in Illinois, and had enjoyed the younger man's company on the journey from Springfield to Washington. John Pope told stories, and Lincoln liked stories. Reticence and modesty formed no part of the character of the hero of Island Number 10. To his brother officers in the regular Army, he was known as a "bag of wind." Montgomery Blair was later to remark to Lincoln that Pope was "a blower and a liar," and should never have been entrusted with the command of the Army of Virginia. His father, Judge Pope, as Gideon Welles heard Blair laboring the point, "was a flatterer, a deceiver, a liar, and a trickster; all the Popes are so." The President "admitted

Pope's infirmity, but said a liar might be brave and have skill as an officer." Lincoln also credited Pope with "great cunning"—a quality which the events connected with Jackson's raid must have taught the President to value in military management.

The loquacious Westerner gave satisfaction to the Republican radicals. Slavery must perish, he told Mr. Chase at dinner, and he added that there should be a change in the command of the Army of the Potomac. He freely disparaged McClellan's operations on the Peninsula, and spoke in favor of a vigorous prosecution of the war. From the capital, he issued orders which bore harshly on the noncombatant population of Virginia. Pope was applauded in Washington, but he had scarcely become acquainted with his command. The Army of Virginia needed to be united, inspired, infused with fresh enthusiasm. The only common bond of its three corps was the exhaustion of fruitless campaigning. The troops felt that they had been hardly used and neglected in the Valley, and their failure had made them sensitive to criticism. They were quick to resent comparison with the Western soldiers, whom everyone was praising, and only by the exercise of the most delicate tact could a Western general have won their confidence. Pope, still in Washington, issued an address to his command, eulogizing the soldiers of the West, "where we have always seen the backs of our enemies." Success and glory, he fatuously declared, were in the advance, while disaster and shame lurked in the rear. With the egoist's want of imagination about other people's feelings, Pope expected that his address would create "a cheerful spirit" in his men. Its effect was to make him an object of dislike and ridicule, not only to the Army of Virginia, but to all the soldiers of the East. The Army of the Potomac despised him for a sneering outsider, and gibed at the boast, attributed to Pope, that his headquarters were in the saddle.

Late in June, the President had surprised the country by making a flying trip to West Point, where General Scott was living in retirement. The object of this visit was kept secret, Lincoln, with a humorous reference to Stanton's "tight rein," merely stating that it had nothing to do with "making or unmaking any general in the country." The curiosity of the country was scarcely satisfied. Whatever had passed between the President and General Scott, it became clear in July that Mr. Lincoln was dissatisfied with the civilian direction of the war. In Virginia, the problem was desperate. The Union had two armies, McClellan's and Pope's, but they could not form a junction, for the entire force of the enemy lay between them. A solution had to be found; brains were needed, expert military judgment. Out of the West, where, far from the capital, heroes were made, the President called still another general—Henry W. Halleck, commander of the Department of the Mississippi. Grant was appointed to replace him in the West, and Halleck was named general-in-chief of the armies of the Union.

Halleck came to Washington in an aura of great prestige. He had been highly respected in the regular Army as a master of military science. Scott had favored him for the chief command, before McClellan's appointment. In civil life, Halleck had proved his ability as a successful lawyer and businessman in San Francisco. His command in the West was a starry record of success.

There was nothing about Halleck's appearance which suggested a hero. His figure and dress lacked military dash. It was the fashion for American generals to leave one or two of their coat buttons carelessly unfastened on the chest—out of six buttonholes above the waistline, four of Frémont's were empty, when he sat for his photograph. Halleck was buttoned up tight, from his double chin to his fat paunch, but he appeared slouchy, rather than neat. He had a stooping posture, and walked with his hands held behind his back, or thrust into the pockets of his trousers. No initiative lurked behind his surly face, with big, bulging, "busy" eyes. Halleck's bald brow was haloed by the victories his subordinate generals had won. "Old Brains," his soldiers had sarcastically called him on the one occasion when he took active command—a snail-like advance on Corinth, Mississippi. Halleck had no capacity for leadership. He was a scholar and bureaucrat, who marshaled files of papers and commanded ranks of facts.

On August 6, a great war meeting was held at the east front of the Capitol. At five o'clock, the park held an expectant throng, facing the portico filled with ladies and the flag-draped platform occupied by the President, the Cabinet, the Washington city councils and other dignitaries. Above their heads, an arch of gas jets, surmounted by a burning star, blazed in futile competition with the daylight. Mayor Richard Wallach, brother of the proprietor of the *Star,* was in the chair, and the President was greeted with uproarious enthusiasm. Lincoln, in a short and informal speech, made light of the widely bruited quarrel between Stanton and McClellan. It was a politician's speech, which painted a veneer of concord and co-operation over the management of the war. The President said that "in the very selfishness of his nature" McClellan must wish to succeed, and added, "I hope he will. . . ."

After visiting the Army of the Potomac, Halleck had advised that it was a military necessity to concentrate McClellan's forces with those of Pope at some point where they could cover Washington while operating against Richmond. Three days before Lincoln publicly uttered his wishes for McClellan's success, he knew that the last stamp of failure had been set on the Peninsula campaign, and that the trail of blood and fever which led from Yorktown to Malvern Hill had been marked to no purpose at all.

X *Lost Leaders*

AMID TOCSINS AND TUMULT, Washington clung to its life as a community. Even during Jackson's raid, many people had gone quietly about their business. The panic, said the *Star*, was almost entirely confined to the abolitionists. Major French, whom the President had appointed Commissioner of Public Buildings, passed the time pleasantly, playing euchre of an evening, or watching the fountain in his garden. It was no surprise to him that Jackson got away scot-free from the Federal forces in the Valley. Like other Washingtonians, French had grown skeptical of good report and evil. He had hardly believed, he wrote, that the *Merrimac* was blown up, until he received "a certified splinter from her"—and then he had doubted whether it hadn't come from his own wood box.

While the Army of the Potomac was engaged on the Peninsula, Washington had felt the war in other ways than the alarm of Jackson's raid. The price of shad was an irritating reminder—fifty and seventy-five cents a pair, because the rebel batteries had frightened off the fishermen and damaged their seines. Speculation had driven gold and silver from circulation, and people went shopping with queer light money that did not jingle in their pockets—Secretary Chase's greenbacks and almost anybody's shinplasters. The small paper notes from Northern cities were of uncertain value, and caused much inconvenience and even distress. For the very best notes, it was hard to get change except at a heavy discount, or when most of the note had been expended. The markets refused to give change on purchases amounting to less than sixty cents. Congress, legislating against the nuisance of the shinplasters, created a worse medium of exchange, the gummy, frail postage stamp, for which Chase promptly substituted a postage currency—facsimiles of stamps, printed on small notes of thick paper, without mucilage. Pending the issue of this scrip, Washington disdained the postage stamps, and made the best of the shinplasters.

In comparison with the preceding summer, the city was free of soldiers, but they were still far too numerous for quiet and serenity.

Children went straying after bands and regiments, and there were many accidents to little boys, whom careless officers asked to hold their horses. The wounded from the Peninsula were painfully borne to the wharves, and captured bands from Jackson's army, in clothing of every shade of butternut dye, coffee-brown, yellow and dust-color, marched to the Old Capitol. Congress had interfered with the District by emancipating its slaves. War disturbed the city's peace with horse thieves and confidence men and harlots. It set brother against brother in the arguments of divided loyalties; but few were more dangerously engaged. The casualty lists in the newspapers were not scanned with agony in Washington, as in other cities of the Union. The First and Second District Regiments were on duty in the vicinity of the capital, and they did not number many men. It was a grievance of soldiers enlisted in the District that, neither privately nor by legislative enactment, did they receive the local pecuniary rewards which were usual elsewhere; while contributions for the relief of their families were equally deficient. The difficulty of filling the regiments was ascribed to this want of patriotic generosity, as well as to the demand for labor in the wartime capital and the employment of many able-bodied men as Government clerks.

Around the Capitol, the atmosphere was sulphurous with the rage of the radical Republicans. The support which the President had given to McClellan had combined with his conservative course on the slavery question to produce a crisis within his party. Like men evacuating a condemned city, the legislators took their departure in July. Ben Wade said that the country was going to hell. Many believed that Congress had met for the last time in Washington. But the outward signs were those of permanence and progress. Work had been resumed on the aqueduct for the city's water supply. Congress had made large appropriations for local improvements: for completing the west wing of the Treasury, five hundred thousand dollars; for adding a new story to the War Department and to the Navy Department, twenty thousand each; for grading and improving Judiciary Square, four thousand; for painting the outside of the old portion of the Capitol, eight thousand; for removing the army bakery from the basement and repairing damage done by said bakery, eight thousand. The Capitol was swarming with stonecutters, bricklayers, painters and laborers. At the east front, the statuary for the pediment of the northern portico was being assembled—the hunter, the Indian, the wheat sheaf, the anchor of hope. Clark Mills had completed the casting of the great bronze figure of Armed Freedom, and piece by piece the sections were carried to the grounds, and set up on a temporary platform until the dome should be ready.

The citizens' pride was puffed by the construction of a street railway. An apparent act of supererogation, workmen had busied themselves in tearing up Pennsylvania Avenue, and gleaming tracks now bisected the rutted street. Two elegant cars had been delivered. One was a large open summer or excursion car, painted in white and cream. The regular passenger car, in a still richer taste, had silk velvet upholstery, windows which combined plain and stained glass, and handsome damask curtains; while the red glass lamp was hung in such a manner that it showed on the outside. Even members of Congress had been pleased to avail themselves of an experimental ride, and the townsfolk rushed to enjoy the free introductory trips which the railway company offered. One mid-July night, at eleven o'clock, a number of gentlemen careened noisily to Willard's, while on the sidewalks the few persons abroad at that hour lustily cheered their progress. The tracks were to be laid all the way to Georgetown, and there were to be branches to the depot and the Navy Yard. When the line was opened, however, it extended only from the Capitol to the State Department. The first car that ran up the Avenue was crowded almost to suffocation, and an extra horse had to be put on before it could proceed around the curve at the Treasury.

The service did not at once give perfect satisfaction. The cars were few and crowded, and crinolines occupied a disproportionate amount of space. Weary business men were aggrieved at being ejected from their seats by conductors "to make room for any female." When the branch lines were opened, the mysteries of the transfer system led to confusions and heartburnings; and, even after weeks of experience, there were unadaptable persons who thought that they could stand on the curb and beckon cars to come up and take them in.

After Congress adjourned, the city all but subsided into its summer languor. Trade was dull, and sutlers and dealers were preparing to follow in the wake of the Army of Virginia. Ladies from the regions of Virginia newly occupied by the Union forces came up to see their friends and do a little shopping. Room rates had been cut in half. The forts, said the *New York Herald*, had a sleepy look, as they sunned themselves on the hilltops. It would need Stonewall Jackson, with half a hundred thousand men, the *Herald* correspondent thought, to wake up Washington.

In late July, all business was suspended in Washington as a mark of respect to the dead ex-President, Martin Van Buren. The capital had paid no tribute to the demise of the rebel, John Tyler; but guns boomed and flags drooped in honor of Little Van, a used up man, a souvenir of a quaintly united nation. Festooned in crape, the city was beginning to feel uneasy. The big war meeting at the Capitol was a disturbing sign. Three days later, there was news of a Federal defeat, not on the distant Peninsula, but just south of Culpeper Court-House. Lee, who had replaced Joe Johnston in command of the Confederate army, had sent Jackson to oppose the advancing Army of Virginia. Banks rashly attacked at Slaughter Mountain—also called Cedar Mountain—and God blessed Jackson's force, which was overwhelmingly larger, with victory. War meetings broke out in Washington, posters and orators calling for volunteers in all the wards. So many of the waiters at Willard's had enlisted that the dining-room was staffed with Negroes. A committee urgently solicited funds to aid the soldiers' families. Department clerks were organizing home-guard regiments.

The President's order for a draft of State militia was a potent stimulus, not only to the capital, but to able-bodied men in all parts of the Union. There was so much migration for the purpose of dodging enrollment that travel was restricted. Foreign-born residents of Swampoodle fled north in numbers, before the guard at the Washington depot began turning them back.

Washington was wide awake by mid-August. Newspaper correspondents at Fort Monroe had telegraphed that transports loaded with troops were moving down the James. The defeat at Slaughter Mountain suddenly seemed ominous. With the withdrawal of the Army of the Potomac from the Peninsula, Lee's army was free to march north in force. Pope, after advancing to the Rapidan, fell back on the Rappahannock.

The 107th New York arrived at the capital, led by two congressmen, Van Valkenburg and Diven. They had vacated their seats before the close of the session to raise soldiers among their constituents, and the regiment was the first to reach Washington under the President's July call. It was the advance of fresh legions from New York, Pennsylvania, Massachusetts, Connecticut, Maine, New Hampshire, New Jersey. In the despondency which followed the Seven Days, it had been hard to whip up patriotism. These were men who had not sprung eagerly to arms, who needed the inducement of cash bounties to serve the Union; men who sang a brave new song, "We are coming, Father Abraham, three hundred thousand more." Again soldiers streamed through the Washington depot. Familiarly, their slouching figures tramped the streets. Their officers took up the conventional positions in the hotel barrooms. They passed across the bridges, and others took their places, to be sent across the river in their turn—a steady procession of raw recruits marching into Virginia. It was all reminiscent of the early days of the war; yet it was not the same. The brash confidence had gone with the bright militia uniforms. There were no more military spectacles and concerts. Regimental bands had been abolished, leaving only the fife and drum corps, and the bands of the brigades. Convalescents replaced army cooks, stewards and messengers. The provost marshal announced that convalescents found at saloons or houses of ill fame would be considered fit for duty. The Secretary of War issued an order revoking all furloughs. The Union needed men. There was a grim urgency in the dispatch of the untrained regiments to Virginia.

Among the thronging soldiers, a white-faced general moved unnoticed. He had a star on his shoulder straps, and his military erectness bespoke a West Point training; but no command awaited him. Charles P. Stone, after nine months in Federal prisons, had returned to the city he had defended. He had been abruptly released, without trial or explanation; and he had yet to see a copy of the charges brought against him. Into the excitement and preoccupation of Washington, he brought his passionate wish to clear his name, to fight once more for his country. But there was no one to listen to one small voice which cried for justice. The Adjutant General's office knew nothing about his arrest. General Halleck had never heard of the case. The President put him off with an evasion that had the ring of a jest. There is no record that he tried to see Mr. Stanton.

The capital was praying for the arrival of the Army of the Potomac. Its fears were not exaggerated. Pope's small and recently organized army had been engaged in constant skirmishes with Jackson. Banks's corps had been badly cut up at Slaughter Mountain, and Pope considered Sigel an unreliable officer. The cavalry of the Army of Virginia was almost useless, for the overworked and ill-fed horses had given out. Straggling had become a serious problem, with which it was impossible for Pope to deal in the field.

Many regiments had been sent from the Washington defenses to reinforce Pope. Sturgis was ordered to the front, and General Barnard, chief engineer of the Army of the Potomac, was placed in command of the fortifications. Hastening back from the Peninsula, Barnard found that the garrisons consisted of less than six thousand men, of whom two thousand had been ordered to march with Sturgis, and two thousand more were nearly ready to be mustered out. Barnard could get plenty of raw recruits to fill their places, but none of them knew how to handle the guns.

The divisions of the Army of the Potomac and of Burnside's command began to land at Alexandria and Aquia Creek. Without wagons or artillery or sufficient ammunition, they were ordered by Halleck to join Pope. The corps commanders, Fitz-John Porter and Heintzelman, reported to Pope, as well as division commanders who had distinguished themselves on the Peninsula—Hooker, Kearny, Meade, and John F. Reynolds, the brave and skillful general who led the Pennsylvania Reserves. In leadership and fighting material, these reinforcements were of first-rate quality; but neither officers nor men had confidence in the bragging Westerner to whose army they abruptly found themselves attached. Pope had a conglomeration of soldiers. Lee's advancing army was a force united by confidence and loyalty, and elated by victory.

Pope was no military genius. He failed to outguess Jackson. His ears were not sharp enough to hear the tread of Longstreet's army. But, for all his gasconade, he was courageous and energetic, and he did his best to carry out Halleck's orders. As late as August 25, he believed that Halleck intended to command the army in person. In the fierce fighting that followed, Lee was in the field. Halleck remained at his desk in the War Department, smoking cigars and rubbing his elbows.

"Old Brains" won no honors as a master of military science in August of 1862. His armchair in the War Department held only an irritable bureaucrat. Halleck detested Washington—it was a "political

Hell," he wrote his wife—and exhibited a petulant evasion of responsibility. He gave indefinite orders, and neglected to answer pressing dispatches. In vain, Pope appealed to him for information about his plans, about the reinforcements. "Just think of the immense amount of telegraphing I have to do," he wired Pope on August 26, "and then say whether I can be expected to give you any details as to movements of others, even when I know them." Through all the bloodshed and wasted heroism of the last days of August, Halleck devoted more than three-quarters of his time to the raising of new troops and to matters in the West.

In the reception of the incoming regiments, Washington showed that it had learned something of the business of running a war. At the large buildings near the depot, the Soldiers' Rest and the Soldiers' Retreat, the men were well fed and lodged, efficiently policed and forwarded. As the troop trains neared the capital, the Commissary Department was notified, and gangs set to work cutting meat, cooking, and laying the tables. Promptly on their arrival, the men sat down to a hot meal. If their orders were to leave at once for the field, a day's ration for each was cut and cooked while they ate. Rutherford B. Hayes, lieutenant-colonel of the Twenty-third Ohio, found that all arrangements connected with army matters in Washington were perfect. His regiment, part of a division ordered from western Virginia to defend the capital, had spent months campaigning in the wilds, and Washington was a revelation to Colonel Hayes. In his regiment, there was a short, serious boy called William McKinley, a commissary sergeant for whom he was to secure promotion.

Alexandria, swamped by troop ships from the Peninsula, presented a less attractive military picture. The streets were filled with loitering soldiers, and there was much drunkenness and disorder. A capable man sat at the little depot, the army's chief of railways, Colonel Herman Haupt. His first duty, to send through the supplies for Pope's army, was attended with many complications. While the animals of the Army of Virginia were dying in their harness for lack of forage, seventy-eight carloads of grain stood on the tracks on Maryland Avenue. The Alexandria tracks were cluttered with other carloads of supplies of every kind. They were too numerous for the quartermaster to unload. Many of the cars that went to the front were not sent back, and Haupt was faced with a shortage of transportation. General Sturgis interfered with the control of the trains, and held up the service for many hours. When Haupt told him that he would delay reinforcements for Pope, Sturgis snapped out, "I don't care for John Pope a pinch of owl dung!" The generals of the Army of the Potomac argued, disputed, gave contradictory orders, each expecting his command to be given the preference. All wanted to go by rail, and remained in camp in preference to marching. There was no organization through which Haupt could be informed of the arrival of regiments, of the location of their camps, or the priority of their rights. Somehow, working night and day, he kept thousands moving to the front—or what he believed to be the front, for the exact whereabouts of Pope's army was uncertain, and Halleck left to the railway chief the responsibility for the destination of the reinforcements.

On August 26, the day that Hayes was looking about Washington with admiration, and Halleck was peevishly disclaiming responsibility, silence fell on the telegraph wires from Pope's headquarters. Next day, the road from Manassas to Alexandria was dark with refugees. Wagonloads of women and children rolled into the small brick town. Sweating Negroes trudged through the dust. All brought stories of a raid of rebel cavalry who had captured the immense army stores at Manassas Junction. Behind them rose the smoke of burning storehouses and freight cars. Bridges were down, and the railroad was torn up.

The severance of Pope's line of communications caused alarm to intrude on Halleck's preoccupation with recruiting and matters in the West. McClellan arrived that evening at Alexandria, and reported for orders next morning. Halleck thankfully shifted to his shoulders the burden of troublesome detail. McClellan was to direct reinforcements to march to Pope's army, and to see that the fortifications on the south side of the Potomac were equipped and fully garrisoned. As many men as possible must be pushed toward Manassas. For, as the hours passed, it was becoming plain that no mere band of rebel cavalry stood between the forces of the Union and Washington. The enemy had flanked Pope's army, and was in his rear. Those were Jackson's ragged men who feasted on the Federal supplies beside the splintered bridges and twisted tracks.

When McClellan made his camp in a field near the river at Alexandria, he was no longer the irrational man he had been at the end of the Seven Days. In a trying and anomalous position, he was calm and self-controlled. He had strenuously opposed the order to withdraw his army from the Peninsula, had begged to be allowed to move on Richmond from Harrison's Landing. Halleck had repeatedly told him that he would have the command of the Army of the Potomac and the Army of Virginia, and the rumor of this appointment still ran persistently in Washington; but McClellan could get no definite information about his status. The duties assigned him were those of a staff officer. Ironically, one of them was to send the troops of his own army to the command of another general—a general whom McClellan distrusted, whose communications were severed, whose situation was unknown.

McClellan went diligently to work. Undoubtedly the defense of Washington was a more congenial task than that of sending reinforcements to Pope. In proposing two alternatives to the President, that of opening communications with Pope or protecting the capital, he used the revealing phrase, "leave Pope to get out of his scrape." It was not hard to deduce the secret wish in McClellan's heart, even if he was too virtuous to acknowledge it to himself. Moreover, the inclination of his nature was toward defensive fighting. He was in the vicinity of Washington, and he feared an attack on its ill-garrisoned fortifications. One corps of the Army of the Potomac had been left at Fort Monroe, but McClellan had two at Alexandria. Franklin's had arrived before him. Sumner's he had promptly ordered up from Aquia Creek. On August 28, the city was tremulous. Muffled reverberations of cannon could be heard from Virginia. Many people were fleeing to Maryland. All night, McClellan was deluged with telegrams from the War Department, disquieted by a rumor that Lee was advancing on the Chain Bridge with one hundred and fifty thousand men. Next day, Halleck willingly agreed to McClellan's suggestion that Sumner should protect the fortifications, and particularly the Chain Bridge. The disposition of Franklin's corps became a matter of dispute. Halleck had wanted to shrug off the whole business of sending the troops forward, telling McClellan to "direct as you deem best." McClellan deemed best, on the ground that Franklin's corps wanted wagons, cavalry and artillery, not to push it toward Manassas, where the enemy was in force. But from the capital unfriendly eyes were watching him. Franklin was known to be one of McClellan's favorites, and the delay was regarded as proof of ill will toward Pope. The tone of Halleck's orders changed. Complaints that Franklin was slow to march were murmured by the frightened people in the streets. On

August 29, the day that his corps plodded nine miles to Anandale, the heavy cannonade from the direction of Manassas told Washington that Pope had fallen back to encounter Jackson.

Late in the afternoon, the War Department received a dispatch from Pope—the first in four days. The next afternoon, another telegram, sent early in the morning, announced that the Federal forces still held the field. All during the sultry Saturday of August 30, the air was shaken by the thunder of artillery. The *Star* said that, when wind freshened from the southwest, it carried an acrid smell of gunpowder. At Alexandria, McClellan heard the noise of battle. All his troops were gone. Sumner's corps had been belatedly ordered to the field by Halleck. McClellan had sent off even his cavalry escort and camp guard. In the field beside the river, the commander of the Army of the Potomac was left with his aides and less than a hundred men.

McClellan had been publicly humiliated, but his enemies were not satisfied. They charged him with imbecility, cowardice and treason because he had been slow in moving from the Peninsula and had withheld support from Pope. Chase carried around a protest, addressed to the President, which he and Stanton had prepared for the signature of the other Cabinet members. It enumerated McClellan's offenses, and demanded his immediate dismissal from the army; but Chase's real opinion was that the general ought to be shot.

In the afternoon, agitated crowds gathered around a bulletin on the Treasury, which announced a great victory. It stated that ten thousand Federal dead and wounded were lying on the old battlefield of Bull Run, and that surgeons and male nurses should gather at five o'clock to go to their assistance. Similar notices were posted by Stanton's order in the hotels, and appeared in the afternoon newspapers, while the telegraph flashed the War Department's appeal to the cities of the North. The medical department of the Army of the Potomac had been disrupted by the removal from the Peninsula, and in the confused movement to Pope's assistance ambulances and almost all medical and surgical supplies had been left behind. At a late hour, it had been realized that there was no adequate preparation for attending or transporting an immense number of wounded.

A throng gathered at five o'clock at the railroad depot on Maryland Avenue. Tracks and bridges had been hastily repaired, and trains were running as far as Fairfax; but they were sorely needed for military supplies and troops, and it was only over Colonel Haupt's protest that cars were sent to Washington. They were freight cars, without seats. Packed to the doors, with some people riding on top, they could accommodate less than a thousand. A few women forced their way among the male nurses, but in the main it was a hard crowd. The nurses had been asked to bring stimulants for the wounded. By the time the cars reached Alexandria, half of them were drunk.

Meantime, from the Surgeon General's office at F and Fifteenth Streets to Willard's, the streets were packed with volunteer attendants, laden with food and medicines, waiting to be conveyed in the ambulances which were to leave from the Treasury. Only a quarter of them could find room in the first train that belatedly rolled up. The rest impatiently waited. More ambulances appeared. The crowd surged forward, and fought for places, and in the crush the doctors and nurses were accompanied by many persons for whom transportation to the front was not intended. In the warm light of a fine sunset, curious citizens, women and children, congressmen who wanted to visit the battlefield, sight-seeing officers, and convalescents from the hospitals went clattering over the Long Bridge; and a number of well-known traitors seized this excellent opportunity to pass freely through the lines.

When all the ambulances were gone, some of those left behind appropriated carriages and horses, while a few hardy individuals started off on foot. Still, there were clamors for conveyances. The Surgeon General produced another group of "excited nurses." At the same time, the Quartermaster's Department began to call for wagons. It is not clear what had happened to all the wagons in Washington. Neither Franklin nor Sumner had been able to get any. Some had gone to carry supplies and ammunition to Pope, during the interruption of the railroad service. McClellan said that most of them were being used for the current supplies of the Washington garrisons. Perhaps the breakdown in the organization of the wagon trains was simply another aspect of the prevailing confusion. The provost marshal was called on to supply transportation, and on this mission a regiment of cavalry and two regiments of infantry scattered through Washington and Georgetown. Charging with drawn sabers on the hack drivers, the cavalry forced their passengers to alight. Strangers, who had just arrived in town, found themselves in the streets with their baggage; and ladies in evening toilette desolately trailed their laces and ribbons through the dirt of Pennsylvania Avenue.

By nine o'clock in the evening, the approaches to the provost marshal's office in the Gwin mansion were "jammed with a variety of vehicles and drivers in every shade of rage and indignation." Not only had the hackmen been deprived of their fares, but they were being impressed for a long night's drive, on uncertain roads, with every probability of accidents. Soldiers carried out the army supplies and piled them on the seats, and the caravans moved off with a detachment of cavalry to keep them in order. Some of the drivers contrived to upset on the way, and "the back of the sabre was used to straighten them."

At midnight, Provost Marshal Doster received a peremptory order to furnish a train for quartermaster's stores by six o'clock in the morning. It was then that the guard began to take the horses from the street-railway cars, and harness them to the discarded omnibuses. At the Western Market, on the Avenue at Twentieth Street, hucksters angrily trundled off their pots and kettles and unsold merchandise in wheelbarrows, while their wagons and drivers departed under military escort. The guard invaded livery stables, private stables and cab depots. At dawn on Sunday morning, the air of Washington was noisy with the curses of reluctant patriots, driving "omnibuses, cabs, market wagons, old family coaches, hay wagons, dog-carts, rockaways, sulkies, coupés, and gigs," to be loaded at the quartermaster's.

With early morning came the shocking news that the report of victory at Bull Run had been false. The capital awakened to rumors of disaster. Some said that the army had fallen back on Centreville, others that the Confederates were at Munson's Hill, preparing to shell the city. A little after seven o'clock, an ambulance with a cavalry escort crossed the Long Bridge, and rattled up to Willard's. It was instantly surrounded. The politician and diplomat, General Schenck, who commanded a division of Sigel's corps, lay inside. He raised himself, and a peering gentleman exclaimed, "Why, General, is it you?" "Yes," said Schenck, uncovering his rudely bandaged arm, "and they have shattered me, too." His words came indistinctly to the bystanders, who flew to repeat their version; and soon it was all over Washington that General Schenck had said that "our army was scattered to the winds." Hundreds of people hastened to vacate the city. At the Old Capitol, the inmates joyfully listened to the stories of a few prisoners who had been captured on the preceding day, and the Fredericksburg hostages were "almost in ecstasies." The President called John Hay from his bedroom—"Well, John, we are whipped again, I am afraid."

With soldiers and civilians milling in the streets, it did not look like Sunday in Washington. Weary, unarmed stragglers and Negro fugitives from Virginia thickened the crowds of pedestrians. The clouds hung heavy. There was a tense silence in the damp air. The only clatter of traffic came from ambulances and hacks, carrying wounded men from Centreville. After all the commotion about the casualties, some of these early arrivals could not obtain admission to the hospitals, and were taken to the City Hall, where they were provided with cots and blankets.

On Saturday night, Pope had sent Halleck a telegram, reporting that the army had withdrawn to Centreville, but adding that the troops were in good heart, their conduct had been very fine, and everything would go well. This was the only knowledge that Halleck possessed on Sunday morning, but McClellan was better informed. Unable to endure the suspense, he had sent to the front one of his German aides—"a cool-headed old soldier," named Hammerstein. Before daylight, Hammerstein had returned with the news that the Federals were beaten—"McDowell's and Sigel's corps broken," Heintzelman's and Fitz-John Porter's "badly cut up, but in perfect order." McClellan was a man of imagination. He must have been able to see it all: the defeated brigades, the abandoned guns, the shamed and weary stragglers; the dead and wounded on the lost field. When he telegraphed Washington that there were twenty thousand stragglers from Pope's army on the road between Centreville and Alexandria, Chase said that it was "infamously false and sent out for infamous purposes."

McClellan hoped that, reinforced by Sumner and Franklin, the army would be able to hold its own; but, in the light of Hammerstein's report, he did not regard Washington as safe against the rebels. "If I can slip quietly over there," he wrote his wife, "I will send your silver off." Passes were once more strictly regulated at the bridges, and he did not care to ask the War Department for so slight a favor as permission to go to the capital. In his "pain and mortification" he had requested permission to be with his troops on the battlefield, even if he were not allowed to command them; but Halleck had telegraphed that it would be necessary to consult the President. Inaction had become torture to McClellan, for Hammerstein had told him that his soldiers wanted him. On Sunday evening, he saw an order, published by Stanton's direction, stating that his command consisted of that portion of the Army of the Potomac which had not been sent to Pope. Save for the troops left at Fort Monroe, all had now been sent. McClellan's anomalous position had at last been defined. He was in command of nothing.

After all, McClellan was not obliged to steal secretly to Washington on a domestic errand. Another telegram from Pope was laid on Halleck's desk on Sunday afternoon. "I should like to know," it inquired, "whether you feel secure about Washington should this army be destroyed?" Halleck had nothing to say. He had crumbled. His nerve was gone; and to the other disasters of Washington was added the disintegration of a bureaucrat. That night, "utterly tired out," he telegraphed to beg McClellan for help.

Next morning McClellan posted to the capital. He said that Halleck asked him to take charge of the Washington defenses and garrisons, actually under the command of Barnard. McClellan urged Halleck to go to the front, and finally succeeded in persuading him to send a staff officer to investigate. Meantime, he strongly recommended that the Army of Virginia should fall back on the Washington fortifications. It was the course which Pope himself advised, and Halleck sent the order. Pope's dispatches no longer mentioned the good heart of his troops, but made sinister allusion to the want of it among the officers. Later, he reported that the enemy was between him and Washington. The fight would be desperate, and he hoped that Halleck would make all preparations for a vigorous defense of the entrenchments.

On that cloudy Monday morning, the early train brought an eager crowd to Washington. Bright, expectant and dedicated, there descended from the cars the country practitioners, professors, undergraduates and nurses whose hearts had been touched by the War Department's call for volunteers to succor the wounded. No one had given another thought to them—no one, in the growing consternation, was prepared to think of them now. The nurses who had gone in the ambulance trains had been unfortunate. They had been set down on a battlefield which was in the possession of the victorious Confederates; and, interrupted in their attentions to the wounded by a body of rebel cavalry, fifty-nine ministering angels from Washington had been taken prisoner. Those who had gone by train had never reached the battlefield at all. After standing all night in the unventilated freight cars, they had been deposited on Sunday morning in the mud of Fairfax Station. There the commanding officer had orders to arrest all who had partaken too freely of whisky. The patriots from the North found that volunteer nurses were not only superfluous, but in bad repute. The War Department had ordered General Wadsworth to place guards at the bridges and wharves to turn back "drunken and other nurses."

Out at Upton's Hill, where the Twenty-third Ohio was on guard duty, Colonel Rutherford B. Hayes wrote his wife an enthusiastic letter. He could see four forts, a number of camps and many fine residences. From the higher elevations, the white dome of the Capitol was visible. Artillery sounded in the distance, troops and army wagons and ambulances were pouring past, and couriers galloped to and fro. It was a relief to get away from the petty skirmishes of western Virginia to "the pride and pomp of glorious war." The soldiers were in ignorance of the results of the fighting. Hayes had seen many wounded, some prisoners, a few paroled men. "Some think we got the best of it, some otherwise. As yet I call it a tie."

But, while there was still hope in the entrenchments, the city was in desperation. A number of male nurses, bewildered and frightened by their experience, had returned with terrifying stories. The Army of the Potomac had refused to fight. McClellan and his officers —Fitz-John Porter and Franklin, in particular—had deliberately caused the defeat of General Pope. McDowell was guilty of treason, one wild rumor ran, and Sigel had shot him on the battlefield. The army was cut to pieces. The routed survivors were fleeing to Washington in panic. They had not eaten for days, and hunger was driving them faster than the great Confederate army which came thundering behind them. The fall of the capital was a certainty.

Hatless, shoeless and ragged, stragglers limped across the Long Bridge. Hysteria mounted in the capital. The solace of whisky was so freely sought that Wadsworth closed down all drinking places. The excitement was not allayed by the provost guard, galloping up and down the Avenue as though Lee's divisions were already at the fortifications. The hacks which had returned from the front were rounded up, and transformed into provision trains. Omnibuses were rushed to wharves and depots to carry the wounded to the hospitals.

Near sunset on Monday, a loud uproar of artillery—from Chantilly, near Fairfax Court-House—seemed to threaten Washington with imminent invasion. It mingled with the roll of thunder, as lightning split the sky and rain came down in torrents. Sidewalks and crossings were flooded. Pedestrians—in other words, practically all who were abroad—waded up to their knees in muddy water. After a stormy night, Tuesday dawned clear and cool. McClellan was at an early breakfast when the President and Halleck came along the wind-swept square to his house on H Street. Halleck's aide had brought back the same story as Hammerstein. The army was badly whipped, and the roads to Washington were clogged with stragglers. Lincoln had come to an important decision. He asked McClellan to take command of the city and of the troops falling back on it from the front.

The President was among those who believed that McClellan had wanted Pope to be defeated. He was influenced by the delay in sending forward Franklin's corps, and the phrase, "leave Pope to get out of his scrape," rankled in his mind. John Hay had the impression that Lincoln thought that McClellan was "a little crazy." In deciding to restore him to command, the President had his political ear to the ground. The general's cause had been espoused by factious and discontented Democrats. He was in close alliance with leading opponents of the administration, and was beginning to be regarded as the leader of the opposition party, on whose support Lincoln depended for recruiting and other war measures. Moreover, in the great emergency, there was no one else to choose. Halleck had gone to pieces. Pope's gasconade was over. It was McClellan, or chaos. "There is no man in the Army," Lincoln said, "who can man these fortifications and lick these troops of ours into shape half as well as he."

The Secretary of War was busy with nervous preparations for the fall of Washington. To prevent arms and ammunition from falling into the hands of the enemy, he had given orders to ship the Arsenal stores to New York. In Stanton's office, the important papers had been gathered into bundles which could be carried by men on foot or on horseback. On Tuesday morning, gunboats were anchored in the Potomac. The steamer *Wachusett* was making her way to the Navy Yard—ready, said McClellan, to take the President and Cabinet to a place of safety. Neither then nor in any other crisis did Lincoln act like a man about to flee in terror. He directed that the department clerks and the employees on the public buildings be organized into companies, armed and supplied with ammunition; and he went to face a great ordeal—the meeting of his Cabinet.

Seward was out of town. It was surmised that he wished to avoid any connection with the scheduled dismissal of McClellan, in which, although he had long sustained the general, he had been induced to acquiesce. The Cabinet members were, for once, in agreement; and on their unanimity there fell like a bombshell Stanton's trembling announcement that the President had placed McClellan in command. Stanton fumed and lowered—he had been looking forward to a court-martial. Chase cried that restoring McClellan was "equivalent to giving Washington to the rebels." The President's manner toward these two was kind, even affectionate. He said that, as a fighting general, McClellan was a failure, but that he had the confidence of the soldiers. The army was "tumbling into Washington," something had to be done. Calmly, but emphatically, he told Stanton that the order was his own, and that he would be responsible for it to the country. Montgomery Blair said that Stanton and Chase would have preferred the fall of the capital to the reinstatement of McClellan.

In the midst of his hasty preparations to go to the front, the general received a message that he should not assume command until the troops were close to the fortifications. It was afternoon when, with a few aides and a small cavalry escort, he rode out to Munson's Hill. Some infantry of McDowell's corps was beginning to come in, and McClellan halted the soldiers and ordered them into position. Soon, a regiment of cavalry appeared, with Pope and McDowell and their staff officers "sandwiched in the midst," as McClellan sarcastically described it. "I never," he wrote, "saw a more helpless-looking head-quarters." Haughtily, by McClellan's own account, he gave the two generals permission to return to Washington, remarking that he himself would go to the artillery firing, which could be heard in the distance. As night fell, the guns ceased. Still, McClellan rode on, far beyond the fortifications where the officers slept in boots and spurs, and the lights of the signal corps flashed from all the heights. On a dark road under the stars, he met the first troops of Fitz-John Porter's corps, which had seen hard fighting and suffered heavy losses. Their cheers aroused the men behind them, and through the lines rang the cry that Little Mac was there. Far down the road, regiments, brigades, divisions roared with a tumult of cheering; and men crowded around McClellan's horse, shouting, crying, thanking God, and begging him to lead them into battle.

The soldiers of the East had not yet seen the backs of their enemies. They had stubbornly waged a long and losing fight—a fight that had been predestined to defeat. In the positions assigned them in the Washington entrenchments, they waited in black resentment, eager to fight again under a general they could trust. There was indignation among the fresh troops of Sumner's and Franklin's commands, who had marched too late to participate in the battle—twenty thousand men, the veterans of the splendid Second and Sixth Corps of the Army of the Potomac. The good old soldier, Edwin Sumner, was enraged when he heard that McClellan had said that his corps had not been in condition for fighting. If he had been ordered to advance right on, he later told Ben Wade's committee, he would have been in that Second Bull Run battle with his whole force. Some of Franklin's soldiers had stood on the Warrenton Turnpike, taunting the retreating Army of Virginia, jeering at the new route to Richmond. Nevertheless, the Sixth Corps had wanted to get into the fighting, had been bewildered by the delay in its advance. In a single evening, these troops had returned from Centreville to Alexandria—a march which had taken them two full days and part of another, when they were going to Pope's assistance.

From Centreville to Washington, the roads and bridges were choked with the ambulances and carriages which bore the wounded and the dying. Strewn across the miles of rain-soaked battlefield lay the host of the Union dead. The officers who wore the scarlet Kearny patch put a black band on their coat sleeves, and mourning draped their colors and their drums. Under a flag of truce, men in gray had carried to the Union lines the body of their lean and daring general, shot in the buttock as he galloped out of a nest of rebel skirmishers. One-armed Phil Kearny would ride no more into the thick of the fighting, with his reins held in his teeth; but his fame was secure, and on the field of Second Bull Run more than one good name had been tarnished.

Pope's brief career in the East was ended, and the hero of Island Number 10 was a hero no longer. No one remembered that he had fought bravely, but only that he had boasted and failed. He was sidetracked in a department of the frontier, and went off very angry, charging his defeat to McClellan and his sneering officers.

Fitz-John Porter, handsome, able and autocratic, was the scapegoat of this campaign. On him Pope's accusations bore most heavily, and he was to serve in September with the shadow of a court-martial and a dishonorable discharge from the army hanging over him. Many years would pass before the passions of that day subsided, and Porter's name was cleared. "Porter was the most magnificent soldier in the Army of the Potomac," John Hay wrote, "ruined by his devotion to McClellan."

Of McDowell's faithfulness to his duty, Pope spoke in praise. But that earnest officer, who could not remember names and faces, and spoke with "rough indifference" to his soldiers, had again been unfortunate as a commander. He had failed too often. His men would no longer fight under him. Calumnies, ranging from treason to drunkenness, assailed him, and he sought to clear himself by asking for a court of inquiry. The court exonerated McDowell, but he did not again receive a command in the field.

Halleck, however, remained at his post. He had not essayed to bear a gallant part, and there was little notoriety in his failure. Whipped at his desk, he lingered on in Washington, exercising tyrannical authority over the mass of army details. He was still nominally the general-in-chief, but actually, as John Hay quoted Lincoln as saying, "little more than a first-rate clerk."

The incapacity of the Union commanders was a scandal over which Cabinet members shook their heads. Mr. Welles ascribed their dilatoriness to their West Point education, which instilled a defensive policy; and, quite overlooking Lee and Jackson, declared that "no efficient, energetic, audacious, fighting commanding general had yet appeared from that institution." Montgomery Blair blamed Stanton for the defects of the generals, and said that he should not give way to narrow prejudices and personal dislikes, but should search out good officers—"should dig up these jewels."

The reputation of the soldiers of the East, as well as of the officers, was blighted. The ranks of the veterans were thinned, not only by death and wounds and capture, but by the dark contagion of desertion. Exhaustion and hunger and loss of faith had demoralized thousands of the soldiers. They flooded back in disorder on the Alexandria road, flopped down to rest, indifferent to the tumult of the retreating infantry and cavalry, artillery and wagons. Their great fires illuminated the whole countryside. Across the bridges, they crowded into the capital, congregated in low groggeries and staggered drunken and loud-mouthed in droves on every street. Hundreds of officers, absent from their commands, were rounded up in Washington hotels

and other public places in "such general hauls . . . as the police of
New York are at times compelled to make of the inmates of the notable
dance houses." Washington saw the dead beats and the shirking
officers, and believed that they represented the armies of the Union.
The backwash of this retreat was not soon forgotten. So many organizations were dissolved, so many men were too sick and jaded for
duty that a convalescent camp was formed for them at Alexandria. It
was an immense, comfortless dump heap for the misfits of the army,
and throughout the war it was a disgrace to Federal management; but
the need for it persisted, and it remained.

Monotonously every day, the incoming volunteers lined up at the
depot. One morning, the Soldiers' Retreat fed over seven thousand
men. "We are coming, Father Abraham." Into a soured and despairing
city, they brought their awkwardly held rifles, their inexperienced
faces that had never looked on war.

The cause of the Union had never seemed so hopeless. To the
people of Washington it appeared that Lee's victorious army would
be faced by a force of drunken stragglers and the legions of the raw
recruits. But the capital had not forgotten the summer of 1861, and,
in spite of the belief that the veterans were demoralized, many eyes
turned with hope to McClellan's house on H Street. The Army of
Virginia no longer existed. All the troops—Pope's, Burnside's, the new
volunteers—were consolidated in the Army of the Potomac. Once more
McClellan went out to inspect the fortifications and the camps, once
more he galloped along the Avenue, with his staff pelting behind him.
There were a few changes. The French princes had gone back to
Europe. One of the aides, appointed on the Peninsula, could ride as
hard as McClellan—a long-haired, reckless lad called Custer.

For over a week, the wounded came back to Washington by train
and boat and in vehicles of every description. The provost guard
commandeered private carriages for service between the wharves and
depot and the hospitals. To the consternation of the State Department,
the Prussian minister, Baron Gerolt, was unceremoniously deprived
of his conveyance and left standing in the street; and, to prevent
diplomatic incidents, Frederick Seward hastened to get safeguards for
all the foreign ministers from Wadsworth. A horrified sergeant rode
up in time to rescue the President's barouche, stopped by one of the
troopers. Lincoln said that the man was doing his duty.

The guard had become the bugbear of the Avenue. When the

hacks were back on their stands, a waggish gentleman at Willard's whispered that the provost marshal was about to send for the drivers. In a minute, the double line of carriages had wheeled and made off "in a cloud of oaths and dust" in the direction of the Island. The alarm spread to the stands at Kirkwood's, Brown's and the National, and soon the Avenue was as empty of hacks as it had been on the night of the battle.

After the army came the long trains of noncombatants—sutlers' men, traders, laborers and other camp followers. Strangers descended on Washington as merrily as though there had been a victory. Volunteer surgeons and nurses continued to arrive until there were more than five hundred in the city. Most of them indignantly made their way home, after a vain attempt to get their expenses paid by the Government; but some lingered in the hope of finding an opportunity to attend the wounded. Washington was so crowded that it was almost as hard to move in the back streets as on the Avenue. The bakers, unprepared for the demand, could not supply enough bread to feed the people.

Meanwhile, Lee's army appeared to have withdrawn. Rumors came that it was crossing the upper Potomac. The President, consumed with anxiety to find and hurt the enemy, ordered Halleck on September 3 to organize an army immediately for active operations. Halleck passed the word along to McClellan.

That week, McClellan performed something very like a miracle. In the camps and fortifications, the broken brigades seemed to re-form by magic. This had been a conglomeration of soldiers. When McClellan spoke the word, it was an army. Its organization was imperfect, its clothing, ammunition and supplies were all in sad condition. No commander ever had more excuse for saying that his men were not ready to fight; but for once McClellan was able to lay aside his desire for a perfection not attainable in human enterprise. He took command on Tuesday. On Thursday, he threw out the advance of his force to the north. On Friday, the army marched.

The bummers had not all been cleared from the streets, and people were still clucking and headshaking over the demoralization of the troops, when the Army of the Potomac came swinging along the Avenue. Washington had known regiments of sturdy boys, American individualists, smartly drilled and perfectly equipped. They had returned as veterans. Every reduced brigade had its iron column of

fighting men. With the tendrils of home and family and small ambitions quick about them, they had learned to subdue their strongest
traditions, and yield uncritical obedience to an arbitrary command.
Scarred by war and weather, with their bleached and scanty uniforms
and their dirty, shredded flags, they wore a look of hard utility. Their
collars had been wilted in the sweat of the Chickahominy, leggings
and gaiters had littered the Peninsula from Mechanicsville to Malvern
Hill. Men marched in shirt sleeves or blue blouses, open at the throat,
with trousers rolled at the ankle, and tucked into gray woolen socks.
There were worn-out caps of every style, and hats of straw and of palm
leaf, of brown and black and soiled white wool. The trappings of the
officers' horses no longer glittered. The gold-embroidered shoulder
straps were tarnished, or replaced by common metal, and the crimson
sashes were faded or gone. It was a shabby and seasoned army that
brought the gaping citizens to the pavements. The troops did not pass
the White House, but turned into H Street, to cheer McClellan
lustily as they went by his house.

By every road the long columns marched, recruits brigaded with
veterans; by Seventh Street, Fourteenth Street, out by the Kalorama,
by Georgetown. Reversing the usual order, soldiers pounded across
the bridges from Virginia into Washington. This was a defending, not
an invading army. It was marching to the north.

Seward's cheerful spirit had been saddened. "Mr. Hay, what is the
use of growing old?" he asked. "You learn something of men and
things but never until too late to use it. I have only just now found out
what military jealousy is." As was his custom in the late afternoon,
when he had dealt with his "croaking, litigious, foreign mail," he went
out for a drive on Friday, and paused by the roadside near Tennallytown to watch the troops go by. At the head of the column, marching
in a brisk route step to the tap of a single drum, came the strong
soldiers, with their eyes on the road ahead; cheering, as now and then
an officer would recognize the silver-haired man by the roadside, but
never slackening their pace. Then came squads that lounged forward
lazily and unevenly, disintegrating here and there into knots of men
who stopped to talk or take a rest. Trailing behind them, with no pretense of order, came a shambling rabble of laggards—old skulkers, convalescents, limping recruits. With furtive glances behind them, they
scrambled over the ditches into the fields, or prowled off toward the
farmhouses. Last of all, sounded the sharp, steady tread of the army

provost guard, coming to pick up the stragglers and deserters. "Those first soldiers are the ones the country must depend on for its victories," Mr. Seward remarked. "These later ones are those that only turn up on pay-day."

McClellan had been expressly informed that his command was confined to the troops defending Washington. Burnside, again offered the active command, had for a second time declined it. The Army of the Potomac was advancing on Lee's forces without a leader. McClellan prepared to follow his men. Halleck said that the President told McClellan to take command in the field. Lincoln said that the responsibility was Halleck's. There was no written order, and McClellan affirmed that he received no directions at all. He thought that, in the excited state of feeling in the capital, he might well be condemned to death, if the army were defeated. Firmly and promptly, he made his decision; but some puerility in his nature persuaded him to disfigure it with a piece of impudence. Like a gentleman leaving a town where he had been hospitably received, he inscribed on three of his visiting cards the initials, P. P. C.—"Pour Prendre Congé." With his staff and personal escort, he rode on Sunday to the White House, the War Office and Seward's house, and left a card at each.

In the evening, while taking a walk with his son, Edgar, Mr. Welles observed a cavalcade on the Avenue near H Street, and remarked that their mounts seemed better than usual. Edgar, with the sharper eyes of youth, reported that this was no squad of cavalry, but General McClellan and his staff. As they dashed past and the Secretary of the Navy raised his hand in salute, the general pulled up his horse, and rode over to the sidewalk to take his leave. Welles inquired which way he was going. McClellan said that he was proceeding to take command of the onward movement. "Well," hinted the Secretary, "onward, General, is now the word; the country will expect you to go forward." McClellan said that it was his intention. "Success to you, then, General, with all my heart," said Mr. Welles. Thus, fortuitously, a representative of the Government sped McClellan on his way.

With the departure of the army and its commander, Cabinet members, senators, and heads of Government bureaus ran from office to office with stories that hostility to the administration was rampant in the Army of the Potomac. These tales were not without foundation. Supercilious West Pointers in McClellan's command had openly sneered at the Government as well as General Pope, and bragged about clearing the Republicans out of Washington and putting the army in power. At Harrison's Landing one night, Burnside had moved into a fire-lit circle with the blunt words, "I don't know what you fellows call this talk, but I call it flat Treason, By God!" Washington called it flat Treason. Senator Henry Wilson assured Gideon Welles that there was a conspiracy among certain generals for a revolution—he had obtained important information from a member of McClellan's staff. Welles reflected that Wilson was "by nature suspicious and sensational"; and as chairman of the Military Affairs Committee he came under Stanton's influence. Most sensible men concluded that the threats were mere bluster and camp talk; but the more excitable politicians trembled at the menace of military dictatorship. McClellan rode in triumph into Frederick, a Union town which pelted him with flowers, and decked Dan Webster's bridle with little flags. The army was filled with confidence and vigor, and even Chase admitted that it might have been hazardous, in view of the condition of the troops, to have dismissed McClellan.

McClellan led his army slowly forward, sending back entreaties to Halleck to reinforce him. He wanted all the troops in Washington, where General Banks had been left in command of the defenses. Even if the capital should be taken, McClellan said, its capture would not compare in importance with the defeat of the Army of the Potomac. Lee sent a large detachment to lay siege to Harper's Ferry. McClellan did not relieve the garrison at the Ferry, which presently surrendered. Neither did he take the opportunity to attack Lee's reduced army. In gloomy depression, Washington awaited the clash of arms from Maryland. Even the secessionists had lost their joyful spirits, for Maryland had not risen in insurrection, as they had fondly expected, on the arrival of the rebel forces.

General Mansfield came in to call on Mr. Chase, feeling himself wronged. Scott had treated him badly, superseding him by McDowell, and at Fort Monroe he had fared no better under General Wool, who did not like him. Now he had been called to a court of inquiry at Washington. Mansfield's beard was white, but he wanted active service. Chase, touched by his story, found himself wishing that the stiff, resentful old soldier were a younger man. After all, Mansfield had his way. He was sent to Maryland, and placed in command of Banks's former corps, the Twelfth, a week after he talked with Chase.

Two days later he fell, mortally wounded, while cheering on his troops.

On September 15, Washington had news of a victory at South Mountain, a spur of the Blue Ridge, beyond which Lee's army was massed. The hotels, public offices and promenades were filled with smiling unionists, and "McClellan stock went up generally." In the evening, a large crowd gathered before the bulletin board at the *Star* office. When a man said that he wanted the news confirmed, for "McClellan was no more reliable than Pope," he was struck instantaneous blows on each side of the head by two bystanders. "Divil take the man who would say a word again McClellan after hearing that news," said an Irishman who was one of the assailants.

Two days later, there was furious fighting at Sharpsburg, along the Antietam Creek. There, in the golden air of September, for fourteen hours the armies contended; and, at the close of day, twenty thousand men from North and South lay dead and wounded in the narrow country lanes, the ripe cornfields and the laden orchards. McClellan claimed a great victory—"a masterpiece of art." Lee called it a drawn battle. The losses of the Union were a little the heavier. But the tide of gray rolled back from Maryland, and the North went wild with joy.

Lee's army made its escape into Virginia. McClellan did not follow. His thirst for battle had been quenched in the blood of Antietam. He had learned to fight aggressively, but he could not pursue or destroy. After South Mountain, he had received a telegram, signed Winfield Scott. "Bravo, my dear general!" it ran. "Twice more and it's done." But once more was all that McClellan was able to manage.

The breach between McClellan and the Government widened. His partisans included not only patriotic members of the Democratic party, but peace advocates, soreheads with a grudge against the administration, secession sympathizers. He was being spoken of as the Democratic nominee for President in 1864. The military proclamation of emancipation which the President issued that month was said to have awakened great dissatisfaction among McClellan's soldiers. There was a story that he did not pursue the enemy because it was not "the game" to destroy the rebel army and end the war, but rather to bring about a compromise settlement which should preserve the institution of slavery. The President traced the report to a major who was the brother of one of McClellan's staff officers, and personally examined and dismissed him from the service as an example.

One early morning, while visiting McClellan's camp, Lincoln climbed a hill from which he could see the white tents stretching for miles in the rising sun. "Do you know what this is?" he asked a friend who accompanied him. "It is the Army of the Potomac," said the gentleman, in surprise. "So it is called," said Lincoln, "but that is a mistake; it is only McClellan's bodyguard."

On his return to Washington, the President sent McClellan orders to cross the Potomac, and give battle to the enemy or drive him south. McClellan did not obey. The dashing rebel commander, General Jeb Stuart, galloped his cavalry completely around the Army of the Potomac—a contemptuous feat he had already performed on the Peninsula. His raid extended into Pennsylvania, where at Chambersburg he took much plunder of stores, horses and cattle.

Washington went to the circus, where P. T. Barnum's famous pygmies were the chief attraction. Tom Thumb was the most admired general in town, and Commodore Nutt was received at the White House and sang "Columbia, the Gem of the Ocean" for the Cabinet. Guns sounded along the Potomac, as sportsmen invaded the marshes. The military occupation had enforced a quiet season the year before, and reedbirds, blackbirds, blue-wing duck and jacksnipe were plentiful.

The fine autumn days went past. The capital grew restless, waiting for Lee's army to be driven from the Valley. Little was said in the Cabinet meetings, clouded by discouragement. Now and then, Stanton's voice uttered a musical sneer; but for the most part he brooded in silence. With McClellan in power, he felt that his importance and influence were gone, and he threatened to resign.

For six weeks, the Army of the Potomac lay in Maryland. The country groaned with impatience and dissatisfaction. Stocks declined. Volunteering lagged. The State ballot boxes gave a verdict adverse to the administration. The President repeatedly begged, persuaded and ordered McClellan to advance. McClellan said that the army was not ready. It was true that his soldiers were in need—like those of General Lee, though not so sorely—of shoes, blankets, clothing, horses and camp equipment. McClellan's mood was one of proud, dark, brooding resentment. His communications with Stanton and Halleck were few and rigidly formal. He regarded himself as the savior of his country, who should be spared interference. Much of his time was spent in controversies with the Quartermaster's Department over his supplies—those supplies that he had been able to forget in his great phase of resolution in September.

At last, he got his army across the Potomac. Moving east of the Blue Ridge, it marched slowly down to Warrenton. Lee was at Winchester. The road to Richmond was open to the Federals. A committee of patriotic ladies, who paid a visit to the President, were shocked by "his introverted look and his half-staggering gait." He shook their hands mechanically. He could give them no encouragement, he told them. There was agony ahead for the people, and they were not prepared for it. The army did not realize that they were in a terrible war that had to be fought out.

General Lee brought his army through the passes of the Blue Ridge, and occupied Culpeper Court-House, between the Army of the Potomac and Richmond. For Mr. Lincoln, it was the deciding factor. On November 7, General Catharinus P. Buckingham, Stanton's confidential Assistant Adjutant General, took a journey by special train on the Orange and Alexandria Railroad. He did not go direct to McClellan's headquarters, but made his way through a heavy snowstorm to Burnside's camp. After all, Burnside was the only jewel that the War Department was able to dig up. For the third time, the command of the Army of the Potomac was offered to him—it was in the form of an order from Halleck. In agitation, Burnside hesitated. Outside his quarters, the November gale whirled the snowflakes. In the thick white twilight, he made his reluctant decision to obey, and rode with Buckingham to McClellan's tent. The two officers stood watching while McClellan read the order which relieved him of command. He made no sign while they were there. "Alas for my poor country!" he wrote his wife when they were gone.

In all that stricken and saddened army, the most unhappy man was its new commander. McClellan pitied him. He thought—or so he later said—that his old friend was not competent to command more than a regiment. Of his own incapacity, Burnside had no doubt. He was an honest man, and he went about telling the other officers that he was not fit for the position.

McClellan declared that there were hotheads in the army who were in favor of his refusing to obey the order, who wanted to march on Washington to take possession of the Government. But, if revolution might have broken out at a word from him, he never spoke that word. For a few days he remained at his headquarters, helping Burn-side with his arrangements. Then he bade farewell to his troops, and quietly took his departure. He had been directed to go to Trenton to await orders. There had been no military operations around Trenton since that icy December morning of 1776 when General Washington had marched from the Delaware to capture a thousand Hessians there. Stanton was not a man much given to smiling, but surely his Cupid's bow upper lip must have widened over his abundant whiskers when he contemplated that order.

XI "The Great Army of the Wounded"

ON A MORNING of late September, the three handsomest people in Washington were gathered in a room in the Insane Asylum. Mr. Salmon P. Chase, the majestic figure of a statesman, had come on an errand of mercy nicely allied with his itching political ambition, and with him on his drive across the Eastern Branch he had brought the belle of Washington, his beautiful daughter, Kate. This girl of twenty-two loved the intrigue of political life, and shared her father's dreams of succeeding the awkward Lincolns in the White House. Her small, golden-bronze head, her elegant toilettes and her imperious manners were more suited to parlors and ballrooms than to the bedsides of the afflicted. But on this September morning, suitably armed with a basket of peaches and grapes, she was paying a visit to an invalid worthy of her attention—Major-General Hooker, who many believed would soon succeed McClellan in the command of the Army of the Potomac.

Hooker, before resigning his regular Army commission, had served with distinction in Mexico; but in the spring of 1861, he had not been received with much warmth at the capital. After First Bull Run, he had called on the President, and told him that he was a better general than any Union commander on that field. Lincoln was sufficiently impressed by Hooker's claims to make him a brigadier. He had borne a gallant part in all the battles of the Army of the Potomac since Williamsburg, where he had won his nickname of "Fighting Joe," which he regretfully thought made him sound like a bandit. He was tall and statuesque, with a noble blonde head—"fit for a model of a war-god," one newspaper correspondent wrote. To be sure, he had the reputation of being excitable, and indiscreet in speech; and it was whispered that he was too fond of whisky to be entrusted with the responsibility of an army. Yet his bravery and his frank and engaging manners won him many admirers. His complexion was ruddy. His lively eyes were blue. He had a charming way of persuading others to share his enthusiastic opinion of himself. To these important callers, the Secretary of the Treasury and his daughter, Hooker talked freely, making the most of a good opportunity to disparage General Mc-

Clellan. If he himself had commanded on the Peninsula, he assured
them, he would have taken Richmond. In the Maryland campaign,
he had led the First Corps, and he expressed the sorrowful conviction
that his premature removal from the field at Antietam had prevented
a sweeping victory for the Union arms. Perhaps he overplayed his
charm that morning. The Secretary of the Treasury, solemnly ap-
praising General Hooker as he lay on his couch in the Insane Asylum,
was aware of a qualm of doubt. Nevertheless, on the whole, Hooker
was a good choice for the command of the army. He looked like a
great general, and he had no political ambitions. The Chase interests
would support Hooker.

The general's mentality was not impaired, he had been shot in
the foot at Antietam. In the autumn of 1862, there seemed nothing
incongruous in the lodging he had selected. It was shared by many
lesser soldiers. Washington, which had been a camp, had been transformed into a hospital—the vast base hospital of the Army of the
Potomac. Clusters of white buildings and tents had changed the aspect
of the city and its surrounding hills. The E Street Infirmary, destroyed
by fire in the autumn of 1861, had been replaced by the rectangular
pavilions of the new Judiciary Square Hospital. Stanton Hospital, at
New Jersey Avenue and I Street, was another modern institution, and
opposite it on Minnesota Row the former mansions of Douglas,
Breckinridge and Rice now constituted Douglas Hospital. Lincoln
and Emory Hospitals were being constructed on the plain to the east
of the Capitol. Near the Smithsonian, beside the open sewer of the
canal, lay the clean, parallel sheds of the great Armory Square Hospital, conveniently accessible from the Maryland Avenue depot and
the wharves. On the distant heights, long one-story buildings, lavishly
whitewashed and encircled by huts and tents, seemed to bloom like
monstrous flowers in the soft Washington light. Several of these big
hospital colonies on the Seventh and Fourteenth Street Roads were
transformed barracks. Contagious diseases were isolated in a pesthouse at Kalorama. Harewood Hospital was situated on the Corcoran
farm, not far from the Soldiers' Home. Columbian Hospital, on
Meridian Hill, took its name from the college which once had occupied its central building. On the summit of the hill where the New
York Seventh had encamped, sprawled the new pavilions of Mount
Pleasant.

A stranger, wandering about the city, might find his way by using the low, pale masses of the hospitals as landmarks. But there were many more which could be recognized only on a closer inspection. In Washington, as well as in Georgetown and Alexandria, sick and wounded men lay in hotels and warehouses, in private houses, schools and seminaries, and the lodges of fraternal orders. On Independence Day of 1862, it had been observed that the church bells could not be rung, because of the suffering that lay beneath them. The seizure of the churches had begun in June, when an officer of General Wadsworth waited on the rectors of Trinity, the Ascension and the Epiphany—three edifices which, the *Star* felt, could be occupied with the least inconvenience to loyal worshipers. Soon, congregations of Union sympathizers were vying with one another in offering their buildings to the War Department. Carpets, cushions and hymnbooks were packed away. Carpenters covered the pews with scantling on which floors were laid, and the pulpits and other furniture were stowed underneath. The mains were tapped to supply water for kitchens established in the basements, or in hastily constructed outbuildings. Presently appeared wagonloads of furniture, drugs and utensils. The flag of the Union was run up. Wardmasters, nurses, orderlies, cooks and stewards arrived. Ambulances began to stop at the church doors. Last of all came the surgeons, with their knives and saws and dirty little sponges.

Since the preceding year, the Patent Office had been used as a hospital. One thousand more beds were placed on the second floor and on the gallery which ran around the lofty hall. At night, in the glare of the gaslight, it was a curious scene. Like some new exhibit of ghastliness, waxy faces lay in rows between the shining glass cabinets, filled with curiosities, foreign presents and the models of inventions. The nurses' heels clicked on the marble floor, and over all lay the heavy smell of putrefaction and death.

Yet, as the wounded came in from Pope's campaign, there was still not room enough. Georgetown College was turned into a hospital; so was the H Street mansion of the rebel sympathizer, Mr. Corcoran. At last, it was found necessary to make a temporary requisition of the Capitol, and two thousand cots were placed in the halls of the House and Senate, in the corridors and the Rotunda.

From the first, many inhabitants of Washington had shown themselves sympathetic to the suffering strangers in their city. Relief associations had sprung up to work for the soldiers and to raise money to purchase comforts for them. The sick of the early regiments and the beaten stragglers of First Bull Run had been charitably treated. Ladies whose hearts were with the Southern cause joined their Northern sisters in sewing and picking lint for the wounded. As the hospitals multiplied in the capital, so did the visitors who came to tend the soldiers and to bring them presents. These ministrations were not invariably welcome. The hospital doors were wide open, not only to relatives and friends and the agents of relief organizations, but to any strangers who chose to call. Some fed improper food to the sick. Others wearied them with impertinent questions. Even desperately ill men were not protected from the intrusions of the tactless and the curious. The haphazard distribution of gifts resulted in much inequality. Some would give only to those from a favorite State. Others selected pets, whom they gorged with delicacies, leaving their neighbors quite neglected. When wounded prisoners began to be sent to Washington from the Peninsula, the more virulent secessionist ladies made themselves a nuisance. To the irritation of doctors and attendants, they strolled through the wards, casting freezing looks at the Union cots, while they showered the rebels with flowers, fruits and clothing.

The constant civilian inspection served the purpose of advertising the defects of the institutions. The shortcomings of old hotels and schoolhouses, of churches and public buildings were glaringly apparent to the most casual caller. The renovated barracks were dark and badly ventilated, and usually lacked municipal conveniences; while their grounds, particularly those of the cavalry barracks, were filthy. Moreover, the administration of the hospitals left much to be desired. There was no trained personnel on which to draw. Where institutions were hastily improvised, it was inevitable that some surgeons should be careless and incompetent, many cooks and stewards corrupt, almost all nurses inexpert. The patients were not supplied with proper clothing. The diet was coarse and not infrequently meager. The dead received scant ceremony. Their thin plank coffins were loaded on a cart and rattled off to the cemetery at the Soldiers' Home, where they were hurriedly dumped into the ground. At the Judiciary Square Hospital, whose management had promptly earned an unenviable notoriety, the naked bodies of the dead were stretched on a vacant lot, and prepared for burial in full view of the populous neighborhood. Almost as soon as the Washington hospitals opened their doors, their abuses became a scandal, to be exposed and deplored by public-spirited citizens. By the autumn of 1862, a local relief society had been formed to investigate them. The chaplains, too, gathered in the Y.M.C.A. rooms to protest against the manner of burial. Its casualness was explained by the fact that the Government had contracted with the undertaker to furnish shroud, coffin, vehicle, team and driver, and to have the grave dug and filled, all for the sum of $4.99 per dead soldier.

Although the scientifically planned pavilions were to expert eyes only partially successful experiments, and although at least two of them, on Judiciary and Armory Squares, were badly situated, these clean and airy buildings were popularly admired. It could not have occurred to anyone that a generation later their fine operating rooms would be considered abominable places. They were scrubbed and odorless. There was running water. Large mahogany boxes held the instruments; and the heavy center table was covered with a freshly wiped rubber cloth. But asepsis was not understood. The surgeon rolled up his sleeves, gave his knife a last flick on the sole of his boot, and the operation began. His exploring hands wore no gloves. The probe carried the infection deep into the torn tissues. If one of the sponges, employed to mop out the wound, happened to drop on the floor, it was squeezed in water and used at once; and, in any case, only a cursory washing had cleansed it of the blood and pus of the last operation. In threading the needle for the stitches, it was customary to point the silk by wetting it with saliva and rolling it with the fingers. Cold water was the sovereign dressing; bad wounds were repeatedly drenched to relieve the burning pain. Sometimes the wound was covered with wax; or ointments were applied on lint which had been scraped from cotton cloth by the patriotic but unsterile hands of women and children. Poultices of flaxseed meal or moistened bread were valued for promoting an abundant flow of pus, for all wounds were expected to suppurate. Blood poisoning, tetanus, secondary hemorrhage and gangrene were familiar visitors in the finest of the shining, whitewashed new pavilions of which Washington was so proud, and helped to fill the pine coffins which went jouncing in the dead carts to the cemetery.

Yet, to the wounded soldier, as to the vast fellowship of the sick, the hospitals of Washington seemed havens of comfort to which he had attained after a long delirium of agony and neglect. In his flesh, he bore the gashes of canister or grape, the rent of the splinter of shell, or the neat hole which marked the entrance of the shattering Minié ball. Frequently, he had undergone a crude amputation at the front; for, during the first years of the war, the field surgeons were ruthless in lopping off arms and legs, which piled in heaps, man-high, about their bloody tables. Before the soldier ever reached a hospital, infection was often far advanced.

Hungry, thirsty and untended, the wounded man at last reached a place where he was fed and washed and cared for. He could lie still on a bed, instead of the floor of a freight car, the deck of a ship, or a shelf in a jarring ambulance. In Washington, he found the stupor of morphine and laudanum, the deep oblivion of chloroform and ether.

The journey by road was the most painful mode of transportation. Yet ambulances in the armies of the United States were a humane innovation; they had never been used before this war. Two years before the outbreak, the Medical Bureau, in an uncharacteristic moment of expansiveness, had decided to fall in with the modern European idea of providing wagons expressly planned for carrying the sick and wounded. The design which met with the greatest favor, because it was light and intended for only one horse, consisted of a square box mounted on the axle of a single pair of wheels. This absurdly tilting rig made an acceptable pleasure carriage for junketing officers, but for more practical purposes it was useless. As frail as gigs, the two-wheeled ambulances cracked at the first strain, and their rocking motion was unbearable to suffering men. Everyone condemned them; but so many had been ordered that it was some time before they were entirely supplanted. The cumbrous four-wheeled ambulances, which required four horses to draw them, were the most comfortable that could be devised. When the wounded traveled by road, only the worst cases could find a place in them. For men with fresh amputations, with faces shot away, or with lead in breast or belly, was reserved the poor luxury of being bumped and jolted, dashed against each other and against the sides of the vehicle, as they hurtled over the rutted Virginia roads.

The journey by rail was mercifully shorter, if the cars were not side-tracked or delayed. When such accidents occurred, the men suffered bitterly. They were closely packed on the floor of the cars, sometimes on mattresses, sometimes on straw, sometimes on the bare boards. The boxcars were dark and noisome. On the open platforms of the flat cars, the sick and wounded were exposed to the blazing sun, or to wind and rain. Often there was a tedious wait for ambulances at the Maryland Avenue depot, the terminus of the trains which crossed the Long Bridge from Virginia. On a Saturday night in June of 1862, four hundred men arrived unexpectedly from Front Royal, where they had already endured much misery because of the disorganized medical service in the Valley. No ambulances came to meet them, and no hospital official appeared. After a fruitless effort to find the Surgeon General, the doctor in charge deserted them, and went off to eat and sleep. Aroused from their beds by the news of the soldiers' predicament, near-by residents of the Island hurried to the depot with hot drinks, food, stimulants and fresh bandages. Grace Church, Ryland Chapel and Potomac Hall were opened, and the wounded were carried in and cared for. Next morning, the congregation of Grace Church, coming to worship, took one look at the figures on the pew cushions, and dispersed to bring a fresh supply of food and drink. This was an exceptional case of neglect, and resulted in the doctor's dismissal from the service; but delays and maladjustments were unending. The citizens of the Seventh Ward repeatedly came to the rescue at the Maryland Avenue depot, and won high reputation for generosity and compassion.

By ship, as well as by train, the Island received the wreckage of the army in Virginia. Throughout June, hospital ships had come up from the Peninsula. In July, the wounded poured in a great tide from the battles of the Seven Days. Crowds gathered at the Sixth and Seventh Street wharves to see the men carried from the ships and loaded on the ambulances. At night, there were fewer spectators. In the flaring light of the torches, the workers of the Sanitary Commission moved about the sheds where coffee and beef soup steamed in cauldrons. The watchman's hoarse voice cried, "Steamers in sight!" Through the mist, loomed the white top-heavy shape of a great river boat. In silence, like a ghost ship, it moved alongside the wharf. There were no lights, no figures at the rails, no stir of arrival or greeting. The passengers lay on the decks, in the cabins and the saloons, even on the stairs and the gangway. The light of the relief workers' candles flickered on beseeching eyes, for these men were pitifully afraid of being stepped on. The business of transferring them to the ambulances went on quietly. There were a few groans. Now and then, a man screamed as he was lifted. For the most part, the passengers were as silent as their companions who lay with covered faces in the bow. The ghost ship moved on, to make way for another. All night, the ambulances rattled out to the hills beyond the city.

Often, when at long last he lay in a quiet bed, the wounded soldier opened his eyes on a strange apparition—the figure of a woman. The example of Miss Florence Nightingale in the Crimea had made seemly the presence of ladies in hospitals devoted to men. In June of 1861, Miss Dorothea L. Dix of Massachusetts had been appointed Superintendent of Women Nurses.

Miss Dix had for many years been known among her compatriots for a remarkable reason; she was a lady who was engaged in public work. She had devoted her life to lunatics, paupers and prisoners. By her revelations of the inhumane conditions in almshouses and jails, particularly in the treatment of the insane, she had brought about reforms, influenced legislation and enlarged the social consciousness of the nation. All this she had accomplished without sacrificing her woman's prerogative of timidity and refinement. Her health was extremely delicate, so were her sensibilities. She wanted to be, in the words of her biographer, "a voice of tender supplication"; and she shrank from the filth and depravity which her investigations forced her to witness, as she did from the vulgarity of the politicians through whom she was obliged to work. There was something formidable in the self-castigation of this fragile and consecrated virgin. She had a low, sweet voice. The knot of hair seemed too heavy for the gentle head set on a long neck. But her mouth and chin were firm, and her blue-gray eyes could dilate with holy indignation. Her fame as a humanitarian was national. Railway companies in all parts of the United States sent her passes. Express companies carried free the packages she forwarded to prisons, hospitals and insane asylums. Her reputation cast a final respectability over the position of female nurse; and on the news of her appointment applications flooded into Washington, while many young women came in person to offer their services.

The majority of these thousands of applicants met with a stern rejection. Miss Dix in 1861 was nearly sixty years old. She considered all persons under thirty disqualified for nursing. She requested the provost marshal, who had been receiving a number of aspiring ladies, to send her only those who were able to turn a full-grown man around in bed, and to do the most menial work. This, he remarked, thinned the ranks of the candidates very much. Good looks met with as little favor as youth. Miss Dix had a detestation of wasp waists. A kindly disposed woman said that, to win the superintendent's approval, an applicant must be "plain almost to repulsion in dress." Certainly, hospital wards were no place for crinolines. The nurses, in their perpendicular skirts, seemed to themselves laughably "angular" and "mediaeval" in appearance. But young and personable women showed that they were able to lay off their hoops, forget their vanity, and do good work in the hospitals; while a number of Miss Dix's elderly frights proved a disgrace to the service for which she had accepted them.

Even in June, 1861, when preparations were being made for a war of only two or three months, Miss Dix needed an organization. In her long career of public service, she had always worked alone, and she had no administrative ability. She was elderly, high-strung and inflexible. In a determination to do everything herself, she was soon involved in a maze of details. She interviewed all candidates, assigned them to their posts, visited hospitals, adjusted disputes, and ferreted out abuses, in addition to supervising the distribution of quantities of supplies. Her authority was ill-defined, and conflicted with that of surgeons. Most of them did not approve of the new-fangled idea of introducing female nurses into the military hospitals. Some conceded that women might have a place in the diet kitchen, the linen room or the laundry. Others would employ only black-robed, disciplined Sisters of Charity, who did not gossip or fuss, and were not given to writing home that the patients were maltreated, or that the surgeons drank and misappropriated the hospital stores.

It was not a time when men were accustomed to having their work interfered with by women. The pious and opinionated Miss Dix, sweeping like an avenging angel through the wards, was soon detested by the medical profession. Under the pressure of her multifarious and unsystematized duties, she grew overwrought, lost her self-control and involved herself in quarrels. In these she was often in the right; but she never showed the graces of tolerance and tact. Some of her feuds were carried to remarkable lengths. The surgeon in charge of the Mansion House Hospital in Alexandria was determined to have none of her nurses. Miss Dix assigned a woman to the Mansion House, instructing her to make no complaint, whatever happened. The hospital informed the nurse that there was no room for her. Miss Dix bade her stay where she had been placed. Resolutely ministering to the wounded by day, this obedient soul passed the nights on the floor between their cots until her presence was accepted. But hers was an unusual fortitude.

Miss Dix remained at her post without a leave of absence throughout the war. Many of the doctors snubbed her, and selected their own nurses, and they were supported by the Surgeon General's order giving them "control and direction" over the attendants of the cases under their charge. The nurses were never organized. One group continued to report to Miss Dix, others to various surgeons. Some gave their services without compensation, and some received the Government allowance of twelve dollars a month and food. There were women sent by State agencies and aid societies, and wives and sisters who came to visit soldiers and remained to care for them. Without training or discipline, they were all set adrift in the hospitals, to learn their duties as best they could. They were overburdened with heavy work because of the infirmity of the male attendants—convalescent soldiers, often too weak to be of any assistance. Women showed courage and initiative in entering this new field of activity, but most of them were of little use. The foolishly sentimental and the incompetent were weeded out. Many fell ill. Only a few heroic women were able to survive the hard work and the bad food, and to conciliate the surgeons and wardmasters.

In her inspection of the hospitals, Miss Dix had fixed her spinster's eye on perfection; but in those hastily devised institutions perfection was nowhere to be found. At the outbreak of war, no general hospital existed in the United States Army. Buildings, nurses, sick-diet kitchens, clothing, a readily available supply of medicines were all wanting. The entire system had to be created in the midst of war. On the Medical Bureau, as on the other War Department bureaus, the dead hand of seniority lay heavily. Its white-haired officers had not kept pace with the improvements made in European armies in the care of the sick and wounded. The Surgeon General's authority was confused by complicated relations with the Commissary Department, which had jurisdiction over food for the hospitals, and the Quartermaster's, which was in charge of ambulances and of hospital construction and equipment. The small medical staff of the regular Army was largely composed of elderly men, unfit for active service. It was necessary to recruit doctors by thousands; and, tying green sashes about their waists, practitioners of every degree of skill and training were transformed into army surgeons. In addition, large numbers of physicians—the so-called "contract surgeons"—were employed as uncommissioned officers in the hospital wards. Underpaid and without incentive to promotion, the contract surgeons were, with notable exceptions, an inefficient and ill-disciplined group. A corps of Medical Cadets was chiefly made up of students who volunteered as dressers and assistants. The duties of druggists, clerks and storekeepers were performed by men who enlisted as stewards.

In the spring of 1861, while everything connected with the army organization was in chaos, ladies' relief societies were devotedly working in every city and town and village in the country. Their boxes of clothing and food overloaded the freight cars on the Washington railroad. Sidetracked to make way for the movement of troops and army stores, these cars frequently yielded moldy cakes, broken glass, and garments stained by fermenting jellies. Even when they were not wasted, the supplies sent in those first days were usually unsuitable. Soldiers at the front were soon obliged to dispense with the luxurious outfits which loving hands had prepared for them; and the hot and cumbersome havelocks carpeted every camp and line of march with soiled white drilling. Even before they had learned that the havelocks were an outstanding example of misapplied energy, the women began to realize that their impulsive generosity should be guided by some information about the soldiers' needs.

In New York City, Dr. Henry Bellows, a popular Unitarian minister, suggested that the information should be sought in Washington; and, in company with three doctors, he made a trip to the capital in the second month of the war. Though their mission had received its impetus from the ladies, these gentlemen were only secondarily concerned with the delivery of comforts for the army. They had been deeply impressed by the appalling loss of life by disease during the Crimean War, and they were determined that the United States should profit by the experience which Great Britain had gained at such fearful cost. They wanted to form a scientific board which should have power to enforce sanitary regulations in the camps. Their hopes were soon dashed by contact with the antiquated machinery of the Medical Bureau. The meddlesome civilians were received with coldness, and discouraged by evasion and delay. But they were prominent gentlemen, and persistent, and at last they were grudgingly granted permission to act as an advisory body.

The office of president of the United States Sanitary Commission fell to Dr. Bellows, and he devoted his eloquence and zeal to the arduous task of raising funds for its work. The chief executive duties were performed by the general secretary of the commission at its central office in Washington; and presently, to fill this post, a frail little man arrived at the capital on crutches. Before the war, Frederick Law Olmsted had traveled widely in the South, and had written books describing social and economic conditions little comprehended in the free States. The vivid and tolerant pages of *A Journey in the Back Country* and *A Journey in the Seaboard Slave States* had given many Northerners their first accurate knowledge of slavery. Aside from his writing, Olmsted's main interest was in farming and horticulture. He was engaged in an unusual profession, that of landscape architect, and he had been made the architect and superintendent of New York City's Central Park, that project novel in America of a large pleasure ground designed for the use of the people. Olmsted had proved to be an able public servant who tenaciously developed the park in the face of unceasing opposition from corrupt politicians. His health had suffered from the strain; and a fall from his horse, while inspecting the work, had given him a badly broken thigh. Yet his leave of absence for patriotic duty brought him no rest for two laborious years. In July of 1861, he shared with a competent doctor the labor of inspecting twenty camps near Washington. That year, the servants often found him still at work when they came to set the breakfast table. In the spring of 1862, he went to the Peninsula to spend himself in untiring service. His wasted, autocratic face, with its feminine features and straggling mustache, burned with the same harsh flame of consecration that lighted the features of Miss Dix. But Olmsted had a genius for organization; and, backed by the gentlemen of his board, he developed the Sanitary Commission into an immense and powerful agency for the relief of suffering among the soldiers.

Theirs were the plans for the new pavilion hospitals; theirs, the monographs which acquainted country practitioners in green sashes with hygiene and vaccination, with the treatment of dysentery and malaria and venereal diseases. They forced the necessity for camp sanitation on the Government's attention. Their barrels of potatoes and onions abated scurvy in many regiments. They equipped and staffed the hospital ships; and, later, built hospital cars, with swinging litters, kitchens and dispensaries.

For all this great work, however, the Sanitary Commission might have remained little known to the general public, had it not been for the secondary phase of its activities—the distribution of supplies. By the sheer force of their patriotic benevolence, the ladies overwhelmed the scientific preoccupations of Dr. Bellows and Mr. Olmsted and their associates. Everywhere the war was bringing women out of the seclusion of domestic life. Timid ones grew bold as lions. Invalids arose from their sofas. To the astonishment of men, they were able to draft constitutions and bylaws, to serve on committees and preside at meetings; even to raise and handle money. From thousands of aid societies in all parts of the Union, a steady stream of stores flowed to the Sanitary Commission. Enriched by large donations, it established enormous storehouses, and administered them efficiently. It organized a relief service for hospitals and camps, and installed its own refreshment saloons. Trained agents, in charge of the commission's wagonloads of supplies, moved with every army. The name, which had been derived from an interest in preventive hygiene, became a household word; and everything sent to the soldiers, from currant wine to canton flannel drawers, went by the name of "sanitary stores."

As the first volunteers marched from the Washington depot, the regiments spilled out ailing and exhausted men. Unless they were desperately ill, they could find no room in the few beds provided by the Government, or the emergency hospitals established by the regiments; and many lay in cars and streets, dependent on the random charity of the passers-by. After the rout of First Bull Run, the number of these derelicts was enormously multiplied; and, for the purpose of giving them food and shelter, the Government allotted to the Sanitary Commission a part of an old cane factory near the depot. This was the beginning of a new field of the commission's work. From the cane factory on North Capitol Street grew the rest house known as the Soldiers' Home. It was a collection of frame structures, enclosed by a picket fence, with the name of the Sanitary Commission flapping on an awning over the entrance. Between the buildings on sunny days, pale soldiers were to be seen lounging against the walls, resting on their crutches or sitting in wooden chairs. It was the first of five lodges established in Washington, in addition to two at Alexandria— one at the depot, and one in the near-by convalescent camp, known to the soldiers as Camp Misery. They served food to the wounded at wharves and depots, gave lodging to their mothers, wives and children, and cared for convalescents who were discharged from the hospitals. Forty rest houses were operated by the commission at various points during the war.

At the outset, there had been no pretense that a sufficiency of any sort of supplies existed in Washington. The surgeons had been so destitute of every necessity that the Sanitary Commission had undertaken to supplement the Government's hospital stores, and also to employ nurses, dressers, laundresses and barbers, until the Medical Bureau should have time to function properly. There were many cases of dysentery, diarrhea and typhoid in the unsanitary camps. The sick lists were lengthened by the frequent acceptance of the unfit for service—men with long-standing disabilities of hernia or consumption. Country boys had little resistance to the epidemics of measles, mumps and smallpox which broke out in the first summer of the war, and autumn ushered in the season of malaria in Washington.

As the months passed, the other War Department bureaus were active, and, in spite of fraud and confusion, the army was in some fashion being fed and clothed and armed. The Medical Bureau remained somnolent. Even for the routine medical work of the camps, no efficient allowance was made. In spite of the smallpox epidemic, the Government ran short of vaccine virus in the autumn, and the Sanitary Commission provided for the vaccination of over twenty thousand men. Although a battle was momentarily expected to take place near Washington in the fall of 1861, the Medical Bureau refused to prepare for it, and informed the protesting Sanitary Commission that it would be time enough to order hospital supplies after the battle had occurred. When a few wounded were brought to the capital after a skirmish in September, the Medical Bureau was obliged to call on the commission for lint and bandages. As late as November, there was no large reserve of hospital stores in the capital. If Ball's Bluff had been followed by a general action on the Potomac, it would have been impossible to care for the wounded.

Indignant at being forced to continue the legitimate work of the Government, Mr. Olmsted and the other members of the commission determined that the Medical Bureau must be reformed. These gentlemen became vigorous lobbyists, and the medical bill which they assisted in preparing was passed by Congress in the spring of 1862—

too late to prevent the frightful neglect of the wounded in the campaigns of that season.

Among the bill's provisions was the appointment of a Surgeon General on the ground of ability, rather than seniority. The incumbent, Dr. Clement A. Finley, placed in office in 1861, was a gentleman of the old school, courteous and fossilized. In his youth, he had been known as the handsomest man in the Army, and he still presented a very fine appearance, with his rosy cheeks, short white hair and spruce beard and mustaches. Although he had been obliged to yield the point, Dr. Finley was opposed to female nurses for soldiers. In Philadelphia, he had an old-maid niece called Martha, a female who tried her hand at writing stories. Before he died, he would see Martha Finley make a success with her *Elsie Dinsmore* books.

Mr. Stanton had had a furious quarrel with Finley over Dr. John Neill, a prominent Philadelphia physician whom the Surgeon General had placed in charge of the military hospitals in that city. The Secretary of War had received a letter attacking Neill, and referred it to Finley, who forwarded it to his friend. Neill instituted a libel suit against his detractor, and Stanton's vengeance fell summarily on the Surgeon General. Packing Dr. Finley off to Boston, he kept him at a distance until the old gentleman asked to be retired.

For some time, the Sanitary Commission had been urging the appointment of Dr. William Alexander Hammond, an assistant surgeon who had attracted attention by his successful work in organizing hospitals and sanitary stations. On Finley's resignation, the President was bombarded with petitions from doctors in favor of Hammond, and in late April, 1862, he was made Surgeon General.

Hammond was big and dark and powerful. A beard and mustache covered the lower part of his heavy, intelligent face. He had a vibrant, masculine voice. His manner was authoritative. With his strong physique and personality, he seemed to fill every room he entered. It was not hard to believe that he was able to hypnotize.

He was only thirty-four years old, but he had every qualification for his post. His professional reputation was high; he had had ten years of Army experience; and he had made a special study of modern hospital construction and management. Into the stultified Medical Bureau, he brought vitality and imagination. His work, however, was embarrassed by the antagonism of the senior officers of the staff whom he had superseded. A still more serious obstacle to achievement was the enmity which speedily developed between him and Mr. Stanton. Dr. Hammond had been the choice of the Sanitary Commission, not the War Secretary. His positive nature clashed with Stanton's, and the resultant controversies blocked many of Hammond's projects. Though the Secretary hampered the Surgeon General, he did not find it easy to be rid of him. Hammond's influence was such that he could not be sent off to cool his heels in Boston, and Stanton was obliged to bide his time.

One of the reforms which Hammond was prevented from making was the creation of an ambulance corps controlled by the medical department of the army. The quartermasters' authority over the ambulances had worked much hardship on the battlefield. The teamsters were unsuitable attendants for the wounded, and often refused to help them. The army had no trained corps of stretcher-bearers. Early in the war, this duty was performed by the members of the regimental bands, supplemented by shirking soldiers who made the assistance of their fallen comrades an excuse for moving to the rear. The Surgeon General's plans for remedying these notorious abuses aroused no enthusiasm in Stanton. Hammond pressed the matter before Second Bull Run, but Halleck opposed any reorganization. Washington at that time was abundantly stocked with everything that hospitals needed—medicines, anesthetics, surgical supplies, good beds. The wards were cleared of convalescents, who were sent to Northern cities, each with a comfortable mattress. Thirty miles away, nearly two thousand wounded lay from Saturday until Wednesday on the field, and many died of starvation and neglect. The want of food was partly caused by the enemy's capture of the first wagon train of provisions which Hammond sent out, and medical stores had also been cut off from the front by rebel raids. The village of Centreville was a scene of horror, most of its houses appropriated for hospitals, some surgeons operating in the streets. There was no chloroform at Centreville, and a shortage of stimulants, tourniquets, splints and dressings.

Hammond could not control the mischances of war, but he was indignant that he was powerless to transport the wounded to Washington. Surgeons were in despair at the conduct of the drunken and insubordinate teamsters, who stole blankets and commissary stores, and loaded the ambulances with forage, camp kettles and personal baggage. Single trips had been made by hundreds of ambulances, omnibuses and hacks, loaded with "pallid passengers"; but there was no proper organization to return these vehicles to the field to bring in the men who remained. Hammond wrote the War Secretary a letter which burned with protest at the frightful disorder, and again urged the formation of an ambulance corps under the direction of the medical department. His letter was returned with a notation by Halleck, reiterating his disapproval on the ground that the army trains were already too large.

Nevertheless, an order for just such an ambulance corps as Hammond desired had already been issued in the Army of the Potomac. Immediately after the Seven Days, Dr. Jonathan Letterman had taken up his duties as the new medical director of that army. He was a small, slight, taciturn man, with the earnest face of a student. Although he was charged with the medical department of a great army, his rank was only that of major; for, until very late in the war, surgeons did not rank as high as the heads of the other staff departments. With General McClellan's backing, this quiet little man rehabilitated the service of the wounded in the Army of the Potomac. His work, barely instituted, was disastrously interrupted during Pope's campaign. At Antietam, the ambulance corps began to demonstrate its value. The hospitals and dressing stations still remained inefficient, and medical and surgical supplies were deplorably lacking at the front. Surgeon Letterman immediately set to work to reorganize these branches of the medical service. In the following spring and summer, his program proved so effective that it was eventually adopted throughout the armies of the Union. The field medical service of the Russian army in 1870 was modeled on Letterman's plan, which forms the basis of the systems used by all modern armies.

At Antietam, the Sanitary Commission first developed its system of relief on the battlefield. The reforms in the army medical department never made civilian assistance superfluous in alleviating the sufferings of the wounded; and to the end of the war the Sanitary Commission continued to labor at the front, as well as in hospitals and camps. Another group, the United States Christian Commission, also went with supplies to Antietam. This organization was an outgrowth of the Y.M.C.A. It had been formed in New York City in the autumn of 1861 at the suggestion of Mr. Vincent Colyer, a pious artist who, as representative of the New York Y.M.C.A., had gone to Washington after First Bull Run to distribute Bibles, tracts and hymnbooks to the soldiers. The aims of the Christian Commission were religious and moral. The society worked in co-operation with army and navy chaplains, to whom Mr. Colyer subscribed himself "Your brother in the Lord." The Christian delegates held services in the camps, and knelt in prayer beside the dying in the hospitals. In addition to their spiritual ministrations, however, they gave comfort to the body as well; and especially in the latter part of the war, when its relief organization was fully developed and large sums of money were raised by the women of the various religious denominations, the Christian Commission did notable work in supplying the Union forces with food, clothing and hospital stores.

Before either of these large organizations had found means of reaching the front, they had been anticipated by a solitary little maiden lady—Miss Clara Barton, who had singlehanded succeeded in forcing her way through official red tape and military restrictions. The April evening of 1861, when she had sprung forward at the Washington depot to dress the wounds of the Sixth Massachusetts with handkerchiefs, had marked a turning point in a hitherto obscure and unrewarded life. The next day she had spread a feast before the Massachusetts soldiers in the Senate Chamber. Through her, they received many small necessities—thread, needles, buttons, towels, handkerchiefs and salves. Standing before them all at the Vice-President's desk, Miss Barton read them the news from home, for somehow, in those days of the capital's isolation, she had secured a copy of the *Worcester Spy*, only two days old. The soldiers saw a small, prim, nervous lady of forty, with brown eyes and hair, a prominent nose and a wide mouth. Miss Barton had many temperamental resemblances to Miss Dix. She, too, was timid, high-strung and willful; but, unlike the other spinster from Massachusetts, she had no national reputation and no background of public service. From school teaching, she had gone to the job of Patent Office clerk at a salary of fourteen hundred dollars a year. It was unusual for a female to be employed by the Government, particularly at a wage which equalled that of a man, but Miss Barton was well qualified for the work by her fine, copperplate handwriting. Although she was morbidly sensitive and shy, suffered agonies of self-consciousness and was subject to nervous breakdowns, the soldiers in the Senate Chamber were only the first of many audiences she would address in a long career as an eloquent and dramatic public speaker.

After First Bull Run, she advertised in the *Spy* for provisions for the wounded. As quantities of boxes were shipped to her from Massachusetts, she established her own distributing agency; but she was not satified with the role of dispensing supplies. In the hospitals and on the wharves, she heard heartbreaking stories of the neglect which had preceded the soldiers' arrival in Washington. Miss Barton began to badger the Surgeon General's office for permission to carry her supplies to the front. In some manner, she secured an authorization from Hammond, who asked the Assistant Quartermaster General, Colonel Daniel H. Rucker, to give her every facility for taking supplies to the sick. Her eloquent plea touched Rucker's heart. He arranged for transportation by boat and train, and helped her with the complicated business of obtaining the various passes necessary to permit her to travel with her stores and a lady companion through the army lines between Washington and Fredericksburg. On a Sunday morning in early August of 1862, Miss Barton, in a plain black print skirt and jacket, climbed over the wheel of an army wagon in full view of the Washington churchgoers; plumped herself down beside the Negro driver, and drove off to take a Government transport for the camps near Aquia Creek. A few days later, she was ministering to the wounded of Banks's corps on the battlefield of Slaughter Mountain.

Clara Barton was a shining exception to the useless civilians who went out from the capital to tend the wounded of Second Bull Run. Few timid women have spent such a week end as that she passed near Fairfax Station. The disgruntled male nurses, drunken and otherwise, who reached that point on the Sunday morning after the battle, might have found plenty of opportunity to be of service on a hillside near the little depot. All day, wagonloads of wounded arrived from the battlefield. The men were laid among the trees on the ground, where hay had been scattered to make an immense bed. That night, in the mist and darkness, Miss Barton, with a little band of helpers, prepared to feed the crowd. She had almost no utensils but she had many boxes of preserves; and as jam jars and jelly tumblers were emptied, she filled them again and again with soup or coffee or bread soaked in wine. Monday brought many wounded who had lain three days without food. To insure that none should be loaded on the cars without receiving nourishment, Clara Barton personally fed that day's arrivals in the wagons, climbing from wheel to brake. By evening, her supplies were almost gone. As the wounded still came in, she stirred the leftovers together; and, in the pouring rain, amid the uproar of the thunder and the artillery at Chantilly, the famished men greedily ate a concoction of hard crackers pounded into crumbs and mixed with wine, whisky, brown sugar and water.

Informed by this experience, Miss Barton made thorough preparation for the next battle. An army wagon, drawn by a string of frisky mules, was assigned to her by the Quartermaster's Department. Her own baggage was contained in a handkerchief, but the wagon bulged with stores. She had even had the forethought to bring lanterns, so that the surgeons could see to work at night. In the middle of September, a solitary woman in the wagon train of an advancing army, she journeyed over the hills of Maryland, slicing bread and passing it out to the stragglers along the road. Progress was slow; and, pushing on at night while the drivers of the other wagons slept, this indomitable lady reached the artillery by morning, and followed the cannon to Antietam Creek.

The work she did on that field caused the Quartermaster's Department to capitulate to her completely. When the Army of the Potomac advanced in Virginia, Clara Barton accompanied the Ninth Corps with her own train of four heavily laden wagons and an ambulance. She treated her rough teamsters like gentlemen, and they became her devoted servants. This shy little lady had overridden the regulations of the army and the conventions of society. Hardship and danger had cast out all her nervous fears; and, in the giddy elation of service and self-sacrifice, she bumped triumphantly to Warrenton and Fredericksburg.

In November, as the news of General McClellan's removal filtered into Washington and began to be believed, there was hot controversy in the streets and the halls of the hotels. One man thought that the change should have taken place long ago—they might now hope to finish the war "some time within the present century." A bystander retorted that "the war would be 'finished' with a vengeance now, à la Pope"; and that McClellan should be kept within call, in case of a Bull Run Number 3. A third man declared that Burnside had caution, as well as energy, and the army would be safe in his hands. A fourth said that Burnside was not to be considered— Hooker was the coming man. Another gave the opinion that Hooker would do well, but he was silenced by an informed gentleman who vowed that Hooker was brave and able, but as vain as a peacock—in fact, he was Pope all over again in his "habit of self-laudation and unprofessional depreciation of his superiors." A wager was laid that, with Hooker in command, the Confederate army would be in Washington within a month. A man wanted to bet on drastic results—the Confederates in the capital or the Federals in Richmond—for Hooker would either "make a spoon or spoil a horn." There was a rumor that Frémont was to be drawn from a richly deserved obscurity, and placed in command of the Army of the Potomac. The *Star* remarked that the capital's secesh were in high glee over this last report.

The army, which had been advancing, was now halted stockstill near Warrenton. Hooker had recovered from his wound, and gone to the front; but the capital and the Chase interests soon learned that it was Burnside who was the coming man, after all. Presently, a presage of activity, the sick began to come up from Warrenton on the cars. The army was marching toward the Rappahannock. On November 18, the *Star* was confident that General Burnside had crossed the river and made his headquarters in Fredericksburg, and would take Richmond in less than ten days. On November 21, that newspaper admitted that the rebels still occupied Fredericksburg; Lee's army was firmly entrenched on the heights around the city. On the twenty-fifth, the *Star* conceded that the rebels apparently designed making serious resistance to the Federal army's crossing the Rappahannock.

Washington was humming with talk of the fearful conditions in Camp Misery near Alexandria—the huge, filthy catchall for the odds and ends of the army. With the onset of cold weather, the mortality had become a scandal, and the Sanitary Commission went to the rescue with hospital tents and woolen shirts. The customary report of Stonewall Jackson's proximity briefly agitated the more nervous inhabitants; but, for the most part, the shortening days found the capital going briskly about its business. Cargoes of hay, potatoes, lumber, coal and ice cumbered the docks and filled the multiplying storehouses. There was a constant arrival and departure of transports and freight boats, plying between Washington and the army base of supplies at Aquia Creek. The war was developing the settlement on the Island into a busy and prosperous section. Smiling faces appeared at every door and window on South Seventh Street, and boys ran shouting beside the cars, as the directors of the city railway formally opened the new line to the wharves.

Wadsworth revoked his order closing the drinking places, and the rejoicing citizens proclaimed him "an agreeable and liberal gentleman," instead of "a horrible ogre." Gladness returned to the gloomy hotels, and Gautier, Wormley, Hammack and Klotz were jubilant. Ladies bustled to the hospitals with hampers of good things for the soldiers' Thanksgiving dinners, and the wagons of the express companies were loaded with turkeys and chickens from the North. The wounded had been removed from the Capitol. The interior had been cleaned and renovated. The old central building shone with fresh white paint. Near the statue of Armed Freedom, surrounded with children squabbling over their mud pies, a derrick was erected to raise the immense columns into place on the wings. Up the rough wooden steps stamped the returning legislators, with perversity in their hearts.

The officers of the Army of the Potomac had been peremptorily ordered to rejoin their commands, but the city was still filled with shoulder straps. There were the officers of the large force left for the protection of Washington under the command of General Heintzelman, who had succeeded General Banks in command of the defenses. Staff officers were legion, as were those of the Commissary and Quartermaster's Departments. There were paroled prisoners and members of courts-martial, convalescents and a multitude of surgeons. Handsome Fitz-John Porter was there, to learn the verdict that would wreck his career. Irvin McDowell had come to hear his name traduced at the court of inquiry which he had demanded. Charles P. Stone, with his prison-bleached face, still went looking for justice.

On Saturday, December 13, the rumbling rumors from Fredericksburg culminated in the report of a heavy engagement. The story unfolded slowly. At first, the *Star* again stated that the Federals had crossed the river and occupied the city. On Sunday, there was an extra, which told that there had been a close and desperate battle, in which forces under General Franklin had been opposed by superior numbers of the enemy. The War Department gave out nothing. The Secretary of the Navy heard only a rumor that the Federal troops had done well, and that Burnside and the other generals were in good spirits. The astute old Yankee was not satisfied by these vague reassurances. "When I get nothing clear and explicit at the War Department," Welles wrote in his diary, "I have my apprehensions. . . . Adverse tidings are suppressed with a deal of fuss and mystery, a shuffling over of papers and maps, and a far-reaching vacant gaze."

The military censorship was suppressing the news of the losses at Fredericksburg; but the War Department was actually uninformed of the outcome of the engagement. From early morning until night, the President sat in suspense in the telegraph office. Burnside, with every one of his generals opposed to him, wanted to renew the assault. The uncertainty at the War Department lasted until the early hours of Tuesday morning.

The border town of Washington had access to firsthand information. On Sunday night, a steamer-load of officers and soldiers arrived from Aquia Creek—men who had been slightly wounded in the battle, who were able to walk, who were able to tell of the hopeless courage and the slaughter of the repeated assaults which Burnside had ordered on the Fredericksburg fortifications. That same evening, the correspondent, Henry Villard, reached Washington from the front. The censor refused to pass his dispatch to the *New York Tribune,* which Villard then represented. He sent it off by messenger on the night train, but the *Tribune,* in advance of confirmation, was afraid to print the full story, which told of the blundering command and the perilous situation of the army. Villard's beat was wasted—a fate which frequently overtook early reports of bad news during the war. When his story was written, Villard went into Willard's to get some supper, and, meeting Senator Henry Wilson, told him that Burnside was defeated. Wilson hurried to the White House. A little before ten o'clock, he came to the *Tribune* office to take Villard to the President. Still in his soiled campaign clothes, the young correspondent answered Lincoln's anxious questions. He spoke of disaster to the army, if the attack were renewed. "I hope it is not so bad as all that," the President said with a sad smile. Senator Wilson was pleased that Villard had spoken so frankly, and, though his report did not cause the Government to take action, Villard felt proud that he had performed a patriotic duty.

From the accounts of eyewitnesses, the Washington newspapers on Monday began to rumor defeat and fearful losses. On Tuesday, the whole Union learned that the battle of Fredericksburg had been a costly proof of Burnside's incapacity for high command. More than twelve thousand Federal soldiers had been killed and wounded, and the Army of the Potomac had staggered back across the Rappahannock in retreat.

The Senate met, but had no heart to do business, and adjourned.

The Republicans gathered in caucus, to air, apart from the Democrats, their criticisms of Lincoln and his Cabinet. At the wharves, the stir of trade ceased, as out of the Potomac mist moved the white and silent transports. Thousand after thousand, men littered the landings, like spoiled freight. First, the lesser injuries arrived; then, the more serious; at length, the frightful cases, the thigh amputations and the belly wounds.

At dawn, in the hospital lodged in the unsavory old Union Hotel in Georgetown, Miss Louisa M. Alcott of Concord, Massachusetts, was aroused by a thundering knock. "They've come! they've come! hurry up, ladies—you're wanted." From the window, she saw forty wagons like market carts lining the dusky street. It was the moment for which, in her three days' experience as an army nurse, she had longed. She had a romantic taste for heroism and "ghastliness"; and under her stout bodice beat a rebellious heart that longed for life and freedom. But, looking down at the sights before the hotel door, she wished for a moment that she were safe at home in Concord again.

In the damp corridors, the smell of wounds began to mingle with the odors of the kitchens, the washrooms and the stables. Some of the arriving guests stumbled in on rude crutches, while others were carried in men's arms or on stretchers. They sat along the wall or lay on the floor of the main hall of the hotel, until the formalities of registration were accomplished and they were assigned to beds. Through coal hods, water pails, and teapots, Miss Alcott made her way downstairs, to her post in Ward Number One. The ancient label, "Ballroom," was fastened on the door.

Forty beds had been prepared in that room. On many of them, men were lying in their dirty clothes. "Round the great stove was gathered the dreariest group I ever saw—ragged, gaunt and pale, mud to the knees, with bloody bandages untouched since put on days before; many bundled up in blankets, coats being lost or useless; and all wearing that disheartened look which proclaimed defeat, more plainly than any telegram of the Burnside blunder." So Louisa Alcott took in the scene, as a nurse briskly put into her hands a basin and sponge, towels and a block of brown soap. It dawned on Louisa that she was expected to wash these soldiers. She was flabbergasted, but she was an intrepid woman, and could take a joke on herself. "I drowned my scruples in my wash-bowl," she wrote, "clutched my soap manfully, and, assuming a business-like air, made a dab at the first dirty specimen I saw. . . ." He was old and Irish, and soon they were both laughing. Louisa scrubbed with a good will after that: faces and necks and ears, breasts and shoulders and feet. The male attendants finished them off, and put them into bed.

The trays of bread, meat, soup and coffee were carried in. There was plenty of everything; for the matron was a motherly woman, and a shortage of food was not among this hospital's deficiencies. When the dishes were cleared away, the dressings began. The surgeon whom Miss Alcott assisted was an expert. "He had served in the Crimea, and seemed to regard a dilapidated body very much as I should have regarded a damaged garment; and, turning up his cuffs, whipped out a very unpleasant looking housewife, cutting, sawing, patching and piecing, with the enthusiasm of an accomplished surgical seam-stress. . . ." The men, revived by rest and food, had begun to talk, but now the ballroom grew quiet. Amputations had been put off until the following day, and no ether was thought necessary. As the sur-geons probed and sliced, sweat stood on the men's foreheads and the beds shook with their agony. One or two Irishmen cursed, or "ordered the Virgin to stand by them." For the most part, the silence was broken only by the doctors' low requests for roller bandages, instru-ments or plaster.

Louisa Alcott had begun to be known as a writer of tales and poems. She had had no training as a nurse and these were the first wounds she had ever seen; but she possessed the qualifications which found favor with Miss Dix. She was thirty, strong and plain—a big, bashful woman, with dark eyes, and a yard and a half of brown hair bundled up in braids at the back of her head. Like the other inex-perienced nurses, she was given to shedding tears, smoothing brows, singing lullabies and laying nosegays on pillows. But, if she was sentimental, she was also very jolly. There was something comical about "topsey-turvey Louisa," armed with a bottle of lavender water, with which to besprinkle herself and the premises in a detestation of bad smells. She was the enemy of blue devils. She joked and gossiped, played games and recited bits from Dickens. Soon she was promoted to the post of night nurse, in charge of her ward in the lonely hours after the ringing of the nine o'clock bell, when the gas was turned low and the day nurses went off duty.

Nursing the soldiers was Miss Alcott's great adventure. All night, she hovered "like a massive cherubim, in a red rigolette, over the slumbering sons of man." Sometimes, hurried steps sounded overhead. Surgeons passed up, or men carried down a stretcher, whose occupant's face was covered. Outside, the cold moonlight fell on the silent figures of the sentinels.

In this strange world where men clung to her for help and comfort, Louisa felt her generous heart expanding with affection for them all. Some she even kissed good-by—"well, why not?"—when they went off to regiment or convalescent camp. She noticed that John, a tall, noble-looking blacksmith, with a hole in his lung, used to watch her with a satisfied expression in his fine eyes. Sometimes, as she tidied the table by his bed, she felt him touch her gown. On the night that John was dying, she sat by his bed, holding his hand. Next morning, the watchman had to help her unlock the rigid fingers.

Miss Alcott cherished dreams of going to the front. She might have had a career like that of Clara Barton, who had crossed the swaying pontoon bridge to Fredericksburg under fire, and had a piece of her skirt shot away, as she stepped down. But in January, Louisa fell ill. Nights of wandering from the overheated ward to the freezing halls had given her a bad cough. The sparse vegetarian fare on which Bronson Alcott had nurtured his children had been poor preparation for a diet of fried army beef. She had been little more than a month in the Union Hotel Hospital when they sent for her father. Miss Dix overwhelmed her with gifts: a basket full of bottles of wine, tea, medicine and cologne; a blanket and pillow; a fan and a Testament. Burning with fever, her great adventure over, Louisa suffered Bronson Alcott to lead her back to Concord. In the delirium of typhoid, she fancied that she had married a stout, handsome Spaniard in black velvet, with very soft hands.

After Fredericksburg, Burnside came to Washington in anguish of mind. He took on himself the full blame for his ill-judged attack; yet the responsibility fell heavily on the administration. Many believed that Burnside was a scapegoat, that his manly and disarming attitude had been assumed to protect the Government. The want of faith which had long been in evidence in Washington had crept insidiously throughout the country. In State after State, the autumn elections of 1862 had gone against the Republicans. The new disaster brought the administration, not only a fear of foreign intervention, but a dread that the Union was losing heart. The Cabinet appeared to be crumbling, as the press announced that Seward and Chase had both resigned.

The crisis was averted, and the two eminent secretaries still sat in the Cabinet meetings. Caleb B. Smith betook himself home to Indiana, attracting little attention by exchanging the post of Secretary of the Interior for that of judge of the circuit court. Before leaving Washington, Mrs. Smith, "a truly philanthropic lady," took charge of organizing the Christmas dinners for the soldiers in the hospitals. Evergreens hung in the wards, and a long train of ambulances and wagons was loaded with the provisions donated by Mrs. Lincoln.

The burden of gloom and suffering dulled the holiday season. The only diversion was the fire at Ford's Athenaeum on Tenth Street. Flaming high in a stormy sky, the conflagration illuminated the city. A gentleman claimed that he had read a newspaper on Capitol Hill by the light. Stanton had provided Washington with its first steam fire engine, with a crew of experienced men, but it bogged in the mud at the Avenue and Thirteenth Street, and the theatre burned to ruins. Fear of a raid of Jeb Stuart's cavalry rose and died with the dying year; and the eggnogs of 1863 were swallowed with little merriment.

Burnside had come again to Washington, in consternation at a telegram from the President, advising him that there was a good reason for him not to order a movement without advising the Government. Recently, two brigadiers of the Army of the Potomac had obtained an interview with Lincoln—John Newton, a loyal Army officer from Virginia, who had worked on the fortifications, and John Cochrane, a former New York congressman. They had alarmed the President with stories of the demoralization of the troops. Lincoln repeated their report to Burnside, without mentioning the names of the two brigadiers. Burnside said that they should have been dismissed from the service, and Halleck agreed with him. Opposed by all his general officers in his desire to make another advance, convinced that neither Stanton nor Halleck had the confidence of the army or the country, Burnside was ready to resign. The command of the Army of the Potomac had unbalanced him, as well as McClellan, but Burnside's obsession took the form, not of procrastinating and blaming the Government, but of planning to move his army at all hazards. At Fredericksburg, he had ordered Hooker, over that officer's protests, to continue useless and costly assaults. Franklin was coming to the conclusion that Burnside was losing his mind.

The official New Year's festivities at the White House took place in the midst of grave and painful perplexity. At noon, after the official calls, the gates were flung open, and the scuffle of the public reception began. In struggling installments, the crowd was admitted to the mansion, whose elegant carpets had been covered to protect them from the mud. In the midst of the melee in the Blue Room, Lincoln stood serene, but his eyes often looked over the heads of the greeters, as though they were fixed on something far away. He had a proclamation to sign, after the crowd was gone.

Vainly, the President tried to induce Halleck to go to Burnside's headquarters at Falmouth on the Rappahannock, to investigate and give the deciding judgment. Halleck was miffed at the tone of Lincoln's letter, which implied that he had failed in the discharge of his duties. He instantly offered to resign. The President withdrew the letter. Nothing was decided, and Burnside went back to his mutinous army at Falmouth. The soldiers, since Fredericksburg, had lost all confidence in their commander, and believed him marked for failure in any undertaking.

The *Monitor* floundered, and went down off Hatteras. From the Army of the Cumberland came word of a severe engagement at Murfreesboro', Tennessee. The Federal commander, General William S. Rosecrans, a former Army lieutenant of engineers who had won reputation in the fighting in the West, claimed a victory and was hailed as a hero; but the tale of dead and wounded silenced the brief clamor of rejoicing. The port of Galveston, which had been taken by the Federals, was recaptured by Confederate forces. Soon from the Mississippi the disheartening news was heard that Grant's expedition against Vicksburg had failed.

McClellan arrived in Washington to give testimony before the Fitz-John Porter court-martial. Such crowds turned out to see him that it was difficult for him to pass from the courtroom to his hotel. The most popular song in the capital was "McClellan Again at the Head of his Men." When it was sung in the music halls, every blue-coat in the audience sprang to his feet, with three times three and a tiger.

Desertions in the Army of the Potomac occurred at the rate of about two hundred a day. Many resulted from loss of morale and discontent over the Government's delay in paying the troops. Other deserters belonged to a new class of soldiers, who had never had any morale to lose—the bounty jumpers, who had enlisted with the in-

tention of seizing the first opportunity to run away, after pocketing
the large State and local bonuses. In the face of all the disaffection,
Burnside stubbornly persisted in a plan he had formed to cross the
Rappahannock a few miles below Fredericksburg. The march began
in a deluge of rain. The army—men, guns, wagons—stuck fast in the
glutinous mud; and, as it struggled back into camp, Burnside's reputation petered out to the sound of the nation's bitter laughter. In agitation, Burnside journeyed again to Washington, with his resignation
in his pocket. As an alternative, he had prepared an order dismissing
the antagonistic generals of his command. It was a sweeping list—
Hooker, Franklin, Newton, Cochrane, Baldy Smith, Sturgis and
others. Lincoln accepted Burnside's resignation. Late in January, the
Chase interests had their way, and Hooker was placed in command
of the Army of the Potomac. Hooker had been one of Burnside's
loudest critics, and he had voiced hostility to the Government, too, and
talked of military dictatorship.

Two competent generals, outranking Hooker, were relieved.
Washington would not see again the good old soldier, Edwin Sumner.
He died on his way to take command of the Department of Missouri.
McClellan's friend, Franklin, whom Burnside accused of disobedience
of orders at Fredericksburg, was severely censured by the Committee
on the Conduct of the War. After months of waiting, Franklin would
return to active service on the Southern coast, but he would not again
receive a command commensurate with his abilities.

While the blond war god, Hooker, rode out on his milk-white
horse, and the heart of the Union rose again with the rise of a new
hero, a big, blowzy fellow in a gray suit was beginning to be known
in the streets and the hospital wards of Washington. He had been
one of a crowd of anxious people who rushed to the capital after
Fredericksburg, as after every great battle of the Army of the Potomac.
His brother, an officer in the Fifty-first New York, had been wounded,
and he was seeking word of him. After a reassuring visit to Falmouth,
he returned to linger in Washington, looking for an office. His life
had given him a varied experience, though he had not made much
of a success of anything. He had been a carpenter, a printer and a
schoolteacher, as well as a newspaper editor and contributor. He had
also published a thin, quarto volume of unconventional verses, called
Leaves of Grass. It had not sold well, and was said to be vulgar.

Even in the heterogeneous company of the capital, Walt Whitman had no counterpart. His scarlet face, bushy beard and wide-brimmed sombrero gave him a delusively robust and rural aspect which caused one politician to tell him that he looked like an old Southern planter. Whitman's home was in Brooklyn, and he loved the life of cities. Though he was stout and gray and slow-moving, with opaque, heavy-lidded eyes, he was only forty-three years old. A friend compared him to "some great mechanic, or stevedore, or seaman, or grand laborer of one kind or another . . ." The word *grand,* with its hint of apotheosis, betrays that the resemblance is not to be taken quite literally. In his youth, Walt had been a dandy. His rough garments were carefully selected. He never wore a tie; but his spotless shirt, with its open collar was Byronic rather than proletarian. There was a queer daintiness about this big, bluff man. He looked as though he had just taken a bath. He wore a flower or a green sprig in the lapel of his coat. His flesh was soft and rosy, like a woman's.

Whitman had letters to important personages, but he did not find it easy to get a clerkship. While he waited, he lived in a miserable room in a tenement across from the Chase mansion, earning a little money by "hacking on the press," and by copying in the Paymaster General's office for a couple of hours each day. On the corner, by the big, five-story house at Fifteenth and F Streets, pale and tattered soldiers were always waiting. The paymaster's office was at the top of the building; and cripples often labored in, faint from the long climb, only to find that there was some hitch in their papers and they could not get their money. It hurt Whitman, watching them from his desk by the window, to see their disappointment. In his strolls about Washington, he was impressed by the low, white buildings that housed thousands of suffering men. Soon, he started to visit the hospitals, to talk with the soldiers and give them little presents.

As Whitman wrote to his family and friends and to the newspapers about his hospital work, people began to send him money. He dispensed it carefully, making it go as far as possible. Through the wards on Sundays and some weekday afternoons, he trudged with his slow, rolling walk. A haversack hung heavy on his shoulder, and the pockets of his cheap gray suit were bulging. To one man he would give an orange, to another an apple or a small quantity of pickles or horehound candy. He brought pens and pencils, writing paper and envelopes. Sometimes he carried a good-sized jar of jelly, and spooned it out to the occupants of a ward. He did not encourage the use of tobacco, but he had a store of cut plugs in his pocket, to dole out to men who craved it. Often he left money, in "bright new ten-cent and five-cent bills." Sick men longed for the fresh milk that was carried for sale through the wards; and Walt thought that it raised their spirits to have a little cash by them.

The penuriousness of his own life was reflected in his tiny gifts; but the recipients were simple men—poor, often destitute. They understood Walt, and were grateful to him. He regarded his presents as a means of making friends with the soldiers. Once a relationship was established, he talked with them, wrote their letters home, read aloud or played Twenty Questions. Between him and some of the very young soldiers, a deep tenderness developed. In gifts of the heart, in love and tact and sympathy, Walt was lavish. As fervently as the most sentimental of the women nurses, he believed in the curative properties of affection. His hands were gentle. His red face bent kindly over the sunken, childish features on the pillow. Sometimes, it pressed close. "Many a soldier's kiss dwells on these bearded lips."

Outside the hospitals, snow eddied in the blustering northeast gale. It was a stormy winter in Washington. Barges and steamers, loaded with quartermaster's stores, were driven aground in the Potomac mud between Alexandria and Aquia Creek. The houses of the capital were roofed in white. Men and women donned their patent arctic gaiters, and the streetcars slid uneasily over tracks sprinkled with salt. Late in February, there was such a heavy snowfall that cutters and basket sleighs sped along the Avenue, their occupants cosily wrapped in fur carriage robes of buffalo, wolf, skunk or tigerskin. To the gratification of the livery-stable keepers, hilarious stag parties joined in the sport; and for two days a glittering capital jingled with bells like any northern town. The thaw darkened the whiteness with rivers of mud. In spite of the efforts of the contrabands who operated the new street-sweeping machine, the Avenue was as filthy as the back streets. The carriage of the Russian minister stuck fast in a hole in I Street, and the coachman, holding desperately to the reins, was dragged from the box into the muck. Drivers and postillions cursed and lashed the six-mule teams that drew the army wagons. The noise of the traffic of war deadened all other sounds. In March, a nurse at the Mansion House in Alexandria wrote that she could hear the birds sing at daybreak, before the wagons began to pass.

Anxiety about the demoralization of the Army of the Potomac

had subsided. Hooker had worked wonders in restoring the spirit and confidence of the troops. He had judiciously administered punishment, and granted furloughs and leaves of absence. Increased drill and field exercise kept the soldiers fit and lively. Their health, under intelligent medical supervision, was excellent. Staff departments were reorganized. The units of cavalry in the various corps were consolidated in one effective force and placed under the command of Major-General George Stoneman. To fix responsibility for straggling and marauding and to stimulate morale, Hooker adopted the idea of the Kearny patch, and assigned to each corps a distinctive device. Its color, red, white, or blue, differentiated the divisions. The emblems were proudly painted on the wagons and ambulances of the respective corps, stenciled on all articles of public property, and sewn on the caps of every officer and soldier. The cloverleaf of the Second Corps, and the Greek cross of the Sixth would, in particular, come to be famous badges of valor.

Early in April, Hooker said that he had "a living army." He was boastfully certain of success, and the reinvigorated troops shared his high spirits. At this time, he received a visit from the President, Mrs. Lincoln, and Tad, accompanied by Attorney General Bates, Dr. A. G. Henry of Washington Territory and Noah Brooks, correspondent of the *Sacramento Union,* a young man whom Mr. Lincoln had known and liked in Illinois. On the pretty little dispatch boat, *Carrie Martin,* the party slowly voyaged in an unseasonable snowstorm to Aquia Creek Landing, now changed from a leisurely point of connection with the Richmond, Fredericksburg and Potomac Railroad to the army's busy base of supplies, filled with new unpainted warehouses and offices, crowded with soldiers, laborers and contrabands, and served by fleets of transports and Government steamers on the one hand and long lines of freight cars on the other. At Falmouth Station, the President was met by an escort of cavalry and Major-General Dan Butterfield, former colonel of the Twelfth New York militia, who was Hooker's chief of staff. For nearly a week, the Presidential party stayed in three hospital tents at Hooker's headquarters. Lincoln, riding at the head of the cavalry, watching the parade of the troops or visiting the hospital tents, was received with tremendous enthusiasm. Before his eyes passed in grand review the six magnificent infantry corps, the large and disciplined cavalry corps and the great reserve artillery force of the Army of the Potomac. The

First Corps was commanded by the Pennsylvanian, John F. Reynolds, one of whose division commanders was James S. Wadsworth. Darius N. Couch had replaced Sumner as leader of the Second Corps. The erstwhile politician, Dan Sickles, commanded the Third. The Fifth was under George Meade, who had distinguished himself at Antietam and Fredericksburg. Franklin's Sixth Corps had been assigned to John Sedgwick, division commander on the Peninsula and at Antietam, where he had been wounded. Oliver O. Howard, who had lost his right arm at Fair Oaks, led the Eleventh Corps, largely composed of German troops, Carl Schurz commanding a soldierly looking division. At the head of the Twelfth Corps, originally Banks's and briefly Mansfield's, rode Henry W. Slocum, severely wounded at First Bull Run and veteran of every field from Gaines's Mill to Fredericksburg.

Seward invited Baron Gerolt, Count Piper, Mr. Schleiden, minister from the Hanseatic Cities, and other diplomats to accompany him on an excursion. With shawls and spyglasses and maps they made a pleasant voyage on the *Carrie Martin* to Aquia Creek, and witnessed a grand review of General Sickles's corps. The fame of Hooker's army circulated in Washington. The entire country, primed by an optimistic press, had grown elated and hopeful. Although disappointed by the failure of a naval attack on Fort Sumter, it looked forward with assurance to a military victory. War industries flourished, business was booming. A prosperous people invested confidently in the new issue of Government bonds.

The upturn in business had conspired with the defeats of the last year and the weariness of the long war to discourage volunteering. The State militia drafts had been a failure. In March, Congress passed the Enrollment Act, applying to men between the ages of twenty and forty-five. New regiments were not needed, but replenishments for the depleted organizations already in the field. The measure, which provided for a military draft when necessary, removed prospective levies from State control, centralizing all authority over them in the Federal Government. The Union was divided into districts, under provost marshals who reported to a Provost Marshal General, at the head of a special bureau of the War Department. Conscription, dreaded by the country, did not affect the man who was well-to-do. If drafted, he could avoid service either by furnishing a substitute or by paying three hundred dollars. This sum, when the first draft was ordered in May, became the purchase price of the substitute soldier, who also received the Federal bounty of one hundred dollars, paid to those drafted and their substitutes, as well as to volunteers. In 1863, able-bodied men were plentiful, and four hundred dollars was a good sum. To obtain it, worthless soldiers crowded into the Federal ranks; while the swindling and extortionate brokers, who traded in men, multiplied and flourished in every State of the Union.

April ran out on a tide of rumors that General Hooker had crossed the Rappahannock. Washington clacked with reports of fighting, all vague, all unofficial. The first five days of May passed in uncertainty, in growing uneasiness, in the fear that victory had been purchased at a terrible price; and still the military telegraph was muffled and the press was jubilant. The War Department was only half informed. The President was feverishly anxious for facts. Gideon Welles picked up tidbits of news from correspondents and naval officers who came up from Aquia Creek. In spite of the general impression that the Federal arms had had a great, if costly triumph, Welles was not satisfied. "If we have success," he wrote in his diary, "the tidings would come to us in volumes." On Wednesday, May 6, the Secretary of the Navy saw a letter from Dahlgren's boy, Ulric, who was on Hooker's staff. He had telegraphed his father that he was "all right," and the message came from headquarters near Falmouth, on the north side of the Rappahannock. Stanton, when Welles questioned him, said that he had no information that Hooker had retired across the river. An hour later, Senator Sumner strode into Welles's room with raised hands, crying "Lost, lost, all is lost!" In a White House bedroom, the President stood, with a telegram from Butterfield in his hand. His face was the color of the French-gray paper on the walls. At Chancellorsville, the Army of the Potomac had paid a terrible price; but it was the price of defeat.

Through the crash of yet another fallen idol, the country heard the devastating story. Hooker, his forces twice as large as Lee's, had moved forward brilliantly, confidently, crossing the Rappahannock thirty miles above Fredericksburg, moving on with four army corps across the Rapidan. Confronted by an aggressive enemy, Hooker had lost his impetus. He ordered the army to fall back, astounding his vigorous corps and division commanders and disheartening the troops. On May 2, Stonewall Jackson attacked the Eleventh Corps, and the German soldiers, surprised and unprepared, were routed. The next morning, Hooker had been knocked insensible by a cannon ball which struck a veranda pillar against which he was leaning. The great defeat of that day was ascribed to the effects of this accident; but, in fact, the battle was already lost. Hooker appeared to have suffered a nervous collapse. It was said that he appeared no more dazed and incapable after being knocked down than he had been before. Some declared that he had been drinking heavily; others, that he had abstained, and missed his accustomed stimulant. Sedgwick's corps, sent across the river at Fredericksburg, had captured the city and the heights, but was not reinforced, and was defeated by Lee. Stoneman's cavalry, sent off on a fruitless raid on Lee's communications, with difficulty escaped to rejoin the army on the north bank of the Rappahannock. Soon after, Stoneman, dining in Washington with the Pennsylvanian, A. K. McClure, gave his explanation of Hooker's failure. "He could play the best game of poker I ever saw until it came to the point when he should go a thousand better, and then he would flunk."

As the tale of incompetence and vacillation unfolded, there was only one detail which might bring comfort to the Union. At Chancellorsville, Stonewall Jackson had been wounded. The week after the battle, it was known that his somber figure would ride no more at the head of his ragged rebel troops.

Though the calamity of this defeat appalled and discouraged the nation, there was not the black despondency that had followed the Seven Days, Second Bull Run and Fredericksburg. Business was good. Factory wheels were turning. There was wild speculation on the Stock Exchange. The humblest man could pocket a large bounty by donning the uniform of his country. If the people of the Union could not win this war, at least they were making money out of it. Two bitter years had made them callous to the loss of thousands of men; and above the sighs and the weeping arose a shrill new noise of laughter. People were beginning to spend money, to give parties, to dine and dance and be merry.

Again, the wounded cumbered the Washington wharves, but few sightseers gathered to see the transports arriving, day after day, with the men from Chancellorsville. Now, each of those prostrate young bodies seemed the very figure of the Union itself, and people turned away from the heartsickening, habitual scene. The compact caravans of the ambulances had become a monotonous part of the pageant of the streets. The procession of the maimed, with their empty sleeves and trouser legs, no longer attracted attention. Even death had grown

commonplace. There had been a time when the loss of one young
Ellsworth had thrown the capital into mourning. Now, from the
silver-mounted rosewood of the higher officers to the cheap pine slats
of the ordinary soldiers, the business of death was plied like any other
prosperous trade. There was a section of the city where the rat-tat
of the coffinmakers' hammers sounded all day, and the stacks of long,
upended boxes rose and fell outside their doors, like a fever chart of
the battles. The capital had had a surfeit of misery; and, if the horror
of blood beat like a wound in the back of every mind, the faces on
the streets were smiling.

The soft spring air carried the plaintive mechanical melodies of
the organgrinders; and on the Avenue, under the huge transparency
which advertised embalming, the promenaders sauntered in the sunshine. Busy hacks rolled among the wagons and the caracoling horses
of the officers. Fashionable ladies drove in barouches, with black
coachmen and footmen. On the sidewalks, salesmen cried the merits
of patent soaps, and proprietors of telescopes and lung-testing machines
clamored for customers. Pineapples, oranges and tomatoes were piled
in colored pyramids, ice-cream dealers were stationed in the shade
of the trees, and Italians roasted chestnuts in little portable stoves.
Children shrieked for pieces chipped from big, variegated rocks of
candy and for the artificial bugs which were swung enticingly up and
down on strings; while sharper children bawled the evening newspapers, and swarmed at the crossings to polish muddy boots.

The Avenue wore a cosmopolitan air. Every nationality seemed
to be represented in the gaudy crowd. The swords and sashes, plumed
hats and riding cloaks of the army officers, the gold lace of the naval
officers, the outlandish dress of the Zouaves gave Washington the
look of a carnival, a huge and lively masquerade. The spring bonnets
of the ladies were fantastic—extravagantly high and narrow, "with
over-hanging balconies of flowers." They were wearing much red
that season, for the color of the Garibaldians' shirts was still the
fashion. There was a shade called Magenta, and another paler red
called Solferino—warm, bright, amusing names. Those smiling ladies
knew that they were the names of battlefields, where alien men had
died for some vague cause. But no one named a shade of red for
Fredericksburg; and the silliest of the officers' trollops would have
shrunk from a scarlet dress that bore the name of Chancellorsville.

XII *Black, Copper and Bright*

IN THE FAUL OF 1856, I showed my show in Utiky, a trooly grate sitty in the State of New York," the President began in his pleasant, high-pitched voice. He was reading from the book which Artemus Ward had sent him. The Cabinet members, summoned to the White House by messenger, listened in silence.

"1 day as I was givin a descripshun of my Beests and Snaiks in my usual flowry stile what was my skorn & disgust to see a big burly feller walk up to the cage containin my wax figgers of the Lord's Last Supper, and cease Judas Iscarrot by the feet and drag him out on the ground. He then commenced fur to pound him as hard as he cood."

Five days had passed since the cannon had roared along Antietam Creek. It had been called a great Union victory, but the end of the war was not in sight. The Federal losses had been more than twelve thousand men. There had been no effective pursuit of the retreating Confederates. The minds of the gentlemen of the Cabinet were troubled on that September day of 1862, when they sat in the room with the view of Washington's unfinished monument.

The President read with evident relish.

"Sez he, 'What did you bring this pussylanermus cuss here fur?' & he hit the wax figger another tremenjis blow on the hed.

"Sez I, 'You egrejus ass, that air's a wax figger—a representashun of the false 'Postle.'

"Sez he, 'That's all very well fur you to say, but I tell you, old man, that Judas Iscarrot can't show hisself in Utiky with impunerty by a darn site!' with which observashun, he kaved in Judassis hed. The young man belonged to 1 of the first famerlies in Utiky. I sood him, and the Joory brawt in a verdick of Arson in the 3d degree."

The worried gentlemen appeared to share the President's enjoyment. This was, after all, the sort of interlude to which habit had inured them. Mr. Smith and Mr. Blair permitted their features to relax. Old Mr. Bates was always courteous. Mr. Seward smiled easily, and Mr. Welles had a wry glint of Yankee humor. Even Mr. Chase's awful solemnity paid its homage to fun. Only that reluctant courtier, Mr. Stanton, was not amused at all.

Mr. Lincoln's persistent indulgence in anecdote had not always served him well in Washington. It was considered unworthy the dignity of his high office that he should jest at serious moments. Conservative Easterners were sometimes shocked by the tang of the soil or the backhouse in his tales. Yet laughter followed this melancholy man. His grotesquely attenuated figure and mournful, yellow face were an introduction to comedy. The face was startlingly mobile. Unexpectedly, the somber mouth pulled a droll grimace, the brooding eyes sparkled. His laugh, one observer thought, was as hearty as the neigh of a wild horse. Gentlemen from New York or Boston might shrink, Mr. Stanton might lower, but many men laughed with Lincoln.

Often the President drew on his stock of salt and homely stories to illustrate a point, to terminate a controversial discussion, or to save himself the embarrassment of a direct reply. But, when he read Artemus Ward to his Cabinet, he was prompted by no wish to speak in parables. The American humor of the period stands revealed in his selection. *High-handed Outrage at Utica* was pure entertainment.

As he put aside the book, his tone changed to one more suited to the frowning face of his Secretary of War. "Gentlemen," he said, "I have, as you are aware, thought a great deal about the relation of this war to slavery. . . ." For, actually, he had summoned his ministers in order to read to them something which was very seriously intended, something of which he himself was the author—a military proclamation of emancipation.

From the beginning, nearly four millions of slaves had shadowed the turmoil of this brothers' war. The blacks had been the brand that had set the nation burning. Yet slavery was not the cause for which Northern men fought. In slogan and speech and rallying cry, this was a war to save the Union.

So closely was slavery bound with the conflict that at the outset even Northerners shuddered at the prospect of a servile insurrection. None took place. Quietly, and without violence, in those voiceless millions a change occurred. News spread among them as mysteriously and swiftly as in the African jungles. With the first movement of the Union armies, they began to straggle into the camps. Feeble old people came, big bucks and scrambling children, women with babies at their black breasts. Their few possessions were tied in ragged bundles.

Their faces, smeared with dust and sweat, were shining with hope. For, whatever might be said in slogan and speech and rallying cry, these dusky people knew that the men in blue were crowned with light and carried freedom on their banners.

A mission of deliverance formed no part of the intention of those first Union troops. They had not enlisted to right the wrongs of the Negro race; and, for the most part, they looked with hesitation and even with aversion on their dark camp followers. Although there were regiments in which abolition feeling ran strong, most of the soldiers, like the great majority of the Northern population, were reluctant to interfere with an institution which they were accustomed to tolerate as a legal, if detestable fact. The commanders in the field were inclined to treat the slaveholders with a punctilious consideration, and many even permitted them to enter the Federal lines to seek their property.

To the nation's capital, as well as to the army lines, the bondmen traveled in the confident expectation that freedom awaited them. Across the Potomac bridges, they trudged into a town where slavery was entrenched. The people of Washington were comfortably used to scowling at the tiny woodcuts of running figures which appeared, among the strayed cows and mules, in the advertising columns of their newspapers. The severe black code, derived from the old Maryland statute books, was the law of the District, never modified by Congress. Under its provision that an unclaimed fugitive could be sold to pay for his imprisonment charges, the District had had an unsavory early history of the kidnaping and sale of free men. Although slave trading had been abolished there in 1850, the participation of magistrates and constables in the fees paid by the runaways' masters continued to degrade the courts and corrupt the police; while it was to the financial interest of the jailers to detain fugitives as long as possible. Slaves who wandered farther than the legally prescribed distance from home were liable to be thrown into jail, even though they had had no intention of escaping. No free Negro, without a certificate of freedom on his person, was safe from arrest. Since his testimony could not be received as evidence against a white person, he was without redress. The city police and the District marshal's deputies gave almost their entire time to hunting and seizing colored people, while unofficial slave catchers were attracted to this business, in which there was much to gain and nothing to lose.

The black code had at an early date been supplemented by re-

pressive city ordinances. Lashes were prescribed for pathetically childish offenses—for setting off firecrackers near a dwelling, for bathing in
the canal and for flying a kite within the limits of the corporation.
More important, in the resultant oppression and extortion practiced by
the police, was the regulation that Negroes found on the street after
ten o'clock at night could be locked up until morning, and fined as
high as ten dollars. Since 1835, when an anti-Negro mob had rioted
in the capital's streets, the relations between the races had been
strained. Washington still remembered the dread of a black insurrection, which had followed John Brown's raid. The few slaves—the census of 1860 counted only eighteen hundred in the city—were not
responsible for the alarm so much as the population of over nine thousand free Negroes, a class which the capital, like all slaveholding communities, regarded with fear and hatred. A disorderly minority of their
number seemed to justify the charge that they were a menace to the
town's security. Drunkenness and brawls were notorious in such
plague spots as Prather's Alley in the Northern Liberties and Nigger
Hill in the Third Ward. Washington made little discrimination between the dregs of the black inhabitants and industrious colored men.
The latter, indeed, aroused the jealous resentment of white workingmen by the very qualities which made them serviceable to the community. In spite of the restrictions, they had flocked to Washington because of the many opportunities for making a livelihood as servants,
hack drivers, bootblacks, barbers, bartenders, waiters and cooks. Livery
stables and restaurants were successfully operated by Negroes. The
well-to-do among them owned property and paid taxes. In their Sun-
day-best attire of gay shawls and satin waistcoats, carrying prayer
books and pocket handkerchiefs, canes and parasols, they appeared so
grand from the back that it was a surprise to see black faces when they
turned. Bonnets as fine as any in Washington, said the *Star* reporter,
were to be seen at the Fifteenth Street Presbyterian Church, where
the colored aristocracy of the District worshiped. This church, which
boasted a famous choir, showed the prosperity of its congregation in its
cushions and carpets, its gold-lettered pews, marble-topped pulpit and
handsome chandeliers. Yet its most respected members could not hold
a gathering in their own houses, without a special permit from the
mayor. Like the rowdies of Nigger Hill, they were liable to arrest if
they ventured out after ten o'clock at night. Even for the children of
colored taxpayers, no public schools were provided. A succession of

private schools, some taught by Negroes, some by sympathetic white people, had persistently defied the prejudices and even the persecutions of the townsfolk.

It was to this place that, in the spring of 1861, the Virginia field hands came in quest of freedom. Many were fugitives, others had been deserted by their decamping masters. In either case, the city and county police were zealous in hustling them off to jail. The police soon had formidable competition from the soldiers of the Union. A slave who had escaped from Mr. Gibson Peach of Alexandria had the misfortune to meet his master in Washington, and fled for protection to the Fourth Pennsylvania Regiment, then quartered at the Assembly Rooms. The guard held him at the point of the bayonet, while Mr. Peach got a carriage and secured him. On the Eastern Branch Bridge, soldiers of the Seventy-first New York caught three fugitives and kept them under guard at the Navy Yard until Mr. Reeder of St. Mary's County, Maryland, came to claim them. Seventy-one runaways, confined in jail during May, had almost all been arrested by soldiers.

On the other hand, a number of escaped slaves made themselves so useful as servants and laborers that they were harbored in the camps about Washington. This condition caused the President embarrassment. As an individual, Mr. Lincoln hated slavery, but, as Chief Magistrate, he had given solemn assurances that the institution would be protected; and he was anxious to avoid giving offense to the slaveholding States which had not joined the Confederacy. Before First Bull Run, an army order excluded slaves from the camps and the lines of the troops around the capital.

But here was an anomalous situation. The young black men were strong and willing, and the army needed laborers. In May, General Ben Butler, commanding at Fort Monroe in his gold-laced militia uniform, had set some runaways to work on his fortifications, instead of permitting them to be reclaimed for similar service on behalf of the enemy. There was a simple logic in the idea that the slaves of the rebels, like their horses and mules, were "contraband of war." The novel use of the term caught the fancy of the North, and people, while they chuckled over it, experienced a great relief. A phrase vindicated a policy. The ludicrous nickname stuck, lost its oddity and became a commonplace of speech, used throughout the war to describe all slaves who had fled from or been abandoned by disloyal masters.

Butler's policy was soon given a legal justification. With the rout of First Bull Run still vivid in their minds, Congress included in the Confiscation Act a section providing that owners should forfeit their claim to slaves used for insurrectionary purposes. As practically interpreted, this was extended to include all slaves whose owners were disloyal. The contrabands in Washington were accordingly placed under the protection of the provost guard. They were lodged at the Old Capitol, and the able-bodied were employed at a small wage by the Government.

The problem of the runaways, however, was by no means settled. The Fugitive Slave Law remained on the statute books, and the bereft masters of the technically loyal State of Maryland visited the City Hall with loud protestations of allegiance. The three commissioners, appointed by the circuit court under the law, duly sat to receive their complaints. The District marshal's office continued to issue warrants to his deputies. Still, that autumn and winter, the little figures ran, black, copper and bright, in the advertising columns of the Washington newspapers. They were almost all very young. The sparse lines of description breathed their half-formed plans, the haste and excitement of their adventure. Jane, seventeen, good-looking, made off in a pink dress and black, flaunting hat. Charles boasted new winter shoes and a suit of claret-colored kersey. Slender Dave Kelly left in a frock coat of gray cassinet, whiskered Ned had a purple jacket and white pants. Madison Booth, in two pea jackets, carried off a large gray horse. Bettie and Ellen Nora Bell clasped their babies in their arms. The boy, Toney, wearing yellow gauntlet gloves and a jacket with U. S. buttons, had a grum face, scarred by the kick of a horse. Lisping Robert Butler limped on an injured foot. Alfred Duckett went with his queer walk, throwing himself back. Special reasons appeared for presuming them to be in the capital. Louise had a husband there; Paul had a free grandmother. Lewis might be lurking near the Island, where his former master lived. Samuel Bungy, supposed to indulge in ardent spirits, had friends on both the Island and Capitol Hill. Edwin Nicholls's mother belonged to Mrs. Burch on Sixth Street.

When in December of 1861 the flags were hoisted on the Capitol for the return of the Thirty-seventh Congress, the radical Republicans had already been angered by the President's action in annulling Frémont's proclamation of emancipation in Missouri. Halleck, succeeding Frémont in the West, had forbidden Negroes to enter his lines. There were reports of generals who treated slaveholders with extravagant courtesy, and helped them regain their property. McClellan was in power in Washington, and the District marshal's constables scrutinized every dark face that passed. The accumulated wrath of the abolitionist politicians found partial vent in the hue and cry after Charles P. Stone.

Immediately after the opening of Congress, an Executive order reminded McClellan of the Confiscation Act. Slaves employed in hostile service were frequently received in the army lines, the order stated. On entering the city, they were liable to be arrested by the police. They were under the military protection of the United States, and persons arresting them should be arrested by the soldiers.

On the day that this order was issued, the Senate Chamber rang with denunciations of the slave system at the seat of Government. Congress was the lawmaking body for the District, and, in the passionate phrases of the radicals, Washington grimly foresaw the emancipation of its slaves. All that winter, like a little kingdom under the heel of a foreign invader, the city sat sullen, smarting and resentful. Loyal or disunionist, its citizens had no sympathy with abolition. Many Republican newcomers to Washington, however, were imbued with the doctrine. In the Hall of Representatives, as well as in some of the churches, anti-slavery sermons were preached on Sundays. The *National Republican* daily exposed the wrongs of the Negro race. The Hutchinson Family tunefully delivered their anti-slavery repertory at the Y.M.C.A. rooms and elsewhere in the capital. Such embattled champions of the blacks as Henry Ward Beecher, Horace Greeley and Wendell Phillips were the speakers at a "popular course" of lectures given at the Smithsonian Institution. When Wendell Phillips spoke, there were colored people in the audience. Professor Henry had reluctantly consented to give the use of the lecture hall, and was much criticized in Washington for having done so. He stipulated that, on every occasion, it should be announced that the Institution was not responsible for the statements made by the lecturers. This announcement became a joke to the large Northern audiences which assembled each week, and its opening words, "I am requested," were greeted with satirical applause.

In the Senate, the county jail had provided a convenient springboard for the slavery question. As early as November, there had been unexpected callers at the dismal lockup north of the City Hall. The detective, Allan Pinkerton—alias E. J. Allen—had gone there to draw up a report for the provost marshal. James W. Grimes of Iowa, radical Republican chairman of the Senate's Committee on the District, had pried into its damp precincts. The rickety old building had long been a disgrace to the community. It was dark, unsanitary and ill-ventilated. From the peculiar dull shade of its walls, it was known as the Blue Jug. For years, the city authorities and the grand juries of the District had been calling it to the attention of Congress, without arousing any great interest in that body. In December of 1861, however, it was suddenly crowded, like an exposition, with notabilities.

The jail was under the control of the District marshal, the President's close friend, Ward Hill Lamon. Soon after the outbreak of the war, he had secured a colonel's commission and for some months he had been absent from Washington, raising troops for his command. Deputy Marshal George W. Phillips acted in his absence. Pending repeal by Congress of the Fugitive Slave Law, it was clearly the marshal's duty to continue to issue warrants for fugitives from loyal masters. There was, however, a pro-slavery atmosphere about the marshal's office that increased the irritation of the radical senators. It had not escaped their notice that Lamon himself was a native of Virginia. Phillips was suspected of sympathy with the slave system, and had been denounced to the Potter Committee by the jailer, Amon Duvall, as a secessionist. Lamon discharged Duvall because of his incessant opposition to Phillips and his friends. On the other hand, Duvall himself was reputed to be pro-slavery. In 1863, the commissions of one hundred and seven constables were revoked by the court on the ground that they had not taken the oath of allegiance and given bond, leaving only twenty-five members of the force who were authorized to act.

There was no doubt that things had been going from bad to worse at the Blue Jug. It had been designed to accommodate from fifty to one hundred prisoners. In the winter of 1861, more than two hundred were crowded into its noisome cells. Among them were burglars, horse thieves and confidence men, as well as unruly soldiers and citizens suspected of disloyalty. Vastly more important to the radicals, Pinkerton had reported that sixty fugitive slaves were detained there. A goodly number of these were contrabands. One, at least, was indubitably a free man, and he had been in confinement for more than six months.

By order of the provost marshal, some of the contrabands were discharged. The howls of outrage in the Senate Chamber had been justified, but no one was taken in by the radicals' outburst of humanitarian feeling. The "Washington slave-pen" was a handy peg on which to hang abolitionist speeches. Soon after the uproar began, Senator Henry Wilson introduced a bill for emancipation in the District.

Colonel Lamon was recalled to his duties as marshal. The big, swashbuckling Virginian hated abolitionists, and he had not the temper to take a challenge meekly. Soon after Grimes on the Senate floor compared the jail to the French Bastille and the dungeons of Venice, it was reported that no one was to be admitted to the Blue Jug without a special permit from the District marshal. Lamon said that the order was prepared by the Attorney General at the President's request. Grimes flew out to test the truth of the rumor he had heard, and the jailer closed the door in his whiskered, official face. He went straight to the White House, but was unable to see the President. In a rage, he "bounced up to the Capitol," and aired his grievance in open Senate. The insult to its dignity fired that highly combustible body. No one's feelings were soothed by the explanation that, after a recent large influx of visitors, chisels and knives had been found in the possession of the prisoners. A resolution was passed that Lamon had been guilty of contempt for the lawmakers' authority. There was a loud demand that "this foreign satrap" should be instantly dismissed.

It was the President himself whom the abolitionists were attacking through his friend. Mr. Lincoln was well aware of this. He loved and trusted Lamon, and firmly refused either to displace him, or to accept the resignation which Lamon proffered to relieve the President from an embarrassing situation. However, an Executive order soon cleared the jail of the remaining fugitives held on suspicion, and instructed Lamon to receive no more of them.

The Senate did not relent in its persecution of Marshal Lamon. Every offense was charged against him, from inhumanity and dereliction of duty to dishonesty in participating in the fees of the jail, which were part of the perquisites of his office. The House, preserving a more nonchalant air, waited for two years before assenting to legislation which reduced his power and emoluments by giving the custody of the jail and prisoners to a warden, and providing a special marshal for the court. The change of custody gave rise to a singular situation. The District court sentenced two men to be hanged for murder, ordering the marshal to carry out the execution on April 1, 1864. In the meantime Congress created the office of warden, and Lamon, glad to be relieved of a painful duty, declared that he had no control over the prisoners, and could not legally execute them. On the appointed day, the gallows erected in the yard of the Blue Jug attracted a crowd to witness the hanging. The President, however, had solved the dilemma by commuting the prisoners' sentence to life imprisonment. The crowd, at first inclined to take the rumor of Lincoln's clemency as "an April 1 hoax," eventually dispersed, and the gallows was taken down. The question arose whether Congress had not virtually abolished capital punishment in the District.

In contrast to the demagogues and fanatics of his party, Lincoln viewed the slavery problem as a statesman. Above all things, he desired to save the Union, and in his mind emancipation was always subsidiary to this great central ambition. Neither sentimentality nor vindictiveness blinded him to the social upheaval which a sudden overthrow of the institution would entail. He had repeatedly voiced his cherished hope that the loyal slaveholding States would voluntarily adopt some plan of gradual emancipation with compensation to the owners from the Federal Government.

In March, 1862, to the accompaniment of heated oratory, the Senate took up the bill for emancipation in the District. The slaves were to be freed immediately, but loyal masters were to receive compensation at an average of three hundred dollars per slave. Moreover, an amendment appropriated money for a project dear to Mr. Lincoln's heart, one to which he strongly adhered and with which he unsuccessfully experimented—the colonization of such freed blacks as might wish to leave the country.

Neither compensation nor the hope that some Negroes might take their departure calmed the anxiety of the capital's citizens. In their eyes, the abolitionists were bent on making the District "a hell on earth for the white man." The Board of Aldermen passed a resolution which urged Congress "to provide . . . safeguards against converting this city . . . into an asylum for free negroes, a population undesirable in every American community." The *Star* indignantly took it for granted that owners of valuable slaves would lose no time in placing them beyond the reach of Congress. According to observers of Republican sympathies, there was a great exodus of blacks by train and wagonload to Maryland. The Baltimore slave-pens were reported to be crowded. A few owners undoubtedly persuaded their slaves to leave. The provost marshal remarked that a number of these apparently compliant chattels seized the opportunity to escape altogether.

The emancipation bill was passed in both Houses, and on April 16, 1862, was signed by the President. In an attempt to atone to ex-Mayor Berret for his summary arrest and detention in Fort Lafayette, Mr. Lincoln offered him a place on the commission to award compensation for the freed slaves; but the honor was declined. Early in May, the commission was receiving the petitions of the owners, while the long lists of itemized human property, to be examined and valued by a Baltimore slave dealer, began to appear in the newspapers. Eventually, about one thousand persons in the entire District presented claims for three thousand, one hundred and twenty-eight slaves. There were a few applications—mainly those of ladies advanced in years—in which the evidence warranted the commissioners in withholding payment. It was refused for one hundred and eleven slaves in all, either because of the disloyalty or the defective titles of the owners. Among those who received their money was a free Negro, who asked compensation for a wife he had purchased, and for the half-dozen children born of the union. At least, this fact was vouched for by Horace Greeley, the pink-faced, goggle-eyed, anti-slavery editor of the *New York Tribune.*

With enfranchisement an accomplished fact, Congress provided public schooling for the Negro children of the District. Meantime, the capital was preparing to stage its own political contest for the election of mayor and members of the city councils. The contenders in the miniature arena of the municipality corresponded with the two branches of the Democratic party in national affairs: the War Democrats, who had rallied to the support of the Union; and the Peace Democrats, who decried the administration and opposed the war. In Washington, the loyal faction was called the Unconditional Union party. Its candidate for mayor was the incumbent, Mr. Richard Wallach, the brother of Douglas Wallach, the proprietor of the *Star.* In the two preceding elections, Richard Wallach had run against Berret and been defeated. At the time of Berret's arrest and enforced resignation, he was serving as president of the Board of Aldermen, and was elected mayor by the city councils for the unexpired term.

The opposition, the Union Democratic party, was, according to the *Star,* made up of "those whose faces are so radiant with joy when

news of a secesh victory reaches the city." Its supporters denounced
the Unconditional Union party as allied with the radical Republicans.
Mayor Wallach himself was assailed as an abolitionist of deepest dye.
He scorned to refute the charge during the campaign, but one of his
adherents disposed of it on the ground that Wallach owned nine
slaves.

Late in May, a mass meeting of Union Democrats on Capitol
Hill was picketed by the police, while a squad of the provost guard
was drawn up across the street. From a stand draped in red, white and
blue, the speakers addressed the crowd "in terms violently patriotic and
desperately pro-slavery." The candidate, Mr. James F. Haliday, was
greeted with shouts of "Damn the abolitionists" and "Send the niggers
to Massachusetts to be educated." Mr. William Mulloy, a member of
the Common Council, whose feelings were for the white man first,
spoke in favor of a humble petition to Congress to set the Democrats
free. More telling in its emotional appeal, which evaded the fact that
Washington citizens had no voice in the issues before Congress, was
the speech of Mr. McNerhany, who inquired if a father would vote
to have his darling boy educated with niggers. "No, by God, no. God
damn it, no," roared the Union Democrats. Carried away by the excitement, this speaker went so far as to recommend that wives should refuse admission to their husbands if—by voting the Unconditional
Union ticket—they were willing to place such a stigma on their little
ones.

On election day, June 2, the voters carried proof of their loyalty
to the Union in their pockets; for, under a recent act of Congress, they
were obliged to produce certified oaths of allegiance, if challenged.
Most of the restaurants were closed, and there were few cases of
drunkenness at the polls. Toward evening, however, "effervescences of
feeling" suggested that some restaurants' side doors had been left open.
The Third Ward was enlivened by a procession of flag-draped hacks,
filled with caroling Baltimore roughs of both factions. Well-known
election strikers in the Fourth Ward were disarmed of concealed weapons, including a bowie, two pistols and a double-headed billy. The
Metropolitan Police—proudly uniformed for summer in navy-blue
flannel frock coats and straw hats—charged to the aid of a badly
beaten Unconditional from the Island, and put down a "skrimmage"
in the Second Ward. A scattering of other fights occurred, but only
one approached the dimensions of a riot. A Wallach crowd near the

City Hall was so enraged by a Haliday supporter that bricks and stones began to fly, and only the timely interference of the mounted provost guard averted serious trouble. The day was conceded to have "passed off with remarkable good order."

The result of the election proclaimed the Union sympathies of the capital—Richard Wallach was chosen mayor by a vote of five to one. But in spite of the increase in the population of the District, the total vote of under five thousand was considerably smaller than that registered at the 1860 election. The *National Republican* was not slow to attribute this fact to the required oath of allegiance; while the *Star* noted that many citizens were absent on military duty, under one flag or another.

In the evening, after the result was known, huge bonfires were lighted in the streets, and the bands of the exultant Unconditionals blared their way to City Hall and to Mayor Wallach's residence on Louisiana Avenue. On succeeding nights, the winning candidates for the city councils were serenaded, and self-congratulation prevailed among the loyal Washingtonians. The secessionist sympathizers, although defeated, were by no means silenced, and Swampoodle was seething with dissatisfaction. Mary Shaunnessy, who lived near the iron bridge on H Street, went to the house of her neighbor, Patrick Quirk; and, "after disposing of her clothing after a singular fashion," knelt down and invoked curses on his head—that his children might be born blind and that purgatory would hold him fast—because he had cast a vote for Mr. Wallach. The irritated Quirk procured a warrant. Presently, two officers visited Mrs. Shaunnessy's house and bore her, half-dressed and tied with ropes, to a baker's wagon, in which she was carried to the justice of the peace. In jail, she was joined by her brother, who had brandished a double-barreled gun and professed an intention to kill any Irishman living between the iron bridge and Seventh Street who had voted the Unconditional Union ticket.

Although the congressional legislation on behalf of the Negroes created so much commotion in the District, it brought little immediate change to the colored people themselves. For the most part, the manumitted slaves continued to work for their masters. They were not assertive in laying claim to their new civil rights. They were not permitted to ride inside the Washington streetcars, although special labeled cars were presently provided for them. This discrimination became nearly a personal issue between Senator Sumner and the street-railway company, and was at length abolished. A year and a half after Congress provided public schools for Negro children, none had been opened in the District. The expected revenues from taxes on Negro property and philanthropic contributions proved disappointing, and the community had no mind to saddle itself with the expense. The Freedman's Aid Society, formed by sympathetic persons in the capital, set up schools in shabby rooms and church basements on the Island and in the Northern Liberties. Teachers volunteered their services. The pupils in the night classes, from ten years old to sixty, supplied their own books and lights.

Prior to ordaining emancipation in the District, Congress had passed an article of war which forbade the Federal forces to be used in apprehending slaves. All during the winter, contradictory orders about the treatment of fugitives had been issued by various generals, some excluding Negroes from their lines, some still using soldiers to hunt them down and return them to their masters. Contrabands in increasing thousands, however, were being employed in the army. In Washington, in the spring of 1862, there was evidence that a year of war had softened the soldiers' attitude toward the fugitives.

Early in April, an attempt to arrest the Negro, Edward Sam, caused wild excitement out on the Seventh Street Road, where two cavalry regiments, the Seventh New York and the Fourth Pennsylvania, were encamped. When two county constables got out of a hack and seized him, Sam's lusty cries brought the Pennsylvania sentinel running, with his saber drawn. Soon soldiers from both regiments were milling around the hack, with shouts of "Hang the damned kidnapers!" and "Shoot the nigger catchers!" The colonel of the Fourth Pennsylvania Cavalry rescued the constables, and sent them off, with an escort, to the provost marshal's office. They were taken before General Wadsworth, who, on learning that they had no warrant, ordered them to be taken to the Central Guard-house.

No abolitionist leanings were needed to revolt at the injustice of Sam's arrest, for he was a free Trinidad man. In their camp north of Washington, however, the soldiers of the Seventy-sixth New York were harboring slaves from Maryland, and refused to admit the District marshal's constables, though they were provided with warrants. In May, the regiment was ordered to the front. As it marched down Seventh Street to the steamboat landing, a pair of constables seized two runaway slaves who were attached to one of the companies as servants. The ensuing rumpus brought people running from the Avenue. Some of the soldiers raised their bayonets and threatened to shoot into the crowd. The officers restored order; and, after examining the constables' writs, permitted them to carry off the two slaves. Seven or eight other fugitives accompanied the wrathful Seventy-sixth to the wharf. Next morning, when a deputy marshal went down to get them, with his warrants and an order from the provost marshal, he was admonished by officers and soldiers that they would see him in hell before they gave the Negroes up.

Emancipation in the District had not abrogated the Fugitive Slave Law. As the restless slaves of Montgomery and Prince George's counties came in hundreds across the Eastern Branch bridge, their disgruntled Maryland masters continued to seek redress at the City Hall. There was much anxiety and complaint in Maryland and the new unionist governor, Augustus W. Bradford, wrote Attorney General Bates of a report that the Government had forbidden the execution of warrants under the law. The radicals of Congress and, increasingly, the army were ready to consider any slaveholder a traitor—an opinion which nullified the necessity of restoring his property. On the other hand, the commissioners of the circuit court and its officer, Marshal Lamon, were disposed to accept the Marylanders' protestations of allegiance, and were therefore bound to return their slaves.

Against the background of a free District, every demonstration of the slave system was sharply etched. The Negro catchers could no longer peacefully drag their captives through the streets. Crowds gathered. There were protests, altercations, brawls. It was a sin and a shame, said the *National Republican,* that men and women could not walk abroad without being liable to witness the struggles and hear the shrieks of the fugitives. Abolitionists made the legal point that the Fugitive Slave Law was not applicable to the District, but only to the States. Judge John Dean of Brooklyn—said to have been engaged by wealthy and respectable citizens of Washington—came down to test the law in the courts. As he made his way out of the City Hall, after volunteering to defend certain runaways, he was followed by ominous shakings of heads and fists. "I'd like to stuff all the niggers down their damned throats," one man remarked. On the points raised by Judge Dean, the decisions of the circuit court were all favorable to a strict enforcement of the law. Senator Wilson introduced a bill to reorganize the judiciary system of the District—or, as everyone clearly understood, to have judges opposed to the slave system appointed.

The conflict had not been smoothed by the appointment of the abolitionist, James S. Wadsworth, as military governor. With the departure of the Army of the Potomac for the Peninsula, the contrabands in the District had come under Wadsworth's charge, together with the control of the provost guard and the military prisons. He had soon moved the blacks from the Old Capitol prison to the near-by houses of Duff Green's Row. To prevent overcrowding, a number of able-bodied men and women were placed in private service in Washington and other cities. In spite of Wadsworth's efforts, conditions at Duff Green's Row were far from ideal. Its constantly changing population lived in miserable poverty. The Negroes had too recently been enslaved to become immediately industrious and self-reliant. They required, not only Government supervision, but philanthropic assistance as well. The Freedman's Aid Association provided them with clothing and sent them teachers. Colored churches in the city contributed to their relief. Missionaries came down from the North to labor among them.

On arrival, each fugitive was examined on the important point of his master's loyalty; and, on his giving evidence against this, he was furnished with a paper, signed by Wadsworth and known as a military protection. As martial law had not been proclaimed in the District, the civil authorities saw no reason for supposing that Wadsworth was either perfectly informed or all-powerful. Although Duff Green's Row was patrolled by a detachment of the Old Capitol guard, Lamon's constables hovered in the neighborhood. One of the contrabands was whisked away to his master in Maryland before the military governor had a chance to act.

The arrest of the mulatto girl, Alethia Lynch, precipitated the conflict between the civil and military jurisdictions. There was a story that she was General Wadsworth's cook. In any case, she carried one of his military protections when the constables seized her. Wadsworth sent a peremptory demand for her release. When this was refused, his aide and a squad of the provost guard marched on the jail, took possession of the keys and delivered Alethia by force. The jailer and Deputy Marshal Phillips were arrested and taken to the Central Guard-house;

while two lawyers who had arrived on the scene—one was the counsel for the girl's Maryland owner—were shut up in the Blue Jug.

News of these highhanded doings reached the District marshal late that night. Under the persecutions of Congress, Lamon's temper had not improved. When he found the President was out of town—it was the occasion of his visit to McDowell's camp on the Rappahannock —he decided to take things in his own hands. Word was sent for the police to assemble, but either they were reluctant to engage in the fray, or Lamon was too impatient to wait for them. Posting to the Blue Jug with a single police sergeant, Lamon personally "recaptured the jail," by disarming the two soldiers who had been left on guard. The lawyers were now released, and the soldiers locked up instead.

In the clear light of day, this melodrama must have seemed a little absurd, even to the leading participants. Both sides set their prisoners free. The honors of the engagement were divided—Lamon had his jail, but Wadsworth had Alethia Lynch.

In his account of the affair, the District marshal stated that Lincoln called on the Attorney General for an opinion, and that Mr. Bates decided that, under existing conditions in the District, the civil authority outranked the military, and that Wadsworth's conduct had been misguided, however kindly his intentions. But, if the gentleman from western New York was rebuked, he was by no means subdued. A few days after the jail episode, according to the *National Intelligencer,* he sent a file of soldiers into Maryland to demand the restitution of a slave recovered by due process of law—though in defiance of a military protection—by Mr. William H. Offutt, a venerable citizen of Montgomery County. The *Intelligencer* stated that the soldiers, on finding that the slave had been sent to another part of Maryland, arrested Mr. Offutt instead, and the venerable citizen was lodged in the Old Capitol as a prisoner of state, until Mr. Montgomery Blair procured his release.

That same month, May, 1862, a proclamation of military emancipation was issued in the Department of the South. It was the act of Lincoln's old friend, Major-General David Hunter, who after serving for some time in the West had been placed in command of the coastal regions of South Carolina, Georgia and Florida, which had passed under Union control as the result of successful military and naval expeditions. The department was under martial law, and the white population had fled, abandoning their slaves. These thousands of blacks were cared for by the Government and by private philanthropy, and it was their freedom which Hunter, in all sincerity exceeding the powers of a military commander, proclaimed. On reading of this order in the press, the President publicly annulled it, with the quiet consistency which allied him in abolitionist minds with the slave-catching Lamon. To Hunter himself, Lincoln expressed no disapprobation, and their friendship was not disturbed by the incident.

At this same time, the President again besought the loyal slave States to adopt gradual and compensated emancipation, "not rending or wrecking anything." Against the conservatism of his course, the radicals of Congress fulminated. The President signed the bill prohibiting slavery in the territories; but when he forced the modification of a second confiscation bill, more drastic and explicit than the first, the relations between Mr. Lincoln and his party leaders were strained to the breaking point.

In public speech or writing, the President made no sign. Yet, after a hopeless conference with the representatives of the loyal slave States, his resolve was taken. The reverses on the Peninsula and the fierce political pressure forced him to the precipitate act of military emancipation of the rebels' slaves. It was designed to weaken the Confederacy by drawing off the Negro laborers who released their men for military service. In July of 1862, Mr. Lincoln had come to believe that this war measure was the alternative to surrendering the Union. He said as much to Mr. Seward and Mr. Welles, as they drove out to the funeral of Stanton's baby, James. A week later, he discussed the subject with his Cabinet. In September, after Antietam, he issued his preliminary proclamation: on the first day of January, 1863, the slaves of persons in rebellion against the Government were to be proclaimed forever free.

The country, in the main, received the proclamation without enthusiasm. Democrats interpreted their gains in the State elections which soon followed as a protest against the President's capitulation to the radicals. Abolitionists, on the other hand, were still dissatisfied with Mr. Lincoln's moderation. His wholehearted support came from the Negroes themselves. From the beginning, his name had been to the race the simple synonym of their deliverance. Colored folk, when crowds gathered at the White House, wildly demonstrated their love for the President, shouting and swinging their hats with abandon. In long columns, the contrabands came toiling over the dusty roads to the city he inhabited. Some were in rags, some wore the rough and sweat-stained garments of the field, some were decked in the antique finery of their masters and mistresses. The pickaninnies who rode their fathers' backs, the tiny black Abraham Lincolns who nuzzled at the breast were scarcely more helpless than those who carried them.

For these were primitive and childlike people, adrift without a plan from the dependence of slavery. They understood nothing of the political complexities in which their destinies were involved. They took no account of the abolitionists who pressed the President to his reluctant decision. They knew only that Lincoln was a man raised up by God to work the miracle of their deliverance. Their simple imagination had its own power. They and other millions like them, flocking to the Union armies of the West and South, or waiting on the plantations of their masters, impressed their faith on a nation's mind. The abolitionists of Congress—Wade, Stevens, Chandler, Wilson, Lovejoy, even the lofty Sumner—have been all but forgotten by their countrymen. The Lincoln who lives in the American legend was shaped in the slave's long dream of a kindly master who should set his people free.

In July, smallpox broke out among the families huddled in the little rooms of Duff Green's Row. The sick were left there, while the rest were transferred to the camp on North Twelfth Street, formerly occupied by the dragoons of McClellan's bodyguard. No Maryland fugitives were allowed in this camp, but Lamon's constables hung around it. In protecting his charges, Wadsworth remained defiantly paternal. He had two county constables arrested as kidnapers. In November, and again in December, there were spectacular jail deliveries of Negroes by the provost guard. The civil and military authorities were as much at odds as ever, when Wadsworth left to take command of a division of the Army of the Potomac, and the post of military governor fell to a less impetuous western New Yorker, General John A. Martindale. Meantime, the windows of Duff Green's Row had been fitted with iron bars, and the block of houses was transformed into Carroll Prison.

In their crowded and comfortless barracks, the contrabands patiently awaited the coming of the day of jubilee. On New Year's Eve, they filled the chapel to overflowing. An old man named Thornton arose to testify. "I cried all night. What de matter, Thornton? Tomor-

row my child is to be sold, neber more see it till judgment—no more
dat! no more dat! no more dat! Can't sell your wife and children any
more!"

Ecstacy mounted with the passing hours, and the silent prayer
enjoined by the superintendent at midnight gave place to fervent
invocations and hallelujah hymns. Young and old wrung one another's
hands, dancing and shouting in a frenzy of joy. Around the bleak,
dark camp, they paraded singing. Many marched until daybreak.

The sun rose on the first day of January, 1863. The air was clear
and brilliant. The President opened his tired eyes on a momentous
day. Since he had issued his preliminary proclamation, the defeat of
his party in the State elections had been followed by the military
disaster of Fredericksburg. The radical senators, demanding the
removal of the conservative Seward, had nearly wrecked his Cabinet.
The thing he was about to do had alienated some of his warmest adherents among moderate men. In Washington, that winter, he seemed
to stand alone, almost without friends.

Threading his way through the mob of New Year's callers about
the White House came the slender, amiable man whom the radicals
hated, with his slender, amiable son by his side. William and Frederick
Seward climbed the stairs to the President's office. There were less
than a dozen persons in the room to witness the signing of the Emancipation Proclamation. Conscious of a moment of history, the President
closed his aching fingers on a pen. His whole right arm was numb
from the ordeal of the morning's receptions. He feared his hand might
tremble; but he signed his name firmly.

All day, while an artificial conviviality surrounded the bowls of
eggnog in the Washington parlors, the wastes of North Twelfth
Street rang with the choruses of the contrabands. "I'm a Free Man
Now," they sang, "Jesus Christ has made me Free." At last, the
beautiful word was spoken, as potent and as incomprehensible as a
magician's spell. At seven in the evening, a bellman made the rounds
of the quarters, to summon them to the chapel for a reading of the
President's proclamation. In droves, they came from the cabins which
surrounded the muddy quadrangle of the camp. A grizzled old Negro
in a military overcoat, known to all as John the Baptist, led them in
prayer. Twin lamps suspended from the low chapel roof and a candle
or two set on a rafter cast a dim light on their dark, expectant faces.
The superintendent, Dr. Nichols, entered, bringing the white man's

quibbling precision to their unclouded jubilance. He explained that the proclamation did not free all slaves, but only those in the States and parts of States which were in rebellion. In Virginia, where this audience had many loved ones, he enumerated, county by county, the sections in which freedom was declared. Joyful cries arose. "Dat's me!" "Dar's where I'se come from!" Some sat in hurt and puzzled silence.

In the city, the Negroes who had been emancipated the preceding April, and the vastly larger group of freedmen received the news without disorderly excitement and with few outbursts of rejoicing. It was a great day for their race. But the intelligent among them were skeptical and disillusioned. The white man's oppression had taught them that freedom might be an empty privilege. That spring, the Reverend James Reed arose in the Fifteenth Street Presbyterian Church to say that he had purchased his liberty years before, but could not say that he had ever felt himself free.

Above all, it was fear that kept the Washington Negroes quiet. Since the emancipation in the District, there had been demonstrations of hostility to them. The Washington guttersnipes had been ready with insults and even with stones. The President's proclamation increased the antagonism of the white rowdies. Apprehensively, uneasy over rumors of a projected disturbance, the colored people gathered in January at the Israel Church near the Capitol, to make plans for a mass meeting in recognition of the proclamation. Stones thumped against the sides of the building. Panic spread, as panes of glass were shattered. The women, clutching shawls and cloaks and furs, hurried to the door. Some of the men huddled close to the wall between the windows. Others stood defiantly brandishing their canes. Even after the arrival of the police, some time passed before order was restored. The *Star* reporter was of the opinion that they would have defended themselves desperately. The proposed mass meeting was not held.

On a Sunday evening in February, the minister of McKendree Chapel announced for his sermon a text which inadvertently contained the word, Ethiopia. Part of his congregation walked in protest from the church. Even this Biblical allusion was interpreted as an alliance with abolitionism. A number of soldiers who had attended the service behaved in a disorderly manner.

Congress, in the preceding summer, had given the President authority to employ Negroes as army laborers or for any other military or naval service, fixing their pay at six dollars a month less than that of the soldiers, and providing that, if they had been slaves of rebel masters, they and their families should win freedom by their service. On the strength of this, Union officers had begun recruiting and drilling blacks in South Carolina and New Orleans. The Emancipation Proclamation explicitly stated that the slaves of rebels would be received into the armed service of the United States; and Stanton in January authorized the governor of Massachusetts to raise two colored regiments. There was widespread antipathy to this new policy of the Government. In the army, the officers warmly shared the men's repugnance to colored troops. This prejudice did not exist in the navy, where Negroes were freely enlisted, with the same pay and allowance as white sailors. In the country at large, save for a minority of extremists, the sentiment was bitterly adverse to arming colored men. It was well known that Negroes had fought bravely in the Revolution and the War of 1812; yet it was repeatedly stated and earnestly believed that they would neither enlist nor fight. Even Lincoln shared this opinion in some measure. In September of 1862, he had told a group of anti-slavery ministers from Chicago that he was not sure that much could be done with the blacks; if they were to be armed, he feared that, in a few weeks, the arms would be in the hands of the rebels.

In February of 1863, the troops in Washington were flagrant in their hostility to Negroes, chasing and stoning them in the streets. Convalescents, returning to duty, beat up the contrabands employed at the Soldiers' Rest. A few days later, convalescents on their way to camp in Virginia attacked every colored person they met along Maryland Avenue. No provocation was necessary. The sight of a dark face was enough; and in Washington dark faces seemed to be everywhere, as, drawn by the Emancipation Proclamation, the contrabands streamed to the capital and to freedom. The camp on North Twelfth Street was so crowded that tents had to be erected outside the enclosure. Its smallpox hospital was crowded, too, and complaints began to be heard about the careless burial of the dead in the graveyard on Boundary Street. The camp held only a fraction of the invading blacks. In April, 1863 it had a thousand occupants, while the contrabands in Washington were estimated at ten thousand, in addition to three thousand at Alexandria. The following month, a new and healthful camp was established at Arlington, and, under the supervision of the Quartermaster's Department, the men were employed in cultivating the abandoned rebel farms between Fort Corcoran and the Long

Bridge. Later, workshops were organized, where the contrabands became skilled blacksmiths, wheelwrights, carpenters, tailors and shoemakers. The Arlington camp developed into a model miniature city, the Freedman's Village, with houses, shops, a church, a school, a hospital and a home for the aged, laid out around a little park. The colony became self-supporting, with several thousand dollars to its credit in the Treasury. The vast majority of the incoming refugees, however, continued to take their chances in the city, which, as its inhabitants had fearfully foreseen, became littered with poverty-stricken settlements of Negroes.

Senator Wilson's bill to reorganize the District judiciary came before Congress early in 1863. Although forty-eight local lawyers petitioned against it, the bill was passed. A supreme court of four judges was created in place of the old circuit, District and criminal courts. The chief justice was David K. Cartter of Ohio—"a coarse, vulgar, strong-minded man," Gideon Welles said. His face was disfigured by smallpox, and he had an impediment in his speech, but his mind was vigorous, and he was in good standing as a Republican having nominated Mr. Chase for Presidential candidate at the Republican convention of 1860. However, the complacency of the radicals was rudely jarred when the question of the application of the Fugitive Slave Law to the District came before the new court in May. To the serious embarrassment of its members, they were unable to agree; and Andrew Hall, the young fugitive from labor who had occasioned their variance, stood before a hopelessly divided bench. He was released by the court, but a division of opinion pursued Andrew, as his Maryland master seized him by the collar, while Judge Dean of Brooklyn tried to pull him away. In the crowded courtroom, there was so much excitement that the police were called, and Andrew, for safekeeping, was taken to the Fourth Ward station house. The provost guard presently removed him to the contraband camp. Meantime, the court had disentangled itself from the slavery question by restoring to office one of the former commissioners of the circuit court. Andrew's status remained precarious, and, as Congress had promised freedom to all who should render military service, he settled the problem by enlisting.

The reappointed commissioner handled the cases of the fugitives precisely as had been done under the circuit court. In the autumn of 1863, runaways from Maryland dwindled with the opening of recruiting stations and the payment to loyal masters of three hundred dollars for every slave permitted to win his freedom by enlisting. In June, 1864, the problem was finally settled by the repeal of the Fugitive Slave Law by Congress.

In spite of antagonism and doubt, in spite of Confederate threats of retaliation, the Government carried out its policy of organizing Negro regiments. In the spring of 1863 Adjutant General Lorenzo Thomas was sent to the Mississippi Valley to promote enlistments from the multitude of slaves, advancing, "like the oncoming of cities," to the Union lines. For service to their country Negroes were not offered the same inducements as white men. They received no bounty. Although the fact was widely misunderstood by the first colored recruits, they were paid less than white soldiers—ten dollars a month without clothing, instead of the customary thirteen dollars in addition to clothing. As a protest against this discrimination, the Negroes of the Fifty-fourth Massachusetts Regiment refused for more than a year to accept pay. In 1864, Congress after much discussion and dispute passed a bill providing white man's pay and bounty for all Negro soldiers who had been free on April 19, 1861. This was, however, construed by the Attorney General to the advantage of all the colored troops.

By the time that the wounded began to come up from Chancellorsville, recruiting for the first colored regiment in the District was under way in Washington. It made slow progress. The available number of able-bodied contrabands was reduced by the fact that many were already employed, as laborers and teamsters, by the Government. The city Negroes, mistrustful, hung back. At meeting after meeting in the colored churches, white speakers and black worked to whip up enthusiasm. At the first of these meetings, Massachusetts soldiers stood on guard at the church doors and in the aisles. In the capital, a Negro recruit not only feared the vengeance of the Confederates if he should be taken prisoner; he was in immediate danger at the hands of his white comrades and the secessionist bullies who loitered in the streets. An army officer told one gathering of blacks that anyone who would insult a colored soldier in his presence had better have his life insured. He also mentioned a report that one of the city police had declared he would put as many bullets through a nigger recruit as he would through a mad dog. This speech caused a great sensation in the audience; but it was scarcely conducive to the military enlistment of a long-oppressed race.

Even among those who braved the community's hostility and signed the rolls, there were many who lingered on the fringes of subsequent meetings, hesitant to come forward and commit themselves. Forty or fifty of them were presently marched along, with red, white and blue badges on their breasts. They seemed to bear their honors well, in spite of the jeers from the sidewalk—some of which, the *Star* remarked, came from persons of their own color. No officers had as yet been assigned them. They had no quarters, no uniforms, no arms. In spite of Mr. Stanton's known enthusiasm for colored troops, there was a dispiriting tardiness at the War Department.

The third week in May, the rolls of the first two companies, mainly composed of contrabands, were made up at a desk set outside the Israel Church on Capitol Hill. Splendid among the shabby field hands, moved Dr. A. T. Augusta, a colored physician of Washington, whom Mr. Stanton had made an army surgeon. The sight of his uniform stirred the faintest heart to faith in the new destiny of the race, for Dr. Augusta wore the oak leaves of a major on his shoulders. The next winter, he would create a hubbub by refusing to ride in the rain on the platform of a streetcar, as he was ordered by the conductor to do. Offended by the disrespect shown to his rank, Dr. Augusta walked. He was very late in arriving at a court-martial, where he was an important witness, and his explanation echoed to the Senate Chamber, already inflamed at the streetcar discrimination.

While the contrabands waited to be mustered in, they drilled in squads in an open lot. The hours dragged on. The mustering officer, sent for in the morning, did not come. At that evening's meeting, the Negroes were assured that there was the most friendly feeling toward them at the War Department; but no more volunteers stepped forward. The enlisted men camped beside the church for the night. Sentries, armed with sticks, patrolled the lot, and a crowd of various complexions stood staring.

When the two companies were at last mustered in, they were hurriedly taken from Washington to Analostan Island, opposite Georgetown. There, out of sight, they were clothed in the army blue. Their removal was a discouragement to the white recruiting officers, who wanted to use them to stimulate enthusiasm and reassure the doubtful. These officers were not permitted, under penalty of arrest, to visit Analostan Island. One of them said that the President himself did not know where the colored soldiers were encamped, but had been driving around Washington with Mrs. Lincoln, trying to find them. No criticism was made of the War Department, but there were hints of outside interference. One theory was that trouble had been caused by a desperate fight to have District citizens appointed as officers of the colored regiment. The strictness and secrecy of the seclusion on the island may have been prompted by a fear of race riots and bloodshed, once the Negroes were armed, for civilians and soldiers continued their persecution of colored men. Early in June, a disorderly gang made an attack on the contraband camp, and seriously wounded several Negroes before a detachment of Massachusetts troops arrived to protect them. So numerous were the assaults on colored soldiers that a special military commission was appointed to examine the cases.

A few days later, a company of blacks was permitted to parade through the city. Fully armed, uniformed and equipped, they attracted a curious crowd. Little boys and an eager following of colored people trailed behind them; and the bearers of advertising banners for places of amusement kept step with their ranks, to engage the attention of the public. Later in the month, five colored companies, almost all jet black—"real Negro," the *Star* commented—marched down the Avenue to attend prayer meeting. There was something formidable in their appearance. No insults or outbreaks were reported in the press. By that time, Washington, scanning the news of the fierce fighting on the Mississippi, had learned that at Port Hudson and Milliken's Bend colored regiments had fought with desperate bravery and suffered heavy losses. The disciplined, dark-faced men in blue were beginning to be accepted as soldiers.

By mid-June of 1863, the capital had cause to welcome new defenders. Louder and more perilous to the city than the distant roar of guns at Vicksburg, an ominous rumble had sounded beyond the Blue Ridge. Raids and skirmishes had at first been ascribed to the rebel guerrillas who hovered in small squads along the Federal lines across the Potomac. But a hundred startling rumors flew along the Avenue. The details were various and contradictory, but they had one constant theme: General Lee was marching north.

The rebel cry of "On to Washington!" echoed up from Richmond. The Federal capital choked on a suspense as stifling as the summer dust. On a Navy Yard streetcar, the passengers spoke of barricades in the streets; and several ladies got out to study a pile of upturned earth on G Street, where a new flag footway was being laid. Jeb

Stuart's troopers wheeled dangerously near. There was a clash of sharp cavalry engagements. Wounded officers and men began to come into Washington. The name of Manassas rose again, like a ghost of old disasters.

To the north, the city looked in fear, as well as across the Potomac. The Shenandoah Valley, guarded by mountain ridges, formed a great fertile corridor to the Cumberland Valley of Maryland and Pennsylvania. Running from southwest to northeast, it brought an invading army closer to Washington with every mile of its advance. Once in Maryland, the enemy could easily descend on the fortifications of the capital.

There was a scare at Harper's Ferry. Somewhere on the upper Potomac, rebel troops had crossed into Maryland. Alarm was spreading in Pennsylvania. June 14 was one of the capital's "rumor Sundays." Some said that Hooker's army was protecting Washington, others that Hooker was retreating. An evening visit to the War Department left the Secretary of the Navy "painfully impressed." Lincoln quietly said that he was feeling very bad. Stanton, uneasy and fussy, communicated nothing. Halleck sat in silence, puffing his cigar. His relations with General Hooker were strained. They had known and disliked each other in California before the war. It had been a long time since Hooker had "enjoyed the confidence" of the general-in-chief.

On Monday morning, there was something close to panic in Washington. Rebel troops were said to be at Hagerstown in Maryland, at Chambersburg in Pennsylvania. There were rumors of a fight at Aldie, in Virginia, east of the Blue Ridge. It was a day of oppressive heat. At the bars, men turned from their long, cold glasses of whisky punch and sherry cobbler to read the President's proclamation, calling out one hundred thousand militia for six months from Maryland, Pennsylvania, Ohio and the new state of West Virginia, formed of the unionist counties beyond the Alleghenies. The week passed in a cloud of menacing reports. The governor of Pennsylvania and the mayor of Philadelphia were appealing for help. Fear gripped Harrisburg. The whole North was in a blaze of excitement. Militia regiments began to pour into Pennsylvania from New York, from New England, Ohio, New Jersey. The rebels were raiding Pennsylvania in force. Save for the cavalry, the Army of the Potomac might, for all the country knew, have vanished into thin air. The arriving boatloads of sick and wounded from the hospitals on the Rappahannock informed

Washington that the Federals had stripped themselves for action.
Washington secessionists said that Hooker's headquarters were at
Fairfax Station. Lee was reported to be at Fairfax Court-House. On
Friday, the capital heard that the fight at Aldie, north of Manassas,
had been a severe cavalry engagement.

On Sunday, June 21, Washington listened to heavy artillery fire
from the direction of the Bull Run Mountains. It gradually receded,
ending at six o'clock. Ambulance trains moved across the Long Bridge
to Virginia, and every day wounded troopers were brought in, many
Ohio men among them. The cavalry of the Army of the Potomac,
led now by General Alfred Pleasonton, boldly engaged Stuart's horsemen in the gaps of the Blue Ridge. So far, it was noted, not a single
Union straggler had limped into Washington. Rebel prisoners arrived
from the mountain passes.

Unexpectedly, Hooker had appeared in town. After a conference
with him at the War Department, the President's face was careworn.
The newspapers spread headlines that Lee's entire army was in
motion, advancing on Harrisburg. The enrollment of Washington
citizens for conscription began in an atmosphere of tension. Confederate cavalry were in Maryland now, seizing horses. It was said that
wagon trains had been seized in sight of the Capitol, that a rebel
scouting party had been seen near Georgetown. On June 28, Montgomery Blair and his father drove down Seventh Street at sunset to
their city residence, thinking it unsafe to stay at Silver Spring, Maryland. One hundred army sutlers tendered their services to General
Heintzelman as a mounted patrol for Washington, to relieve the
cavalry for action. Mechanics and laborers at the Capitol formed a
company for the defense of the city. Troops were moving into
Maryland, many of them men just out of the hospitals. With rattling
sabers, a veteran regiment of bearded, sunburned young troopers rode
up Fourteenth Street, bound for the Susquehanna. The menace had
moved from Virginia, was concentrated in the North. The Army of
the Potomac had advanced to meet it.

The announcement came abruptly that Hooker had been relieved
of his command, and replaced by General George G. Meade. A little-
known commander, with a bleak, scholar's face, was to lead the Federal forces in the imminent battle on which the safety of the East
depended.

Above the line which halved the hard, gray boulders of the

Maryland-Pennsylvania border, the Union cavalry moved through the dusty, green hills in search of the enemy. They found them on the outskirts of the comfortable, red-brick town of Gettysburg. On Thursday morning, July 1, the battle opened; and, before a rainstorm swept across the ridges on Saturday night, a hundred and sixty thousand men had fought with rifles and rocks and bayonets and new, long-range British cannon among the wheat fields and the peach orchards. Outnumbered and bleeding, Lee's army fell away southwest, along the Hagerstown Road. In the seminary yard, in the cabbage patches and among the graves of the hillside cemetery of Gettysburg, boys of the Army of the Potomac lay bloating in the rain. For a second time, they had thrown back the invasion of the North. The gallant soldier, General John Reynolds, had fallen on the first day. He had been born near Gettysburg.

For three days, Washington had held its breath, waiting for the outcome of the thunder and the slaughter on the free soil of Pennsylvania. All during the evening of July 3 and for the most of the night, the burning of firecrackers, squibs and rockets ushered in the celebration of Independence Day, and early on the morning of the Fourth powder was exploding all over Washington. Excitement was fanned by whispers that Lee's army had been terribly whipped. At ten, a bulletin put out at the *Star* office on the Avenue announced the victory, and the city was aroused to an enthusiastic rejoicing which it had not known for years. Crowds gathered in the grounds south of the White House—citizens, volunteer regiments, veterans of 1812, the Odd Fellows, the mayor and the members of the city councils. The Declaration of Independence was read, there were speeches, and Mayor Wallach gave out the *Star's* bulletin of the stirring news from Meade's army. The hot air shook with three times three and a tiger, and the Marine Band played "The Star-Spangled Banner."

The District militia regiments assembled on Monday, in response to the President's call, but the emergency was past, and they were permitted to disband. Dan Sickles came to Washington on a stretcher, one leg shot off and amputated above the knee. Bystanders marveled at his imperturbable face, as he lay with folded arms on the stretcher.

Next day, there was news that on July 4 Vicksburg had fallen to the forces of General Grant. The double victory sent the nation reeling in a heady celebration. Across the North boomed the salutes of the guns. Bells rang, buildings flared with garish illuminations, and people cheered the name of Grant and his right-hand general, Sherman. Headed by the band of the Thirty-fourth Massachusetts, thousands went to the White House to serenade the President, surged on to Stanton's residence on K Street, to Seward's on Lafayette Square.

But the first exultation was succeeded by a soberer mood. In Washington, doubt began to dull the hope that, abetted by the flooded Potomac, General Meade would destroy Lee's army. The Federals crept forward under hesitant and cautious leadership. Meade, after his magnificent success, seemed to be cut from the very pattern of all generals of the Army of the Potomac, and memories of past delays came back to haunt the capital. The fall of Port Hudson brought the assurance that throughout its length the Mississippi was open to the Union; but by the middle of July the noise of riots racketed down from the North, as the enforcement of conscription was resisted. New York was possessed by mobs, which burned and pillaged, and murdered innocent Negroes. In the uproar of anarchy and faction, the Union learned that General Lee's forces, with all their guns and all their plunder, had splashed across the Potomac.

For a moment, the North had dared to hope that the end of the rebellion was in sight. As the Secretary of the Navy walked slowly across the White House lawn, the President overtook him. They stood talking at the turnstile gate. Mr. Welles would never forget Lincoln's voice and face, as he said that he had dreaded, yet expected Lee's escape. "And that, my God, is the last of this Army of the Potomac!" the President cried, in the first pain of his disappointment. "There is bad faith somewhere. . . . What does it mean, Mr. Welles? Great God! What does it mean?"

"Your golden opportunity is gone," Mr. Lincoln wrote General Meade; but he did not send the letter. That conscientious soldier had been so offended by the criticisms of his delay that he had asked to be relieved of his command. His request was refused, but his achievement at Gettysburg had been permanently clouded by a dilatoriness that painfully recalled McClellan's after Antietam.

The Union was not yet saved, either from the armies of the Confederacy or from those more insidious enemies who spread disaffection at home. But, in spite of Copperheads and peacemakers and narrow partisans, there was a growing confidence in the country. The Emancipation Proclamation was increasingly popular. The Army of the Potomac had an awakening loyalty to the administration, did not like to hear it censured. The relation of slavery to the war no longer seemed remote. It was coming to appear the hateful source of the division of the country and the wastage of men and money. Before the need of replenishing the depleted armies—the losses at Gettysburg had been over twenty-three thousand men—the prejudice against enlisting Negroes faded. Late in the summer, General Grant wrote the President that the arming of the Negro, with the emancipation of the slaves, was "the heaviest blow yet given the Confederacy."

A disillusioned nation had lost its capacity for easy optimism; but it had learned to hold a grim and steadfast resolve. By the time that Mr. Lincoln journeyed up to Gettysburg in November, to read his short and simple speech over the vast graveyard of the battlefield, the Union was strong in the determination that, at whatever cost, white and black together, they would win this brothers' war.

AUTUMN LEAVES were bright along the Eastern Branch, as the jolly procession of carriages rolled across the Navy Yard Bridge. There were parties of sporting men in lively waistcoats, and smart, brass-buttoned officers on horseback. Mr. John Usher, the Secretary of the Interior, was driving out; and so were Marshal Lamon, Mayor Wallach and young Mr. John Hay. Everywhere ladies, in fall costumes of redundant skirts and sugar-loaf beaver hats, gleamed with scarlet like the maples. Chickamauga had been another costly blunder. General Rosecrans had been relieved of his command. The Army of the Cumberland, besieged at Chattanooga, might be starved into surrender, and the concentration of troops in Tennessee portended still more desperate fighting. But the war had lasted a long time; Tennessee was far away; and, in October, 1863, Washington was going to the trotting races.

By two o'clock, the stands at the new National Race-Course near the Insane Asylum were packed. The plank enclosure was blue with standees drawn from the rank and file of the near-by military posts; while carriage-loads of spectators covered an area of ten acres. In front of the judges' stand, the purse of one thousand dollars swung in its wire cage. The band played, the bell clanged, and the three contestants were driven onto the track: Butler, a slashing black gelding; a bay gelding called Prince; and Hartford Belle, a bay mare. Butler was the favorite. His name was actually General Butler, but he had been deprived of rank because military titles led to difficulties at the Washington track. The soldiers who formed a great proportion of the crowd had recently displayed passionate insistence that a horse named General McClellan should be permitted to win.

The race was for three heats out of five. At the second stroke of the bell, the track was cleared. There was a drum tap, and the sulkies went twinkling around. Butler won the heat. His backers greeted his success with deafening cheers, but he seemed to blow pretty hard, and there was speculation over his staying qualities. In the second heat, Prince struck out briskly, and was nearly at the home stretch, when Butler shot forward and came in a length ahead. Hartford Belle was withdrawn, and the two geldings got away splendidly for the third heat. Prince had a slight lead, but Butler passed him, and opened a bad gap. Prince closed up and the black gelding broke. To the excitement of the crowd, the bay won by two lengths.

The odds on the favorite dropped. He appeared to be a dull horse when not in motion. But the Butler backers were noisily confident. His driver had removed his coat; and his businesslike appearance in shirt sleeves was received with shouts. The tap for the fourth heat sent the geldings flying neck and neck. Suddenly Butler made a dash. Prince gradually drew upon him, and lapped him. For a dozen rods, the two ran beautifully together. Butler swung into the homestretch ahead. The bay pulled up, shutting out the daylight between them. Butler coquetted a little. Neck and neck, they neared the judges' stand. Then Butler went like great guns, and made the goal a neck and a half ahead. There was wild cheering as the black was driven up to the post of honor. The cage of greenbacks was lowered, and, with an air of nonchalance, Butler's driver crammed them into his pocket.

The excitement was over. It was time to go home to dinner, but it was long before the race track was deserted. The road was wedged with traffic, and thousands were obliged to sit waiting for their turn to move. In the clear evening air, it was a sight to see the dense train of carriages and horses dark along the sweep of road down by Foxtown and on across the bridge, winding at last up through the Sixth Ward. They would have preempted the whole width of the bridge, but the sentries kept them to the right, to leave room for the Government wagons and the droves of led horses, moving, eternally moving, even in trotting week, to the big cavalry depot at Giesboro' Point.

At least one incident enlivened the tedium of the homeward trip. Sarah Austin, the proprietor of a popular fancy house, chanced to drive alongside a carriage in which were seated two professional rivals, Fannie Lee and Fannie Dennis. One of them called out that the Austin equipage contained a "tub of guts." Madam Austin summoned the police; and the Fannies were hailed before a justice, and fined two dollars and a half each.

The press deplored the conduct of two army officers, who, returning from the races in an open barouche, sat hugging and kissing their "fair but frail" companions in full view of a regiment on dress parade.

It was not a new complaint. From the first, the *Star* had crusaded against the public consorting of officers and bawds. After Second Bull Run, it had sternly condemned the uniformed idlers who went "gallanting the painted Jezebels with which the city is stocked." But protests had been ineffectual. In 1863, the women of the town were as much a feature of the Washington scene as the soldiers themselves.

The *Star* was no prude. There was a sophisticated wink in its reporting. It was far too worldly-wise ever to have supposed that a great army could exist without women. Camp followers were a part of the military show, and so were the traipsing girls in soldiers' uniforms. The *Star* chuckled over a "handsome, fat little Zouave," with burnt cork imperial and mustache. The damsels of the District were bound to walk out with the volunteers. McClellan's army had fathered many an infant before it left for the Peninsula. Some of the mammas had wedding rings, but some, of course, had not. A number of them had left their squalling encumbrances on the doorsteps of the city. When the Seventy-first New York revisited its old encampment at the Navy Yard, the *Star* had its little joke about the wise babies who knew their own fathers; and it quoted an old pauper's jibe that the abandoned infants at the poorhouse were "the natural consequences of the rebellion."

In those pious but practical days, allowance was made for the weakness of sinful flesh, and prostitution, under proper restraints, was accepted as a necessary evil. The *Star* was wont to treat the wenches with a roguish masculine indulgence; called them by euphemistic names—Cyprians, fallen angels, daughters of Eve, the g'hals, gay young ducks. When it used harsher epithets, it had been provoked, like the rest of Washington, to righteous anger by the irresponsible volunteer officers who lost all sense of decency in their freedom from family restrictions. The spectacle of their concupiscence was not only subversive of military discipline, it was an affront to the chaste womanhood of the community. Tolerance of vice was strictly a masculine attitude. Ladies, hermetically sealed in their own virtue, might not even recognize its existence, and were permitted only a glacial unawareness of their fallen sisters. But, by 1862, if they ventured on Pennsylvania Avenue, they met on every hand the gaudy courtesans, promenading with the officers or lolling in their carriages. Painted equestriennes, in riding dresses and gaily feathered hats, galloped beside their spurred and booted cavaliers. In satin and pinchbeck, the women of the town staggered boisterously into the restaurants; and the attendance of respectable citizens at the theatre was disturbed by scenes of bawdry in the audience. One officer attended the Campbell Minstrel Show at the Odd Fellows' Hall with a harlot on each arm. The *Star* remarked that it would astonish the good wives, sisters, daughters, mothers and sweethearts of many volunteer officers, if they could see the female companionship they unblushingly indulged in at the capital.

Washington, with its population of unattached males, had always been noted for its prostitutes; but the *Star* estimated that, before the war, there had been not more than five hundred in the entire District of Columbia. The fallen angels of wartime had been recruited, like the soldiers, from the States. In New York, Philadelphia and Baltimore, and even in Chicago and St. Louis, ambitious madams had closed their houses; and, shepherding a choice selection of their misses, had entrained for the Washington market. The invasion was so sensational that it was easy to exaggerate its numbers. Major Doster, who as provost marshal kept a list of the houses and had them under surveillance, said that in 1862 there were four hundred and fifty registered houses in the capital. In 1863 the *Star*, after an investigation, made the considered statement that the city had about five thousand prostitutes, while there were half as many more in Georgetown and Alexandria. This estimate included streetwalkers, who were said to comprise at least one-third of the number, but did not account for the concubines, often demure little women, who were set up in their own establishments by officers and men, and sometimes passed as their wives.

On scrofulous hillsides in the Northern Liberties and in a scramble of mean passages on the Island, whites and blacks had opened a multitude of resorts. Nigger Hill and Fighting and Tincup Alleys welcomed teamsters and laborers and the riffraff of the volunteers to hovels where pleasure was dispensed in bare and dirty rooms, sometimes the abode of families with small children. Soldiers were often robbed of their pay, or pawned their uniforms and blankets to pay for drink. The poisonous tanglefoot whisky, illicitly dispensed, led to brawls, shootings, stabbings and riots. Most of the crimes for which soldiers were arraigned were committed in the dives of Washington.

Police Superintendent Webb openly stated that the principal

obstacle to the control of crime was found in the courts of the District. His report was made in late September of 1863, when the judicial system had been reformed, and the District supreme court had been sitting for over five months. Bail was easily procured, and the cases were postponed from term to term. Moreover, the District had no adequate prisons. The county jail was in such a state of decay that enterprising malefactors easily bored their way out of "the iron cage" in which serious offenders were confined, and, wrapping their chains in rags, ran off to freedom. The so-called workhouse was a part of the poorhouse, a charitable institution, where prisoners loafed at ease. The District Penitentiary, situated near the Arsenal on the Island, had been taken over by the Government as a storehouse for ordnance and ammunition. After the outbreak of war, criminals convicted in the District courts served their terms in the penitentiary at Albany, New York. Juvenile offenders were sentenced to the House of Refuge in Baltimore. Pending their trial, Washington had no suitable place in which to lodge the members of its own youthful gang of robbers, the Forty Thieves, or the runaway boys and delinquent girls who came trailing after the soldiers.

On the formation of the Metropolitan Police in 1861, vice and crime were so prevalent in Washington that there was no possibility of restraining the disorder with a force of one hundred and fifty patrolmen. The provost guard, which had acted as city police while the force was being organized, continued to combine military and civil duties. At first, there was some friction between the police and the guard. In the autumn of 1861, under the headline, "The Provost Guard Hitch Their Horses at Madame Duprez's" the *Star* grew satirical over the onerous duties of the soldiers in the brothels of Marble Alley. A police sergeant had reported that he had found an officer of the guard in bed at the Duprez house, while his squad was "cutting up high" in the neighborhood. The delinquents must have been promptly purged, for no subsequent irregularities were publicized, and the provost guard became the terror of the lawbreakers. Washington welcomed military protection, and arbitrary methods of handling crime were accepted as a necessary part of the wartime emergency. In 1863, the guard began a system of summary roundups of criminals and vagrants who showed their faces in the capital. Handcuffed and labeled with large red placards, bearing the words, "Pickpocket and Thief," they were paraded on the Avenue. Behind them followed a fife and drum corps, playing "The Rogue's March," and a jeering troop of men and boys. The undesirable visitors were then hustled on board the cars. This medieval procedure attracted much attention from the Washington populace; but it failed to reduce crime. The capital continued to swarm with underworld characters from all parts of the Union. A gang of robbers made their headquarters in the Smithsonian grounds, and pickpockets flourished in every public gathering; while gambling hells, illicit liquor houses and brothels were declared by Superintendent Webb to be "fearfully on the increase."

Night after night, among the thieves, the bullies and the roistering soldiers, the drabs bedizened the police courts. The charge of prostitution was lightly treated. Many cases were dismissed, others were let off with a small fine. Sometimes the girls were locked up for the night; and, if they were drunk and made trouble, they were sent to the workhouse for a short term. Rarely, the magistrate ordered women to leave town, and a few were sent to New York by the provost marshal. As the houses multiplied, the police and soldiers began to raid and close them. That the system did not act as a deterrent was illustrated in the annals of the Lights, a family indigenous to the District. There were five Lights, father, mother and three daughters, and they had made themselves notorious in every unsavory section of the capital; an alley on English Hill, in the Northern Liberties, was named for them. Early in the war, the father enlisted, and, after several carousals with his family, his name disappeared from the police records. The mother ran the "house," where Kate and Anna and Matilda purveyed their charms to the soldiers. Life for the Lights was a kind of squalid lark. Once, they engaged an organ-grinder and monkey, and danced their clothes off to the rhythm of mechanical melodies, until the racket brought the police, and they were carried, monkey and all, before the magistrate. Noisy, quarrelsome and outrageously profane, the sisters were repeatedly sent to the workhouse. They were chased from the Island, from English Hill, from an empty barracks on North Seventh Street. Then they crossed the boundary line to occupy a shanty near Cliffburne Hospital. There was a fracas between two groups of visitors—some boys of the Second District Regiment and a party of Pennsylvania Bucktails—and they were again evicted. In early July of 1863, while the guns roared over Gettysburg, Kate, Anna and Matilda were reluctantly torn from a free-for-all fight with eighteen soldiers. They were arrested, as usual. In the autumn, they were back on the Island, incorrigibly open for business in new quarters in Pear Tree Alley.

If the Lights and their various neighbors had made up the whole tale of Washington's vice, respectable people might still have slept in peace. But the ambitious madams of the Union had no intention of setting up their establishments in sordid surroundings. They liked fine mansions with gardens, and discreet little brick residences which fronted on tree-shaded streets. In addition to high rents, they were willing to pay the large premiums demanded in Washington during the war, and agents and landlords winked at their "boarding-houses," which soon spread through all parts of the city. Entire blocks on the south side of Pennsylvania Avenue were devoted to the business. Marble Alley, where Sal Austin and Julia Deane had their high-class resorts, lay between Pennsylvania Avenue and Missouri Avenue, a good residential section. Brothels were numerous in the First and Second Wards, to the east and west of the White House and Lafayette Square. Twelfth and Thirteenth Streets had a large quota, and so had D and E Streets. One whole section of the Second Ward was christened Hooker's Division. A large establishment known as the Club House immediately adjoined the First Baptist Church on Thirteenth Street. In this godly vicinity, the hacks of the sporting men were thickly ranked, and saucy women flounced in and out in full view of the horrified churchgoers on Sundays.

The outrage of the capital's citizens was vented on the volunteer officers. All night, before the fancy houses stood long rows of saddled horses. Even when the gas lamps paled in the daylight and honest persons began to be abroad, the tired orderlies were still waiting. In one locality, the residents threatened to make up a list of officers who frequented "notorious places of infamy," and report them to the commanding general, and to their families at home. Brazen misconduct in public places was bad enough; it was intolerable to find it rampant at the very doors of decent folk. Shrieks and revelry rent the midnight air; and respectable ladies suffered the extreme mortification of having their homes entered by a rabble of men who had mistaken the address.

In the expensive resorts, there were luxurious furnishings, and the pretty young hostesses were dressed in silk. One fashionable establishment maintained a summer place at Great Falls, twelve miles up the Potomac, as a retreat for the personnel when business was dull.

Yet the red-plush houses had many resemblances to the cheap and barren dives. The privy at Sal Austin's, like many another in the Northern Liberties and on the Island, gave up the body of a new-born infant. Whisky was illicitly sold. Drunken men grew rough and excited. Pistol shots rang on the midnight air, and frightened girls bawled from the windows for the police. A roundsman was stabbed in Marble Alley.

By the spring of 1862, the columns of the *Star* were lively with the "descents" of police and provost guard on the town's bordellos. The soldiers knew the names: the Ironclad (also known as the Monitor and the Post-Office), Fort Sumter, Headquarters U. S. A., the Devil's Own, the Wolf's Den (kept by Mrs. Wolf), the Haystack (kept by Mrs. Hay), the Cottage by the Sea, the Blue Goose, Madam Wilton's Private Residence for Ladies, Madam Russell's Bake Oven. Fanatical in his devotion to his work was Lieutenant W. G. Raymond of the provost guard. In civil life, he had been a clergyman. He was not strong, but he spent many arduous nights before he was forced to take up the less exacting duties of hospital chaplain. Men in army blue—and a few in broadcloth, as well—scurried before the tramp of Raymond's squad in the street below. There were often eagles and oak leaves on the shoulders of the coats they hastily donned. Sometimes they escaped. Otherwise officers and men were taken to the police station. The madams met the guard with prompt co-operation, ordered every room to be thrown open. "They made it a kind of point of honor," wrote Major Doster, "to obey with alacrity what they could not help." The girls from the high-class houses were never detained. From fat purses the madams slapped down the money for their fines. The brothels were locked and declared to have been "broken up." As the provost marshal and the superintendent of police well knew, they had merely been moved on. The same method was employed in "breaking up" gambling houses, and liquor shops which were either unlicensed or failed to observe the early closing hour. In these cases, however, the system was somewhat more effective, for raiders confiscated the gambling paraphernalia, and poured the whisky into the gutter. The stock in trade of the madams packed their tinsel belongings and fluttered unimpaired to a new address.

Equally unavailing in reducing the social evil was the provost marshal's order which prohibited the employment of "pretty waiter girls" in lager beer and concert saloons. These well-known places of assignation were cleaned up; but the girls took to the Avenue, to swell the throng of street-walkers who greeted the routed Federals after Second Bull Run. "Quinine may be the need of the Confederate army," wrote the *Star*, "but copavia [i.e., *copaiva*, a balsam then used in treating affections of the mucous membranes] is certainly the necessity of ours."

Occasionally, the Washington prostitutes made excursions in the wake of the advancing army, notably at the time of Antietam; but their places were quickly filled. Only one exodus made any impression on the community—the departure early in 1863 of certain females, notorious not only for their want of chastity but for their Southern sympathies. Like the Episcopalians, the gentlefolk and the Irish denizens of Swampoodle, the Washington bawds had a strong secessionist element. In hilarious mood, they were wont to drive about the streets, tipsily cheering for Jeff Davis, singing "The Bonnie Blue Flag," and shouting that Stonewall Jackson was coming to blow the city to hell. When the Government arranged to send Southern ladies from the capital to their friends in Richmond, seventy of the six hundred applicants were prostitutes. A large party was loaded on a steamer which left the Sixth Street wharf on a cold January day. All night, the officers had been examining baggage, taking out dry goods, shoes, medicines, pins, needles and thread sorely needed in the blockaded Confederacy. Among the stiff-necked dames of the capital moved the painted daughters of Eve, as warm for Dixie as the best of them. Fort Sumter, the Monitor, Headquarters U. S. A., Gentle Annie Lyle's, Mary Hall's, The Cottage by the Sea and Number 10, Marble Alley, all had their representatives. A French Creole girl from Sal Austin's tearfully begged an officer to let her keep the articles in her trunk, saying that she would befriend him if he came to Richmond. The officer was not to be bribed. Mademoiselle was obliged to leave without many small possessions which were difficult to obtain in the Confederate capital. The whistle sounded. An exasperated squad of the Tenth New Jersey shooed off the visitors, trying to smuggle letters to the South. Handkerchiefs waved. There were calls of farewell. The assembled admirers of the fancy girls saluted them with a burst of applause. "It is better to give than to receive," remarked the *Star*, "and Washington sends the party greeting to Richmond. . . ."

There is no record of the reception of the fair but frail seventy on their arrival in Virginia. Presumably, they were met by their friends and went about their business. They were not prisoners, and were probably never seen by the Confederate exchange agent, Robert Ould. For, a few months later, the arrival at City Point of a mere pair of unseemly women in a group of exchanged civilians, sent the former Washington attorney into a state of chivalric apoplexy. In a letter beginning, "Sir: I send back to you two strumpets," he assailed the Federal exchange agent with reproaches justified by "holy feelings," "the sanctity of a pure woman's character," and even "the purity of a flag of truce." There was a solemn reminder of the Southerner's code of honor: "If I did not believe you were imposed upon I would be justified in taking this matter as a personal affront." The Federal agent was far too overwhelmed with shame to make the point that a woman might be light in morals and still adhere to Dixie. He meekly sent the secesh strumpets back to Washington, where they were confined in the Old Capitol.

When the party of Southern ladies embarked for Fort Monroe, they were not accompanied by soldiers, but by Colonel La Fayette C. Baker and his detectives. Baker had had his finger in a wide variety of pies since his appointment. People called him a cheat and a liar and a tyrant, but no one had ever been able to lay against him a charge of inactivity. With his large force of agents—popularly said to number two thousand men—he was hot on the trail of traitors, war speculators, counterfeiters, fraudulent contractors, and bounty jumpers in all parts of the country. In addition, Baker had time to spare for police duty in Washington. He seized contraband supplies of medicines, morphine and quinine, and arrested stewards and nurses who were robbing soldiers in the hospitals. The dirty gutters behind the Capitol ran with liquor spilled by his detectives. He charged into gambling hells and bawdy houses, ruthless in arresting guests as well as inmates. Washington was grateful. Baker's methods were highhanded, but the citizens of the capital, weary of lawbreakers, had nothing but praise for his energy.

While the gambling hells were a scandal to the good people of Washington, they did not as a rule create disturbance in their neighborhoods. There was a hush of secrecy about the large establishments. At the door, the applicant for admission was scrutinized through a grated window before he was permitted to enter "the carpeted, elegant jungles of the modern 'tiger.'" The rooms were dazzlingly lighted, richly curtained and hung with "voluptuous paintings." A buffet held decanters and cigars, and champagne and sherry and claret flowed freely. There was a supper of boned turkey, ham, chicken salad and other delicacies. As all refreshment was free, a careful gentleman might enjoy the worth of a few greenbacks lost at play in the evening's entertainment. Some volunteer officers, however, saw large sums—not always their own money—disappear under the long, white, be-diamonded fingers of the faro dealers. Recurrent irregularities in the accounts of paymasters and quartermasters caused the military authorities to notify Colonel Baker that the gambling hells must be closed.

Baker, however, was no more successful than the police and the provost guard in cleaning up Washington. Gentlemen continued to fight the tiger in luxurious surroundings, and drown the disappoint-ment of their losses in glasses of Veuve Cliquot. The brothels, the city's chief abomination, seemed to flourish under the raids of three separate forces.

In the autumn of 1863, the District supreme court joined in the campaign against the bawdy houses, and the grand jury began to take evidence against the proprietors. They had seldom been indicted in the District. An outstanding exception was Mrs. Wolf, the landlady of the Wolf's Den, who in the preceding spring had sat in the court-room, closely veiled, with downcast eyes, "looking the very picture of a modest and disconsolate widow." Although Mrs. Wolf was found guilty, she had continued to operate successfully at her new house, the Band-box. At her second trial, her penalty—a year in prison or a fine of a thousand dollars—was the heaviest given to any of the madams brought to justice.

The grand jury spread a wide dragnet over the houses of ill fame, and a tremor ran through the Washington underworld. Keepers of prosperous resorts were threatened with arrest and trial, with heavy fines and possible imprisonment. Superintendent Webb gave damning information against them. Mortified witnesses reluctantly made an appearance at the City Hall. An employee of the Quartermaster's Department, who had patronized a Negro resort in Bates' Alley, testified in green goggles "to defy recognition." The evidence accumu-lated. Twenty indictments were found in a single day. The police were called on to aid Marshal Lamon and his deputies in serving the warrants. Vice was by no means suppressed in Washington, but the business of prostitution was transacted with less flagrant offense to the community thereafter.

Only one of the ensuing trials received sensational publicity— that of H. C. Burtenett and Maude Roberts, jointly indicted for keeping a bawdy house on D Street, a block away from the President's Park. Burtenett reduced the antics of the shoulder straps to the final depths of degradation and absurdity, for he himself had been a volunteer officer. Although his name was variously spelled and the record is not clear, he had apparently served for a brief time as lieutenant-colonel of a New York regiment. After being discharged, he had obtained an appointment as major on Frémont's staff, and was subsequently dismissed for a second time. He was still often called Major Burtenett. In the dock, he wore an undress uniform, with staff buttons on coat and vest.

Maude Roberts was a young and smart brunette, and the courtroom was well filled with men, whose eyes rested with interest on her headgear—"rather an inflamed bonnet of red." Otherwise, with her "sober, virtuous-looking dress of black," her pure white sleeve cuffs and modestly checked shawl, Maude was a picture of discretion. The glances of her beautiful dark eyes awakened the sympathy of the masculine onlookers, and Maude was pitied rather than condemned.

Her paramour, Burtenett, did not fare so well. He looked elegant and complaisant, even rather distinguished. His face was intelligent, and a slight baldness and a pair of black-rimmed eyeglasses lent dignity to his appearance. He was, in short, a man of the world, a mature and fascinating villain, who could worm his way into the affections of an innocent girl and seduce her to a life of shame. The newspapers, raking up stories of Burtenett's dismissals from the service and charging that he had robbed the Government, had deeply prejudiced Washington against him before the trial was well started.

The drabs filed up to the witness stand to bear testimony. They painted, in part, a cosy picture of Burtenett's helpfulness in laying down oilcloth and putting up shades, helping out with the cooking, and serving "the family" at meals from his place at the head of the table. He had been zealous, too, for Maude's financial interests; had sold gin cocktails to the patrons at eight cents apiece; rowed with the four female boarders over payments of bed money, and found fault because they asked for second helpings of meat. Other testimony of a less domestic character firmly established the ex-major's connection with the management of the house. The counsel for the defense was Thomas H. Ford, lieutenant-governor of Ohio during Chase's gubernatorial term. He wasted no pains on attempting to exonerate either of his clients. He made a few indecent jokes about Burtenett, and pleaded Maude's youth and the discreditable character of the witnesses who had aspersed her. Burtenett addressed to the court a protest that the press had been his judge and jury.

The District Attorney, Edward C. Carrington, Virginian, Mexican War veteran and brigadier-general of militia during the Buchanan administration, had been chosen by Mr. Bates in the spring of 1861. At that time, the claims of the rival candidate, Mr. Edwin Stanton, had been strongly urged by Seward; and, save for Bates's strong feeling that he could work more freely with Carrington, who was a courteous gentleman and his friend, Stanton might have been making the speech for the prosecution of Burtenett and Roberts, instead of exercising a tyrannical rule in the War Office. Carrington developed to the full an opportunity for an oratorical arraignment of vice. Fixing his eye on Burtenett, "he photographed the character of the fornicator and the paramour of a prostitute." At times, the former major's composure was shaken, and he winced. The crowd in the courtroom was quite overcome by the District Attorney's eloquence. Handkerchiefs appeared in the jury box, as Burtenett's peers snuffled over the tale of his iniquity. It took them only ten minutes to bring in a verdict of guilty, with a recommendation of clemency for Maude. The judge let her off with a fine of fifty dollars, expressing the hope that she might mend her ways. The ex-major was sentenced to a month's imprisonment and a fine of five hundred dollars, in default of which he was to suffer a further imprisonment of five months. Burtenett was unable to pay the fine, but he was pardoned by the President some four months later.

In his charge to the jury, Judge Olin administered a rebuke to the city newspapers which had given publicity to the proceedings. Mr. Forney's *Daily Chronicle,* just celebrating its first birthday, was gratified. The *Chronicle* had refused to pander to "morbid and impure readers" for the sake of gaining circulation. The *Star* and the *National Republican,* on the other hand, had reported the case with what one citizen described as "reprehensible gusto." Their sales must have been very heavy to make the *Chronicle* so bitter over their "polluted columns." The stately old *National Intelligencer* had, of course, been oblivious of the whole thing. It seldom stooped to notice even the respectable news of Washington; and was preoccupied, that first week of November, 1863, with the siege of Charleston, military interference in the Maryland elections, and the situation of the Army of the Cumberland, still beleaguered at Chattanooga.

The scene of war had shifted to a safe distance from the earth-works that ringed the capital. Since Gettysburg, Washington had enjoyed a surcease from apprehension, if not from annoyance. Virginia was infested with bands of guerrillas who attacked isolated pickets, stole horses, threw trains off tracks and captured Government and sutlers' wagons. During the preceding spring, their leader, Major John S. Mosby, had performed the notable feat of creeping through the Federal lines at Fairfax Court-House and seizing a brigadier-general, as well as a hundred other prisoners and many horses. Mosby was a skinny, caustic, taciturn trooper who had served as a scout for General Jeb Stuart, and still reported to him. His hard-riding band was prin-cipally composed of Virginia citizens and Confederate deserters, some of them dressed in gray uniforms, some in the Union blue. Between their raids, they scattered, assembling at a signal, and their professedly innocent character when out of uniform combined with their dashing horsemanship to make their capture difficult. From the viewpoint of Washington and the Federal soldiers, the guerrillas were no better than highway robbers, a character that was substantiated by the fact that they were permitted to retain their spoils. They were, however, recognized by the Confederate government as Partisan Rangers, and received the same pay as cavalry. Mosby's horsemen appeared to be as plentiful in Fairfax County as Union troops, and much more active. Stories of raids at Bailey's Crossroads, Munson's Hill and Falls Church kept Washington in a state of perpetual vexation at the audacity of the rangers.

After Gettysburg, General Lee had retired behind the Rapidan. For three quiet months the two armies had confronted each other south of Washington. Late in September, after the defeat at Chicka-mauga, the War Department had taken the unprecedented step of depleting the Army of the Potomac to strengthen an army distant from the capital. The Eleventh and Twelfth Corps had been sent, under General Hooker, to the Army of the Cumberland. Hooker's impulsive request to be relieved of high command on the eve of battle had been prompted by resentment against Halleck. He still wanted active service; and, on receiving no reply to his report for orders, he had gone to Washington, where he was placed under arrest for visiting the capital without leave. In spite of this ungracious treatment, Hooker persisted in applying for subordinate duty with the Army of the Potomac, but his appointment was opposed by Meade, with whom he was on bad terms. The detachment of the Eleventh and Twelfth Corps offered an opportunity of giving Hooker a suitable command. This force of sixteen thousand men was rushed by rail to the danger point in Tennessee—a victory for Stanton's energy and decisiveness over the apathy of General Halleck. No mention of the movement was permitted to appear in the newspapers; but Washington, watching the passing of large bodies of troops, hearing the constant rumble of trains and screaming of whistles, understood what was happening, and was strengthened in the opinion that Tennessee was to be the scene of important action.

In mid-October, Washington heard of sharp skirmishes on its immediate front, as General Lee began a flanking movement, and Meade's army retreated all the way to Centreville. The rear guard was the Second Corps, which had fought gallantly at Gettysburg, under the command of General Winfield Scott Hancock. Hancock was a Pennsylvanian, handsome and magnetic, one of the ablest generals in the army. He had been dangerously wounded at Gettysburg, and the Second Corps had been temporarily assigned to General Gouverneur K. Warren of New York State, a topographical engineer, who had done his country great service by seizing Little Round Top, the key to the Federal position at Gettysburg. At Bristoe Station the soldiers who wore the cloverleaf now inflicted a signal defeat on Lee's advancing column. Lee fell back on the line of the Rappahannock. The gratification over the Confederate retreat was threaded with criticism of Meade's cautiousness in withdrawing the army to Centreville. The rumor circulated in Washington that Sedgwick would succeed him in command.

The popular impression that the Army of the Potomac was doomed to inactivity for the winter was increased by the passing of New York troops, furloughed to vote in the State elections. At the end of the first week of November, however, there was news of a successful Federal attack under Sedgwick at Rappahannock Station. Twice within a month, the Federal arms had met and mastered the enemy in Virginia, and the *Star* proudly called Rappahannock Station one of the most signal victories of the war. The capital cheered the prowess of the Army of the Potomac, but its movements caused scarcely more excitement in the city than the raids of the marauding guerrillas. Washington comfortably accepted the protection of the great army which formed a buffer between the enemy and the fortifications, where the regiments of the preceding summer were becoming expert artillerists. People in the capital, as elsewhere in the Union, turned first to the news from Tennessee in their morning newspapers. In command of the Army of the Cumberland, General Rosecrans had been succeeded by General George H. Thomas, the able Virginian who had remained loyal to the Union; and late in October General Grant had ridden into Chattanooga. Washington was like a tiny concert hall, vacated by a great orchestra. The music could still be heard; but it was no longer deafening.

In its respite from distraction, the capital had many concerns besides the bawdy houses and the crime wave which war had brought to the city. The provost guard was busy intercepting the female smugglers who carried liquor to the army. A female detective employed at the Seventh Street ferryhouse searched Mary Welsh and Catherine Hartnett, and found canteens fastened to their legs after a manner which the *Star* was not prepared to describe. "The unusual size of Mary's lacteal fountains" had already inspired the guard to draw two large bottles from her bodice. Soldiers had become expert in scrutinizing any departure from the normal in the female figure. An "extensive and unseemly bustle" had led to the discovery of a tin contrivance on one woman's posterior—a vessel composed of four sections, each holding one and a quarter gallons of "rot-gut whiskey."

The subject most seriously discussed in Washington was conscription. A gentleman who made a daily trip to and from Georgetown on the streetcars observed that it had almost replaced dollars and contracts in the conversation of his fellow-travelers. Early in August, in the courtroom at the City Hall, a blind man had drawn the names from the wheel. One-third of the drafted men were Negroes. William Johnson, barber and bootblack to the President, was among them, and so was George Washington, "the gorgeous headwaiter" at Willard's, and another "good-natured shiny-faced darkey" who was John Hay's special favorite. Southern sympathizers found themselves among the conscripts, and some Government employees were drawn; a clerk in the War Department committed suicide on hearing he was drafted. It was a farcically ineffective business. The District's quota was 3863 soldiers. By October the draft had procured 960, of whom 675 were substitutes, paid by well-to-do men to go to war in their stead. The white conscripts were sent to the camp on Analostan Island, while the Negroes went to the colored encampment at the contraband farms across the river.

Conscription, in general, raised but a small number of men for the armies. Its principal value was in stimulating enlistments, all volunteers being credited to the draft quotas. The Government bounty had been raised to three and four hundred dollars, and States, counties and cities frequently offered more than double additional premiums. A Washington committee, frantically seeking to fend off another draft in the District, solicited funds for bounties during the winter, but the citizens showed no liberality in contributing. In the autumn and again in the winter, the President called for volunteers, but on February 1, 1864, the District had been assigned no quota, and Mayor Wallach wrote Provost Marshal General James B. Fry to inquire the reason. Fry answered that it was because of the unsettled state of the population and the division of feeling on the subject of the war. The explanation, giving Washington a similar status to that long held by the border slave States of Kentucky and Missouri, rankled in the minds of loyal residents. The entire District quota, including deficiencies under former calls, was presently set at more than twelve thousand men. Reduced by credits for volunteering and conscription, nearly five thousand were still to be furnished by March 1, and soon after Lincoln called for two hundred thousand more men. Wallach, persistently assailing the District enrollment as excessive, succeeded in having it based on the census of 1860, instead of the greatly increased population of Washington in wartime.

During the winter, the annoyance of the capital was vented on recruiting agents and substitute brokers who quietly made their way into town, and, in spite of the vigilance of the provost marshal's detectives at the depot, carried off a number of contrabands to fill the quotas of Northern States. The Negroes, attracted by large bounties, were willing to go. The indignant District called it kidnaping. A Washington citizen might be averse to educating Negroes or sitting next to them in the streetcar; but his heart yearned toward his black brother as a man who could shoulder a gun.

An enormous increase in desertion was one of the notable results of conscription. Substitutes, when not professional bounty jumpers, were mercenary soldiers with no heart for a poor man's war. From the Army of the Potomac, they began to flee across the river below Washington in boats and canoes and on rafts. Many of them escaped, but there were arrests of soldiers, black and white, from New York, Pennsylvania, Maine, Michigan, Maryland, the District. In most cases, they were sent back to their regiments, but at Forrest Hall in Georgetown a prison had been established especially for deserters. Stone Hospital on Fourteenth Street was reserved for the sick and wounded among them. Washington began to hear the dismal detonations of the firing squad on execution days. The District provost marshal received an anonymous letter, threatening him with harm if he arrested any more deserters. An attempt was made to burn his house, and the stable was actually set on fire.

During the third autumn and winter of the war, there was much anxiety over the growing labor unrest among Government employees, as well as in private industry. The high cost of living in Washington—estimated at $1333 per year for a family of five—caused clerks to form a society to promote a plan of emigrating to Baltimore, and making a contract with the railway for a special train, with commutation tickets. The increased wages in private industry had not been matched by the Government, and there were protests over the ten-hour day at the Navy Yard and the Arsenal. Labor suddenly loomed as a factor in national affairs, not only because its supply had been reduced by the army, but because it had become self-conscious and exigent. Mechanics and laborers employed on the Treasury Extension were threatened by the chief architect with a decrease in pay unless they complied with a new regulation cutting their lunch hour in half. Nearly a thousand men laid down their tools, held a meeting in Temperance Hall and appointed a committee to wait on Mr. Chase with a memorial of their grievances. The Secretary of the Treasury urbanely heard them out, and then informed them that this was an unusual mode to adopt in obtaining the opinion of a department head. He requested the committee to advise the laborers and mechanics to go back to work, and trust to him that justice would be done. In the afternoon, the men returned to the Extension, and were on hand next morning at seven; but, on learning that the half-hour lunch period was still in force, they again stopped work. Although Mr. Chase deprecated the strike as a coercion of the department and informed the workers' committee that he could not treat with them as strikers, about three-quarters of the men voted to go back to work, taking an hour at noon, while they awaited his decision. About two weeks later, the Secretary rescinded the chief architect's rule. He later made an announcement that all strikers would in future be discharged.

In November, the bookbinders created consternation by calling a strike, and the bindery at the Printing Office was gloomy and deserted. They had been receiving sixteen dollars a week for a ten-hour day, and demanded either an eight-hour day or an increase of two dollars a week, promising that they would perform as much labor in eight hours as in ten, while the employer would be saved the expense of gas. Private binderies acceded to both higher pay and shorter hours, and soon after the Government reached an agreement with the workers' association. Meantime, the compositors at the Printing Office had briefly stopped work in sympathy with the bookbinders. This strike was called without action on the part of the Typographical Society, which, however, adopted a resolution that the rate of wages was insufficient.

The drivers of the street railway struck for higher pay. They had recently been raised from a dollar and a half a day to a dollar seventy-five, wanted three dollars, would settle for two. Conductors and hostlers replaced them, and the business of the road was not materially interrupted. Committees of strikers, posted on Seventh Street and the Avenue, attempted to persuade the substitutes to quit, and were sufficiently demonstrative to demand the interference of the police, but, at a meeting held by the drivers, coercion was frowned on as bad policy. The railway company granted the twenty-five cents raise. Both at the Navy Yard and the Arsenal, petitions for shorter hours were complied with. Stanton ordered the bureau heads to make inquiry regarding a reasonable increase in wages. Welles appointed an investigating board composed of one commissioned officer and three workmen, and in the spring higher pay was given to ships' carpenters and mechanics at the Yard. Other department employees, the Metropolitan Police, bricklayers, plasterers, carpenters and cabinet-makers all petitioned for higher pay during the winter and spring, and there was agitation over the starvation wages of the Washington schoolteachers.

On the whole, there was a disposition to sympathize with the just grievances of labor in Washington, and an effort was made to equalize the hours and pay of Government workingmen with those prevalent in private industry. In the readjustment, the women workers fared badly. There was an inexhaustible supply of them, and they were without standing, precedent or basis for comparison. Female clerks had been almost unheard of in the departments when Clara Barton obtained an appointment at a man's wage. As time went on, their numbers became one of the notable effects of the war. The "Treasury girls" alone constituted a sizable group. Women were employed on the Government printing presses and at the bindery, and in making cartridges at the Arsenal and Navy Yard. Their remuneration was usually much lower than that of the men they replaced. The Treasury girls were comparatively well paid at fifty dollars a month; but Major Doster remarked that it was little enough, when an ordinary room cost twenty dollars and board was hard to get at thirty. In 1862, female press feeders had been audacious enough to strike for an increase from five dollars a week to a dollar a day, and had won their raise because of the heavy pressure of work. When women at the Printing Office again struck almost two years later, they were unsuccessful in obtaining higher pay, and some, according to the *Star*, found that their places had been filled. Many girls, earning a pittance in the factories and shops of other cities, bending over sewing machines in lofts to make uniforms for the soldiers, would have envied their sisters in the Printing Office. The *Sunday Chronicle*, in a thoughtful editorial, discussed the low prevailing scale of female wages, and came to the conclusion that the Printing Office women were still underpaid. The pertinent question was whether a woman should receive enough for her daily toil to rescue her from want and preserve her from shame. The *Chronicle* had never believed that "what are called 'strikes' are always oppressive and unjust."

Belle Boyd, back in Washington from August to December, was untroubled by the high cost of living in the capital. She had been given one of the best rooms in Carroll Prison, the Old Capitol annex. Both of the rambling jails were crowded. Over two thousand Confederate captives from Rappahannock Station jammed every hole and corner of the Old Capitol, and stood in the yard, "packed as closely as apples in a barrel." It had become impossible for Washington to hold the large and growing numbers of prisoners of war, whose exchange had been blocked by acrimonious disputes between the Federal and Confederate authorities. As fast as possible, the captives were sent off to the big prison camp at Point Lookout in Maryland and the officers' camp at Johnson's Island, Ohio. In spite of omnipresent military commissions, the cases of political prisoners, smugglers, blockade runners, defaulting contractors and Federal military offenders were slowly disposed of. One of Belle's fellow inmates was a prominent Washington banker, Mr. William T. Smithson. It was his second arrest on a charge of corresponding with the enemy. The proceedings of the court-martial were not divulged, but the banker was sentenced to five years' imprisonment, and went off under guard to the Albany penitentiary.

The iron rule of Stanton, Watson and Baker had not succeeded in obliterating Southern sympathy in the capital city. The places of the six hundred ladies who had gone to Richmond were being filled in the autumn of 1863 by former residents who were stealing back through the army lines. Living was high in Washington, but in Richmond conditions were growing intolerable. Faces that had been missing since the spring of 1861 reappeared in the streets—halfhearted fire-eaters, tired of the pinch of the blockaded Confederacy. "Rats Leaving the Sinking Ship," headlined the *Star*. The Union victories of Gettysburg and Vicksburg had subdued their spirits, but they nodded and signaled toward Belle Boyd's window, as they walked by Carroll Prison. Government clerks and boardinghouse keepers gathered behind the Capitol park in the evenings, while she plaintively sang, "Take me back to my own sunny South." After an attack of typhoid fever, Belle obtained permission from General Martindale to walk in the park for a half-hour each evening, under guard. So many ladies and gentlemen congregated to watch her, uttering pitying expressions as she passed, that the permission was revoked by Mr. Stanton.

One night, a fine new flag which had been raised on top of Grover's Theatre was torn down and carried off. The incident aroused the wrath of the loyal population. The loss of a single Union banner was felt in Washington, which still made little festive show of red, white and blue, even in time of victory. The *Sunday Chronicle* deplored the unpatriotic aspect of the streets, and urged that the flag should float all day every day on the public buildings of the Government and the District—on the departments, at the provost marshal's office and Colonel Baker's headquarters, over every courtroom and at the police stations. The example, the *Chronicle* hoped, would spread to other buildings, to private dwellings and places of amusement. The newspaper was gratified that Manager Grover was prompt in purchasing another mammoth flag, to replace the one that had been stolen; and that Manager Ford had promised that his theatre would shortly fly the Stars and Stripes.

The theatres could well afford to show patriotism. The war was making the managers rich. The Varieties Theatre, on Ninth Street near the Avenue, invariably concluded its performances with a national song and a patriotic tableau, profusely decorated with flags—loudly cheered by the bluecoats in the audience. The big auditorium was like a barn, with roughly plastered walls and bare rafters. It had, however, been renovated at considerable expense, and a wheel of colored lights revolved in kaleidoscopic brilliance above the entrance. Canterbury Hall, located in the old Assembly Rooms behind the National Hotel, illuminated Louisiana Avenue with its powerful calcium light. Like the Varieties, it was nightly crowded with "soldiers and roughs, screeching, catcalling, smoking and spitting." Drinks, at ten cents apiece, were sold in the bar, and the entertainment was a potpourri of scantily dressed ladies, Negro comedians, acrobats and contortionists, broad jokes, farce, sentimental songs and satires on the management of the army. Matinee performances, suitable for women and children, were sometimes offered on holidays, but otherwise, save for a possible spree, family men did not frequent the music halls.

A year after the outbreak of war, respectable Washington had been provided with an unprecedented wealth of theatrical entertainment because of the enterprise and rivalry of the two managers, Mr. John T. Ford and Mr. Leonard Grover. Ford, an amiable gentleman of high reputation, was manager of the Halliday Street Theatre in his native city of Baltimore. He made frequent trips to Washington, where his two brothers were in charge of his business. Before the war, Ford had been president of the Baltimore city council, and had served as acting mayor for two years. He had also managed the Richmond Theatre, knew that city well and had close relatives there. His Union sympathies were of the ultra-Democratic variety prevalent in Maryland and the District. Leonard Grover said that Ford's political opinions differed little from his own, and that they were both chary of expressing them, but on the record Grover made a better impression of loyalty to the administration. He had been born and reared in western New York, and had a friendly acquaintance with Mr. Seward. At the outbreak of war, he had been employed on a Baltimore newspaper; and, before coming to Washington, he had taken an active part in raising the First and Second Maryland Regiments.

Both Ford and Grover were keen young men who saw an opportunity for making money out of the theatre business in the capital. As was customary, they organized resident stock companies, to support visiting stars during their engagements of one or two weeks—or, in a few instances, longer periods—of repertory. Popular actors were entitled to a benefit night as a part of their contract, but the managers also took an annual benefit performance for their own profit. The greatly increased population of Washington readily supported two new theatres, in addition to the music halls and the occasional good bills still offered at the old Washington Theatre on C Street. Ford's first house, the Athenaeum, was a remodeled Baptist church on Tenth Street, between E and F. Grover, with his partner, C. D. Hess, assumed the management of a new theatre on E Street, between Thirteenth and Fourteenth. It was billed as Grover's, but some people called it the National, because it stood on the site of an old theatre of that name, which had burned down several years before the war. Although, in these high-class places of amusement, propriety was observed in the sections reserved for ladies, the rear seats and benches were occupied, like the music halls, by rowdies. If a gentleman were forced to sit in the back of the house, he needed, said the *Sunday Chronicle*, an umbrella and a life preserver to protect him from the sluices of tobacco juice, which ran under his feet in a yellow sea, laden with peanut and chestnut shells. There were vulgar fellows who laughed and sneered at pathos and tragedy, and some disturbed their neighbors by rushing out before the close of the last scene. Nevertheless, since the stars were famous and the bills well selected, there were seldom empty seats in either of the theatres.

After the Athenaeum was destroyed by fire, Ford had had no difficulty in getting financial support from wealthy Washington citizens to erect another theatre on the same site; and in August, 1863, the "magnificent new Thespian temple" had opened in a blaze of gaslight with the performance of the dramatic pageant, *The Naiad Queen*. There was a fine drop curtain, decorated with a bust of Shakespeare and a landscape. In ventilation, acoustic properties and optical advantages, the house was locally pronounced to be superior to any theatre in America. It contained fire hydrants with hose attachments, and accommodated twenty-four hundred persons. The admission was twenty-five, fifty and seventy-five cents. Painted Jezebels were barred from the audience by police officers stationed at the door.

Ford had learned that there was a greater demand for private boxes in Washington than in almost any other city; for, though they did not afford as good a view of the stage as the orchestra or center balcony, they were fashionable for entertaining theatre parties. At both ends of the balcony or dress circle, he had provided a number of boxes, in addition to four boxes built in double tiers on either side of the apron of the stage. The two boxes of the upper right-hand tier, from the point of view of the audience, were divided by a movable partition which permitted them to be thrown into one, forming a double box for the use of the President. Both were papered in dark red, carpeted and hung with Nottingham lace curtains. In October, Mr. Lincoln attended the new theatre for the first time, to see Maggie Mitchell in *Fanchon, the Cricket*. The double box was decorated with flags and flowers, and the President occupied an upholstered rocking chair, with a carved frame, which was part of a handsome set of furniture purchased for the reception room. Two weeks later, while John Wilkes Booth, the youngest of the famous family of actors, was playing his first engagement at Ford's, the President went to see his performance in *The Marble Heart*, which John Hay pronounced "Rather tame than otherwise."

In December, James H. Hackett played for a week at Ford's. He was a veteran of the theatre, soon to retire, and large audiences gathered to see his famous impersonation of *Falstaff* in *Henry IV* and *The Merry Wives of Windsor*. It was a role which especially interested the President, who had seen it presented on the stage for the first time during Hackett's visit to Washington the year before. Lincoln had written Hackett, inviting him to call, and on the Sunday which preceded his opening, the actor and the President sat down for an evening's discussion of *Falstaff*. The *Chronicle* said that Mr. Lincoln went to Ford's four nights running, while Hackett was playing. John Hay noted two nights in his dairy.

Leonard Grover, not to be outdone by his competitor, had altered and improved his theatre, increasing its capacity by a thousand seats. It reopened in October with the appearance of a team of stars, E. L. Davenport and J. W. Wallack, who were very popular in Washington. The celebrated tragedienne, Miss Charlotte Cushman—always Mr. Seward's house guest when she came to the capital—played *Lady*

Macbeth with Davenport and Wallack in a benefit which netted two thousand dollars for the Sanitary Commission. The President, Mrs. Lincoln and Tad were part of the enthusiastic audience.

Both Grover's and Ford's were launched on a highly successful season, when the opening of Congress brought the rush of winter visitors. Politicians and contractors and hangers-on crowded into hotels already busy with officers on leave and sutlers with an eye on the movements of the army. Tourists came in droves, with money to spend. Northern capital had been invested in District enterprises and business in Washington was thriving as never before. Government contracts for mattresses, iron bedsteads, hardware and stoves had enriched many of the citizens. Merchant tailors, saddlers, blacksmiths, stationers and hotelkeepers had amassed fortunes from the war. On Saturday nights, the Avenue, illuminated by blazing shops and hotels, surged with pleasure-seeking people. Along the street went brass bands and shining transparencies, announcing "Po-ca-hon-tas and the Webb Sisters" and "The star of Canterbury never sets." "This way to Ford's Theatre," bawled a boy stationed at the corner of Tenth Street.

To foreign visitors, Washington still appeared an outlandish place. Mr. George Augustus Sala, looking it over that winter as correspondent for the London *Daily Telegraph*, expended a deal of turgid and contemptuous rhetoric on the capital of the Union. He called it "a vast practical joke," "a hydrocephalous hamlet," and a "great, scrambling, slack-baked embryo of a city basking in the December sun like an alligator on the mud-bank of a bayou in July." But its residents, in the flush of a new prosperity, gazed on Washington with honest civic pride and felt a warm faith in the future of the city. The doubts of the spring of 1861 had vanished with the leisurely Southern aspect of the streets. The abundance of money and the demand for housing had sent up the price of real estate. All over town, shops and houses were being erected. The Navy Yard docks were filled with vessels under repair. Blacksmiths hammered, carpenters sawed and planed. Guns, howitzers, copperplate, bullets, caps, fuses, rockets and cartridges were manufactured. Frigates were built and launched. The vast main reservoir of the Washington waterworks was opened with appropriate ceremonies. The public buildings, whose prone pillars and scattered ornaments had once recalled the ruins of antiquity, were being pushed to completion in the midst of war. There were brand-new carpets in the Hall of Representatives, and a splendid bronze door, depicting the history of Columbus, was set up at the entrance of the corridor leading from the old Hall to the new. In the Senate wing, painters were frescoing the walls, and workmen were heaving the marble columns into place on the portico. Over all, the great dome grew round beneath its scaffolding.

Although the President had been criticized for continuing the work on the Capitol when men and money were needed for the war, he had been convinced that its moral effect was good. "If people see the Capitol going on," he had told a caller, "it is a sign we intend the Union shall go on." On the December day when the statue of Armed Freedom was raised to the top of the dome, there were no speeches or public ceremonies. A battery of artillery was stationed east of the Capitol, and thousands gathered on the desolate hill. The grounds had been disfigured by the tracks of the street railway to Georgetown, and the dazzling white wings rose from a waste of mud and litter, brick walks and workmen's sheds. Through opera glasses, the crowd watched the tiny figures moving on the dome, and saw the tug on the wire cable as the pulley turned, hoisting the swinging bronze head, with its eagle's crest. For a moment, it hung above the torso, then settled into place to the metallic tune of hammer taps. Majestically, Armed Freedom rose in the cage of the scaffolding, leaning on her shield and her sheathed sword. The Stars and Stripes waved over her head, and cheers split the keen air. The battery fired a salute of thirty-five guns, one for each State, and thirty-five resolute times the iron voices of the forts replied.

The President had issued a proclamation, recommending that the last Thursday in November—long observed in New England and other Northern States—should be set apart as a national day of Thanksgiving. An abundant harvest had increased the prosperity induced by the boom in industry and trade. The country around Washington had a peculiar reason for fruitfulness that autumn. With the withdrawal of many encampments, farmers had returned to plow land enriched by the wastage of camps and corrals. Enormous deposits of manure in the city were, moreover, offered free to all who would haul it away. Fine houses were desolate, trees had been cut down and the litter of the abandoned camps marred the landscape; but the fields had never been so green.

To complete its thankfulness, the Union wanted news that its armies were moving; and, before the last Thursday in November, there was action in Tennessee. Grant's plans had been firmly made. When Sherman's army joined him, he attacked the rebel forces besieging Chattanooga. Across the nation, the newsboys screamed success. The story grew, swelling to a paean of triumph—Lookout Mountain, Missionary Ridge. In Washington, on the unaccustomed holiday, people scanned the extras which proclaimed such timely reason for thanksgiving. The heroism of the Army of the Cumberland and the Army of the Tennessee brightened the faces in churches and theatres and streetcars. Sherman, Thomas and Hooker were names pronounced with pride; and, above all, like an echo from the hoarse throats of the armies at Chattanooga, sounded the name of Grant.

Hard on this glorious news came word that the Army of the Potomac had advanced across the Rapidan. The nation looked for a crushing victory over Lee's weakened forces, and the old rallying cry of Richmond went up like a challenge and a prayer. But this time the story faltered. While the gold market nervously fluctuated, there were rumors of a reverse. The press, familiarly, grew reassuring—insisted that Meade was merely delayed, that there could have been no disaster. In fact, there had not been a major engagement. The Federals had intended to storm the Confederate position at Mine Run. On discovering that the fortifications were formidable, Meade had withdrawn his troops to their former encampment on the south bank of the Rappahannock. It was not a disaster, but a fiasco.

Not even the loyal *Star* tried to palliate this failure. The deep disappointment brought biting censure of Meade. Had he achieved even a partial success, his earlier delays would have been forgotten. Now they were all sharply recalled. Meade was denounced as another hesitating general, and rumors again circulated that he would be displaced from command.

But on the pleasure-seeking capital, the news of Mine Run made little impression. The social season had a diversified extravagance that winter, as the official set, the Washington parvenus and the rich visitors made merry. There was so much wealth in the city that several affairs took place on the same night, with plenty of sumptuous toilettes left over to decorate the boxes of the theatres. Mr. Seward gave his small dinners and his grand receptions at his residence, the Old Clubhouse. Schuyler Colfax—the blond and genial little Speaker of the House, whose nickname was "Smiler"—had a series of delightful parties, and so did Congressman Fernando Wood, former mayor of New York City, who had become the leader of the Peace Democrats. Thin and elegant, with dyed hair and mustache, Wood was a new and conspicuous figure in Washington. Although he was openly allied with the secessionists, he attempted to maintain a clandestine relation with the administration, and lost no opportunity to ingratiate himself at the White House.

One of the most important social events of the winter had preluded the brilliant season—the marriage of Miss Kate Chase to William Sprague, lately the Boy Governor of Rhode Island, now United States Senator. With her endowment of beauty and wit, Kate Chase would have shone in any society; but accident, too, had aided her to take an unrivaled place in the official gaieties of Washington. Since the semi-invalid Mrs. Seward seldom came to the capital, the Secretary of the Treasury's daughter was the first lady of the Cabinet. Willie's death had darkened the White House and there were no functions to contest the pre-eminence of the dinners, receptions and *matinées dansantes* at the Chase mansion. Kate's marriage, like that of a young princess, cast a radiant reflection far beyond the circle of exalted personages who were invited to attend the ceremony. Her starry career lighted the rooms of tired workingwomen. Many who had never seen her or had briefly glimpsed her in the street thought of her marble-white skin, her proud eyebrows and her glittering auburn hair; knew that pink was her favorite color. Simple lives were enlarged by the description of the long white velvet train of her wedding gown, and the lace veil clasped to her brow by a parure of diamonds and pearls, the gift of the groom.

Perhaps the groom seemed not quite worthy of this radiant girl. There was nothing very impressive in his insignificant figure, or his amiable face, marked by dissipation; but his patriotism was remembered in his favor. In his yellow-plumed hat, he had been among the first to come to the defense of the capital. He had gone with the Rhode Island troops to First Bull Run and the Peninsula. Above all, he drew importance from the bright stream that flowed from his grandfather's cotton mills. "Few young men have such advantages as he," old Gideon Welles had noted, "and Miss Kate has talents and ambition sufficient for both." Under her loveliness, Kate's core of purpose was as hard as her father's. Her wedding would cost four thousand dollars, and Mr. Chase was in debt. Senator Sprague would buy the house at E and Sixth Streets, and his father-in-law would continue to live there, paying board.

The Secretary of the Treasury's inordinate ambition for the office of President was an open secret. The *New York Herald* had suggested the probability that Mrs. Lincoln, "with her usual good nature," would permit Miss Chase to hold her wedding reception in the East Room, "in order that in view of a certain possible event she may have an opportunity of judging how its associations suit her." Mrs. Lincoln did not even attend the wedding; it was said, because she was still in mourning. The President took his stovepipe hat and stepped into his carriage.

Soon after dark, the people of Washington had gathered on either side of the roll of matting that ran from the carriage steps to the door of the Chase residence. It was an American crowd, patient, impudent, good-natured. On E Street, the long line of carriages moved slowly forward. The personages descended: the gentlemen of the Cabinet, the gold-laced diplomats; Generals Halleck, McDowell, Stoneman and Schenck, Senator Wilson, and the Honorable Simon Cameron. Laces and feathers swirled over the matting to the entrance, and jewels gleamed in the light of the carriage lamps. There were vivid beauties—young Miss McDowell and the daughter of the Brazilian minister. Still, the people in the street were not satisfied. They wanted to see the President. It was eight-thirty, the hour set for the marriage ceremony, when at last he came, solitary, without escort. Once in the streets of the capital, scarcely a head had turned to mark the prairie lawyer who had made his awkward way into the highest office of his country. Now people pressed and scrambled for a sight of his good, ugly face. Between their ranks, he walked to the door of his jealous Cabinet minister: a tired man, racked by a thousand anxieties, sick at the price of a nation's survival; a man with too much to do, too many people to see, who had to go up to Gettysburg the next week to make a speech.

In the parlors, draped with the national colors, the marriage vows were spoken, and the guests surged jubilantly around the bride and groom. The scene was invisible to those who lingered in the street; the window frames had been fitted with large mirrors to reflect and enhance the festive show inside. But strains of dance music came from the house, as beside the vertical gentlemen the circular ladies began to revolve like planets. E Street heard the "Kate Chase Wedding March," composed expressly for the occasion. The mansion trembled with a high-keyed explosion of laughter and tinkling glasses, toasting long happiness to the young couple; and Mrs. William Sprague, with a languid smile on her beautiful lips, swept confidently into a life whose misery not the poorest girl in the Printing Office, not the weariest of the superannuated trollops would have envied her.

In December, Washington society was fluttered by the advent of the Russian naval officers. Russia had sent her fleet into American waters for the winter. Smarting under the enmity of England and France, the Union rejoiced to have a powerful friend in Europe, and the officers had been feted in every great port. Anchored near Alexandria, the vessels which visited Washington sent groups of bearded sailors, with queer lettering on their caps, wandering through the holiday streets, to the marvel of newsboys and soldiers and belles in spoon-shaped bonnets. In the windows of the shops, they saw the gaudy and expensive trifles which pleased the capital of a nation at war: marble and china ornaments, cigar cases, slippers and smoking caps, cloaks and opera hoods, military and mechanical toys, hobby horses and pearly-toothed dolls that spoke and sang and even walked. The markets in Washington had never been so well supplied with grouse, venison, luscious oysters, quail, swan, juicy reedbirds and tender four-dollar turkeys.

The citizens of Washington had been mortified because the Board of Aldermen had refused to concur in the Common Council's resolution, offering the hospitalities of the city to the Russian naval guests. The officers were entertained by Mr. Seward, by the Russian minister, Baron Stoeckl, and by Mr. Welles, who gave a large evening party, with all the legations represented, although it had been rumored that some would refuse to attend. The admiral and several officers attended a lecture by Bayard Taylor, and, with a throng of diplomats, occupied flag-draped boxes at Grover's Theatre. Congressmen and their wives lunched with ceremony on one of the visiting frigates, and feasted on the choicest viands, washed down with champagne and Russian punch. Muskets served as candlesticks, and the banquet tables were adorned with pyramids of flowers furnished by the White House florist, John Watt. Every day a steamboat carried excursionists from the Seventh Street wharf on a sight-seeing tour of the fleet.

It had been hoped that Mrs. Lincoln would give a grand ball for the Russian officers; but the only entertainment at the White House was a reception given on the eve of their departure. The President had been prevented by illness from attending any of the functions in honor of the strangers. He had returned from Gettysburg in poor health. At first, he was thought to be bilious; but, by the time he was ready to submit his congressional message to the Cabinet, he was aware that he was suffering from a mild form of smallpox. His advisers did not flinch from the summons to the White House, but their meeting was a proof of patriotism, for smallpox was epidemic in Washington, and not all the cases were light. The scare spread, while the capital celebrated the holidays with eggnogs and feasting, and thronged shops and theatres and parties. People fled in terror from the streetcars at the sign of a mottled complexion. Many of the sick were carried to Kalorama Hospital, but there was no systematic program of isolation. Delirious Negroes stumbled through the streets, and died on doorsteps and in police stations. Senator Bowden of West Virginia died of smallpox, and Congress grew alarmed. Whispers that one of the House reporters had paid a visit to the pesthouse caused such excitement in the press gallery that Speaker Colfax asked the man to leave. Physicians offered free vaccination to all who were unable or unwilling to pay for it. The smallpox hospital at the abandoned contraband camp on Twelfth Street was set on fire as a precautionary measure.

Still, in the new year of 1864, the trains of Government wagons rumbled through the streets, pigs and cows meandered on the slushy sidewalks, and dead horses lay stinking in the winter sun. On hospital cots, men languished and died. Abandoned infants wailed in alleys. Recruiting agents ran off contrabands, and deserters stealthily paddled across the Potomac. Peculating contractors and quartermasters went to jail. There were robberies and murders on the Island. The grand jury brought fresh batches of indictments against the bawdy houses. The destitute starved and shivered, and the underpaid workers scrimped.

But Washington society flocked more merrily than ever to balls, private theatricals, tableaus, dinners and levees. In the third year of the war, a new spirit was abroad in the land. The whole prosperous Union was *en fête*—drunk, some people said, in its crazy pursuit of pleasure. The Sanitary Fairs, which raised millions of dollars for war relief, were mammoth centers of amusement in the big Northern cities. Washington ladies split into two factions, and the Sanitary Fair was not a financial success. A grand fair at the Patent Office, however, netted twenty-five thousand dollars for the benefit of the Christian Commission and the families of District volunteers, and offered Washington a week of diversion on a grand scale. Mrs. William Sprague had returned from her wedding journey to entertain more lavishly than before. Many secession sympathizers were coming out of their seclusion to mingle in the new world of fashion that had replaced the old. Banker Riggs gave a magnificent party in his baronial mansion, which in other days had received the Southern aristocracy. "Gayety has become as epidemic in Washington this winter, as gloom was last winter," wrote Frederick Seward. ". . . A year ago the Secretary of State was 'heartless' or 'unpatriotic' because he gave dinners; now the only complaint of him is, that he don't have dancing."

For dancing was the rage, and in crimson velvet and purple *moire antique,* in pink and green silk and white tarletan, the ladies tossed their cataract curls in the mazes of the polka and the lancers. Besides the private parties, there were the great Patent Office Ball and the Enlistment Fund Ball and the monster hops at Willard's and the National. The entire company was on the dance floor. No gentlemen lounged along the wainscoting, no spinsters sulked on settees. Young and old, plump and lean, pretty and plain, the ladies all found partners. Grave statesmen and stout generals capered as friskily as boyish lieutenants on leave, while the capital celebrated the third winter of civil strife with laughter and music and the soft bombardment of champagne corks.

Faintly, through the rhythm of the orchestras sounded the President's calls for troops. A second draft was ordered. On the summits of the Blue Ridge, the snow was growing thin and gray. The time was approaching when Meade must cease his dawdling before the capital, and march his army on Richmond and put an end to the war. Stretched in the mire along the Rappahannock, the Army of the Potomac had given Washington a welcome season of security. But a man cannot win a fight with his hands held before his breast. In Virginia, the Union needed a sword as well as a shield. The spring sun dried the mud with a portent of blood and death, as fashionable Washington laughed and flirted and danced, spinning like the colored, kaleidoscopic wheel in front of the Varieties.

WITH THE NEW YEAR, Mrs. Lincoln laid off her heavy mourning. She wore diamonds and pearls, and garlanded her hair with white flowers; draped her handsome black lace shawl around new dresses of purple and lilac and white and silver-colored silk. At the big public receptions, people saw the same richly gowned and artificially gracious little woman who had first appeared at the White House in the spring of 1861; but three years had worked a change in Mary Lincoln, no less than in the capital. She had reached the pinnacle of worldly success, only to find it rotten with pain and fear and hatred. Always of unstable temper, she had come to feel the jerk of panic, as well as anger, in her blood. A sudden noise made her turn pale, and put her hand to her heart. Her nights were startled by visions.

Mary Lincoln had come to Washington in the flush of gratified ambition. Her husband's election to the Presidency had justified her marriage to an uncouth and self-educated lawyer. It had never been a happy marriage. Mr. Lincoln had not been an eager or romantic lover, and he was an abstracted, if kind and patient husband. Against his unpossessable spirit, Mary Lincoln's craving nature spent itself in rages, productive only of further gentle withdrawal on his part, "Jesus, what a home Lincoln's was!" wrote his Springfield partner, Herndon. "What a wife!"

As Madam President, Mary Lincoln had attained power of another kind; but even in the first enjoyment of her exalted place she also encountered a partial frustration. In Springfield, she had accepted gifts in return for her influence on behalf of office seekers; and there was a story that a fit of hysterics over a diamond brooch had induced Mr. Lincoln to give in on one appointment. She was credited with great political influence. Possibly she may have favored the bestowal of the office of Commissioner of Public Buildings on one W. S. Wood, who had acted as courier for the Presidential party on the journey from Springfield. Wood had originally been recommended to the President by Mr. Seward, but in the gossip of Washington society he was spoken of as a "person connected with the establishment." Ladies tittered over the fact that he had been "dismissed because he would not put down the expense of a certain state dinner to the public account, and charge it under the head of 'Improvement to the Grounds'." Wood accompanied Mrs. Lincoln on at least one trip to New York, and gave her carte blanche to order any quantity of expensive wallpaper for the White House. He was soon replaced by the solid old Washington Republican, Major French, who had already held the office during the Pierce administration. Mrs. Lincoln nagged her husband into giving minor posts to her family connections, but she was forced to learn that her wishes were not paramount in the distribution of appointments, from postmasters to Cabinet ministers. She detested both Seward and Chase, and was at loggerheads with Stanton.

Socially, Mary Lincoln's position in Washington was a difficult one. As the wife of the Republican President, she incurred the enmity of the secessionist ladies of the capital; while, as a Southern woman, with the speech and manners of her native Kentucky, she was an alien among the Yankee matrons. With the greatest tact and graciousness, she could not have avoided criticism.

It had been taken for granted by strangers that Abraham Lincoln's wife would be unused to polite society. Kindly disposed Republican ladies showed her that they were ready to offer advice and assistance. She quickly sensed the implied reproach to her breeding, and never forgave them. Mary Lincoln had grown to womanhood among proud and hospitable people, the slaveholding aristocracy of Lexington. By the standards of the day, she had received a good education, had a smattering of French and could turn a graceful phrase in writing a letter. Her manners were not vulgar, but genteel; the manners of the provinces, more elaborate than the casual, easeful ways of cosmopolitan people. After the custom then still prevalent in the South, she addressed gentlemen as sir, using the word to punctuate her conversation, like a comma. This old-fashioned mannerism seemed affected, but it was by no means ill-bred. Mary Lincoln's stilted airs matched those of many a Washington dame who refused to call on her. Her stepmother had kinsmen in the capital. John C. Breckinridge and the Blairs called her Cousin Mary.

Nevertheless, the ladies of Washington society persistently jeered at Mrs. Lincoln as an outrageous vulgarian. Prejudice was partly nourished by her ostentatious way of dressing, by her unfortunate

choice of intimate friends and her arrogant assumption that they constituted a "court," and her quick resentment of even a formal courtesy
paid by her husband to another woman. Above all, it fed on an often
unconscious perception of the dark tides of her personality. There was
a look "very like cunning" in the smiling face under the artificial roses;
an almost coarse tone in the affable, company voice. Mary Lincoln had
been an attractive girl, plump, blue-eyed and animated. Greed and
jealousy and rage leave their marks on the face of a woman of forty-
three. When she had her headaches, as people in Springfield knew,
she lost all control, picked quarrels, railed at servants and screamed
like a fishwife. John Hay called her "the Hell-cat." If Mrs. Lincoln
appeared to be acting an unnatural part when she politely received
her callers in the Blue Room, it was not for the reason the gossips
whispered, that she had wanted gentle training, but because her emotional instability was too great to be concealed by the mask of acquired
discipline.

On the morning after the inauguration, four mantuamakers had
waited at the White House while Mrs. Lincoln finished breakfast.
One of them was colored—a former slave, Mrs. Elizabeth Keckley, who
had been highly recommended to the President's wife. Mrs. Lincoln
had a pattern of bright rose *moire antique* which she wanted to have
made up immediately for the first evening levee at the Executive
Mansion. She engaged Mrs. Keckley with the stipulation that they
were poor; if the mulatto seamstress would work cheap, she would
give her plenty to do. Only four days remained in which to cut and
fit and finish the dress, and Mrs. Keckley also had an order to make
a waist of blue watered silk for Mrs. Lincoln's cousin, Mrs. Grimsley.
When she came with the garments on Friday evening, shortly before
the hour appointed for the levee, she found Mrs. Lincoln in an angry
and perverse temper. It was so late, she said, that she had no time to
dress and go down; but Mrs. Keckley tactfully persuaded her. The
seamstress combed Mrs. Lincoln's hair, and arranged red roses in it,
and smoothed and adjusted the bright rose dress and the point-lace
trimming. Mrs. Lincoln was pleased. There was deference and kindness in Mrs. Keckley's manner. She was colored, and the Kentucky
woman felt at ease with her. She often acted as Mrs. Lincoln's personal maid; and she made her many dresses, cutting the evening
bodices to reveal the firm neck and rounded arms, fitting the rich

materials deftly to the dumpy figure. Mrs. Keckley became the only intimate friend that the President's wife had in Washington.

Although Mrs. Lincoln's tantrums were often vented on her husband, she was an indulgent mother. She had borne four sons, the second of whom—Eddie, named Edward Baker after Lincoln's friend, who fell at Ball's Bluff—had died eleven years before the family left Springfield. Willie and Tad, then respectively aged ten and nearly eight, were lively youngsters whom no one had even been at pains to correct. Lincoln was a doting father, blind to his children's faults, pleased by their racket and intrusions, and ready to throw himself full-length on the floor for a wrestle and romp. Willie, good-looking and blue-eyed, had been idolized by his parents for his frank and intelligent manners, and his cleverness at his studies. Their love for Tad was warmed by an intense and protective compassion, for he had a defective palate, and spoke in a halting baby talk which was hard for strangers to understand. Whether because of overindulgence or actual mental deficiency, Tad did not learn to read or write during the four years he spent in the White House, and he was still dressed by a nurse. In appearance, he was not stupid, but sparkling with mischievous enterprise. He was a forward, self-willed brat, given to asking impertinent questions and banging his drum in the ears of clerks and Cabinet ministers. Yet there was something winning in his impetuous, stormy personality. He had a tender heart, and his queer, muted little face was lighted by "dark, loving eyes." All the White House employees were his friends. After Willie's death the devotion of both parents was concentrated on Tad. The mother was also deeply attached to Robert, made many trips to Cambridge to visit him, and fiercely opposed any suggestion that he should become a soldier.

Two characteristics of Mrs. Lincoln's divided nature immediately became the subject of critical comment. She was at once avaricious and wildly extravagant. "All manner of stories about her were flying around," wrote young Charles Francis Adams, after attending a fashionable reception in Washington; "she wanted to do the right thing, but, not knowing how, was too weak and proud to ask; she was going to put the White House on an economical basis, and, to that end, was about to dismiss 'the help,' as she called the servants; some of whom, it was asserted, had already left because 'they must live with gentlefolks.' . . ." The Commissioner of Public Buildings was responsible for appointing and paying the doorkeepers, night watchmen, furnace men and gardeners, while others of the White House employees, including a coachman and footman, received their wages from the President. The secretaries disbursed about twenty thousand dollars a year for the upkeep of the mansion. Mrs. Lincoln's conception of "an economical basis" was to discharge members of the staff, and demand their wages for her own pocket. A year after her arrival in Washington, she was badgering John Hay to pay her the steward's salary. She engaged in controversies with the secretaries over the feed for their horses, which were kept in the President's stable, and sent the doorkeeper of the Executive office, Stackpole, to "blackguard" Hay on the subject, making no concealment of her opinion that there was cheating in the accounts.

Mrs. Lincoln had never had much spending money, but her shopping expeditions soon brought her wide publicity. Two months after the inauguration, she paid a visit to New York with Mrs. Grimsley, and purchased a solferino and gold dinner service, with the arms of the United States emblazoned on each piece. She also selected some handsome vases and mantel ornaments for the Blue and Green Rooms, and ordered a seven-hundred-piece set of Bohemian cut glass. These were but the premonitory signals of a great renovation of the White House. All its elegance was concentrated in the parlors, where the furniture, which dated from the time of Monroe, was handsome in its antique way; but even in these much admired rooms the decorations were soiled and shabby. At the session preceding an inauguration, it was customary for Congress to make an appropriation, to be expended under the direction of the President, for refurnishing the Executive Mansion. Mrs. Lincoln had twenty thousand dollars to use as she pleased, in addition to the purchases which she expected to charge to the Commissioner of Public Buildings, and she luxuriated in samples of costly damask and lace and wallpaper, and placed orders for carpets and materials to be imported from Europe.

During the first summer of the war, the President's family did not follow Buchanan's example of moving out to the cottage at the Soldiers' Home. All during June and July and even in the insalubrious heat of August, the White House levees continued. "Private soldiers in hodden grey and hobnailed shoes," wrote Mr. Russell, "stood timorously chewing on the threshold of the state apartments, alarmed at the lights and gilding, or, haply, by the marabout feathers and finery of a few ladies who were in ball costume, till, assured by fellow-citizens that there was nothing to fear, they plunged into the dreadful revelry." The President seemed in good humor, but Mrs. Lincoln, in the midst of her bevy of ladies, appeared less contented.

The state dinner for Prince Napoleon Jerome Bonaparte was the most important function of the summer of First Bull Run. Leaving the Princess Clothilde on his yacht in New York harbor, the Prince had come to see Washington and the encampments of both the Federal and the Confederate armies. In spite of a startling resemblance to his uncle, Napoleon I, he was known to have very advanced political ideas, and the capital was agreeably fluttered by his visit.

On the Saturday evening of August, when the dinner party took place, Mr. N. P. Willis, proprietor of the successful magazine, the *Home Journal*, was in the White House grounds, enjoying the open-air concert of the Marine Band with the rest of the Washington crowd. Willis was a foppish, middle-aged gentleman, admired for the grace of his literary style in prose and verse, and recently noted for dancing attendance on Mrs. Lincoln. Though he disclaimed any intention of catching a glimpse of royal entertainment, he had his eye firmly fixed on the mansion. He was rewarded only by the sight of the President, who, with his knees to his chin, was reading his letters at the window in full view of the south lawn. At half past six, Mr. Willis began to wonder whether "Abe" would be able to change his gray coat in time for a seven o'clock dinner. At that moment, a servant entered the room, draped a napkin around the President's throat, expeditiously shaved him, and shook the napkin out of the window. Mr. Lincoln's long arms moved about his head. He stooped—"for biforked disencumberment," Mr. Willis guessed. Presently, there came a gleam of white linen. The President's elbows shot out as he tied his cravat. He donned his black coat, and Mr. Willis checked the time by his watch—twenty-two minutes flat.

Mrs. Lincoln was elegantly attired in white grenadine over white silk, with a long train. The only other lady at the dinner party was Mrs. Grimsley, who had been staying at the White House for over five months. She wore a salmon tulle dress with natural flowers, and sat on the President's right. On his left was General Scott, while Mrs. Lincoln had the Prince Napoleon and Secretary Chase on her right and left respectively. Lord Lyons, M. Mercier, General McClellan and the Sewards, father and son, were also present and there was a retinue of aides, attachés and secretaries. As they entered the dining-room, the Marine Band struck up the "Marseillaise," under the inno-cent impression that any French tune was appropriate for compliment-ing a Frenchman. The Prince was said to have observed good-naturedly, *"Mais oui, ici je suis républicain."*

Like many sharp-tongued and destructive critics of human char-acter, Mrs. Lincoln lacked capacity for judging it. Young Charles Francis Adams heard that "she had got hold of newspaper reporters and railroad conductors, as the best persons to go to for advice and direction." Mr. Russell observed that she had "permitted her society to be infested by men who would not be received in any respectable private house in New York." "She allowed herself to be approached and continuously surrounded," wrote Henry Villard, "by a common set of men and women whose bare-faced flattery easily gained control-ling influence over her." Flattery was the unfailing means of winning Mrs. Lincoln's regard, but not all of the sycophants who made up the White House coterie were common. Mr. Willis was almost unbear-ably elegant. At one reception, a newspaper reporter satirized the elderly dandy by noting a wrinkle on the back of his coat as an attempt to set a new fashion. He was, however, well endowed with the qualifi-cations of a courtier. In the *Home Journal,* he gushed over Mrs. Lincoln as "unaffectedly happy," and declared that "the presence of a . . . most motherly and kindly woman . . . gives a home character to the great White Palace. . . ." Challenged by a correspondent for his use of the word "motherly," Mr. Willis tactfully amended it by ex-plaining that "the Lady President is at the most florescent point of her 'thirties,' and in the calmest repose of her noon of beauty. . . ."

Another well-mannered member of Mrs. Lincoln's circle was the disreputable Henry Wikoff, secret representative of Mr. James Gordon Bennett's *New York Herald.* Wikoff was a clever and polished man of the world, who had inherited a large fortune, gone everywhere and known everyone. It was said that no other American was ac-quainted with so many of the notables of Europe as the Chevalier Wikoff, as he was usually called, because of a decoration given him by Queen Isabella of Spain. He had been intimate with several mem-bers of the imperial family of France. While attaché of the United States legation at London, he had performed a mission for Joseph Bonaparte, carrying to him from Paris the valuables of Napoleon I, and receiving a silver drinking cup as a reward. Louis Napoleon, whom Wikoff visited during his imprisonment in the fortress at Ham, gave him the cross of the Legion of Honor. Lord Palmerston, on meeting Wikoff, offered him a connection with the British Foreign Office, and for a year the Chevalier served as its secret agent in Paris. According to Wikoff himself, he thoroughly antagonized the British. Soon after his work for the Foreign Office ended, he found himself in a little scrape. He was in love with an American lady, living in London, and claimed to be engaged to her. When she left for Italy, the Chevalier pursued her, and attempted an abduction, as a result of which he landed in a Genoese dungeon. It was Wikoff's contention that his long imprisonment—over fifteen months—was enforced through British influence.

This was the social spy whom the *Herald* planted in the White House—a glittering, middle-aged scapegrace, who had enjoyed all the gifts of life save stability of character. Villard ascribed Mrs. Lincoln's admiration of him to the fact that she had been accustomed only to Western society; yet Palmerston and Louis Napoleon had moved in wider circles. It is easier to understand Wikoff's attraction for Mrs. Lincoln than his own willingness to engage in a shabby employment, whose remuneration he did not need. On the other hand, he was in such disrepute that ordinary discretion should have prevented the President's wife from an intimate association with him.

> Wikoff showed the utmost assurance in his appeals to the vanity of the mistress of the White House [Villard noted]. I myself heard him compliment her upon her looks and dress in so fulsome a way that she ought to have blushed and banished the impertinent fellow from her presence. She accepted Wikoff as a majordomo in general and in special, as guide in matters of social etiquette, domestic arrangements, and personal requirements, including her toilette, and as always welcome company for visitors in her salon and on her drives.

The *Herald* paid Mrs. Lincoln's social career the dubious compliment of columns of unctuous drivel.

> At the capital [one story ran], she was thrown suddenly among a number of old-time fashionables, to whom her simplicity seemed rustic and her cordiality ill-bred, and who would gladly have patronized and controlled her. Without any apparent effort, how-

ever, the President's lady quietly ignored her would-be mentors, and took the lead of society with as easy grace as if she had been born to the station of mistress of the White House. Soon after, she came to the metropolis, visited the most modish stores, and —like the Empress Eugénie, who was as suddenly elevated in rank—displayed such exquisite taste in the selection of the materials she desired, and of the fashion of their make that all the fashionable ladies of New York were astir with wonder and surprise. Returning to Washington, the President's lady received and entertained the most polished diplomats and the most fastidious courtiers of Europe with an ease and elegance which made republican simplicity seem almost regal. Her state dinner to the Prince Napoleon, on Saturday last, was a model of completeness, taste and geniality; and, altogether, this Kentucky girl, this Western matron, this republican queen, puts to the blush and entirely eclipses the first ladies of Europe—the excellent Victoria, the pensive Eugénie and the brilliant Isabella.

In August, Mrs. Lincoln was tired, and took a holiday at the seaside. "Thus having burst upon the fashionable world as suddenly and as brilliantly as the last comet did upon the celestial," said the *Herald*, "Mrs. Lincoln is now about to leave Washington for a time to enjoy the purer air and more healthful breezes of Long Branch, and to achieve new triumphs in a brief summer campaign. Let all of our best society prepare to follow in her train."

Bob Lincoln, who in company with John Hay had preceded his mother to the resort, proved to be too moderate and quiet for the reporters of a sensational newspaper. The belles were "all aflutter to be introduced to, to dance and talk with Mr. Lincoln," and the *Herald* thought it a "strange infatuation."

He does everything very well, but avoids doing anything extraordinary. He doesn't talk much; he doesn't dance differently from other people; he isn't odd, outré nor strange in any way. . . . In short, he is only Mr. Robert Lincoln. . . . He does nothing whatever to attract attention, and shows by every gentlemanly way how much he dislikes this fulsome sort of admiration, but it comes, all the same. . . . Mr. Robert is happier when smoking a pipe, student fashion, and doing his share in a good laugh than among all the doings of the Branch.

Day after day, the *Herald* ran a column headed "Movements of Mrs. Lincoln." It was devoted to her doings at the seaside resort, where, in truth, she made little display, and seemed to desire seclusion and rest. She was not, however, offended by the *Herald's* cloying paragraphs. In October, she wrote Bennett to thank him for defending her against unkind comment in other newspapers. She explained that she did not want notoriety, and that her nature was very sensitive, and said that she hoped to welcome him and Mrs. Bennett to Washington.

In her first year at the White House, Mrs. Lincoln received more personal publicity in the Northern press than the President, and most of it was unfavorable. Several Republican newspapers made her the target of malicious attacks. She was assailed for her political interference, her extravagance and her Kentucky origin. Slanderous accusations were made against the loyalty of the President's wife. She was called "two-thirds pro-slavery and the other third secesh." It was noted that she had two brothers in the rebel army, and that one of them, David Todd, had treated Yankee prisoners at Richmond with brutality. Rumors had begun to spread that she was not only a traitor at heart, but that she was acting as a spy communicating the secrets of the Union generals, as she learned them from the President, to the Confederate authorities.

As a measure of self-protection, Mrs. Lincoln ceased to open her own mail. The second assistant secretary, William O. Stoddard, read every letter that came to her, even from her sisters, and examined every package. He could testify that there was no treasonable matter in any of them. Stoddard was a rather stuffy fellow, whom Nicolay and Hay disliked. He admired Mrs. Lincoln, and was angry at the injustice of the charges of disloyalty. Standing at the window of Mrs. Lincoln's sitting-room, the Red Room, he sarcastically reflected that this must be the scene of her betrayal of the Union plans. "The Confederate spies work their way through the lines easily enough, fort after fort, till they reach the Potomac down yonder. The Long Bridge is closed to them, and so is the Georgetown Bridge, but they cross at night in rowboats, or by swimming, and they come up through the grounds, like so many ghosts, and they put a ladder up to this window, and Mrs. Lincoln hands them out the plans."

Reports of Mary Lincoln's treason were persistent enough to cause the Senate members of the Committee on the Conduct of the War to gather in secret session to consider them. On the morning they assembled, they were startled by the appearance of the President in the committee room. Without explanation, he formally stated that he positively knew it to be untrue that any member of his family was holding treasonable communication with the enemy. The senators, astonished and uncomfortable, dropped the subject.

At the first levee of the winter season in December, 1861, Mrs. Lincoln faced her enemies in a figured silk brocade with her head brightly wreathed in flowers. She was beginning her own levees early, and she gave the secretary, Stoddard, to understand that she was willing to do her duty "while her smiling guests pull her in pieces." Her pride was soothed by the splendor of the transformed mansion. All the old furniture had been freshly varnished, and the chairs and sofas were upholstered in crimson satin brocatelle, tufted and laid in folds on the backs, "rendering a modern appearance." The changes in the East Room were striking. A heavy cloth velvet paper, in the Parisian style, covered the walls with a pattern of crimson, garnet and gold. A new carpet, of Glasgow manufacture, ingeniously made all in one piece, had designs of fruit and flowers in vases, wreaths and bouquets. The inner curtains, imported from Switzerland, were of white needle-wrought lace, and over these French crimson brocatelle draperies, trimmed with heavy gold fringe and tassel work, hung from massive gilt cornices.

The Green Room had also been completely renovated. The Blue Room had a new carpet and fresh paper. In the Red Room, the only familiar object was the old painting of General Washington. Upstairs, the state guest room was papered in light purple, with a golden figure of a rose tree, while the huge bed was cushioned and canopied in purple figured satin, trimmed with gold lace. The private apartments had acquired some modern furniture, and the Executive Chamber had been freshly papered. The *Herald* correspondent found the shabby old chairs and desks in the office "too rickety to venerate," but he remarked that "Mr. Lincoln don't complain." The only new article of furniture was the big rack that held the war maps, which the amateur strategists of the Government studied in earnest perplexity.

The President was innocent about the cost of the luxurious things which his wife was fond of purchasing. He was quite unaware that she was using the credit obtained by her position to run up large bills for wearing apparel. It did, however, come to his attention that she had exceeded the congressional appropriation for furnishing the mansion. After all the funds were gone, there remained a bill of some seven thousand dollars, for which a Philadelphia decorator named Carryl was demanding payment. About half of this amount was due for the handsome wallpaper, for which Carryl had made a trip to Paris, advancing the money for the purchases himself. The East Room paper alone had cost over eight hundred dollars. Papering the "President's Room" (probably the office), which including scraping the walls and furnishing gilt moldings, came to more than four hundred.

On hearing of the outstanding bill, the President said that he would pay it himself, and in extremity Mrs. Lincoln sent for the Commissioner of Public Buildings, Major French. Since his appointment, he had had ample opportunity to become acquainted with Mrs. Lincoln's love of money, and spendthrift ways with it. The opening of the winter social season had, moreover, put him "on the most cosey terms" with her because of his duty of presenting the visitors to the President's wife at the White House receptions. French was a stout, choleric old gentleman. With his arrogant mouth and his bristling gray side whiskers, brushed to the front, he resembled a cartoon of a Victorian papa. He kept a weather eye on Mrs. Lincoln, and winced suspiciously when she flattered him; but he was very patient with the Republican Queen.

Mrs. Lincoln was not up when French arrived at the White House at nine in the morning; but she presently appeared in a wrapper to implore him, with tears and promises of future good conduct, to get her out of trouble. She asked him to tell the President that it was "common to over-run appropriations." French obligingly went to Mr. Lincoln's office, and, without involving Mrs. Lincoln, said that Mr. Carryl had presented a bill in excess of the congressional appropriation, and that he would have to have the President's approval before asking for the money.

"It can never have my approval," French wrote that Lincoln told him—"I'll pay it out of my own pocket first—it would stink in the nostrils of the American people to have it said that the President of the United States had approved a bill over-running an appropriation of $20,000 for *flub dubs* for this damned old house, when the soldiers cannot have blankets." He asked how Carryl came to be employed. Major French declared he knew nothing about it, but thought perhaps Mr. Nicolay did. The President jerked the bellpull, and demanded Nicolay's presence. "How did this man Carryl get into this house?"

"I do not know, sir," said the discreet Nicolay.

"Who employed him?"

"Mrs. Lincoln, I suppose."

"*Yes,*" French heard the President say—"Mrs. Lincoln—well, I suppose Mrs. Lincoln *must* bear the blame, let her bear it, I swear I won't!"

Nicolay fetched Carryl's bill, and Lincoln read, "'elegant, grand carpet, $2,500.' I should like to know where a carpet worth $2,500 can be put," he said. Major French ventured that it was probably in the East Room. "No," said Lincoln, "that cost $10,000, a monstrous extravigance." (The spelling is French's.) It was all wrong to spend one cent at such a time, the President went on; "the house was furnished well enough, better than any one we ever lived in. . . ." He said that he had been overwhelmed with other business, and could not attend to everything. In his agitation, Lincoln arose and walked the floor, and he ended up by swearing again that he *never* would approve that bill.

In his interview with the President, French disclaimed all official connection with the bill, but he was not as uninformed as he implied. He well knew that his predecessor, W. S. Wood, had authorized the purchase of the wallpaper, and that it was chargeable to an annual appropriation of six thousand dollars, disbursed by the Commissioner of Public Buildings for repairs on the Executive Mansion. This money had been used for painting the outside of the house and other necessary work, and French did not want to be saddled with Wood's mistakes. On taking office, he had told Carryl that there were no funds to meet his bill, and he had also vainly advised Mrs. Lincoln to put off papering the rooms until the following year. In the end, French managed to get the cost of the wallpaper tucked into an appropriation for sundry civil expenses. Presumably, this also covered the "elegant, grand carpet," as well as a charge of over twenty-five hundred dollars for new silver and replating of cutlery which Mrs. Lincoln had ordered without any authorization at all.

French privately admitted that Mrs. Lincoln was "a curiosity" and a very imprudent woman, but he thought her an accomplished lady, and he knew that many of the stories circulated about her were false. There were few in Washington who did her equal justice. Holding her beflowered head high, facing slander and malice with an appearance of indifference, Mrs. Lincoln met the world with pride, even with a well-bred reticence. She could not muster the discipline to control her mania for display. It led her, in the flaring prejudice and deep anxiety of the first winter of the war, to issue five hundred invitations for a splendid private party. The entertainment was rendered doubly conspicuous by the fact that it ran counter to social traditions, for at the White House the state dinners were the only large functions which had a restricted guest list; all receptions were open to the general public. The innovation caused great indignation among those who had not been invited, and additional invitations were sent out to appease some of them. The President was said to have good-naturedly remarked that he didn't "fancy this pass business."

Whether from ignorance or defiance, Mrs. Lincoln had given her enemies excellent grounds for berating her. Extravagance and gaiety were in clashing contrast to the mood of Washington in February, 1862. Abolitionists bitterly criticized the merrymaking at the White House, and many declined to attend. Ben Wade's regrets were said to have been harshly worded. "Are the President and Mrs. Lincoln aware that there is a civil war? If they are not, Mr. and Mrs. Wade are, and for that reason decline to participate in feasting and dancing."

The *New York Herald,* always the back-stabbing friend of the President's wife, defended her in a series of editorials which brought the ill-timed function wide notoriety. According to the *Herald,* Mrs. Lincoln had two motives for giving a grand *soirée.* One was her spirited desire to show the "haughty secessionist dames," who had closed their houses and refused to go out, that there was a fashionable society among the loyal residents. The other explanation was far more damaging, and the *Herald* hammered it with enthusiasm. Mrs. Lincoln, by limiting the guests, was "trying to weed the Presidential mansion" of "the long-haired, white-coated, tobacco-chewing and expectorant abolitionist" politicians. "Mrs. Lincoln is responsible to Congress for the Presidential spoons," said the *Herald,* "and it is not safe to trust an ice cream thus manipulated in the itching fingers of these sweet smelling patriots." The President's wife was thus advertised as having aimed an intentional insult at the powerful and vindictive radical faction of the Republicans.

Lincoln paid for the party out of his own purse, but his wife spared no expense. Not content with the local caterers, she engaged Maillard of New York to prepare the supper, and he arrived several days in advance with a retinue of waiters, cooks and artists in confectionery. On the great night, Mrs. Keckley dressed Mrs. Lincoln's hair, and arranged her low-cut white satin evening gown, lavishly flounced with black lace. At her bosom and in her Parisian headdress were bunches of crape myrtle, and her only ornaments were pearls. Prince Albert had died in December, in the midst of the bruit of war between England and the United States, and Mrs. Lincoln had adopted half-mourning for her *soirée* as a mark of respect for Queen Victoria, whose representative, Lord Lyons, was among the expected guests. The long train of her dress drew a comment from her husband, "Whew! our cat has a long tail tonight!" Mrs. Keckley also heard the President say that he thought it would be in better style if some of that tail were nearer the head.

As she stood with the President in the center of the East Room, while the guests presented their cards at the door, and streamed through the flower-decked parlors, Mrs. Lincoln enjoyed a social triumph. Her party had been savagely attacked, but all the important people had come to it. The diplomatic corps made a brilliant group— Lord Lyons, M. Mercier, M. Stoeckl, M. von Limburg, Señor Tassara, Count Piper, Chevalier Bertinatti and the rest. A patter of languages sounded in the Blue Room, where General McDowell, conversing in perfect French, was made much of by the Europeans.

There were Cabinet members, senators, representatives, distinguished citizens and beautiful women from nearly every State. Few army officers were present below the rank of division commander. The French princes had come, and Prince Felix Salm-Salm, a Prussian nobleman and cavalry officer who was serving on General Blenker's staff. Hostility lurked beneath some of the smiling faces which passed the President and his lady. General and Mrs. McClellan were present, the center of curious observation. General Frémont attended, with his fascinating wife, Jessie, who had roundly assailed the President for not supporting her husband's disastrous reign in the West. Miss Kate Chase, said to have incurred Mrs. Lincoln's animosity by holding her own court at White House levees, was exquisite in a mode-colored silk.

Before them all, at eleven o'clock, Mrs. Lincoln led the promenade around the East Room on the President's arm. The Marine Band played in the vestibule, but, as a bow to the national tribulation, dancing had been omitted, although many young people, including Bob Lincoln, were present. There was great hilarity when at suppertime it was discovered that a servant had locked the door of the state dining-room, and misplaced the key. "I am in favor of a forward movement!" cried one. "An advance to the front is only retarded by the imbecility of commanders," said another, parroting a recent speech in Congress. General McClellan, struggling in the throng, laughed as heartily as anybody.

When at last the key was found, and the merry guests poured in, Mrs. Lincoln had reason for pride in the magnificence of the repast. Costly wines and liquors flowed freely, and the immense Japanese punch bowl was filled with ten gallons of champagne punch. There was nearly a ton of turkeys, duck, venison, pheasants, partridges and hams, and the tables were loaded with the confectionery inspirations of Maillard. A fountain was held aloft by nougat water nymphs. Hives, swarming with lifelike bees, were filled with charlotte russe. War was gently hinted by a helmet, with waving plumes of spun sugar. The good American frigate "Union," with forty guns and all sails set, was supported by cherubs draped in the Stars and Stripes. Fort Pickens sat in sugar on a side table, surmounted by deliciously prepared birds. At two o'clock the party was still going on, and Mrs. Lincoln's triumph had only one flaw. Her two little boys had taken cold, and Willie had a worrisome fever. Several times during the evening, both the mother and father went upstairs to bend over his bed, where Mrs. Keckley was in attendance. Lincoln's face was grieved and anxious, and in greeting General Frémont he spoke of Willie's illness.

The fever, which had been diagnosed as a cold, developed into typhoid, and for over two weeks the agonized parents watched the boy's condition become critical, dangerous, hopeless. The mother scarcely left him, but her enemies accused her of heartlessness, and said that the boy had been dying while the house rang with the music and laughter of her great party. In retrospect, the memory of that triumphant evening must have been blotted with anguish. Save for the official functions which she could not avoid, Mrs. Lincoln never again gave any large entertainment. Both parents were desolated by the loss of the blue-eyed boy in whom they took such pride. Lincoln repeatedly gave way to uncontrollable expressions of sorrow. The mother was prostrated and hysterical. Months later, she was unable to restrain her paroxysms of grief. Mrs. Keckley said that she could not bear to look at Willie's picture, and never again entered the guest room where he died, or the Green Room, where he was embalmed. Once, the seamstress saw the President kindly bend over his wife, take

her by the arm and lead her to the window. Pointing to the battle-
ments of the Insane Asylum beyond the Eastern Branch, he said,
"Mother, do you see that large white building on the hill yonder? Try
and control your grief, or it will drive you mad, and we may have to
send you there."

During Willie's illness, the animosity of the radical politicians to
the President's wife flashed into scandalous publicity. In December,
1861, Congress had been disquieted by the fact that a portion of the
President's message had been reported in the *New York Herald* in
advance of its communication to Congress; and the House Committee
on the Judiciary had been directed to investigate "the alleged censorship over the telegraph." The chairman of the committee was John
Hickman of Pennsylvania, a sharp and skillful politician who had
emerged from affiliation with the Democratic party to become an extreme anti-slavery Republican, notably unfriendly to Lincoln. Hickman subpoenaed the Chevalier Wikoff, who admitted that he had
filed the dispatch to the *Herald,* but refused to give the source of his
information. Charging into the House in irritation, Hickman induced
his colleagues to adopt a resolution that Wikoff should be arrested.
The sergeant-at-arms brought the Chevalier to the bar of the House
to answer to a charge of contempt. Wikoff remained discreet. He told
the Speaker that he had received his information "under an obligation
of strict secrecy," and he was sent to the Old Capitol prison. Wikoff's
intimacy with Mrs. Lincoln was well known, and the impression prevailed that she had shown him the President's message, and permitted
him to copy portions of it for the *Herald.*

The distinguished counsel for the prisoner was General Dan
Sickles. He was haled before the Judiciary Committee, and quarreled
so hotly with his former associates that, according to the journalist,
Ben: Perley Poore, he nearly landed in the Old Capitol along with
Wikoff. The arrest of the tarnished courtier had been generally regarded as a joke, but the imprisonment of a prominent Democrat,
wearing the uniform of his country, would have been a serious matter,
and in the end the Judiciary Committee concluded to exercise self-
restraint.

After consulting his counsel, Wikoff made a surprising confession. He said that John Watt, the head gardener at the White House,
had been his informant. Watt, appearing before the committee in his
turn, told a tale of having peeped at the President's message in the

library. He explained that the extraordinary tenacity of his memory had enabled him to repeat portions of it verbatim to Wikoff on the following day.

From this sensational story, the *New York Herald* extracted every drop of news value. In the face of all the evidence, it disowned any connection with Wikoff, held him up to ridicule, and blandly professed that its foreknowledge of the President's message had been "a shrewd surmise." The *Herald* also derided Hickman and "his kitchen committee," and righteously declared that the abolitionists were resorting to "an infamous attempt to break up the domestic relations of the President, and sow misery in his family." In another editorial, headed "The Satanic Element of the Abolitionists Assailing the President Through His Family," it was stated that "they invade the sacred privacy of his home, and seek to infuse poison into his domestic relations by scandalous insinuations." However dastardly the intentions of the House Judiciary Committee, in the invasion of privacy and the dissemination of scandal, they were amateurs in comparison with James Gordon Bennett. After receiving a letter from Wikoff, the *Herald* hinted that "a lady had called on him in prison." The newspaper further asserted that Congressman Hickman, at the introduction of Watt's name, had asked in disappointment, "Then it was not one of the President's family, after all?"

Years later, Ben: Perley Poore made a statement which must have reflected the information current among newspapermen at the time of the Hickman investigation. ". . . Mr. Lincoln had visited the Capitol, and urged the Republicans on the Committee to spare him disgrace, so Watt's improbable story was received and Wikoff was liberated."

Events had combined to end Wikoff's usefulness as the *Herald's* spy at the White House, and he disappeared from Washington, though not from Bennett's employment. A faint odor of intrigue with the Confederacy clung around the Chevalier. In the first summer of the war, he had besought Mrs. Greenhow to help him get to Richmond so that he might send back "a peace letter" from that city—a plan which he assured Mrs. Greenhow had met with Seward's approval. Shortly after his encounter with the Judiciary Committee, Mrs. Morris wrote Colonel Thomas Jordan of the Confederate army, "Mrs. Lincoln gave Wycoff the message you saw when they arrested him to make him tell."

John Watt was a petty thief who had been making a profit for years by padding his expense accounts for the White House grounds. He had been appointed head gardener in the time of President Pierce, with whom he had much influence, perhaps because he had been a protégé of the horticulturist, Andrew J. Downing. When Major French, nearly seven years before the war, had caught Watt forging pay rolls, he had had to carry the matter, not only to the Secretary of the Interior, but to Pierce himself. It was concluded that Watt had made errors through inexperience in handling money. Later, French obtained indubitable proof that Watt was a cheat and a liar, and he laid it before Pierce, without succeeding in having the gardener discharged. Watt retained his place through the Buchanan administration, and became captain of a company of District militia. W. S. Wood, during his brief term as Commissioner of Public Buildings, discovered and reported his peculations, and gravely angered Mrs. Lincoln, who wrote Secretary Caleb B. Smith that the gardener was "rigidly exact" in all his accounts. She turned spitefully against Wood, informing Smith that he was the last man who ought to bring a charge against any one, that he was either deranged or drinking. At the time of French's second appointment, he found Watt still basking in White House favor, and still signing pay rolls and bills for cart hire and other expenses.

In the eyes of Washington unionists, Watt was under a cloud because of his reputation as a sympathizer with secession. Several witnesses, including the Washington postmaster, Lewis Clephane, had testified to his disloyal associations before the Potter Committee in the late summer of 1861. After First Bull Run, he was reported to have said that the South could never be conquered, that Jeff Davis was the best and bravest man in America and that the Federal army was composed of rubbish and cowards. Charges of disloyalty were also made to the Potter Committee in the cases of three White House attendants. One of them, old Edward, was a genial little Irishman, who had been on duty at the north entrance for many years. Though Edward was regarded as a Washington fixture and celebrity, there is confusion about his last name, for he was called McManus, and borne on French's pay roll as Burke. He incurred Mrs. Lincoln's displeasure early in 1865, and lost the post of doorkeeper, but French did not discharge him until June of that year.

Thomas Burns and Thomas Stackpole, likewise accused before

the Potter Committee, were doorkeepers at the main entrance and the President's office respectively. Burns was dismissed in the last winter of the war. Stackpole was at that time apparently acting as steward, and in May, 1865, was formally appointed to the position by French. He was subsequently called to account by French for lending the White House punch bowl to a Baltimore saloon.

None of the White House employees suffered because of the accusations of disloyalty, but the favors shown to Watt were astounding to Potter, who had hastened to communicate the evidence against the gardener to the President. Soon after, Watt was given a lieutenant's commission in the regular Army. The historian, George Bancroft, heard that "Madame wished a rogue who had cheated the government made a lieutenant," and that the President forced the reluctant Cabinet to approve, telling them, "Mrs. Lincoln has for three nights slept in a separate apartment." The story is representative of the gossip of Washington, not of Lincoln's habit of speech. It was also said the gardener had "been specially detached to do duty at the White House, where he superintends the cooking." Mrs. Lincoln had discharged the steward, and Watt appears for some time to have held that position, in addition to his work in the grounds.

In February, 1862, shortly before Watt publicly took the blame for giving Wikoff the President's message, his Army commission was revoked. At the end of the month, his name disappeared from Major French's pay roll; but he was still employed at the White House. "Hell is to pay about Watt's affairs," John Hay wrote Nicolay in the following November. "I think the Tycoon begins to suspect him. I wish he could be struck with lightning. He has got William and Carroll turned off, and has his eye peeled for a pop at me, because I won't let Madame have our stationery fund. They have gone off to New York together."

In the summer of 1863, Watt was a corporal in the Thirteenth New York Artillery, although the *Star* mentioned him, months afterward, as in charge of the White House conservatories. The singularly close alliance between the President's wife and the dishonest gardener probably came to an end when Watt tried his hand at blackmailing the President. The story was hushed up. John Hay heard it later from Isaac Newton, a rotund farmer whom Lincoln had placed at the head of the new Agricultural Bureau. Newton was a stupid old fellow. Ben: Perley Poore said that he once made requisition for two hydraulic rams, because he had been told that they were the best sheep in Europe. But he was honest and kind, and he befriended Mrs. Lincoln, preventing, he told John Hay, "dreadful disclosures." When he learned that Watt was involved in a conspiracy to extort twenty thousand dollars from the President in return for three of his wife's letters, Newton sent for Simeon Draper, a New York politician. Draper "went to Watt in his greenhouse on 14th Street," as Hay wrote down the story, "& told him he was come to take him to Fort Lafayette, with much bluster & great oaths as Simeon's wont; . . . Watt fell on his literal marrow bones & begged, & gave up the letters & the conspiracy got demoralized & came down, down, to 1500 dollars which was paid, and the whole thing settled."

Not the least curious aspect of Mary Lincoln's character was her tolerance of a lack of protection. In the semi-public mansion, there was a want of security and privacy which would have been unthinkable in other residences of the crime-ridden capital. There was no watchman on duty in the parlors, and costly furnishings were stolen and defaced by the sight-seers who roamed at will on the first floor. The front door was open all day and late into evening. The attendant was often absent from his post, especially after office hours and on Sundays. On many occasions, people walked into the house at night and wandered about the rooms, and sometimes even went upstairs, without finding anyone to direct them.

Politicians and army officers, alarmed by repeated threats against the President's life, were agitated by these conditions. They urged Mr. Lincoln to have a guard of soldiers; but for a year and a half after the spring of 1861, when Stone had concealed a squad of District militia in the shrubbery every night, there were no armed men within hail of the Executive Mansion.

The President was indifferent to his own protection, either at home or abroad. Washington citizens had always been cautious about walking in the dimly lighted streets after dark. In Springfield, it had been natural for Lincoln to step out after supper to do an errand or talk with a friend, and he did not change his habits in the capital. During the great military campaigns, it was his habit to pay late visits to the War Office. By night, as well as by day, he took the short cut which led through the turnstile in the White House grounds, heavily planted with trees and shrubbery. Often he went with a secretary or friend, uneasily mindful that the President's attenuated figure, topped by a stovepipe hat, was an unmistakable target, even in the dark. Lincoln sometimes walked out alone at night on informal visits to the theatre, dropping in for a half-hour of diversion at Ford's or Grover's.

In the summer of 1862, the Lincoln family had moved to the isolated cottage at the Soldiers' Home over the protests of the President's friends, advised of secret service reports of assassination plots. They were especially alarmed by Lincoln's habit of riding unaccompanied, frequently after nightfall, along the three miles of lonely road which lay beyond the city limits. Stanton and Lamon both urged him to have a military escort, but the President laughed at the idea. One night in August, as he jogged along through the dark, he was startled by the report of a rifle and the whistle of a bullet. Next morning, in his office, Lincoln told Lamon the story as a great joke, describing the speed with which his horse had bounded home, and lamenting the loss of his eight-dollar plug hat.

On another summer evening, when Mrs. Lincoln was in New York, a detective turned in a report which thoroughly frightened Lamon for the President's safety. After searching for Lincoln everywhere in Washington, he went for his brother, Robert, who was serving as deputy marshal, and the two men drove rapidly out to the Soldiers' Home. Near the entrance, they met and challenged a carriage, attended by a horseman. It proved to be Stanton, with one of his orderlies. He also had received a threatening report, and had hurried to the suburban cottage, to which Lincoln had not returned. The Lamon brothers had given Stanton the greatest scare of his life, for he took them for the assassins.

On returning to Washington, the Lamons found Lincoln walking across the White House lawn. There was much laughter over Stanton's false alarm. But Marshal Lamon insisted on the President's sleeping at his house for the remainder of Mrs. Lincoln's absence. Soon after, Lincoln was induced to accept military protection when he rode or drove around Washington.

The President's first cavalry escort consisted of random details made from day to day from Scott's Nine Hundred, a New York regiment which had earned much derision in Washington because of its pretentious name and its raw and rowdy character. Later, a guard from one company was expressly assigned to the President, and remained in attendance on him for more than a year. Its place was taken by a squadron of Ohio cavalry, the Union Light Guard.

The President was irked by the cavalry escort, thought military show unbecoming to the Chief Executive of a democracy, and was sensitive about appearing to be fearful of danger. He complained to General Halleck that he and Mrs. Lincoln "couldn't hear themselves talk" when they took a drive, because of the clatter of sabers and spurs, and professed to be more afraid of being shot by one of the green troopers than by a lurking guerrilla. He repeatedly sent the escort away, and frequently at night still rode unattended between the White House and the Soldiers' Home.

At about the same time as the appointment of the first details of cavalry, the President also yielded to the importunities of his friends on the point of having an infantry guard at the Soldiers' Home. For a short time, a detachment of regulars was placed on duty there, but they were soon succeeded by two companies of the 150th Pennsylvania Regiment, a newly organized addition to the famous Bucktail Brigade, so-called because the soldiers wore bucktails in their hats. Possibly because it was less ostentatious, the infantry guard was far more acceptable to the President than the cavalry escort. He grew to like the Bucktails, especially Company K, with whose captain he became so friendly that he invited him to share his bed on autumn nights when Mrs. Lincoln was away from home. When the question arose of a guard at the White House on the family's return to town, the President especially requested that Company K continue on duty. The congenial captain was presently transferred to another command, but the soldiers remained with the President throughout the war.

In the late autumn of 1862, the Bucktails were encamped on the lawn south of the White House, and two sentinels paced their beats on the east and west sides of the mansion. The sentinels, however, were in no sense doorkeepers, and the same casual system of admission to the house continued to prevail. Lincoln had no bodyguard, either on his walks or in the house. At one time during the third winter of the war, a cavalry guard was placed at the gates of the mansion, but the President "worried until he got rid of it." There were continual muttering rumors that the President's life was in danger, and a queer story of an abduction plot was twice reported in the *New York Tribune* in the spring. It was said that the President was to be carried down to the Maryland town of Port Tobacco, and thence across the Potomac into Virginia. Lincoln never listened seriously to any of these rumors. He spoke only once of fearing harm from any man—and that was the old Polish bear, Count Gurowski, who took out all his animosity in his snarling manners and badly written diary.

Some of the alarming stories may have been concealed from Mrs. Lincoln, but she was not without apprehension about her husband's nocturnal walks. One night, crossing to the War Department with Noah Brooks, the President carried a heavy walking stick, "in deference to his wife's anxious appeal." Mrs. Keckley heard her telling him that he should not go out alone because he was "surrounded with danger."

At least one warm friend of the President could not help thinking that Willie's death had not been an unmitigated tragedy. Mourning had cut short Mrs. Lincoln's pretentious social career, and removed occasion for publicity. During her two years' mourning, she attracted public attention chiefly by her visits to the hospitals. She showed much kindness to sick and wounded soldiers, carrying them presents of fruit and wine. Southerners satirized her as "the Yankee nurse," but Union people saw nothing to criticize in her benevolence. Mrs. Lincoln never was well liked, but the early hostility to her subsided. In her retirement, she was almost forgotten. Few people knew her. Among the ladies of official society, only Mrs. Gideon Welles was on pleasant terms with the President's wife. Time, moreover, befriended her. Her extravagant dress and countrified airs became an old story, and people tired of repeating the rumor that she was a spy, sending information to the South.

Behind the screen of an outwardly quiet life, Mary Lincoln raged, wept, intrigued and purchased expensive mourning. She selected new jewelry, demanded the finest straw and the sheerest crape veiling for her bonnets, and ordered dainty sets of collars and undersleeves for her rich black silk dresses. "I have your money ready for you," she wrote significantly on one order. Her credit was already being questioned.

In the summer of 1862, Washington grumbled because Mrs. Lincoln refused to allow the concerts of the Marine Band to be given at the White House during her absence at the Soldiers' Home. Her strict observance of mourning interfered with one of the city's pleasantest customs, and a year later, when permission was again withheld, there was so much discontent that Gideon Welles felt obliged to mention it to the President. Mrs. Lincoln was still adamant in her refusal, and a compromise was arranged by offering military concerts twice a week in Lafayette Square.

Eleven months after Willie's death, the public receptions began again at the White House, and the President's wife in her heavy crape faced the ordeal of greeting crowds of strangers. She had one small private reception during the winter, to entertain General Tom Thumb and his bride. Attended by an agent, a private secretary, a valet and a French maid, the tiny couple made a short stay at Willard's on their wedding tour. It was the occasion for a reunion with Mrs. Thumb's brother, a soldier in the Fortieth Massachusetts, on duty in the Washington defenses. At a hop at Willard's, General Thumb was dressed in a black suit, patent-leather boots, snow-white kid gloves and a faultless necktie with a breastpin of brilliants. Mrs. Thumb wore rich white satin, sprinkled with green leaves and looped with carnation buds, and diamonds sparkled on her wrists and bosom. Cabinet members and other notables went to the White House to meet the bride and groom. Mrs. Lincoln's next levee was a *"crusher,"* wrote Major French, and the lady herself remarked, "I believe these people came expecting to see Tom Thumb and his wife."

While the mother's grief had been criticized as excessive, it was a licensed and respected sorrow. Always, in the sight of curious and hostile eyes, she was obliged to conceal her distress for her Southern kinsfolk. Sometimes, she vehemently denied she felt it. One full brother, three half brothers and three brothers-in-law had joined the Confederate army. Alec had fallen at Baton Rouge, and Samuel Todd at Shiloh. David, hated by Northerners for his treatment of prisoners, lingered on, weak from wounds received at Vicksburg. A brother-in-law, handsome young Ben Hardin Helm, who had visited the White House in the spring of 1861 and turned down a commission as Federal paymaster, was killed at Chickamauga.

The dead were real to Mary Lincoln. The winter after Willie died, she drove out on New Year's Eve with her old protector, Isaac Newton, to visit a spiritualist called Mrs. Laury in Georgetown. Mrs. Laury made wonderful revelations about Willie, Mrs. Lincoln told Senator Browning. She also had information about earthly matters. The spirits had told her that the Cabinet members were all enemies of the President, and would have to be replaced before he had success.

There were other mediums whom the President's wife consulted. She was not alone. Spiritualism, the accompaniment of long and wasting wars, was rampant in the capital in the third winter of conflict. People sat hand in hand around tables in the dark, to hear bells run and drums thumped and banjos twanged. A public meeting at Odd Fellows' Hall, conducted by Father Beeson, the patriarchal friend of the Indian, drew crowds to hear a communication from the spirit of Judge Dean, for the Brooklyn lawyer who had come to the defense of the fugitive slaves had recently succumbed to pneumonia. Father Beeson lost a part of his audience, when he read a message from a dead colored man which revealed that Negroes occupied the chief seats in Paradise. The janitor of Odd Fellows' Hall, Beeson complained, had followed the Washington custom of ordering them into the gallery. There was, however, no controversial matter in Judge Dean's communication. His spirit visited Father Beeson—with whom in life he had had the barest acquaintance—merely to inform him that he had seen him at his own funeral, and that things in the other world were more comfortable than he had expected. The message, in the *Star's* opinion, "seemed to indicate that the practical business turn of mind of the Judge had rather deteriorated. . . ."

The converts, however, were not critical. The mediums were coining money in the capital. One of the most successful was a young and personable man called Colchester, who claimed to be the illegitimate son of an English duke. Mrs. Lincoln received him into her home, and hopefully listened to the scratches and taps which were supposed to represent messages from Willie. Presently, Colchester wrote Mrs. Lincoln an insolent letter asking her to get him a pass to New York from the War Department, and suggesting that "he might have some unpleasant things to say to her" if she refused it. This attempt at blackmail was settled by the President's friend, the correspondent, Noah Brooks. In a skeptical mood, he had recently attended one of Colchester's séances, and had risen in the dark to grasp a hand beating a bell against a drum. Brooks called for lights, but, before a match was struck, the drum hit him on the head. The flaring gaslight revealed the correspondent, bloody of brow, tenaciously holding on to Colchester. When Mrs. Lincoln frantically appealed to Brooks to help her, he arranged a meeting with the medium at the White House. He confronted Colchester with the unhealed scar on his brow, denounced him as a swindler and ordered him to leave town on pain of imprisonment in the Old Capitol. Colchester gave Mrs. Lincoln no further trouble, though Brooks's empty threat did not frighten him away from Washington, where his fascinating personality and wonderful demonstrations of occult powers continued to attract large numbers to his séances.

The world of the living reached in to pluck with rough fingers at Mary Lincoln's jangled nerves. In the summer of 1863, while she was driving in her carriage, the coachman's seat broke, throwing him to the ground. The frightened horses ran away, and Mrs. Lincoln jumped out, striking the back of her head. She was ill for some time afterward. Later, her carriage ran over a little boy and broke his leg. Her husband had smallpox, and Tad caught scarlatina. She was frantically afraid that Robert would enlist, that she might lose him, too. At night, she started up from her restless sleep, sensing a presence in her bedroom overlooking the Potomac. Without benefit of taps and scratches, Willie came back to his mother. She could see him, sweetly smiling, at the foot of her bed. Sometimes, her dead baby, Eddie, was with him; and sometimes Alec, her youngest half brother, the redheaded one, who had died in gray in a skirmish at Baton Rouge.

Mary Lincoln was so strange and shaken that her husband was thankful to have her half sister, Emilie, come for a visit at the White House. In Illinois, she had three full sisters who might have given her companionship, but Mrs. Lincoln did not like them. She was naggingly critical even of Mrs. Ninian Edwards, in whose house she had paid long visits, meeting and marrying Lincoln there. Frances was jealous, and ungrateful for the commission of paymaster which Mary Lincoln had had "a hard battle" to get for her husband, Dr. William Wallace, for whom Willie had been named. Ann, Mrs. C. M. Smith, she venomously detested for her "false tongue." Emilie, eighteen years younger, had had no opportunity to become embroiled with the President's wife. She was the widow of the Confederate general, Ben Hardin Helm.

Traveling with her little daughter from Alabama to her mother's home in Kentucky, Emilie Helm had been stopped at Fort Monroe because she refused to take the oath of allegiance. The President telegraphed the military authorities to send her to Washington, and on a winter day she trailed into the White House in the desolation of her young widowhood. The hangings of the state guest chamber oppressed her with their gloomy, funereal purple, and she shrank from the inquiring glances which strangers directed at her deep crape. She was tenderly received. Hand in hand, not talking much, she and Mary Lincoln wept together. The President called her "Little Sister," and shed tears, as he took her in his arms and said that he hoped she felt no bitterness toward him.

Perhaps, to a man of simple and magnanimous nature, there appeared nothing incongruous in having Emilie Helm as a house guest; perhaps his judgment was influenced by worry over his sick and lonely wife. For nearly a week, in the midst of war, the President entertained a passionate adherent of the enemy, and he invited her to spend the summer at the Soldiers' Home. The fact that the rebel visitor called the President "Brother Lincoln" aggravated the offense of her presence to people who saw her there. Taddie was annoyed by a little cousin who shouted "Hurrah for Jeff Davis!" on a hearthrug of the White House, and contradicted him, when he said that his father was President. Although Emilie tried to slip away when people called, they sometimes asked to see her, hoping for news of friends in the Confederacy. One of these was Senator Ira Harris of New York, who came in with General Dan Sickles, to inquire about John C. Breckinridge, now a general in the Confederate army. Emilie Helm faced a Republican politician and a Union soldier who had lost a leg at Gettysburg. She had no information about Breckinridge. There were questions about the South, which she evaded. Senator Harris may have made Breckinridge an excuse for looking over the President's sister-in-law, or he may have been suddenly stung to resentment by her mourning and her silence. "We have whipped the rebels at Chattanooga," he burst out, "and I hear, madam, that the scoundrels ran like scared rabbits." Emilie Helm choked out, "It was the example you set them at Bull Run and Manassas." Mrs. Lincoln tried to change the subject, and Harris turned on her. "Why isn't Robert in the army?" The President's wife blanched, and bit her lip. She said that Robert was anxious to enlist. The fault was hers, because she had insisted on his staying in college.

Shivering and weeping, Emilie Helm stumbled out of the room. The President, who was not feeling well, was resting on his bed, but Dan Sickles stumped up the stairs on his crutches, and insisted on seeing him. Emilie understood that the President was amused at

Sickles's angry account, and told him "the child has a tongue like the rest of the Todds." "You should not have that rebel in your house," Sickles shouted.

Emilie Helm felt that her visit was an embarrassment, and she left for Kentucky on a pass the President gave her, not requiring the oath of allegiance. She did not accept the invitation to stay at the Soldiers' Home. Lincoln privately interested himself in trying to help her sell six hundred bales of cotton, but she was the occasion of no public scandal.

The next spring, Lincoln was assailed in the press on the ground that his wife's half sister, Martha—Mrs. Clement White of Alabama—had carried merchandise to the South on a pass given her by the President. He frankly explained the matter to Welles and others, saying that Mrs. White had repeatedly called, and that both he and Mrs. Lincoln had declined to see her. He had sent her a pass to go South, and refused to permit her to take her trunks without examination. She had "talked secesh" at her Washington hotel, and finally Lincoln told one of her intermediaries, Brutus Clay, that he would send her to the Old Capitol, if she did not leave at once.

The Todd family legend was that Martha White was a frequent visitor at the White House during the war, that she carried South a little quinine only for her own use; but that, on one occasion, she was mortified to have a Federal inspector find a splendid sword and a rebel uniform, placed by Baltimore friends without her knowledge in her trunk, which she nevertheless transported to the Confederacy, and presented to General Lee.

Mary Lincoln had turned a gentle face to Emilie Helm. The young widow understood Lincoln's worry when he told her that Mary's nerves had gone to pieces, that the strain had been too much for her mental, as well as physical health. Emilie saw Mary start and go white when a bell rang or a book dropped. She was appalled, when she suddenly came into the room, by the look of fright in her sister's eyes—those blue eyes that grew wide and shining when she spoke of Willie, relating that he said he loved his Uncle Alec, and was with him most of the time.

Mary Lincoln put on a smooth mask of civility in the Blue Room, dipped in little curtseys and said, "How do you do?" and sometimes to acquaintances, "I am glad to see you," touching their hands with the tips of her white kid fingers. Her afternoon levees were crowded.

On a stormy day she apologized to Major French for not releasing him, since surely no one would come. French had "quite a cosy talk" with her in the servants' room, where she was seated "in full rig." Senator Sumner was announced, and Mrs. Lincoln and French marched into the parlor to receive him. There was more chat on the Blue Room sofa, and the President came in and was "pleasant and funny as could be." They were relaxed and unexpectant until old Edward came and told them that the hall was filled with people. When the doors were opened, the stream of callers almost equalled a New Year's reception. There were people in traveling costumes and country clothing, and soldiers in muddy boots; but elegant ladies came, too. The successes of the Union had made the White House levees fashionable, and in 1864 the Blue Room was awash with French bonnets and ermine muffs and pelerines. At the gates, a pair of unkempt troopers marshaled the line of carriages with their swords. Edward stood in the vestibule, cracking nuts.

Like a child begging for treats, the President's wife made demands on Major French, who did his best to help her. "Mrs. Lincoln is boring me daily," he wrote in May, 1864, "to obtain an appropriation to pay for fitting up a new house for her and the President at the Soldiers' Home and I, in turn, am boring the Committee of Ways and Means. If Thaddeus, the worthy old chairman, did not *joke me off,* I think I should get it. . . ."

After she laid off her mourning, Mrs. Lincoln was often seen with the President at the theatre, especially when there was opera, of which she was very fond. She would invite a party of friends, and send a messenger to reserve either the big upper box at Ford's, or the lower box which the President habitually occupied at Grover's. On these occasions, flags were placed on the front of the boxes, and the entrance of the party was usually greeted with the strains of "Hail to the Chief." The cavalry escort seldom accompanied the President's carriage on these short drives. Leonard Grover told of a disagreeable incident which occurred one evening, as the Lincolns left his theatre, accompanied by Schuyler Colfax. Grover's was in a neighborhood of saloons and disorderly houses, frequented by secessionist roughs whose antipathy to the administration had been increased by the Emancipation Proclamation. A jeering crowd gathered around the President's carriage. The coachman, Grover said, was drunk, and fell sprawling on the sidewalk, as Mr. and Mrs. Lincoln entered the carriage. The crowd gave a threatening shout. There was only a one-armed drummer boy on the box, and Grover was frightened. He sprang to the box himself, took up the reins, and drove to Colfax's residence and then to the White House. Both the President and Mrs. Lincoln warmly thanked him for a very great service.

Grover may have exaggerated the hostility of the rowdies, for Mrs. Lincoln was not discouraged from going to the theatre. It had become one of her chief amusements to make up little box parties. Externally, her life had agreeable moments. The big state dinners were duly held, and she was complimented on the taste of her appointments. She had a coy admiration for the handsome bachelor, Senator Sumner, and showered him with invitations, notes and flowers. To the furious indignation of Mr. Stanton, she was also very attentive to the Copperhead, Fernando Wood, whose residence blossomed at the expense of the White House conservatories, when he gave his grand receptions. There were quiet times, when the Lincolns drove in their carriage, talking like any companionable, affectionate couple, drawn together by years of habit and shared sorrow.

Yet Mary Lincoln's fits of temper were uncontrollable. She spoke sharply even to her favorite, Sumner, and wrote him an abject letter of apology. Her rages at her husband burst all bounds of decorum and pride. She could not hold her tongue in front of other people. After attending the Patent Office fair, she lashed out at Lincoln for the stupidity of his speech, to the mortification of General Richard Oglesby of Illinois, who was with them in their carriage. The President's speech had been a rather facetious little tribute to the ladies for their work for war relief. The mere reference by her husband to women drove Mary Lincoln wild. Her jealousy had become a mania. On a visit to the army in the spring of 1865, she carried on like a crazy woman, insulting General Ord's wife until she burst into tears, because she had ridden beside the President.

All the while, like a drug for her tortured nerves, she indulged in her orgies of buying things. She hoarded her old possessions in innumerable trunks and boxes, keeping even outmoded dresses and bonnets she had brought from Springfield. The charge accounts for her purchases mounted to appalling sums—things she could never use, for which she could never hope to pay. A Washington merchant sent in a bill for three hundred pairs of gloves ordered in four months. At A. T. Stewart's New York department store, she bought furs, silks, laces, jewelry; three thousand dollars for earrings and a pin; five thousand for a shawl. In the summer of 1864, she told Mrs. Keckley that she owed twenty-seven thousand dollars. The seamstress asked her if Mr. Lincoln suspected this. "God, no!" said Mrs. Lincoln. During the Presidential campaign of that year, she grew hysterical with fear of exposure and bankruptcy, if her husband should fail to be re-elected. As long as he was in office, rich Republicans might be induced to dig into their pockets to save the party from scandal. She sat wailing to old Isaac Newton, "shed tears by the pint," while she begged him to help her pay her debts.

Her dress for the second inauguration ball cost two thousand dollars. She was back on her unsteady pinnacle of arrogance, while the clouds gathered that would darken her brain, and send her stumbling out of the White House, a sick and haunted woman with eyes that would never again be wide and shining, that would tremble with fright for the rest of her life. With all her trunks and boxes of old rubbish and the finery for which she had not paid, she would be bundled on the cars with only Mrs. Keckley to befriend her, and a policeman who was fond of Tad.

NEAR THE DOOR of the Blue Room the advance of the column of callers was suddenly checked. The President, after cordially wringing the hand of one visitor, detained him in conversation. He was a short, scrubby officer, stooped and sunburned, with rough, light-brown whiskers, and he appeared scarcely worthy of signal attention. There was something seedy about him; the look of a man who is out of a job, and takes too much to drink. The stars on his shoulder straps were tarnished. But a buzz ran through the Blue Room. Everyone began to stare at the man who stood awkwardly looking up at the President, while arriving guests jostled in confusion outside the doorway. General Grant and Mr. Lincoln were meeting for the first time.

Seward hurried to the rescue. He presented the general to Mrs. Lincoln, and led him through a lane of eager faces into the crowded East Room. Grant's entrance turned the polite assemblage into a mob. Wild cheers shook the crystal chandeliers, as ladies and gentlemen rushed on him from all sides. Laces were torn, and crinolines mashed. Fearful of injury or maddened by excitement, people scrambled on chairs and tables. At last, General Grant was forced to mount a crimson sofa. He stood there bashfully shaking the thrusting hands that wanted to touch success and glory—Donelson, Vicksburg, Chattanooga—personified in a slovenly little soldier, with a blushing, scared face.

The Union had had some queer heroes, but none as unlikely as the one on whom, after three years of war, its ardent hopes were fixed. Grant had been a taciturn boy, who liked farming, and went to West Point only because his domineering father got him the appointment. He had never enjoyed military life. In the Mexican campaign, he had served as a quartermaster, hating the war. It was in Mexico that he began to drink. He was not a boon companion, but took his whisky in morose solitude. Later, in the desolate life of a western Army post, the habit had grown on him until it became subversive of discipline, and he was forced to resign. Grant found himself a penniless civilian. He made fumbling attempts at farming, and then at business in St. Louis. The disgraced ex-soldier was going downhill fast, when his father made a place for the family failure in the family leather store in Galena, Illinois. Grant did not like the work, but he had a wife and four children, and he was glad to get it. He was there, thirty-nine years old, when the fall of Sumter awoke the Union to civil war.

Captain Grant, as he was called, assisted in drilling the Galena volunteers, but was not elected an officer in the company. He followed the boys to Springfield in his civilian clothes, and got a clerkship at the State capital. Having received his education at the Government's expense, he felt it his duty to offer his services, but the letter he wrote to Washington, rather diffidently suggesting that he was fit to command a regiment, was never answered. At last, he was given a chance in Illinois. A regiment of mutinous volunteers behaved so badly that they drove their colonel to resign, and Grant was put in his place. He soon whipped the regiment into shape. His former neighbor, Congressman Washburne, got him a brigadier's commission. The "unconditional surrender" at Fort Donelson made him a national figure.

Accidentally, in middle age, Grant discovered his one great aptitude: for dogged and obstinate fighting. He had a superstitious aversion to retracing his steps. It was not always an advantage in his military campaigns, but it was a new fault in Federal generals. The sentence in his dispatch to the Confederate commander at Donelson, "I propose to move immediately upon your works," is one of those phrases which echo coldly down the aisles of history, without seeming to have earned the right to be remembered. It thrilled a nation in the spring of 1862.

The clamor for his removal after the slaughter at Shiloh was drowned in the cheers for Vicksburg, and Chattanooga made him the unrivaled military leader of the Union. Although, when he was nobody, Grant's character had not seemed in any way remarkable, it became invested with power as soon as he was famous. His very ordinariness appeared marvelously sound. He was the apotheosis of the plain man, and the plain man admired and trusted him. His uncouthness was no handicap. Grant was in the American tradition. He had pluck and persistence and common sense, qualities which a young country understood and respected. There was no nonsense about him. He had no airs or falderols or highfalutin talk. He had, in fact, very little to say, either in speech or on paper. The Union, surfeited with boastful promises, liked his reticence. During a serenade at Willard's in March of 1864, Congressman Washburne introduced

Grant as a "man of deeds, and not of words." The crowd cheered the inarticulate soldier to the echo.

Grant had come to Washington by order of the War Department. He had never before set foot in the capital; hated and feared the place, and did not mean to tarry there. Sherman had dinned into his ears the dangers of its intrigues, and the corrupt moral atmosphere of its politics. "For God's sake, and for your country's sake," Sherman wrote his friend, "come out of Washington." Grant did not need this plea to stiffen his resolution. He was too diffident to find enjoyment in public receptions and ovations. He had no taste for a fine office with a Brussels carpet, preferring a wall tent, with a narrow bed and a rude pine table for his maps and papers. He was accustomed to planning his own campaigns and keeping his own counsel. With a soldier's dread of political interference, he, as well as Sherman, had marked the influence of Washington on other military men—McClellan, Pope, and Halleck.

On the day after Grant's arrival, he was formally presented with the commission of lieutenant-general. The grade had been revived by recent act of Congress, with the tacit understanding that it would be bestowed on Grant. It was high military honor from a republic which had been chary of permitting its heroes to place a third star on their shoulder straps. To witness the presentation, Grant brought along his son Fred, a boy of fourteen, who had been through the siege of Vicksburg. He was also accompanied by two aides and by General Halleck, who had all but forced him out of the service in 1862. The President and the gentlemen of the Cabinet assembled, and, in reply to Mr. Lincoln's short speech, Grant painfully stammered out a few lines he had penciled on a half sheet of note paper. In his embarrassment, he seemed scarcely able to read his own writing; but the composition, with its reference to his heavy responsibilities, the noble armies of the Union and the favor of Providence, was entirely original with himself. He had omitted the compliments to the Army of the Potomac, which the President had asked him to pay.

The next day Grant paid a visit to General Meade's headquarters at Brandy Station. Mr. Welles, observing him at the Cabinet meeting on his return, found him deficient in military bearing and dignity, but more businesslike than he had formerly appeared. Grant had been fortified by a great decision. He had completely changed his plans, abandoning his cherished intention of leading the Western armies on a campaign to Atlanta. The President had told him that the country wanted him to take Richmond. Grant said that he could do it, if he had the troops. In his stubborn heart, he felt the strength to resist the political pressure of Washington, and he had resolved that his place was with the Army of the Potomac. On the third evening after his arrival in the capital, he left for Nashville, to sever his relations with the troops which he led to victory. As he traveled westward on the cars, the orders were issued which placed him in command of all the armies of the Union.

Grant's trip to Brandy Station disappointed the Washington public, for it had been advertised that he would accompany the President to a grand gala performance in his honor at Grover's, where the famous tragedian, Edwin Booth, was playing a four weeks' engagement. The theatre was lavishly decorated with flags. The names of Grant's victories, elaborately inscribed, were hung on the boxes and the dress circle, and across the front of the stage ran a banner painted with the golden words, "Unconditional Surrender," adorned with the flag and the eagle. On a stormy night, Booth gave his admired impersonation of *Richard III* to a house packed to the doors, with standing room sold out. The President and Mrs. Lincoln and Secretary Seward sat in the flag-draped boxes, but the crowd had come to see Grant. Leonard Grover stepped on the stage to explain that the military chieftain had been obliged to leave town, but would positively attend Booth's performance of *Hamlet* the next evening. The *Chronicle* understood that Grant telegraphed this assurance to Grover, and reported that throngs again rushed to the theatre on the following evening, only to meet with a second disappointment, as Grant had left for the West. Mrs. Lincoln had arranged a military dinner in his honor, and it was said that the President had urged Grant to stay.

Two rooms on the second floor of Winder's Building were fitted up for the commanding general, but he spent little time in them, making his headquarters with the Army of the Potomac, far from the center of the military telegraph. He left the multifarious details of the army headquarters to General Halleck, who on Grant's elevation to the chief command assumed the position of national chief of staff. From the field, Grant made four flying trips to Washington in late March and early April, for conferences at the White House and War Department. Each of these visits was the occasion for an outbreak of deputations, receptions, presentations and serenades. Crowds tailed

Grant, whenever he went out. In the hall of Willard's, where he lodged, men avidly stared at his ordinary face, with its protruding stump of cigar. No uninformed stranger could have imagined that this plain-looking soldier was the commander of nearly nine hundred thousand men. He had, however, gained composure. There was a reassuringly quiet and self-possessed look about him. His cold blue eyes were clear, and his features wore the impassive expression which had become familiar to his soldiers on the battlefield.

Throughout the Union, the news that Grant was commander-in-chief had inspired a joyful expectation that the war would soon be won. The national morale needed this vitalizing hope in the early months of 1864. An attempt to occupy the interior of Florida had proved unsuccessful. A movement up the Red River in Louisiana, under command of General Banks, was a failure, and a sudden fall in the river imperiled the fleet which co-operated in the expedition. Fort Pillow on the Mississippi was captured by the Confederates, and the massacre of Negro soldiers and their white officers set the Union calling for retaliation. Reports of the sufferings of Federal prisoners of war in the South added urgency to the desire for decisive military action.

On the political horizon, the clouds were dark and heavy. It was election year. Washington was in a ferment as the nation, in the midst of war, became embroiled in the distractions of the Presidential canvass. On the floor of the House, Copperheads clamored for a change of rulers and a peaceful settlement of the war, demanding the recognition of the independence of the Southern States. Citizens of the Union had been shut in military prisons for uttering sentiments far less treasonable than those which the people's representatives boldly shouted at the Capitol. The acrimonious debates recalled the days of secession excitement, and the galleries were again crowded with spectators. Motions were made to expel some of the more reckless Democratic extremists, but they dwindled, after heated oratory, into resolutions of censure.

Although the State elections of the preceding autumn had sustained the Republicans, the opposition was formidable. Copperhead cries for peace found sympathetic listeners in the war-weary nation. Secret orders, actively engaged in discouraging enlistments and agitating resistance to the draft, had mustered a large membership. Many viewed with alarm the President's assumption of war powers. The great hope of the Democrats lay in the division within the Republican party. The powerful radical leaders, though informed of Lincoln's popularity in the country, were passionately opposed to his renomination. The President had repeatedly proved too strong for them. He had emancipated the slaves when and how it pleased him. Worst of all, he had issued a proclamation of amnesty to rebels who should take the oath of allegiance. For Chief Magistrate during the next four critical years, the anti-slavery cabal wanted a man of their own faction who, once the war was ended, would carry out a vengeful program of abolition and subjugation in the Southern States. Lincoln's views on reconstruction were infused with moderation and generosity to the vanquished. He was as incapable of vindictiveness toward the Southern people as toward his own Secretary of the Treasury, that pious double-dealer, Mr. Chase.

Even Lincoln could no longer pretend to be unaware of the Presidential aspirations of his radical Cabinet minister. While Chase sat, irritably and intermittently, in Lincoln's council, a circular advertising his claims went broadcast over the country, and eventually appeared in the press. A great silence greeted the movement for Chase's nomination. From Republican caucuses and conventions in various States came expressions of loyalty to the President. The radical politicians of Congress read the portents with mounting blood pressure. Republicans vied with Democrats in railing against Lincoln. In the anteroom of his office, the President was openly assailed by senators of his party, while they waited for an interview with him. Washington Republicans shared in the stormy altercations which preceded the holding of the party's convention—designated, not the Republican, but the National Union Convention. The delegates from the District were chosen in an atmosphere of quarrelsome debate. Lincoln supporters maintained that Washington delegates, the constant witnesses of the President's patriotism, should speak with an unwavering voice; but they went uninstructed to the convention at Baltimore in early June.

In the midst of the commotion, an artist had set up a studio in the state dining-room of the White House. Mr. Francis B. Carpenter, a portrait painter from New York, had been granted permission to carry out his ambitious project of depicting the President with his Cabinet at the first reading of the Emancipation Proclamation. Pencils, brushes and paints littered the dining-room table, and a large canvas was stretched to catch the light from the windows. In the blaze of the great chandelier, Mr. Carpenter often labored until dawn.

The artist had also been given the freedom of the official chamber, which was to form the background of his painting. There he sat for hours on end, making pencil studies of "accessories" and staring at Lincoln's face. Sometimes a caller who wanted a private word with the President would look hesitantly in Carpenter's direction. "Oh, you need not mind him," Lincoln would call out heartily; "he is but a painter."

Lincoln took an innocent pride in Carpenter's work. He was devoid of aesthetic appreciation, but this was a picture he could understand. He found the painter congenial, too. Carpenter was painfully earnest and humorless, but he was a gentle, thoughtful fellow, and he conceived a worshipful admiration for the President. Though he spelled art with a capital A, Carpenter was predominantly concerned with its moral purpose. He was also a stickler for historical accuracy: pen and paper, books and chairs all had to be painstakingly represented; and he even tossed into one corner of his picture a newspaper "studied" from a copy of the *New York Tribune*. He tried to explain his artistic aims to the President, but did not capture his attention. For Lincoln, the painting was a point from which to take off on reminiscences of the Emancipation Proclamation. The moralist in Carpenter reveled in the rattle of breaking chains. Conscious that this was history and a noble thing, he listened more eagerly than a better artist might have done, and wrote down everything he heard.

Only second in interest to the President in the artist's mind were the gentlemen of the Cabinet. Caleb B. Smith was missing from the roster of the historic occasion. He had died in Indiana. His pictured face was dim, but scarcely dimmer than the part he had played in Washington. His successor, Mr. John Usher, must have felt quite left out, as the others sat for their portraits and hurried down to Brady's to have their photographs taken. Mr. Carpenter enjoyed meeting them all, and faithfully transcribed their conversations. He could not fail to be aware that serious differences existed among them, but he did not permit facts to intrude on his idealistic conception of his subject. The President's advisers, who had never acted in harmony, were now in the snarling temper of a cage of wildcats. Carpenter united them on canvas for posterity, like Sunday-school children grouped around their teacher. Old Mr. Bates, somberly ruminating, and Mr. Seward, the profile of an antique dictator, were well enough. But the stormy petrel, Montgomery Blair, looked as acquiescent as the wraith of Mr. Smith. Cross Mr. Welles seemed to have his eyes fixed on a vision of the Apocalypse. Mr. Stanton sat slumped in a benevolent collapse; while, behind the President's chair, as firm as the rock of ages, stood Mr. Chase, ready to die for his leader.

Chase was almost never at the Cabinet meetings as the National Union Convention approached. His position was an equivocal one, and his relations with the President were growing strained. He had many worries. His greenbacks had depreciated as, in a wild wave of speculation, gold mounted sky-high. The Treasury Department was the subject of other criticisms than the animadversions of sound-money men. Stories were circulating of fraudulent operations, of flagrant improprieties. Chase had felt constrained to make an inquiry, and he had asked the War Department to assign Colonel L. C. Baker to him for this purpose. As Treasury officials were clapped into the Old Capitol, Chase must have rued the day he invited the highhanded detective to wash his dirty linen. The scandal did not stop with exposures of dishonesty. The most sensational charges were those of immoral relations between certain Treasury employees and their female clerks. Congress appointed an investigating committee, which included enough Republicans to insure a majority report favorable to the department. Baker was charged with conspiracy against the officials he had named. The publicity, however, could not be recalled. While Washington held its breath, waiting for the thunder of guns from Virginia, barroom loafers sniggered over the means by which the Treasury girls augmented their earnings. The shining walls of the Extension—as white as Mr. Chase's personal life—were popularly believed to shelter a kind of Government house of ill fame, where pretty women toiled until morning over ale and oyster suppers.

Early in April, General Grant wrote his orders for the simultaneous advance of all the armies of the Union. The two main movements were those of the Armies of the Cumberland, the Tennessee and the Ohio, united under the command of General Sherman, against the forces of General Joe Johnston in Georgia; and of the Army of the Potomac under General Meade against the forces of General Lee. Primarily, on the latter movement rested the hope of a decisive victory for the Union. It had become evident that the war must be won in Virginia. Three years' fighting had produced little change in the relation of the opposing armies. Stubbornly facing each other across the Rapidan, they still defended the terrain which lay between them and their respective capitals.

Grant's plans were laid in strict secrecy. The censored newspapers were silent. Government officials had never been so reticent. At one of the Washington parties, a lady frivolously asked Mr. Seward which way the army was going. "Madame," the Secretary of State is said to have replied, "if I did not know, I would tell you." Mr. Seward, however, was actually not so wise as he appeared. For the first time, the Government had completely entrusted its military operations to a military man. Grant had carte blanche to act, without political interference, advice or consultation. The President was done with meddling in army matters, and assured the commanding general that he did not want to be informed of his plans. Mr. Stanton and General Halleck had both cautioned Grant against confiding in Lincoln, on the ground that the President might be amiably indiscreet. Grant made no confidences to Stanton or Halleck, either.

That spring, Washington saw for the first time a scrawny little Irish general, called Phil Sheridan. He was only thirty-three, and looked younger. His legs were short, and his chest and shoulders enormously wide. He wore a mustache and imperial on his red, coarse-featured face. In the West, Sheridan had made an excellent record, and he was a favorite with Grant. He paid his respects at the War Office and the White House, and went off to take command of the cavalry corps of the Army of the Potomac.

The great Federal armies toed the mark, like runners waiting for the pistol shot. The recent mercenary recruits were not of the caliber of the earlier volunteers. Yet, though bounties and substitute fees had put criminals and vagrants in uniform, money had also enlisted marching regiments of country boys, Canadians and sturdy European immigrants. After Gettysburg and Vicksburg, these men swelled the ranks of armies which—as even the most prejudiced West Pointers acknowledged—had become professional. Tardily, at terrible cost, the democracy had developed an efficient fighting machine. There was no military nattiness about the rank and file of the Army of the Potomac in the camps along the Rapidan. The soldiers were dirty, bearded and long-haired, and they had the hard-bitten look of a band of desperadoes. It was a young army, but boys in their teens had the grim faces of veterans. In brigades, divisions and corps, they were superb implements of battle, and they were now commanded by officers whom war had turned into experts. Something the Union had lost: the first patriotic whoop and hurrah, the quick allegiance of generous hearts, the tide of unsuspected ardor for the flag. But disorganization and ineptitude were nearly gone from the battlefield. The war of amateurs was over.

Uninformed and tense with expectation, the country waited. In Washington, there was news which no censor could efface. It was written on the streets, in the halls of the hotels, on wharves and at the railroad depots, and in the scrubbed wards of the hospitals. Civilians, superfluous on the Rapidan, were returning to the capital—officers' wives and sight-seers, and newspaper correspondents who were not registered at the War Department. Back came the sutlers, purveyors of pies, cakes, lollipops, tobacco and Hostetter's Bitters. Sure premonition of action, the sick were being carried in from Meade's army; men wasted by enteric complaints, the victims of long endurance of pork, hard biscuit and exposure. It was plain that they were not the only guests whom the Washington hospitals expected. Stewards and matrons and nurses were laying in supplies and opening rooms like people preparing for a party—the vast levee of the maimed.

To the south went men with guns. Squads and companies on detached duty in Washington were ordered to join their regiments. Their places were taken by the soldiers of the Veterans' Reserve Corps, wounded men fit for light duty, who wore a distinguishing uniform of pale blue. The movement into Virginia seemed as resistless as a force of nature. Deserters marched, under escort, from their prison cells. Convalescents stumbled into line in front of the hospitals. Men returning from furlough passed through town in a steady procession.

Late in April, Washington watched General Burnside's command, the Ninth Corps, stream down Fourteenth Street—infantry, cavalry, artillery, twenty-five thousand strong. There were five fine new regiments of Negro troops, prepared since the news of Fort Pillow to fight savagely. All the rest were veterans. Two companies of Indian sharpshooters were part of a Michigan regiment. There were the showy troopers of the Third New Jersey Cavalry, with new cloaks and gold-braided breasts, and some of the officers were as superbly uniformed as those who had gone to the Peninsula. The rank and file were like their comrades on the Rapidan—worn, sunburned, high-spirited boys. Their equipment was light: thin bundles, knapsacks, tin cups, frying

pans, guns that shone like silver. Under their grime and sweat, these
soldiers looked as hard and handy as a mechanic's tools, which have
been used, and will be used again.

Burnside stood beside the President on the balcony of Willard's,
reviewing the troops. The President's head was uncovered, and Walt
Whitman, watching him from the other side of the street, thought it
looked funny to see him with his hat off when the colored soldiers
passed. Whitman had posted himself at the corner, with his new
bosom friend, John Burroughs, a young teacher and naturalist, who
had come down to Washington and secured a clerkship in the
Treasury. Walt had to wait three hours before the Fifty-first New
York came along, and he had a chance to speak a few words with his
brother, George. But there were many other soldiers who called and
waved when they saw Walt standing there. Sometimes, a man would
break out of the ranks and kiss his red, bearded face, and draw him
along a few steps, before he let him go.

Day after day, the flatcars that pulled out of Washington were
loaded with men in blue. In the mild April air, they jolted down
through the desert of Virginia. Farms, gardens, churches, schools,
wayside taverns and turnpike roads were obliterated. In Washington,
the tulip trees were green, and the silver poplars dropped their plumes.
Daffodils danced in the gardens. Along Rock Creek, the redbuds were
in flower. Only stumps and stunted undergrowth remained of the
forests of northern Virginia. Only some dock and watercress told of
spring along Bull Run. The cars lurched through the naked country,
carrying desolation to the south.

On the early morning of May 4, the Army of the Potomac crossed
the Rapidan, and entered the dense thickets of the Virginia Wilderness. Meade had, in addition to Sheridan's cavalry, three full infantry
corps, re-formed and consolidated: the Second Corps, Hancock commanding; the Fifth under Warren; and the Sixth, led by Sedgwick.
Burnside's Ninth Corps, until recently detached, had rejoined the
strong army with which Grant meant to find and follow Lee, to fight
and disable his forces. If the defeated Confederates should retire
within the entrenchments of Richmond, the Army of the Potomac
would then cross to the south side of the James River and lay siege to
the Confederate capital. Meantime, that city was to be threatened
by the Army of the James, commanded by General Ben Butler.
Butler had a great opportunity in early May. Richmond was feebly

defended. If he had taken it by a prompt and vigorous assault, he would have been a great hero. He was one of the few political generals who still remained in the Federal armies in 1864. His attack on Richmond was a prime example of military mismanagement.

When the news first came up from Virginia that the Army of the Potomac had crossed the Rapidan, the country was in a torment of suspense. Its state of mind was like that of a man pacing the floor in a hospital where an emergency operation is being performed by a skillful surgeon. Blood and danger were implicit in the program indispensable to recovery. The Union expected no military jaunt, no easy victory; knew that a price must be paid for every mile of the disputed terrain of Virginia. It took without faltering the tidings of the grapple in the tangled Wilderness. In Washington, the war extras were on the streets on Saturday, May 7. That afternoon, for the first time since 1861, the Marine Band played on the lawn south of the White House. There was an immense gathering. Loud calls greeted Mr. Lincoln when he appeared on the portico. He proposed three cheers for Grant and his armies, and roar after roar came, in a release of pent-up emotion, from the throats of the crowd.

The next day, Sunday, brought further word of terrific fighting. The story was inconclusive. There was as yet no official report. But it was known that the quartermaster of the Army of the Potomac had telegraphed for forage; and a city, grown wise in the ways of war, realized that this imported an advance. That day, Washington sweltered in a premature blast of hot weather. As though news might be read in the quiet streets, people leaned from their windows and hovered in their doorways. Many went out to wander restlessly in the burning sunshine. Colonnades and porticoes, lampposts and awning poles were rendezvous for discussion. There was deep feeling, but no alarm. The long hours of suspense were, said the *Sunday Chronicle,* "the ides of the national trial."

Monday passed in a maze of rumors of still more heavy fighting, thankfully received since they brought no intelligence of disaster. About four o'clock in the afternoon, Stanton sent an official dispatch stating that Grant was on to Richmond. Lee was in retreat with Hancock, Sedgwick, Warren and Burnside close on his heels. In the evening a crowd again gathered at the White House. There was more music, more cheering, as the band of the Twenty-seventh Ohio Regiment, on its way to the field, serenaded Lincoln. The President made a short speech. There were black rings under his eyes. He had scarcely slept since the advance of the Army of the Potomac. At night, in a long wrapper, he paced the big hall on the second floor of the White House, with his head dropped on his breast. But his tone was sanguine, as he spoke of the gallant officers and soldiers, and said he was "exceedingly gratified to know that General Grant had not been jostled from his plans. . . ." He said, too, that much more remained to be done. The crowd went on cheering. That night, the first boatload of wounded came in at the Seventh Street wharf.

The news of Saturday, Sunday and Monday had strained men's nerves; but on the rugged hills of Spotsylvania the hurricane still howled. For five more days, the people of the Union arose from their beds to read the same story—a nightmarish prolongation of battle and slaughter. On Wednesday, May 11, the *Star* printed a telegram which General Rufus Ingalls, quartermaster of the Army of the Potomac, had sent from Spotsylvania to a friend in the capital. They had been fighting all the time, he said. The losses were heavy. They were about to attack again. "The world never heard of war before."

Two days later, another dispatch from Spotsylvania was published in the press. It came from General Grant, and contained one of his blunt sentences, clipped and made more forceful before it reached the people in Stanton's bulletin: "I propose to fight it out on this line, if it takes all summer." The President read it to a deliriously joyful crowd that surged around the White House in the evening. The words resounded through the nation. Stark resolution had been rare among its generals. Memories were still vivid of the grand attacks which McClellan, Pope, Burnside and Hooker had made in Virginia. All had fought bloody battles, all had fallen back in defeat. The Union accepted the new toll of dead and wounded, and cheered the grit of a commander who advanced.

The newspaper accounts of the Wilderness campaign marked in accuracy and moderation of tone a great improvement over the early war correspondence. The reporters sent to the front by the great dailies and the Associated Press were picked and experienced men, registered by the War Department. Moreover, the press now had access to official bulletins which Mr. Stanton sent to General Dix, who had been made commander of the Department of the East, with head-quarters in New York City, after the draft riots of the preceding summer. Inevitably, there were some exaggerations of success. On the whole, with due allowance for the changing and confused conditions of active military operations, the news was well presented. Every day, the Washington newspapers carried a concise resumé of "The Situation." The staunch resistance of the Confederates and the heavy Federal losses were neither minimized nor viewed with alarm, but soberly and frankly stated. Editorial comment was temperate, counseled patience and resolution and deprecated hasty reliance on rumor.

When the news of the terrible eight days was all in, there was a lull. Torrents of rain had mired the Virginia roads, and offensive operations were discontinued for a week. The country waited for the final decisive battle. Every sign was good. Fresh veteran troops were marching south to repair the losses of the Army of the Potomac. Ben Butler was nearing Richmond, throwing its population into a panic. Phil Sheridan's cavalry had inflicted a smashing defeat on the Confederate horsemen. Sherman was advancing in Georgia. Sigel, appointed to the command in West Virginia, was charging through the Valley. These reports were all true. Only one thing was misunderstood by the people. Lee was fighting prudently, protecting his army behind breastworks. Grant was throwing his troops against them with great slaughter. After Spotsylvania, he still went ahead, moving to the left, striking farther south. He was advancing; but he had not defeated Lee's army.

Only the strong belief in Grant and the confidence of approaching victory nerved the country to sustain the shock of the casualties. The exultation over the approaching end of the war was deep and solemn. The President had recommended a day of thanksgiving and prayer, and in their homes and churches people bowed their heads in gratitude to God, looking toward peace humbly, like children chastened by punishment. In a mood of religious faith, men in Washington discerned in the sunshine and blossoming flowers the signs of a loving Providence. They read an augury of good in the statue of Armed Freedom, cleared of its last veil of scaffolding on the Capitol dome. Washington saw the marching lines of reinforcements, and the shabby gray backwash of rebel prisoners and deserters; but it saw also the results of an unprecedented carnage which staggered even a war-hardened city.

During the week that the news of Spotsylvania pounded in the nation's ears, the wounded from the Wilderness were coming back to Washington. The Sixth Street wharf was as lively by night as by day. The torches made dancing puddles in the black Potomac waters, as the ambulances rumbled into line. Cookhouses clattered and steamed, and ladies hovered over refreshment stands. The silent steamers came in, wafting the smell of wounds like a greeting.

There were three days and nights in which the procession of ambulances never ceased. The hospital lists darkened long columns in the newspapers. The *Chronicle,* on May 21, reported eighteen thousand cases, including the slightly wounded and prisoners of war. To Washington, staring at the jolting caravans, it seemed that Grant's whole army was being carried back to the city.

Hundreds of men and women went to the wharves to deal out food and drink, and to pour water on the dressings, which had dried and stiffened on the journey. Little darkies ran beside the ambulances with drinking water. Along the route to the hospitals, people set tables in the street before their houses, and offered tea, coffee and sandwiches as the trains moved slowly past. The hospitals were surrounded with volunteer nurses and friends of the wounded. Crowds of strangers added to the turmoil of the city—anxious people, hurrying through the streets, scanning the newspapers, bending over rows of stretchers and cots, each looking for one certain face, hoping and dreading to find it.

There was no want of preparation for receiving the wounded in Washington. Tents had multiplied around the big hospital buildings. Long ranks of clean beds were ready. There were plenty of surgeons and nurses. The city was stocked with instruments, medicines, bandages, food and drink. Boxes and bales of supplies, ordered for the emergency, overflowed the storerooms of the commission houses, and were piled high on the sidewalks. But many miles separated the comforts of the capital from the lonely battlefields of the Virginia Wilderness; and there the handling of the wounded, with all the experience the Union had gained, was bungled with frightful mismanagement, inadequacy and neglect.

The first intention had been to send the casualties direct to Washington over the Orange and Alexandria Railroad. When that line was for military reasons abandoned, they were taken to Fredericksburg, and thence transported to the steamers at Grant's new base of supplies, the little landing of Belle Plain, south of Aquia Creek. On the hot Sunday when Washington tremulously awaited the news from the Wilderness, the Secretary of War and the acting Surgeon General were informed that a hospital was being established at Fredericksburg for the reception of the wounded. Trains of ambulances and army wagons were already pouring into the Virginia town when Meade sent off his telegram. The *Star* stated that the wounded lay so thick in the streets that a cavalry patrol could not perform its duty, for fear of trampling the helpless men.

Fredericksburg had been occupied by Union forces on the night before the wounded began to arrive. It was impossible to organize comfortable hospitals on a moment's notice. Surgeons and medical and commissary stores were all urgently needed at the front. The town had been abandoned by most of its inhabitants, and those who remained were without pity for their suffering enemies. There were still, however, comfortable residences and a supply of food in the occupied town. Federal officers did not commandeer them. From the streets, the wounded were carried into stores, churches, stables and deserted houses, and laid in rows on bare and dusty floors. Without room to stretch or turn, they were pushed into the corners of halls, and huddled on stairways. One severely injured man was glad to find a place on a closet shelf. A day's rations for the Fredericksburg "hospitals" consisted of a single cup of coffee and a piece of hard tack. Many men died from want of treatment, and many, it was said by those who witnessed the conditions, from starvation. Only the ministrations of the Sanitary and Christian Commissions saved thousands of others.

It was to Washington that General Meade and the medical director of the Army of the Potomac sent appeals for surgeons, nurses, ambulances and supplies. Fredericksburg was only seventy miles from the capital. In a few hours, a representative of the Medical Bureau could have verified the truth of the frightful conditions, could have started off shiploads to relieve them. There was the excuse that transportation was delayed on the road from Belle Plain to Fredericksburg, but it did not prove an insuperable obstacle to the Sanitary and Christian Commissions. Without recognizing any emergency, the Medical Bureau gave routine orders for attendants and medical supplies and food to be sent to the wounded. All were fatally slow in reaching them. From its big storehouse on F Street, the Sanitary Commission was sending enormous shipments, not only of articles of diet, but of things which it was the business of the Medical Bureau to provide—morphine, chloroform, opium, scissors, forceps, chloride of lime.

The Medical Bureau had been disrupted for months. Surgeon General Hammond was no longer in office. For weeks, in a dreary courtroom on Fourteenth Street, he had been on trial for fraud and malpractice in office. Mr. Stanton had found a means of relieving himself of a brilliantly capable subordinate, whose forceful personality antagonized him. In the autumn of 1863, he had ordered Hammond away from Washington on a prolonged tour of inspection. In his absence, a commission examined the affairs of his office, and reported irregularities in the award of contracts for hospital supplies. Hammond demanded a trial by court-martial. He was acquitted. But, while the wounded were languishing in Fredericksburg, the wheels were already turning which would reconvene the court, and dismiss Hammond from the service in disgrace.

Meantime, Colonel Joseph K. Barnes was the acting head of the Medical Bureau. He was Mr. Stanton's choice for the place, the man whom he would make Surgeon General, as soon as the formalities of ousting Hammond were over. Stanton was far too upright and patriotic to put a worthless favorite in office. Barnes was a man of ability. In the light of his subsequent record, his incapacity in the spring of 1864 might be explained by the fact that, although he had been in charge of the Medical Bureau for nine months, he had not yet received his appointment.

The extraordinary hardships of the wounded did not end when they were removed from Fredericksburg. Between the town and the Belle Plain landing lay nearly ten miles of narrow, roughly made road, cluttered with the ceaseless, southbound movement of reinforcements and supplies. For want of sufficient ambulances, springless wagons were used for transportation. Behind the trees, rebel guerrillas carried on desultory attacks on the slow-moving trains. Mules took fright, reared and plunged in wild confusion. Sometimes, wagons overturned, spilling bandaged men on the roadside.

During the week of heavy rains which interrupted Grant's offensive, the road to Belle Plain became a strip of bottomless swamp. The wagons went jolting across fields and stumps. Often men were bruised so severely that they died on the way. Around the landing, the clay soil was a mass of soft, pink mud, in which the heavy vehicles sank to the hub, and stuck fast. One of the first tasks assigned to the Christian Commission delegates was to carry fresh bread to Belle Plain. The workers kindled fires and boiled coffee; rolled up their trousers, and waded among the ambulances to feed the famishing men inside. The Sanitary Commission established a refreshment station at the landing, and three others along the route to Fredericksburg.

With the improved administration of the Washington hospitals and the increasing efficiency of the two relief commissions, Clara Barton had begun to feel that her usefulness was ended. Stanton had refused to give her passes to move at her discretion among the troops. With the news of the casualties in the Wilderness, however, Miss Barton received her passes. From Belle Plain, with its bogged ambulances, she went on to Fredericksburg. She rushed back to Washington, and told Senator Henry Wilson what she had seen. Wilson went to the War Department at ten o'clock in the evening. Clara Barton understood he said that either they would send someone that night to correct the abuses, or the Senate would send someone the next day. Wilson got action. In the small hours, Quartermaster General Meigs and his staff galloped to the Sixth Street wharf. The next morning, there was a reorganization in Fredericksburg. Meigs ordered the houses of the citizens opened to the wounded, and arranged for them to receive food from the supplies in the town. Soon after, the water route to Fredericksburg and the railroad to Aquia Creek were both opened, and the distressful transportation to Belle Plain was at an end.

Late in May, all judged able to endure the journey had been sent to the Washington hospitals. Those who remained behind were the men with amputations and breast and belly wounds. As Grant advanced south, his base was removed from Belle Plain. Fredericksburg was to be abandoned to the guerrillas, and it became necessary to evacuate all the wounded. It was then that Washington received boatloads that surpassed, in multiplied dreadfulness of suffering, all that had gone before. Crowds gathered at the Sixth Street wharf to meet the steamers. Even the gangways were lined with people. Women wept aloud, as the litters passed. Two by two, bearers went through the streets, carrying men too far gone to be placed in the ambulances. The death rate in the hospitals began a fearful ascent.

Although the numbers of Grant's casualties had not been minimized, the Washington press had depreciated the severity of the wounds. Serious cases were said to be unusually few, because little use had been made of artillery in the campaign. There must have been War Department authority behind the repeated statements that a large proportion of the patients in the hospitals would be ready to return to the field within thirty days. The invasion of prostrate men was not, it was emphasized, made up entirely of Federal casualties. There were many wounded prisoners among them. Moreover, there were the usual cases of sickness. Finally, there were always malingerers and deserters. They were well known to mingle with the wounded, especially the first arrivals after a battle. Some went hobbling along, with sound limbs swathed in bandages. Others pleaded sunstroke. Examining officers turned them over to the provost guard to be sent back to their regiments. Washington grew ready to look with suspicious eyes on any soldier who was able to drag himself about, even though he went on crutches, had a broken head, or carried his arm in a sling. Sarcastically, the newspapers declared that wounds were slight indeed, if they permitted a man to lounge about the hotels or promenade on the Avenue.

Yet all the palliation of the casualties could not persuade a population which, by day and by night, witnessed the passing, not only of agony, but of death. Boxed in rosewood and in pine, officers and men of the Army of the Potomac mutely answered the statement that their wounds were trivial. The coffin-loads from the hospitals traveled a new route. The cemetery at the Soldiers' Home was full, and at Arlington fresh graves began to blot the green acres which surrounded the mansion of Robert E. Lee. While death rattled across the Long Bridge, every incoming steamer carried its consignment of corpses. Fatalities among officers were heavy. All ranks were represented in the sheeted forms in the bows. Even major-generals fell in Grant's campaign. For a day, John Sedgwick, late commander of the Sixth Corps, lay in Dr. Holmes's embalming establishment on the Avenue, to receive the last tribute of respect and curiosity. His body had been brought to Washington the second night after he was killed, and the embalmers were proud of their work. Many soldiers wept, as they stood beside his bier, for Sedgwick had been beloved by his men. A lady, pertinacious in her desire for souvenirs, was with difficulty prevented from clipping two buttons from his uniform.

James Wadsworth's hearse moved with ceremony to the depot,

accompanied by a military guard and a delegation of New York congressmen; but no man looked again on his handsome face. His body did not reach Washington for almost two weeks after he fell in the Wilderness. It was found and disinterred on the battlefield, where it had been given rude burial by a Virginian who lived in the vicinity. He was a former prisoner in the Old Capitol, to whom Wadsworth had shown kindness when he was military governor.

Like the living, the dead were usually long delayed in transportation. The weather grew hot. Filled with shipments of corpses, Washington stank like a charnel house. The people, who could not accuse the dead, vented their horror on the embalmers. On every hand, flaunting signs advertised their prosperous business. The mortuaries were situated next door to private houses, restaurants and markets. "It insults the meanest animals," said the *Chronicle*, "to have their dead and food in juxtaposition." Washington cried that the embalmers were purveyors of pestilence, and must be cleared out of town. Dr. Holmes, the proprietor of the leading establishment, was arrested for creating a nuisance on Pennsylvania Avenue.

It was the murmuring of people whose faith was beginning to be shaken. Faint hints of adversity had trickled through the news. Sigel had been defeated at New Market in the Valley by a smaller force under John C. Breckinridge. The capital had not been alarmed, but enraged at Sigel as "a chronic lagger." The accounts of Ben Butler's movements south of the James had lost their first elation. Plenty of people on the Avenue were eager to take bets that Fort Darling, below Richmond, had fallen. Pessimists were denounced as bulls in gold, and secession sympathizers. There were days of uncertainty and depression, as the country waited for Grant's decisive victory north of Richmond, and heard only of sharp cavalry clashes and heavy skirmishing—costly in casualties, but inconclusive. Yet Grant was still advancing, and hope rang valiantly in loyal hearts, when June came in with a racket of guns ten miles northeast of Richmond. The Union read accounts of a severe battle at Cold Harbor. The optimistically worded bulletin carried no hint of defeat, but there was ill omen in the very neighborhood. Cold Harbor brought back memories of the Peninsula campaign. It was near Mechanicsville and Gaines's Mill. Grant's base of supplies was at White House on the Pamunkey. Once more, the reports stated that only the Chickahominy lay between the

Army of the Potomac and Richmond. There was a rumor that Grant was retreating to Harrison's Landing.

Cold Harbor had been a disaster. It shook the morale of the Army of the Potomac. These were superbly disciplined soldiers, but they were human. There had to be an end to dashing them against Lee's breastworks. Grant had intended to fight it out on that line, if it took all summer; but the suns of mid-June found his troops sidling down to the south of the James River. When his obstinacy yielded, the Army of the Potomac had lost over fifty thousand men: more than half the force that had crossed the Rapidan in early May; nearly as many effectives as Lee's whole army had then comprised.

In the middle of June, the news that the campaign north of Richmond had ended in a stalemate was officially endorsed, and could no longer be labeled an invention of the timid and disloyal. Petersburg occupied the headlines, reported in the old way, a success story in reverse. First, the Federal forces gloriously captured the city. Next, the outworks were taken, with heavy losses. Finally, a gradual approach and regular siege would be necessary before the army took possession of Petersburg.

It was a moment of sickening anticlimax. The nation, expecting the end of war, was offered the siege of Petersburg. In staunch and sensible editorials, the Washington press strove to mitigate the disappointment. There had been excessive hopefulness, the vice of the American people. Grant would in time get Richmond. "We need," said the *Chronicle,* "something more of the old Roman temper that grimly welcomed a triumph, and in the darkest hour never despaired of the Republic." All signs were plain that the Union, with its vastly superior resources and man power, needed only good heart and patience to defeat the Confederacy. In June of 1864, it had little left of either.

Shortly before the defeat at Cold Harbor was understood, the National Union Convention had gathered in Baltimore, and renominated Abraham Lincoln for the Presidency. For his running mate, they chose a Democrat and a Southerner, Andrew Johnson of Tennessee, who for over two years had been military governor of that reclaimed State. The White House was the center of visiting delegations, there were serenades and congratulatory speeches. A grand ratification meeting was held on the south portico of the Patent Office, just as the tide of the country's confidence was turning. Decked in evergreens, huge transparencies celebrated Lincoln and Johnson and Grant, and the name of Stephen A. Douglas was resurrected to stimulate the adherence of the War Democrats. In the soft darkness of the June night, the Patent Office blazed like a many-faceted beacon, and the Post-Office glittered brightly across the way. Rockets streamed and burst across a sky hung with the constellations of illuminated balloons. Military music and sonorous oratory stirred the crowd of loyal citizens in F Street. From the fortifications, the guns saluted, not the victories of the Union arms, but the discomfiture of the Republican radicals.

THERE HAD BEEN an impatient expectation that Grant might signalize Independence Day by making a successful sortie, but no news came from Petersburg. Instead, Washington heard that Sigel had again been defeated in the Valley, and was retreating to Harper's Ferry. Sigel appeared to be played out. The War Department began casting around for able major-generals who were not on active service. Stanton spoke of sending for Alex McCook, of the famous Ohio family of "Fighting McCooks." His brave record as a corps commander in the West had been blurred in the recriminations which followed the Union disaster at Chickamauga, but a court of inquiry had exonerated him. Halleck's thoughts turned toward Quincy A. Gillmore, a capable young engineer who had succeeded in reducing Fort Sumter, though not in taking Charleston. Lately commanding in the Army of the James, Gillmore had been relieved, with angry accusations, by General Ben Butler.

The capital's streets were cluttered with crowds of destitute contrabands, sent back from Virginia by the army. Depression over the military situation was deepened by doubts of the national solvency, stirred by the abrupt announcement that Mr. Chase had resigned from the Cabinet. An explosion in the cartridge department of the Arsenal had killed seventeen District girls, and mutilated many others. Washington, smothered in hot yellow dust, showed scant enthusiasm for the celebration of July 4, 1864. A new school building was dedicated. The Peace Democrats held a meeting. Congress adjourned.

Only in the White House grounds was a spirit of carnival evident. Washington colored folk had been given permission to hold a grand Sunday-school picnic on the lawn between the mansion and the War Department. Congress had at last provided revenues for their education, and the gate receipts were to be applied to constructing a school. In hacks drawn by brightly caparisoned horses, prosperous Negroes drove through the White House gates. It was a well-dressed crowd, plentifully besprinkled with fair skins and blue eyes. Men sported ivory-headed canes, and women carried gay parasols. With irreproachable decorum, barbers and waiters and house servants promenaded on the walks, clustered around the speakers' platform to hear the fervid periods of the orators, and enjoyed the motion of the swings which had been suspended from the shade trees. White passers-by paused to stare at the unprecedented scene, some with laughter, some with curses, some with shrugs of resignation to the processes of revolution. One observer was reminded of the palace gardens of Haiti. "The blacks are right," he noted in his diary. "They and they alone, freed by accident, have lost nothing and gained everything." Along the curb, outside the grounds, sat a dejected row of figures—contrabands in butternut, aliens and inferiors.

The next day, the Navy Department hung out its big flag in honor of a victory at sea. The rebel pirate, *Alabama,* had been sunk off the coast of France by the Yankee steamer, *Kearsage.* Loyal Washington stirred in the heat to applaud the news, slipped back into the lassitude of July. The legislators, the lobbyists and the hangers-on had all taken their departure. Many families had left for the seashore and the mountains. Quiet rested on the halls of the hotels and the sunscorched pavements. There were empty seats in the streetcars. Hack drivers nodded on their boxes.

Rumors of a rebel raid penetrated the city's siesta like a disturbing dream. It had already occurred to a number of people that General Lee might make a movement to the north, with the view of loosening Grant's hold on Petersburg. The Army of the Potomac, south of the James River, no longer shielded Washington. Moreover, the Shenandoah Valley, the broad route to the back door of the capital, now lay open wide to the invader.

Sigel, operating with a small force in the lower Valley had since May held only a subordinate command in the Department of West Virginia. After his defeat at New Market, he had been superseded by General David Hunter. With the main body of the troops in the department, Hunter had made a vigorous campaign to the south, investing Lynchburg in mid-June. To drive him away, Lee had dispatched the Second Corps of his army—Stonewall Jackson's former command —under a stout, round-shouldered old war horse, General Jubal Early. Hunter had been forced out of the Valley, and obliged to retreat by a westerly route that carried him all the way across West Virginia to the Ohio River. Soon after the withdrawal of his army from the Shenandoah, alarms had begun to rumble beyond the Blue Ridge. Out of a cloud of contradictory reports, the facts emerged that Confederate troops were advancing down the Valley, and that Sigel's force—the only Federals in their path, save for a small number at Harper's Ferry—had been routed.

There was panic in the fertile Cumberland Valley. Excited refugees from the western counties of Maryland poured into Baltimore with frightening stories. Washington, however, remained calm. Invasion had become an old story to the capital. Every summer of the war, the Confederates had approached the city in force. Mosby's rangers and other marauding detachments of rebel cavalry had sounded a hundred alarms. Habit had dulled the edge of apprehension. The *Star* contemptuously referred to the first rumor of an attack on Hagerstown, Maryland, as "a scary Harrisburg report." The Confederate force was variously estimated at from five thousand to forty thousand. Washington, used to war and its alarms, inclined to a conservative view. Even when it was definitely established that the enemy had crossed the upper Potomac, most people in the capital believed that this was merely an incursion of swooping roughriders, who would vanish as suddenly as they had appeared.

As early as July 2, the telegraph at the War Department had begun to sound signals of distress from worried generals and railroad officials in the Valley. There were warnings of torn-up tracks, burned bridges and severed telegraph wires. The War Office could not dismiss the enemy's advance as a mere cavalry raid. It was informed that the Confederates were moving in force, with artillery. Halleck complained that he could get no reliable estimate of the numbers of the invaders. In the first days of July, he was repeatedly advised that the enemy had between twenty and thirty thousand men. The lower figure was approximately correct.

On July 4, Washington was cut off from telegraphic communication with Harper's Ferry. From the railroad company, the War Office learned that the Ferry had been evacuated by the Federals stationed there. Together with Sigel's force, they had shut themselves up in entrenchments on Maryland Heights across the river. Halleck hustled off a scrambled collection of Ohio militia, dismounted cavalry and light artillery, armed as infantry, under command of General Albion P. Howe, who was in charge of the artillery depot in Washington. Though the railroad was interrupted, Howe managed to get through to Maryland Heights. He replaced Sigel, now finally relieved of command, at Harper's Ferry, which was reoccupied by the Federals, after the enemy had crossed into Maryland. The break in the telegraph also inspired a scouting expedition. A detachment of the Eighth Illinois cavalry, a veteran regiment which was on patrol duty in Washington, was sent up the Potomac to Point of Rocks. Moving two bodies of troops away from Washington exhausted General Halleck's capacity for action. In a crisis which called for decision, he appeared to be "in a perfect maze." For once, Mr. Stanton, too, showed no initiative. As a rule, the threat of danger sent him into a furor of nervous energy; but on this occasion, subdued and casual, he was inclined to pooh-pooh all alarming reports. Like a secret cult, the War Office was wrapped in impenetrable mystery. It had no information to give to anyone about the invasion, and seemed to find the subject faintly distasteful.

This reticence did not cover a resolute plan. Though aware that the Baltimore and Ohio Railroad was badly damaged, both Stanton and Halleck relied on the hope that General Hunter would be able to move his forces all the way from the Ohio River in time to confront the invaders. Meantime, Stanton made the spacious, if wasted gesture of asking the governors of Pennsylvania and New York to call out their militia. On July 5, Grant suggested sending up an army corps from Petersburg, in case the enemy should cross the upper Potomac. Halleck telegraphed that he thought this unnecessary. He had "no apprehensions," though he conceded that he might make use of the dismounted cavalry of the Army of the Potomac. That same day, however, Grant became rather tardily convinced that a Confederate army corps was gone from his front. In spite of Halleck's reassurances, he ordered to the relief of Washington not only three thousand dismounted cavalry, but the third division of the Sixth Corps, under General James B. Ricketts. These troops landed at Baltimore on July 8.

In the autumn of 1862, Stanton had sought expert advice on the Washington fortifications. A commission of distinguished army engineers had spent two months in examining them. The defenses, then still being enlarged and strengthened, formed a complete circuit of thirty-seven miles. Over fifty forts occupied commanding positions north and south of the Potomac, with emplacements for field guns and connecting lines of trenches between them. The commission had reported that they required garrisons of thirty-four thousand men—twenty-five thousand infantry and nine thousand artillerists—in addition to a force of three thousand cavalry for outpost duty. The figure for the garrisons was over twice as high as that set by McClellan's corps commanders in the spring of 1862. On the point of a covering army for the field, in case the capital were threatened, the Army engineers agreed with the earlier estimate of twenty-five thousand men.

Early in 1863, a Department of Washington had been re-created, absorbing the military entity of the District, and reducing the office of military governor to little more than an honorary position. In command of the department, the troops of which were designated the Twenty-second Corps, Heintzelman had been replaced by General Christopher C. Augur, who had seen service both in Virginia and Louisiana. Augur, in July of 1864, reported an aggregate of thirty-one thousand men in the department. General Barnard, who had been made chief engineer on Grant's staff, was in Washington in early July. He stated that a little over twenty thousand men of the Twenty-second Corps were in the vicinity of the capital; but that a large number of them—dismounted troopers, guards at the bridges and buildings, and novices at the artillery camp—were unavailable for defense. The garrisons, according to Barnard, the acknowledged expert on the subject of the Washington fortifications, numbered not thirty-four thousand, but ninety-six hundred soldiers.

Even this figure gives no conception of the military impoverishment of Washington. In May and June, the troops defending the capital had been reduced in quality, as well as in numbers. Nearly all able-bodied and disciplined soldiers had been sent to reinforce the Army of the Potomac. The infantry on guard duty in the city was composed of the semi-invalid Veteran Reserves. The Army engineers had advised Stanton that heavy artillery regiments, once trained, should remain permanently in the forts. This counsel had been followed until the losses of Grant's campaign were realized. Then most of the experienced gunners were ordered to the front as infantry. A number of dismounted batteries of field artillery, brought in to man the ordnance, had also been sent away to Petersburg and, more recently, to Harper's Ferry. Their places had been taken by the Ohio National Guard. In late April, the governors of several western States had offered to raise seventy-five thousand volunteers for one hundred days' service on guard and garrison duty during the campaign season. The Ohio regiments in the Washington fortifications were militia, corresponding in want of training and length of service to the first troops which had come to the capital at the outbreak of war. They were, however, far less numerous. The dispatch of one regiment to Harper's Ferry reduced by one third the infantry on duty in the northern defenses of Washington.

The lethargy of the War Office was based on no illusions about the caliber of these soldiers. Halleck was well aware that the Ohio militia could "scarcely fire a gun." By July 6, this fact was beginning to worry General Augur, and, on his prompting, Halleck suggested to Grant that one regiment of heavy artillery should be returned to Washington. The infantry around the capital, he later assured Grant, could do nothing in the field, as one half of the men could not march at all.

At this time, it occurred to General Halleck to inquire about conditions at the bridges across the Potomac. He received a prompt report from Colonel B. S. Alexander, a brusque and corpulent officer who had been Barnard's assistant in Washington in the early days, and had recently been appointed chief engineer of the defenses. All three bridges were guarded by insufficient detachments of Veteran Reserves, Alexander stated. At the Washington end of the Long Bridge, there was no artillery at all; while, at the Virginia end, Fort Jackson had fallen into dilapidation as a result of being traversed by the railroad tracks. The Aqueduct was protected on the Virginia side by three blockhouses and a stockade, with gates at the approach. The blockhouses were unoccupied. The captain of the guard declared that he would close the gates, in case of attack. He had, however, never tried to close them, and did not know if the bars fitted, or indeed if there were any bars at all. The batteries at the District end of the Chain Bridge were in charge of an Ohio militia sergeant, who knew nothing about ordnance. He merely cleaned the guns, aired the ammunition and swept the platforms. No one at the bridge knew how the guns were loaded. The officer of the guard believed that the bridge was mined, and could be blown up in an emergency; but Colonel Alexander remarked that this was not the case.

The character of the troops which had been left in the capital would have permitted a raid from any direction. This was not understood by the people of Washington. They knew that many regiments had been sent away, and viewed with some consternation the departure of Halleck's reinforcements for Harper's Ferry; but they were convinced of the excellence of the city's defenses, which for the preceding year and a half had been so strongly garrisoned that they had induced a comfortable tradition of security.

On July 6, the day that Alexander made his report, boatmen were coming down the Chesapeake and Ohio Canal to Georgetown, with news that the rebels were crossing the Potomac at nearly every fordable point between Harper's Ferry and Muddy Branch, less than twenty miles above the Washington suburb. The boatmen were too frightened to return upriver, and their empty barges lay huddled around the Aqueduct.

Even the most skeptical persons were obliged to admit that the raiders were extraordinarily bold. They were plundering and stealing horses in the border counties of Pennsylvania. Fifty miles of Baltimore and Ohio tracks had been torn up. Their forces levied requisitions of money on Hagerstown and Frederick.

Commanding at Baltimore was General Lew Wallace, the Indiana officer who would one day write a novel called *Ben Hur*. He had a small body of troops, as weedy as those in Washington. He had no more accurate information than Halleck or Augur. An army, apparently of twenty thousand men, had crossed the upper Potomac, and was moving toward the gaps of South Mountain. Wallace promptly moved out to meet the enemy. On the Monocacy River, where the railroad and the pikes to Washington and Baltimore converged, he concentrated his command of twenty-five hundred men. There he was providentially joined by Ricketts's division of the Sixth Corps, which, on landing at Baltimore, made haste to follow him on the cars. Wallace had little hope of defeating the Confederates, but he suspected that they meant to march on Washington, and he thought that he might delay them. With the reinforcements that reached him, he had about six thousand men on Saturday, July 9, when he fought a sharp engagement. The defeated Federals fell back to the east on the Baltimore road. General Early did not pursue them. At dawn on Sunday morning, the gray-clad troops—Early's corps and another division under General John C. Breckinridge—were marching south along the Georgetown Pike. They camped that night above Rockville, a town within ten miles of the District line.

In the northern defenses of Washington, the regulations had been tightened. No man was permitted to leave his post. Four hours a day were given over to artillery practice. The garrisons were busily employed in chopping down the brush, which was growing high on the approaches. The spirit of the Ohio soldiers was good. They were prepared to fight for the capital. But the Confederates, if they had not been held up on the Monocacy, could have walked past them on Sunday. In the northern works, the infantry consisted of two regiments of raw militia, spaced out in earth-banked forts, between which the rifle pits were unoccupied. Early's was an army of veterans.

Strong reinforcements, as the War Office knew, were starting for the capital. On Saturday evening, Halleck had received permission from Grant to order up the Nineteenth Corps from Fort Monroe, where it was expected by ship from the Gulf of Mexico. Late that

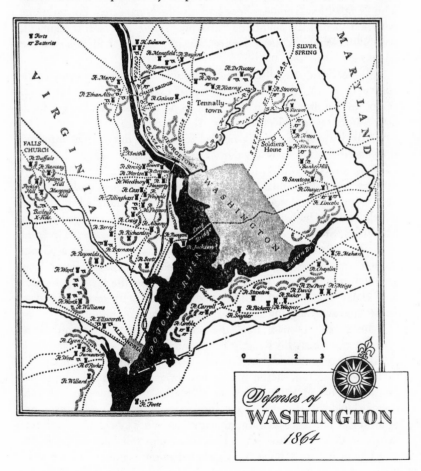

Defenses of
WASHINGTON
1864

night, mulling over Washington's predicament, the old bureaucrat aroused himself to send off another telegram, asking Grant for the rest of the Sixth Corps. Fortunately, Grant had already given the order, and the two remaining divisions embarked at City Point on Sunday.

None of these troops could arrive before Monday. Meantime, the additions to the defense of Washington were negligible. Sheridan's force of dismounted cavalry, forwarded from Baltimore, proved to include twenty-five hundred sick, and yielded but five hundred serviceable men, mainly the residue of the Twenty-fifth New York Cavalry. The Ninth New York Artillery had also been expected, but only one battalion turned up on Sunday afternoon. The rest of the regiment, with its colonel, William Henry Seward, Junior, had gone to the Monocacy.

Halleck and Augur kept the wires busy, rounding up every available man in the department. Orders clicked to outlying forts and camps in Virginia. Augur's eye fell hopefully on the broken-down inmates of the stragglers' camp at Alexandria.

Cavalry was desperately needed for outpost duty. Eight hundred troopers, including some regulars, had been hastily organized at Falls Church, and sent out on the Rockville Road to meet the enemy. On Sunday, they skirmished briskly with Early's advance, and did their best to impede its progress. The detachment of the Eighth Illinois which Halleck had sent to Point of Rocks had been engaged on the Monocacy. Six other companies of this regiment were scattered in front of the line of the northern defenses. The commanding officer at Camp Stoneman, the rendezvous for dismounted at Giesboro' Point, was assembling equipment and drawing horses from the Cavalry Bureau on Sunday, but the men could not be made ready for service that day. Some, however, were ordered into the defenses as infantry.

Inside the District line, the strong earthworks of Fort Reno guarded the Rockville Road. The battalion of the Ninth New York Artillery was encamped at Tennallytown on Sunday afternoon. In this exposed section of the line, a new brigadier, General Martin D. Hardin, who had graduated from West Point only two years before the outbreak of the war, took command late on Sunday evening. Hardin did not leave Washington until eleven o'clock, and reinforcements of Veteran Reserves reached Fort Reno still later in the night.

General Alex McCook was assigned to the command of a reserve camp on Piney Branch Creek, midway between the city and Fort Stevens, the northernmost point of the defenses, which guarded the great thoroughfare of the Seventh Street Road. The dearth of infantry was shown by the fact that the 150th Ohio garrisoned and picketed the entire line from Rock Creek east to Bladensburg. One company of this regiment occupied Fort Stevens, supplemented by a battery of artillerymen and a few convalescents—two hundred and nine men in all. On Sunday night, the Second District Regiment, a regiment of Veteran Reserves and two batteries reported to McCook's camp. The general had made a hasty survey of the northern defenses, which he had never before set eyes on. He took command of them next day.

Quartermaster General Meigs had been ordered by Mr. Stanton to report for field service. The clerks of his office and the various quartermaster's employees in the District and in Alexandria formed a sizable body of men, and Meigs was champing to lead them on active service. His ardor was dashed by General Halleck, who directed him merely to relieve the guards at the depots and corrals. This paltry duty could be performed by a battalion of two hundred and fifty clerks. Meigs was also counting on leaving a number of teamsters in the city for the accommodation of Grant's reinforcements, who would arrive without wagon trains. Even with these deductions, the Quartermaster General could still command a movable force of nearly two thousand men, and he spent a busy Sunday, organizing them and procuring arms from the Arsenal. He offered their services to General Augur, who gladly accepted them.

The news of the defeat on the Monocacy startled Washington out of its complacency. The rumors rivaled those which had preceded Gettysburg. It was said that Lee's whole army was again invading the North. People could not fail to be impressed by the sudden bustle of activity at the hitherto somnolent War Office. The movement of soldiers was of small military significance, but invalids and dismounted artillerists and troopers raised the dust, as they tramped to the northern works. Long trains of horses were being led in all directions. In some of the vacant lots, squads were drilling in linen coats. It was a noisy and excited Sunday.

Whatever the private emotions of the War Office, it remained uncommunicative. Gideon Welles was disgusted. To the Navy Department on Sunday came a well-authenticated report that rebel pickets had been seen near Georgetown. It was disdainfully dismissed at the

War Office as a mere street rumor. That night, however, Mr. Stanton sent a carriage out to the Soldiers' Home, with positive orders that the President and his family should return to the White House. It was after midnight when John Hay was awakened by Bob Lincoln's coming into his room and getting into bed.

On Monday morning, the Federal cavalry again skirmished with the Confederates on the Rockville Road. From the signal station at Fort Reno, it was presently observed that clouds of dust were moving to the right. Out beyond Silver Spring, a courier of the Eighth Illinois threw himself on his horse, and galloped back to McCook's reserve camp behind Fort Stevens. The enemy was advancing on the Seventh Street Road.

McCook abandoned the reserve camp and pushed his meager command into Fort Stevens and the adjacent rifle pits. He was joined by a third National Guard regiment and a few invalids and dismounted during the morning. Some of the dismounted he threw out with Ohio militiamen in a skirmish line before the fort.

In the meantime, news of invasion had burst on Washington with the arrival of a horde of refugees from Tennallytown in the District and from Rockville and Silver Spring and other Maryland towns. Down the roads they came flying before the rebels, with their household goods stacked crazily on their wagons. This was no cavalry raid, they told the city. The country to the north was swarming with gray uniforms.

Washington, with its pelting couriers and marching squads and trains of army wagons, wore quite a military aspect. It was entirely illusory. The authorities were at the end of their resources. Convalescents had been called from the hospitals. Three companies of useless stragglers had been sent to Tennallytown. Even the President's guard of Bucktails was ordered to the fortifications, where they smelled gunpowder for the only time in their service. As a last forlorn expedient, the District militia and volunteers were called out on Monday morning. The militia now consisted of three-year-old lists of names, and loyal citizens were urged to fill up the companies. Republican clubs, the recently formed Union Leagues, stepped forward, but they had no military organization. The only existing volunteer companies were those in the Government departments, and they had to be armed and equipped and mustered in, before their services were available. While Washington resounded with frenzied calls to arms, and military orders rattled like hailstones, the dust of Early's advance arose before Fort Stevens.

The Confederates were within sight of the gleaming dome of the Capitol. Behind the firm, but ill-garrisoned fortifications lay the Treasury and the Arsenal and the rich manifold storehouses. The raiders were not in sufficient force to hold the place, once reinforcements from Petersburg should arrive; but the sack of the capital would bow the Union's head in humiliation before the world, and General Early, hunched in his saddle before Fort Stevens, knew a flash of hope more dazzling than the noonday sun.

Early had won the race to the Washington defenses. He saw that the forts were "feebly manned," and he gave orders to attack. As a strong fan-shaped line of Confederate skirmishers moved into the valley before the fort, McCook ordered his picket line to fall back slowly, fighting, while a fresh force of six hundred men, made up of the Twenty-fifth New York Cavalry, some of the 150th Ohio National Guard and a company of the Second District, made ready to go out and drive the skirmishers back. The New Yorkers were a skeleton command of unhorsed troopers, but they were veterans, and looked the part. The sight of them made Early change his mind. He feared that reinforcements from Petersburg were already in the defenses, and gave orders to reconnoiter before attacking.

At half past one, a heavy, growling detonation startled the city. Another followed, and another. Washington, recognizing the sound of artillery from the northern forts, was informed that it was besieged.

The President had spent the morning at Tennallytown, but in the heat of midday he was driving down to the Potomac. At the foot of Sixth Street, an eager crowd pressed forward. Steamers were landing at the wharf which, for more than two months, by day and night, had received the prostrate and agonized soldiers of the Army of the Potomac. The new arrivals were not like the comrades who had preceded them. Erect and armed, three brigades bounded down the gangplanks. Greek crosses gleamed in the summer sun, and the crowd hailed the Sixth Corps with jubilant, tumultuous cheers, incongruous in a beleaguered city. Traditions are quickly made in wartime. The corps, organized two years before, was already hailed as the old Sixth.

The column quickly formed, and went swinging up Seventh Street. General Horatio Wright, a precise and formal officer of engineers who had been made corps commander on Sedgwick's death, was not immediately advised of the need for concentrating at Fort Stevens. One of his brigades was starting toward the Chain Bridge before Halleck sent word to Augur to "stop General Wright's movement up the Potomac. . . ." The rhythm of tramping feet brought people running to the sidewalks to welcome back the Army of the Potomac. The city had had its queasy fill of militia and invalids and odds and ends in uniform. Washington knew veterans when it saw them. "It is the old Sixth Corps!" the soldiers heard voices exclaim. "The danger is over now!"

By late afternoon, the three brigades had marched out beyond the city limits, and were in the vicinity of Fort Stevens. Three more brigades arrived on Tuesday morning, bringing to Washington the entire first and second divisions of the corps—ten thousand effectives. For many of them, it was almost a home-coming. In these defenses, boys from New England, New York, Pennsylvania and New Jersey had learned to be soldiers. To some, the ordnance was as familiar as the rifles on their own shoulders. Wright himself, as one of Barnard's assistant engineers, had taken part in constructing the fortifications.

Hard on the arrival of the first three brigades of the Sixth Corps, the advance of the Nineteenth Corps steamed up the Potomac. The sight of the sun-browned campaigners from Louisiana brought added reassurance to Washington. They were, however, a small force—only six hundred and fifty effectives—and the rest of the corps came too late to aid in the defense of the capital. Those who landed on Monday were sent out the Old Bladensburg Road to Fort Saratoga. General Gillmore, summoned from New York by Halleck, was placed in command of them.

From newspaper extras, the capital learned that a considerable force of Confederates, swerving east from the Rockville Road, had reached the Blair family's farm at Silver Spring. Headlines announced fighting on the Seventh Street Road. Washington had been reading for years about that shifting and crucial area, the Front. Twice, on the plain of Manassas, thirty-odd miles away, it had lain uncomfortably close to the capital. But now it was as accessible as a suburban residence. The Front was a place which people could approach by taking the North Seventh Street cars; and pell-mell, out to the end of the car line and thence on foot, as well as in carriages and on horseback, went the Washington population, pardonably curious to discover what was going on. The confusion they witnessed told them little more than they already knew. Even the privileged officials who were permitted to visit Fort Stevens returned home scarcely wiser than they went. Yet to the sight-seers of that Monday evening, the trip out the Seventh Street Road must have been an unforgettable experience. The moon sailed in a tranquil sky, and from forests and fields came the ripe scents and murmuring sounds of a summer night; but along the road the breath of war blew like a hurricane to shatter the rural quiet. Toward Washington flocked the frightened refugees, men, women and children, trudging behind their laden wagons. Candles, stuck on fences along the way, lighted agitated dooryards where people were packing their household goods, loading muskets, piling up rude barricades. Fires, kindled by the roadside, hemmed the route with flame; and, in the distance, blazed the roaring bonfires of burning houses. On past the sentry post, squads of soldiers and galloping horsemen moved toward the flaring lights and flashing rifles in the forts. An armed host of patients from the hospitals shambled forward. Quartermaster General Meigs led out his sturdy force of employees, shouldering guns instead of whips and shovels. Through clouds of thin dust, silver under the moon, the teamsters and laborers marched to fill the rifle pits on either side of Fort Slocum, east of Fort Stevens. That night, Meigs slept in no humdrum quartermaster's bed, but in an orchard, under a poncho, with his horse tethered to an apple tree.

Washington, awakening on Tuesday to the noise of artillery, found itself without mails or newspapers from the North. The railroad had been badly damaged above Baltimore. During the day, rebel cavalry struck the tracks between Baltimore and Washington. At noon, the telegraph wires to the North were cut.

The city's isolation could be marked, not only in the absence of news, but in the destitution of the markets. Only the supply of beef was plentiful. Herds of cattle, driven south to escape Early's cavalry, stampeded into town, and were freely offered for sale. Some grocers, in hopeful anticipation of a prolonged siege, set famine prices on flour and potatoes. Agents of Baltimore firms were closing their accounts with the local merchants and refusing to take more orders, because of the precarious situation of the capital.

The Washington secesh, after a long period of glum repression, went flying about in high glee. They glibly assured the rest of the residents that the city was doomed. The Confederates had made a successful assault, they said, and the President had been wounded.

Loyal inhabitants were conscious of an enemy within, as well as without the gates. Young men were stealing through the lines to join the
invading army. A few of the quartermaster's employees had been conspicuously absent during the call to military duty. Some of the Navy
Yard workmen, ordered to take up arms on Tuesday, refused to obey.
Confederate flags were being secretly manufactured to celebrate
Early's triumphal entry, and at least one of them was found and confiscated. It was firmly believed in Washington that spies, by means
of a signal service, were keeping the rebels informed of conditions in
the northern defenses.

The capital, in 1864, was too sophisticated for panic. No city ever
heard the noise of cannon in its suburbs with a greater appearance
of *sang-froid*. People were eager to learn the facts. They bought and
devoured every newspaper extra. "The city shows no signs of alarm,"
wrote Doster, the former provost marshal, "except being as subdued as
children in a thunderstorm, listening and waiting for the issue. It
seems funny to hear the rumbling of street cars mixed with the rumbling of hostile cannon. . . ." Sight-seers were still thronging out toward Fort Stevens, some of them seeking word of relatives and friends
in the Second District Regiment. They were so numerous that they
interfered with the movement of the army wagons, and orders were
issued to turn them back. The varied business of the city went on as
usual. Both on Monday and Tuesday, according to schedule, premiums were distributed at the Smithsonian to meritorious pupils of
the public schools. Shoemakers hammered, said Doster, clerks copied,
lawyers pleaded and ladies shopped. Perhaps some of the indifference
to danger was affected. Nonchalance had become the fashion in
Washington. Major French said that he was chiefly discomforted by
the heat. He supposed that the "ugly mugs" of the rebels were in front
of Washington; but he also supposed that there were "brave men
enough to give 'em hell," if they tried to come in.

The brave men on whom the capital was relying were the soldiers
of the Army of the Potomac. It would have needed a superhuman
optimism to derive reassurance from the military goings on within
the city itself. Under the direction of Brigadier-General Peter Bacon,
the worthy grocer who commanded the District militia, companies
were being ordered to assemble at the City Hall, in Franklin Square
and in various vacant lots which served as parade and muster grounds.
To arms! bawled the *Chronicle*, as, in flamboyant editorials, it im-

plored able-bodied citizens to die to a man in the trenches, rather than permit the rebel flag to float from the Capitol dome. Major Doster went into Bacon's grocery store, and asked where the militia headquarters was. "Damned if I know," said Bacon's brother.

The War Office still lacked definite information about the Confederate force and, for want of fresh cavalry, was unable to procure it. The enemy appeared to be massed at Silver Spring, but it was by no means certain that Fort Stevens would be their main point of attack. The War Office was also fearful of an assault on the fortifications south of the Potomac. Reports that Early's soldiers were moving east from Silver Spring caused the muster-in of the Navy Yard workmen. The defenses in the northeastern section of the line, which guarded the railroad and the approaches from Bladensburg, were ill-prepared to meet an attack. Halleck gratefully accepted the services of several naval officers who happened to be in town, and the super-annuated sea dog, Admiral Goldsborough, was placed in command of the Navy Yard carpenters and mechanics, who were sent to fill the rifle pits at Fort Lincoln.

Assistant War Secretary Charles A. Dana telegraphed Grant, begging for orders. Grant should appoint a head in Washington, Dana said. Augur commanded the defenses of the city, "with McCook and a lot of brigadiers under him," but he was not permitted to move from Washington. Wright commanded the Sixth Corps, and Gillmore had been temporarily assigned to the arrivals from the Nineteenth. Advice and suggestions were not enough, Dana bluntly informed Grant. "Unless you direct positively and explicitly what is to be done, everything will go on in the deplorable and fatal way in which it has gone for the past week." Without mentioning Halleck's name, Dana could scarcely have made more plain the reason for the muddle in Washington. The city, which had no love for the grouchy bureaucrat, spitefully criticized Halleck. At his residence on Georgetown Heights, he kept great military state, with a guard of invalid soldiers and nightly bugle-blowing of tattoo and taps. Irritable persons suggested that it would be no serious loss if the rebels marched down Rock Creek and captured him.

All day Tuesday, there was skirmishing in front of Fort Stevens. White puffs of smoke rose from the entrenched line of Federals in the valley, and from the groves and orchards and farmhouses where the Confederate sharpshooters were posted. At intervals, the discharge of musketry was drowned by the booming of guns from Fort Stevens and its neighboring strongholds, De Russy and Slocum. Over the green meadows and waving cornfields, solid shot whistled, and shells shrieked defiance to the invaders. As the Confederates did not show themselves in heavy force, the artillery did little execution. It was mainly directed at demolishing the trees and houses which sheltered the enemy's skirmishers.

The Federal skirmish line was made up of soldiers of the Sixth Corps, who, at McCook's request, had relieved his pickets on Monday evening. This was in contravention of War Office orders that Wright's command was to be held in reserve. It was McCook's understanding that he had been ordered to take command of the entire line of northern defenses, Gillmore commanding under him on the right, Meigs in the center and Hardin on the left. The War Department had no clear-cut idea of the commands, and from various contradictory reports it is apparent that McCook did not actually control the northern line. Conflict of authority between him and General Wright made for further inefficiency. The Sixth Corps was eager for action. Wright, if he had not been deterred by Augur, would have advanced to clean out the enemy's skirmishers as soon as his men came up on Monday evening. The veterans, encamped on either side of Rock Creek, in the vicinity of Fort Stevens, found it irksome to remain in the rear, while militia, invalids and quartermaster's employees were on active duty. Some of them went into the rifle pits between Forts Stevens and De Russy, creating disorganization in this section of the line, because of the intermingling of troops under different commanders. On the other hand, heavy artillerists of the Sixth Corps were, to their mortification, not permitted to touch the ordnance, though Forts Stevens and Slocum needed skilled reinforcements so badly that they welcomed feeble gunners from the Washington hospitals.

Late on Tuesday afternoon, a brigade of the Sixth Corps was ordered to make an assault for the purpose of driving Confederate sharpshooters from two houses, situated on either side of the Seventh Street Road. A number of notable civilians had congregated in Fort Stevens: the President, some members of the Cabinet and of Congress, and other Government officials. Mrs. Lincoln had driven out with her husband, and several other ladies had accompanied General Wright and his staff. The hill beside the fort was occupied by other spectators, influential enough to secure passes and sufficiently ad-

venturous to tolerate, from the shelter of trees and bushes, the whiz-
zing of bullets from the enemy's long-range rifles.

Presently, a small brigade of veterans approached, with their
portly commander, Colonel D. D. Bidwell, at their head. They
marched past the fort into the valley, and formed behind the Federal
skirmish line. The batteries of Forts Stevens and Slocum opened on
the Confederate positions. As the firing ceased, General Wright gave
the signal for the charge from the parapet of Fort Stevens. Bidwell's
brigade dashed forward. The Confederates obstinately held their
ground. The crack of the rifles turned to a rattle, then to a continuous
roar. As the rebels at last gave way, the civilians at Fort Stevens
clapped their hands and shouted.

This sharp skirmish was the President's only opportunity of
seeing troops in action. He had no concern for his personal safety.
Both on Monday and Tuesday, with nearly half of his tall form exposed above the parapet, he was under fire at Fort Stevens. During
the charge of Bidwell's brigade, he clambered on top of the parapet,
where General Wright and a few others were standing. A surgeon was
killed by a sharpshooter's bullet within three feet of Lincoln. The
President remained, after Wright had cleared the parapet of everyone
else, and the general ordered him to withdraw. Wright's remonstrance
was couched in dignified, if peremptory terms; and it was left for his
exasperated young aide, Lieutenant-Colonel Oliver Wendell Holmes,
to shout at the Chief Executive, "Get down, you fool!"

Dusk began to shadow the distant valley. There was little more
to be seen, and the spectators looked for their carriages. Still, on the
evening air, the noise of musketry sharply sounded. The enemy's line
had been reinforced, and the contest continued until dark. Bidwell's
brigade, which numbered only about one thousand men, lost nearly
three hundred killed and wounded. Men, borne on stretchers or leaning on the shoulders of their comrades, passed slowly to the rear of
Fort Stevens, where the barracks had been turned into a hospital. The
scattered dead, New Yorkers and Pennsylvanians, were laid that night
in rude graves on the common. There they awaited a more ceremonious burial in a little cemetery presently established on the right
of the Seventh Street Road.

At sunset, military men had remarked that dense clouds of dust,
in the rear of the Confederates, appeared to be receding toward the
northwest. The streets of the Northern Liberties were lively all eve-

ning with small boys and females, pressing as close as possible to the
scene of action. Vendors of ice cream and cake did a rushing business.
The lights from the signal tower at the Soldiers' Home streaked brilliantly across the sky, and Washington expected a night attack. In
the morning the suspense was over. The enemy was gone.

The dust settled behind the last skedaddling rebel pickets on the
Rockville Road. The siege of Washington had not been such an important matter, after all. The main body of the Confederates had
never appeared before the defenses, but had remained encamped at
Silver Spring and beyond. They had about forty pieces of artillery,
and there were newspaper reports that a battery was erected near
Fort Reno, and that another rebel gun was placed near the Bladensburg station. These, however, were said to have done no damage.
Early himself stated that not a piece of his artillery was fired in front
of Washington. The Federal casualties, aside from those of Bidwell's
brigade, were less than a hundred killed and wounded by sharpshooters.

It was only in contemplation of what might have been that
Wallace's stand on the Monocacy assumed the proportions of a deliverance. Remembering the confused disorder of Sunday, Washington shuddered at a narrow escape. The ineptitude of the War Department had been made as crystal-clear as the folly of confiding in
staunchly built earthworks. The final disillusionment was the turn-
out of the District militia on Wednesday morning, after the enemy
had departed. Only one company of the National Rifles had succeeded in recruiting to full strength. A few companies of volunteers
were sworn in. War Department clerks went on guard duty; and two
companies of the Treasury Guard and a battalion of Union League
members spent a night at Fort Baker across the Eastern Branch. The
quartermaster's men were the only Government employees who saw
service at the front.

On Wednesday morning, the suburbs north of Washington lay
serene in the haze of July. The soldiers of the Sixth Corps lay encamped "in a loafer-like, gipsy style among the trees." Some slept
under the shelter of their little tents. Squads were filling their canteens
at the farmers' pumps. A smell of coffee and frying meat came from
the campfires. Muskets stood in pyramidal stacks, and the fences
fluttered with flags and banners. From the Seventh Street Road, the
alarms of war had vanished overnight, leaving a scene as empty of

initiative as the brain of General Halleck. Early's forces were well on their way toward the upper Potomac, before General Wright received his orders, and the Sixth Corps started in pursuit.

Beyond the line of the defenses, the countryside was defaced by breastworks, riddled trees and scarred and trodden fields. Smoldering ruins of houses were reminders of the guns which yesterday had thundered from the forts. Severely wounded Confederates had been left behind. Stragglers were marched back to the Washington prisons. Gray uniforms lay sprawled here and there in the grass, and a squad of contrabands went out to bury the rebel dead.

The houses behind the Confederate skirmish line had been occupied by the enemy. Horses had been picketed in the orchards, and fences had been torn down for firewood. Soldiers had ransacked the wardrobes, leaving in exchange the tattered remnants of butternut uniforms. Books and letters and women's clothing strewed the grounds. In one family's mansion, the crockery was broken, and the furniture smashed; even the piano had been split up. Among the obscene drawings on the walls was scrawled a reminder of the devastation in the Valley. There had been destruction of property during Hunter's campaign to Lynchburg. He had ordered the burning of the residence of Governor Letcher, as well as of the Virginia Military Institute. The Confederates made persistent retaliation for the former offense. They had destroyed the house of Governor Bradford of Maryland on their way to Washington. Only blackened walls remained of the country seat of Postmaster General Blair at Silver Spring. At the end of the month, when the Confederates raided Chambersburg, Pennsylvania, Early ordered the whole pretty town laid in ashes.

The fine old house of the elder Blair, situated not far from his son's, had been the headquarters of the Confederate army. On the lawn, where Mr. Lincoln had played with the Blair grandchildren, his coattails sailing out behind him as he ran, Early and Breckinridge had briefly lain to dream of the glittering prize of Washington. All the liquors had been consumed, the papers were ransacked and only the hems remained of old Mrs. Blair's linen sheets; but the house had not been wantonly despoiled, and the shrubbery and the fields of fine corn were spared. Protection of the property was attributed to Breckinridge's former friendship with the elder Blair. Washington, unimpressed by this gesture of sentiment, was bitter against John C. Breckinridge. Four months after the outbreak of war, he had been in his seat at the Capitol, paying lip service to the old flag. Jubal Early was merely a rebel name, one of the enemy's generals; but, with the sourness of spoiled friendship, Washington held Breckinridge to be a traitor who had returned to assault a city where he had been held in honor.

Both the War Office and the city's secesh had changed their tune, the former lugubriously exaggerating the seriousness of the invasion, the latter minimizing Early's numbers and tittering at the ease with which they had laid siege to the capital. The President, wanting the rebel force destroyed, remained firm in the decision he had formed on Grant's appointment to the chief command, that he would take no hand in the direction of the army. In an aftermath of rage at the audacity of the raiders, Washington longed for vengeance. Wright, with his two divisions and the advance of the Nineteenth Corps, did not start until noon on Wednesday. With all their booty and their droves of stolen cattle, Early's men escaped across the upper Potomac. There was no effective pursuit, though Hunter's force, too, was back in the Valley. In a confusion of contradictory orders from Washington, the Union troops marched helplessly to and fro, and loyal citizens bowed in shame at the exhibition of Federal bungling.

General Early had no reason to feel elated at the success of his expedition. He had lost his chance of plundering Washington. He had not been able to carry out his intention of releasing the Confederate prisoners at Point Lookout. Most important of all, his move-ment had not accomplished Lee's main purpose of forcing Grant either to weaken his hold on Petersburg or to attempt a costly attack. Yet Early's raid had the vastly important result of shaking the already unsteady confidence of the Union. Again, as often in the past, the Shenandoah had been, in the words of the *Intelligencer*, "the valley of our national humiliation." Once more, under trusted leadership, after a ruthless expenditure of men, the old pattern of Federal im-potence was repeated; and the country in bitter disgust cursed the administration and its generals. Even Grant fell from the pedestal on which his countrymen had placed him, and was reviled as no better than a bloody-handed butcher.

Volunteering had virtually ceased. Over the protests of his friends, who feared that the step would ruin his chances of re-election, the President issued a call for five hundred thousand more men.

Drearily across the land fell the shadow of the hated draft, which would be set in operation to complete the unfilled quotas.

The Union camps no longer rang with "Cheer, Boys, Cheer," and "The Battle-Cry of Freedom." From the bivouacs came strains of weariness and death—"When This Cruel War Is Over," "Just Before the Battle, Mother," "The Vacant Chair," and the nostalgic "Tenting Tonight," written by a New Hampshire conscript.

> We are tired of war on the old camp ground,
> Many are dead and gone . . .

Down in front of Richmond, skirmishing with the First Massachusetts Cavalry, was Andrew J. Clement, the Chelsea boy who had driven out beyond Centreville to find his brother on the morning of First Bull Run. Andrew had seen a lot of war since then. He was a hard-riding trooper, veteran of a dozen bloody fields. He had a curved Chicopee saber and a silver-bright carbine and a tight-buttoned blue jacket, piped in yellow, with the three chevrons of a sergeant on the sleeve. Sometimes, in the shattered Virginia woods, he thought of the hot July Sunday of 1861, when he had lingered with the soldiers at the front, innocently hopeful of an excursion to Richmond. After three years' fighting, he hadn't quite got there yet.

XVII *Portents of a Second Term*

THE RAINY ELECTION DAY of 1864 found the White House nearly deserted. After the conferences and the hullabaloo of the canvass, Mr. Lincoln quietly awaited the news of the people's choice. It lay between him and an old friend, recently estranged. Copperheads and pacifists had rallied to the standard of George B. McClellan, once the military idol of the Union, who had been nominated for the Presidency on a platform that the war had proved a failure and must cease.

The loyal people of the nation were no longer united, but in Mr. Lincoln's phrase, "divided and partially paralyzed by a political war among themselves." While the Confederacy hopefully watched and intrigued, the Union had become embroiled in an internal feud. Its two contending clans, Republican and Democratic, were subdivided by angry family quarrels.

The discord in the household of the National Union party threatened to bring down the roof on the administration's head. Dissatisfaction with the conduct of the war had been increasing during late July and August. False hopes held out by unofficial peace missions had unsettled the country. Early's forces had again swooped up from the Valley to raid Maryland and Pennsylvania. Sherman's army, engaged in severe fighting, appeared to be blocked before Atlanta. To deepen the gloom, August had brought news of a futile attack on Petersburg, where a mine, laid by the Federals, had been exploded with disastrous bungling and great loss of life.

The widespread murmuring against the administration had emboldened the President's enemies in the Republican party. The Wade-Davis Manifesto blazoned to the public the radicals' opposition to their leader. There was a movement in New York to force Mr. Lincoln to withdraw in favor of a more promising candidate. Grant and Ben Butler were hailed as men who could save the Union party. Even Lincoln's friends became infected with belief in a great popular reaction against him. The President himself, in August, despaired of re-election.

In expectation of profiting by the delay, the Democrats had postponed their national convention until the end of August. It took place only a few days before the fall of Atlanta revived and inspirited the country. In early August, Farragut's victory in Mobile Bay—a stirring story of an old admiral lashed to the mast of his flagship—had not been enough to offset the prevailing depression. After Atlanta, the two great successes were triumphantly bracketed together. The Union remembered its superior man power, and grew confident again.

Before the Democratic convention, the Republicans had scarcely begun their campaign. With brighter prospects, they set to work in September. In opposition to McClellan and his party's platform, the radical leaders ceased their machinations and sullenly fell into line to work for the President's re-election. Even a group of malcontents, who had bolted the party and nominated Frémont, were pacified. Montgomery Blair, target for radical detestation, resigned from the Cabinet at Mr. Lincoln's request. Frémont withdrew from the race. The Republican party was, for campaign purposes, united.

The opposition remained irreconcilably split into Copperhead and pro-war factions. The former had dictated the peace plank in the platform, while the latter had been appeased by the choice of McClellan, a military hero who had been persecuted by the administration. However, as McClellan's popularity rested on his war record, the Copperhead sentiments of the platform placed him in an anomalous position; and, at the cost of antagonizing a section of his adherents, he promptly repudiated the peace plank. To his standard flocked a host of loyal Union men, alarmed by Federal centralization and incensed by the draft, the heavy taxation, the censorship and the arbitrary arrests.

As the political canvass grew spirited in September, events in the Shenandoah Valley brought further aid to the Republicans, for whom a victory in the field spoke more eloquently than any campaign speech. In August, the blundering interference of the War Department had moved General Grant to make a drastic reorganization in the Valley. Hunter resigned, and the cavalry commander, Phil Sheridan, was placed at the head of a force, presently to be known as the Army of the Shenandoah, which included the Sixth and Nineteenth Corps and heavy cavalry reinforcements from the Army of the Potomac. With this fine army, Grant expected Sheridan not only to defeat Early, but to blast the fertile Valley so that it should no longer supply provisions for Lee's forces and never again subsist an army of invasion.

Grant had discovered that he could not depend on Halleck and

Stanton to transmit his orders to troops in the vicinity of Washington. Without stopping in the capital, the general-in-chief went in mid-September to the Valley and personally directed Sheridan to attack. Soon the country vibrated with the news of great Federal victories at Winchester and Fisher's Hill. Down the bountiful Valley, the Army of the Shenandoah swept like a blight, seizing and destroying the crops, driving the cattle before them. The young Irish general's exploits fired the imagination of the Union. In derision of pacifist efforts, he was called Peace Commissioner Sheridan.

Although citizens of the District were debarred from voting in the Presidential election, partisans of both sides carried on a demonstrative campaign in the capital. The zealous Washington Democrats were the first to organize, but by the middle of September Lincoln-and-Johnson clubs were sprouting in all the wards of the city. Immediately after McClellan's nomination, a campaign flag bearing his name and that of Pendleton, his Copperhead running mate, was suspended across the Avenue at Seventh Street, outside Democratic headquarters at Parker's Hall. Nearly two weeks elapsed before the Republicans hung out their Lincoln-and-Johnson banner from the Union League rooms at Ninth Street. Thereafter, the cheers of passing troops were eagerly noted, as an indication of the army's political sentiments.

In the clamorous animosities of the pre-election weeks, only the draft meetings found the Washington citizenry united, irrespective of party affiliations. After the new draft was in operation, the capital, eternally protesting the injustice of its quota, continued to make a frenzied effort to raise subscriptions for bounties. The President set a good example by paying the bounty for one soldier, credited to the Third Ward, out of his own pocket. Mr. Lincoln's representative recruit, as he was called, was John Summerfield Staples, a twenty-year-old veteran of nine months' service in the Pennsylvania militia. Before joining the Second District Regiment in early October, Staples went uniformed to the White House, where the President shook his hand, and told him that he was a good-looking, stout and healthy man, who, in Lincoln's opinion, would do his duty.

Even before the wheel had begun to turn in September, when substitutes had been plentiful and cheap, it had not been possible to raise a sizable exemption fund in the capital. Once the draft had started, substitutes suddenly disappeared, and black looks were turned on the brokers who now asked from eight to nine hundred dollars per man. Washington, fulminating and protesting, refused to pay the price of release from Federal oppression. The draft continued to function, arousing an amount of hostility out of all proportion to its effectiveness in producing man power.

The October elections in Pennsylvania, Ohio and Indiana were crucial in determining the drift of political sentiment. Soldiers from the first two States were enabled by law to vote in the field; and, in polls opened in the barracks and hospitals of the capital, ballots were gathered in boxes which had once held cigars and paper collars. These showed heavy majorities for the Union party, although Carver Hospital registered a substantial opposition vote.

Some ten thousand Pennsylvania soldiers were also rushed home from Sheridan's army to swell the Republican vote in that doubtful State. It was carried by only a small majority, but Republican gains in Ohio and Indiana were sufficiently impressive to give promise that Lincoln would be re-elected in November.

Of close importance to Washington was the election in Maryland which adopted, by a slender majority, eked out by the soldiers' vote, a new State constitution abolishing slavery. Loyal Marylanders marched to the White House to serenade the President, and the Washington colored people made ready for a grand jubilee at the Fifteenth Street Presbyterian Church.

In the midst of the October rejoicing, Chief Justice Taney appropriately breathed his last. He had long outlived his day, lingering on to the age of eighty-seven in a world of change and crisis. His long and honorable service to his country was stamped across with the name Dred Scott, and there was little pomp of official mourning as his coffin moved to the Washington station, on the way to a burying ground in the now free soil of Maryland.

Guerrillas swarmed along the Manassas Gap Railroad, turning the eyes of the capital to a tiny theatre of war. Railroad employees were killed, and pickets of the Second District Regiment were captured by Mosby's daring riders. Augur was at last permitted to take the field, under orders to clear the bushwhackers from the railroad line. Quartermaster's employees were also dispatched to cut down the timber which afforded shelter near the tracks; but forty-seven of them refused to go, and were clapped into the Central Guard-house.

Soon, there was action on a larger scale in the neighborhood of Washington. Before daybreak on October 19, Early's forces made a

surprise attack on the Army of the Shenandoah. Phil Sheridan was not
with his command. On his way to rejoin it, after a conference at the
War Office, he was sleeping that night at Winchester, twenty miles
north of Cedar Creek, where the army was encamped.

As Sheridan rode out of Winchester in the morning, he heard
the sound of heavy firing. Blue-clad fugitives welled out of the south,
panting the news that his army was routed. Sheridan put spurs to his
horse, and, calling on the men to follow him, galloped to the front.
He rallied his forces, and in the afternoon made a counter-attack
which ended in a decisive Federal victory. In the speeding figure of
the little Irishman on his big black horse, there was drama useful to
the Union party. Before the end of the political campaign, the florid
stanzas of "Sheridan's Ride"—Sheridan twenty, fifteen, ten, five miles
away!—were thrilling the country with patriotic fervor.

Cedar Creek was a momentous victory for the capital. The pursuit
and devastation which followed it drove the enemy forever from the
Shenandoah. The final crushing battle would not be fought until
spring, but alarms had vanished from the Cumberland Valley, and
Maryland and Pennsylvania farmers slept peacefully in their beds. On
the hills surrounding Washington, the game birds flocked near the
fortifications and fed under the silent guns.

All through the autumn, captured Confederate battle flags were
borne to Washington from the Valley. With the eloquence of inanimate objects, the torn and dusty standards cried the defeat of their
cause. Stanton received the flags at the War Department, and, with
unwonted effusiveness, wrung the hands of prideful sergeants and
privates and thanked them for their gallantry. After three months'
interruption, the Baltimore and Ohio trains again traversed the Valley;
and, following the success at Cedar Creek, young General George A.
Custer—the former lieutenant of cavalry who had been made one of
McClellan's aides on the Peninsula—took the cars for Washington
with ten rebel battle flags flying from the engine. A quantity of Confederate artillery was also sent by rail to the capital. Accompanied by
a band, the guns were drawn through the streets to the grounds in
front of the War Department. However, the discovery that the ammunition boxes were filled with powder proved too much for Mr. Stanton's nerves, and during the night these alarming trophies were
whisked away to the Arsenal.

In an atmosphere of military excitement, the political campaign grew heated in Washington. The greatest demonstration was a Republican torchlight procession which took place two days after Cedar Creek. The night was weirdly lighted by the blue fire which burned in the streets and on the roof of the Patent Office. Through the city went the jubilant parade, horses, wagons, howitzers and marching men, with thousands of torches, lanterns and lighted transparencies. Soldiers, Metropolitan Police, quartermaster's employees and delegations from the hospitals were in line with Lincoln-and-Johnson clubs from the Washington wards and from some of the States. Five ambulances were loaded with the maimed. The members of the Elephant Club of the Northern Liberties had a large transparency of their mascot mounted on a wagon. The New Jersey club carried a portrait of McClellan, labeled "Great Failure of the War." As the procession passed the President's House, Mr. Lincoln appeared with Tad at an upper window. Rockets flashed and torches waved. There were loud calls for a speech. Lincoln disliked making impromptu addresses, at which he was ineffective, and he responded only by asking for cheers for the Union's commanders, soldiers and sailors.

This gala occasion was marred by an unfortunate incident. As the torchbearers marched past Parker's Hall, the Democratic banner above the Avenue somehow caught fire, and the names of McClellan and Pendleton were consumed before the infuriated Democrats could pull it in. In consternation, the local Republicans met to express regret for this occurrence, and to arrange to pay for a new flag. Their generosity did not silence the charges of vandalism made by their opponents. Democrats loudly jeered at Republicans, not only as "dirty niggers," but as "damned flag-burners." Lincoln-and-Johnson men responded to the challenge. A Democratic street meeting was broken up by the racket of the fist fights, and McClellan's supporters were showered with bricks and stones. Large details of police were on hand at all political demonstrations after the torchlight procession. They succeeded in keeping order when the new McClellan flag was raised above the Avenue, though the Democrats flaunted a transparency inscribed "Burnt by negro abolition traitors." Lincoln, who commented sadly on the rancorous character of the campaign, must have seen plentiful evidence of its bitterness in Washington.

The power of the War Department had been turned into the service of the President's re-election. Officers looked in vain for promotion, if it came to Stanton's ears that they were admirers of

McClellan. Republican soldiers were furloughed by thousands, to return to doubtful districts. On the War Secretary's order, three Democratic commissioners from New York, headed by a prominent citizen, Colonel Samuel North, were cast into Carroll Prison and held *incommunicado*. The commission had been appointed by Governor Horatio Seymour, an outstanding critic of the administration, to aid the Democratic soldiers around Washington in casting their votes. Stanton treated the New Yorkers as prisoners of state, aired charges of fraud against them, but made none to the unfortunate gentlemen themselves. Emissaries, sent by Seymour to investigate, denounced the War Department's methods. There was difficulty in finding military officers who dared to administer the oath to soldiers who wished to vote the Democratic ticket. Democratic ballots were seized and prevented from reaching New York in time to be counted. North and his associates, after a long and disagreeable confinement, were found not guilty by one of Stanton's military commissions.

A week before Election Day, the exodus from the armies began. The Washington depot milled with Republican soldiers, pushing their way aboard the northbound trains. They rushed the gate and fought for standing room in the aisles and on the platforms of the cars. It was observed that no important action could be expected before Petersburg, because of the depletion of Grant's army. Government clerks and other employees were so freely granted leaves that the business of the departments was crippled. The last of them went on Monday night, and Tuesday found Washington, in a sudden lull, waiting for evening to bring the telegrams to the War Department.

The dull November rain beat down on the White House grounds. Mr. Lincoln, in the restlessness of suspense, seemed unable to settle down to work. On Tad's insistence, he stood at a south window, to watch his guard of Bucktails lining up in the wet to cast a unanimous vote for him. Most of the afternoon he spent chatting with Noah Brooks, who had called at midday. It was seven o'clock when, in company with John Hay and a policeman, he splashed to the side door of the War Department.

Almost before the gaslights gleamed through the fog, men with rolled-up trousers had begun plowing along the muddy streets in search of news. By eight o'clock, there was a furious bobbing of umbrellas around the political clubrooms and the hotels. On the ground that no man could fight under a spread umbrella, the *Star* gave the weather credit for abating the excesses of Election Night.

Both Parker's Hall and the Union League rooms were packed with partisans, early on hand to hear the first returns. The storm had delayed the reception of telegrams, and for a time there were only reports of the anticipated Union majorities in the barracks and hospitals. The announcement that Bladensburg had gone overwhelmingly for McClellan was received with cheers by the Democrats, and with howls of derisive laughter by the Republicans. Soon, however, telegrams began to come in from New York, Philadelphia, Boston and Baltimore. By ten o'clock, the returns were so favorable to the President that bands of Union party adherents began trooping through the streets, singing "The Battle-Cry of Freedom." At Parker's Hall, it was suggested that no confidence should be put in the dispatches, as they came from Republican sources. Someone raised the cry of "fight." McClellan men went tumbling down the stairs, shouting "Democrats to the rescue!" Spread umbrellas were forgotten, and there was a free-for-all scuffle at the Metropolitan Hotel.

Colonel Eckert, the superintendent of military telegraphs, had provided a little supper at the War Department, and late at night Mr. Lincoln "went awkwardly and hospitably to work shovelling out the fried oysters." Though the returns were incomplete, his election seemed assured. He acknowledged, without exultation, the congratulations of the company. Still in the rain-swept streets, his supporters called on the boys to rally 'round the flag. In the early morning hours, the President was serenaded by a crowd of Pennsylvanians, jubilant over Republican majorities in their State. He responded with a felicitous little speech. "If I know my heart," he told them, "my gratitude is free from any taint of personal triumph."

General Grant sent his congratulations to Lincoln, with the message that the orderly passing of Election Day was a victory worth more to the country than a battle won. In two or three days, it was known that the Republicans had carried every State but Delaware, New Jersey and Kentucky. Clubs, replete with bands and noisy howitzers, went serenading the President and the Cabinet members. The resignation of George B. McClellan as major-general in the United States Army was accepted.

Between the election excitement and Christmas, Washington was

in the doldrums which held the whole country. There was uneasiness
over the conspiracies of the Confederate agents in Canada, headed by
Jacob Thompson, formerly Buchanan's Secretary of the Interior. During the summer and autumn, they had worked with disloyal secret
societies in the North, tried to foment revolt in the West, plotted for
the forcible liberation of Southern prisoners of war, and laid plans
for incendiary attempts on a number of cities. On the night after
Thanksgiving, several New York hotels were set on fire by rebel
agents, in an effort to start a general conflagration. Washington, in
alarm, increased the guards at Government warehouses and shops, and
called out the department volunteers for patrol duty.

The desperate intrigues of the failing Confederacy were, however, overshadowed by military affairs. In late November, the attention of the Union was fixed, not on Petersburg, where Grant still
stubbornly hammered, but on Georgia. An unprecedented thing had
happened. An army—Sherman's army of sixty thousand hardy veterans
—had cut its communications, and disappeared into the deep South,
leaving the opposing Confederate army in its rear. For thirty-two days,
the Government received its only news of Sherman from the Southern press. Richmond and Savannah newspapers, with an overtone of
panic, carried rumors of a countryside laid waste; but the Union
waited in suspense for word of the whereabouts of the army, of its
progress and its fate.

December came, with still no definite news. Like a cold blast
from the North, Congress assembled. Old Judge Bates, disgruntled
with proceedings in the capital, resigned from the Cabinet, and took
his precise lawyer's mind and his old-fashioned Whig principles to
the scarcely less turbulent scenes of Missouri. Lord Lyons, in impaired health, sailed for England. His horses, carriages, wines and
brandies were sold at auction, the mulatto caterer, Wormley, securing
some of the best sherries. Salmon P. Chase, nominated by the President for the office of Chief Justice of the Supreme Court, took his
seat on the bench with his usual majestic air of rectitude. Washington grumbled over the muddy abyss of F Street, where a new street
railway was being constructed. Harvey's served Rappahannock oysters,
the first received since the outbreak of war. Holiday boxes for the
soldiers in the field began to pile up on the Sixth Street wharf.

Over all, like a miasma of anxiety, hung the fears for Sherman's army. In the silence, rumors spread that it would be starved out, surrounded, forced to surrender. By the middle of the month, the suspense was relieved by news that Sherman had, at long last, reached the sea, and was in communication with the navy at Savannah. Meantime, the Confederate army, which Sherman had left in his rear, had invaded Tennessee. Late at night, Colonel Eckert, on duty at the military telegraph office, received messages that General Thomas had attacked the enemy with success at Nashville. With two telegrams in his hand, Eckert ran downstairs, and jumped into the ambulance which was always kept at the door of the War Department. His shout of good news at the War Secretary's house on K Street brought hurrahs from Mr. and Mrs. Stanton and the children. Stanton and Eckert drove to the White House, to call the happy tidings to the President, standing tall and ghostly in his nightshirt at the stairhead, with a lighted candle in his hand.

Thomas had won a smashing victory. The Confederate army was routed, and fleeing to the mountains. Headlines proclaimed the close siege of Savannah, as Washington did its Christmas shopping. The only cloud on a joyous holiday season was a new call for three hundred thousand volunteers, the prospect that the pestiferous draft would never come to an end.

On the evening of Sunday, December 25, the President received Sherman's dispatch, "I beg to present to you as a Christmas gift the city of Savannah. . . ." Guns boomed next day in Franklin Square, flags and bunting blossomed in a cold drizzle of rain, and there were patriotic celebrations at all the hospitals. Almost without opposition, Sherman had slashed and burned a track through Georgia. Loyal Washington waded, rejoicing, in the mud, sure at last that the power of the Confederacy was broken.

With high hearts, the New Year's Eve merrymakers went singing, "When This Cruel War Is Over." The New Year's reception at the White House—held on Monday, January 2—was a surging crush of people. Ladies and children were lifted in the arms of their escorts to escape the suffocating pressure of the crowd. One lady reached the door of the Blue Room with her bonnet so smashed and her shawl so torn that she was ashamed to enter. When the ordeal of the handshaking was over, the weary President rallied his forces to welcome a crowd of colored folk who had lingered around the mansion in the hope of being admitted. For a little time, the trampled reception room knew laughter and tears and cries of "God bless Abraham Lincoln!"

A constitutional amendment to abolish slavery, repeatedly urged on Congress by the President, had already passed the Senate, and in January Washington echoed with the debate in the House. Floor and galleries were filled with tense spectators, and Copperheads were sour of face, as the "ayes" rang out in response to the roll call. With cheers and mutual embracings, the Republicans hailed their victory; and the batteries of the Union saluted the end of slavery.

Within the ranks of the Republicans, however, there were signs that complete harmony did not prevail. Criticisms of the arbitrary arrests flared up on the floor of the House, when a resolution was adopted that the Committee on Military Affairs should be directed to inquire into the detention without trial of persons in the Old Capitol and Carroll Prisons. In the preceding session, Congress, after prolonged wrangling, had passed a bill requiring that lists of political prisoners should be furnished to the judges of civil courts within whose jurisdiction they came; and that, if the lists were not promptly furnished, the prisoners should have legal redress. This act of Congress had been ignored by the War Department, and the Washington prisons, in particular, were filled with the languishing victims of Colonel Baker's summary arrests. The resolution to investigate took unconditional supporters of the administration by surprise, and Thad Stevens was soon on his feet with a motion to reconsider it. He was opposed by a young Republican member of the Military Committee— James A. Garfield of Ohio, who after winning the rank of major-general for gallantry on the lost field of Chickamauga, had taken his seat in the House at the request of the President and Mr. Stanton. Another Republican, Henry Winter Davis, Maryland radical, also broke through party discipline to speak on behalf of civil rights. The House sustained Davis and Garfield, and the inquiry proceeded, resulting in a sweeping clearance of the military prisons, though not in the termination of Stanton's favorite form of court, the military commission.

On the policy of reconstruction, the Republican party had been sharply divided since the President's amnesty proclamation of 1863. The radicals were fiercely at odds with Lincoln's attitude toward the rebellious States which had come under Federal control. In war, as in politics, his watchword was, "We must not sully victory with harshness." Looking to a future of union and peace, he wanted to see the nation gradually rebuilt during the progress of hostilities. In July of 1864, he had enraged the radicals by pocketing a rigorous reconstruction bill.

Under the President's direction, provisional State governments had been set up in Tennessee, Louisiana, Arkansas and Virginia, but they had been excluded by Congress from the electoral count, with Lincoln's reluctant assent. To Louisiana he had given especial interest and support, and in the debate over the recognition of the new State government the radicals found an opportunity to retaliate for the President's disposal of their harsh reconstruction bill. The loyal minority of citizens, required by Lincoln's plan, had adopted a constitution which provided for the abolition of slavery. The radicals, however, were no longer satisfied by emancipation. In a determination to crush and humiliate the South, they were demanding suffrage for Negroes. The measure for the recognition of Louisiana failed in the House; and Sumner, by a threatened filibuster, succeeded in defeating it in the Senate.

This deadlock between the President and Congress foreshadowed the conflict over reconstruction which the end of the war would shortly bring. In January, there had been a smell of peace negotiations in the air. Old Mr. Blair aroused great curiosity by making two trips to Richmond. Then Mr. Seward journeyed to Hampton Roads to confer with commissioners from Jefferson Davis. When the President followed the Secretary of State, the radicals were angrily prepared for the worst. In any negotiations undertaken by these two moderate men, they fearfully foresaw the sacrifice of all the fruits of victory. The alarm, however, blew over. In response to the demands of Congress, Mr. Lincoln gave an account of his doings at Hampton Roads. The stern silence of the House, as his reply was read, gradually yielded to smiles of relief and approbation, and at length to applause. The President had listed, as terms indispensable to peace negotiations, the restoration of the national authority, the disbandment of the rebel forces, and the abolition of slavery. The conference had ended without result.

Though the Confederacy had been merely seeking an armistice and was not yet ready to capitulate, its downfall by force of arms was drawing nearer every week. The thin gray line at Petersburg was weakening. In January, there had been rejoicing over the fall of Fort Fisher, guardian of Wilmington, North Carolina, the last open port of the South. February prolonged the celebration, as Sherman came smashing up through South Carolina. Columbia fell. Charleston was evacuated. Washington's Birthday found the capital *en fête,* red, white and blue by day, sparkling with lights by night. The vessels in the river were gay with bunting. People crowded the roof tops to view the pretty scene, while from the hills the guns welcomed the return of Fort Sumter to the Union. That same day, Federal troops entered the city of Wilmington.

Prisoners of war came into Washington in a steady procession. For the most part, they were familiar figures in shabby butternut, but Washington had stared at natty officers from the captured rebel pirate, *Florida,* sporting gold watch chains and diamond rings, "the proceeds," sneered the *Star,* "of their piratical career." Among the prisoners, too, had been a figure once well known at the Capitol and on the Avenue, Roger A. Pryor, former United States Representative from Virginia. Those were dark days for a man who had fired on Fort Sumter, a man whose home was at Petersburg; but the *Star* found him little changed. The hotspur of 1861 was a hotspur still, as uniformed in defiance as in Confederate gray, his long hair hanging under his stiff-brimmed hat. After some weeks' imprisonment in Fort Lafayette, he was released in February by the President. The secretary of the Senate, Colonel Forney, cherished a grudge against the Southern leaders, his enemies in ancient quarrels within the Democratic party. Having been induced to put in a good word for Pryor's release, he was dismayed to find that Mr. Lincoln had saddled him with the Confederate. Pryor had been ordered, pending his exchange, to report to Forney's lodgings on Capitol Hill, where for over a week the gentleman from Petersburg held court for the Washington chivalry. Lincoln enjoyed the joke; and Thad Stevens daily tantalized the unwilling host with his greeting, "How's your Democratic friend and brother this morning?"

Gray uniforms, rather than blue, now predominated in the capital. There were increasing numbers of Confederate deserters. Twilight was settling over Richmond. Lee's losses of starving and disheartened men could be counted by brigades. Two or three times a day, the ragged bands were encountered on their way through the streets. Twelve hundred and thirty-nine of them came to Washington alone in February. In March, twenty-eight hundred and sixty arrived in the capital. Men lost to a losing cause, they flocked around Augur's headquarters on Lafayette Square, eager to take the oath of allegiance to the Union.

With the imminent victory of the Union, the vindictive spirit of the radicals was a portent of trouble in the second term on which the President would enter in March. At the White House, there were other portents, small changes to which people gave little heed, not comprehending their significance.

The depredations of the sight-seers in the public rooms were aired in the press in the autumn of 1864. Paper had been pulled from the walls, and large pieces of brocade and damask slashed from draperies, sofas and chairs. In the East and Green Rooms, the heavy cords and tassels had been snatched from the draperies. The gilded ornamental shields in the East Room had almost all been stolen; an entire lace curtain was gone, and others hung in rags. Designs of flowers had been clipped out for the purpose, it was supposed, of covering pincushions. The *Star* said that ladies and gentlemen of high standing had been caught in the act of collecting souvenirs, and that one lady had fainted when discovered.

In the absence of ushers to protect the costly public property, the craze for mementoes had led to wanton vandalism, and it seemed natural and desirable that special officers should be assigned to the Executive Mansion. Late in November, the press began to report arrests. The *National Republican* stated that it had been requested to give notice that Marshal Lamon had detailed officers to the White House under orders to apprehend all persons detected in larcenies. Four members of the Metropolitan Police had, in fact, been assigned to duty there. However, their primary function was not to arrest memento seekers, but to protect the person of the President.

Two of them, on day duty from eight until four, guarded the approach to the official chamber or other room occupied by Mr. Lincoln, and accompanied him on his walks. The night shift, divided between the two remaining policemen, was charged with escorting the President to and from the War Department and the theatre, and patrolling the corridor outside his door while he slept.

Lincoln had a bodyguard at last, but the fact, masked by the publicity given to the vandals, was not generally understood. The policemen were armed with .38 Colt revolvers, but they were not in uniform. They did not walk behind the President, but at his side, like any casual friend or office seeker. Although they were inconspicuous, their presence must have been highly distasteful to Lincoln. Sometimes he succeeded in getting rid of the armed attendants at his elbow. Extraordinary pressure must have been used to induce him to consent to the arrangement at all.

Marshal Lamon's anxiety about the President had flamed into acute alarm in the autumn. He was convinced that Lincoln's life was in grave danger. Armed with pistols and bowie knives, Lamon had passed Election Night on the floor outside the President's bedroom door. Even after the appointment of the bodyguard, the marshal frequently went to the White House during the night. Other measures for Lincoln's protection were taken during the winter. Two policemen went on duty as doorkeepers, in place of Burns and old Edward. By cutting doors and constructing partitions, a private passageway was made on the second floor of the mansion, so that the President could pass from his bedroom to his office without meeting the crowds of strangers in the hall. Moreover, at the evening receptions, all persons were required to leave their wraps outside the Blue Room. Cloakrooms had been built in the corridor the preceding year, while the dining-room was fitted up for the ladies, but many people had preferred to retain their outer garments. When the new rule was introduced in January, Thomas Crook, a young policeman who had just joined the White House detail, was charged with enforcing it. Flabbergasted by the brilliance of the scene, he did not find his task an easy one. The innovation was resented by many of the guests, notably the lovely Mrs. William Sprague, who in a few months would become a mother.

Crook was well aware that the reason for the regulation was that weapons might easily be concealed in the folds of voluminous cloaks and shawls. No mention of solicitude for the President's safety was made, however, in the press. Just as the Washington newspapers had veiled the purpose of the police detail at the White House, so they explained the compulsory removal of wraps as a matter of propriety. To enter the Blue Room divested of outer garments was, the *Star* declared, a rule of etiquette, and a mark of respect to the President and his lady.

To Marshal Lamon, the theatre appeared to be a place of especial danger for the President. Keeping a close watch on the White

House, Lamon knew that Lincoln did not always take his bodyguard to the play, but went unattended on several occasions during the early winter. On a December night, Lamon's exasperation at this carelessness reached a climax. The President had been at the theatre in company only with Charles Sumner and a foreign minister— "neither of whom," as the District marshal heatedly wrote Lincoln at one-thirty in the morning, "could defend himself against an assault from any able-bodied woman in this city." It was an angry and offended letter, in which Lamon stiffly offered to resign the marshalship, if the President doubted his honesty in warning him of danger.

It seems probable, though the evidence does not exist, that Lamon's concern about the theatre was based on some warning contained in a secret service report. If it had no such basis, it was a curious coincidence that at this very time a young man was plotting to abduct the President from the theatre. It was a play actor's idea, and the young man was a play actor—John Wilkes Booth. He was a Marylander, who sympathized with the South and was obsessed with hatred for Lincoln. Like everyone else, he knew that the great need of the Confederacy was man power. Grant, with reserves on which to call, had in the spring of 1864 adopted the ruthless policy of putting a complete stop to exchanges of prisoners of war. Booth had conceived the plan that, by kidnaping the President and turning him over to the Confederate authorities to be held as a hostage, he could force the Union to release its many thousands of Southern captives.

Booth was scarcely the figure of a conspirator. He looked handsome, vain, prosperous, exhibitionistic. As he strolled in and out of the National Hotel many feminine eyes followed him. He was twenty-six years old, with a dark romantic beauty that was fatal to women— the beauty of ivory skin, silky black hair and mustache, white teeth and lustrous, heavy-lidded eyes. In his dress, he was the picture of nonchalant dandyism. His loose greatcoat, with its flowing cape, was collared in fur. There was a velvet collar on his braid-bound jacket. He wore a seal ring on his little finger, and a stickpin was thrust in the center of his fine cravat. His hair was as perfectly waved as though he used a curling iron.

Fluttering, sighing ladies packed the theatres when John Wilkes Booth was on tour. There were showers of love letters in his mail. He carried the photographs of several lovely actresses in his pocket diary. He also had a photograph of Miss Bessie Hale, the plump, mature-looking daughter of the prominent Republican senator, John P. Hale, who had just failed of re-election in New Hampshire, and would shortly be appointed minister to Spain. Bessie was infatuated with Booth, and he had given his family to understand that they were engaged to be married. During his visits to Washington, he also found time for his mistress, Ella Turner, a blond, rather pretty little woman, whom he kept in her sister's parlor house on Ohio Avenue. Booth did not carry her photograph, but Ella Turner loved him.

The actor was not a soft and lazy Lothario. He was an athlete—a fencer, an expert horseman and a crack pistol shot—and his big, powerful hands contrasted oddly with his fine-drawn head and face. Men, as well as women, felt Booth's fascination. In spite of his fits of temper and love of playing practical jokes, he was popular among his fellow-actors. Bartenders liked a word with young Mr. Booth, who enjoyed his glass of brandy and was always ready to stand treat. Doormen and stagehands and hotel clerks were attracted by his winning manners.

In his profession, both because of his own overweening aspirations and the high standard expected of him, John Wilkes Booth had suffered the handicap of his famous name. His father, Junius Brutus Booth, had been the greatest tragedian of his day. Both of his older brothers, Edwin and Junius Brutus, Junior, were prominent in the theatre, when John Wilkes started his career. He showed signs of brilliant talent, but he was too vain and undisciplined for study, and vaulted brashly into stardom. Metropolitan audiences raised their eyebrows, but on the road he played to packed houses and earned a large income, about twenty thousand a year. People in the provinces got their money's worth from his romantic looks, impassioned gestures and ranting eloquence, from his spectacular sword play and the great, bounding leaps by which he was fond of entering the stage.

Before the war, he had been very popular in the South. Folk in Richmond had cheered him in 1859, when he put on a militia uniform and went to stand guard while old John Brown was hanged. It was, however, the only time that Booth wore a uniform. He was one of many natives of the Union's border slave States who sentimentalized over the Confederacy without caring to join its fortunes. There was nothing out of the way in a Marylander who hated the Republican administration, and no one paid much attention to Booth's excited talk.

His first professional appearance in Washington was made in April of 1863, when he played a week's engagement at Grover's Theatre, billed as "The Youngest 'Star' in the World." His opening in *Richard III,* a role in which his father had been famous, was greeted with unbounded applause by a fashionable audience. At that time, the Washington newspapers had no dramatic critics, and touted all entertainments which were advertised in their columns. Business was sufficiently good to warrant Booth in prolonging his stay, for at the end of his brief engagement at Grover's he leased the inconvenient old Washington Theatre and starred, under his own management, for two weeks more.

The following November, he again appeared in Washington, playing for two weeks at Ford's. He offered a familiar dramatic diet: *Richard III, Romeo and Juliet, The Merchant of Venice, The Apostate, The Lady of Lyons, The Marble Heart, The Robbers.* His engagement was hailed by the *Star* as "brilliant and lucrative."

The *Sunday Chronicle,* however, was then beginning to print occasional pieces of dramatic criticism, the best of which were signed *Bizarre.* This was the pseudonym of a witty and erudite old gentleman who aroused great irritation among simple-minded playgoers by his sarcasms about the "moral drama" and the low standards of taste among Westerners employed as Treasury clerks. *Bizarre* hailed Booth's advent with skepticism. "We do not regard Mr. Booth as an eminent tragedian," he wrote on November 1, 1863; "we can scarcely call him a tragedian. Unless he has improved very much since we last saw him, he is little more than a second-class actor, who, as the possessor of a great name, and with a fine presence, sweet voice, and much natural and uncultivated ability, has seen proper to come upon the stage as a representative of tragedy. It is possible that Mr. Booth will in time become a great actor. . . ."

A week later, the critic had not revised his opinion. He commended Booth's performance as *Shylock* in the trial scene, and thought that it showed him to be an actor of promise, in spite of his traditional, violent and noisy rendition of the other scenes of *The Merchant. Bizarre* was disgusted by the introduction of sentimental modern songs into the production. "Mr. Booth," he satirically observed, "might make a greater success in Richard III, if he permitted his Richmond to sing 'When this cruel war is over' on the morning of the battle. . . ."

Bizarre, however, was a voice crying in the wilderness. Booth ranted and bounded before packed houses during his two weeks at Ford's.

A year later, when he returned to the capital, he had no professional engagement there, and was making few appearances anywhere. His brother, Junius Brutus, more successful as a manager than as a tragedian, had just completed an engagement at Ford's. All over the North, theatre business was booming, and John Wilkes had to answer many questions about his absence from the stage. He talked grandly about his investments in oil lands, and his friends hooted with laughter, for these risky speculations had become a stock joke of the day. In fact, though Booth had bought land in western Pennsylvania, it was entirely valueless, and he had closed out his holdings. He had at first hoped to bring off his abduction plot before the election, and talked of seizing the President on the road to the Soldiers' Home. However, while he was settling his business affairs, the Lincoln family returned to the White House for the winter.

All during the winter, Booth made the National his headquarters, leaving on occasional trips to Maryland and New York, but always returning to Washington. One of the places he visited was Charles County in lower Maryland. The old stage road which ran through Charles County had been since 1861 the main route traversed by Confederate spies, mail carriers and blockade-runners on their way between the capital and the secret ferries on the Potomac. Booth made many inquiries among the local residents about roads, relay stations and ferries. It was a district of Southern sympathizers, formerly prosperous slaveholders, and some of them were undoubtedly informed of Booth's abduction scheme. He talked, however, of investing in land and buying horses, and did actually purchase one horse through the good offices of Dr. Samuel Mudd, a gentlemanly physician of the region, whose acquaintance Booth made at church.

In the meantime, he was forming a band of conspirators. If there were prominent Washington secessionists among them, their names are unknown. Booth's closest associates were a shabby group of men, over whom he was able to maintain an ascendancy by fanatical determination and the promise of pecuniary rewards from a grateful Confederacy. The first two whom he interested in his scheme were friends of his Maryland school days, Confederate deserters in poor circumstances, on whom Booth flashed back in an aura of money and success.

Samuel Arnold was a decent-appearing clerk, who, for want of other employment, was working off and on as a laborer on his brother's farm in Maryland. Michael O'Laughlin was a dark, slender fellow, who looked like a Cuban. With his long black hair and whiskers and his loud and fashionable clothes, O'Laughlin made a dashing appearance, but he was engaged in the humdrum occupation of taking orders for his brother's feed business in Baltimore, and his prospects were no brighter than Arnold's.

On one of his trips to Charles County, Booth probably heard of John Surratt as a man well informed about the underground route to Richmond. Surratt was a tall, sandy-haired, foolhardy boy of twenty, another Marylander, who had served since the autumn of 1861 as a spy and dispatch carrier for the Confederacy. Recently, he had moved to Washington with his mother and younger sister, Anna. Mrs. Surratt, left a widow, had leased her Maryland property, a village tavern some thirteen miles from Washington, and set up a boarding-house in the capital. It was a small, drab-painted, high-stooped house on H Street, and Mrs. Surratt had no trouble in filling its few rooms. John took a job clerking in the Adams Express Company; but he was unstable and adventure-loving, and Booth was able to talk him into joining the conspiracy. Soon after the New Year, Surratt gave up his job, and devoted all his time to the plans for Lincoln's abduction.

To carry the kidnapers and their captive across the Potomac, Surratt suggested George Atzerodt, one of the secret ferrymen on the underground route. He was a droll, disreputable little German-American, who worked at the trade of carriage maker at the Maryland town of Port Tobacco, and was eager to earn a large fee for a night's work. Booth also annexed a Washington acquaintance of the Surratts, an idling, rosy-cheeked boy named Davy Herold. He had worked off and on as a pharmacist's assistant, and had once charged up a bottle of castor oil for Mr. Lincoln. Simple and immature, with his buck teeth perpetually exposed in a silly smile, Davy had nothing to offer but a good knowledge of the Maryland countryside, where he had often gone on shooting trips.

In laying his plans to kidnap the President from the theatre, Booth had several reasons for preferring Ford's to Grover's. He had played in both Washington houses, but his relation with the first was closer because of his friendship with John T. Ford, under whose management he had appeared in other cities. Booth was also friendly with Ford's younger brother, Harry Clay, and was on agreeable terms with the employees and stock-company actors at the Tenth Street playhouse. He had, moreover, plausible excuses for frequently visiting the theatre, since his mail was addressed there and he kept two horses in a small stable which he had rented in the back alley.

Booth badly wanted an accomplice on the stage, and tried to induce a friend named Chester, who was an actor in Edwin Booth's company in New York, to get a job at Ford's. He offered to pay Chester's salary, if Ford would engage him. However, Chester was a family man, and wanted no part in the conspiracy, and he did not come to Washington.

Among the stagehands at Ford's, Booth had a humble admirer, a carpenter who had worked on the elder Booth's house in Maryland when John Wilkes was a boy. This man, Edward Spangler, was now middle-aged—a hard-drinking, good-natured fellow, who had helped to repair the stable in the back alley, and looked after Booth's horses. The actor did not pay Spangler for his hostler's work, but the two were often seen drinking together, like cronies. There is no evidence that Spangler knew anything about the abduction plot; but Booth must have been glad of his devotion and counted on it to serve him in a crisis.

By early January, Booth had brought Arnold and O'Laughlin to Washington, but he was unable to infuse them with enthusiasm for abducting the President from the theatre. Arnold was vehemently opposed to the plan, and tried to talk Booth out of it. On two occasions, he claimed that favorable opportunities were lost for kidnaping Lincoln on a country road, because of Booth's obsession with the theatre. He was still sufficiently under the actor's influence to pass most of his time loitering in Washington. Booth was irritated by Arnold's criticisms and introduced neither of his boyhood friends into the Surratt boardinghouse, to which he frequently went to confer with John. Mrs. Surratt had become very fond of the fascinating actor, who caused quite a flutter among the ladies in her simple parlor. It is probable that she knew something of the reason for the long secret discussions between him and her son. She was a kind, motherly woman, a pious Roman Catholic; but she was firmly devoted to the Confederacy, and had an older son in its army, and her sympathies would naturally have been drawn to a project for helping the South.

One of the boarders at Mrs. Surratt's was a War Department

clerk, Louis Weichmann, who worked in the office of the Commissary General of Prisoners. He was a big, timid, scholarly student for the Roman Catholic priesthood, who had been at school with John Surratt, and shared his bed at the H Street house. Weichmann's job entailed membership in the War Department Rifles, but he did not appear to be out of place in the secessionist atmosphere of the boardinghouse. Although he was a native of Pennsylvania, he was pining to go to Richmond to continue his theological studies. Sojourning blockade-runners found him a safe and congenial companion. He himself admitted that he "talked secesh very often . . . for buncombe. . . ." He was friendly with Atzerodt, often going out with the Confederate ferryman, and even lending him his clothes.

Booth was obsessed with his plan, but he did not find it easy to execute it. One of its serious disadvantages was the necessity of knowing well in advance when Lincoln was expected at Ford's, in order to perfect the organization for carrying him off. To seize the President in his box was not the hardest part of the undertaking. The stage boxes at Ford's were not open to the view of the whole house, but were covered alcoves, whose back walls were set at such an angle to the auditorium that the interior could be seen only from the opposite side of the dress circle. The President's box, moreover, was partially veiled by the Nottingham lace curtains.

The removal of Lincoln from the theatre was the principal difficulty. The upper boxes had no stairway, and were reached by a passage from the dress circle. The only feasible way of getting the captive to the street was to lower him onto the stage and carry him through the back door into the alley. To the gymnastic actor the jump of about twelve feet from the box did not present a problem, but he was absurdly underrating the strength of his victim. A man of fifty-six years, in failing health, the President was still no weakling. He was a man of muscular arms, who had in youth been a powerful wrestler. Even if he had been alone with Charles Sumner and an effete foreign minister, it is inconceivable that he could have been trussed up and bundled onto the stage in full view of the audience, without a struggle that would have prevented the accomplishment of the kidnaping.

There is evidence that Booth was prepared to make the attempt in January. The story runs that it was set for the night of the 18th, but was frustrated because the President failed to attend the theatre.

The veteran tragedian, Edwin Forrest, was filling a leisurely month's engagement at Ford's. Lincoln admired Forrest sufficiently to see him three or four times, in January and March, when he returned for an additional week. On January 18, Forrest appeared in the popular play, *Jack Cade,* which dealt with the Kentish insurrection of 1450, but was held to be a timely piece because of its hostility to slavery. If Booth had succeeded in kidnaping the President at *Jake Cade,* he would have canceled a professional engagement in Washington two nights later, when he played *Romeo* to the *Juliet* of Miss Avonia Jones, who had been running the gamut of tragedy at Grover's.

A week later, Booth left for New York for the purpose, Arnold said, of raising money. During his absence of nearly a month, the abduction plot was at a standstill. Lincoln serenely continued to attend the theatre. Twice during February, he went to Ford's to see the popular comedian, J. S. Clarke, who was brother-in-law to the Booths. On one of these occasions, the President was accompanied by General Grant. The performance, which had already begun, was suspended on the entrance of the two leaders, while the audience cheered and the band played "Hail to the Chief."

On February 23—though no Washington newspaper noted the fact—it was just four years since that gray morning when Abraham Lincoln, guarded by Lamon and Pinkerton, had slipped into a capital tense with fear of revolution. Across those four years, Washington had seen, in blood and labor and confusion, the progress of the Union cause toward its approaching triumph. In 1861, the country town had been startled by the arrival of a handful of soldiers. In 1865, geared for war on a grand scale, the capital remembered those few bristling guns as "far more war-like" than any preparations that were being made for Lincoln's second inauguration.

Lincoln-and-Johnson clubs, local and State, met to discuss their participation in the ceremonies. The marshal-in-chief, Daniel R. Goodloe, prescribed the regalia which was to bedizen the black frock coats and pantaloons of nearly a hundred marshals with orange, blue-and-gilt, cherry-color, yellow, pink and white. Mrs. E. Lowe on Pennsylvania Avenue did a rushing business in scarfs and batons. Messrs. Topham and Company on Seventh Street sold gaudy saddlecloths. Hammers pounded on the wooden platform rising at the east portico of the Capitol. Workmen cleared a clutter of building material from the park, and laid plank flooring over the marble blocks which still obstructed the grounds. Major French, busy with preparations for the inauguration ball, found time to have an iron table made for the President's address, out of some leftover fragments of the Capitol dome. The trickle of strangers, coming to beg immunity from taxation, solicit appointments or ask for passes to the front, turned to a stream of early arrivals for the inauguration. Congress was holding evening sessions, trying to clear its program before adjournment. The galleries were filled.

On the evening of March 1, Andrew Johnson of Tennessee arrived in Washington. The Vice-President-elect had the air of a Southern statesman of the old school. With his massive head and deep chest, he looked dignified and defiant. He dressed in broadcloth and fine linen. A yellow manservant stood behind his chair while he ate. Yet his was not the face of the planter, fine-drawn, haughty, born to command. It was another pride which his grim features wore—the pride of the poor white, the illiterate tailor boy, who had fought his way to place and power against the hated aristocrats. The struggle was written in his coarse, strong, stubborn countenance; and new scars of bitterness had been burned around eyes and mouth by the fires of reconstruction in Tennessee. In fierce devotion to the Union, Andy Johnson had braved danger and hardship and hatred. His health had suffered, his swarthy face was worn. In the winter, he had been ill with typhoid, and had been slow to recover from the fever. He came to Washington under pressure, feeling unfit to leave his home in Nashville.

The inauguration rush was on. Special trains roared and smoked over the double tracks of the Baltimore and Ohio. The arrivals thronged the newly decorated depot, shining with fresh paint. The *Star* thought that the influx was not so great as it had been four years earlier. Many, because of the difficulty of finding lodgings, were said to have stopped in Baltimore, intending to come to Washington only for the day. The *Sunday Chronicle* blamed the recent rainstorms for the absence of numerous delegations which had been expected. Yet, under the sullen skies of March 3, the streets were alive with carpetbagged and blanket-wrapped sojourners, picking their way through the fog and mud in search of rooms. Willard's had cots and mattresses in its halls and parlors. The National and the Metropolitan were filled. Lincoln-and-Johnson clubs lodged a thousand visitors, and local fire companies entertained a swarm of firemen from Philadelphia. There were enough strangers in the capital to give General Halleck bilious apprehensions of mischief, and he nervously advised Mr. Welles that the Navy Yard should be closed.

In the evening, the town was musical with the bands of the serenaders, while on the Avenue the torches of the firemen's procession burned through the mist with a silver light. High into the fog, the roof lights of the Capitol threw a white halo, in which the flag floated in splendor. Inside the building, the closing scenes of Congress had attracted many visitors, who moved in a jostling vibration between the Senate Chamber and the Hall of Representatives. Mrs. Lincoln and John Wilkes Booth were among the spectators. The President and the Cabinet were also at the Capitol on official business. Andy Johnson was at one of the stag parties which the hospitable Colonel Forney was fond of giving at his chambers on Capitol Hill.

Saturday, March 4, dawned with rain and a heavy, damaging gale. Clouds still rolled darkly in the sky as the paraders began to gather. It was a diminished procession, almost entirely local in character. Marshal Lamon had arranged to have thirteen United States marshals and thirteen citizen aides in attendance on the President's carriage, as it moved from the White House to the Capitol. During the morning, however, Lincoln drove off to the Capitol by himself, and was occupied in signing bills while the procession was forming. The special marshals and the President's Union Light Guard escorted Mrs. Lincoln.

The military patrols sat their horses at the street intersections. A squad of police formed a line along the pavements on either side. Vehicles were cleared from the Avenue. The parti-colored marshals rode madly up and down on last-minute errands. The streetcars were stopped, the bands blared, and a squad of Metropolitan Police marched out to clear the way for the marshal-in-chief and his aides. There were a few soldiers, cavalry, artillery, Veteran Reserves and marines. Floats drove into line: a muslin Temple of Liberty, decorated with flags and flowers; a model of a monitor, rending the air with salutes from the howitzer in its revolving turret; a portable printing press, operated by members of the Typographical Society, scattering broadsides of the day's program. The corporate authorities of Washington escorted a municipal delegation from Baltimore. Out stepped the Lincoln-and-Johnson clubs, a battalion of Negro troops and a colored lodge of Odd Fellows. Philadelphia and Washington firemen paraded their apparatus. Under brightening skies, along a street ankle-deep in mud, the procession went slithering and wading and splashing to the Capitol.

Meantime, the senators, squeezed into one half of their chamber to leave room for the representatives, were engaged in a lopsided transaction of business. At half past eleven, the doors of the gallery were opened, and the ladies rushed in. Gasping and screaming after their race through the halls and up the stairways, they settled above the solemn assemblage like a flock of brilliant, noisy birds. With spirits undamped by the mud on their voluminous skirts, they "chattered and clattered," while the presiding officer futilely tapped his gavel, and senators protested that they could not hear what was going on.

The chamber grew packed with personages. Military and naval officers appeared. All eyes turned to Admiral Farragut and General Hooker, heroes whose uniforms vied in gorgeousness with the gold lace and decorations of the diplomatic corps. Eight black-gowned old men followed the new Chief Justice, Salmon P. Chase, who looked very young and queer in his silk robe, with his stovepipe hat in his hand. The Cabinet members took their places. Mrs. Lincoln seated herself in the diplomatic gallery.

Shortly before twelve, Andrew Johnson entered, arm in arm with Hannibal Hamlin. Johnson must have been glad of that sturdy arm, as he walked to the dais of the presiding officer. The party at Colonel Forney's had been too much for a man still convalescent. He had just doctored his shaky nerves with three stiff drinks of whisky, and in the overheated Senate Chamber his swarthy face was turning crimson.

The House, led by Speaker Colfax, made its entrance when Johnson was fairly launched on the speech which preceded his taking the oath of office. Shortly after, the President arrived with the Senate committee in charge of the ceremonies. Mr. Lincoln's face wore an expression of deep sorrow, as he took his seat. Johnson, a man who could take his whisky or leave it, was on this occasion indubitably drunk. His dignity was gone, only his defiance remained, while he hoarsely delivered a confused harangue, half stump speech, half egotistical ranting. The word "plebeian" rang like a refrain, as, with that insistent pride which is the most embarrassing form of shame, he harped on his lowly origin.

The mortified Republicans sat in agony. Hamlin kept nudging

Johnson from behind. Senators turned and twisted in their chairs. Welles muttered to Stanton that the new Vice-President was either drunk or crazy. Stanton, looking petrified, muttered back that there was evidently something wrong. Seward, as always, contrived to appear serene, but the new Cabinet members were unequal to exhibiting composure. Postmaster General William A. Dennison went red and white by turns. Attorney General James Speed kept his eyes closed, whispering to Welles that it was all "in wretched bad taste." Judge Nelson of the Supreme Court had his jaw dropped down in horror. When Johnson turned to take the oath, Chief Justice Chase gave Nelson such a look that he closed his mouth. "I kiss this Book," bawled Andy, like a bad actor, to the assemblage, "in the face of my nation of the United States."

After the newly elected senators had been sworn in, the dignitaries lined up for the procession to the east front of the Capitol. Their progress through the Rotunda was guarded by the Capitol police, who held back the crowd which, in spite of orders to the contrary, had gained access to the hallways. After the President had passed, a man broke through the police line, and started toward the inauguration platform. He was seized by Lieutenant Westfall of the Capitol police. There was a scuffle, the east door was slammed shut, and police hustled the intruder off to the guardroom. The incident was not taken seriously at the time, for the man was released as soon as the ceremonies were over. Cranks were common in Washington. The next day, the military authorities looked into the case of a bibulous lunatic named Thomas Clemens, who said that he had intended to kill the President on Inauguration Day.

The incident at the Capitol, however, took on great importance in retrospect. According to an affidavit made by Robert Strong, a policeman who had been stationed with Major French at the east door of the Rotunda, a photograph of John Wilkes Booth was some weeks afterward recognized by Westfall, as well as by French and Strong himself, as that of the intruder. This identification came too late to be convincing. Booth did not need to rush the police lines. Through his sweetheart, Bessie Hale, he had secured a ticket of admission to the inauguration platform. He told a friend that he was close to the President during the ceremonies, and had an excellent chance to shoot him, if he had wished to do so.

There was, however, no disturbance at the east front of the

Capitol. The door slammed shut behind the dignitaries, silencing the noise of the scuffle in the passage. Before them, as they stepped into the daylight, they saw the mighty assemblage of the people, spreading back, back from the acclaiming faces near the portico to the blurred and tiny dolls' heads among the distant trees. In a thunder of cheers, Lincoln advanced to Major French's iron table, with its lonely tumbler of water. The last clouds rolled away, flooding the scene with sudden sunshine, and the multitude hushed to hear Lincoln's short address, which spoke of malice toward none, of charity for all. In the tumult of applause which greeted its conclusion, many people were seen to be in tears. Chief Justice Chase, his right hand raised, administered the oath of office. The President bent his head to kiss the open Bible. Artillery mingled with the salvoes of the people, as he bowed and retired.

The close-packed park of humanity stirred, seethed, began to disintegrate. John Wilkes Booth sauntered back along the Avenue with Walter Burton, the night clerk at the National, an enthusiastic admirer of Lincoln. Handkerchiefs fluttered from windows and balconies as the President, with Tad at his side, drove to the White House, escorted by the gaudy-scarved marshals and the motley retinue of the procession.

XVIII *Star-Spangled Capital*

THE PRESIDENT was looking not only old, but feeble. The long strain had worn him almost to the breaking point. His weariness was too deep to be eased by an hour's diversion or a night's rest. He was thirty pounds underweight, and his hands and feet were always cold. On the evening of March 4, he faced a public reception, his last levee of the season, set for Saturday in honor of the inauguration.

Two thousand people, massed in the streets about the White House, stampeded at eight o'clock through the opened gates. There were the usual casualties in the free-for-all of entering the mansion. The vestibule presented a doleful exhibit of battered finery. Shrieks of females in pain punctuated the music of the Marine Band. Some were carried swooning over the heads of the mob. Others, caught in the wrong stream of traffic, were helplessly dragged to the exit, without ever having had a chance to pay their respects to the President. Still, as the front door opened and closed, fresh batches of callers struggled in. Still, faces jerked past Lincoln, as, in the suffocating atmosphere of the Blue Room, he mechanically stretched out his big, cold, aching hand.

One dark-skinned man dared to bolt past the detaining policemen at the entrance. Frederick Douglass, the famous Negro orator, had presumed on his reputation and his acquaintance with Mr. Lincoln to attend the reception of the public. Inside the house, he was seized by two more policemen, and all but hustled through the East Room window, before his appeals were carried to the President. While white handshakers waited, Lincoln stopped the flustered colored man for a chat.

When the last footsteps had clattered down the plank, when the music had died and the rooms were empty, Mr. Lincoln looked about him in distress. The receding tidal wave of the people had left wreckage behind. Almost a square yard of red brocade had been cut from one of the East Room window hangings. Another great piece was gone from a drapery in the Green Room. Lace curtains gaped with fresh rents of snipped-out flowers. "The White House," wrote the bodyguard, William Crook, "looked as if a regiment of rebel troops had been quartered there—with permission to forage." The arrests were a sorry ending to Inauguration Day.

In the city streets, befuddled celebrants went staggering. The *Star* bragged that the night was the most orderly to succeed an inauguration since Jackson's first term. There were a few, but only a few assaults, robberies and riots.

The inauguration ball was scheduled for Monday night. As a measure of economy, the supervisory committee, of which Major French was chairman, had decided to hold it in the Patent Office, in lieu of erecting a temporary structure. After the expenses had been paid, the proceeds were to be devoted to the aid of soldiers' families, and there had been a brisk sale of ten-dollar tickets, which admitted a gentleman and two ladies, with no extra charge for an elegant supper. The committee, however, had been obliged to issue an emphatic denial that tickets had been sold to colored people.

On Monday morning, while "representative belles" of the Union drove from the depot with their Saratoga trunks, sight-seers gathered at the bustling Patent Office. Hampers whirled through the doors. The ballroom band was holding a rehearsal. A ticket office was open for business in the Rotunda. In the recently finished north saloon, which in 1862 had been a hospital, workmen were attaching lines of gas jets and draping the walls with flags. Blue and gold sofas were carried to the raised dais provided for the Presidential party. As only a few visitors were admitted to the ballroom, the preparations made rapid progress. In the supper room in the west wing, curious crowds impeded the labors of Mr. Balzer, the confectioner. By afternoon, it was found necessary to exclude them, and carriage-loads of ladies departed, grumbling, from F Street.

Mr. Balzer had a gargantuan assignment, the hearty delectation of over four thousand people. His elegant supper comprised beef, veal, poultry, game, smoked meats, terrapin, oysters (prepared by T. M. Harvey), salads, jellies, ices, tarts, cakes, fruits, nuts, coffee and chocolate. The long table, designed to accommodate three hundred persons at a time, grew festive with flags and pyramids and ornaments. Waiters labored in with the monuments of confectionery which were the crowning glory of the feast. The piece in honor of the army had six sculptured devices, including a combat between infantry and cavalry, and a mounted general with his field glass in active use. It was balanced by an equally elaborate tribute to the navy, surmounted by Farragut's flagship, with the admiral lashed to the mast. The centerpiece was a mammoth sugar model of the Capitol, with all its statuary and gas lamps. Its supporting pedestal was adorned with scenes ranging from the Revolution of 1776 to Fort Sumter, surrounded by ironclads, as it appeared when recaptured by the Union troops.

Early in the evening, the promenade halls, lined with cabinets of patents and curios, began to fill with strolling couples. The band from Finley Hospital discoursed military music until ten o'clock. Then the ballroom band, under the baton of Professor Withers, Junior, orchestra conductor at Ford's,—receiving one thousand dollars for forty pieces for the evening—sounded off with a quadrille. In the bright, flag-draped saloon, where wounds and death had been, the couples took their places, and the tessellated marble floor was covered with revolving flounces. Fashion was as pale as the crocuses. There were lilac and pearl-colored and light yellow silks, fitted tightly to the throat; and an abundance of frail white tarletan, festooned with tinted ruches. Under their flowered headdresses, the ladies all wore curls, and some had powdered their hair with golden or silver dust.

At half past ten, the military band played "Hail to the Chief," and a path was cleared through the throng, as the President walked to the dais, accompanied by Speaker Colfax. Mrs. Lincoln, in her costly white silk and lace, with a headdress of white jessamine and purple violets, and a fan trimmed with ermine and silver spangles, followed on the arm of Senator Sumner. Their appearance caused a buzz, for it was supposed that, since his successful fight against Lincoln's reconstruction plan, Sumner was *persona non grata* at the White House. The President had chosen to make this public demonstration that there was no breach between them. On Sunday, he had sent Sumner a ticket to the ball, with a note of invitation which, for all its gentle courtesy, had a hint of royal command.

In the swirl of arriving guests were many distinguished persons: the gentlemen of the Cabinet, generals and diplomats; Admiral Farragut in person, as well as in sugar; the rich eccentric, George Francis Train and his beautiful wife; the novelist, Mrs. E. D. E. N. Southworth. Bob Lincoln, in the army at last, had come up from Petersburg, where he was serving on Grant's staff, and attended the ball with the lovely daughter of Senator Harlan of Iowa on his arm. Lancers, waltzes, schottisches and polkas drew an increasing throng to the unresilient marble tiles, until the floor became so jammed that dancing was almost impossible.

At this point, shortly after midnight, supper was announced. Mr. Balzer had provided accommodations for three hundred at a time, but over four thousand hungry guests were determined to eat at once. There was a moment when his splendid table appeared in its full perfection. Before the onslaught of the crowd, it was soon in ruins. Parties, picnicking in corners and alcoves, were served by foraging gentlemen who snatched whole *pâtés*, chickens, legs of veal, halves of turkeys, and ornamental pyramids. Ladies shuddered for their dresses as the greasy trophies wobbled overhead and the supper-room floor was covered with a paste of trampled carcasses and cakes. To the tune of smashing glasses, while the waiters rushed in fresh supplies of delicacies, souvenir hunters tripped over piles of dirty dishes to attack the decorations. A confectionary Ship of State was carried away in fragments. One young lady triumphantly bore aloft an entire sugar horse. Only the model of the Capitol, fortunately removed at the outset, was preserved from destruction.

After this wild party, Washington returned to normal preoccupations—the draft, the guerrillas and the locust swarm of office seekers. Four policemen at the White House had been conscripted, but their cases had been "fixed." Policemen of less influential connections were scurrying for substitutes, but these brought eight hundred and a thousand dollars each, and agents were active all over the District. A series of subscription parties were given for the benefit of drafted men, while the capital fretted at the boldness of the rebel rangers who had entered the Federal lines, dressed in Union blue, and stolen six horses at Munson's Hill.

The dawn of a second term had again packed the White House with insistent suppliants. Seeking time for official business and sorely needed rest, the President was obliged to limit his appointments. On Tuesday, March 14, he spent the day in bed, holding the Cabinet meeting in his room. Though the press spoke of influenza, it was generally understood that Mr. Lincoln was suffering from exhaustion. On Wednesday, he was back at his desk. The announcement had been made that his health prevented him from receiving visitors, but the passages and rooms on the second floor of the mansion were filled with "political vultures." In the evening, he accompanied Mrs. Lincoln to the German Opera Company's performance of *The Magic Flute* at Grover's.

About the middle of March, John Surratt took a theatre party to Ford's, occupying part of the President's double box. The pass had been given to Surratt by Booth. John T. Ford's brother, Harry, who was treasurer of the theatre, said that Booth engaged this same box three or four times that season; it was the only one that he ever engaged.

Two of the people whom Surratt invited to accompany him were boarders at his mother's house; Miss Honora Fitzpatrick, a girl of seventeen, and a child called Appolonia Dean. The third guest was a strange occupant of a fashionable seat at the theatre. He was a youth like a Roman gladiator, with a moron's face, low-browed and dull, and an erect, powerful, magnificently muscled body. This was Lewis Powell, an Alabama soldier who had deserted the Confederate army, and now passed as Lewis Paine, the name under which he had signed the oath of allegiance at Alexandria. He went to Ford's muffled in a blue military cloak which belonged to Louis Weichmann.

Somewhere, somehow, the Alabama boy had once seen Booth on the stage. He had been spellbound, had sought Booth out afterward and pleased him by his simple hero worship. Paine's brief intimacy with the actor had remained a bright memory across years of fighting, wounds, captivity, escape, more fighting. On the last day of February, a ragged and penniless deserter in the streets of Baltimore, Paine had met a willing benefactor. Booth's smiling face must have appeared like a miracle before him. For the actor, too, there was something wonderful in the chance encounter. Here, ready to his hand, was a tool far more serviceable than the wavering Arnold and O'Laughlin, than timid Atzerodt and silly Davy Herold, even than foolhardy John Surratt. Paine, in 1865, was a logical development from a stupid, strong, nerveless recruit, who at seventeen had been given a gun and taught the trade of killing. War had given him a disregard for human life and the habit of implicit obedience. Attaching himself to Booth, he called him "captain." The actor fed and clothed Paine, but the soldier followed him out of no mere venality. He was Booth's creature, his henchman, ruthless, unquestioning and ferociously loyal.

While the odd party sat in the President's box, Booth came to the door and called Paine and Surratt outside. They conferred for some time in the passage, while the two girls remained seated.

The time had passed when Booth and his accomplices could talk in terms of holding Lincoln as a hostage for Southern prisoners of war. In midwinter, negotiations for exchange had been resumed, and large numbers of Confederate captives were passing to City Point. Booth, however, no longer needed a rational justification for his hatred of the President. It had burned until it lighted all his mind with a blaze in which he walked in glory, the hero and the avenger of the South. One early March day, in spurs and gauntlets and military hat, he sat in his room at the National before a table on which were spread a map, a knife and a pistol. His intimate friend, John McCullough, an actor in Edwin Forrest's company, suddenly entered the room. Booth seized the knife and went for him. At McCullough's cry, "John . . . are you crazy?" he stopped, put his hands over his eyes, seemed to come out of a dream.

Either after Surratt's theatre party or late the following evening, the conspirators gathered in a private room in a restaurant for the only general meeting which they ever held. Severally, Booth had governed them, seeing them one or two at a time in bars, bedrooms and livery stables. Except for the new man, Paine, they were nervous over the long delay in the execution of their design. They had grown apprehensive that the Government had been informed of the plot. John Surratt advised throwing up the project altogether, and he thought that the others agreed with him. Only Booth "sat silent and abstracted," until at last he rose to crash his fist on the table, and burst into a violent altercation with some of his accomplices. The meeting, which lasted all night, ended on an amicable note, Surratt remembered. Booth apologized for his temper, making the excuse that he had taken too much champagne.

Arnold, in a confession which he made in 1867, also gave a description of this all-night meeting. He said that Booth began by assigning the part that each was to play in the abduction. Paine was to assist Booth in seizing Lincoln, while Arnold was to jump on the stage and lend a hand, as they lowered their victim. O'Laughlin and Herold were charged with putting out the gas, controlled at Ford's by a mechanism situated near the prompter's box. Surratt and Atzerodt, posted beyond the Eastern Branch, were to guide the party to the boats which were ready on the upper Potomac.

This program precipitated an excited discussion of the feasibility of the whole scheme. Arnold declared that he made outspoken objections, and that Booth threatened to shoot him. The quarrel was patched up, but Arnold remained firm in his expressed resolve to withdraw from the conspiracy, unless action were taken that week.

Apparently, the disaffection of his followers persuaded Booth to make an attempt in another setting than the theatre. Information was received that the President was planning to attend a theatrical matinee performance at a hospital on the Seventh Street Road. It was quickly resolved to kidnap Mr. Lincoln as he drove through the suburbs in his carriage. Herold, with arms and ammunition, was sent ahead into Maryland. The rest of the band rode out in pairs—Booth and Surratt, Paine and Atzerodt, Arnold and O'Laughlin—to lie in wait for the President's barouche. Surratt said that they were confident of success. They had fast horses, and knew the country. That the President might be accompanied by his cavalry escort seems not to have entered their minds; for Surratt thought that, by the time the alarm could be given, they would be well on their way through southern Maryland.

On the afternoon of Friday, March 17, Davenport and Wallack, who were playing an engagement at the Washington Theatre, appeared at Campbell Hospital on North Seventh Street in Tom Taylor's *Still Waters Run Deep.* The sick and wounded men at Campbell were under the charge of Dr. A. F. Sheldon, a surgeon who believed in mental as well as physical rehabilitation, and his efforts to provide amusement for the soldiers were seconded by the hospital chaplain. A hall, with a capacity of five hundred persons, had been erected expressly for entertainments. A dramatic company had been formed among the patients, and performances were given every Friday. On March 10, several actors from the Washington Theatre and Grover's had volunteered to offer a program in this unique hospital theatre. The appearance the following week of the two stars in a full-length comedy, which was one of the most popular plays in their repertoire, was an event of importance at Campbell Hospital, and the hall was filled with convalescents, officers, ladies and other invited guests.

In later years, an unidentified actor wrote for a Boston newspaper the account of an incident which E. L. Davenport had related to him. Davenport said that in the early spring of 1865 he had played in *Still Waters* at a theatre some distance out of Washington. The President and Cabinet had been invited, but Lincoln was unable to be present. During a long wait, Davenport strolled outside, and was enjoying a cigar in a sort of garden behind the theatre, when John Wilkes Booth appeared. He was elegantly dressed, but wore riding boots and spurs, and Davenport thought that he seemed rather excited, as he bade him "Good-evening, Ned," and inquired who was in the house. Davenport, according to his friend's recollection, mentioned Stanton, Seward, Chase and others. "Did the old man come?" Booth asked. When he heard that Lincoln was not there, he turned on his heel. To Davenport's remark that he seemed in a great hurry, he replied with the explanation that he had a new horse that was rather restive.

Meantime, at the boardinghouse on H Street, Mrs. Surratt was weeping bitterly. Louis Weichmann, returning from the War Department at four-thirty, learned from the colored servant, Dan, that John Surratt had gone off on horseback with six other men. The unhappy mother sent Weichmann down to his dinner without her. At half past six, however, as the young man sat in his room, Surratt came rushing in with a pistol in his hand. In agitation, he gabbled that his hopes were blighted, and asked Weichmann to find him a clerkship. Paine, also armed, soon followed. He was flushed and excited, but taciturn. Last came Booth, his face chalk-white. He strode around the bedroom, with his riding whip clenched in his hand, too disturbed to notice Weichmann's presence.

The disappointment of the conspirators was a severe reaction to the confidence they had placed in the information that the President was going to Campbell Hospital. Either in their haste they had not seen, or they had refused to credit a report which appeared in both the *Chronicle* and the *National Intelligencer*, that Mr. Lincoln was expected to attend a little ceremony on the Avenue on the afternoon of Friday, March 17. At Fort Anderson, near Wilmington, North Carolina, soldiers of the 140th Indiana had captured a fine rebel garrison flag, which they were presenting to their State through the governor, Oliver P. Morton, then on a visit to Washington. Morton and some Indiana officers, released after long confinement in Southern prisons, gathered on the veranda of the National, where they were joined by the President, who addressed the assembled crowd. By a curious irony of events, Lincoln was at Booth's hotel at the very time that the actor was lying in wait for him on North Seventh Street.

As in January, the successful accomplishment of the kidnaping attempt would have interfered with a stage appearance which Booth had promised to make. The following night, he played *Pescara* in *The Apostate* at Ford's in a benefit for his friend, John McCullough.

The Lincolns heard *Faust* at Grover's that evening. On Tuesday, they went to the E Street theatre again, attending the German Opera Company's performance for the third time in a week, while Booth was traveling to New York.

Arnold and O'Laughlin, thoroughly discouraged, had returned to their homes. Paine went to Baltimore, and thence to New York. John Surratt left for Richmond to resume his dispatch-carrying. On Thursday, March 23, the President himself departed from Washington. In response to an invitation from General Grant, he embarked for City Point on the steamer, *River Queen*, accompanied by Mrs. Lincoln, Tad and the bodyguard, William Crook. When Booth returned to the capital that week end, Lincoln was out of reach.

Two motives were assigned for the President's visit to the front. For many, a release from the pressure of business was the obvious and sufficient explanation. The state of Lincoln's health had been the subject of anxious comment in the press. His haggard appearance had been remarked. The *National Republican*, denouncing the herd of office seekers, had recommended driving them from the city to save the President from breaking down. The *New York Tribune*, in an article which was reprinted in the *Star*, had struck a doleful, graveyard note, referring to Lincoln's death or disability as a national calamity, and declaring that his energies must be spared, if he were to outlive his second term. The fate of Harrison and Taylor was recalled, and it was suggested that the Union might have to mourn another dead President, this time "killed by the greed and impudence of bores."

Yet, in spite of all the publicity given to Lincoln's need of a holiday, the rumor was persistent in Washington that his excursion was a forerunner of peace; and, among those close to the President, it was understood that the approaching end of hostilities had made him wish to insure that severe terms should not be exacted from the insurgents. The last crucial days had come at Petersburg and Richmond. Sheridan's army, its work in the Valley done, had swung to the south and joined Grant. In North Carolina, near the Virginia line, Sherman's army was massed with the troops from Fort Fisher and Wilmington. Sherman and Sheridan, as well as Grant, conferred with Lincoln on board the *River Queen*.

The President had frequently made flying visits to the army. If he anticipated a protracted absence from the capital on this occasion, no one was aware of it, not even Mr. Seward. On the Monday after their departure, the *Star* printed a notice that the President and Mrs. Lincoln had secured boxes for several performances of the Italian opera at Ford's, and on Tuesday heralded their impending return. Mrs. Lincoln had certainly expected that they would be home on Wednesday, March 29, for before leaving she had invited Senator Sumner to accompany them to *Ernani* on that evening.

Booth, easily aware that Lincoln was expected at Ford's, went into action on Monday. He telegraphed O'Laughlin in Baltimore, urging him to come to Washington on Wednesday, with or without Sam Arnold. "We sell that day sure. Don't fail," the message ran. Neither of his boyhood friends responded to the summons. The President remained with the army. On March 29, with thoughts far from the Italian opera, he was watching the launching of Grant's grand assault on the Petersburg lines.

On Sunday, April 2, an extra *Star* cried the news of Lincoln's telegrams to Stanton—furious fighting, great successes. Lee's entrenched lines were broken. Grant was crushing him on the east. Sheridan was sweeping down from the west, carrying everything before him. The next morning, another telegram from Lincoln told that Petersburg was evacuated. Grant was confident that Richmond, too, had fallen. He was pushing forward to cut off Lee's army.

Shortly after this message was received, the operators at the War Department were startled by a new signal. For the man who bent over the instrument, the dots and dashes that spelled "From Richmond" were enough. Leaving Willie Kettles, a boy of fifteen, to copy the dispatch, he ran into the cipher room with the news. Operators hung from the windows, bawling "Richmond has fallen!" and soon, from all the bureaus, the War Department employees dashed cheering into the street. As the exultant cry echoed through the town, it was at first received with incredulity. People stormed the newspaper offices, snatched the thousands of extras which speedily appeared with official confirmation of the victory. "Glory!!! Hail Columbia!!! Hallelujah!!!" screamed the *Star*. "Richmond Ours!!!"

From Fourteenth and M Streets sounded a deafening salute of eight hundred guns—three hundred for Petersburg and five hundred for Richmond—and one hundred more boomed from the Navy Yard wharf. Every Government building spilled out shouting clerks. The circuit and criminal courts adjourned. Workers tumbled out of banks and offices and shops. Gleeful colored folk came running, convalescents panted out of the hospitals, and children skipped from the public schools to swell the holiday crowds. By noon, in streets dizzy with clanging church bells and waving flags, the entire population of Washington seemed to be abroad, shaking hands and embracing, throwing up their hats, shrieking and singing, like a carnival of lunatics.

Oratory burst spontaneously from the steps of public buildings and hotels. Most impressive of all was the scene at the War Department, where Secretary Stanton faltered out a solemn speech to the multitude that packed the park. In a phrase that might have been Lincoln's, he asked his hearers to beseech Providence "to teach us how to be humble in the midst of triumph." The crowd yelled applause for his pious sentiments, though some called "Let her burn!" at the news that Richmond was on fire. There were tears in Stanton's eyes, as people rushed forward to grip his hand, even to try to throw their arms about him. He had suddenly become the most popular man in Washington. "I forgive ye all yer sins, ye old blizzard!" a soldier shouted. Young Willie Kettles was brought forward to make a modest bow, and Secretary Seward, as nonchalant in victory as in defeat, delivered an amusing little address.

As though by prearrangement, bands turned out, blaring the national airs, and the crowds marched in time to "Yankee Doodle" and "Rally 'Round the Flag." Two squadrons of cavalry and a brigade of Veteran Reserves formed a parade, and found themselves being reviewed by General Augur in the grounds south of the White House. Carriages, draped with flags, went rolling along the Avenue. The fire departments galloped through town, blowing off blasts of steam.

Black and white, the people of Washington whooped it up through the whole delirious afternoon. Fraternizing patriots went arm in arm to drink together, and nightfall failed to quiet their exuberance. That evening, the celebrated comedienne, Miss Laura Keene, opened a two weeks' engagement at Ford's in a composition of her own, *The Workmen of Washington,* a moral drama directed at exposing the evils of intemperance. It was a timely, if uninfluential, production. Champagne corks were popping all over Washington, and the drinking saloons were jammed. To assist the night force, the day police remained on duty until eleven. The patrolmen looked with tolerance on boisterous parties of songsters, escorting helpless drunks home, and arrested only flagrant offenders.

The next day, the propeller, *Rebecca Barton,* proudly cleared for

Richmond from the Sixth Street wharf. The steamer, *Thomas Powell,* came in from City Point with some three hundred wounded, chiefly from Sheridan's cavalry. They had heard the big guns at Fort Monroe and had glimpsed bunting on the ships in the roads, but these men did not know that Richmond had fallen until the *Thomas Powell* docked. The newsboys who scrambled on board were soon sold out, and for once the pale voyagers to the hospitals were smiling.

The State Department had recommended a grand illumination for Tuesday evening in honor of the victory. All day the public buildings swarmed with workmen. The White House and its neighboring departments grew gay with decorations. Patriotic mottoes embellished the State Department. The War Department was smothered in flags and ensigns. The Navy hung out a large model of a full-rigged ship. Over the main entrance of the Treasury was a transparency of a ten-dollar, interest-bearing United States note.

The big Treasury, with its many windows, was bound to outshine the rest in concentrated splendor, and Mr. Stanton bestirred himself to make a striking effect at the War Department. Though it was a diminutive structure, it had overflowed into eleven buildings, some of which, like Winder's and the Corcoran Art Gallery, were of imposing size. As the dark-blue evening fell, a man was stationed, matches in hand, in every window. Other men stood ready at a row of fireballs in the department park. There was a trumpet blast, a band crashed into "The Star-Spangled Banner," and instantaneously, "like lighting gas-jets by electricity," the branch offices gleamed in a comet's tail along Seventeenth Street, while the little War Department swam in colored flame.

From basement to dome, the Capitol burned like a beacon on its hill. Over the western pediment, Major French had contrived a great, gaslighted transparency, printed in enormous letters. The words could be read far up Pennsylvania Avenue: "This is the Lord's doing; it is marvellous in our eyes." There were illuminations at the Patent Office and the Post-Office, at all the army headquarters, the Marine Barracks, the Navy Yard, the National Conservatory and the hospitals. Superintendent Wood had been at pains to make the First Street prisons brilliant. The Insane Asylum glittered like a star.

The community participated in the national celebration. The City Hall was lighted. Spangled hotels, restaurants, banks, offices and shops bordered the length of the Avenue. Grover's Theatre was crowned with "Victory" in gas jets. Dr. Holmes's funeral establishment was festive. Not only the Government officials, but numbers of private citizens had decorated their residences. Secesh had never been so little in evidence. Even the most virulent and obstinate, said the *Chronicle,* rejoiced to see the war drawing to a close. Relief and self-interest prompted many of them to illuminate their houses and display the Union flag in honor of the fall of Richmond.

All Washington turned out to see the show. Throngs gathered in the Capitol grounds, and around the furnace glow of the Treasury. There were music and fireworks in F Street, where thousands stood wedged before the Patent Office at a Republican mass meeting. Under the gas jets which spelled "Union," Judge Cartter of the District supreme court stepped forward on the Patent Office portico to speak of Jefferson Davis, "the flying rascal out of Richmond." He made dark allusions to the national military institution which educated traitors to cut the nation's throat, and hesitated not to say "that those who have been fed, clothed and taught at the public expense ought to stretch the first rope." F Street rang with cheers for Judge Cartter, and for Vice-President Johnson, who dwelt on the same theme. Jefferson Davis, Andy ranted, had plunged the sword given him by his country in his mother's bosom. Calls of "Hang him!" rose from the crowd; and Johnson shouted yes, hang him twenty times, for treason was the greatest of crimes.

The President was at Richmond, watching the last struggles of Lee's hard-pressed and starving troops, and Washington could hear no word from him on that night of celebration.

Mrs. Lincoln had returned to Washington on Sunday, but on Wednesday she again left for City Point with a party of notables. That same day, an accident occurred in Washington which was influential in hastening the President's return. While Mr. Seward was taking his afternoon drive, his horses became frightened, and bolted. The Secretary jumped from the carriage, and was violently thrown to the ground. He was picked up unconscious, suffering from concussion, a broken right arm and a shattered jaw.

While the capital was concerned about Seward's injuries, the tide of excitement was too strong to be checked by this one unhappy event. People moved that week in a dazzle of anticipation of still more triumphant news from Virginia. On Friday, April 7, there was great enthusiasm—more salutes, more flags—over the information that

Sheridan had headed Lee off, attacking and routing his army. Washington saw a queer sight that day, when a rebel band serenaded Mr. Stanton. The musicians, bearing their instruments, were part of an arriving boatload of Confederate deserters. From the moment of leaving the wharf, they obligingly performed, and Washington was delighted with the novelty. So many gathered to hear them at the War Department that traffic was stopped. Those were unfamiliar tunes which serenaded the War Secretary of the Union; not "Rally 'Round the Flag, Boys," not even "Yankee Doodle"; but "Dixie," "Jordan" and "Aint we glad to get out of the Wilderness." On Stanton's behalf, Adjutant General E. D. Townsend welcomed the deserting musicians beneath the folds of the Star-Spangled Banner. Several expressed regret that they were unable to play a national air.

The *River Queen* docked early on the evening of Palm Sunday, April 9. Lincoln went immediately to Seward's residence, and was admitted to the sick chamber. Seward lay on the side of the bed away from the door, precariously stretched along the edge, so that his painful broken arm projected, free from any pressure. His face, swathed in bandages, was so swollen and discolored as to be nearly unrecognizable. He managed to whisper, "You are back from Richmond?" "Yes," the President told him, "and I think we are near the end, at last." Lincoln sprawled across the bed, resting on his elbow with his face close to Seward's, and related the story of the last two weeks. At last, the Secretary of State fell into a feverish sleep, and Lincoln slipped softly from the room.

Before he went to rest, the President learned from Stanton that Lee's army had surrendered that morning at Appomattox. Few were abroad in the dark and damp to join the jollification of the newspaper reporters. Most people in the capital were informed of the surrender when, at daybreak next morning, their beds were shaken by the repercussions of the guns. The battery was stationed on Massachusetts Avenue, behind Lafayette Square, and cracking windowpanes in that aristocratic neighborhood provoked some of the residents to wish an end to the Union's rejoicing. A large crowd of patriots was soon hurrahing in the bleak dawn. Many loyal persons, however, remained abed, satisfied to know that the tongues of the guns proclaimed victory for General Grant.

The morning newspapers brought full details to Washington breakfast tables. Lee's officers and men were paroled, and permitted to return home, the officers keeping their side arms and horses. The rainy April morning was lighted by the promise of peace. The capitulation of the Southern chieftain foretold the end of the rebellion, for it must quickly be followed by the surrender of Joe Johnston's army to Sherman and the collapse of the other scattered remnants of the Confederate forces. For a second time, Monday was given over to celebration. At an early hour, flags were waving in the rain. The Government offices and many business firms granted their employees another holiday, and again the capital was in an uproar of salutes, bells, music, cheers and speeches.

There was not the wild hysteria that had greeted the fall of Richmond. Popular emotion had been too freely spent to repeat that outburst in a single week. Yet there was one new factor which made for the strongest excitement on April 10. The President was back in Washington, and to the White House, from breakfast time on, people went running like joyful children eager to see their father. Several times, Lincoln, hard at work in his office, sent out word to disperse the crowds, but twice he appeared briefly at the window. In the forenoon, a procession followed in the wake of the Navy Yard workmen, who had been rampaging through the streets with bands and noisy boat howitzers. While the little show-off, Tad, waved a captured rebel flag, there were shouts for a speech. The President's appearance was the signal for pandemonium. Throwing their hats in the air again and again, men gave vent to throat-splitting yells of exultation. Lincoln briefly excused himself. He supposed that there would be some general demonstration, and he would say something then. He called on the musicians to play the good old tune of "Dixie," which he declared had now become the lawful property of the Union. Late in the afternoon, he again responded to rousing calls by saying that he would defer his remarks; preferably until the following evening, as he would then be better prepared.

The President's features had lost their look of illness and fatigue. His thin face was shining. The burden of "this great trouble" was about to be lifted from his shoulders; but there was no elation in his happiness. Absorbed in thoughts of rebuilding the Union, his joy was sobered by the heavy responsibilities of victory.

It was announced that the Government buildings would again be illuminated on Tuesday evening, and Washington prepared to give the President a grand ovation on the occasion of his promised speech. Its general tenor should not have been hard to anticipate. The President had become widely beloved as a man of mercy. Charity for all had been the keynote of his recent inaugural address. His conferences with Grant had been followed by generous terms to the defeated enemy. On Tuesday evening, across the Potomac, General Lee's mansion blazed with lights, and a host of freedmen trampled the lawn, chanting "The Year of Jubilee." But, to spare humiliation to the rebels, the Army of the Potomac had scarcely been permitted to enjoy its triumph at Appomattox. Grant had fed Lee's officers and men, before allowing them to return home.

While the illuminations turned a shrouding mist to gold, an immense throng gathered before the White House, filling the grounds and obstructing the sidewalks on Pennsylvania Avenue. As Lincoln stepped to the window, cheers surged and broke, and surged again. An observer felt that "there was something terrible in the enthusiasm. . . ." The crowd was vibrating with emotion, which a word from the President could have turned to frenzy.

Lincoln, however, scarcely dwelt on the victory which was the reason for the demonstration. At this jubilant moment of his country's history, his mind was fixed on the resumption of the relations between the Union and the rebellious States. As though he were addressing a persuasive message to the Congress which had already rejected his policies, he read from a carefully prepared manuscript an elucidation of his views on reconstruction, and their practical application in the case of Louisiana. His address was a defense and a plea; reasonable, expository, lacking in eloquence. It was a noble speech, and one quite unsuited to the humor of his auditors. Some reporters heard cheers, and cheers there must have been—for a personality and an occasion. Others said that the serenaders stood silent, surprised at finding their elation punctured by the arguments of statesmanship. On the subject of Negro suffrage, the President's opinions were far too moderate to suit the radicals of his party; yet his statement that he favored giving the vote to certain colored men, the very intelligent and the soldiers, must have fallen with chilling effect on a part of his audience.

There was at least one man who listened to the President's speech with rage and sickness of heart. Booth, seared by the news from Richmond and Appomattox, was in the White House grounds. The tall figure in the lamp-lighted window made a good target; and perhaps for the first time, as Booth watched it, the thought of assassination burst, like an explosion, in his brain.

Senator James Harlan of Iowa, designate for the post of Secretary of the Interior, followed the President at the window, and evoked an outburst by asking what should "be done with these brethren of ours." "Hang 'em!" cried the crowd. There were shouts of "Never! never!" when he suggested that Mr. Lincoln might exercise the pardoning power. The crowd, however, sustained Harlan in supposing the mass of the rebels innocent. It was only the punishment of the leaders that they cheered; and there was great and prolonged applause for Harlan's concluding statement, that he was willing to trust the future to the President.

Calls for other speakers were interrupted when a band struck up "The Battle-Cry." The misty drizzle thickened into raindrops, and the multitude began to disperse. Large numbers went off to Franklin Square to serenade Secretary Stanton.

It was Holy Week, and on Wednesday the bells of religious mourning tolled incongruously in a city still occupied with celebration. Even the arrival of the wounded from City Point did not subdue the spirits of the capital. As though they had not already experienced ten days of carnival, the citizens were making elaborate preparations for still another jamboree.

Rather spitefully the *Chronicle* had speculated on Monday whether Lee's surrender would arouse the municipal authorities from their indifference to the successes of the Union. Gettysburg, Vicksburg, Savannah, Charleston and Richmond had failed, remarked the *Chronicle*, to startle them out of their lethargy. Although Mayor Wallach was loyal and the City Hall had been lighted for the fall of Richmond, there was some justice in the *Chronicle's* attack. The dart struck home. By noon of Monday, Wallach had borrowed a battery which fired two hundred guns in front of the City Hall, breaking many of its windows in honor of Appomattox; and the city councils, goaded into enthusiasm for the winning side, requested by joint resolution a grand illumination for Thursday, April 13.

The proposal met with prompt Federal co-operation. Illuminations were ordered in all the departments, and some fine new embellishments were added to the earlier displays. The Treasury hung out a second huge transparency, representing the popular issue, the fifty-dollar, seven-thirty bond. At the Post-Office, there was a striking display of a courier with the United States mail, and the words, "Behold I bring you good tidings of great joy." Over thirty-five hundred candles were required for the Post-Office windows, and nearly six thousand for the Patent Office.

Primarily, however, this jubilee was the affair of the community, rather than the Government. The city councils had inspired the residents with a belated fervor of loyalty. Some there must still have been who closed their houses and wept, as Weichmann said that Mrs. Surratt did; but there was every indication that most Southern sympathizers were ready to turn their coats. Down from New York came boxes of lanterns and fireworks and Union flags. Candles were sold by thousands. Dealers advertised the merits of special "illuminating candle-sticks." Competitive in their patriotism, private houses, as well as shops and offices and hotels, were arranging prodigious spectacles. The supply of flags was exhausted, and the president of the Board of Aldermen had to send to Alexandria to procure suitable decorations for his residence on H Street.

In the midst of Thursday's excitement, General Grant arrived in the capital. It was a dramatic moment for the advent of the commander-in-chief, but Grant was not thinking of ovations. He was preoccupied by military details; and he was especially anxious to confer with Mr. Stanton, for his main purpose in hastening to Washington was to curtail the enormous expeditures for the army. In spite of the acclaiming throngs at Willard's, he was simple enough to suppose that he could quietly walk over to the War Department, and the police had to rescue him from the crowd.

As Grover's partner, C. D. Hess, was going over a manuscript with the prompter, Booth entered the office, seated himself and began to chat about the evening's festivities. Did Hess intend to illuminate? he inquired. The manager told him, yes, to a certain extent. His great night, however, was to be the following one.

Friday, April 14, was to be observed with appropriate ceremonies at Fort Sumter as the fourth anniversary of the surrender. Undoubtedly realizing that the entire population would be gaping on the streets on Thursday evening, Grover's had cannily decided to hold a patriotic gala on Friday. It was, of course, Good Friday, a poor night for places of amusement; but people were in a merrymaking mood, and on that evening the theatres would suffer no greater competition

than a torchlight procession of the Arsenal employees. Grover's was
going to have fireworks, and the current attraction, *Aladdin; or, The
Wonderful Lamp*—a Grand Oriental Spectacle—was to be diversified
by the singing of a new patriotic song, and the recitation of "The Flag
of Sumter," an original poem by Major French.

Was Hess going to invite the President to attend? Booth asked.
For several days, the manager had been meaning to do so; and, after
this reminder, he addressed a note of invitation to Mrs. Lincoln.

Booth often dropped in at Grover's, but Hess and the prompter,
working over their manuscript, were a little jarred by his interruption.
They were evidently busy, and Hess had not invited Booth to come
in and take a seat. Aside from the intrusion, there seemed nothing
remarkable in the little interview. On the actor's handsome face, there
was no sign of the purpose in his heart; and Hess could not guess
that Good Friday had been chosen as the ides, or that this was Brutus
who conversationally lounged in Grover's office.

By seven o'clock on Thursday evening, the last candle was burning. "The stars," said the *Star,* whose proprietor was brother to the
mayor, "twinkled in a sort of faded way, as if . . . earth had become
the great luminary." Ostentatiously, the City Hall sat dressed in gas
jets, with as many as sixty candles apiece in some of its windows;
while, from the square, the radiating streets seemed to stretch in
unbroken vistas of flame. On the Avenue, the south side vied with
the north in grandeur, and Seventh Street was dazzling.

"Union" and "Grant" were the words that the gaslights flashed
on every hand. "Victory brings peace," proclaimed the transparencies;
"Stand by the flag," and "God wills that we remain united." Lengthy
Biblical and patriotic quotations covered many shops and houses.
Others had original mottoes. "Glory to God, who hath to U. S.
Grant-d the Victory" was suspended on the banking house of Jay
Cooke and Company, opposite the Treasury. "God, Grant, our Coun-
try, Peace" was the contribution of the Y.M.C.A. on Seventh Street.
The clothing store of E. L. Seldner queried "How are you, Lee?"
"How are you, Johnny Bully?" slyly inquired Lowenthal and Com-
pany, opposite Willard's.

In all the seven wards, from Rock Creek to the poorhouse, from
the Arsenal to the Northern Liberties, there was no section which
lacked its patriotic display. At the mansions of the rich and prominent,
the great windows were brilliant, and fireworks played on the fes-

tooned flags. Lonely suburban streets shone with illuminations in the tenements of laboring men. The broken shanties of the Negro settlements and the poorest alleys showed humble flickers of candlelight.

Down the Avenue, with music and transparencies, went a parade of workmen from the Government repair shops. The pavements eddied with people, staring at the lights until their eyes ached. Many out-of-town visitors had come to see the show. A party of young men from Baltimore included Michael O'Laughlin, tricked out in a dahlia-colored coat, and a double-breasted vest and pantaloons of purple and green Scotch plaid. He was working in Baltimore now, while Sam Arnold had gone to Fort Monroe to clerk in a sutler's store. O'Laughlin stopped in at the National to call on Booth, but he spent the rest of the time with his party, gallivanting in his flashy new suit in the populous barrooms along the Avenue.

There were fireworks in Franklin Square, and serenaders gathered around the residence of the Secretary of War. Mr. Stanton was holding a reception that evening, and Grant was among the guests. The city blazed and echoed with the military chieftain's name, but Grant remained in Stanton's parlor, making but one inconspicuous appearance in the midst of a group on the steps, while the Secretary of War responded to the serenade. Stanton, fearful that a tragedy might occur in this season of popular agitation, was opposed to any public appearance on the part of either the general-in-chief or the President. David Bates, manager of the War Department telegraph office, said that extra precautions were taken to protect them both because of secret service reports that attempts might be made to kidnap or kill them during the excitement. Marshal Lamon, in recent weeks, had repeatedly told one of Lincoln's friends that he believed the President would be assassinated. Seward, though he was of the opinion that assassination was not an American practice, had some reason for thinking that the President should not expose himself at this time.

Terrified that he might be implicated in the disloyal activities at the Surratt boardinghouse, Louis Weichmann had talked. In March, he had confided the story of the abduction plot to a fellow-clerk at the War Department, Captain Gleason, whom he begged to keep the matter secret, lest his friends discover that he had betrayed them. Gleason, however, promptly gave the information to an assistant provost marshal on Augur's staff. Weichmann, on learning of the disclosure, hastened to put himself in the right by making a report to another officer. The

War Department authorities had thus been thoroughly advised of
Booth's conspiracy. Gleason thought that the reports were made before
the inauguration, and that an attempt was planned for that day—a
contention supported only by the case of the man, later recalled as
resembling Booth's photograph, who broke through the police lines
at the Capitol. Weichmann said that he did not confide in Gleason
until the day after the attempt on the Seventh Street Road.

Lincoln must have taken the warnings of danger more seriously
than he admitted. He had confessed to his wife and Lamon that he
had lately dreamed of a corpse, lying in the East Room on a catafalque
surrounded by a guard of soldiers. The sound of people sobbing had
drawn Lincoln, in his dream, from bed. "Who is dead in the White
House?" he asked one of the soldiers. "The President," was the answer.
"He was killed by an assassin!" A loud outcry of grief had awakened
Lincoln. He had not slept again that night. Even in recalling the
dream some days afterward, he was grave, pale, visibly disturbed.

In view of the threatening rumors, the fantasy might well have
frightened a less nervous woman than Mrs. Lincoln, but she had taken
it very sensibly, merely making the remark that she was glad that she
did not believe in dreams, or she would be in terror after hearing this
one. She proceeded to behave in a manner which showed no great
concern for her husband's protection. On Thursday, she invited Grant
to take an evening drive around the city with her and the President
to see the illuminations. Aside from the fact that Mr. Lincoln was
suffering from a severe headache, there was every reason against
proposing this excursion. The streets were blocked with people, there
was much drunkenness, and the sight of Grant would have caused
the President's carriage to be mobbed.

There was no mention of Mrs. Grant in the invitation. One of
Grant's aides said that the general took a drive with Mrs. Lincoln
during the day. There was no excursion from the White House in the
evening. The lights glittered on the wreathing evergreens, the corps
flags and the guidons and the cavalry standards. Crowds, gathering at
the mansion, were not rewarded by the appearance of the President.

Marshal Lamon, who had been sent on an errand to Richmond,
had asked Lincoln not to go out at night during his absence. He
wanted the President to promise, in particular, not to attend the
theatre. Lincoln had made an evasive reply. The fears that troubled
his dreams did not influence his actions, and he acceded to his wife's

proposal for a theatre party on Friday night. Instead of attending the patriotic gala at Grover's, the tickets for which were turned over to Tad, Mrs. Lincoln planned to go to Ford's, where Miss Laura Keene was offering, as her benefit and closing performance, Tom Taylor's comedy, *Our American Cousin*. For years, this flimsy piece had been a favorite with the public, who enjoyed a good laugh at the shrewd Yankee, *Asa Trenchard,* and the ridiculous Englishman, *Lord Dundreary*. Its first run in New York, before the war, had brought stardom to Joe Jefferson and Sothern, and *Florence Trenchard* was the outstanding success of Miss Keene's theatrical career. Much repetition, however, had diminished the comedy's popularity, and in 1865 it was only a fair box-office attraction.

The suggestion apparently came from Lincoln that Grant and his wife should be asked to go to Ford's. Perhaps he had some thought of atoning for the discourtesy of Mrs. Lincoln's omission of Mrs. Grant from the invitation to drive around the city. He himself extended the theatre invitation to Grant, when he saw him on Thursday. Grant remembered making the answer that they would go if they were in town, but that, if he could get through his work, he was anxious to leave on Friday to see his children. Although the children later became fixed in Grant's mind as a plausible excuse for an early departure, it is improbable that his reply to the President was expressed in the vague and conditional terms which he recalled. Caught unawares by the verbal invitation, he must have blundered out a half-hearted acceptance; for it was certainly Lincoln's understanding that the Grants were going to the theatre, and the White House messenger so informed Ford's, when he went to reserve the President's box at ten-thirty on Friday morning.

Grant must soon have regretted that he had not been quick-witted enough to refuse the invitation outright. It was impossible that Mrs. Grant should enjoy the prospect of an evening in Mrs. Lincoln's society. At City Point, she had recently been a pained witness of Madam President's wild tempers, and had even received an angry insult or two herself. Grant, on his own account, was impatient to get away from Washington and its embarrassing ovations. A visit to the theatre would be the occasion for a grand demonstration in his honor. The year before, he had broken an engagement with the President and disappointed the audience at Grover's, and he was ready to do it again at Ford's.

When Stanton got wind of this theatre party, which controverted all his admonitions, he vehemently opposed it. The telegrapher, Bates, said that he urged Grant not to go to Ford's because of the danger of assassination. Grant willingly agreed, telling Stanton that he only wanted an excuse; but he did not use the excuse which the War Secretary had given him, nor try to dissuade the President from attending the theatre, as Bates said that Stanton had asked him to do. He offered the same rather lame excuse that he had had all along, that he wanted to visit his children. He did not bring himself to utter a decisive refusal until about two o'clock in the afternoon, when the afternoon papers were appearing with announcements that he would be at Ford's.

Grant went to the White House at eleven on Friday for the Cabinet meeting. It was a prolonged session. The President was confidently anticipating the news of Johnston's surrender to Sherman, and three hours passed in the discussion of plans for the harmonious restoration of the Union. One of Grant's aides, Colonel Horace Porter, heard the general make some apologies to Lincoln, emphasizing his wife's disappointment, if the visit to the children were delayed. The President pressed him a little, Porter said, reminding him of the pleasure it would give the people to see him. The appointment still hung fire, until a note from Mrs. Grant was handed to the general, expressing anxiety to leave on the late afternoon train. Thus fortified, at the close of the meeting, Grant firmly told the President that he must decide not to remain.

Frederick Seward, attending the Cabinet meeting in his father's place, verified the time of the definite refusal. At about two o'clock, young Seward heard Lincoln speak to Grant about the theatre, understanding the general to excuse himself on the ground of a previous engagement.

Grant himself attributed his vagueness about fulfilling the engagement to uncertainty about finishing his work in time to leave on Friday. "I did get through," he wrote, "and started by the evening train on the 14th, sending Mr. Lincoln word, of course, that I would not be at the theatre." Although there is a want of candor in Grant's casual treatment of the whole episode, and his pretext was disingenuous, since he had little time to work on Friday, he plainly acknowledged that he made a last-minute decision.

Nevertheless, on the basis of two accounts, one by Speaker Colfax and the other by the telegrapher, Bates, it has been said that Lincoln knew of Grant's intended departure at an early hour on Friday. By internal evidence, Colfax's conversation with the President could not have taken place during his morning call, at about nine o'clock, at the White House. The President asked Colfax to go with him to the play, adding that Grant had promised to do so, but had gone north; and he also said that he supposed that he himself must put in an appearance, in order that the people might not be disappointed. Not only was Grant in town until early evening, but the White House messenger did not reach Ford's until the middle of the morning. These remarks were undoubtedly made during a second conversation which Colfax had with the President at seven-thirty in the evening.

Similarly, although Bates thought that Lincoln spoke of the broken engagement in the morning, he probably did so during an early evening visit which he paid to the War Office. Both Noah Brooks and the guard, Crook, substantiate Colfax's statement that the President went to Ford's out of a sense of duty to the public. For some reason, he did not want to go, after the Grants had backed out. It was the advertisement of the plan which induced him to carry out his intention. Ford's did not send the notice to the evening papers until very late in the forenoon. If Grant had given a plain refusal either on Thursday or early on Friday, the President would have been able "to give up the whole thing," as he told Brooks he had felt inclined to do.

The news that Grant would accompany the President to *Our American Cousin* threw the Tenth Street theatre into a furor. John T. Ford had hastened down to Richmond to see his relatives, but his brothers, James and Harry, bestirred themselves to prepare for a gala evening, well aware that the presence of the commander-in-chief would completely eclipse the patriotic doings at Grover's.

The usual company rehearsal was prolonged to practice a new song, "Honor to Our Soldiers," the music for which had been composed by Professor Withers, Junior. The costumer, Mr. Carland, went shopping for ribbons to make badges for the gentlemen of the cast to wear during the rendition of this song. Fresh playbills were ordered. Spangler helped to remove the partition which separated the two stage boxes, and young Harry Ford arranged the decorations. This work was the duty of Mr. Raybold, the upholsterer of the theatre, but he was suffering from a severe neuralgia of the face, and the responsibility fell on Harry. Flags were tied at the sides and the middle column of the lace-curtained double box, while across the railing was draped the big blue flag of the Treasury Guard, which had been borrowed for the evening. Harry introduced a novel touch, which had never occurred to Raybold, by hanging a picture of General Washington in the center of the Treasury flag.

To furnish the box with suitable elegance, a sofa and some easy chairs were brought from the property and reception rooms. Among them was the upholstered rocking chair which the President had occupied on his first visit to Ford's new theatre. Harry entertained a respectful admiration for this fine chair; and, as the ushers "had greased it with their hair," he had had it removed to his own bedroom in an adjoining building. It had not been used in the box that season. This, Harry felt, was an occasion worthy of the rocking chair, and a colored boy, Joe Simms, carried it on his head through the alleyway, and set it in place for the President.

One more chair was needed. It was put in the narrow passageway which led from the dress circle to the box, for the bodyguard to sit in.

On Friday morning, according to one story, Booth engaged a box for the evening's performance at Grover's. He did this surreptitiously, through one of his cronies, John Deery, who was the proprietor of a large billiard saloon, situated over Grover's front entrance. The excuse that Booth gave Deery for not going direct to the ticket office was that he did not want to be under obligations to the management for complimentary seats. Deery said that the box he engaged for Booth adjoined the one which was reserved for the President.

There is also a story that Booth was in Grover's office on Friday morning, and there heard the news that the President would not accept Grover's invitation, but Ford's. In any case, he was informed of Lincoln's plans at noontime, when he visited Ford's to collect his mail.

Booth sat on the steps of the Tenth Street playhouse, reading a letter. Now and then, he looked up and laughed. Perhaps he laughed at the thought of the favoring stars which preside over a hero's destiny. Ford's was the very place he would have chosen for the President on Friday evening. There was no need for the actor to engage a box in that theatre, or to explain his presence there, front or back, at any hour.

Many people afterward remembered seeing Booth that day, as he went about Washington, making his final arrangements. None of these people, however, were Government agents. Booth was as unobserved by the authorities as though Captain Gleason had never informed the War Department of the abduction conspiracy.

Under the smooth glaze of his easy manners, he was concealing a feverish excitement. For a week, Deery had noticed the enormous quantity of liquor which Booth consumed at his bar, sometimes taking a quart of brandy in less than two hours. The editor of the *Constitutional Union,* a recently founded Democratic organ, had a short conversation with him on the Avenue in the afternoon. He remembered that Booth, though he appeared sober, seemed abstracted, and moved his arms and body nervously, as though anxiously thinking of something. His nervousness was plainly noticeable to one of his friends, John Matthews, an actor in Ford's stock company. Matthews was standing near Willard's, watching the passing of a group of Lee's officers, who had been taken prisoner by Sheridan before the surrender, when Booth came riding down the Avenue, and reined in to speak to him. Matthews spoke of the captive officers, and Booth placed his hand on his forehead. "Great God!" he cried. "I have no longer a country!" Then he took Matthews's hand, and holding it, asked him as a favor to deliver a letter for him to the *National Intelligencer* next morning. He might be leaving town that night, he said.

As Matthews took the letter and thrust it in his pocket, a carriage, which had just pulled away from Willard's, drove past. "John, there goes General Grant," Matthews exclaimed; "I understood he was coming to the theatre tonight with the President." Booth turned in anxious haste, squeezed his friend's hand tight, and galloped off down the street.

Mrs. Rucker, the wife of the Assistant Quartermaster General, had called to drive the Grants to the station. Mrs. Grant and Mrs. Rucker occupied the back seat, while the general was perched up front beside the driver.

As the Grants started along the Avenue, a horseman rode past them, staring into the carriage. Presently, he turned and rode back, attracting the occupants' attention by his close scrutiny. Later, they thought that a photograph of Booth resembled this intrusive stranger. Whether or not Booth followed the carriage, he must have seen the piled-up baggage, as it rolled in the direction of the depot, and realized that Grant's advertised engagement with the President would not be fulfilled.

Booth had three accomplices left. His program of vengeance for the South had widened. He now meant to bully Atzerodt into murdering Vice-President Johnson. Paine could be depended on for bloody work. He would go that night to Seward's bedroom. Davy Herold, who was no killer, would act as Paine's guide in escaping through Maryland. The elaborate organization for abducting the President from the theatre had ceased to be required. A derringer needed no accomplices. Booth would go alone to Ford's.

About three o'clock on Friday afternoon—so Stanton later told a party of gentlemen, of whom Charles Dickens was one—Mrs. Stanton came into the War Office to ask her husband how she should reply to an invitation from the President to go to the theatre that evening. The Stantons were an unlikely pair of guests. The hard-working War Secretary had no interest in the theatre. The only time that he ever entered Grover's was to hold a whispered conversation with Lincoln in his box during the play. Mrs. Stanton was not on friendly terms with the President's wife; she did not even call on her. They had frequently been invited to join the Lincolns' theatre parties, Mr. Stanton said, but they had always refused because he disapproved of the President's exposing himself. On this occasion, as might have been expected, he again instructed his wife to send regrets.

After a long afternoon drive with Mrs. Lincoln, the President spent an hour in his office with some friends from Illinois. He had a bite of dinner at six o'clock, and then crossed over to the War Department. Passing some quarrelsome drunkards, Lincoln said to the bodyguard, Crook, that he believed there were men who wanted to take his life. He quietly expressed the conviction that they would do it, commenting that, if it were to be done, it was impossible to prevent it.

It was probably on this visit that Stanton renewed his expostulations about the theatre party, as described by the telegrapher, Bates. Warnings of danger had influenced the President's actions on only one occasion, the secret journey to Washington in 1861. During Lincoln's recent stay at City Point, Stanton had telegraphed to caution him against going to the front, but the next day the President had calmly walked into the tumult of Richmond, a place which certainly appeared to present far greater hazards than a Washington theatre.

Stanton glowered and protested in vain. Finding the President unimpressed, he told him that he ought to have a competent bodyguard. This was a curious remark. Lincoln himself had perfect confidence in his guard, as he had just assured Crook on the way over to the War Department, saying that he knew that no one could assassinate him and escape alive. If Stanton had any good reason to doubt the efficiency of the policemen on duty with the President, it was his plain duty to have taken some action, instead of tossing off an oblique criticism.

. Lincoln countered by asking Stanton to let him take Eckert, the superintendent of military telegraphs, to the theatre. On one occasion, in Lincoln's presence, Eckert had demonstrated the poor quality of some cast-iron pokers, purchased for the War Department, by breaking them over his arm. The President, recalling this feat, declared that Eckert would be the kind of man to go with him that evening.

There was a teasing quality in Lincoln's request. Not only did it smack of levity, but it invaded Stanton's domain of authority. The Secretary shortly replied that he had important work for Eckert and could not spare him. Though he had implied doubts of the competence of the President's guard, Stanton was far too huffy and disapproving to encourage the theatre party by furnishing Lincoln with an able protector. The President pressed the invitation on Eckert himself, but the superintendent knew better than to offend Stanton by accepting.

On Stanton's behalf, however, it must be said that the President was apparently to have adequate protection at the theatre; far better, at least, than he had had on many previous occasions. Though the Lincolns had had much trouble in making up their party—even Robert, just home from the front, had begged off because he was tired—Mrs. Lincoln had secured a young engaged couple, Miss Harris and Major Rathbone, the daughter and the stepson of Senator Ira Harris of New York. Rathbone was an able-bodied man. The armed guard would also be in attendance in the passageway of the box.

The sky was overcast and the air had turned raw and chilly as Lincoln walked back from the War Department with young Crook at his side. Crook should properly have gone off duty at four o'clock, but the relief guard, John F. Parker, a shiftless native of the District who had had a poor record on the Metropolitan Police, was late in showing up. It was long past Crook's dinnertime and he was tired and hungry, when he left the President at the door of the White House.

On Tenth Street the theatre was awakening from the darkness and disuse of late afternoon. At six-thirty, Spangler and the other stagehands were at work, while the ushers, with their well-oiled heads, busied themselves in the lighted auditorium. The stage-door attendant, Peanut John, went to his post. Soon the actors sauntered into the gloomy alley, cluttered with Negro shanties. A smell of grease paint floated from the dressing-rooms. Miss Laura Keene adjusted her costume. Mr. Harry Hawk, her principal comedian, prepared to impersonate the Yankee, *Asa Trenchard*. Mr. E. A. Emerson donned the copious whiskers of *Lord Dundreary*. Mr. John Matthews took off his frock coat, with Booth's letter in the pocket. Professor Withers arrived, nervous over the performance of his song.

The carriages began to roll up Tenth Street to the wide plank platform which bridged the gutter in front of the theatre. The doorkeeper, Mr. Buckingham, a Navy Yard carpenter by day, stood at the entrance to take the tickets. The crowd thickened, the tickets flashed faster into Buckingham's hands, the ushers hurried up and down the aisles. John Parker arrived to meet the President. He had walked over from the White House, and, perhaps, as he waited, he scanned the bills with interest. Parker's duty was not supposed to include an interest in the drama. His chair in the passageway did not command a view of the stage. But Parker wanted to see the play.

The theatre was nearly filled. Only the stage boxes were empty. The eyes of the audience turned expectantly toward the flags and lace curtains on the upper right. Professor Withers lifted his baton, and the orchestra played. Then the house-lights dimmed, and two colored boys raised the curtain, with the landscape and the bust of Shakespeare, on the first act of *Our American Cousin*. Still, the curtains of the state box did not stir. It was ten minutes after eight when Lincoln reluctantly rose, and, bidding his last callers good night, started off through the gusty April evening on the drive which ended at Ford's Theatre.

Although Stanton had given an impression of great activity at the War Office, he did not work after dinner that evening. Instead, he went to pay a call on Seward. The Secretary of State was still a sick man, suffering much pain, unable to bear the slightest pressure on his broken arm, and all but speechless from the injury to his jaw. Though his doctors, in their frequent consultations, expressed satisfaction with his progress, the family continued to feel anxious. Two convalescent soldiers had been detailed as nurses; but his delicate wife, who had hastened down from Auburn, divided the night watches with two of her children, Fanny and Major Augustus Seward, a West Point graduate who was serving as paymaster in the army.

In the early evening, the Old Clubhouse was humming with the inquiries and attentions inevitable at a house where an important man lies ill. Gentlemen sat in the red and yellow parlors where Mr. Seward had often received his guests, showing them his collection of portraits of the world's sovereigns and their ministers, whom he laughingly called "my tormentors." Stanton stayed on, chatting with the other visitors, until about nine o'clock, when the sound of music reminded him that he was to be serenaded by the torchlight procession from the Arsenal. Gradually, the callers took their leave. The family physician, Dr. Verdi, called. An army surgeon paid a late visit. By ten o'clock, Mr. Seward had fallen into a doze on the edge of his bed. The mansion was hushed, like any house where a loved one's sleep is precious. The gaslights were turned low. Mrs. Seward had retired. Frederick and his wife whispered softly in their bedroom. Augustus was napping in preparation for his turn to watch beside his father. Fanny was on duty with the male nurse, Robinson. In the yellow parlor, Mr. Seward's tormentors smiled secretly from their frames.

The doorbell rang, and William Bell, the colored second waiter, went to answer it. A big, red-faced man, with his hat pulled down over one eye, walked into the hall. He had a little package in his left hand. It was medicine, he informed Bell. Dr. Verdi had sent him to direct Mr. Seward how to take it, and he must deliver it personally. Bell told him that he could not see Mr. Seward. It was against his orders to let anyone go up.

While Bell was expostulating, the stranger was walking slowly toward the stairs. His right hand was in the pocket of his overcoat. He was very tall and broad-shouldered, nicely dressed, with a fine voice, and he "looked pretty fiery out of his eyes" at the colored boy. He seemed so determined that Bell was afraid that he had gone too far in his refusal to admit this authoritative person. He asked the man to excuse him, and led the way up the two flights of stairs. Once he turned and cautioned the stranger not to "walk so heavy."

In the dim and quiet third-floor chamber, where Fanny hovered near her father's bed, the tramping feet sounded loud. Fanny indignantly whispered to Robinson that whoever was coming was not very careful for one approaching a sickroom. Then the girl and the nurse heard a mumble of argument in the upper hall. Frederick was remonstrating with someone. His voice grew peremptory. There was a moment of silence. Robinson could not hear the click of a pistol, missing fire; but, at the noise of a scuffle and pounding blows, he sprang to the door. Two men wrestled there. One was Mr. Frederick, Robinson saw his bloody head. A bowie knife flashed, slicing the nurse's brow and knocking him over, as the other man plunged into the bedroom.

Painfully, in the half-dream of an invalid's awakening, Mr. Seward raised himself. For a moment, as the intruder punched Fanny aside and bounded across the bed, the Secretary of State must have wavered in his belief that assassination was not an American practice. The last thing he remembered was Fanny's scream. He did not feel Paine's knife, gashing his face and throat, tumbling him from the edge of the bed to the floor.

Augustus, aroused from sleep, ran into his father's room in shirt and drawers. He saw two men grappling at the foot of the bed, but in the dim light he did not recognize Robinson, and did more to hinder than to help the nurse. "I'm mad! I'm mad!" Augustus heard Paine say, before he broke away, and dashed down the stairs, slashing Mr. Hansell, a State Department messenger, who was on the first floor.

It had all happened quickly. There was a slouch hat on the floor, and the pistol which had been broken over Frederick's head. Seward lay unconscious beside his bed, his bandages running crimson. Frederick, with two gaping holes in his skull, was sinking into a coma. Robinson was severely wounded. Hansell had a deep cut in his side. Augustus's injuries were not serious, but they were bloody. There was blood even on the handles of the doors of the Old Clubhouse. Fragile Mrs. Seward would live only a little over three months after that night of horror. Fanny would be dead in a year and a half.

William Bell, aghast at the stranger's sudden attack on Mr. Frederick, had dashed down the stairs and into the street, hallooing murder. General Augur's headquarters were next door, at the corner of Fifteen-and-a-half and Pennsylvania Avenue, but Bell could not find the guard. Possibly the routine had been upset because the building had been damaged by fire two weeks before, and Augur had been occupying temporary headquarters on Fourteenth Street. Three soldiers came running out, as Bell pelted back to the Old Clubhouse. He saw Paine mounting his horse, and he shouted to the soldiers, but they did not go in pursuit. Paine rode away so slowly that Bell was able to keep after him on foot as far as I Street, where he lost sight of him. When the servant returned to the house, Major Seward was standing at the front door with a pistol. Augustus seems to have been extraordinarily slow of comprehension. He had been in a fog during his struggle with Paine, and, until he spoke with Bell, he had still not realized that the man who had turned his home into a shambles was an assassin.

A crowd was gathering around the mansion. Physicians, hastily summoned, raced up the stairs. Soldiers and citizens pushed through the door of the Old Clubhouse. Representatives of foreign legations hurried in with anxious inquiries. By the time Gideon Welles got over from the north side of Lafayette Square, the office and the big lower hall were thronged. Two frightened servants were holding the people back from the stairs. They seemed relieved to see Welles, and let him go up.

Stanton, after making a speech to the serenaders, was undressing, when a man came to his door with the news that the President was shot, that Seward was murdered. Humbug, Stanton told his wife; he had left Seward only an hour ago. But people came rushing in with wild and dreadful stories. Stanton took a hack to Seward's house, entering the bedroom almost as soon as Welles.

Surgeon General Barnes had been sent for, but he was late in coming. As he was passing Willard's, an officer had told him that the President had been shot, and, before hurrying to the White House, he had stopped at his office to get assistance. There he had found the call to attend Seward, and supposed the other report a mistake. He was dressing Frederick's injuries when a frightened Negro hack driver came to the door with an insistent summons to Tenth Street.

The city shook with rumors of murder in the streets. Newcomers told the crowd around Seward's house that the President was dying. Welles had scoffed at the improbable tales brought by the messenger who had called him, but now he had seen Seward, unconscious on his scarlet bed. As they went down the stairs, he questioned Stanton, who told him that the rumor about the President was true. He had seen a man who had been at Ford's Theatre.

In the lower hall, Quartermaster General Meigs begged Stanton not to go to the President. Others pressed around, remonstrating with the War Secretary. Welles thought that Stanton hesitated, and he urged him impatiently through the crowd to the carriage. Meigs got in with him. Eckert posted up on horseback, to protest against Stanton's exposing himself. Meigs called for an escort of soldiers. At last the carriage started, and through the traffic of running people the Secretaries of War and of the Navy drove into the mutter of the mob in Tenth Street.

A NEWSPAPERMAN picked up a silver-mounted pistol from the floor of the double box at Ford's. There was a tear in the Treasury flag that draped the railing, and a spur had fallen on the stage. Blood darkened the buttoned-in back of the rocking chair which Harry Ford admired.

When the President had been carried across the street, when the surging aisles were empty and the frightened actors had slipped away, Ford's settled into a dreary disuse which no morning rehearsal would enliven. Never again would the orchestra play, or the footlights flare as the curtain rose. A vast, inanimate accomplice, the playhouse was marked with guilt. Mr. Hess dashed off a telegram to Leonard Grover in New York. "President Lincoln shot tonight in Ford's Theatre. Thank God it wasn't ours." In the streets, the mob was yelling, "Burn the theatre!"

A sullen dawn dimmed the bleak gaslight after a night of such horror as Washington had never known—the shuddering fear of secret assassins, creeping with knife and pistol through the city.

The entire Cabinet had been wiped out, the people heard; Johnson was another victim; Grant had been murdered on the train. Men wept and cursed and seized their arms, while the long roll beat in the barracks and the startled troops turned out. All night, patrols pounded through the streets, and guards stood tense at the homes of the Government officials.

Rain beat on waiting crowds, as in the early morning the dignitaries filed out of a little bedroom in an obscure lodginghouse in Tenth Street. A doctor laid silver half-dollars on Lincoln's eyelids. Mrs. Lincoln was led to her carriage, crying, "Oh that dreadful house! that dreadful house!" at the sight of Ford's. At seven-thirty, the bells tolled, and the flags drooped to half-mast. A long coffin was edged down the narrow lodginghouse steps. A group of army officers, walking bareheaded, followed Lincoln to the White House. Along the route, men, women and children stood in a silence broken only by the noise of sobs and the tramp of the soldiers' feet.

Washington seemed stunned, paralyzed by a pistol shot. There were guards on all the roads that led from town. Market wagons, milk carts and mail riders were turned back from the suburbs. Drinking places had been shut by the police. Government departments and business houses were closed. Theatres and music halls canceled their engagements. Concerts and social functions were postponed. Societies called meetings to arrange for participation in the funeral services.

The community felt the disgrace of the crimes, and hastened to disown them. The city councils assembled to eulogize the dead President, and to arrange to wear mourning badges, and cause the buildings of the corporation to be draped in mourning. They also passed a bill offering a reward of twenty thousand dollars for the murderers. Another reward of ten thousand was announced by General Augur on behalf of the Department of Washington.

At an early hour, the gala decorations began to disappear behind lengths of black. The columns of the White House were shrouded, and somber folds were looped on the Federal buildings, and on residences and places of business in all parts of town. Sorrow seemed universal among the poor. Hovels and huts had their scraps of black cloth or ribbon. On the Avenue before the White House, hundreds of colored people stood wailing in the rain.

"Oh, Mr. Welles, who killed my father?" Tad sobbed, as the Secretary of the Navy came down the stairs of the mansion. Welles and his companion, Attorney General Speed, could not restrain their tears. They did not know how to give the boy a satisfactory answer.

All Washington, by this time, knew the answer. Actors and members of the audience had recognized Booth, as he jumped from the box and ran across the stage, and many witnesses had identified him before midnight. His name, however, did not appear in the first orders and dispatches. The guards who watched the roads and the troopers scattered at dawn along the Virginia side of the Potomac had been directed to arrest any suspicious person who tried to leave the city. The announcement of Booth's identification was nearly the only definite fact to emerge from a maze of hearsay. Cavalry and mounted police went galloping into Maryland to search for him. Because of a fancied resemblance to Booth, a man just arrived from Kansas was arrested on Saturday morning. There was a taint and a dreadful importance in having been his associate. During the night, police had paid a visit to the Surratt house. There were rumors that John Surratt was "the man who cut Mr. Seward." Weichmann went early to police headquarters to aid in the investigation. In her sister's fancy house on Ohio Avenue, Ella Turner took chloroform. Booth's picture was under her pillow, and she did not thank the doctors who revived her.

A name, bright with gaiety and talent, had overnight become that of an outcast. That the actor had murdered the President on his own responsibility seemed too fantastic to be believed. People sprang to the conclusion that Booth and his unknown accomplices were the agents of a powerful organization, which had instigated a program of murder, which still might strike again. Memories of the enemy's conspiracies, to spread revolt in the Union, to deliver prisoners of war and fire Northern cities, flashed hot and bitter in men's minds. Behind the figure of Booth loomed the Confederacy, plotting, since force of arms had failed, to disrupt the Federal Government by assassination.

The Washington press was quick to charge the South with the blame for Lincoln's murder. The *Chronicle,* recently filled with conciliation and forgiveness, declared in an editorial written at dawn that treason had culminated in this crime. It foretold a widespread demand for vengeance on the authors of the rebellion. The *Star* spoke of "the terrible act committed by the conquered South yesterday, through its representative, the assassin of President Lincoln." Even the *Constitutional Union,* which had been antagonistic to Lincoln, now talked of retribution for the honored dead, and called on God to save the republic.

Under a subdued and mourning aspect, the capital was agitated by a mob spirit of revenge. Men stood murmuring on every crape-hung corner, and loitered in groups before the shop windows where Lincoln's portrait was displayed. Their hostility drove Confederate soldiers into hiding. The only gray uniforms to be seen, those of prisoners under guard, started riots. The appearance of two Confederate officers, escorted by cavalry, shattered the quiet of Sunday afternoon. At first, there were shouts of "guerrilla"—some said Mosby himself—but the cry soon changed to "Booth." There was such a clamor outside the provost marshal's office that Senator Hale and General Spinner were sent for. They vainly addressed the mob with persuasions to disperse. Eventually, the Confederates were whisked through a rear door to the security of the Old Capitol. A similar demonstration occurred on Monday, when one prisoner was mistaken for Booth, and another for John Surratt. With yells of "Shoot them! Hang them!" a crowd surged around the prisoners, whose seizure was prevented only by the firmness of the guard of Veteran Reserves.

Prudent secessionists hung mourning on their houses. Only a few reckless persons dared to oppose the popular feeling, and found themselves in jail. Among these were several women of Hooker's Division, charged with exulting over the murder of the President, and pulling mourning emblems from the windows of their neighbors. A warrant was issued for the arrest of Miss Mary Jane Windle, chronicler in prewar days of the doings of Washington society, who had recently returned after a long absence in the South. Miss Windle was accused of maliciously tearing down flags from her boardinghouse, and throwing them into the street. At the Mission Church in the First Ward, a preacher made some slurring comment on Lincoln in the course of his Sunday sermon. Veteran Reserves in the congregation seized him, and dragged him from the pulpit. Outside the church, he was put under arrest.

For the most part, the capital's ministers, hastily revising their Easter sermons, exhorted their congregations to resignation to bereavement. The sun shone bright, and birds sang in the blossoming trees, as people trailed dejectedly to church to hear the soothing platitudes. One hospital nurse would remember the smell of the lilacs, and the weeping soldiers coming to ask for bits of crape and ribbon to fasten on their sleeves. At the New York Avenue Presbyterian Church, the President's pew was draped in black, and Dr. Phineas D. Gurley spoke of the chastening hand of a wise God. The Unitarians, however, heard a challenging discourse from their pastor, Dr. William H. Channing. He denounced the ruling class of the South, saying that they must either totally submit, or be brought as criminals before the law, and be condemned as guilty. His listeners repeatedly broke into applause, and several persons muttered "Hang them!"

The agitation was calmed by no official counsels of moderation and suspended judgment. In the despair and hysteria of Friday night, Mr. Stanton had grasped the reins of Government in his strong and trembling hands. He had been told of a prowler, skulking at his house on K Street, and believed that he, too, had been marked for assassination. Fearful of a vast murderous conspiracy, he had called Grant back to defend the capital. At the prisons he ordered special vigilance over rebel officers and soldiers. As though an invading army were marching on the city, he directed that the forts be alert and the guns manned. But, though the Secretary of War was frightened, he was not impotent. The wheels of Government turned, as he dictated his orders. All night, while Lincoln lay dying, mounted couriers had dashed from the boardinghouse to the War Department. With blanched faces, the telegraph operators had sent out Mr. Stanton's dispatches. They spread the terror of Washington over the nation, but they also carried the reassurance of authority in the crisis.

On Saturday morning, the Union had a new President. Andy Johnson, hastily inducted into office in his guarded rooms at the Kirkwood House, was a silent figurehead. Seward lay speechless on his bed. Stanton was still in power. He was convinced that the crimes had been deliberately planned by the rebels to avenge the South and aid the Confederate cause, and he would turn the great resources of the War Department into proving it.

Stanton's rage against the South was to become remarkable for its blind and passionate persistence; but on the day that Lincoln died it was representative of the wild revulsion of feeling that swept the capital and the nation. Even Grant was swayed by prejudice. On Saturday afternoon, he telegraphed to Richmond, "Extreme rigor will have to be observed whilst assassination remains the order of the day with the rebels." Although he later changed his mind, his first drastic order was to arrest the Confederate officials in Richmond, as well as all paroled officers who had not taken the oath of allegiance. The virulent reaction of the Federal army was reflected in a dispatch from General Horatio Wright, advising that rebel officers within control of the Army of the Potomac should be closely confined with a view to retaliation on their persons.

The frail shoots of good will to the defeated enemy had been blasted in a night. All over the Union, a hoarse cry of vengeance sounded a discordant requiem for Lincoln.

The preparations for the funeral were a somber diversion which served partially to abate the excitement in the capital. The services, set for noon on Wednesday in the East Room, were to be followed by a grand procession to the Capitol. The War Department issued orders for the military escort, and Lamon's office nominated the marshals for the civic procession of dignitaries, delegations, societies and clergy. Boswell's Fancy Store advertised its readiness to make up sable sashes, batons and rosettes. Shops sold quantities of black gloves, crape for hat and arms, and badges, adorned with Lincoln's portrait. Large supplies of mourning draperies had been rushed down from New York, and were offered at bargain prices. Every train disgorged a load of visitors. Tenth Street swarmed with sight-seers, staring at Ford's, which was guarded by soldiers, and invading the lodginghouse to see the room where Lincoln had died.

On Monday afternoon, the embalmers had finished, and Lincoln lay in his new black suit in the White House guest room. Officials came to bow beside the four-poster bed, whose pillow was strewn with flowers. Mrs. Lincoln did not leave her room. As though in death Lincoln belonged not to his family, but to the nation, the funeral arrangements were made with official impersonality. The total expenses amounted to thirty thousand dollars.* Carpenters and costumers had come and gone past the military guard around the White House. In the middle of the East Room towered a catafalque, festooned with black silk. The domed canopy, lined in white, rose so high that it had been necessary to remove the central chandelier. The two remaining chandeliers were swathed in mourning. The frames of the mirrors were similarly darkened, and white material was stretched over the glass. A series of steps, which had been built around three walls of the room, were covered in black, as were also the chairs provided for the press. Black draperies, concealing the lace and crimson damask at the windows, gave the room the gloom of a vault. When all was ready, Lincoln's body was laid in the casket, braided and studded and starred with silver.

On Tuesday, Lincoln lay in state on the catafalque in the East Room, just as he had dreamed. Officers stood, rigid and severe, at his head and feet. The sepulchral light glinted on the veiled mirrors and the silver trimmings of the casket, as the people ascended the steps of the catafalque for a lingering look at his dim face. There were many soldiers and colored folk in the sorrowful procession which all day wound through the entrance, through the Green Room, slowly through the East Room, and over the black-draped platform which led from one of the windows. In the late afternoon, when the doors were closed, a long line was still waiting on the Avenue.

The hotels were as crowded as they had been for Lincoln's first inauguration, and it was said that six thousand persons spent Tuesday night in the streets and in depots and outbuildings.

* Detailed accounts paid by the Government are listed in the Appendix.

At sunrise on Wednesday, a Federal salute awakened the capital to the most solemn day in its history. All places of business had been voluntarily closed, and nearly every house was deserted, as families, servants, boarding-house keepers and lodgers hurried to find vantage points from which to view the funeral procession. From the White House to the Capitol, the Avenue was bordered by two thick, dark stripes of humanity. Spectators gathered on roof tops, and weighted trees. Lafayette Square and the Treasury colonnade were packed. As the morning passed, fresh arrivals filled the town to overflowing— soldiers who had managed to slip away from the army, travelers by boat and train, and country people in hay wagons, donkey carts and dearborns.

The sun beamed from a cloudless sky, and a gentle breeze stirred the draperies on the buildings. The hush of the crowds was penetrated by the minor strains of the bands, as they took their places in line. Officers, with mourning knots on their sword hilts, led out the military escort. Black-gloved civilians were forming in every side street. Delegations from outside cities swirled around the City Hall. At noon, the church bells tolled, and the minute guns began to boom.

The press had arrived early in the fragrant stillness of the East Room. Flowers carpeted the platform of the catafalque, and were scattered on the coffin top. A cross of lilies stood at Lincoln's head, and an anchor of roses at his feet. General David Hunter silently paced the room, his buttons and twin stars and crape-hung sword faintly gleaming. Now and then he spoke to the other officers of the guard, before they all went to stand like statues beside the catafalque. The upholsterers softly drove the last nails, and smoothed the draperies, and the guests began to arrive. Tickets had been limited to six hundred, and the Treasury Department, which was in charge of the admissions, had been besieged. Clergymen, governors, mayors and councilmen, and the corporate authorities of Washington took their places on the tiers of steps, together with the Cabinet, the justices, senators and representatives, the diplomatic corps and many officers. President Johnson stood on the lowest step, facing the middle of the coffin, with his hands crossed on his breast. Grant, in white gloves and sash, was seated alone at the head of the catafalque. At the foot sat Robert and Tad and a few Todd relatives. In all the room, there were but seven ladies: Mrs. Welles, Mrs. Stanton, Mrs. Usher, the two daughters of Chief Justice Chase, and Mrs. Dennison and her daughter.

Dr. Gurley preached the funeral sermon, and, when the closing prayer had been spoken, the casket was closed. A detachment of Veteran Reserves carried it to the high, black-canopied hearse, drawn by six gray horses. Propped on the pillows of his bed near a window on Lafayette Square, a sick man vaguely saw the moving, plume-decked structure. Mr. Seward was too weak to understand its meaning, but he would keep a dreamy memory of those black, nodding plumes.

The dirges of the bands mingled with the tolling bells, and the minute guns repeated their methodical punctuation, as the military escort started down the Avenue. Regiments and battalions marched in slow time, with arms reversed and draped banners. Heavy artillery rumbled behind them. Hundreds of army and naval officers went on foot. There was one unforeseen change in the line of march. The Twenty-second Colored Infantry, just landed from Petersburg, found itself unable to proceed up the Avenue from Seventh Street. Wheeling about, the Negro soldiers headed the procession to the Capitol.

Block after block, grief moved along the sidewalks at the sight of the casket, followed by Lincoln's horse, with his master's boots in the stirrups. Dignitaries, delegations and societies filled the wide street, on foot or in their carriages. Thirty thousand people took part in the funeral pageant, which ended with the colored lodges. When Welles drove back along the Avenue after the service at the Capitol, he met the broad platoons, still marching.

For one more day, Lincoln's corpse lay on view in a catafalque under the high dome. The walls were heavily draped, and the pictures and statues were covered, save only the figure of General Washington, on which a black sash was tied. From early morning until dark, soldiers marshaled the visitors into a double line which passed on either side of the casket.

At six on Friday morning, there was another brief service in the Rotunda. Stanton drove up in great haste, attended by Lincoln's guard of cavalry. Grant was present with his staff, and there were other officers, several members of Congress, and the Illinois delegation. Followed by this small cortege, the casket was removed to the railroad depot before Washington was well awake. It was placed on the funeral train, and Willie's smaller coffin, brought from the cemetery vault, was placed at its foot. The officers of the guard of honor, headed by General Hunter, took their places. The Illinois delegation and other friends and political associates climbed aboard. From the railroad yard came a melancholy clangor of engine bells. Crowds, which the early service at the Capitol had been designed to avoid, struggled to pass the lines of soldiers around the depot.

At eight o'clock, the funeral train pulled out of Washington on the slow and circuitous journey which would carry the prairie lawyer home to Springfield. By day and night, along the railroad tracks, in wayside stations and in the pomp and pageant of mourning cities, Lincoln's countrymen would pour forth to do him honor. Seven million people would gaze on his coffin. Over a million and a half would have a fleeting glimpse of his face. Back to the capital, for twelve days more, would come the noise of a nation's weeping. It would echo in a city distracted by changing events, by anger and excitement. On April 15, a new day had dawned in Washington and, after the lull of the obsequies, it blazed forth in noontide heat.

The Republican radicals had wasted no time in hypocritical lamentation for Lincoln. The assassination had done them the double service of removing a merciful Chief Executive and inflaming the country to rage against the Confederacy. A few hours after Lincoln's death, they had gathered in caucus to map out a stringent policy toward the South. The next day, the Committee on the Conduct of the War had called on the new President. "Johnson," said Ben Wade, "we have faith in you. By the gods, there will be no trouble now in running the government."

In the first days after taking office, Johnson accepted Wade as his chief adviser. He was surrounded by anxious politicians, extremist and conservative alike, all frantically contending to influence him and win his favor. Before Lincoln's body left Washington, Johnson was the center of visiting delegations of every kind. The growing crowds of courtiers and suppliants disgusted the friends of the late President. Johnson welcomed all comers, shook their hands, and repetitiously conveyed his view that treason was a crime, and crime must be punished. The radicals were confirmed in their first opinion, that the Tennessee Democrat's accession seemed "a godsend to the country."

The last act of the rebellion was drawing to a close during the third week of April. In North Carolina, Joe Johnston's war-weary soldiers had laid down their arms, and Sherman sent Grant the terms of the surrender. While they were in consonance with Lincoln's ideas, Sherman had exceeded his authority by including political questions in the agreement. His action had a tang of military arrogance. Sherman was warm with pride in his army's exploits, and believed that generals knew more than civilians about making peace, as well as war. Lincoln would have known how to deal with him firmly and tactfully, but Lincoln on April 21 was no more than a sacred image, receiving the reverent homage of Baltimore.

The Cabinet, hastily convened, could not approve the terms. Grant himself did not; but he loved and honored Sherman, and listened with mounting indignation while Stanton denounced his friend. Here was no orderly process of correcting the error in judgment of a brilliant commander, second to none in his services to the Union. Stanton's words were lurid with suspicion of Sherman's motives, even with insinuations of treason.

Attorney General Speed had apprehensions which were reminiscent of McClellan's day—that Sherman, at the head of his army, designed to usurp the powers of the Government. The others did not go so far; but all had been influenced by Stanton. Welles later thought that he understood the reason for their unsteadiness of mind. They had been shocked by information which the War Secretary had recently given them, that there was proof that Jefferson Davis and other Southern officials were involved in the assassination conspiracy. Appalled at learning that high-minded men had connived at murder, the Cabinet was ready to believe anything.

Stanton published the news of Johnston's surrender simultaneously with the announcement that the terms had been rejected by the Government. The story was presented in a form so prejudicial to Sherman that he was unanimously condemned in the press. At best, he was depicted as a simpleton from whom concessions had been adroitly wheedled by the "arch-conspirators," as all Southern leaders were now described. Grant, immediately sent to Sherman's headquarters to supersede him, remained in the background, and Sherman concluded another agreement with Johnston on the same terms as those offered to Lee. But, in his moment of triumph, Sherman's fame had been tarnished, and his great popularity impaired. Peace came at last, shabby and disfigured, under the new regime.

In his determination to implicate the Southern leaders, Stanton had the assistance of his former colleague in Buchanan's Cabinet,

Judge Advocate General Holt, head of the Bureau of Military Justice. Hints of the Government's stand whipped up the ill feeling in Washington. Like a growling accompaniment to mourning, the mutter of hatred had penetrated the solemn lull of the obsequies. Twice during the week, the *Chronicle* had renewed its attack on the Confederate authorities, involving them in the assassination and calling for their blood as atonement for their crimes. Loyal citizens met to protest furiously against the marshals who had been selected for the funeral procession. It was asserted that many of them had been Lincoln's enemies, while in a number of cases their "secret sympathies were understood to be with the infamous rebellion, the prime moving cause of the assassination of our President." A committee was appointed to wait on Lamon, and found that he had left on the funeral train. He had also been away when the obnoxious list was prepared, and Deputy Marshal Phillips attempted to mollify the enraged unionists by taking full blame for the blunder and offering to resign.

Soon after, Stanton publicly declared that Lincoln's murder had been originated in Canada and approved in Richmond. On May 3, a Presidential proclamation announced the connivance of Jefferson Davis, Jacob Thompson, Clement C. Clay and other Southern gentlemen, and offered rewards for their arrest. The names of the officials were blazoned, like those of common criminals, opposite the prices set on their heads. Many, until then incredulous of their guilt, were convinced by the statement that the evidence was in the possession of the Bureau of Military Justice. Davis, for whom one hundred thousand dollars was offered, was the object of scathing attacks. "His unscrupulous hand," said the *Star*, "has guided the assassin's trigger and dagger. . . . The tragedy-cracked player who did the deed . . . was no such criminal as was the cold-blooded politician who laid out the work."

In Washington, as elsewhere in the Union, the proclamation caused a thrill of horror, and inflamed the rage against the South. The shame of its association with crime had made the city vociferously loyal. The members of the city councils, wearing their mourning badges, had organized a group which was raising funds for a local monument to Lincoln. Washington, eager to bury its secessionist past in oblivion, was rudely jarred by the return of a host of former residents from Richmond, the disunionist émigrés of 1861. They

did not appear to feel disgraced, but walked the streets with a comfortable air of home-coming—went into the departments, shook hands
and received welcomes all around. The blood of loyal inhabitants
boiled at the sight. A meeting of the Common Council was the scene
of a violent altercation over "unscrupulous traitors and assassins who
left their homes and business at the threshold of rebellion . . . and
now Judas-like return. . . ." It was proposed that the board resolve,
for the preservation of the public peace, to warn such persons to stay
away from Washington. The resolution, however, was referred to a
committee. Some of the councilmen were opposed to it, while others
thought it futile—"only puffing against the wind." The *Star* took up
the fight against the "National Volunteers Redivivus," recalling their
treacherous activities and railing against their "brassy impudence" in
expecting "to be taken to the arms of loyal citizens whose throats they
hoped to cut." Sectional animosity raged in Washington, and a large
mass meeting was held in front of the City Hall to protest against
the presence of dangerous and defiant rebels.

While pursuing his cherished plan of arraigning the Confederacy
on a murder charge, Stanton had not neglected the actual perpetrators
of the crimes. Behind the mourning scenes of the capital, the War
Department had launched on a program of inquisition and terror, in
which the Metropolitan Police and detectives from other cities participated. Prisons were filled with suspects and witnesses and their
friends and relatives. The haul included liverymen who had rented
horses to Booth and his associates; Ella Turner and other inmates of
the fancy house on Ohio Avenue; the Ford brothers, and actors and
employees of the theatre; Mrs. Surratt and her sister, and the two
girls, Anna Surratt and Honora Fitzpatrick. The most important
arrest, that of Lewis Paine, had been fortuitously made on the night of
April 17, when he returned to the Surratt house after hiding out in
the woods near Fort Lincoln. O'Laughlin had been picked up in
Baltimore the same day, and Sam Arnold was taken into custody at
Fort Monroe. Later in the week after the assassination, Atzerodt was
arrested in his cousin's house in Maryland. These four men and the
sceneshifter, Spangler, were loaded with double irons and thrown
into the hold of monitors anchored off the Navy Yard.

The public, avidly curious about the inquiries and arrests, was
able to learn almost nothing. Scanty newspaper reports testified to the
censorship of the War Department. It was best for the ends of justice,

said the *Star*, that no publicity be given to the facts elicited in the investigations. By publishing that Arnold and Atzerodt had been brought to Washington and committed to "a safe place," newspapers earned a reprimand from the War Department, and in subsequent editions printed Colonel Eckert's peremptory request that such publications be not made.

Six days after the assassination, Mr. Stanton proclaimed rewards of fifty thousand dollars for Booth, and twenty-five thousand each for Herold and Atzerodt. Liberal rewards were also offered for information conducing to the arrests. The anxiety under which the War Secretary was laboring was revealed in the language of his proclamation. It dramatically opened with the words, "The Murderer of our Beloved President is still at large!" It closed with an appeal that "the stain of innocent blood be removed from the land," and exhorted "all good citizens to aid public justice. . . ."

This proclamation also announced the harsh authority which the War Department would exercise in the coming trials. Stanton's statement, that all persons harboring or aiding Booth, Atzerodt or Herold would be subject to trial before a military commission and to the punishment of death, forecast the grim fate in store for the accused conspirators themselves. The War Secretary had no intention of relinquishing them to the delays and uncertainties of separate trials by jury in the civil courts of the District. He did not hesitate to prejudge the accused, referring to them as "the above-named criminals" and "the murderers."

The delay in finding Booth was a cause of frantic exasperation, not only to Stanton, but to the people. Flickering rumors of his capture repeatedly lighted up excitement in the capital. As one after another they proved to be false, the despairing belief spread that the large search parties were incompetent, and the assassin had escaped. It was not known that, in jumping from the box at Ford's, Booth had caught his spur in the Treasury flag, and had landed on the stage with a jarring fall which broke his leg. He had been forced to turn out of his way to have the bone set by his Maryland acquaintance, Dr. Samuel Mudd. Almost helplessly crippled, he hid out for many days with Herold in southern Maryland before he succeeded in crossing the Potomac to Virginia.

One cause for the inefficiency of the search was the lack of cooperation among the pursuing forces. Soldiers, police and detectives, organized into a number of independent expeditions, jealously guarded important clues from the knowledge of their competitors. Stanton's offer of prize money sharpened their rivalry, and cupidity brought new batches of detectives, as well as ex-soldiers and adventurers, posting to the capital to join the man hunt.

Immediately after the assassination, Stanton had sent an urgent summons to Colonel Baker, who was on business in New York. Baker said that the War Secretary tearfully greeted him with the words, "My entire dependence is upon you." He did not, however, give any coordinating authority to Baker, who entered the field merely as another investigator. He was cold-shouldered at Augur's headquarters, where he was informed that a positive clue had been obtained and that his services were not required.

Baker did not explain why Stanton tolerated this insolence to the head of the War Department's detective force. According to his two most trusted subordinates, his cousin, Lieutenant L. B. Baker and Lieutenant-Colonel E. J. Conger, their chief was obliged to take up the case from the beginning, "with such slender information as was then in the personal possession of the Secretary of War." Information was slender on the day after Lincoln's death, but there is something ludicrous in the implication that Stanton was also being snubbed by Augur and his officers.

Colonel Baker did not make much progress during the first week. He sent a few detectives on an unavailing trip to lower Maryland, and he circulated some hand bills, containing photographs and descriptions of Booth and Surratt, and offering a reward of thirty thousand dollars, of which twenty thousand was the amount already announced by the Washington city authorities. Other cities and States were also publishing rewards, and Baker's hand bills were entirely overshadowed by the large sums offered by the War Department.

On Monday, April 24, Baker had information that Booth and Herold had crossed the Potomac, and were in Virginia. The source of this knowledge is mysterious. It certainly did not come from the anonymous colored man, to whom it was ascribed in Baker's own fishy story. However, the Washington provost marshal, Major James R. O'Beirne, who was in charge of one of the search parties, was hot on Booth's trail in Virginia. O'Beirne was at this time recalled, and Baker took charge of the pursuit. The detective chief sent for Conger and

L. B. Baker, both of whom had been officers in the First District Cavalry. Pointing out on a map the place where the fugitives had crossed and the route which, with "quick detective intuition," he expected them to take, he ordered his subordinates to leave by boat for Belle Plain, and scour the country around Port Royal on the Rappahannock. A supporting force of soldiers was necessary, and Colonel Baker was assigned a detachment of the Sixteenth New York Cavalry. Eager, not only for a personal triumph but for a generous cut of the reward, he took the precaution of placing the expedition under the command of Conger and L. B. Baker.

Two days later, Conger reported back. In Baker's ear, he whispered a few words which sent the imperturbable chief of detectives springing to his feet and across the room. Calling a carriage, the two men quickly drove to Stanton's house. The War Secretary was lying on a sofa, when Baker rushed into the room. "We have got Booth," he cried.

Stanton put his hands over his eyes, and lay for a moment in silence. Then he arose and coolly put on his coat. Baker was arranging some articles on a table: two pistols, a knife, a tallow-encrusted compass, a pipe and a small red-leather diary. These were, he explained, the things found on Booth's body. Thus the War Secretary learned that Lincoln's assassin had not been taken alive.

Colonel Conger related the story of the preceding night, when Booth and Herold had been surrounded in a tobacco barn on a farm near Port Royal. One dead and the other a prisoner, they were being brought to Washington on a steamer, which Stanton instructed Baker to meet at Alexandria. Late that night, Herold joined O'Laughlin, Atzerodt and Spangler on the monitor *Montauk*. The body, sewn in a gray army blanket, was placed on a bench on the forward deck. Downstream, the monitor *Saugus* held Paine and Arnold, as well as Dr. Mudd, who had recently been arrested, and Mrs. Surratt, who had been transferred from the Old Capitol.

While Baker was stealing off to Alexandria, Washington had been thrown into an uproar by a rumor that Booth, disguised as a Negro woman on crutches, had entered a building near the Kirkwood House. Soldiers made a house-to-house search of the neighborhood. The story that Booth had injured his leg was being buzzed about Washington, which understood that he had been hurt in falling from his horse. Another leakage of inaccurate official information appeared in the description of his dress, for the War Department had been told that Booth was disguised as a woman.

Next morning, Washington gasped at the headlines, and avidly read the story of Baker's successful pursuit, and Booth's ignominious end in the burning barn. That the assassin had been shot was the cause of general disappointment. Vengeance would have been better satisfied with a living captive. The crowds which rushed to the Navy Yard were strictly excluded. Stanton dreaded that Booth's corpse might be made "a subject of glorification by disloyal persons," and had ordered Baker to place a strong guard on the *Montauk* to prevent Southern sympathizers from securing relics. Barnes, Holt, Eckert and a few other officials were permitted to go aboard. There was an autopsy, and the body was formally identified, photographed and sewn into a sack.

Baker said that, in spite of all precautions, "persons of high position, and some of secession proclivities" succeeded in boarding the *Montauk*. Returning after an absence on shore, the detective chief found them gathered around Booth's body. The seam of the sack had been ripped open, and a lady was in the act of cutting off a lock of the actor's black, curling hair. Baker forcibly wrested the souvenir from her hands, and cleared the visitors from the deck.

Even this dramatic incident would scarcely account for Stanton's excessive anxiety to hide Booth's remains. As though in superstitious fear that the corpse might arise and strike again, the War Secretary ordered an immediate, secret burial. With his cousin, the lieutenant, Colonel Baker snatched the body so suddenly from the *Montauk* that the officers were taken completely by surprise. Not even the commandant of the Navy Yard was informed of the removal, and the box in which he had been ordered to seal the remains was left on board the vessel.

A shallow hole was scraped in the floor of a ground-floor room of the old Penitentiary, used since the outbreak of war as a storehouse for ammunition and other Arsenal property. At midnight, by the light of a single lantern flickering over gun boxes and packing cases, Booth's body was dropped in the hole. After the dirt had been packed down and smoothed over, there was no trace of the interment. The storage room was locked, and the key was delivered to Mr. Stanton. The few men who knew of the burial place were sworn to secrecy.

The sudden disappearance of the body gave rise to wild conjectures. There were rumors that it had been thrown into the swamps around Giesboro' Point, a dumping ground for the carcasses of horses and mules. Other accounts contended that it had been burned, dismembered, sunk in the Potomac. The melodramatic mystification of the public eventually aroused suspicions that the identification of Booth's remains had been a hoax, and that the assassin had actually escaped.

Soon after the burial, the decayed old Penitentiary became a place of notorious importance. The accused conspirators were incarcerated there. Once more the jail in the Arsenal grounds heard the tramp of guards and the rattle of chains, as the eight prisoners, seven men and one woman, were lodged in cells on the third floor. They were transferred to the custody of General Hancock, who had been ordered with strong reinforcements to the command of the defenses of the capital. A special provost marshal for the trial, General John F. Hartranft, guarded the prison with a brigade of soldiers and a detachment of Veteran Reserves. The prisoners were placed in solitary confinement. Their guards were forbidden to converse with them, and they were also under the surveillance of a force of detectives. Every man, on his arrest, had been heavily ironed, hand and foot. In the old Penitentiary, they were manacled with stiff shackles, handcuffs joined by a rigid iron bar.

In his severe treatment of the accused, Stanton had not balked at torture. While they were held on the monitors, he had given directions that "for better security against conversation," their heads should be placed in canvas bags. The male prisoners had been shrouded in heavy, stifling sacks, which extended over the chest, and were tightly tied about the neck and body. They were obliged to push their food through an air hole at the mouth, a difficult feat for blinded and manacled men. They were not permitted to remove the bags even to wash their swollen faces. In the Penitentiary, the bags were changed for tight-fitting hoods, padded with cotton an inch thick. The medical officer of the Arsenal, who was in attendance on the prisoners, feared that the hoods would produce mental derangement, and stated that his representations and those of a specialist on insanity persuaded Stanton to remove the headpieces. This may have been true in the case of other suspects, who the surgeon said were similarly treated in prison, but the accused conspirators wore their hoods throughout the trial, being relieved of them only during the proceedings in the courtroom.

The exacerbated feelings of the time gave the War Department a free hand. The prisoners were regarded as outcasts, beyond the pale of human sympathy. Even secession sympathizers turned away from them. "The rebels," wrote William E. Doster, ". . . eager to think with the triumphing side in a cordial way . . . found, in the appearance of a forlorn lot of conspirators, a most timely subject of common reprobation—a most agreeable means of being identified with the loyal side. . . ." Only the case of Mrs. Surratt aroused uneasiness. The trial of any woman before a military tribunal would have been shocking to the community. Mrs. Surratt bore the record of a blameless character, respectable and devout. She was spared some of the hardships of the male prisoners, but not the relentless prosecution of the War Department. It was the contention of the Bureau of Military Justice that her missing son, John, was second only to Booth in importance in the assassination plot. The boarder, Weichmann, shut up in Carroll Prison and fearful for his own neck, would give evidence implicating John's mother.

Stanton had personally assumed the direction of the investigation. Night after night, he labored until dawn, driven by a fantastic ambition to see the accused condemned and executed before Lincoln's funeral should take place at Springfield. In preparing the case, he worked with Colonel H. R. Burnett, an energetic young judge advocate, who had made such a good record in securing death sentences in the West that he had been summoned to Washington. When he arrived on the day of Lincoln's funeral, Burnett had not found even the evidence against Booth conclusive. A cavalry squad sent out by Provost Marshal O'Beirne was then suspiciously watching Dr. Mudd; and, two days later, a riding boot was found in the physician's house, with Booth's initials inside. The identification of this boot by its maker in New York was, in Burnett's opinion, the first positive proof that Booth was the assassin.

Aside from this point, however, Burnett proved to be no stickler for conclusive evidence. He entered enthusiastically on a case based on the kind of evidence which Colonel Baker could be relied upon to secure—extorted, perverted and, when necessary, manufactured. It was the intention of the prosecution to find the prisoners guilty in a mass trial on the general and loosely worded charge of conspiracy. By this means, participation in the abduction plot was identified with the assassination, and it was possible to involve Mrs. Surratt, as well as Arnold and Dr. Mudd, both of whom could establish that they were not in Washington on the night of April 14. From the articles placed in evidence, Booth's pocket diary was eliminated. The notations plainly showed that the original design had not been murder.

Although Stanton did not succeed in disposing of the defendants in the space of three weeks, preparations for their trial were nearly complete, when on May 4 Washington heard the minute guns and the national salute in honor of the funeral at Springfield. Attorney General Speed had legalized the War Department's procedure with an opinion that the prisoners were lawfully triable before a military commission, and the President had ordered nine officers detailed for this duty. Colonel Baker had assembled his array of witnesses. A room on the third floor of the old Penitentiary had been made ready for the court. Divided lengthwise by three pillars, and poorly ventilated by four grated windows, this apartment's only suitability lay in the fact that it was connected by an iron door with the block of cells in which the prisoners were confined. A narrow, railed platform had been built across this wall for the dock. The room had been freshly whitewashed, carpeted with coconut matting, and provided with tables and chairs and a witness stand.

On May 10, the trial opened, and the charges were read to the prisoners. They were jointly and severally accused of having conspired with Booth, Surratt, Jefferson Davis and other Southern officials to murder Lincoln, Johnson, Seward and Grant. There was a clear case against Paine, who had been identified as Seward's assailant, and against Booth's companion, Herold. Atzerodt was charged with lying in wait for Johnson, with intent to murder. O'Laughlin's junket to see the illuminations had brought on his head the specific accusation of lying in wait for Grant at Stanton's reception. Spangler was charged with having assisted Booth in his preparations at Ford's and in his escape. The death penalty was demanded for all. The prisoners communicated with their counsel in court, whispering through the bars of the dock. All pleaded not guilty, and made motions for separate trials, which were in each instance refused.

That the eight pariahs had been able to secure reputable counsel was remarkable. The most distinguished name was that of Reverdy Johnson, senator from Maryland, who headed the defense of Mrs.

Surratt. Before that court, however, his services were nullified by his Southern sympathies. He soon withdrew, leaving the case to a pair of inexperienced youngsters. General Thomas Ewing, Sherman's brother-in-law, was one of the defense lawyers, and the former provost marshal, Doster, undertook the hopeless task of defending Atzerodt and Paine.

The first intention, to hold the sessions of the commission in secret, had brought outcries of military highhandedness from the press, and the courtroom was presently opened to reporters and to visitors who could procure passes. As the warm May days passed, sightseers congregated at the old Penitentiary.

"A perfect park of carriages stands by the door to the left," wrote George Alfred Townsend, correspondent of the *New York World*, "and from these dismount major-generals' wives in rustling silks, daughters of congressmen attired like the lilies of the milliner, little girls who hope to be young ladies and have come up with 'Pa' to look at the assassins; even brides are here, in the fresh blush of their nuptials . . . they chatter and smile and go up the three flights of stairs to the court-room, about as large as an ordinary town-house parlour."

The spectators were herded in confusion in the space to the left of the pillars, where a long table had been set up for the press. The continual whispering of the ladies caused much annoyance to the reporters, who were intently following the evidence. Counsel for the prisoners sat at the foot of the press table, and were frequently cut off by the crowd from a view of the court, which occupied the space on the other side of the pillars.

At the head of a long, green-covered table sat the president of the commission, General David Hunter, flanked by his fellow-officers, two major-generals, four brigadiers and two colonels, all of unimpeachable loyalty to the Republican party. Hunter, newly released from his post of honor at the head of Lincoln's casket, combined the virtues of radical sympathies and long devotion to the dead President. General Albion P. Howe had been in charge of the artillery depot in Washington. Colonel Clendenin was attached to the Eighth Illinois Cavalry, which had long been stationed at the capital. General Lew Wallace was known for his stand on the Monocacy.

A table adjoining that of the nine officers of the commission was occupied by Judge Advocate General Holt and his two assistants, Colonel Burnett and the Honorable John A. Bingham, who under military rules were members of the court. Bingham was a former Republican congressman from Ohio, and a successful criminal lawyer. He was conspicuous in this trial for his bullying of defense counsel.

The army officers were in full uniform, but, as they negligently lounged in their chairs, they presented an appearance neither correctly military nor solemnly judicial. The whispering ladies had not come to stare at the unimpressive gentlemen who comprised the court. The eyes of all spectators were fixed on the prisoners' dock at the end of the room.

When the iron door opened, there entered a clanking file of seven men, like inhuman figures from a nightmare, with padded hoods for heads. Each was escorted by a soldier in the light-blue uniform of the Veteran Reserves. Two of them—Paine and Atzerodt —had their legs weighted with heavy iron balls, which their guards carried, as they shuffled to their places. As soon as the prisoners were seated, their hoods were pulled off, and the glare of the spring sunlight struck their habitually darkened eyes. Flinching and squinting, with disheveled hair and whiskers, they gave the scribbling reporters inspiration for lurid paragraphs about their wild and bloodthirsty aspect.

Four of the prisoners appeared crushed by their terrible predicament. Atzerodt was demoralized by fear. Sam Arnold sat brooding, inattentive to the proceedings. O'Laughlin, still wearing his gaudy suit, moved his chained feet, and rolled his large black eyes uneasily. Spangler's fingers incessantly twitched up and down his thighs. Davy Herold, on the other hand, smiled vacantly as he pulled at his budding mustache, and seemed pleased at the notice he attracted. Dr. Mudd, whose mild, intelligent face was tragically out of place in the prisoners' dock, looked sure of himself. Paine, a towering figure with muscles bulging under a tight, knitted shirt, sat bolt upright, with his head against the wall, staring at the crowd. His splendid physique and defiant bearing inspired a reluctant admiration in the spectators. Paine's dim brain had mastered one lesson, that of being a good soldier. He had obeyed orders, and he was ready to die.

Last of all in the procession which passed through the iron door was Mrs. Surratt. As she shambled to her place at the end of the row, a little apart from the rest, many people in the courtroom heard the clank of chains under her skirts. Her face, with its expression of motherly innocence, was heavily veiled; she kept it turned to the wall, and fanned herself constantly. One observer reported that she kept up a pitiful moaning and called for water. Mrs. Surratt was ill, greatly weakened by disorders incident to the menopause.

From the beginning, the trend of military justice was plain. The lounging officers of the commission obediently aligned themselves with the prosecution. The trial would go all one way, Stanton's way, toward the ultimate verdict which on a July day would hang Mrs. Surratt, along with Paine, Atzerodt and Herold, on a scaffold in the Arsenal yard, and exile the others to the barren rocks of the Dry Tortugas.

Outside the whitewashed courtroom, the fragrant streets were washed with Union blue. The muster-out of a million men had begun at the end of April. Divisions, awaiting disbandment, were arriving at the capital. Three corps and Sheridan's cavalry had come from the Army of the Potomac, and four corps from Sherman's army. Miles deep, on every slope and ridge, their camps radiated from the city, "musical by day, smoky and twinkling by night. . . ." Many of the soldiers spoke vehemently against the military trial of the conspirators. They had had their fill of killing; and they had given their blood and sweat for another ideal than the justice meted out in the old Penitentiary. On the two days of late May, when they marched in triumph on Pennsylvania Avenue, the streets were so crowded that witnesses could not reach the Arsenal grounds. Fittingly, the military trial was suspended during the grand review of the armies of the republic.

The spirits of the capital had revived, as it made ready for the last and greatest pageant of the war. The emblems of mourning were taken down, and once more the city was bedecked with the national colors. In all the display of celebration, there was but one tragic reminder—the blue regimental flag of the Treasury Guard, which bore, like a battle scar, the tear made by Booth's spur.

Before the White House rose a covered pavilion, decorated with flags and flowers and evergreens and surmounted by the names of the great battles of the war. Here the President and General Grant would review the armies, in company with the Cabinet members, the diplomatic corps and other notables. Across the Avenue was a large stand for governors, members of Congress and the Supreme Court judges. Other stands afforded space for officers of army and navy, the press, invited guests, State delegations and disabled soldiers, and there were ranks of seats extending down both sides of the Avenue.

After four years of teeming crowds, Washington was staggered by the invasion. Lodgings were all engaged, and a party of young ladies from Boston, one of whom would become Mrs. Henry Adams, gladly occupied a single attic room in a house near Willard's. On the day before the grand review the girls drove out to Georgetown, hailing the passing troops, "What regiment are you?" "Michigan!" the boys would shout, or "Wisconsin!" or "Iowa!"

At sunrise on May 23, the spectators were gathering. The sky was blue, a soft breeze stirred the roses, and from the Capitol to the White House the Avenue was aflutter with waving flags and handkerchiefs, when at nine o'clock the signal gun was fired, and General Meade rode out on his garlanded horse at the head of the Army of the Potomac.

The bands blared, and around the corner of the Capitol came the cavalcade of Sheridan's troopers, filling the street for an hour with the racket of hoofs and the clash of sabers and the sharp whine of the bugle call. Before his division of horsemen, scarfed like himself in red, rode the dashing figure of Custer, with long, yellow hair and buckskin breeches, "half general and half scout." The crowd near the White House gasped when a thrown wreath frightened Custer's horse, and the young general galloped madly past the reviewing stand, brandishing his saber in salute. There were cheers, as he reined in and wheeled gracefully back to the head of his column.

After the Provost Marshal General's and the engineer brigades, the first of three proud and famous infantry corps went swinging toward the White House—the Ninth Corps, Burnside's former command, with its badge of a shield, with anchor and cannon crossed. It was followed by the Fifth, which wore the Maltese cross, and the Second, whose emblem was the cloverleaf. Brigades and divisions, preceded by generals and their staffs, marched with mechanical precision. There were mounted artillerymen, with their cannon; pioneers hauling pontoons and boats; gaudy Zouaves; Irish regiments, with green sprigs in their hats. These were but variations in the steady lines of blue, sixty men abreast, in tight-fitting coats and jaunty kepis, their bayonets shining in slanted rows of steel.

Massed on stands and housetops, hanging from windows and balconies, the people had forgotten their disappointments: that Sheridan, sent to the Rio Grande, was not there to ride with his cavalry; that the Sixth Corps—the Greek crosses of grateful memory—

had been detained in Virginia. They sang the choruses of the tunes the bands were playing, "Tramp, Tramp, Tramp" and "When This Cruel War Is Over" and "When Johnny Comes Marching Home." Showers of bouquets and garlands festooned the officers and their horses, banked the cannon, adorned the flags and carpeted the street. The crowds shouted with exultation, which caught, like tears, in their throats. For this was Washington's own army. The capital had seen it grow from a muddle of untrained boys. It had built the city's fortifications, and formed a living barrier in the Virginia mud. It had stopped Lee at Antietam and at Gettysburg, had taken the slow and bloody path to Appomattox. People wept as the battle flags went by, and many rushed into the street to kiss their shredded folds.

Through the plaudits and the flowers and the singing, the brigades marched past the Treasury and swung right to pass the reviewing stand in front of the White House. As corps and division commanders went by, the President and General Grant and Mr. Stanton and the rest stood up, and swords were lowered in salute and the colors dipped. General Meade had taken his place on the reviewing stand, as did the corps commanders in their turn—Merritt and Parke and Griffin and Humphreys, generals who had won high honors in the Wilderness. All day, Meade's spectacled scholar's face looked down on the pageant of the army he had led to victory, with glory overshadowed by Grant. It was late afternoon, when the hoarse cheers were silent, and the last cloverleaf badges of the Second Corps disappeared beyond the reviewing stand.

Early next day, with enthusiasm increased by vivid curiosity, the crowds burst out to welcome the strangers from the West. Again the sun was bright, as the signal boomed and General William Tecumseh Sherman rode on Pennsylvania Avenue. Most onlookers saw for the first time this tall, wiry, nervous soldier, with deeply wrinkled face and grizzled red beard and a smile of unexpected sweetness. His loss of popularity had been transient. That day, Sherman was again a hero, wreathed like his horse in flowers, almost fiercely acclaimed, while the bands played a jubilant new air, "Marching Through Georgia." His countrymen had forgotten the wrong done to his reputation, but Sherman had not. On the reviewing stand, when Stanton held out his hand, Sherman's face clouded and grew scarlet, and he turned brusquely away.

One-armed General Oliver O. Howard, who rode with Sherman,

had once commanded the Eleventh Corps of the Army of the Potomac, and Washington knew him now as commissioner of the Freedmen's Bureau. Until recently he had commanded the Army of the Tennessee, and he had been succeeded by the former congressman, John A. Logan, whom Washington recognized and hailed, as it did Francis P. Blair, Junior, who led the Seventeenth Corps. General H. W. Slocum, commander of the Army of Georgia, had formerly headed the Twelfth Corps of the Army of the Potomac. The few familiar faces were exceptions in a procession of soldiers whose very badges were strange to the capital—the cartridge box of the Fifteenth Corps, the arrow of the Seventeenth, the five-pointed star of the Twentieth, the acorn of the Fourteenth.

Taut with pride in his army, Sherman had feared that it might suffer unfavorable comparison with the Eastern troops. As he topped the rise before the Treasury, he had turned in his saddle for one backward glance, then had ridden on, well satisfied. On review as well as in the field, the soldiers of the West could challenge any army in the world. They wanted the neatness of dress and precision of movement which were McClellan's legacies to the Army of the Potomac on parade. Most of them wore loose blouses instead of trim jackets, black slouch hats in place of tilted kepis. Some were in rags, some wanted shoes. They had a gaunt, rough look about them, like frontier soldiers, taller and bonier than Eastern men. There was something bold, aggressive and magnificent in their rolling, cadenced stride. It seemed to shrink the length of the Avenue to a step, reminding people of the hundreds of miles those long, strong legs had ranged, through swamps and over mountaintops. For a second day, Washington shouted applause, pelting the Westerners with blossoms. Their torn and dingy battle flags bore the legends of Donelson, Shiloh, Vicksburg, Chattanooga, Atlanta, Savannah, the Carolinas—names that told the story of victory for the Union.

There were cheers, too, for novel spectacles, more entertaining than any provided by the ranks of the Army of the Potomac. Mother Bickerdyke, devoted nurse of the Western troops, rode sidesaddle in a calico dress and sunbonnet. Pioneer corps of huge Negroes, with picks and spades and axes, marched ahead of each division. The Bummer Brigade, preceded by a darky on a tiny donkey, was composed of the foragers of Sherman's army. They had a train of wagons loaded with pots and pans and kettles, and pack mules carrying turkeys, geese and chickens. There were cows, sheep, goats, dogs, raccoons, a poodle and a monkey, all flocking along the Avenue with a motley horde of contrabands, who at first tried to preserve their dignity, but were soon grinning with the hilarious spectators.

"Hurrah! Hurrah! We bring the jubilee!" In Georgia and the Carolinas, Sherman's men were reviled as vandals and marauders. Most of the excesses of the march through the Confederacy had been committed by undisciplined stragglers. Yet among the foragers and the troopers, and among the striding infantrymen, too, were some who had danced in the blaze of the pillared mansions of the South. Now the orgy of war was over, and these few went bravely along the Avenue with the rest, as purged as lynchers whose hysteria has been spent. The bummers had become merry boys with innocent trophies of war. They did not brandish their silver spoons, or the rings they had torn from women's fingers.

The sun slanted in the west, as Sherman's men dispersed, to get drunk and disturb the peace of Washington, to fight with Eastern soldiers in the saloons, and blast the name of Stanton. The grand review was ended. For two days, Washington had forgotten the demagogues; forgotten dissensions and military tyranny; ceased to remember the prisoners, sweltering in their hoods, while they waited to be condemned. Once more, the Cause shone bright, as the blue-clad legions swept up Pennsylvania Avenue. The hard young faces and the flags and the brassy, sentimental tunes had revived, like some tender reminiscence of youth, the faith and the courage that had kept the nation united. One hundred and fifty thousand veterans had marched, but even the unimaginative had seen a greater passing. The decimated regiments, the youthful appearance of the general officers, the scarcity of the field officers—all had been reminders of the shadowy army of the Union dead, nearly half a million strong. In unsubstantial ranks, they seemed to form behind the ragged flags: nameless boys who had drilled and caroused in Washington; white-haired Mansfield and Edwin Sumner; Kearny, with his empty coat sleeve; Wadsworth, fingering his grandfather's sword. And on the reviewing stand, behind the concrete shapes of Andy Johnson and the beaming notables, another misty figure seemed to rise, and Lincoln's face look kindly down on the pomp of the Union's triumph.

In that golden light of afternoon, a fanciful man might have seen other ghosts on Pennsylvania Avenue. There, in some grand review of memory, passed a parade of holiday soldiers, profiteers, foreign adventurers, bounty jumpers, prisoners in butternut, spies, detectives and harlots. Mr. Buchanan took his constitutional with his head drawn stiffly to one side. General Scott lumbered by, supported by two young aides. Anxious McDowell trudged obscurely on his errands. McClellan posted through the dust, with his staff hard-pressed to follow him. Blenker flaunted his red-lined cape, and Stone went looking for justice. John Pope posed in his saddle, the military idol of an hour. Among the madams in their carriages and the painted girls on horseback, went haughty Mrs. Greenhow, and gay Belle Boyd, and Mrs. Lincoln, with madness in her eyes. Living and dead, the wind of time had blown them all from Washington. In the streets were only tired people, wandering home through dust and manure and trampled garlands.

Major French had rather regretted the decision to hold the grand review. Washington had had excitement enough, he thought; he would be glad when the city again subsided into "its old jog trot way of life." But French was an aging man. The old jog trot would not come again in Washington. It had vanished forever with the pleasant provincial society, the grinning slaves and the broad-brimmed hats of the planter-politicians. Not in the bustle of Yankee efficiency had war left its supreme mark on Washington, not in the tumbling contraband huts, or the wreckage of men in the big white hospitals; but in the great centralization of Federal authority which had transformed a country town, reserved for the business of Government, into the axis of the Union. The capital of a reconstructed country would not yield an unblemished page for the history books. In days to come, a moral man would find more cause for sadness there than in the tragic streets of Richmond. But, North and South, there was strength in this conglomerate people, at once willful and steadfast. With the tenacity which had carried it through four years of internal war, the country would survive the bitterness of peace. Out of pain and chaos and corruption, Washington was securely established as the capital of a lusty nation; and no one, looking on the public buildings, spoke of the ruins of antiquity any longer.

In the warmth of the late spring days of 1865, the city felt the rush of the receding tide of the armies. For a little time, it suffered racket and thronging men and the uproar of Sherman's crazy fellows. Still, for a space, feet tramped and wagons rumbled, and the bivouacs glinted like fireflies on the darkening hills. War Department clerks were totting up muster and pay rolls. Day after day, the cheering troops departed. The countryside began to wear the aspect of a deserted fairground, and quiet descended on the city's battered streets.

All over the nation, in blue uniforms and gray, soldiers were going home: to take up the threads of small ambitions; to know their wives and kiss strange babies fathered on furlough; to ride their horses to the store and mill, and hitch them to the buggy and the plow. Experts whose skills were useless, they must forget the lessons they had mastered; think of guns as things to shoot at quail and squirrels, and of artillery as a salute for Independence Day; remember discipline and obedience as transitory virtues, foreign to the American way of individual enterprise.

Across the Potomac, the guns had fallen silent. The guards were gone from the Washington bridges. Virginians were no longer enemies, but farmers who trundled their crops to the city markets. Rich with the wastage of armies, the perennial fields were green. On the Capitol dome, Armed Freedom rested on her sheathed sword.

Appendix

Bills for President Lincoln's Funeral

PAID BY THE COMMISSIONER OF PUBLIC BUILDINGS

To Drs. Brown and Alexander
To Embalming remains of Abraham Lincoln late President of
the United States .... $ 100.00
To 16 Days services for self and assistant at $10.00 per day 160.00

$ 260.00

To Sands & Harvey
To coffin covered with fine Broadcloth lined with fine white
Satin & silk trimmed with fine mountings heavy Bullion fringe
& tassells, Lead inside lining fine silver plate & walnut outside
Box for Abraham Lincoln, late President of U. S. $1,500.00
700 yds white silk at 3.75 pr. yd 2,625.00
257 yds. black silk at 3.50 .... 899.50
132 yds. white cambric at 1.00 .... 132.00
90 boxes fine crape at 7.50 per box 675.00
24 yds white swiss at 1.50 yd 36.00
158 pair blk kid gloves at 3.00 .... 474.00
126 pair white silk gloves at 1.00 .... 126.00
84 pair black silk gloves at 1.00 ....   84.00
170 boxes white thread at 3.25 per 552.50
Removing remains of Willie 10.00
23 days attendance 3 men at 5.00 per day each 345.00

$7,459.00

To John Alexander, Dr., Penna. Avenue, between 12th and 13th
Sts.
Putting front of Presidents [House] in Mourning .... $ 50.00
Putting East Room in Mourning 30.00
Upholstering Catafalque in East Room 75.00
Upholstering funeral Car 50.00
Upholstering Rail Road Car 85.00

$ 290.00

Bought of George R. Hall
To making Hearse body [and] Burnishing .... $ 350.00

To A. Jardin
For flowers for the Funeral of the President April 18, 1865:
Rose buds .... $ 9.00
Other white flowers 1.00

$ 10.00

1865. To Phillip Ghegan Dr.
April 18th For Flowers for decorations for funeral of the Presi-
dent of the United States ....$ 20.00

Other Incidental Bills

To James W. Callam 1865 April 14th.
Articles furnished on the occasion of the assassination of the
late President viz.—
3 Packages Taylors Pat. Lint. ...... $ 3.00
2 Pounds Ground Mustard 2.00
6 Oz. Tinct. Camphor (ad) ...... .90

$ 5.90

Bought of Harper & Mitchell [Mourning for Mrs. Lincoln]
1 Mourning dress & trimmings ...... $ 60.00
1 Mourning Shawl 25.00
1 Crape Veil 10.00
5 yds. Blk. Crape 4.00 per yd 20.00
Gloves & Hdkfs 7.50
5 pr. Hose 5.00
1 Crape Bonnet 15.00

$ 142.50

To B. H. Stinemetz,
Apr. 18
2 Silk Hats for Coachmen at 8.00 each ...... $ 16.00
Mourning Bands for same 1.00
1 Silk Hat for Capt Robt Lincoln 10.00
Mourning Band for same ...... .75
Apr. 21
1 Blk felt Hat for Tad Lincoln 4.50
Mourning Band for same ...... .50

$ 32.75

To Elizabeth Kickey [Keckley]
To Services as first Class Nurse & attendant on Mrs. Lincoln
from April 14th to May 26th, 1865. 6 weeks at $35.00 per
week ...... $ 210.00
Traveling & incidental expenses in attending Mrs. Lincoln to
her home in Chicago Ill & return trip to Washington 100.00
Amount expended in requisite mourning apparel 50.00

$ 360.00

Chronology of the Main Events

1861

Apr. 13—Surrender of Fort Sumter

Apr. 15—Presidential proclamation, calling out State militia, and summoning a special session of Congress

Apr. 17—Ordinance of secession adopted by the Virginia convention

Apr. 18—Harper's Ferry abandoned by Federals

Apr. 19—Lincoln proclaims blockade of the Confederate States from South Carolina to Texas

—Sixth Massachusetts reaches Washington after fighting a mob in Baltimore

Apr. 20—Railroad communications with the North severed by Marylanders, isolating Washington

Apr. 25—Seventh New York reaches Washington, the vanguard of many militia regiments arriving via Annapolis, Maryland

Apr. 27—Lincoln extends blockade to include Virginia and North Carolina

—Lincoln suspends writ of *habeas corpus* along the military line from Washington to Philadelphia

May   3—President's proclamation calling for three years' volunteers, and increasing the Army and Navy

May   8—Richmond made the capital of the Confederate States

May 10—Lincoln suspends writ of *habeas corpus* on portion of Florida coast

May 13—Railroad service with the North resumed by way of Baltimore

—Union troops occupy Baltimore

May 23—Virginia votes to ratify secession

May 24—Federals take possession of Alexandria and the Virginia heights and shore opposite Washington, and begin fortifications for the protection of the capital

May 27—McDowell takes command in northeastern Virginia

June 10—Harper's Ferry abandoned by the Confederates

—Engagement at Big Bethel, Virginia

July   2—Lincoln suspends writ of *habeas corpus* from Philadelphia to New York

July   4—First Session of 37th Congress assembles

July 11 —13—Federals under McClellan win victories in western Virginia

July 16—Federals under McDowell begin advance on Confederate position at Manassas

July 21—Federals routed at battle of First Bull Run or Manassas

July 27—McClellan assumes command of Union forces in Washington and Virginia

Aug. 6—Confiscation Act passed by Congress, seizing property of insurgents, including slaves

—Congress adjourns

Aug. 29—Forts Hatteras and Clark, North Carolina, surrender to the Federals

Aug. 30—Martial law and emancipation of slaves proclaimed by Frémont in Missouri

Sept. 11—Lincoln revokes Frémont's proclamation

Oct. 21—Federal defeat at Ball's Bluff, Virginia
Nov. 1—Scott's resignation accepted and McClellan made commander-in-chief
Nov. 7—Port Royal, South Carolina, taken by the Federals
Nov. 8—Mason and Slidell, Confederate envoys to Great Britain and France, seized on the British steamer *Trent*
Dec. 2—Second session of 37th Congress assembles
Dec. 9-10—Senate and House resolve on the appointment of a joint committee to inquire into the conduct of the war
Dec. 28—Mason and Slidell surrendered by the Government

1862

Jan. 19—Federal victory at Mill Springs, Kentucky
Feb. 6—Federals capture Fort Henry, Tennessee
Feb. 7—Federals capture Roanoke Island, North Carolina
Feb. 16—Fort Donelson, Tennessee, surrenders to Federals
Feb. 25—Confederates evacuate Nashville, Tennessee
Mar. 6-8—Federal victory at Pea Ridge, Arkansas
Mar. 8-9—Confederate ironclad *Merrimac* (re-christened the *Virginia*) destroys Union ships in Hampton Roads, but is forced to retire by the ironclad *Monitor*
Mar. 9—Confederate forces abandon Manassas, withdrawing south
Mar. 11—McClellan removed from chief command
Mar. 17—The Army of the Potomac begins to embark for Fort Monroe
Mar. 23—Federals repulse Stonewall Jackson's attack at Kernstown, Virginia
Apr. 2—McClellan arrives at Fort Monroe to begin campaign of Virginia Peninsula
Apr. 3—Recruiting for volunteers discontinued in every State by order of Secretary Stanton
Apr. 4—McDowell's corps detained for the protection of Washington
Apr. 5—McClellan lays siege to Yorktown, Virginia
Apr. 6-7—Battle of Shiloh or Pittsburg Landing, Tennessee
Apr. 7—Federals take Island Number 10 in the Mississippi
Apr. 16—Slavery abolished in the District of Columbia by act of Congress
Apr. 25—New Orleans captured by a Federal naval expedition
May 4—Yorktown evacuated by Confederates
May 5—Battle of Williamsburg on the Peninsula
May 8—Jackson wins victory in mountains west of the Shenandoah Valley
May 9—Hunter proclaims the emancipation of slaves in the Department of the South
     —Confederates evacuate Norfolk, Virginia
May 11—Confederates blow up the *Merrimac* (*Virginia*)
May 18—McClellan receives word that McDowell's corps has been ordered to march to his assistance
May 23—Jackson takes Front Royal in the Valley
May 24—McDowell's advance suspended
May 25—Jackson routs the Federals at Winchester
May 30—Federals occupy Corinth, Mississippi
May 31—June 1—Battle of Fair Oaks or Seven Pines on the Peninsula
June 6—Stanton resumes recruiting

June 8–9—Jackson defeats the Federals at Cross Keys and Port Republic, and escapes from the Valley
June 20—Slavery prohibited in the territories by act of Congress
June 26—Pope placed in command of the Army of Virginia
June 26–July 2—Battles of the Seven Days culminate in the retreat of the Army of the Potomac to the James River
July 11—Halleck made commander-in-chief
July 14—Pope joins his command
July 17—Congress passes act authorizing a draft of State militia, and empowering the President to accept Negroes for military and naval duty
        —Congress passes second Confiscation Act
        —Congress adjourns
July 22—Halleck arrives in Washington
Aug. 3—Halleck orders McClellan to withdraw the Army of the Potomac from the Peninsula
Aug. 9—Federals defeated at Slaughter (Cedar) Mountain, Virginia
Aug. 14–16—McClellan's army withdraws from Harrison's Landing
Aug. 28–30—Battles of Gainesville and Groveton precede Second Bull Run, in which the Federals, under Pope, are routed
Sept. 1—Battle of Chantilly, Virginia
Sept. 2—Pope relieved, and McClellan placed in command of all troops around Washington
Sept. 4–5—Confederates cross the Potomac and invade Maryland
Sept. 14—Battle of South Mountain, Maryland
Sept. 15—Harper's Ferry surrenders to Confederates
Sept. 17—Battle of Antietam or Sharpsburg, Maryland
Sept. 18–19—Confederates retire across the Potomac
Sept. 22—President issues preliminary proclamation of emancipation of slaves of rebels, to take place January 1, 1863
Sept. 24—President suspends the writ of *habeas corpus* for all persons arrested by military authority
Oct. 8—Battle of Perryville, Kentucky
       —Galveston, Texas, captured by Federals
Oct. 10–12—Confederates raid Pennsylvania
Oct. 26–Nov. 1—McClellan crosses the Potomac into Virginia
Nov. 2—Lee begins to interpose his army between the Federals and Richmond
Nov. 5—McClellan relieved of command of the Army of the Potomac, and replaced by Burnside
Dec. 1—Third session of 37th Congress assembles
Dec. 11–12—Army of the Potomac crosses the Rappahannock to attack Lee's forces, strongly fortified at Fredericksburg
Dec. 13—Army of the Potomac defeated at Fredericksburg
Dec. 31—West Virginia admitted as the thirty-fifth State of the Union
       —Battle of Murfreesboro' or Stone River begins

1863

Jan. 1—Emancipation Proclamation
       —Confederate forces retake Galveston, Texas
Jan. 1–3—Battle of Murfreesboro'

Jan.   3—Failure of expedition against Vicksburg, Mississippi
Jan. 20—Burnside begins his "mud-march"
Jan. 25—Resignation of Burnside accepted, and Hooker appointed to command
        the Army of the Potomac
Mar.   3—Congress passes the Enrollment Act
Mar.   4—Congress adjourns
Apr.   7—Federals attack Fort Sumter without success
May   2-4—Army of the Potomac defeated at Chancellorsville
May   22—Grant fails to take Vicksburg by storm and determines on a siege
June   3—Lee's army begins movement to invade the North
June 15-26—Confederate troops cross the Potomac
July 1-3—Army of the Potomac victorious at Gettysburg, Pennsylvania
July   4—Fall of Vicksburg
July   8—Fall of Port Hudson, Louisiana
        —Federals begin siege of Charleston, South Carolina
July 13—Lee's army retreats into Virginia
July 18—Federals repulsed at Fort Wagner outside Charleston
Aug. 17-24—Fort Sumter heavily bombarded
Sept. 2—Knoxville, Tennessee, occupied by Union forces
Sept. 7-8—Federals take Fort Wagner
Sept. 15—President suspends writ of *habeas corpus* throughout the Union
Sept. 19-20—Federals defeated at Chickamauga, Tennessee
Nov. 23-25—Federal victory at Chattanooga, Tennessee
Nov. 26—First national observance of Thanksgiving
Dec.   7—First session of 38th Congress assembles
Dec.   8—Presidential proclamation of amnesty to Confederates who return to
        their allegiance

1864

Feb. 20—Federal expedition defeated at Olustee, Florida
Mar.   9—Grant made lieutenant-general
Mar. 12—Grant made commander-in-chief
Apr.   8—Federal defeat at Sabine Cross Roads, Louisiana, forecasts the failure
        of the Red River expedition
Apr. 12—Confederates capture Fort Pillow, Tennessee, and massacre the Negro
        garrison
May   4—Army of the Potomac crosses the Rapidan
        —Western armies advance into Georgia
May   5-12—Battles of the Virginia Wilderness
May   9-July 17—Almost daily battles in Georgia in Sherman's slow advance
        toward Atlanta
May   15—Federals defeated at New Market in the Shenandoah Valley
May   16—Butler suspends his advance on Richmond and bottles up the Army
        of the James in entrenchments at Bermuda Hundred
May   31—Frémont nominated for President by a convention of Republican
        bolters
June   3—Battle of Cold Harbor, Virginia
June   7—National Union convention renominates Lincoln for President, select-
        ing Andrew Johnson of Tennessee for Vice-President

June 12–16—Army of the Potomac moves south of the James
June 16–18—Federals assault Petersburg, Virginia, without success, and Grant
        determines on a siege
June 19—U. S. Steamer *Kearsage* sinks Confederate cruiser *Alabama* off the
        coast of France
June 28—Congress repeals the Fugitive Slave Law
July 2–3—Early leads Confederate forces down Shenandoah Valley
July 4—Lincoln pockets the drastic congressional reconstruction bill
        —Congress adjourns
July 9—Battle of the Monocacy in Maryland delays Early's advance
July 11—Early's army arrives before the Washington fortifications
        —Three brigades of the Sixth Corps reach the capital
July 12—Three more brigades of the Sixth Corps reach Washington
        —Battle of Fort Stevens
        —Early's forces begin to retire
July 13—Early escapes across the upper Potomac into Virginia
July 20–28—Battles before Atlanta
July 30—Explosion of Federal mine at Petersburg
        —Confederates burn Chambersburg, Pennsylvania
Aug. 5—Federal victory in Mobile Bay
Aug. 29—Democratic convention nominates McClellan and Pendleton for
        President and Vice-President
Sept. 1–2—Fall of Atlanta
Sept. 19–22—Sheridan defeats Early at Winchester and Fisher's Hill
Sept. 22—Frémont withdraws from the Presidential contest
Oct. 19—Battle of Cedar Creek ends in decisive victory by Sheridan over Early
Oct. 31—Nevada admitted as the thirty-sixth State of the Union
Nov. 8—Lincoln re-elected President
Nov. 15—Sherman begins his march to the sea
Dec. 5—Second session of 38th Congress assembles
Dec. 10—Sherman's army arrives before Savannah
Dec. 15–16—Confederates routed at Nashville, Tennessee
Dec. 21—Fall of Savannah

1865

Jan. 15—Fort Fisher, North Carolina, captured by Federals
Jan. 31—Passage of Thirteenth Amendment to the Constitution, abolishing
        slavery
Feb. 1—Sherman starts north on the campaign of the Carolinas
Feb. 3—Peace conference held at Hampton Roads
Feb. 17—Surrender of Columbia, South Carolina
Feb. 18—Charleston, South Carolina, abandoned
Feb. 22—Wilmington, North Carolina, captured
Mar. 3—Freedmen's Bureau established by Congress to care for Negroes
        —Congress adjourns
Mar. 4—Lincoln's second inauguration
Mar. 21–23—Troops from Wilmington and Fort Fisher join Sherman's army at
        Goldsboro, North Carolina
Mar. 26—Sheridan joins Grant before Petersburg

Mar. 29–Apr. 2—Grant's grand assault on Petersburg
Apr.   2—Fall of Petersburg
Apr.   3—Fall of Richmond
Apr.   9—Lee surrenders to Grant at Appomattox Court-House
Apr. 11—Mobile, Alabama, evacuated
Apr. 12—Capture of Montgomery, Alabama
Apr. 14—Booth shoots President Lincoln at Ford's Theatre
        —Lewis Paine attacks and seriously wounds Secretary Seward and his son, Frederick
Apr. 15—Death of President Lincoln
        —Andrew Johnson inaugurated as President
Apr. 19—Funeral services of President Lincoln
Apr. 21—Lincoln's funeral train leaves Washington
        —Sherman's peace agreement with J. E. Johnston rejected by the Government
Apr. 26—Booth found and shot near Port Royal, Virginia
        —J. E. Johnston's surrender concluded
May 10—Jefferson Davis taken prisoner in Georgia
May 10–June 30—Trial of the Lincoln conspirators
May 22—Mrs. Lincoln leaves Washington for Chicago
May 23–24—Grand Review of the Union armies at Washington

Some Biographical Notes

ADAMS, HENRY 1838–1918 Grandson of Presidents, and heir to a formidable tradition of family importance, young Henry spent seven years in London as private secretary to his father, Charles Francis Adams, who was minister to England. He taught history at Harvard for a time, but, after moving to Washington in 1876, he devoted himself to study and writing. A novel, *Democracy*, was descriptive of postwar life in the capital. His most serious work was a scholarly nine-volume *History of the United States* during the Jefferson and Madison administrations. In 1885, he and his friend, John Hay, built adjoining houses on H Street, across from St. John's Church. The Adams house was immediately darkened by the suicide of his wife, the former Marian Hooper of Boston, who poisoned herself by drinking potassium cyanide, which she had used in the preparation of photographic plates. After the completion of his major historical work, Adams spent much time in travel with his friend, John LaFarge. *The Education of Henry Adams* and *Mont-Saint-Michel and Chartres* were both issued in privately printed editions before their publication.

ALCOTT, LOUISA MAY 1832–1888 The daughter of the eccentric New England philosopher, Bronson Alcott, she grew to womanhood in Concord, Mass., in an atmosphere of transcendentalism, communistic experimentation, poverty, cheerfulness and abolitionism. Her letters from the Union Hospital in Georgetown were published in 1863, and the following year her novel, *Moods*, appeared. Her reputation was made with the publication of the first volume of *Little Women* in 1868. It was followed by a long series of stories for girls which brought her sufficient means to establish her father in comfort at Concord. She exhausted herself by overwork, and survived Bronson Alcott by only two days.

ANDERSON, ROBERT 1805–1871 Born Kentucky; West Point, '25; veteran of Indian wars and the Mexican War. A major of artillery, pro-slavery in sympathy, he assumed command of the forts in Charleston harbor in November, 1860, when the secession crisis was acute in South Carolina. He was appointed brigadier in the regular Army after the fall of Fort Sumter, and later assigned to command the Union forces in his war-divided native State. The strain of conflicting loyalties proved too much for Anderson's health. He saw no active service after the autumn of 1861. In April, 1865, he emerged from retirement to participate in the ceremonies at Fort Sumter by raising the same flag which four years earlier he had lowered in defeat.

BAKER, LA FAYETTE CURRY 1826–1868 Acrimonious disputes over the distribution of the reward for Booth's capture ended in the detective chief's receiving only $3,750. He was promoted brigadier-general, but early in 1866 he was retired from the service, and left the War Department. Baker had been denounced in the press for his over-zealous activities, especially for his spying on President Johnson, who had ordered him out of the White House. In 1867, the publication of his book, *History of the United States Secret Service*, made public for the first time the existence of Booth's suppressed diary. Called before the House Judiciary Committee, Baker insinuated that the diary had been mutilated by Stanton. The detective was a witness against President Johnson in the impeachment investigation.

BANKS, NATHANIEL PRENTISS 1816–1894 A native of Massachusetts, Banks started out as a bobbin boy in a cotton factory, studied law and entered politics. He was Speaker of the House in 1856, and Republican governor of Massachusetts in 1858. Hastily made a major-general, Banks was not a skillful soldier, though he was brave and energetic. In November, 1862, he sailed with a strong force to New Orleans, where he succeeded Butler in command. He attempted in the spring of 1863 to storm Port Hudson on the Mississippi, laid siege to it, and received its surrender after the fall of Vicksburg. The next spring he made an expedition, supported by a fleet of gunboats, up the Red River for the purpose of gaining control of western Louisiana, but was defeated at Sabine Cross Roads. The expedition was undertaken on Halleck's orders, but Banks was censured for its failure, was relieved of command, and resigned his commission. He later served a number of terms in Congress, and was United States marshal for Massachusetts.

BARNES, JOSEPH K. 1817–1883 Born Philadelphia; University of Pennsylvania medical school, '38; assistant army surgeon, 1840; brigade medical officer in Mexican War. In May, 1862, he was assigned to duty in Washington; promoted medical inspector, with the rank of colonel in 1863, and in September of that year was made acting Surgeon General. Barnes became Surgeon General with the rank of brigadier in August, 1864, and was brevetted major-general in 1865. He succeeded in bringing the military hospitals, as well as the transportation of the wounded, under the control of medical officers. His friendly relation with Secretary Stanton fostered the establishment of the army medical museum and library, and the compilation of the medical and surgical history of the war. He dressed Seward's wounds on the night of April 14, 1865, and was in attendance at Lincoln's deathbed. He also attended President Garfield after he was shot by an assassin.

BARTON, CLARA 1821–1912 In 1864, she was appointed superintendent of nurses of the Army of the James. After the war, she directed a bureau of records at Washington to aid in the search for missing Union soldiers, identifying thousands of graves at the prison at Andersonville, Georgia. Her eloquence attracted crowds to her lectures on her war experiences. While on a visit to Switzerland in 1869, Miss Barton became interested in the International Committee of the Red Cross, and, on the outbreak of the Franco-Prussian War, assisted in organizing military hospitals, and superintended relief work in Strasburg and Paris. In 1873, Miss Barton returned home and after four years' endeavor succeeded in establishing the American Red Cross. She became the first president of the organization, representing the United States at many international conferences in Europe. She visited Turkey after the Armenian massacres in 1896, carried supplies to Cuba in 1898, and at the age of seventy-nine worked for six weeks among the flood sufferers at Galveston, Texas. Temperamental differences with her fellow-workers in the Red Cross and Miss Barton's inefficient methods of accounting, which shook pubic confidence in the organization, led to her resignation in 1904. She founded a rival society, The National First Aid of America.

BEAUREGARD, PIERRE GUSTAVE TOUTANT 1818–1893 Born Louisiana; West Point, '38; participated in all the battles of the Mexican War, being twice wounded and brevetted major. Beauregard was briefly superintendent at West Point in 1861, resigning on the secession of Louisiana. After the surrender of Sumter, he was ordered from Charleston to Virginia, and for his services at Manassas was made one of five full generals of the Confederacy. In 1862, he was sent to the West, and took command at Shiloh upon the death of the Confederate leader, A. S. Johnston. Beauregard fell back on Corinth, Mississippi, which he was finally compelled to evacuate. Later in the year, he was again assigned to Charleston, and defended it against prolonged attacks from military and naval forces. In the spring of 1864, Beauregard defeated the Army of the James under Butler, and held Petersburg until Lee's arrival. In the autumn, he served in the West, and later was second in command to J. E. Johnston in the campaign of the Carolinas. After the war, he was railroad president, adjutant-general of Louisiana, manager of the Louisiana lottery and superintendent of public works in New Orleans.

BINGHAM, JOHN A. 1815–1900 From 1855 until 1873, with the exception of the Thirty-eighth Congress, he served as representative from Ohio. Failing of re-election in 1863, he was appointed judge advocate by President Lincoln, and later solicitor of the court of claims. As special judge advocate in the trial of the Lincoln conspirators, he was conspicuous for his severity toward defense counsel, and vociferously proclaimed the guilt of Jefferson Davis in his summary of the evidence. On his return to Congress, Bingham took a leading part in the radical reconstruction measures, and was one of the managers of President Johnson's impeachment trial. He was appointed minister to Japan in 1873, and held the post for twelve years.

BLAIR, FRANCIS PRESTON, JR. 1821–1875 He was a leading backer of Frémont for the Missouri command, but soon turned against him, and in the ensuing quarrel was arrested and put in prison. He was made a brigadier-general in 1862, and fought well in the Vicksburg campaign and in other engagements in the West. He was promoted major-general, and proved to be one of the most successful officers who entered the Union army from civil life. Sherman withheld the highest confidence from him as from Logan, regarding both as able military leaders, but primarily interested in politics. Blair resumed his seat in the House in 1864 to lend support to the administration, but his factious belligerence proved embarrassing, and he returned to his command. He opposed the reconstruction policies of Congress, which twice refused to confirm appointments for which he was nominated by Johnson. In 1868, he was candidate for Vice-President on the Democratic ticket, and later was chosen senator from Missouri. His brother, Montgomery (1813–1883), also acted with the Democratic party after the war.

BLENKER, LOUIS 1812–1863 His military career, which opened so promisingly, dwindled into failure after his division was attached to Frémont's Mountain Department in the spring of 1862. He saw no active service after the battle of Cross Keys, in which Frémont's forces were defeated by Stonewall Jackson. He was injured by a fall from his horse, and, after being mustered out of the service, died on his farm in Rockland County, N. Y.

BOYD, BELLE 1843–1900 In the spring of 1863, she sailed for England from Wilmington, N. C., on a blockade-runner, but the ship was overhauled by a United States vessel and Belle was imprisoned at Fort Warren and condemned to death. With the aid of Samuel Hardinge (or Harding), an officer on the boat which had captured her, she won her freedom and proceeded to England by way of Canada. In August, 1864, she was married in London to Hardinge, who had recently been discharged from the Federal service. He went back to the United States soon after the marriage and died without rejoining Belle. According to some reports, he was arrested and confined in a Federal prison. Left in want in London, Belle went on the stage, opening in the *Lady of Lyons* at Manchester in 1866. Returning to America, she starred on tour in the South. In 1868, she was seen in New York in *The Honeymoon,* and later played in stock in Ohio and Texas. Belle began, in 1886, a successful career as a dramatic *diseuse,* presenting her adventures as a spy for the Confederacy. Her second husband, whom she married in 1869, was a former British army officer, John Hammond. In 1885, she became the wife of Nathaniel High of Toledo, Ohio.

BRECKINRIDGE, JOHN CABELL 1821–1875 In December, 1861, the Senate declared the Kentuckian a traitor, and went through the formality of expelling him, although he had joined the Confederate army months earlier. As a brigadier, Breckinridge fought at Shiloh the next spring, and was promoted major-general. He commanded a division at Murfreesboro', Chickamauga and Missionary Ridge. In May, 1864, he defeated Sigel at New Market in the Shenandoah Valley, later joining Lee. After participating in Early's raid on Washington, he was ordered to southwest Virginia. In February, 1865, he became Davis's Secretary of War. On Lee's surrender, Breckinridge fled South with the Confederate cabinet, eventually escaping to Cuba and thence to Europe. The Government in 1869 permitted him to return to his home at Lexington, where he was received with popular acclaim.

BUCHANAN, JAMES 1791–1868 He had forty years of public life, serving successively as U. S. congressman, minister to Russia; U. S. Senator, Secretary of State, minister to England and President. After Lincoln's inauguration, Buchanan returned to his country seat, Wheatland, near Lancaster, Pa., and passed his declining years in rural peace. He prepared a vindication of his administration, and consistently supported the war for the restoration of the Union.

BURNSIDE, AMBROSE EVERETT 1824–1881 Born Indiana; West Point, '47; resigned, '53. He engaged in manufacturing a breech-loading rifle of his own invention in Rhode Island, where he became a major-general of State militia. Burnside failed in business, and through McClellan secured a position with the Illinois Central Railroad. Early in 1862, he gained national reputation by the capture of Roanoke Island, which led to the occupation of New Berne and Beaufort, and later to the capture of Fort Macon. Part of his North Carolina command—organized as the Ninth Corps—was engaged at Second Bull Run. At Antietam and during his ill-starred command of the Army of the Potomac, Burnside was criticized for military incapacity. In the spring of 1863, he took charge of the Department of the Ohio, where he embarrassed the President by causing the arrest and court-martial of the Copperhead politician, Clement L. Vallandigham. In the late summer, Burnside moved into East Tennessee, and occupied Knoxville where he was besieged for a month in the autumn. Once more commanding the Ninth Corps, he rejoined the Army of the Potomac in the spring of 1864. He designed the Petersburg mine, which was exploded with unfortunate results for the Federals. Meade blamed Burnside, and the censure was sustained by a court of inquiry. Burnside left the army, and resigned toward the end of the war. Always personally popular, he was three times elected governor of Rhode Island. In 1874, he was elected United States Senator, and served until his death.

BUTLER, BENJAMIN FRANKLIN 1818–1893 In August, 1861, Butler led the expedition from Fort Monroe which captured Forts Hatteras and Clark. He then recruited an expedition for the Gulf of Mexico, and after Farragut's capture of New Orleans, occupied the city. His drastic and flamboyant administration was criticized in the North and abroad, and he was recalled in December, 1862. His most notorious order was that providing that any woman insulting a Northern soldier should be treated as a woman of the town. He executed a rebel for tearing down the United States flag, and was declared an outlaw by Jefferson Davis. In the autumn of 1863, Butler took charge of the Departments of Virginia and North Carolina. He showed little military ability, either in his command of the Army of the James in the spring of 1864, or in his ineffectual expedition against Fort Fisher, N. C., in the following December. Though Butler had a large following in the country, he made bitter political enemies. He was charged with personal corruption at New Orleans and in Virginia and North Carolina. After the war he served several terms in Congress, supported the Republican radical program of reconstruction, and, as one of the managers of Johnson's impeachment trial, took a prominent part in denouncing the President. During Grant's administration, Butler was regarded as the President's spokesman in the House. After being twice defeated for governor of Massachusetts, he was elected in 1882 on the Democratic ticket. In 1884, he was the Presidential candidate of the Greenback and Anti-Monopolist parties.

CAMERON, SIMON 1799–1889 He served as minister to Russia for less than a year. Returning home in 1863, he continued his manipulation of Pennsylvania politics, and built the Republican machine which was to control the State for many years. Although he had been chagrined by his removal from the Cabinet, he remained Lincoln's staunch friend and supporter. He was elected to the Senate in 1867, and retained his seat for ten years, succeeding Sumner as chairman of the Committee on Foreign Relations. During Grant's second administration, he had his son, James D. Cameron, appointed Secretary of War. Cameron resigned from the Senate on a pledge from the Pennsylvania legislature that his son would be elected to replace him.

CARNEGIE, ANDREW 1835–1919 In the autumn of 1861, after organizing military transportation and telegraphic service in the vicinity of Washington, Carnegie returned to his duties as superintendent of the Pittsburgh division of the Pennsylvania Railroad. He soon made profitable investments in Pullman sleeping cars and western Pennsylvania oil wells, laying the foundation for the immense fortune he amassed in the iron and steel industries.

CHANDLER, ZACHARIAH 1813–1879 An active abolitionist, who helped to organize the Republican party in Michigan, Chandler served in the Senate from 1857 until 1875. During the reconstruction period, as during the war, he was a prominent member of the radical Republican faction, opposed to the moderate policies of both Lincoln and Johnson. From 1875 to 1877, he was Secretary of the Interior in Grant's Cabinet. As chairman of the Republican national committee in 1876, he directed the Presidential campaign of Rutherford B. Hayes. He was re-elected to Congress in 1879.

CHASE, SALMON PORTLAND 1808–1873 As Chief Justice of the United States, he did not relinquish his ambitions for the Presidency, but early in 1868 he lost the friendship of the Republican radicals by his dignified and impartial conduct as presiding officer at the trial of Andrew Johnson before the Senate. He had hopes of receiving the Democratic nomination in 1868, and was much disappointed when he failed to do so. In spite of his enthusiasm for civil rights and suffrage for Negroes, Chase was too moderate to support the vindictive program of reconstruction. He showed reluctance to preside at Jefferson Davis's trial for treason, and favored quashing the indictment. Chase was bitterly criticized in 1870 for handing down the opinion that the Legal Tender Act of 1862, which had authorized his issue of greenbacks as Secretary of the Treasury, was unconstitutional. Although he had a stroke of paralysis in 1870, his name was once more brought forward as a candidate for the Presidential nomination at the Liberal Republican convention in 1872.

CLAY, CLEMENT CLAIBORNE 1816–1882 He served as U. S. Senator from Alabama from 1853 until his withdrawal in 1861, on the secession of his State. After two years in the Confederate Senate, he was sent on a secret mission to Canada in the spring of 1864. Clay was engaged in planning raids on the frontier and in attempting to promote informal peace negotiations with the United States Government. Returning to the Confederacy shortly before the close of hostilities, he was listed as one of the conspirators accused of participation in Lincoln's assassination. On learning of the reward offered for his arrest, he surrendered to the Federals in Georgia, and was taken to Fort Monroe, where he was confined for nearly a year. In the autumn of 1865, Clay's wife went to the capital, where she had once been a famous belle, and beset President Johnson with appeals for her husband's release. She had a futile interview with Stanton, but was kindly received by General Grant, who wrote a letter recommending that Clay should be freed. Senator Henry Wilson voluntarily called on Mrs. Clay to assure her of his belief in her husband's innocence, and wrote a recommendation similar to that given by Grant. In April, 1866, Clay was at last released, without trial, his delicate constitution seriously impaired by his confinement.

COBB, HOWELL 1815–1868 On resigning in early December, 1860, as Secretary of the Treasury, Cobb immediately returned to Georgia to give all his efforts to promoting the secessionist movement in that State. He was chairman of the provisional congress which organized the Southern Confederacy. He later became colonel of a Georgia regiment, was promoted brigadier, and, in 1863, with the rank of major-general, he commanded the District of Georgia. He surrendered at Macon after the fall of the Confederacy.

COLFAX, SCHUYLER 1823–1885 From 1863 until 1869, he was Speaker of the House, supporting during the postwar period the radical reconstruction program. He was elected Vice-President on the ticket with Grant in 1868, but four years later failed to be renominated. Colfax, like many other prominent Republicans, was accused of being implicated in the Crédit Mobilier scandal, and his reputation suffered from charges of corruption. He passed his later years as a popular lecturer.

CORCORAN, MICHAEL   1827–1863   The son of a captain in the British army, he served for a time in the Irish constabulary, but resigned in 1849, and emigrated to the United States. After nearly a year in Southern prisons, Corcoran was exchanged in the summer of 1862. He was promoted brigadier, and received welcoming ovations in Washington and New York. He organized the Corcoran Legion, which saw service in Virginia in 1863. After Gettysburg, the legion was attached to the Army of the Potomac. In December, 1863, Corcoran was thrown and killed while riding near Fairfax Court-House.

CORCORAN, WILLIAM WILSON   1798–1888   His warm sympathy for the South led the Washington banker to go abroad in 1862. He remained in Europe until the close of the war. The Government's attempted seizure of his Washington residence was at first prevented by the fact that it had been leased to the French minister, who claimed the right to occupy it. However, it was occupied for a time as a military hospital and another hospital was erected in the grounds of his summer home near the capital. The art gallery, which Corcoran later deeded to the city, was used as an army clothing depot during the war. On his return to Washington, Corcoran founded many charitable organizations, and was responsible for having the remains of John Howard Payne brought from Tunis to Georgetown.

CUSTER, GEORGE ARMSTRONG   1839–1876   He was the youngest officer to attain high rank and reputation in the Civil War, graduating from West Point in 1861, in time to join his regiment on the field of First Bull Run. Singled out by McClellan for his energy on the Peninsula, Custer served as the general's aide until Burnside took command of the Army of the Potomac. In July, 1863, with the rank of brigadier, he commanded Michigan cavalry at Gettysburg, and distinguished himself under Sheridan in the heavy cavalry actions in the Wilderness and the Shenandoah Valley, and in the final assaults on Petersburg and Richmond. At the end of the war, he was promoted major-general of volunteers, and brevetted with the same rank in the regular Army. He remained in the service, as lieutenant-colonel of the Seventh U. S. Cavalry. In 1866, he accompanied Hancock's expedition against the Cheyenne Indians. While engaged in an expedition against the Sioux in 1876, Custer and two hundred and sixty-four men of the Seventh advanced on a large band of Indians, and were massacred.

DAHLGREN, JOHN ADOLPHUS BERNARD   1809-1870   Promoted rear-admiral in 1863, he was eager for active service, and was given command of the South Atlantic Blockading Squadron. He co-operated with General Gillmore in the prolonged and unsuccessful attempt to take Charleston. Dahlgren was chiefly distinguished as a scientific officer and inventor. After holding various commands, he was appointed chief of the Ordnance Bureau in 1868, and the following year again commanded the Washington Navy Yard. His son, Ulric (1842–1864), served with great distinction in the Union army. In the pursuit of Lee's forces after Gettysburg, he received a severe wound, which resulted in the amputation of his leg. He returned to active service on crutches, and was killed in an attempt to release Union prisoners at Richmond.

DANA, CHARLES ANDERSON 1819–1897 After performing confidential missions for Secretary Stanton, he was made second Assistant Secretary of War in 1864. He acquired a part interest in the *New York Sun* in 1868, and edited that newspaper until his death.

DAVIS, JEFFERSON 1808–1889 After the collapse of the Confederacy, he fled from Richmond and was captured by Federal cavalry in Georgia on May 10. He was imprisoned at Fort Monroe, where he was at first placed in irons. His health suffered from his confinement, and he was later less severely treated, and permitted to have his family with him. Davis's case was involved in disputes over the jurisdiction of his trial. After two years in military custody, he was handed over to the civil authorities, indicted for treason and released on bail of $100,000. Davis was never brought to trial. He was included in the proclamation of general amnesty which President Johnson issued in December, 1868. His last years were passed on a country estate in Mississippi, where he wrote the two-volume story of his career, *The Rise and Fall of the Confederate Government*. Davis might have resumed his place as United States Senator from Mississippi, but declined to ask for a Federal pardon.

DENNISON, WILLIAM 1815–1882 As governor of Ohio in 1861, he enthusiastically supported the administration and in 1864, he was president of the National Union convention which re-nominated Lincoln for the Presidency. On Montgomery Blair's resignation in the following autumn, Dennison was appointed Postmaster General. He continued in office under President Johnson, resigning in 1866.

DIX, JOHN ADAMS 1798–1879 As a boy, he took part in the War of 1812, won a lieutenant's commission, and remained in the Army until 1828, when he resigned with the rank of captain. Dix was active in Democratic politics in New York State, and was U. S. Senator, 1845–1849. By a flirtation with the Free-Soil movement, he estranged Southerners, and injured his political prospects, and Dix was thereafter a strongly reactionary Democrat. He was postmaster of New York City when, in January, 1861, he became Buchanan's Secretary of the Treasury. He staunchly supported the Union, and in the early months of the war was active in organizing and forwarding New York regiments. Appointed major-general of volunteers, he anticipated a command in Virginia, but to his indignation was sidetracked in Baltimore in July, 1861. In May, 1862, he took command at Fort Monroe, being transferred in July, 1863, to New York, as commander of the Department of the East. Dix was minister to France for four years after the war, and in 1872 served one term as Republican governor of New York. He was a lawyer, editor and railroad president; a man of much culture, prominent in the affairs of the Episcopal Church. His son, Morgan Dix, was for many years rector of Trinity Church, New York.

EARLY, JUBAL ANDERSON 1816–1894 Born Franklin County, Va.; West Point, '37. He resigned from the Army to practice law, but served as a major in Mexico, returning to civil life when the war was over. In 1861, he entered the Confederate army, and was promoted brigadier-general in 1862, after receiving severe wounds on the Peninsula. The rout of his forces by the Army of the Shenandoah impaired the confidence he had won by his successful leadership in previous engagements, and he was relieved of command in March, 1865. Early went abroad after the war, but later returned to the United States. He remained until the end of his life an unreconstructed rebel.

ECKERT, THOMAS THOMPSON 1825–1910 The chief of military telegraphs performed many confidential offices for Secretary Stanton. During the investigation of the assassination conspiracy, he devoted himself to detective work, to examining witnesses and especially to trying to get a confession from Lewis Paine, whom Stanton placed in Eckert's custody. Eckert was made Assistant Secretary of War in July, 1866, resigning early in 1867 to become superintendent of the eastern division of the Western Union Telegraph Company. In 1875, he became president of the Atlantic and Pacific Telegraph Company. After its merger with Western Union, he was successively vice-president, president and chairman of the board.

FARRAGUT, DAVID GLASGOW 1801–1870 He was born near Knoxville, Tennessee, the descendant of Spanish dons whose estates were in the Balearic Islands, and received his midshipman's warrant before he was ten years old. He saw active service in the War of 1812. In April, 1861, he was an elderly captain with a long record of honorable service. Virginia was the State of his adoption, through his marriage and long residence there, but he did not hesitate to cast his fortunes with the Union. He became its great naval hero with the capture of New Orleans, and was commissioned rear-admiral. He assisted in opening the Mississippi to navigation, and in 1864 won the victory of Mobile Bay. With the vigor and adaptability of a younger officer, Farragut met new and complicated conditions of naval warfare, damned the torpedoes, shelled casemented forts, and handled ironclads, rams and fire rafts. A grateful nation loaded him with gifts and honors. Congress created the grade of vice-admiral for him, and in 1866 that of admiral, a rank never previously held in the navy of the United States.

FESSENDEN, WILLIAM PITT 1806–1869 In the forties, he became nationally known as a lawyer and anti-slavery congressman, and took his seat as senator from Maine in 1854. He was recognized as one of the ablest members of the Republican party, and in 1861 was made chairman of the important Finance Committee. On Chase's resignation in 1864, he reluctantly consented to accept the position of Secretary of the Treasury, but early in 1865 withdrew to re-enter the Senate, and was replaced in the Cabinet by Hugh McCulloch. Fessenden again became chairman of the Senate Finance Committee, and also headed the powerful Joint Committee on Reconstruction. He disapproved of Johnson's conduct and policies, but placed integrity before party loyalty, and voted against the President's impeachment.

FLOYD, JOHN BUCHANAN 1806–1863 Buchanan's Virginian War Secretary administered the affairs of his department with great incompetence. He was accused of having participated in the abstraction of funds from the Department of the Interior, but was exonerated of responsibility by a committee of the House. It was charged by Republicans that Floyd used his office to aid the cause of secession, dispersing the Army, and transferring arms from Northern to

Southern arsenals. After the secession of Virginia, Floyd was made a brigadier in the Confederate army, and was in command of Fort Donelson at the time of Grant's assault. He withdrew his brigade, and left the surrender of the fort to be made by the Kentuckian, Simon Buckner, who had known Grant well at West Point and in the Army. Floyd was censured by Jefferson Davis, and relieved of his command.

FORD, JOHN T.   1829–1894   After being confined for thirty-nine days in the Old Capitol, he was released for lack of evidence of any complicity in Lincoln's assassination. For the rest of his life he was active in the theatre and other business enterprises, as well as in philanthropic work. He produced the popular operetta, *Pinafore,* in Philadelphia in 1879, and was unique among American managers in sending royalties to Gilbert and Sullivan. In the season of 1879–1880, when Gilbert and Sullivan visited the United States with the D'Oyly Carte Opera Company, they engaged Ford as their manager, and he leased the Fifth Avenue Theatre for the production of *The Pirates of Penzance.* His management was so satisfactory that Gilbert and Sullivan gave him the exclusive rights to their productions in America. In compensation for the seizure of Ford's Theatre in Washington, the Government paid John T. Ford $100,000. The building was a scene of another tragedy in 1893, when the front wall collapsed, killing twenty-eight Government workers who were employed there.

FRANKLIN, WILLIAM BUEL   1823–1903   Born York, Pa.; West Point, '43. He was graduated at the head of the class of which Grant was an undistinguished member, and served as a staff officer in Mexico. Franklin was a topographical engineer, but in 1861 showed ability as a commander in the field, and was made a major-general of volunteers in July, 1862, commanding the Sixth Corps from the time of its formation on the Peninsula. He fought at South Mountain and Antietam, and commanded the left grand division of the Army of the Potomac at Fredericksburg. The censure which he received from Burnside after this last battle increased a prejudice already awakened by Franklin's close friendship with McClellan and by his slowness in advancing to Pope's assistance at the time of Second Bull Run. After awaiting orders for several months, Franklin, in August, 1863, was sent to Louisiana and placed in command of the Nineteenth Corps. His last active service was his participation in the ill-fated Red River expedition of 1864. He was wounded at Sabine Cross Roads, and granted leave of absence. On July 11, while traveling on the Philadelphia and Baltimore Railroad, Franklin was taken prisoner by a detachment of Early's forces, but succeeded in making his escape the next night. He resigned from the Army in 1866, and became vice-president of the Colt fire arms company at Hartford, Conn.

FRÉMONT, JOHN CHARLES   1813–1890   Born Savannah, Georgia; mathematician and surveyor; 1838, appointed second lieutenant of topographical engineers. Through the influence of his father-in-law, Senator Thomas H. Benton of Missouri, Frémont was entrusted with important explorations of the regions between the Mississippi and the Pacific. His romantic and hazardous expeditions won him the admiring nickname of the Pathfinder. He took a prominent and somewhat dubious part in the conquest of California in 1846, eventually being tried by court-martial for disobedience of orders, and sentenced to dismissal. His sentence was remitted by President Polk, but Frémont resigned from the

Army. He served a short term as one of the first United States Senators from California. His opposition to slavery and his personal popularity made him the first Presidential candidate of the Republicans. In 1861, his administration of the Department of the West proved to be so extravagant, ostentatious and inept that Lincoln was obliged to remove him. His appointment to the Mountain Department was a gesture of conciliation to the anti-slavery faction. He was ordered to co-operate against Stonewall Jackson during the Valley raid of May, 1862, but showed no military ability, and was defeated at Cross Keys. Shortly after, he retired from active service, and was little heard of, save for the passing attention he attracted in 1864 as Presidential candidate of a group of Republican radicals. A career of railroading in the West led to bankruptcy and a damaged reputation. In 1878, he was appointed governor of the territory of Arizona. Early in 1890, he was restored to the rank of major-general in the Army.

FRENCH, BENJAMIN BAKER 1800–1870 He was born in Chester, N. H., and was called major because of his early service in the State militia. His first marriage, an elopement which was kept secret for six months, was performed outdoors on a snowy, moonlight night. In 1833, French went to Washington as assistant clerk of the House, and was made clerk in 1845. He was interested in the Magnetic Telegraph Company, and served for three years as its president. Pierce appointed him Commissioner of Public Buildings in 1853. French had meantime built himself a house on East Capitol Street, on part of the site of the present Congressional Library, and took much pleasure in his grounds and gardens. He was active in Masonic circles and in Washington civic affairs, serving on the Common Council and as president of the Board of Aldermen. On the formation of the Republican party, French became one of its leading adherents in the capital. Lincoln made him Commissioner of Public Buildings in the autumn of 1861, and he remained in this position during two years of the Johnson administration. Left a widower in the spring of 1861, he consoled his loneliness by taking a young wife, Miss Mary Ellen Brady. He was the uncle of the sculptor, Daniel Chester French.

GARFIELD, JAMES ABRAM 1831–1881 A teacher and lawyer, Garfield had already made his mark as an anti-slavery man in Ohio politics at the outbreak of war. He commanded a regiment in Kentucky during the first winter of the war, and was made a brigadier. He fought at Shiloh, and early in 1863 was assigned to the Army of the Cumberland, becoming Rosecrans's chief of staff. His bravery and initiative at Chickamauga won him the rank of major-general. He had been elected congressman from Ohio, and in December, 1863, gave up a promising military career to support the administration. During Johnson's term, he joined in the Republican opposition to the President's reconstruction policies. By 1877, Garfield was the leader of the Republicans, then in a minority in the House. Early in 1880, he was elected senator, but received the Republican nomination for the Presidency a few months later. Four months after his inauguration in March, 1881, he was shot in the Washington station by Charles J. Guiteau, a disappointed office seeker. He lingered for more than ten weeks before he died.

GILLMORE, QUINCY ADAMS 1825–1888 Born Ohio; West Point, '49. Gillmore was graduated at the head of his class, and was one of the most brilliant engineers in the Army. With the rank of captain in 1861, he was chief engineer of the Port Royal expedition, and commanded the force which invested Fort Pulaski, Ga., in April, 1862. His success in breaching the masonry fortifications with rifled cannon brought him wide fame as an artillerist. During the second half of 1863, Gillmore, promoted to major-general, commanded the Department of the South. His skillful operations around Charleston, S. C., were partially successful in reducing the defenses of the city, and won him the brevets of brigadier and major-general in the regular Army. Early in 1864, he was transferred to the Army of the James. Ben Butler, easily provoked against West Point officers, brought charges of disobedience and military incapacity against Gillmore, removed him from command and ordered his arrest. Gillmore was, however, relieved from arrest by Grant. While aiding in the defense of Washington during Early's raid, he was severely injured by a fall from his horse. In 1865, he again commanded the Department of the South. He served on many boards and commissions, acting as president of the Mississippi River Commission in 1879. He was the author of authoritative treatises on engineering.

GOLDSBOROUGH, LOUIS MALESHERBES 1805–1877 His father, a Marylander, was chief clerk of the Navy Department, and the boy was given a midshipman's warrant at the age of seven. He took part in the Mexican War. From 1853 to 1857, he was superintendent of the Naval Academy, and at the outbreak of civil war, with the rank of captain, commanded the Brazil Squadron. Although he was overage, he continued on active duty and commanded the fleet which co-operated with the Burnside expedition in the spring of 1862. Goldsborough's squadron was ordered to assist McClellan during the Peninsula campaign, and held the *Merrimac* in check. It was, however, one of McClellan's main grievances that the navy did not co-operate in the capture of Yorktown. After the destruction of the *Merrimac*, the James River flotilla attempted to take Richmond, but was repulsed at Drewry's Bluff, May 15, 1862. Goldsborough was promoted rear-admiral in July, but as he had been much criticized in the press, and the James River flotilla had been made an independent command, he was relieved at his own request in the autumn. He did administrative work in Washington, and had a brief military career in the defenses during Early's raid. In 1865, he took command of the European Squadron, and was again on duty in the capital from 1868 until his retirement in 1873.

GRANT, ULYSSES SIMPSON 1822–1885 Born Ohio; West Point, '43. After the war, the Union showered the commander-in-chief with gifts and honors. In 1866, he was promoted by act of Congress to the rank of full general. Grant was without political experience or perspicacity. He had only once in his life cast a vote—for Buchanan in 1856. Both the Democratic and Republican parties began to court his favor. President Johnson, believing Grant his friend, appointed him Secretary of War *ad interim*, after suspending Stanton in the summer of 1867. Grant promptly left the War Department when the Senate refused to concur in Stanton's removal, and was accused of bad faith by the President. In the resultant controversy, Grant was evasive and lacking in candor. It was his first embroilment in politics, in which he now became identified with the radical Republican faction. Grant forgot the advice of his friend, Sherman, to which he had willingly listened in 1864: "For God's sake, and for your country's sake, come out of Washington." In 1868, he was elected President on the Republican ticket by an overwhelming majority, and in 1872 was re-elected. His two administrations presented the picture of a limited, be-

wildered and foolishly trusting man, caught in a maelstrom of political complexities and corruption. His great popularity declined, as the country wearied
of the scandalous dishonesty in Washington and in the carpetbagger regime in
the South. At the end of his second term, Grant made a world tour, and was
received with high honors in Europe. In 1880, an attempt to re-nominate him
for the Presidency was defeated by the popular prejudice against third terms.
The following year he moved to New York, and became a partner in a banking
house. He trusted his interests to unreliable associates, and lost all his property
with the bankruptcy of the business in 1884. Penniless and suffering from
cancer of the throat, Grant wrote his *Personal Memoirs* in order to provide for
his family. He labored courageously on the work during the increasing agony
of his illness, completing it only four days before his death at Mount McGregor
near Saratoga.

GREENHOW, ROBERT   1800–1854   The distinguished Virginian who married Rose O'Neal studied medicine in New York and Paris. He was an excellent
linguist, and in 1828 he was appointed translator at the State Department. He
went in 1850 to California, where he became a law agent for the U. S. land
commission. Greenhow is remembered for his scholarly *History of Oregon and
California*, based on original sources in Spanish, French and English.

GREENHOW, ROSE O'NEAL   18 ?–1864   After being escorted to the
South, Mrs. Greenhow stayed for a time in Richmond, and paid a visit to
Beauregard at Charleston. She then sailed on a blockade-runner for France,
where she was received with great respect and had a private audience with
Napoleon III. Having placed little Rose in a convent in Paris, she enjoyed a
social triumph in London and was presented to Queen Victoria. Her book, *My
Imprisonment*, attracted much favorable attention. It was said that she was
betrothed to a peer and planned to make her permanent home in England. In
August, 1864, she sailed on a trip to the Confederacy on the steamer, *Condor*,
which ran the blockade off Wilmington, N. C., on the night of September 30.
In the darkness, the *Condor* hit a bar, and stuck fast. Fearful of the Federal
ships, Mrs. Greenhow and two Confederate agents asked to be set ashore. As
their boat was lowered into the surf, it was overturned by a wave. Mrs. Greenhow, weighted down by a bag of gold sovereigns which she had fastened around
her waist, was drowned. Her body was washed ashore next day, and buried in
Wilmington with the honors of war. Little Rose became an actress, and later
married and settled in California.

GRIMES, JAMES WILSON   1816–1872   In 1854, he became governor of
Iowa, aligning himself with the opposition to slavery, and soon taking a stand
on behalf of the new Republican party. He first took his seat in the United
States Senate in 1859. He was chairman of the committee on the District of
Columbia, and served on a number of other committees, including that on Naval
Affairs, of which he became chairman in 1864. During Johnson's impeachment
trial, Grimes was one of seven Republican senators who had the courage to vote
"Not guilty." As a result of the strain, he suffered a stroke of paralysis, and
was carried into the Senate Chamber to cast the ballot which brought on his
head an avalanche of abuse, even in his home city of Burlington. He returned
to Congress in the winter of 1868, but his failing health forced him to go
abroad, and the following year he resigned.

GWIN, WILLIAM McKENDREE 1805–1885 His term as a pro-slavery senator from California expired in March, 1861. Soon after, while on board a vessel in the Bay of Panama, he was arrested on charges of disloyalty. In 1863, he went to Paris, where he interested Napoleon III in a plan for establishing a settlement for Southerners in Mexico, but he was unsuccessful in enlisting the co-operation of Maximilian. After a second visit to Mexico in 1865, Gwin was arrested when he attempted to re-enter the United States, and was imprisoned for eight months. After his release, he went to New York, where he died in obscurity.

HALLECK, HENRY WAGER 1815–1872 Born Oneida County, N. Y.; West Point, '39; lecturer and writer on military science. He served capably as an engineer and administrator on the Pacific Coast during the Mexican War; and resigned in 1854, with the rank of captain, to become a successful lawyer, mine director and railroad president in San Francisco. His works on international law proved his high attainments as a jurist. On Scott's recommendation, he was made major-general in 1861, and in November was placed at the head of the Department of the West. His command was marked by administrative ability, conservatism on the slavery question and, early in 1862, by the victories of his subordinate generals. In March of that year, Halleck's authority was greatly extended by the addition of the Departments of Kansas and Ohio to his command, thereafter known as the Department of the Mississippi. The only campaign in which he took active part was the advance on Corinth. He moved with exaggerated caution, and permitted Beauregard's forces to escape. As general-in-chief (July, 1862-March, 1864) he devoted himself to military minutiae. Shortly after Lee's surrender, Halleck was transferred from the post of national chief of staff to the command of the Division of the James, with headquarters at Richmond. He angered Sherman by issuing orders prejudicial to the latter general, after the Government's rejection of his first terms to Johnston. Halleck later commanded on the Pacific and in the South.

HAMMOND, WILLIAM ALEXANDER 1828–1900 Born Annapolis, Maryland; graduated University of the City of New York, 1848; assistant Army surgeon, 1849. After ten years at frontier stations, he resigned to teach at the University of Maryland; but re-entered the service as assistant surgeon in 1861. Suspended as Surgeon General in 1863 and charged with irregularities in the award of contracts, Hammond appealed to the President to be restored to his position or tried by court-martial. After a session of many months, a military court found him guilty in the summer of 1864, and sentenced him to dismissal. His means had been exhausted by the expense of the trial, and only the financial help of medical friends enabled him to move from Washington. Hammond soon established himself as a leading physician in New York City, and was a pioneer in the practice and teaching of neurology, holding the professorship of nervous and mental diseases at Bellevue Hospital Medical College, and subsequently at the University of the City of New York. In 1878, his case was reviewed, the verdict of the court-martial was reversed, and he was honorably retired. In addition to numerous medical articles, Hammond was the author of several novels. *The Son of Perdition,* a fictional treatment of Judas Iscariot, published when he was seventy years old, attained considerable popularity.

HANCOCK, WINFIELD SCOTT 1824–1886 Born Montgomery Square, Pa.; West Point, '44. He was a veteran of Scott's campaign in Mexico, and at the outbreak of civil war was a captain and quartermaster in California. He asked for active service and, on McClellan's recommendation, was commissioned brigadier, serving on the Peninsula and in the Maryland campaign. With the rank of major-general, Hancock performed gallant service at Fredericksburg, Chancellorsville and Gettysburg. Disabled by wounds received in the last engagement, he was again on active service in the Wilderness, where he commanded the Second Corps. Grant considered Hancock the most conspicuous of the general officers who did not exercise a separate command. After the war, he was commissioned major-general in the regular Army, and commanded in the West and South. His moderate views on reconstruction led to his being transferred to the East. In 1880, he was unanimously nominated Presidential candidate by the Democratic convention, defeated by Garfield in the ensuing campaign. Hancock, as military commander in Washington in the summer of 1865, was obliged to order the execution of the Lincoln conspirators. He suffered for the rest of his life from malignant criticisms for his part in the hanging of Mrs. Surratt.

HARLAN, JAMES   1820–1899   Iowa politician and college president, Harlan became identified with the Free-Soil movement, and served in the United States Senate from 1855 until 1865. He resigned to accept the office of Secretary of the Interior, proffered him by Lincoln, who was Harlan's close friend. However, as John Usher's resignation did not take effect until May 15, Harlan actually entered the Cabinet a month after Johnson had taken office. He was opposed to the new President's policies, and resigned in July, 1866. Harlan made many enemies in office, and was charged with improper appointments and corruption in the disposal of lands. He was immediately returned to the Senate, and was aligned with the radical Republicans in supporting Johnson's impeachment. In 1868, his daughter, Mary, was married to Robert Lincoln. Defeated in the Iowa senatorial campaign of 1872, Harlan was not again elected to office.

HAY, JOHN   1838–1905   Twice, in the course of his secretaryship, he performed quasi-military duty, but never saw active service. In the spring of 1863, he was a volunteer aide on Hunter's staff in South Carolina. Early in 1864, Lincoln commissioned him major and assistant adjutant-general, and sent him, in the capacity of aide to Gillmore, to enroll loyal citizens in Florida, with the view of restoring a legal government in the State. Hay soon found that his mission was premature. It brought charges from Lincoln's enemies that the hapless Florida expedition of that season had been undertaken with a political motive. Weary of life in Washington, Hay welcomed in March, 1865, an appointment as secretary of legation at Paris. Seward later made him chargé d'affaires at Vienna, and in 1869 he was secretary of legation at Madrid. For a time, he was connected with the New York Tribune, returning in 1878 to Washington as Assistant Secretary of State. Hay had married a rich wife, and become solemn and dignified. His literary reputation was based on the publication of Pike County Ballads and Castilian Days. Lincoln's biography, on which he labored with Nicolay for ten years, was serialized in the Century, which paid the authors fifty thousand dollars. Hay and his friend, Henry Adams, built fine houses on Sixteenth Street—the Hay mansion standing on the site of Mrs. Greenhow's former home. In 1897, he was appointed ambassador to Great Britain by McKinley, and in 1898 he became Secretary of State, remaining in office under Theodore Roosevelt until his death. He directed the peace negotiations which followed the Spanish-American War, sponsored the "open door" in China, and helped to prevent the dissolution of China after the Boxer rebellion of 1900. With Great Britain he made the treaty which ultimately permitted the fortification of the Panama Canal, and arranged the settlement of the Alaskan boundary dispute.

HAYES, RUTHERFORD BIRCHARD 1822–1893 After his service in the Washington defenses in August, 1862, Hayes took part in the Maryland campaign and was severely wounded at South Mountain in September. He was later attached to the forces in western Virginia. Joining the Army of the Shenandoah in 1864, Hayes fought at Winchester, Fisher's Hill and Cedar Creek, and was made a brigadier-general, and brevetted major-general for gallantry. Before the war, Hayes had been an Ohio lawyer of some experience in local politics, and during his absence in the field in 1864 he was elected Republican congressman, taking his seat in December, 1865. He followed the party line on reconstruction, and was in favor of President Johnson's impeachment. From 1867 to 1869 and again in 1875 he was governor of Ohio. In 1876, he received the Republican nomination for the Presidency. The election resulted in the acrimonious Hayes-Tilden controversy, in which the Democrats charged fraud. Three days before his inauguration, Hayes was declared to have been elected. During his administration, the worst excesses of military carpetbag rule in the South began to be abated. Hayes was an honest and mediocre President, who earnestly tried to bring about reforms in the civil service. His wife was much commended by teetotalers for her refusal to permit wine to be served on the White House table.

HITCHCOCK, ETHAN ALLEN 1798–1870 In November, 1862, he returned to Washington to serve on the commission for the exchange of prisoners. He published *The Sonnets of Shakespeare and Spenser's "Colin Clout" Explained* in 1865, and *Notes on the Vita Nuova of Dante* in 1866.

HOLT, JOSEPH 1807–1894 Appointed Judge Advocate General in September, 1862, the former Democrat from Kentucky became the ally of the Republican radicals and was widely criticized for his extension of the judisdiction of military commissions. The popular reaction to the execution of Mrs. Surratt covered Holt with obloquy. In condemning her to death, the military commission had petitioned the President for clemency. When this fact came into the open during the trial of John Surratt in 1867, President Johnson declared that he had not been shown the recommendation for mercy when the record of the case was brought to him by Holt. The accusation of having suppressed the petition embittered Holt's later years. In 1873, he published his *Vindication,* and became embroiled in a controversy with Johnson, who consistently maintained that no information regarding the recommendation had ever been given him.

HOOKER, JOSEPH 1814–1879 Born Hadley, Mass.; West Point, '37; resigned, 1853. Hooker's personality involved him in many quarrels. He made an enemy of Scott in Mexico, of Halleck in California, and of Burnside and Meade in the Army of the Potomac. By his leadership at Lookout Mountain and Chattanooga, he regained the reputation which had been dimmed at Chancellorsville. He was made a major-general in the regular Army, and in the spring of 1864 did good service in Sherman's campaign in Georgia. He was disappointed at not receiving the command of the Army of the Tennessee, and asked to be relieved from duty when the appointment was given to Howard. Hooker saw no more active service in the war. He commanded various departments until his retirement in 1868.

JOHNSON, ANDREW 1808–1875 His love feast with the Republican radicals was of brief duration, as it soon appeared that the new President, in spite of his early vindictive utterances, would favor a lenient plan of reconstruction in the seceded States, and was opposed to a sweeping program of Negro suffrage. Early in 1866, he began a desperate fight with Congress, which refused to admit representatives from the provisional governments which Johnson had set up in the seceded States, and passed several important measures over his veto. The partisan struggle between the executive and legislative branches resulted in a sorry paralysis of governmental functions. Johnson, insulted and slandered, showed a high order of courage and statesmanship, but he lost respect by undignified public appearances, especially in his "swing around the circle" in the congressional campaign of 1866. Congress, in 1867, threw out the President's reconstruction plans, and passed harsh legislation, enforcing military rule and Negro suffrage in the South. The Tenure of Office Act, which prohibited the President from dismissing a Cabinet officer without the Senate's consent, was tested by Johnson's attempt to remove the hostile Stanton from his Cabinet, and became the chief ground for the President's impeachment trial before the Senate in 1868. The congressional raid on the executive office failed by a single vote, seven Republican senators breaking party discipline to vote against conviction. In 1869, Johnson returned to Tennessee. He was elected to the Senate shortly before his death.

JOHNSTON, JOSEPH EGGLESTON 1807–1891 Born Virginia; West Point, '29; gallant service in Mexico, where he received two severe wounds and three brevets; Quartermaster General, with rank of brigadier, 1860. Johnston, commanding insurgent forces in the Valley in 1861, made a rapid and skillful junction with Beauregard at Manassas, and, as senior officer, took command on that field. He was made a full general, and assigned to the command in northern Virginia. In the spring of 1862, he transferred his main army to the Peninsula, and superseded Magruder at Yorktown on April 17. He recommended the evacuation of Yorktown and the concentration of the army before Richmond. After partially recovering from the wounds received at Fair Oaks, he took command in the southwest, and in May, 1863, he was placed at the head of all the Confederate forces in Mississippi, opposing Grant's movement on Vicksburg, the siege of which he tried unsuccessfully to relieve. In December, 1863, after Chattanooga, he was transferred to the command of the defeated Confederate Army of Tennessee, with headquarters in Georgia, and in May, 1864, skillfully resisted the advance of Sherman's much larger army. He was relieved of command on July 17, but restored by Lee in February, 1865. In his able service to the Confederate cause, Johnston was constantly at cross-purposes with Jefferson Davis. After the war, he settled in Richmond, and served one term in Congress in 1878. He later moved to Washington, and was appointed commissioner of railroads by President Cleveland.

KEYES, ERASMUS DARWIN 1810–1895 Born Brimfield, Mass.; West Point, '32. As a young officer Keyes served as Scott's aide for four years, and was well acquainted with the old General's foibles when he became his military secretary in January, 1860. In April, 1861, he incurred Scott's displeasure by assisting without his chief's special consent in the plans for the relief of Fort Pickens. He left for New York on business connected with the expedition, and Scott soon appointed another officer in his place. Keyes obtained a colonelcy, and commanded a brigade in Tyler's division at First Bull Run. Lincoln appointed him commander of the Fourth Corps of the Army of the Potomac before the Peninsula campaign. He was promoted major-general in May, 1862, and brevetted brigadier-general in the United States Army after the battle of Fair Oaks. When the Army of the Potomac was withdrawn from the Peninsula, Keyes's corps, to his great chagrin, was left behind at Yorktown. He felt that his career had suffered because of McClellan's antagonism. He became engaged in a controversy with General Dix, and was disappointed at being refused an official investigation. Convinced that his military usefulness was over, he resigned in 1864.

LANDER, JEAN MARGARET   1829–1903   After the death of her husband, General Frederick W. Lander, in 1862, she took charge of the Federal hospitals at Port Royal, S. C., and worked there with her mother for over a year. In 1865, she returned to the stage at Niblo's Garden, New York, in *Messalliance*, a play which she herself had translated from the French. She was seen as *Queen Elizabeth* at the National Theatre in Washington in 1867. Other roles which she successfully enacted were *Hester Prynne, Peg Woffington, Mary Stuart* and *Medea*.

LANE, JAMES HENRY   1814–1866   The senator from Kansas raised two regiments in his State, and during the first autumn of the war served in western Missouri, holding for a time a commission as brigadier-general. Although he was much attached to Lincoln, he allied himself with the radical faction in the Senate. After Johnson's accession, however, he deserted his former political associates to give strong support to the new President. In the summer of 1866, Lane shot himself. It was the second suicide within a year among Johnson's adherents, for Preston King, his closest friend and adviser, had drowned himself by jumping from a New York ferryboat. Some people saw significance in the fact that King and Lane had guarded the White House stairs when Mrs. Surratt's daughter, Anna, vainly sought to see President Johnson to obtain a pardon for her mother.

LEE, ROBERT EDWARD   1807–1870   Born Stratford, Virginia; West Point, '29. With the rank of captain, he was engaged in the Mexican War, winning three brevets for bravery. On his return, while employed in engineering work near Washington, he lived at Arlington, the estate of his wife's father, George Washington Parke Custis, the grandson of Martha Washington. After three years as superintendent of West Point, he became lieutenant-colonel of the Second Cavalry, on duty in Texas. While at home on leave in 1859, he was sent to Harper's Ferry to subdue John Brown's raid. In February, 1861, he was ordered to Washington from Texas, and the following month, after Lincoln was in office, Lee was made colonel of the First U. S. Cavalry. He tendered his resignation on April 20, and, before it had been accepted, took command of the Virginia insurgent forces. On June 8, Lee's army was transferred to the Confederate States. He was made a full general in the late summer, but his first important command dated from May 31, 1862, when he replaced J. E. Johnston at the head of the Confederate Army of Northern Virginia. From that time on, he repelled Federal attacks with brilliant success, but his two attempts at invading the North ended in retreat, after Antietam and Gettysburg. Lee did not assume the chief command of the Confederate armies until February, 1865. After the surrender at Appomattox, he urged on the Southern people the submission which he himself had yielded to the Federal Government. In the following August, he accepted the presidency of Washington College at Lexington, Virginia, and remained in this position until his death.

LINCOLN, MARY 1818–1882 Although her husband's personal estate amounted to over one hundred thousand dollars and she received gifts of money, the President's widow was obsessed with the idea that she was destitute. In a Chicago boardinghouse, she bewailed her homeless state, railed at the niggardliness of the Republicans and jealously begrudged all generosity shown to military leaders of the Union. She declared that her old friends, B. B. French and Isaac Newton, were working against her, and specifically accused French of embezzling money which should have been hers. In the autumn of 1867, to the mortification of the Republicans and the horror of her son, Robert, she created a scandal by arranging a public sale of part of her wardrobe and jewelry in New York. Letters advertising her poverty and denouncing prominent Republicans were printed in the Democratic New York World. Thurlow Weed assailed her in a bitter reply, which declared that she had tried to have a padded bill—$900 for the dinner to the Prince Napoleon—charged to the Government, and had eventually included it in "a gardener's account." Mrs. Lincoln received so much adverse publicity that the sale of her effects was a failure. In the latter part of 1868, she went abroad with Tad, and remained until the spring of 1871. Senator Sumner presented to the Senate her petition for a pension, and in July, 1870, finally succeeded in having a bill passed which awarded Lincoln's wife $3,000 a year. Soon after Mrs. Lincoln returned to Chicago, Tad fell ill, and died in July, 1871. Her mental disturbances became so alarming that Robert felt obliged to have her followed in the street by Pinkerton detectives, and, in 1875, on his petition, she was adjudged insane. She attempted suicide, and was confined in a private sanitarium. After three months, she was permitted to visit her sister, Mrs. Ninian Edwards, in Springfield, and the following year the court declared that she was restored to reason. The next few years were spent by Mrs. Lincoln in solitary wanderings in Europe. Her financial situation was again aired in the press with agitation for the increase of her pension, which Congress in 1882 raised to $5,000, voting an additional gift of $15,000. In July of that year, she died at the Edwards home. The last months of her life she spent in a darkened room, dressed in her widow's mourning.

LINCOLN, ROBERT TODD 1843–1926 On entering Harvard in 1859, he carried a letter of introduction to the president of the university from Senator Stephen A. Douglas, identifying Robert as the son of his friend with whom he had been canvassing Illinois. A year and a half later, the boy was the center of popular attention and flattery. On his mother's solicitation, he remained at college, and spent four months at the Harvard Law School, after his graduation in 1864. There was much criticism in the country because the President's son bore no part in the war. In response to his father's request, Grant appointed him to his staff with the commission of captain, and Robert joined the army before Petersburg in 1865, and saw service in the closing scenes of the war. He returned to Washington on April 14, and for the remainder of his life suffered from remorse because he had refused to accompany his parents to Ford's Theatre that evening. Robert went with his mother to Chicago, and resumed his law studies. In 1868, he married Mary Harlan, the daughter of his father's friend, Senator Harlan of Iowa. His mother's eccentric behavior caused him great distress, and he was at length obliged to ask the courts for a hearing, that he might have her committed for insanity. For the most part, Lincoln held aloof from public affairs, though he supported the movement for Grant's third term in 1880. In the Garfield administration, he served as Secretary of War, and in 1889 President Harrison appointed him minister to England. Robert Lincoln's name became largely associated with big business through his work as counsel for railroad and corporate interests, and his presidency of the Pullman Company. In his advancing years, he lived in semi-seclusion, and was almost forgotten by the public. His influence over the preparation of his father's biography by Nicolay and Hay resulted in the suppression of almost all material about Abraham Lincoln's obscure and poverty-stricken origin. Near the end of his life, before sending his father's private papers to the Library of Congress, he burned a number of them.

LOGAN, JOHN ALEXANDER 1826–1886 Democratic congressman from southern Illinois at the outbreak of war, he became one of the ablest officers who entered the army without training. Logan was actively engaged in the western campaigns, being made a brigadier after Fort Donelson, and a major-general after Vicksburg. In November, 1863, he took command of Sherman's corps, the Fifteenth. He fought in the Georgia campaign, and after General McPherson's fall in the fighting before Atlanta, commanded the Army of the Tennessee. He was disappointed at not retaining the command, and ascribed Sherman's recommendation of O. O. Howard to West Point prejudice. He took an active part in the presidential canvass of 1864, but again commanded the Fifteenth Corps in the campaign of the Carolinas. After Howard was called to Washington in the spring of 1865, Logan was placed in command of the Army of the Tennessee, and served until it was disbanded. He then returned to politics, serving as congressman and later as senator. Logan had become a violent Republican radical, and was one of the managers of Johnson's impeachment trial. He was three times president of the Grand Army of the Republic, and was responsible for the observance of Decoration Day. In 1884, he was nominated for Vice-President on the Republican ticket with James G. Blaine.

McCLELLAN, GEORGE BRINTON 1826–1885 Born Philadelphia; West Point, '46. He was one of the few Northern officers who saw active service in Mexico, where he was twice brevetted. In 1857, he resigned his captain's commission to become chief engineer of the Illinois Central Railroad, of which he became vice-president the following year. At the outbreak of civil war, he was president of the Ohio and Mississippi Railroad, residing in Cincinnati. Governor Dennison of Ohio appointed him major-general of the forces of that State. In May, 1861, he was appointed major-general in the United States Army, and given the command of the Department of the Ohio. The successful advance of his troops into western Virginia was responsible for McClellan's appointment, after First Bull Run, to command the forces which he soon organized as the Army of the Potomac. After finally being relieved of his command in November, 1862, he gained increasing ascendancy in the Democratic party. His nomination for the presidency in 1864 brought him much embarrassment because of the large Copperhead element in his party. He carried New Jersey, Delaware and Kentucky. The only elective office which he ever held was the governorship of New Jersey, 1878–1881. His son, George Brinton McClellan, Junior (1865–1940), was a Tammany politician, who was elected congressman, and mayor of New York City. He later lectured on public affairs at Princeton University, and was professor of economic history from 1912 until his retirement in 1931.

McCOOK, ALEXANDER McDOWELL   1831–1903   Born Lisbon, Ohio; West Point, '52. He was the best known of the clan of "Fighting McCooks," which included his father, Daniel McCook, his seven brothers, his uncle and five cousins. He fought at Shiloh, and in July, 1862, was promoted major-general and placed in command of the Twentieth Army Corps, serving in the campaigns in Kentucky and Tennessee. Blamed for the Union defeat at Chickamauga, McCook was relieved of command, but was exonerated by a court of inquiry. After his service in the Washington defenses in 1864, he commanded in Arkansas, receiving the brevets of brigadier-general and major-general in the regular Army the following year. As a lieutenant-colonel of infantry, he remained in the Army after the close of the war, rising to the grade of major-general before his retirement for age in 1895. From 1875 until 1881, he was aide-de-camp to General Sherman.

McDOWELL, IRVIN   1818–1885   Born Ohio; West Point, '38; acting adjutant-general of Wool's column in Mexico. While the criticisms of McDowell after Second Bull Run made it unwise to give him another command in the field, he was entrusted with important administrative work. In 1864, he commanded on the Pacific coast, subsequently heading departments in the East and South, before returning to the Pacific. In 1872, McDowell was made major-general in the regular Army. In his last years, he served as a park commissioner of San Francisco, bringing to the development of the Presidio reservation his interest in landscape gardening.

MAGRUDER, JOHN BANKHEAD   1810–1871   Born Winchester, Va.; West Point, '30; captain of artillery in Mexico, twice brevetted for gallantry, and severely wounded at Chapultepec. "Prince John" made his reputation for elegance and social grace during his command at Fort Adams, Newport, R. I., where he gave many fashionable parties. In April, 1861, he was placed in command of the insurgent forces on the Virginia Peninsula. He was promoted brigadier-general after the engagement at Big Bethel in June, and became major-general in the autumn. The following April, Magruder succeeded in stopping the Army of the Potomac before Yorktown with a small force. In the battles of the Seven Days, he was censured by Lee for tardiness and inefficiency. He was transferred to Texas in the autumn of 1862, and on January 1, 1863, recaptured Galveston and succeeded in temporarily dispersing the blockading squadron. At the close of the war, Magruder refused to ask for a parole, and went to Mexico, where he served as a major-general under Maximilian. After the emperor's execution, he returned to the United States and lectured on his experiences in Mexico.

MEADE, GEORGE GORDON   1815–1872   Born Cadiz, Spain; West Point, '35. Meade resigned, but re-entered the Army in 1842, with the grade of second lieutenant of topographical engineers; served in the Mexican War, and was brevetted for gallantry. In 1861, he was a captain mainly experienced in light-house construction and geodetic surveys, but he was soon promoted brigadier, and commanded on the Peninsula, where he was severely wounded during the Seven Days. He recovered in time to join his brigade at Second Bull Run, and did such good service at Antietam that he was placed in command of the First Corps, after Hooker was wounded. He distinguished himself at Fredericksburg, was made a major-general and given command of the Fifth Corps, which he led at Chancellorsville. His relations with his superior officer, Hooker, had become so strained that Meade anticipated his own removal and arrest, when he was handed the order appointing him to the command of the Army of the Potomac. After Gettysburg, he was made a brigadier-general in the U. S. Army, but his dilatoriness in pursuing the enemy and his inactivity in the succeeding autumn and winter detracted from the reputation he had earned by his great victory. After the spring of 1864, Grant's presence with the Army of the Potomac cur-tailed Meade's authority as a commander, and he received little mention in the press, with whose representatives he was unpopular. Promoted major-general in the U. S. Army in 1864, Meade was later disappointed at not winning the highest military honors, which Grant reserved for his favorite officers, Sherman and Sheridan. After the war, he commanded departments in the East and South.

MOSBY, JOHN SINGLETON 1833–1916 The guerrilla leader disbanded his men on April 21, 1865. After surrendering himself in June, he opened a law office in Warrenton, Va. He had great admiration for Grant, and in 1872 pub-licly supported his candidacy for President—a surprising course which reduced Mosby's popularity in the South. Faithful in his new allegiance to the Repub-lican party, Mosby supported Hayes in 1876, and was rewarded by being ap-pointed consul at Hong Kong. He was removed by President Cleveland.

MUDD, SAMUEL 1833–1883 The military commission sentenced Dr. Mudd to life imprisonment for his alleged participation in the Lincoln con-spiracy. On July 5, 1865, President Johnson directed that, with the other pris-oners whose lives had been spared—Arnold, Spangler and O'Laughlin—he should be sent to the Albany penitentiary. On the fifteenth, however, the order was changed in accordance with Stanton's wishes to the military prison at the Dry Tortugas, off the coast of Florida. On a report from L. C. Baker that an attempt would be made to rescue the prisoners, they were treated with in-creased severity. In August, 1867, yellow fever broke out on the barren island. After the surgeons of the garrison had succumbed to the epidemic, Mudd offered his services, and did heroic work in caring for both soldiers and prisoners. O'Laughlin caught the fever and died. The officers of the post sent an appeal for Mudd's pardon to the President, and in February, 1869, Johnson signed the papers which freed the doctor. Arnold, also sentenced to life imprisonment, and Spangler, who had been given six years for aiding Booth in his escape, were likewise pardoned. Dr. Mudd returned to his home in Maryland, and gave refuge to Spangler, who lived but a short time after his release. Mudd him-self was buried in the cemetery at Bryantown Church, where he had made a casual acquaintance with Booth in the autumn of 1864.

NICOLAY, JOHN GEORGE 1832–1901 After Lincoln's death, his secre-tary served as United States consul at Paris for four years. From 1872 until 1887, he was marshal of the Supreme Court, collaborating meanwhile with John

Hay on their ten-volume biography of Lincoln. The two secretaries also edited Lincoln's writings. Nicolay wrote two books on the civil war, *The Outbreak of Rebellion* and *Campaigns of the Civil War*.

OLMSTED, FREDERICK LAW 1822–1903 His first travels, made largely on horseback, in the South occurred in 1852, when he was commissioned by the *New York Times* to write his impressions of conditions in the slave States. His letters were published as *A Journey in the Seaboard Slave States*, and later trips resulted in *A Journey Through Texas* and *A Journey in the Back Country*. After his resignation as secretary of the Sanitary Commission, he returned to his work as landscape architect, a profession in which he was a pioneer, and took a prominent part in developing parks and parkways in New York, Brooklyn, Chicago, Washington, Boston and many other cities. In 1872, he became president of the department of parks in New York. During the reconstruction period, Olmsted aided in distributing food in the South. He was active in organizing the New York State Charities Aid Association, the Metropolitan Museum of Art and the American Museum of Natural History.

PINKERTON, ALLAN 1819–1884 He resigned after McClellan's removal from the command of the Army of the Potomac, and was afterward employed by the Government in examining claims. In the spring of 1864, he was transferred to New Orleans for the purpose of investigating cotton claims. After the war, he returned to his detective work in Chicago, establishing branches of his agency in Philadelphia and New York. His agency was responsible for securing the evidence which led to the disbandment of the Molly Maguires, a secret organization of Pennsylvania coal miners. After 1869, when Pinkerton was enfeebled by a stroke of paralysis, he left the management of his business largely to his two sons.

PRYOR, ROGER ATKINSON 1828–1919 Soon after the close of the war, the fire-eating Virginian moved to New York. Before entering Congress, he had been admitted to the bar, and had had newspaper experience in Washington and Richmond. He supported himself by working on the *New York Daily News*, while he prepared for the practice of law in his adopted State. In this he was eminently successful. Pryor was appointed judge of the court of common pleas in 1890, and six years later became a justice of the supreme court of New York.

SCHURZ, CARL 1829–1906 Promoted major-general, he was criticized after Chancellorsville, where the German regiments of the Eleventh Corps bore the brunt of Stonewall Jackson's attack and were routed. Schurz defended his compatriots against violent abuse and charges of cowardice in the press, and engaged in a controversy with General O. O. Howard, whom he succeeded in command of the Eleventh Corps. After Gettysburg, the Germans were again criticized. The corps was sent to Chattanooga, where Schurz failed to agree with General Hooker. He was appointed to a corps of instruction, but asked to be relieved, and campaigned for Lincoln's re-election in 1864. After the war, he engaged in journalism. He was United States Senator from Missouri from 1869 until 1875, the first German-born member of that body. Breaking with Grant's administration, he started the Liberal Republican movement in 1870, and presided over the convention which nominated Horace Greeley for the Presidency in 1872. He supported Hayes in 1876, became his Secretary of the Interior, and did much for civil service reform. During the last two decades of his life, Schurz was celebrated as an independent in politics, a forceful orator and an able editorial writer.

SCOTT, THOMAS ALEXANDER 1823–1881 Appointed Assistant Secretary of War in August, 1861, he was the first ever to hold that office. Early in 1862, he was engaged in organizing transportation in the West, resigning in June to return to his duties as vice-president of the Pennsylvania Railroad. In the autumn of 1863, he was called by Stanton to Washington to superintend the transportation of the two corps of the Army of the Potomac, sent under Hooker to Chattanooga. Halleck had estimated that the movement would take three months. Scott carried it out in eleven and a half days, and his accomplishment was regarded as a brilliant feat. He became president of the Union Pacific Railroad, and subsequently of the Pennsylvania.

SCOTT, WINFIELD 1786–1866 Entering the War of 1812 as a lieutenant-colonel of artillery, he rose to the rank of brigadier-general, and was presented with a gold medal by Congress for his services. He was the most admired military figure in the United States, and in 1841 was placed in command of the Army. His achievements in the Mexican campaign added to his laurels, another gold medal was struck for him by order of Congress, and in 1852 the brevet rank of lieutenant-general was created for him. A feeble old man when he retired from the chief command in the autumn of 1861, he lived to see the rise and fall of many military heroes, the capitulation of the Confederacy and the assassination of Lincoln. For a time, he lived at Delmonico's in New York, but later removed to West Point. In 1865, he inscribed a gift to Grant, "from the oldest to the greatest general."

SEWARD, WILLIAM HENRY 1801–1872 In May, 1865, he was able to leave his bed—a shattered old man, his head covered with a close-fitting cap and his jaw supported with wire appliances, fastened inside his mouth. In June, he had recovered sufficiently to take his place in the Cabinet, in which he remained until the close of Johnson's administration, thus completing eight years as Secretary of State. He supported Johnson in his contest with Congress over reconstruction. The most important act of his later years was the purchase of Alaska from Russia in 1867. His son, Frederick (1830–1915), after a long illness, resumed his duties as Assistant Secretary of State, and served in the same capacity from 1877 until 1881.

SHERIDAN, PHILIP HENRY 1831–1888 Born Albany, N. Y.; West Point, '53. During the first year of the war, when Sheridan was an infantry captain and quartermaster in Missouri, there was no indication of the rapid advancement which awaited him. In the Corinth campaign, he was given the colonelcy of a cavalry regiment, and his skillful maneuvers and bold attacks soon won him the command of a brigade. Sheridan successively commanded divisions in the Army of the Ohio and the Army of the Cumberland, and was made a major-general after Murfreesboro'. He distinguished himself at Chickamauga, and his exploits at Chattanooga so impressed Grant that he placed Sheridan in charge of the cavalry corps of the Army of the Potomac. He was engaged in constant raids on the enemy forces and communications during the Wilderness campaign, and inflicted a crushing defeat on the Confederate cavalry at Yellow Tavern. His brilliant successes as commander of the Army of the Shenandoah confirmed Grant's great belief in Sheridan's ability. He was made a major-general in the U. S. Army after Cedar Creek. Sweeping south in a great raid, Sheridan joined Grant before Petersburg in late March, 1865, and took a leading part in the final assaults on the Confederate lines, and in the pursuit of Lee's army. In the reconstruction period, Sheridan commanded with severity at New Orleans, and was recalled by President Johnson, and assigned to the West. When Grant became President, Sheridan was promoted to the grade of lieutenant-general. On Sherman's retirement, he became general-in-chief of the Army. In middle age, Sheridan married the daughter of General Daniel H. Rucker, Assistant Quartermaster General during the war.

SHERMAN, JOHN   1823–1900   In 1867, he succeeded Fessenden as chairman of the Senate Finance Committee. Opposed to the drastic program of congressional reconstruction and to the impeachment of President Johnson, he submitted on both points to the discipline of the radical faction which controlled the Republican party. During Grant's administrations, Sherman led in shaping the financial policy of the country, and Hayes, in 1877, appointed him Secretary of the Treasury. He discharged the duties of this office with high ability at a time when the country was suffering from a reaction to wartime inflation. Sherman again served in the Senate from 1881 until 1897. His name was associated with the anti-trust and silver purchase acts. He was made Secretary of State by McKinley, but resigned his office in 1898.

SHERMAN, WILLIAM TECUMSEH   1820–1891   Born Lancaster, Ohio; West Point, '40; resigned, 1853. After First Bull Run, he was chosen by General Robert Anderson to accompany him to Kentucky, and succeeded to the command in October, when Anderson's health broke down. The position was uncongenial to Sherman, who believed that a large force would be needed to drive the rebel forces from Kentucky, and he was relieved in November at his own request. Sherman's nervous temperament, his prophecies of the magnitude of the struggle and his hostility to newspaper reporters gave rise to widely circulated stories that he was insane. The turning point in his career came the following spring when his brilliant service at Shiloh won great praise from Grant and Halleck. He was made a major-general and distinguished himself in the Vicksburg campaign and at Chattanooga. When Grant became commander-in-chief in 1864, he placed Sherman at the head of the Western armies. From May until September, Sherman skillfully conducted the fierce campaign which ended in the fall of Atlanta. He had become a military hero, second in popularity only to Grant, before his march to the sea forced the surrender of Savannah, and his armies plowed their way triumphantly through the Carolinas. Unlike Grant, Sherman positively declined to permit a movement for his nomination for the presidency at the Republican convention in 1884. When Grant was appointed full general in 1866, Sherman was promoted lieutenant-general, and he succeeded Grant as general when the latter became president. He was placed on the retired list in 1883.

SICKLES, DANIEL EDGAR   1825–1914   The former New York congressman covered himself with military honors by his vigorous leadership at Chancellorsville and Gettysburg. In spite of the loss of his leg, he remained in the service until 1868. As commander of the district of the Carolinas, he carried out reconstruction so drastically that he was recalled by President Johnson. He was placed on the retired list of the U. S. Army with the rank of major-general. In 1869, Grant appointed Sickles minister to Spain, where his conduct of diplomatic affairs was energetic rather than adroit. He later held various offices in New York, and from 1893 to 1895 again served in Congress. In 1912, he was removed from the chairmanship of the New York State monuments commission on a charge of mishandling funds.

SPEED, JAMES 1812–1887 A native of Kentucky, he was the brother of Lincoln's intimate friend, Joshua Speed, and was appointed Attorney General, after Bates's resignation in 1864. He fell under Stanton's influence, and after Lincoln's assassination acted with the radical Republicans. He resigned from Johnson's Cabinet in 1866.

SPRAGUE, KATE CHASE 1840–1899 Her social endowments enhanced by the immense fortune of her husband, the senator from Rhode Island, she dazzled Washington society by her splendid entertainments and her beautiful gowns and jewels. Kate's bond with her father, Chief Justice Chase, remained close, and she campaigned vigorously for his nomination for the Presidency at the Democratic convention of 1868. It had become evident that her marriage was unhappy. Senator Sprague was often drunk, and Kate's many masculine admirers had started the gossips talking. Prominent among her friends was Senator Roscoe Conkling of New York, whose wife did not accompany him to the capital. The year, 1873, saddened for Kate by her father's death, held other tragedies. The financial panic of 1873 swept away the Sprague fortune at about the time that she gave birth to her fourth child, a little girl who was mentally defective. Kate separated from her husband, but later returned to his home. In 1879, Sprague's jealous rages caused scandalous newspaper publicity. He attacked Roscoe Conkling with a gun, while the New York senator was a guest in his home. After securing a divorce in 1882, Kate went abroad with her three daughters, leaving her son in the father's custody. Four years later, a faded and shabby woman, she returned to take up her residence at Edgewood, an estate which her father had purchased outside Washington. Her last years were spent in bitter poverty. She eked out a living by raising chickens and selling milk. Her son committed suicide in 1890.

STANTON, EDWIN McMASTERS 1814–1869 Remaining at the post of War Secretary at Andrew Johnson's request, he plotted with the Republican radicals in opposition to the President's reconstruction policies. His inimical relation with Johnson reached a crisis in the summer of 1867, after the passage of the Tenure of Office Act, which prevented the President from removing a Cabinet officer. As Stanton refused to resign, Johnson suspended him, and appointed Grant Secretary of War *ad interim*. Stanton had made emphatic objections to the Tenure of Office Act, but resumed his place the following winter, after the Senate had declined to approve his removal. Johnson, nevertheless, dismissed him in February, 1868, appointing Adjutant-General Lorenzo Thomas. Stanton literally held his office by remaining, under guard, at the War Department day and night for several weeks. He resigned after the attempt to impeach the President failed. In broken health, he resumed the practice of law. His friends in December, 1869, succeeded in persuading President Grant to make him a justice of the Supreme Court, but his death occurred a few days after he received the appointment. An unfounded rumor that he had taken his own life was widely believed. It was said by his enemies that his suicide was prompted by remorse over the execution of Mrs. Surratt.

STEVENS, THADDEUS   1792–1868   A well-known figure in Pennsylvania State politics, Stevens first took his seat in Congress at the age of fifty-seven as a Free-Soil Whig. After serving two terms, he retired to the practice of law in Lancaster, Pa. In 1858, he was returned as a Republican, and from that date until his death was the most brilliant and dominating figure in the House, the tireless proponent of emancipation and subsequently of full political rights for Negroes. Sharply antagonistic to Lincoln's policies, he gave strong financial support to the administration as chairman of the Ways and Means Committee. He was a leading advocate of confiscation of Confederate property, and, as chairman of the House Committee on Reconstruction, he opposed amnesty, and urged that the seceded States should be treated as "conquered provinces." Bitterly set on Johnson's removal from office, Stevens reported the impeachment resolution on the day after the President dismissed Stanton from his Cabinet. He was a member of the committee which reported the articles of impeachment, and was chosen as one of the seven managers of the trial. His failing health prevented him from bearing an active part. A dying man, deeply chagrined by Johnson's acquittal, he lingered on in Congress until the end of the session in late July. His death occurred in Washington two weeks after the adjournment. It was said that his mulatto housekeeper, Lydia Smith, was his mistress.

STONE, CHARLES POMEROY   1824–1887   Born Greenfield, Mass.; West Point, '45. In January, 1863, Hooker applied for Stone for his chief-of-staff, but the appointment was refused. In May, however, the disgraced brigadier-general was given an appointment under Banks in Louisiana, and suffered the additional misfortune of being associated with the disastrous Red River expedition. In April, 1864, for no given reason, he was mustered out of the volunteer service. He still retained his colonel's commission in the regular Army, and was later assigned to the Army of the Potomac, but resigned in the autumn of 1864. He accepted an appointment in the Egyptian army in which he served from 1870 to 1883, attaining the grade of lieutenant-general and acting as chief-of-staff. In 1886, he was chief engineer of the construction of the pedestal for the Statue of Liberty in New York harbor.

SUMNER, CHARLES   1811–1874   A fervent crusader for Negro suffrage, he was one of the strongest opponents of Johnson's reconstruction plans, and urgently favored the President's conviction and removal from office. In 1869, he was the leader of the Senate fight against the annexation of Santo Domingo, a project favored by President Grant. Two years later he was deposed from the chairmanship of the Committee on Foreign Relations. Long regarded as an inveterate bachelor, Sumner, at the age of fifty-six, married a young and pretty woman, Mrs. Alice Mason Hooper. The bride was soon observed to be receiving attentions from a young attaché of the Prussian legation. Within a year the marriage ended in a separation, and later in divorce. Sumner died suddenly of a heart attack in Washington after twenty-three consecutive years of service in the Senate.

SURRATT, JOHN H.   1844–1916   After Lincoln's assassination, he succeeded in eluding the Federal officers who were sent in search of him. Fleeing across the Canadian border, he was concealed for five months by a Roman Catholic priest. About three months after his mother was hanged, he sailed for England, and made his way to Rome, where he joined the Papal Zouaves under the name of John Watson. In the spring of 1866, he was recognized by a fellow soldier, Henri Ste.-Marie, who had been at school with him in Maryland. Ste.-Marie gave information against Surratt, without producing immediate action on the part of the United States authorities, who had been similarly lethargic in response to a report of Surratt's identity, communicated by the surgeon of the ship on which he had crossed the Atlantic. By order of the Pope's chancellor, Surratt was arrested in November, 1866, but broke away from his captors, and, leaping over a thirty-five foot ravine, landed on a ledge, and escaped. At Naples, he persuaded the British consul that he was a Canadian, and obtained permission to go to Egypt. He was arrested by the American consul-general in Alexandria, and sent back to the United States. His trial, held in 1867 in the civil courts of the District of Columbia, resulted in a hung jury, and the question of Surratt's presence in Washington at the time of Lincoln's assassination remains a matter of dispute. He was kept in prison until June, 1868, and three months later the charge against him was nolle-prossed. He settled in Maryland, where he took a humble clerkship, and passed the rest of his life quietly and without adventure. He planned a course of lectures on the Booth conspiracy, but his first address, given at Rockville, Maryland, in 1870, did not prove a success, and he abandoned the project.

THOMPSON, JACOB   1810–1885   In 1864, Buchanan's Secretary of the Interior was sent to Canada as a secret agent of the Confederacy, and engaged in conspiracies to foment rebellion in the loyal States and free Confederate prisoners of war. He supported plots to burn several Northern cities. Thompson's name figured after that of Jefferson Davis in the charge that Southern officials were implicated in Lincoln's assassination, but he escaped arrest and lived in Canada and Europe for a number of years after the war. In 1876, when he was living in Memphis, Tennessee, an attempt was made to sue him for the moneys stolen from the Interior Department during his administration. It was, however, a political move; Thompson had already been exonerated by a congressional committee. At the time of his death, the Georgian, L. Q. C. Lamar, was Secretary of the Interior in Cleveland's Cabinet, and caused the United States flag to be flown at half mast over the department buildings in Washington.

TRUMBULL, LYMAN   1813–1896   At first allied with the radicals in their conflict with President Johnson, he was gradually alienated by the severity of the congressional reconstruction program. He opposed the trial of the President, and was one of the seven Republicans who voted against Johnson's conviction. His conservative stand cost him his leadership in the Republican party.

VILLARD, HENRY   1835–1900   Born Ferdinand Heinrich Gustav Hilgard, he assumed a new name when he emigrated from Germany after a quarrel with his father in 1853. He soon mastered the English language, and became a newspaper correspondent, reporting the war for the *New York Herald,* then for the *New York Tribune,* and finally for an agency which he himself established in Washington. In 1866, he married Fanny, daughter of the abolitionist, William Lloyd Garrison, and went to Europe as correspondent for the *Chicago Tribune.* Villard's career as a railway financier and organizer began in 1871.

He was active in developing western railroads, and was president of the Northern Pacific and later chairman of the finance committee. In 1881, he purchased
the *New York Evening Post* and the *Nation*. He was succeeded in the management of these publications by his son, Oswald Garrison Villard (1872-19—).

WADE, BENJAMIN FRANKLIN 1800-1878 Elected to the Senate from
Ohio in 1851, he served continuously until 1869. Wade soon made his mark as
an anti-slavery leader, participating with much force and belligerence in the
debates of the era that preceded secession. He was one of the foremost of the
Republican radicals who urged Lincoln to a drastic policy on confiscation, abolition and more vigorous military action. His antipathy to Lincoln's conservatism
was sharpened by the proclamation of amnesty of December, 1863. With the
radical Marylander, Henry Winter Davis, he prepared a bill which embodied a
severe program of reconstruction, under congressional control, and succeeded in
having it passed by both houses. This move Lincoln checkmated by a pocket
veto, inspiring in August, 1864, the publication of the Wade-Davis Manifesto
which vituperatively assailed the President and denounced "executive usurpa-
tion." At first delighted with Johnson's accession to the Presidency, Wade
reacted violently against his moderate reconstruction program, and became Johnson's uncompromising enemy. In March, 1867, Wade was elected president *pro
tempore* of the Senate, and would have become Chief Executive if Johnson had
been convicted in the impeachment trial. During the proceedings, Wade began
to select his Cabinet. In spite of his personal stake in the trial, he was permitted to cast his vote for conviction. He failed of re-election in 1869, and returned to Ohio.

WALWORTH, MANSFIELD TRACY 1830-1873 After his release from
the Old Capitol, he returned to his wife and children at Saratoga Springs. His
father, Reuben Hyde Walworth, the learned and pious chancellor of New York,
died in 1867. Mansfield Walworth had attained some reputation as the author
of sensational novels, among them *Mission of Death, Lulu* and *Hotspur*. After
his adventures in Washington, he published *Stormcliff, Warwick, Delaplane, or
the Sacrifice of Irene*, and in the year of his death *Beverly, or the White Mask*.
He was engaged in preparing the lives of the chancellors of New York, when
he was shot by his son. The boy was acquitted on the ground of insanity, and
placed in an asylum.

WASHBURNE, ELIHU BENJAMIN 1816-1887 Entering Congress in
1853, he served for sixteen years in the House. He had long been Lincoln's
friend, and fostered the military advancement of Grant, whom he had known in
his home town of Galena, Illinois. Washburne was one of Johnson's most violent
detractors. Grant rewarded his loyalty by making him Secretary of State in his
Cabinet, a post which he resigned five days after assuming it, to accept the
appointment of minister to France. He remained in Paris through the siege and
the Commune, returning to the United States in 1877. Washburne's friendship
with Grant terminated in 1880, when a movement for his nomination for the
Presidency at the Republican convention had an adverse effect on Grant's hopes
of a third term.

WEICHMANN, LOUIS J. 1842-1902 After the conspiracy trial was ended,
he went to Philadelphia, where his father was a merchant tailor, and at first

took a job as a newspaper reporter. Through Stanton, he secured a position in the Philadelphia customhouse, and was employed there for seventeen years. He was obliged to return to Washington in 1867 to give testimony in the trial of his former intimate friend, John Surratt, whose mother he had been instrumental in sending to the gallows. Weichmann's appearances in court brought him great notoriety. He received threatening letters, was fearful of bodily harm and at times was under the protection of Government detectives. In middle age he moved to Anderson, Indiana, where he had a brother, a Roman Catholic priest. There, living with his two sisters, he opened a business college. The fears which had haunted him since 1865 did not diminish, and at the age of sixty he died, a nervous, broken old man. On his deathbed, he dictated and signed a statement that the evidence he had given at the conspiracy trial was absolutely true.

WELLES, GIDEON 1802–1878 At the beginning of Lincoln's second term, only he and Seward remained from the original Cabinet chosen in 1861. Like Seward, Welles continued as a member of Johnson's Cabinet throughout his administration. Always moderate and conservative, he detested the radicals' postwar program, and vigorously defended Johnson's policies, and supported him during his impeachment trial.

WHITMAN, WALT 1819–1892 Over two years after the poet came to Washington, he at last secured a clerkship in the Department of the Interior, but in June, 1865, he was dismissed by Secretary Harlan, who was unwilling to give employment to the author of the indecent book, *Leaves of Grass*. Whitman soon obtained another appointment in the Attorney General's office. He continued his association with the naturalist, John Burroughs, but his most intimate friend was Peter Doyle, a former Confederate soldier who was a conductor on the Washington horse cars. Whitman's love letters to Doyle were later published under the title, *Calamus*. His writings had won recognition, especially in Europe, when in 1873 he had a stroke of paralysis and left Washington to make his home with his brother, George, in Camden, N. J. The death of Whitman's mother, which occurred shortly after the onset of his illness, was an added shock from which he never completely recovered. His salary was paid by the Attorney General's office for a year and a half after he was forced to leave his clerkship. The deep admiration for Lincoln, which Whitman expressed in his poems, created the impression that they had been friends, but Whitman never met the President, and knew him only as a passer-by in the Washington streets.

WILSON, HENRY 1812–1875 Wilson, whose real name was Jeremiah Jones Colbath, was the son of a New Hampshire farm laborer, and was almost entirely self-educated. He settled in Massachusetts, where he supported himself by manufacturing shoes and was known on political platforms as the "Natick cobbler." He was a Free-Soiler and abolitionist, and soon after taking his seat in the U. S. Senate in 1855 made a speech in favor of the repeal of the Fugitive Slave Law and the emancipation of the slaves in the District. He was a pioneer in the formation of the Republican party, and took a leading part in the debates in the Senate, serving for four years on the Committee on Military Affairs, before he was appointed to the chairmanship in 1861. He had a vigorous and prejudiced mind, had been identified with the Know-Nothing party, an antiforeign political organization, and in 1861 gave vent to anti-Semitic utterances on the Senate floor. Wilson introduced the bill for emancipation in the District, and was chiefly responsible for the preparation of the Enrollment Bill. During the reconstruction period, he advocated granting full political rights to Negroes, but was more conciliatory toward the Southern people than his radical confreres. He was nominated for Vice-President on the ticket with Grant in 1872, and took office the next spring, after eighteen years' service on the floor of the Senate. He was soon disabled by a paralytic stroke, and remained infirm until his death. Wilson published many addresses and several books, including a three-volume work, *History of the Rise and Fall of the Slave Power in America.*

WOOD, WILLIAM P. 1820–1903 He assisted in the search for John Wilkes Booth, and took issue with Stanton and the Bureau of Military Justice on the question of the guilt of the accused conspirators, especially of Mrs. Surratt. In a series of articles, published in the *Washington Sunday Gazette* in 1883, Wood affirmed that he had been empowered by Stanton to promise Mrs. Surratt's brother that she should not be executed. After she had been sentenced to death, he vainly tried to see Johnson on her behalf, and declared that he was informed by Colonel L. C. Baker that Stanton had particularly ordered Wood's exclusion from audience with the President. Wood's close association with the War Department terminated in 1865, when he became chief of the secret service division of the Treasury, and engaged in capturing counterfeiters and other malefactors. He contributed to the Stanton legend by describing the late War Secretary on the day before his death, as a man broken and haunted by remorse over Mrs. Surratt's execution.

WOOL, JOHN ELLIS 1784–1869 Born in Newburgh, N. Y.; he entered military service as an officer of volunteers in 1812, and was commissioned U. S. captain of infantry. He distinguished himself during the war, was severely wounded and promoted major. In the Mexican War, with the rank of brigadier, Wool was General Zachary Taylor's second in command at Buena Vista. He was two years older than Scott, but in 1861 he was less feeble than the General-in-Chief, and could still sit a horse. In the first summer of the war, he superseded Butler at Fort Monroe, taking command of the Department of Virginia. In June, 1862, he succeeded Dix at Baltimore, commanding what was then the Middle Department. Wool was placed at the head of the Department of the East, with headquarters in New York City, in January, 1863, but after the draft riots in July he was replaced by Dix. The infirmities of old age forced his retirement from active service shortly after.

Bibliography

GENERAL REFERENCE WORKS

Appleton's Annual Cyclopaedia and Register of Important Events, 1876-1903.
Appleton's Cyclopaedia of American Biography, 1888.
Cullum, G. W. *Biographical Register of the Officers and Graduates of the United States Military Academy*, 2 Vols., 1891.
Dictionary of American Biography, 1936.
Dyer, Frederick H., compiler. *A Compendium of the War of the Rebellion*, 1908.
Encyclopaedia Britannica, Eleventh Edition, 1910-11.
Heitman, Francis B. *Historical Register and Dictionary of the United States Army*, 2 Vols., 1903.
Official Records of the War of the Rebellion, 128 Vols., 1880-1901.
United States Military Academy, Association of Graduates. Annual Reunions.

Abbott, Lemuel Abijah. *Personal Recollections and Civil War Diary*, 1908.
Adams, Charles Francis. *Charles Francis Adams*, 1915.
Adams, Henry. *The Education of Henry Adams*, 1918.
————. *The Great Secession Winter of 1860-61*, Massachusetts Historical Society Proceedings, 1909-1910, Vol. 43, 1910.
Alcott, Louisa May. *Life, Letters, and Journals.* Edited by Ednah D. Cheney, 1889.
American War Songs. Privately printed for the Colonial Dames, 1925.
Arnold, Isaac N. *The Life of Abraham Lincoln*, 1885.
Arnold, Samuel B. "The Lincoln Plot," *New York Sun*, 1902.
Atkins, John Black. *The Life of Sir William Howard Russell*, 2 Vols., 1911.
Auchampaugh, Philip. "James Buchanan, the Squire from Lancaster," *The Pennsylvania Magazine of History and Biography*, Vol. 56, 1932.
————. "James Buchanan, the Squire in the White House," *The Pennsylvania Magazine of History and Biography*, Vol. 58, 1934.

Badeau, Adam. *Grant in Peace*, 1887.
Baker, L. C. *History of the United States Secret Service*, 1867.
Baltimore, Its History and Its People, 3 Vols., 1912.
Bancroft, Frederic. "The Final Efforts at Compromise 1860-1861," *Political Science Quarterly*, Sept. 1891.
————. *The Life of William H. Seward*, 2 Vols., 1900.
Barnard, J. G. *A Report on the Defenses of Washington*, 1871.
Barnes, Joseph K., editor. *The Medical and Surgical History of the War of the Rebellion*, 6 Vols., 1870.
Barrus, Clara. *Whitman and Burroughs, Comrades*, 1931.
Barton, William E. *Abraham Lincoln and Walt Whitman*, 1928.
————. *The Life of Clara Barton*, 2 Vols., 1922.
————. *The Women Lincoln Loved*, 1927.
Basso, Hamilton. *Beauregard, the Great Creole*, 1933.

Bates, David Homer. *Lincoln in the Telegraph Office,* 1907.
Battles and Leaders of the Civil War, 4 Vols., 1884-1888.
Beale, Howard K., editor. *The Diary of Edward Bates 1859-1866,* Vol. 4, Annual Report of the American Historical Association, 1930.
Bellows, Henry W. *The United States Sanitary Commission.*
Benedict, G. G. *Vermont in the Civil War,* 2 Vols., 1886.
Benjamin, Marcus, editor. *Washington During War-Time.* Thirty-Sixth Annual Encampment of the Grand Army of the Republic, 1902.
Beymer, William Gilmore. *On Hazardous Service,* 1912.
Bigelow, John. *Retrospections of an Active Life,* 5 Vols., 1909-1913.
Blaine, James G. *Twenty Years of Congress,* 2 Vols., 1884.
Bohn, Casimir. *Bohn's Hand-Book of Washington,* 1861.
Bowers, Claude G. *The Tragic Era,* 1929.
Boyd, Belle. *Belle Boyd in Camp and Prison,* 1865.
Brockett, L. P. and M. C. Vaughan. *Woman's Work in the Civil War,* 1867.
Brooks, Elbridge Streeter. *The American Soldier,* 1899.
Brooks, Noah. *Washington in Lincoln's Time,* 1895.
Brown, Henri Le Fevre, compiler. *History of the Third Regiment, Excelsior Brigade,* 1902.
Brown, Harvey E. *The Medical Department of the United States Army from 1775 to 1873,* 1873.
Browne, Charles Farrar. *Artemus Ward His Book,* 1862.
Browning, Orville Hickman. *The Diary of Orville Hickman Browning,* 2 Vols. Collections of the Illinois State Historical Library, Vol. 20, Lincoln Series, Vol. 2, 1925.
Bryan, Wilhelmus Bogart. *A History of the National Capital,* 2 Vols., 1914.
Buchanan, James. *Administration on the Eve of the Rebellion,* 1866.
Bucke, Richard Maurice. *Walt Whitman,* 1883.
Buckingham, J. E. *Reminiscences and Souvenirs of the Assassination of Abraham Lincoln,* 1894.
Burnett, Henry L. *Assassination of President Lincoln and the Trial of the Assassins.* The Ohio Society of New York, 1906.
Burnside, Ambrose E. *Memorial addresses,* 1882.
Burroughs, John. *Wake-Robin,* 1871.
――――. *Whitman,* 1896.
Butler, Benjamin Franklin. *Butler's Book,* 1892.

Carnegie, Andrew. *Autobiography,* 1933.
Carpenter, Francis B. *Six months at the White House,* 1866.
Chamberlin, Thomas. *History of the 150th Regiment, Pennsylvania Volunteers,* 1895.
"Zachariah Chandler: An Outline Sketch of His Life and Public Services," Detroit *Post and Tribune,* 1880.
Chase, Salmon P., *Diary and Correspondence,* Annual Report of the American Historical Association, 2 Vols., 1903.
Chesnut, Mary Boykin. *A Diary from Dixie,* 1905.
Clark, Allen C. *Abraham Lincoln in the National Capital,* 1925.
――――. *Richard Wallach and the Times of His Mayoralty,* Records of the Columbia Historical Society, Vol. 21, 1918.

Clarke, Asia Booth. *The Unlocked Book*, 1938.
Clarke, Mrs. Grace Giddings. *George W. Julian*, Indiana Historical Collections, Vol. XI, Biographical series, Vol. 1, 1923.
Clement, Edward Henry. *The Bull-Run Rout*, Proceedings of the Massachusetts Historical Society, March 1909.
Clements, Bennet A. *Memoir of Jonathan Letterman*, 188?.
Coggeshall, E. W. *The Assassination of Lincoln*, 1920.
Coolidge, Louis A. *Ulysses S. Grant*, 1917.
Cox, Samuel S. *Three Decades of Federal Legislation*, 1886.
Cox, Walter S. "Reminiscences of the Courts of the District," *The Washington Law Reporter*, Vol. 23, 1895.
Cox, William V. *The Defenses of Washington. General Early's Advance on the Capital*, Records of the Columbia Historical Society, Vol. 4, 1901.
Crawford, Samuel Wylie. *The Genesis of the Civil War*, 1887.
Croffut, W. A. and John M. Morris. *The Military and Civil History of Connecticut during the War of 1861-65*, 1868.
Crook, William H. *Through Five Administrations*, 1907.
Curtis, George Ticknor. *Life of James Buchanan*, 2 Vols., 1883.

Dana, Charles A. *Lincoln and His Cabinet*, 1899.
————. *Recollections of the Civil War*, 1899.
Davis, Henry E. *Ninth and F Streets and Thereabout*, Records of the Columbia Historical Society, Vol. 5, 1902.
Davis, Varina. *Jefferson Davis*, 2 Vols., 1890.
De Leon, T. C. *Belles, Beaux and Brains of the '60's*, 1907.
Dennett, Tyler. *John Hay*, 1933.
————. *Lincoln and the Civil War in the Diaries and Letters of John Hay*, 1939.
Dewitt, David Miller. *The Assassination of Abraham Lincoln and Its Expiation*, 1909.
————. *The Judicial Murder of Mary E. Surratt*, 1895.
"Diary of a Public Man, The," *The North American Review*, Vol. 129, 1879.
Dicey, Edward. *Six Months in the Federal States*, 2 Vols., 1863.
Doster, William E. *Lincoln and Episodes of the Civil War*, 1915.
Du Bois, W. E. Burghardt. *Black Reconstruction*, 1935.
Dyer, Oliver. *Great Senators of the United States*, 1889.

Early, Jubal A. *A Memoir of the Last Year of the War*, 1866.
"Early's Raid on Washington," *The Republic*, Vol. VIII, No. 3, March 1877.
Eaton, John. *Grant, Lincoln and the Freedmen*, 1907.
Edge, Frederick Milnes. *Major-General McClellan and the Campaign on the Yorktown Peninsula*, 1865.
Edmonds, S. Emma E. *Nurse and Spy in the Union Army*, 1864.
Eisenschiml, Otto. *Why Was Lincoln Murdered?*, 1937.
————. *In the Shadow of Lincoln's Death*, 1940.
Ellet, Charles, Jr. *The Army of the Potomac and Its Mismanagement*, 1861.
Ellet, Elizabeth F. L. *Court Circles of the Republic*, 1869.
Elliott, Charles Winslow. *Winfield Scott, the Soldier and the Man*, 1937.
Ellis, John B. *The Sights and Secrets of the National Capital*, 1869.

Ely, Alfred. *Journal*, 1862.
Epler, Percy H. *The Life of Clara Barton*, 1915.
Evans, W. A. *Mrs. Abraham Lincoln*, 1932.

Fay, Frank B. *War Papers*, 1911.
Ferguson, W. J. "Lincoln's Death," *The Saturday Evening Post*, Feb. 12, 1927.
Flower, Frank Abial. *Edwin McMasters Stanton*, 1905.
Foote, Henry S. *Casket of Reminiscences*, 1874.
Ford, Worthington Chauncey, editor. *A Cycle of Adams Letters, 1861-1865*, 2 Vols., 1920.
Forney, John W. *Anecdotes of Public Men*, 1873.
Freeman, Douglas Southall. *R. E. Lee*, 4 Vols., 1934.
French, B. B. Diary and Correspondence, (Privately printed).
Fry, James B. *McDowell and Tyler in the Campaign of Bull's Run*, 1884.

Garrison, Fielding H. *John Shaw Billings; a memoir*, 1915.
Gleason, D. H. L. "Conspiracy Against Lincoln," *Magazine of History*, Vol. 13, Feb. 1911.
Gobright, L. A. *Recollections of Men and Things at Washington*, 1869.
Golder, Frank A. "The American Civil War Through the Eyes of a Russian Diplomat," *The American Historical Review*, Vol. 26, April 1921.
Gorham, George C. *Life and Public Services of Edwin M. Stanton*, 2 Vols., 1899.
Grant, Jesse R. *In the Days of My Father, General Grant*, 1925.
Grant, U. S. *Personal Memoirs*, 2 Vols., 1885.
Greeley, Horace. *The American Conflict*, 2 Vols., 1869.
Greenhow, Rose O'Neal. *My Imprisonment*, 1863.
Grover, Leonard. "Lincoln's Interest in the Theater," *Century Magazine*, April 1909.
Gurowski, Adam. *Diary*, 3 Vols., 1862-66.

Hamlin, Charles E. *The Life and Times of Hannibal Hamlin*, 1899.
Hammond, William Alexander, editor. *Military, Medical and Surgical Essays*, 1864.
Hammond, William Alexander. Record of a Memorial Meeting. New York Post-Graduate Hospital, Feb. 23, 1900.
Hard, Abner. *History of the Eighth Cavalry Regiment, Illinois Volunteers*, 1868.
Harper's Weekly, 1861–65.
Harris, Elisha. *The United States Sanitary Commission*, 1864.
Harris, T. M. *Assassination of Lincoln*, 1892.
Hart, Albert Bushnell. *Salmon Portland Chase*, 1899.
Haupt, Herman. *Reminiscences*, 1901.
Hawthorne, Nathaniel. "Chiefly About War-Matters," *Atlantic Monthly*, Vol. 10, July 1862.
Hay, John. "Ellsworth," *Atlantic Monthly*, Vol. 8, July 1861.
———. "A Young Hero," *McClure's Magazine*, March 1896.

Hayes, Rutherford Birchard. *Diary and Letters.* The Ohio State Archaeological and Historical Society, Vol. 2, 1922.

Hayward, John A. and George C. Hazleton. *The Reports of the Circuit Court of the District of Columbia,* Vol. 2, 1895.

Helm, Katherine. *The True Story of Mary, Wife of Lincoln,* 1928.

Henderson, G. F. R. *Stonewall Jackson and the American Civil War,* 2 Vols., 1902.

Herndon, William H. and Jesse William Weik. *Herndon's Lincoln,* 3 Vols., 1889.

Hertz, Emanuel. *The Hidden Lincoln. From the Letters and Papers of William H. Herndon,* 1938.

Hesseltine, William Best. *Civil War Prisons,* 1930.

Hillard, G. S. *Life and Campaigns of George B. McClellan,* 1864.

Hitchcock, Ethan Allen. *Fifty Years in Camp and Field,* 1909.

Hoge, A. H. *The Boys in Blue,* 1867.

Hollister, O. J. *Life of Schuyler Colfax,* 1886.

Holt, W. Stull. *The Office of the Chief of Engineers of the Army,* Institute for Government Research, Service Monographs of the U. S. Government— No. 27, 1923.

Home Journal, 1861.

Howe, Julia Ward. *Reminiscences,* 1900.

Humphreys, Andrew A. *The Virginia Campaign of '64 and '65,* 1883.

Hunter, David. *Military Services During the War of the Rebellion,* 1873.

Hutchinson, William T. *Cyrus Hall McCormick,* 2 Vols., Vol. 1, 1930, Vol. 2, 1935.

Hyde, Thomas W. *Following the Greek Cross,* 1894.

Illustrated London News, The, 1861-65.

Impeachment Investigation. Second Session 39th Congress and First Session 40th Congress, U. S. House Reports, 1867.

Ingraham, Charles A. *Elmer E. Ellsworth and the Zouaves of '61,* 1925.

Johnson, Albert E. H. *Reminiscences of the Hon. Edwin M. Stanton, Secretary of War* Records of the Columbia Historical Society, Vol. 13, 1910.

Johnston, R. M. *Bull Run. Its Strategy and Tactics,* 1913.

Joinville, Prince de. *The Army of the Potomac,* 1862.

Julian, George W. *Political Recollections,* 1884.

———. "Journal," *Indiana Magazine of History,* Vol. XI, 1915.

Kauffmann, S. H. *Equestrian Statuary in Washington,* Records of the Columbia Historical Society, Vol. 5, 1902.

Keckley, Elizabeth. *Behind the Scenes,* 1868.

Keen, William W. *The Contrast Between the Surgery of the Civil War and That of the Present War,* 1915.

———. *Papers and Addresses,* 1922.

———. *Selected Papers and Addresses,* 1923.

Kelley, William D. *Lincoln and Stanton,* 1885.

Kelly, Howard Atwood and Walter L. Burrage. *American Medical Biographies,* 1920.
Keyes, Erasmus Darwin. *Fifty Years' Observation of Men and Events,* 1885.
Kimmel, Stanley. *The Mad Booths of Maryland,* 1940.
King, Horatio. *Turning on the Light,* 1895.
King, Horatio Collins. *The Army of the Potomac,* 1898.

Lamon, Ward Hill. *Recollections of Abraham Lincoln,* 1911.
Laughlin, Clara E. *The Death of Lincoln,* 1909.
Lawrence, George Alfred. *Border and Bastille,* 1863?
Leale, Charles A. *Lincoln's Last Hours,* 1909.
Frank Leslie's Illustrated Newspaper.
Leslie's Illustrated Weekly, 1861-65.
Letterman, Jonathan. *Medical Recollections of the Army of the Potomac,* 1866.
Lewis, Lloyd. *Myths After Lincoln,* 1929.
————. *Sherman. Fighting Prophet,* 1932.
Livermore, Mary A. *My Story of the War,* 1888.
Lockwood, Mary Smith. *Yesterdays in Washington,* 2 Vols., 1915.
Lomax, Virginia. *The Old Capitol and Its Inmates,* 1867.
Lossing, Benson J. *The Pictorial Field Book of the Civil War in the United States of America,* 3 Vols., 1874-1881.

McBride, Robert W. *Lincoln's Body Guard.* Indiana Historical Society Publications, Vol. 5, No. 1, 1911.
McClellan, George B. *McClellan's Own Story,* 1887.
McClune, H. H. *The Old Capitol Prison and the Dry Tortugas,* 1865.
McClure, A. K. *Abraham Lincoln and the Men of War-Times,* 1892.
McCulloch, Hugh. *Men and Measures of Half a Century,* 1888.
Macartney, Clarence Edward. *Lincoln and His Cabinet,* 1931.
————. *Lincoln and His Generals,* 1925.
Mackey, Franklin H., reporter. *Reports of the Supreme Court of the District of Columbia. 1863-1868,* District of Columbia Reports, Vol. 6, 1889.
Mahony, D. A. *The Prisoner of State,* 1863.
Malet, Sir Edward. *Shifting Scenes,* 1901.
Marshall, John A. *American Bastile,* 1872.
Meade, George, editor. *The Life and Letters of George Gordon Meade,* 2 Vols., 1913.
Meigs, M. C. "Gen. M. C. Meigs on the Conduct of the Civil War," *American Historical Review,* Vol. 26, January 1921.
Meneely, Alexander Howard. *The War Department, 1861,* 1928.
Michie, Peter S. *General McClellan,* 1901.
Milton, George Fort. *The Age of Hate,* 1930.
Monroe, J. Albert. *Reminiscences of the War of the Rebellion,* Soldiers and Sailors Historical Society of Rhode Island, No. 11, 2nd Series.
Moore, Frank, editor. *The Civil War in Song and Story,* 1882.
————. *The Rebellion Record,* 12 Vols., 1861-1865.
Morrison's Stranger's Guide and Etiquette for Washington City and Its Vicinity, 1862.
Moses, Belle. *Louisa May Alcott,* 1933.

Moss, Lemuel. *Annals of the U. S. Christian Commission,* 1868.
Moss, M. Helen Palmes. "Lincoln and John Wilkes Booth As Seen on the Day of the Assassination," *Century Magazine,* April 1909.
Myers, William Starr. *General George Brinton McClellan,* 1934.

Nevins, Allan. *Frémont,* 2 Vols., 1928.
Newton, Thomas W. L. *Lord Lyons,* 2 Vols., 1913.
Nicolay, Helen. *Our Capital on the Potomac,* 1924.
————. *Personal Traits of Abraham Lincoln,* 1912.
Nicolay, John George. *The Outbreak of Rebellion,* 1882.
Nicolay, John G. and John Hay. *Abraham Lincoln,* 10 Vols., 1904.

O'Connor, William Douglas. *The Good Gray Poet,* 1866.
Oldroyd, O. H. *Assassination of Abraham Lincoln,* 1901.
Olnhausen, Mary Phinney von. *Adventures of an Army Nurse in Two Wars,* 1903.

Paine, Albert Bigelow. *Thomas Nast,* 1904.
Paris, Comte de. *History of the Civil War in America,* 4 Vols., 1875.
Pearson, Henry Greenleaf. *James S. Wadsworth of Geneseo,* 1913.
Pendel, Thomas F. *Thirty-Six Years in the White House,* 1902.
Phelps, Mary Merwin. *Kate Chase,* 1935.
Philp's Washington Described, 1861.
Photographic History of the Civil War, 10 Vols., 1911.
Pierce, Edward L. *Memoir and Letters of Charles Sumner,* 4 Vols., 1877–1893.
Pilcher, James Evelyn, editor. *Journal of the Association of Military Surgeons of the United States,* Vols. 14-15, 1904.
————. *The Surgeon Generals of the Army of the United States of America,* 1905.
Pinkerton, Allan. *The Spy of the Rebellion,* 1883.
Pitman, Benn, compiler. *The Assassination of President Lincoln and the Trial of the Conspirators,* 1865.
Plum, William R. *The Military Telegraph During the Civil War in the United States,* 2 Vols., 1882.
Poore, Ben: Perley, editor. *The Conspiracy Trial for the Murder of the President,* 2 Vols., 1865.
————. *Reminiscences of Sixty Years in the National Metropolis,* 2 Vols., 1886.
Porter, David Dixon. *Incidents and Anecdotes of the Civil War,* 1885.
Porter, George Loring. "How Booth's Body Was Hidden," *The Columbian Magazine,* April 1911.
Porter, Horace. *Campaigning With Grant,* 1897.
Pryor, Sara Agnes (Mrs. Roger A.). *Reminiscences of Peace and War,* 1904.

Randall, J. G. *The Civil War and Reconstruction,* 1937.
————. "The Newspaper Problem in Its Bearing Upon Military Secrecy During the Civil War," *American Historical Review,* Vol. 23, 1918.
Raymond, Henry J. *The Life and Public Services of Abraham Lincoln,* 1865.

Read, John Meredith, Jr. "Military Affairs of New York State," *Magazine of American History*, Vol. 14, 1885.

Reed, William Howell. *Hospital Life in the Army of the Potomac*, 1866.

Report of the Joint Committee on the Conduct of the War, 3 Parts, 1863.

Report of the Joint Committee on the Conduct of the War, 3 Parts, 1865.

Reports of the Committees of the House of Representatives, Sec. Session, 37th Congress, 1861–1862, Vol. 3, No. 16, Loyalty of Clerks and Other Persons Employed by the Government.

Reports of Committees of the Senate of the United States, for the *Third Session of the Thirty-Seventh Congress*, Vol. 3, Part 2, No. 108, 1863.

Rhodes, James Ford. *History of the United States*, 7 Vols., 1904.

Rice, Allen T., editor. *Reminiscences of Abraham Lincoln. By distinguished men of his time*, 1886.

Richardson, Albert Deane. *The Secret Service*, 1865.

Richardson, Francis A. *Recollections of a Washington Newspaper Correspondent*, Records of the Columbia Historical Society, Vol. 6, 1903.

Riddle, A. G. *Life of Benjamin F. Wade*, 1886.

———. *Recollections of War-Times*, 1895.

Roman, Alfred. *The Military Operations of General Beauregard*, 2 Vols., 1884.

Ropes, John Codman. *The Army Under Pope*, 1891.

———. "General McClellan," *Atlantic Monthly*, April 1887.

———. *The Story of the Civil War*, 1894.

———. *The Story of the Civil War* (Campaigns of 1862), 1898.

Russell, William Howard. *My Diary North and South*, 2 Vols., 1863.

Sala, George Augustus. *My Diary in America in the Midst of War*, 2 Vols., 1865.

Salter, William. *The Life of James W. Grimes*, 1876.

Sandburg, Carl and Paul M. Angle. *Mary Lincoln, Wife and Widow*, 1932.

Schlegel, Carl W. *Schlegel's German-American Families in the United States*, 2 Vols., 1916.

Schuckers, J. W. *The Life and Public Services of Salmon P. Chase*, 1874.

Schurz, Carl. *Reminiscences*, 3 Vols., 1909.

Scott, Winfield. *Memoirs*, 2 Vols., 1864.

Seward, Frederick W. *Reminiscences of a War-Time Statesman and Diplomat*, 1916.

———. Seward at Washington, 3 Vols., 1891.

Shannon, Fred Albert. *The Organization and Administration of the Union Army 1861–1865*, 1928.

Sheridan, P. H. *Personal Memoirs*, 2 Vols., 1888.

Sherman, William T. *Memoirs*, 2 Vols., 1875.

Singleton, Esther. *The Story of the White House*, 2 Vols., 1907.

Smith, A. P. *History of the Seventy-Sixth Regiment, New York Volunteers*, 1867.

Smith, George Williamson. *A Critical Moment for Washington*, Records of the Columbia Historical Society, Vol. 21, 1918.

Smith, Thomas West. *The Story of a Cavalry Regiment. "Scott's 900,"* 1897.

Stanton, Hon. Edwin M. Proceedings in Reference to Death of. Union League Club of New York, 1870.

Starr, John W. *Lincoln's Last Day,* 1922.
———. *New Light on Lincoln's Last Day,* 1926.
———. *Further Light on Lincoln's Last Day,* 1930.
Stedman, Edmund Clarence. *Army Correspondence of the New York World,* 1861.
Stephenson, Nathaniel Wright. *Lincoln,* 1922.
Sterling, Ada. *A Belle of the Fifties. Memoirs of Mrs. Clay,* 1904.
Stern, Philip Van Doren. *The Man Who Killed Lincoln,* 1939.
Stevens, George T. *Three Years in the Sixth Corps,* 1870.
Stillé, Charles Janeway. *History of the United States Sanitary Commission,* 1866.
Stimmel, Smith. *Personal Reminiscences of Abraham Lincoln,* 1928.
Stoddard, William Osborn. *Inside the White House in War Times,* 1890.
Stone, Charles P. "Washington on the Eve of the War," *The Century Magazine,* Vol. 26, July 1883.
———. "A Dinner with General Scott," *Magazine of American History,* Vol. 11, June 1884.
———. "Washington In 1861," *Magazine of American History,* Vol. 12, July 1884.
———. "Washington in March and April, 1861," *Magazine of American History,* Vol. 14, July 1885.
Storey, Moorfield. "Dickens, Stanton, Sumner and Storey," *Atlantic Monthly,* April 1930.
Stryker, Lloyd Paul. *Andrew Johnson, A Study in Courage,* 1930.
Sunderland, Byron. *Washington As I First Knew It,* Records of the Columbia Historical Society, Vol. 5, 1902.
Swinton, William. *Campaigns of the Army of the Potomac,* 1882.

Taft, Charles Sabin. *Abraham Lincoln's Last Hours,* 1934.
Tarbell, Ida M. *The Life of Abraham Lincoln,* 4 Vols., 1895.
Thayer, William Roscoe. *The Life and Letters of John Hay,* 2 Vols., 1915.
Thorndike, Rachel Sherman, editor. *The Sherman Letters,* 1894.
Tiffany, Francis. *Life of Dorothea Lynde Dix,* 1890.
Townsend, E. D. *Anecdotes of the Civil War in the United States,* 1884.
Townsend, George Alfred. *The Life, Crime and Capture of John Wilkes Booth,* 1865.
———. *Washington, Outside and Inside,* 1874.
Tremain, Mary. *Slavery in the District of Columbia,* 1892.
Trial of John H. Surratt, 2 Vols., 1867.
Trobriand, Regis de. *Four Years With the Army of the Potomac,* 1889.
Trollope, Anthony. *North America,* 1862.

Usher, John P. *President Lincoln's Cabinet,* 1925.

Van de Water, Frederic F. *Glory-Hunter. A Life of General Custer,* 1934.
Van Rensselaer, M. G. "Frederick Law Olmsted," *The Century Magazine,* October 1893.

Varnum, Joseph Bradley Jr. (Viator, pseud.). *The Washington Sketch-Book,* 1864.

Villard, Henry. *Memoirs,* 2 Vols., 1904.

Vincent, Elizabeth K. *In the Days of Lincoln,* 1924.

Vincent, Thomas McCurdy. *Abraham Lincoln and Edwin M. Stanton. An Address, April 25, 1889,* 1917.

Walker, Aldace F. *The Vermont Brigade in the Shenandoah Valley,* 1869.

Warden, Robert Bruce. *An Account of the Private Life and Public Services of Salmon Portland Chase,* 1874.

Waterman, A. N. *Washington At the Time of the First Bull Run,* Military Essays and Recollections, Commandery of Illinois, Military Order of Loyal Legion, Vol. 2, 1894.

Watterson, Henry. *"Marse Henry," An Autobiography,* 2 Vols., 1919.

Webb, Alexander Stewart. *The Peninsula,* 1881.

Weed, Harriet A. and Thurlow Weed Barnes, editors. *Thurlow Weed,* 2 Vols., 1884.

Welles, Gideon. *Diary,* 3 Vols., 1911.

———. *Lincoln and Seward,* 1874.

Weston, David. *Among the Wounded,* 1864.

White, Horace. *The Life of Lyman Trumbull,* 1913.

Whitman, Walt. *Collected Works,* 1902.

Wikoff, Henry. *The Adventures of a Roving Diplomatist,* 1857.

Wilkeson, Frank. *Recollections of a private soldier in the army of the Potomac,* 1887.

Willets, Gilson. *Inside History of the White House,* 1908.

Williams, George W. *History of the Negro Race in America,* 2 Vols., 1883.

Williamson, James J. *Prison Life in the Old Capitol,* 1911.

Wilson, Francis. *John Wilkes Booth,* 1929.

Wilson, Henry and J. S. Black. *Edwin M. Stanton,* 1871.

Wilson, William Bender. *History of the Pennsylvania Railroad Company,* 2 Vols., 1899.

Windle, Mary Jane. *Life in Washington,* 1859.

Winthrop, Theodore. *The Canoe and the Saddle,* 1913.

———. *"Our March to Washington," Life in the Open Air and Other Papers,* 1876.

———. *"Washington as a Camp," Atlantic Monthly,* July 1861.

Woodbury, Augustus. *Ambrose Everett Burnside,* Soldiers and Sailors Historical Society of Rhode Island, No. 17, Second Series.

Woodward, W. E. *Meet General Grant,* 1928.

Woolsey, Jane Stewart. *Hospital Days,* 1870.

Wormeley, Katharine Prescott. *The Other Side of War,* 1889.

———. *The Sanitary Commission of the United States Army,* 1864.

Wright, M. J. *General Scott,* 1894.

NEWSPAPERS

Washington, D. C.
    Constitutional Union
    Congressional Globe

Daily Chronicle
Daily National Intelligencer
The Daily Record (Law and economics periodical)
Evening Star
National Republican
Sunday Morning Chronicle
New York, N. Y.
Herald
Times
Tribune
Spirit of the Times

MANUSCRIPTS

Private papers of B. B. French—Library of Congress
Official papers of B. B. French, Commissioner of Public Buildings—National Archives
Intercepted correspondence of the Civil War, 1861—National Archives
Record of the Hearings of State prisoners before the Dix-Pierrepont Commission in Washington, 1862—National Archives

Index

592

Library of Congress Cataloguing in Publication Data

Leech, Margaret, 1893-1974
Reveille in Washington.
(Time Reading Program)
Reprint of the 1962 ed. published by Time Inc.
in series: Time Reading Program
Bibliography: p.
Includes index.
1. Washington, D.C. — History — Civil War 1861-1865.   I. Title
[E501.L4   1980]   975.3'02   80-16429
ISBN 0-8094-3556-X
ISBN 0-8094-3557-8